ZANGRANDO

D1532339

THE NEW AFRICANS

A GUIDE TO THE CONTEMPORARY HISTORY OF EMERGENT AFRICA AND ITS LEADERS

Written by Fifty Correspondents of Reuters News Agency
Edited by Sidney Taylor

PAUL HAMLYN · LONDON

Published 1967 by Paul Hamlyn Ltd
Drury House, Russell Street, London WC2

© Copyright in 1967 by Reuters Ltd

Maps © 1967 by Geographia Ltd, England

Filmset by Rugby Photoset Plates Ltd
Rugby, England

Printed in England by Richard Clay
(The Chaucer Press) Ltd, Bungay, Suffolk

✳ FAST-CHANGING AFRICA

While this book was being printed, the following events took place:

Dahomey, Gabon and Upper Volta Changes in the Government.

Ghana Lieutenant-General E. K. Kotoka, Commander of the Armed Forces, who led the military overthrow of Dr Kwame Nkrumah, was killed in an abortive *coup* by dissident soldiers on April 17, 1967.

Nigeria Eastern Nigeria took over all Federal installations in the Region (April 18), including ports, railways, radio stations, posts and telegraphs.

Sierra Leone Colonel Andrew Juxon-Smith became leader of the ruling National Reformation Council which had seized power in March from the two rival political leaders, Sir Albert Margai and Mr Siaka Stevens.

Togo Lieutenant-Colonel Etienne Eyadema, Army Chief of Staff, took over as President (April 14), dissolving the National Reconciliation Committee set up after the military *coup* he led in January. Colonel Kléber Dadjo, outgoing President, was named Minister of Justice.

April 25, 1967

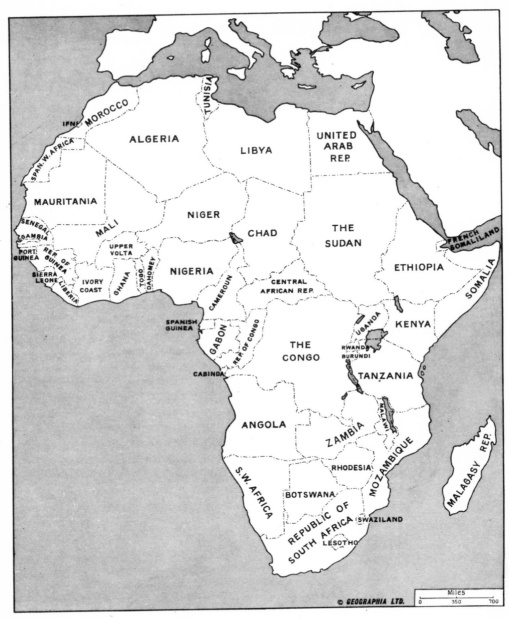

This map of Africa in 1967 shows what has happened since the surge towards national independence began. French West Africa and French Equatorial Africa have vanished as such; they are now divided between a number of separate republics. Spain and Portugal have retained their possessions. Small French Somaliland had its independence referendum early in 1967. Until October, 1966, Botswana was Bechuanaland and Lesotho was Basutoland. A third British protectorate, Swaziland, expects full independence by 1970.

Introduction

1 Men who transformed Africa

The story of Africa's sudden surge to nationhood – 200 million people have won independence within the past decade – is told by the lives of Africa's leaders. Their careers provide a fascinating story of success and failure, sudden rise to power, and equally sudden overthrow or death.

Today black independent Africa and the racially distinct island of Madagascar comprise 33 countries.

Nationhood has done much to raise the standard of living, and push back forest and bush. No doubt much more could have been done but for lack of money, techniques and experience. But the path has not been smooth. Since the spring-tide of African nationalism in 1960, six years of power-struggles and political and racial jealousies have swept away many of the leaders who led their countries to independence.

Vast problems remain, and new men have emerged to take the place of the first wave of leaders.

Still watching closely from the wings are the European powers who once owned the new states as colonies, obtained during the 19th century division of the continent. These countries – France, Britain, Belgium, Germany, Portugal, Italy and Spain – gave Africa the frontiers within which the new nations were born. Now they have been joined as interested parties by the giant powers of the era following World War II – the United States, the Soviet Union and the People's Republic of China.

From about 1880 the rich nations of Western Europe hunted for colonies over almost all the eleven and a half million square miles of Africa. Only Ethiopia, ruled by an emperor of ancient lineage (though occupied by Italy for five years, 1936–41) and Liberia (independent since 1847

and founded as a home for American Negroes freed from
slavery) were left untouched by the European descent on
the Continent.

By far the largest share went to France, over four million
square miles, though about three-quarters of it was the
Sahara Desert. Britain took between two and two and a half
million square miles. Broadly speaking, France occupied
most of North Africa, a large area of the west coast and
Madagascar, off the east coast. Britain gained control over
much of the west and east coasts and the south.

Belgium raised her flag over only one territory – the
million square mile Congo, but it was the third largest
share. After that came Portugal, Germany, Italy and Spain.
The German territories – Tanganyika, South West Africa,
Togoland and Cameroun – were taken over by the
victorious powers of World War I.

When World War II ended in 1945 only four nations on
the vast African continent were independent – Liberia,
the Union of South Africa, Egypt and Ethiopia. In 1955
four-fifths of Africa's population was still under European
rule.

The first to be free was a British colony – Ghana, the
former Gold Coast (1957). One of France's followed–
Guinea in 1958.

In September, 1958, France and all her overseas possessions
had gone to the polls to approve or reject General
de Gaulle's proposed constitution for the Fifth Republic.
As far as the overseas territories were concerned, approval
of the constitution, expressed by voting 'yes' in the
referendum, meant the continuation of links with France
within the French Community in one way or another.
Voting 'no' meant immediate secession and independence
at their 'own risk and peril', to use General de Gaulle's
phrase. In a speech in Brazzaville, capital of the then
French Equatorial Africa, he explained that even if a
territory voted 'yes' it would not have closed the door for
ever on full independence. If at some future date a
member-state felt it was ready to exercise 'all the charges
and duties of independence', it would have the chance to
decide on this through its elected assembly, and, if
necessary, by popular referendum. General de Gaulle
proved as good as his word.

All but one of the 18 overseas territories voted in favour
of the new constitution, the exception being Guinea, which

Sir Abubakar
Tafawa Balewa

Patrice Lumumba

Sylvanus Olympio

acquired immediate independence, followed by the
withdrawal of French aid and technical assistance. Twelve
out of the 13 which voted 'yes' subsequently chose the
status of member-states of the Community. In 1960 all
twelve requested and obtained independence; they were
preceded by the French-administered trust territories of
Cameroun and Togo.

'Freedom year', as 1960 became known, was ushered in
with a remarkable speech by Britain's Prime Minister,
Mr Harold Macmillan. Addressing both Houses of
Parliament in Cape Town (February 3, 1960) he warned
the Nationalist Government of South Africa of 'the wind
of change' blowing through the Continent and served
notice that Britain could no longer support their policy of
apartheid (separation of races according to colour). His
Government rejected the idea of any inherent superiority
of one race over another, believing that 'individual merit
alone is the criterion of man's advancement, political
or economic'.

'The wind of change' became a gale, especially for France,
and Belgium lost the Congo. Eighty-five million Africans
became masters in their own homelands, where white rule
vanished.

But the first years of freedom can be dangerous.
Independence does not solve many problems, and brings
others of its own. Almost every country ran into trouble
of some kind.

Between 1960 and 1966 there were military *coups* or
mutinies in 14 countries – the Congo Democratic
Republic, Ethiopia, Togo, Dahomey, Zanzibar,
Tanganyika, Uganda, Kenya, Gabon, Burundi, Central
African Republic, Upper Volta, Nigeria and Ghana.
Plots and counter-plots often led nowhere but left virile,
dynamic nations ripe for further change.

Men whose names are synonymous with their countries'
fight for independence were deposed, exiled or murdered.
Among the victims were Patrice Lumumba, the first
Prime Minister of Congo Kinshasa, as it became known,
President Sylvanus Olympio of Togo, Crown Prince
Louis Rwagasore of Burundi, Sir Abubakar Tafawa
Balewa, Federal Prime Minister of Nigeria, and two of
his regional Premiers, Sir Ahmadu Bello (the Sardauna
of Sokoto) and Chief Samuel Akintola.

The young African states had ambitious development

plans and few were able to exist without substantial aid.
Probably the biggest aid-giver was France, which provided
direct budgetary contributions to some countries for a few
years after independence, as well as technical assistance
and advisers to ministries, aid for economic projects and
specially subsidised prices on the French market for the
raw materials of French-speaking Africa.

Britain, too, had to provide substantial aid, especially to the
countries of East Africa which won their independence
later than the West African territories.

The United States had to perform a financial rescue
operation in the Congo.

The Soviet Union, other Eastern European countries and
the People's Republic of China joined in on the
Socialist side. Despite this aid the less well-endowed
countries had to face almost annual austerity campaigns
as governments grappled with widening budget deficits.

The European colonisation of Africa, which lasted a
relatively brief period, has tended to cause the European
influence upon the continent to be overstated.

Africa is often divided up into 'French-speaking' or
'English-speaking' areas, although a very small percentage
of the continent's population speak either language.

The years since independence have seen a very real
movement towards African unity, although not at the pace
that the more passionate proponents of pan-Africanism,
such as Kwame Nkrumah, would have wished.

Africans discovered in themselves a positive genius for
settling what looked like dangerous border disputes,
mainly through the Organisation of African Unity. The
continent also found a common culture of oral traditions
and dance and music rhythms.

The passage towards African unity was a stormy one. It was
beset by arguments caused by differing political ideologies,
but at the end of 1966 the OAU was still very much in
existence and gaining wide support.

A factor likely to trouble the continent for some time
is white domination of the southern part of Africa. *Apartheid*
in South Africa and the rule of white minorities in
Rhodesia and the Portuguese territories, where the Africans
often outnumber the Europeans by as much as 30 to 1,
continue as an affront to African nationalism and a
disturbing element in the affairs of the Continent as a whole

2 Uniting the African Continent

The leaders of the 36 member countries of the Organisation
of African Unity face the future with a solid framework
for Continental cooperation, built up at four 'summits'
and at many other conferences.

Though not always agreed on how best to operate, they
have been unanimous in their resolve to maintain the
OAU as an instrument of common policy, and it continues
to play a powerful role in African affairs.

When, in May, 1963, thirty African leaders signed the
Charter they immediately drew sceptical comments from
nations on other continents which had tried the same idea
and did not believe it could work. Indeed, the founding
conference itself was marred by complications arising from
the assassination of President Sylvanus Olympio of Togo,
which had just taken place.

Every conference since then has had its troubles, some of
which threatened to tear the Organisation apart. But time,
reason and goodwill have blown away many clouds and
reconciliations between African leaders have been as
frequent as their quarrels.

The idea of African unity goes back to the early days of
pan-Africanism—a movement originated in the last
century by American and West Indian negroes. It is deeply
rooted in the belief that Africans have a destiny and a
personality of their own, share the same cultural and
spiritual heritage and have a common stake in the future of
their continent. It is further strengthened by the conviction
that Africa's disunity was the cause of the misfortunes
which fell upon them in pre-colonial and colonial days.

Immediately after World War II the centre of
pan-Africanism moved to Britain and new political leaders
from Africa took over from the American and West
Indian Negroes. The sixth Pan-African Congress, held in
Manchester in October, 1945, was dominated by young,
unknown Africans soon to become great figures in their
own countries—Jomo Kenyatta (Kenya), Kwame
Nkrumah and Joe Appiah (Ghana), Nnamdi Azikiwe
and Chief S. L. Akintola (Nigeria), Wallace Johnson
(Sierra Leone) and many others.

Almost as soon as African territories became free their
leaders set out to implement the ideas of African unity.
The first conference of African states, held in Accra in
April, 1958, was attended by representatives of all the

eight countries which by then were governing themselves –
Egypt, Ethiopia, Ghana, Liberia, Morocco, Sudan and
Tunisia. It set the pattern for the score of conferences held
in subsequent years. The leaders fully agreed on both the
aims and principles of African unity, with all their
political, social, economic and cultural implications. They
pledged themselves to assist in the liberation of all other
African territories. They differed, however, in their
proposed methods.
Their divergent opinions became more apparent at the
second conference of African states, held in Addis Ababa in
June, 1960, with 15 countries now attending. Two
groups emerged, subsequently labelled 'radicals' and
'moderates'.
The one, led by Ghana and Guinea, called for an organic
integration of African states under a Continental
government. The other group, led by Nigeria, advocated
a phased, pragmatic approach, beginning with a
coordination of effort in every field, including foreign
affairs, economic development, health and education.
Both groups stood for non-alignment and for a joint
diplomacy with a view to Africa speaking with one voice
to the rest of the world.
The formal split occurred six months later when the
'radicals' – Egypt, Ghana, Guinea, Mali and Algeria
(represented by her provisional government-in-exile) as
well as Libya and Morocco – held their own conference
in Casablanca in January, 1961, and became known as
the Casablanca Group. Their proposed charter for African
states fell short of calling for a political union, but
provided for the establishment of an African Consultative
Assembly, 'as soon as conditions permit', and a Joint
High Command.
Meanwhile Ghana, Guinea and Mali had decided to
establish a 'union' of their three states, but did little to
implement it.
Shortly after the Casablanca conference, seven countries
sponsored an all-African 'summit' at which it was hoped
to reconcile the two schools of thought. The conference
was held in Monrovia, the Liberian capital, in May, 1961,
and was attended by 20 heads of state or government
who became known as the Monrovia Group. Six of the
seven Casablanca countries boycotted the meeting at the
last moment after saying they would attend; these included

Guinea and Mali, who had co-sponsored the conference. Twelve moderate French-speaking states, most of them members of the Monrovia group, had in the meantime formed another association – the African and Malagasy Union (UAM), which became known as the Brazzaville group.

The Monrovia conference defined the short term aim of African unity as 'not the political integration of sovereign states, but unity of aspiration and of action, considered from the point of view of African solidarity and political identity'.

The next attempt to find a concept of African unity acceptable to all independent countries on the continent (except, of course, South Africa) was at Lagos, the Nigerian capital, in January, 1962. The Casablanca countries again intimated their intention to attend but failed to so on the grounds that the Algerian government-in-exile had not been invited.

The Lagos conference adopted a charter for a proposed African unity organisation. However, it deliberately refrained from formally setting up the organisation so that the absentees could join as founder members at a later meeting.

In the following year, Emperor Haile Selassie of Ethiopia attempted for a third time to bring together all African heads of state and reconcile their divergent views on unity. The Emperor's diplomacy, backed by his personal prestige as head of Africa's oldest independent state, proved an unqualified success.

The Addis Ababa conference, held in May, 1963, was attended by the leaders of 30 African countries, the remaining two – Togo and Morocco – supporting it in principle. It achieved what a few months earlier had seemed to the world a Utopian dream – an association of all independent states in Africa. In the process it demonstrated the unanimous wish of African leaders to strive for unity and be prepared for compromise.

The charter was a slightly modified version of the document approved in principle by the Lagos conference. It incorporated five principles enunciated at Monrovia – absolute equality of all states, non-interference in internal affairs, respect for the sovereignty of each state, condemnation of subversive action by neighbouring states, and promotion of cooperation based on tolerance and non-acceptance of any leadership.

It pledged its signatories to a definite line of conduct both towards each other and towards the rest of the world. This included non-alignment with power blocs and cooperation in such fields as economic development, education, communications, health, internal security and defence. But it also made some concessions to 'revolutionary' or radical thought. These included a stronger line on South Africa and Portugal and the decision to bring the word 'unity' into the name of the new body, provisionally styled at Lagos the Inter-African Organisation. But Dr Nkrumah's proposals for steps leading to a Union government were given little consideration.

The establishment of the OAU involved the official winding up of both the Casablanca and Monrovia groups. The French-speaking UAM was also eventually wound up and turned into a regional economic grouping with cultural sidelines known as OCAM (Common Afro-Malagasy Organisation).

Perhaps the most important were the provisions of the charter dealing with relations and cooperation between member states. These included the establishment of a Commission of Mediation, Conciliation and Arbitration, to which member states pledged themselves to submit their disputes. It was instrumental in settling a number of border conflicts.

In the realm of diplomacy and foreign affairs, the African states agreed to coordinate their actions and set up an African Bureau at the United Nations with a view to taking a joint stand on both African and world issues. This made it possible, among other things, to increase the diplomatic pressure on Portugal and South Africa and bring about economic and arms' sanctions and other restrictions. It aimed at ostracising these two countries on a world scale by securing their exclusion from most international gatherings and organisations.

The conference also agreed to add military pressure to the diplomatic and political offensive against the two enemies of African nationalism, measures which were later extended to Rhodesia. These included a decision to encourage the training of young Africans from white-dominated countries on the territories of member states and to set up a nine-member Liberation Committee endowed with adequate funds to speed the downfall of racist regimes.

These fundamental aims were often obscured at later
meetings by splits over current disputes. The 1964 Cairo
meeting was nearly wrecked by the appearance of Moise
Tshombe at the head of a Congolese delegation. What
President Tubman described as Dr Nkrumah's 'hobby
of a Continental government' divided the 1965 meeting,
which was boycotted by five French-speaking states.
Ghana's detention of a Guinean delegation and President
Sekou Touré's subsequent refusal to attend the 1966
conference once more appeared to bring the Organisation
to the brink of catastrophe.

As with the United Nations, sessions of the OAU have
ended in uproar. Speakers have launched fierce attacks on
fellow delegates and there have been angry walk-outs.
Most of the leaders have on one occasion or another
expressed keen disappointment at some aspect of the
Organisation. Yet they all continue to give it their support.

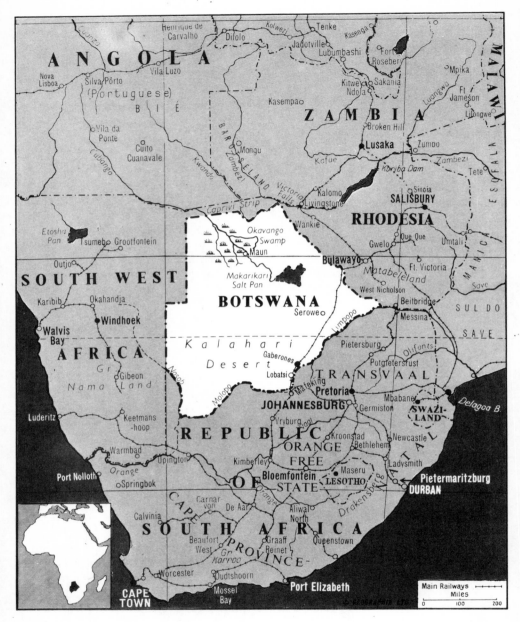

Botswana is 225,000 square miles of desert, swamp and scrubland completely land-locked, with a population, not evenly distributed, of 550,000. In the south and east it shares a long border with the Rep. of South Africa; in the north it borders on Rhodesia, a current focal point of the black-white struggle, and in the extreme north touches independent Zambia. In the west lies South West Africa, under the guardianship of South Africa. The capital is Gaberones. The economy of Botswana depends almost entirely upon cattle which provide about 85 per cent of its export earnings.

16

Botswana

Botswana is an African state almost entirely surrounded
by white-ruled countries in southern Africa.
Formerly the British Protectorate of Bechuanaland, it
became an independent republic within the Commonwealth
on September 30, 1966.
The country became a British Protectorate in 1885,
following an appeal to Queen Victoria by Khama III,
Christian Chief of the Bamangwato, when the lands of the
Batswana were menaced by the Boers advancing out of
the Transvaal.
The executive power of the Republic is vested in an
elected President (Sir Seretse Khama) who is head of
state and commander-in-chief of the armed forces.

A vast, arid, sparsely populated country, with
communications difficult and distances great, Botswana
has problems of poverty, hunger and lack of trained
personnel and equipment.
It is in the cockpit of the struggle between the forces of
black independence and white men determined to stay
and rule the land conquered or occupied by previous
generations.
Like Lesotho it is obliged to live within the currency and
customs area of South Africa, whose markets are
indispensable. Sir Seretse Khama would like Botswana
to become a bridge and a moderating influence between
two Africas. A remarkable feature of Botswana's political
progress has been the harmonious race relations between
the Africans and the relatively small European
population.
At the time of the 1964 census, the population of 550,000
included 535,275 Africans, 3,921 Europeans, 3,849
persons of mixed race and 420 Asians. The population
density is about 2·5 per square mile, compared with 12
for Zambia, 100 for Malawi and 34 for the Republic
of South Africa.
The Africans, with the exception of some 25,000 Bushmen,
are Batswana of Southern Sotho stock and are related to
the peoples of Lesotho. There are eight principal Batswana
tribes and Tswana is the most common African tongue,
the official language being English.
The bulk of the people live in the east, though one large
tribe inhabits the north-western corner. The Batswana

Government office blocks in the fast-growing new capital of Gaberones

The great sand-wastes of the Kalahari Desert which fan over most of western and southern Botswana

tribes are inclined to confine themselves to large villages or towns with names beginning with a 'B' – Bakgatla, Bakwena, Bangwaketse, Bamalette, Bamangwato, Barolong, Batawana and Batlokwa. About one half live in towns of more than 1,000 people.

The central, western and southern areas of the territory, consisting mainly of the Kalahari Desert, are very thinly populated. The desert is made up of vast expanses of sand-belts that rise and fall, with outcrops of limestone. Under the limestone, at a depth of between 30 and 100 feet, water is occasionally found and untapped reservoirs may lie there awaiting exploration.

19

Independence was preceded by a disastrous drought which destroyed 30 per cent of the national herd of cattle and caused great hardship to the people.

The hope that the country will not want for water is expressed in the light blue background on the national flag and the traditional greeting on the coat of arms – *Pula*, which means 'Let there be rain'.

The new capital, Gaberones, traditional meeting place of tribal chiefs, arose in startling modern style on the fringes of the Kalahari Desert. When the first construction team arrived there at the beginning of 1964 it was only a little known village. It was soon an impressive growing city with about 6,000 inhabitants. Britain paid £1,500,000, the cost of the white administrative buildings and nucleus for the virtually non-existent commerce and industry. The central lay-out is fan-shaped, with the Ministries grouped together and a prestige Parliament housed in the centre with curved canopy and gleaming metal doors.

There are offices, banks, schools and hospitals and a traffic-free business and shopping precinct. Only one hotel was open when the independence celebrations were held in the presence of representatives of about 40 nations. There were no bars or restaurants and only five telephone lines to the outside world.

Gaberones has the great advantage of a water supply. This is expected to continue even in the worst drought as a result of a dam across the Notwani River.

The largest towns are Kanye and Serowe, each with some 34,000 inhabitants, Molepolole with 29,000 and Mochudi with 17,700. The principal business centres are Lobatsi and Francistown. Mafeking, in South Africa, 40 miles away, was the capital until South Africa left the Commonwealth in 1960.

CHIEF BATHOEN II

The newly-born Republic of Botswana, as it emerges slowly from its ancient feudalism, has come face to face with a common African problem: resistance to change in the land tenure system which vests control in the tribal chief.

At the head of this resistance stands a small, bespectacled, sparrow-like chief, Bathoen II of the Bangwaketse, who believes that Sir Seretse Khama's Government is breaking down the old, traditional tribal structure too quickly.

Chief Bathoen rules his 71,000-

Sir Seretse Khama

strong Bangwaketse from Kanye –the largest town in the Republic even including Gaberones, the capital.

As Botswana's senior tribal chief and head of one of the country's strongest tribes, he wields great influence in the House of Chiefs, without whose cooperation the Government cannot change laws affecting tribal matters, such as land ownership.

'I have seen many changes, and not all of them are good,' he said late in 1966. 'Our tribal way of life is giving way to what people call Western civilisation, and this will have a seriously disruptive effect throughout the country.'

The Chief has seen his own powers eroded in common with those of other chiefs and fears that the Government intends eventually to eliminate the chieftaincy from the country's administration. Power over tribal lands constitutes his last effective weapon in the fight for survival, and he is using it with grim determination.

Born at Kanye, in Botswana's southernmost tribal area, in 1916, Chief Bathoen received his secondary education in the neighbouring Republic of South Africa. He has visited Zambia, Rhodesia, Kenya, Uganda, Tanzania, Nigeria and Britain.

SIR SERETSE KHAMA

The first President of Botswana, Sir Seretse Khama was born on July 1, 1921, to a position of feudal power.

He was less than five years old when he inherited the chieftainship of the Bamangwato tribe, to which more than a third of the population belong, following the brief reign of his father, Sekgoma II.

His uncle, Tshekedi Khama, who was 21, became Regent. It was decided to give the small boy an education fitting him to play an important part in modern Africa and world politics. He went first to University College at Fort Hare, South Africa, and then to the University of Witwatersrand before going to England to read law, politics and economics at Balliol College, Oxford.

In September, 1948, while completing his law studies at the Middle Temple, London, he married an English girl, Ruth Williams. Now Lady Khama, she was formerly a secretary at Lloyds, the world-wide marine insurance organisation.

Their marriage precipitated a bitter and stormy racial controversy which lasted seven years. Tshekedi and many of the Bamangwato elders were sure it would split the tribe and place the chieftainship in jeopardy. The British Government, administering the Protectorate from Mafeking, across the border in South Africa, was considerably embarrassed, and for six years Seretse was exiled from Bechuanaland.

Seretse eventually renounced for himself and his children all right to the chieftainship and in 1956 was allowed to return in the tribe's interest, it being agreed that he should be allowed to take part as a private person in political life.

He concentrated upon the welfare of the tribe before founding five years later the Bechuanaland Democratic Party. The aim of this party was to achieve an African share of government that would reflect the racial ratio and foster cooperation between African and European.

It swept the polls in the first

Quett Masire

general election under universal suffrage on March 2, 1965. Seretse thus won back as a political leader what he had lost as an hereditary ruler.

He has four children, one girl and three boys, and is a comparatively wealthy man, owning large herds of cattle.

In 1963 the Bamangwato tribe agreed that Seretse's sons should not be excluded from assuming the chieftainship if they wished to do so when they came of age.

The policy of his Government is to maintain a non-racial democratic state in which, he has said, 'no form of discrimination, whether political, social or economic, will be permitted against any racial group'.

This multi-racialism is represented in the design of the national flag with its black and white bands.

Well aware of the grave difficulties ahead of the new Republic, Sir Seretse Khama said in an Independence Day message that his country had been receiving aid for many years and it was perfectly clear that for many years to come they should continue to be dependent on the generosity of the United Kingdom and others.

QUETT MASIRE

Quett Masire, Botswana's Deputy Prime Minister, is a slightly-built, athletic, self-styled 'amateur politician' whose main preoccupation in life is farming.

He has a ready smile and is quick to laugh. His approach to life is honest and forthright. 'I am an amateur politician and can therefore afford to have principles. In a sense, my farm guarantees my principles,' he said late in 1966, when he was 41.

A personal friend of the President, Sir Seretse Khama,

Masire helped him found the Bechuanaland Democratic Party in 1962 and at the inaugural meeting, held at Gaberones under the shade of a giant marula tree, he was appointed first secretary-general of the party.

Mr Masire is in a very real sense the 'shadow' of the President. Talking politics, building the party, winning the pre-election in-fighting, planning for independence – Quett Masire has been at his chief's side throughout.

He carries the brunt of the political hustings and shoulders the main burden in Parliamentary debates.

Born at Kanye, on the fringe of the Kalahari Desert on July 23, 1925, Quett Masire was educated at Tiger Kloof, in the Transvaal, South Africa. He was in turn a school teacher and a journalist before entering politics. 'But,' he explains, 'I am really a farmer who has been drawn into politics.'

As a farmer he achieved the distinction of being the first man in Botswana to be awarded the Department of Agriculture's official 'Master Farmer' certificate in 1957.

Of his first love, Mr Masire says, 'The earth is all we have here; it is the basis of our economy.'

PHILIP MATANTE

Philip Parcel Goannwe Matante, leader of Botswana's attenuated Parliamentary Opposition, is a pan-Africanist whose private interpretation of African nationalism has led him to a theory of racial separation.

Matante, known in his Bechuanaland People's Party as 'the Lion of Botswana', is the firmest friend in Botswana, and possibly in all southern Africa, of the pan-Africanist movement which used to be headed by Ghana's ex-President, Dr Kwame Nkrumah.

As with many other southern African politicians, little is known of Matante prior to his entry into politics. Even his date of birth and birthplace are unknown, although it is said he comes from the Republic of South Africa.

An enigmatic blend of extreme affability in private and of violent statements in public, Mr Matante is anathema to many of Botswana's whites, especially to the Afrikaners among them.

He vehemently denies being anti-white, but his statements sometimes disturb the people concerned. In 1964 he said: 'We (the BPP) say that Africa is the land of the Africans, from the Cape to Cairo, from Morocco to Malagasy. Does this suggest that we are racialists? We believe that we are all one race: the human race.

'We say to hell with multi-racialism, because it seeks to en-trench racialism in our country.'

A gifted orator, Matante is superb in the way he handles a crowd and has a shrewdness which stands out in Botswana politics. But these gifts have proved of little avail against the strongly entrenched traditionalism of the Botswana people, and at the 1965 general elections his party managed to return only three candidates against the ruling party's 28.

Pessimistic about his party's chances at the next general elections, Matante was occupying himself late in 1966 with helping political refugees arriving almost weekly at the famous 'White House' refuge near his Francistown home. These consisted mainly of Africans from South Africa, South West Africa and Rhodesia.

'The Lion of Botswana' bided his time, pinning his political hopes on traditionally agricultural Botswana's slowly increasing number of industrial workers, from whom he was drawing his main support.

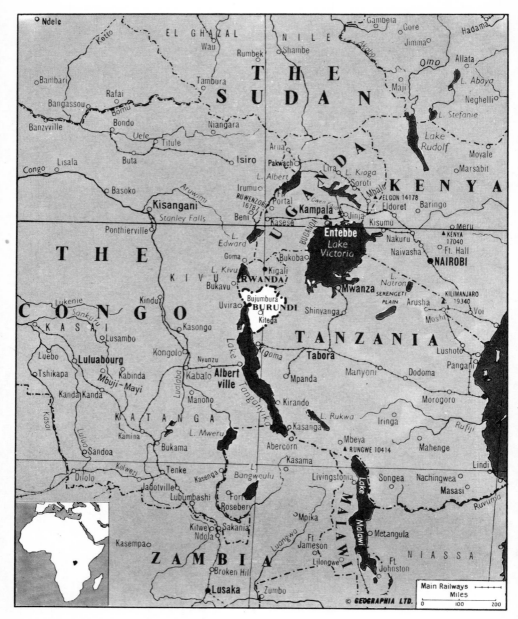

One of Africa's smallest states, landlocked Burundi covers an area of 10,747 square miles and has a population of about three million. Tanzania lies to the east and south, Rwanda to the north and Congo Kinshasa to the west. It has the advantage of being able to use Lake Tanganyika for its trade with the outside world via Dar es Salaam. The capital is Bujumbura.

Burundi's economy is based on agriculture, with coffee the main crop. Other products include cotton, rice and sugar cane. Beneath Lake Tanganyika is one of the world's richest deposits of natural gas.

24

Burundi

On July 1, 1962, Burundi became independent of the trusteeship granted to Belgium by the United Nations in 1918.
King Mwambutsa IV was deposed by his 19 year-old son, who became Ntare V, in July, 1966.
King Ntare was overthrown by Captain (later Colonel) Michel Micombero, aged 26, on November 28, 1966. A Republican Government was established by the 12-man National Revolutionary Committee.

The tiny Republic of Burundi was for 42 years part of the Belgian-administered trusteeship territory of Ruanda-Urundi which became independent as the separate states of Rwanda and Burundi.

It is a beautiful country, especially in the mountains from which there are magnificent views over Lake Tanganyika. Bujumbura is a pleasant city set in a corner of the lake between high peaks, emerald green with luxuriant vegetation.

The Kings (Mwamis) of the Tutsi race traditionally ruled the country now known as Burundi as early as the 16th century. In modern times it has experienced occupation by both Germans and Belgians.

The first Europeans to reach the fabled 'Mountains of the Moon', thought by the ancients to be the source of the Nile, were the explorers Sir Richard Burton and John Hanning Speke (1858). In 1871, Sir Henry Morton Stanley and David Livingstone arrived at the source of the Nile and Lake Tanganyika. The White Fathers of Cardinal Lavigerie followed in 1879.

The Duke of Mecklenburg began his conquest of Rwanda and Burundi in 1892. He incorporated the territories in German East Africa.

In 1918, at the end of World War I, the German colonies were dissolved by the Allies and the League of Nations gave Belgium the trusteeship of Rwanda and Burundi. The United Nations confirmed the mandate in 1946. In 1959 the Belgian Government decided to prepare the territories for independence by granting internal autonomy. In the following year commissariats were created as a basis for future ministries and the first communal elections.

Legislative elections were held in 1961 and independence declared on July 1, 1962.

Opposite:
Modern administrative
buildings in
Bujumbura.
Below: On the outskirts
of the capital stands
the Jesuit College of
the Holy Spirit, built
largely through
Belgian aid; in the
foreground, a group of
traditional dwellings.

Burundi's population is split up into two main ethnic
groups – the Hutu (85 per cent) and the giant,
conquering Tutsi (14 per cent) – with the pygmy Twa
making up the remaining one per cent.

Power has always been in the hands of the Tutsi
and their princes, but the country has been plagued
continuously by rivalries between different royal families
for the succession to the throne, with the former Mwamis
(Kings) attempting to exterminate rival clans.

As independence approached, and influenced no doubt
by the Rwanda social revolution, members of the Tutsi
tribe opposed to the reigning Mwami (of the Ntare clan)
founded the Christian Democratic Party ('Parti
Démocratique Chrétien'), known as the PDC, which they
tried to persuade the Hutu to join.

The Belgians supported the PDC. It obtained a majority
at the general elections in January, 1961, defeating the
conservative 'Uprona' ('Parti de l'Unité et du Progrès
National') and numerous small Hutu splinter parties.

But at the legislative elections in September, 1961, under
the control of the United Nations Organisation, Uprona,
which had campaigned in support of the Mwami
Mwambutsa IV, still revered and feared as a god by the
people, obtained its revenge.

It obtained a majority of the votes and the Mwami's son,
Prince Louis Rwagasore, the main force behind the
Uprona, became head of the Government.

Only one month later, however, the Prince was assassinated
at a lakeside restaurant, allegedly by a paid henchman of
his political opponents, Joseph Biroli and Jean-Baptiste
Ntidentereza, members of the PDC and Ntare clan. They
were first sentenced to life imprisonment and later, after
independence, were tried again and executed. The actual
assassin, a Greek-born shop assistant, had been sentenced
and executed by a firing squad.

The Prince was succeeded by a member of the Uprona
party, M. Muhirwa, son-in-law of the Mwami.

The Government took severe repressive measures against
the opposing Tutsi clans and leaders of the popular
parties and trade unions. The president of the Christian
trade unions and several of his colleagues were assassinated.
Other Hutus were imprisoned or fled the country.

But the Uprona party itself continued to be divided
between Tutsi leaders of different tendencies, some of whom

Spear dance to
the throb of
Burundi drums

remained loyal to the reigning royal family, while others
adopted extreme leftist views.

In the four years between 1962, when the country
became independent, and 1966, seven Governments
followed each other in rapid succession, all of them in
Opposition to the Parliament in which the Hutu had a
majority.

The Mwami Mwambutsa IV, who spent most of his time
in Europe, went home from time to time to give
decisions and to replace his Ministers.

The second and the third Prime Ministers, both of them
Hutu, Ngendandunwe and Bamina, were assassinated.

An abortive uprising in September, 1965, was followed by
extremely severe repressive measures by the Commander-
in-Chief of the Army, Captain Michel Micombero, who
was appointed Secretary of State by the Mwami.

The Mwami left for Europe immediately after the
attempted *coup d'état* and refused to go back to Burundi.
After all attempts to persuade him to return had failed,
his young son, brought up in Switzerland, was recalled to
succeed him with the title of Mwami Ntare V. Micombero
was given the post of Prime Minister.

But new dissensions quickly arose between the young
Mwami Ntare and certain members of the Government. In
October, 1966, some of them were imprisoned or fled
and a new Government was formed by Ntare.

Ntare ordered the dissolution of Parliament and tried in
vain to get rid of his military prime minister. On
November 28, 1966, Captain Micombero overthrew the
king while the latter was on an official visit to Kinshasa
and proclaimed a republic with himself as President.

A 12-man National Revolutionary Committee set up to
rule the country later promoted Micombero to colonel.
The property of the two deposed kings was sequestrated
and nationalised. There were changes in the flag,
national emblems and the national anthem. Street names
were altered.

The National Revolutionary Committee said, 'The epoch
of idleness is over. The era of the bicycle and of walking
is instituted.'

Radio Burundi, re-christened 'Voice of the Revolution',
said ex-King Mwambutsa received an allowance of
500,000 francs (£2,000) a month, plus 5,000 francs (£20)
a day expenses.

Col Michel Micombero

Mwambutsa IV

COLONEL
MICHEL MICOMBERO

Colonel Michel Micombero, President of Burundi, head of the Government and Commander-in-Chief of the Army, was born in 1940. He is a Tutsi, a member of the Hima clan.

He became Burundi's first president after ousting Mwami (king) Ntare V in a military *coup* (November 28, 1966).

Educated at the Catholic College of St Esprit in Bujumbura, where he was a brilliant pupil, Micombero proved to have a determined and tenacious character even at so early an age.

He went on to spend two years at the Brussels Military Academy, but when his country became independent in 1962 he and his fellow countrymen at the Academy were recalled to help maintain order in Burundi. They never returned to Belgium.

A police officer with the rank of captain, he soon became Minister of National Defence.

After the abortive uprising of September, 1965, he was appointed chief of the secretaries of state by the Mwami Mwambutsa IV and took severe repressive measures against the Hutu leaders of the rebellion.

Micombero surrounded himself with members of his own clan and region as well as young Tutsi who had been educated abroad.

His first measures included the reduction of ministerial salaries, stringent steps to stop diamond smuggling, and forcing politicians to work.

Appointed Prime Minister on the accession of the young Mwami Ntare V in July, 1966, Micombero dissolved Parliament in agreement with the Mwami and replaced elected communal representatives, most of them Hutu, by appointed administrators mainly of Tutsi origin.

But Micombero soon clashed with Ntare, whom he accused of following the worldly ways of his exiled father.

Ntare tried to gain the upper hand by changing some of his Ministers, but this proved of no avail. During a visit by Ntare to Kinshasa, Micombero seized power and set up a military revolutionary council. He also dismissed the provincial governors and replaced them by military governors.

Shortly after his *coup*, Micombero liberated a number of Hutu political prisoners but kept in prison several former Ministers.

Since he became President of the Republic, Colonel Micombero has expressed liberal views which show that he wants to put an end to the tribal feuds which have plagued Burundi. In his inaugural address he made clear that he was opposed to the feudal clans and favoured popular progress.

MWAMBUTSA IV

Mwambutsa IV was on the throne during the long period of Belgian trusteeship which ended with independence in 1962. He was 55 when he was ousted by his son.

Born in 1912, he was only three years old when he began his reign during World War I. He is a member of the giant Tutsi race, once undisputed feudal lords of the country. Unlike his fellow tribesmen, however, Mwambutsa is only of average height. He maintains a private apartment in a fashionable residential quarter in Geneva. Elegantly attired in European style, sometimes in a dazzlingly white uniform, he dines in fashionable hotels and visits winter sports resorts.

Ntare V

During his reign King Mwambutsa was described as a moderate and enlightened ruler, popular both with the Tutsi and the majority of the Hutu tribe, who constitute 85 per cent of Burundi's population. He seemed to be holding a balance between the aristocratic Tutsi and their former serfs. But as Belgian trusteeship neared its end and independence came closer, strife between the two tribes led to bloodshed.

In 1961, the Mwami's eldest son and heir to the throne, Prince Louis Rwagasore, became Prime Minister but within months of taking office on October 14 was shot dead as he dined at a lakeside restaurant.

The turmoil of 1965 led to an unsuccessful army revolt in Bujumbura, in which the Mwami was forced to flee his besieged palace and escape into the nearby Congo, never to return.

On November 6, 1965, King Mwambutsa arrived in Geneva. The accompanying official described his visit as a private one, expected to last only two or three weeks. There was no official welcome at the airport for the king and his suite before they drove off in two taxis along the road to exile.

Mwambutsa had just been on a holiday trip to Brussels and Madrid when he received the news, on his return to Geneva, that his son had deposed him.

The Crown Prince had been studying in nearby Lausanne until he flew back via Paris to Bujumbura to seize power.

During the period between the prince's announcement that he had taken over in Burundi and his enthronement, Mwambutsa contacted him several times both by telephone and letter, asking him to change his mind.

NTARE V

Ntare V was enthroned on September 1, 1966, after deposing his father, King Mwambutsa IV.

Better known as Crown Prince Charles (Ndizeye), he assumed the name of his country's first monarch, who reigned in the 16th century and was reputed to have once killed a lion with a single stroke of an axe.

He seized power from his father, who was living in Geneva, at the beginning of July, 1966. He dismissed the Government of M. Léopold Biha, the Prime Minister, and gave further notice that he planned reforms for the country.

Mwambutsa maintained that he was still ruler and that his 19 year-old son was being tricked into an internal power struggle by scheming extremist politicians who were profiting from his inexperience.

In a newspaper interview the young prince had expressed advanced views on reform, pledging that he would ensure justice and social welfare, create work and fight corruption. After the takeover, he explained that his action was because of the continued absence of his father and the necessity to give direction to the country. He promised a new constitution as soon as possible and formed a new Government under Premier Michel Micombero.

In March, 1966 Mwambutsa, while in Europe, had conferred special powers on his son and set up a royal commission to draft a new constitution. One of the decrees said that because the King was obliged by health reasons to prolong his stay in Europe, the Crown Prince was authorised to control and coordinate governmental activities.

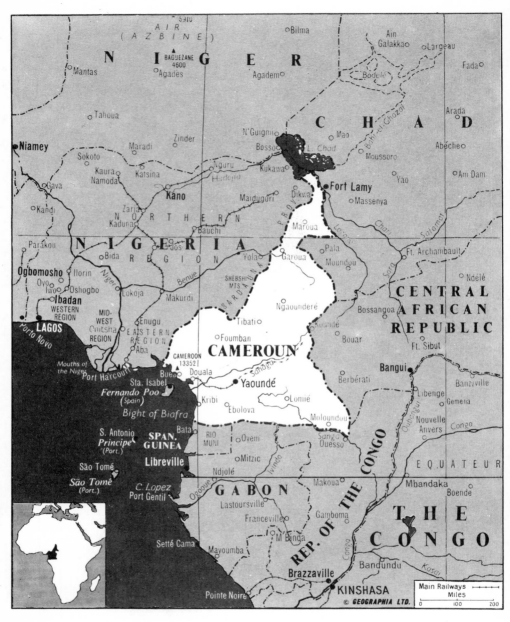

About six million people (1965 estimate) live in an area of 183,381 square miles. With a coastline on the Atlantic, the Federal Republic of the Cameroun has frontiers with Nigeria in the north, the Central African Republic in the east and Spanish Guinea, Gabon and Congo Brazzaville in the south. The Federal capital is Yaoundé. The country's main income is derived from exports of cocoa, coffee, bananas and timber. The major growing industry is the processing of bauxite to alumina.

32

Cameroun

The Cameroun became an independent republic on January 1, 1960, after 75 years of German, French and British rule.

Kamerun, a German colony since 1884, was occupied by French and British troops in 1916, during World War I. When peace came the colony was divided (1919), as a League of Nations mandate between Britain and France, the latter receiving the greater part. The mandate became a United Nations trusteeship after World War II.

The portion assigned to Britain consisted of two parts (northern and southern). A plebiscite in the northern part (February, 1961), which had been administered as part of Nigeria, decided in favour of joining the Federation of Nigeria (145,265 votes) and against joining the Cameroun Republic (97,654 votes).

The people of Southern Cameroon decided in a plebiscite to join the Cameroun Republic (135,830 votes to some 30,000). In October, 1961, the territory combined in the Federal Republic of the Cameroun.

Under the federal constitution, the President is chief of state and commander of the armed forces. He is elected for five years. He appoints the premiers of the two provincial assemblies. There is a Vice-President for the Federation and a Cabinet whose members must not be members of Parliament. The National Federal Assembly, elected by universal adult suffrage, consists of 40 representatives for East Cameroun and ten for West Cameroun.

Born under the threat of violence, the Cameroun Republic has shown itself a moderate and moderating force in African affairs.

Within its frontiers exist many of the diverse elements that make up the character of Africa, and the Republic's history constitutes a model exercise in African unity. French-speaking and English-speaking Africa joined forces there (until the end of World War I, British and French Cameroon were both part of the German Kamerun) and the Moslem-dominated north and Christian-dominated south work together within the country's ruling party, the 'Union Camerounaise'.

Geographically the country varies through some of the thickest rain forest in Africa on the southern coast to arid, sub-Saharan grasslands in the north.

It maintains good relations with France, which has

subsidised much of its post-independence development, and cooperates with the other former French African territories in such collective organisations as OCAM (the Common Afro-Malagasy Organisation) and UDEAC (the Equatorial Africa Customs Union).

Much of the credit for transforming the Cameroun from a country racked in its southern regions by terrorist incidents to the almost completely peaceful land it is today must go to its first President, Ahmadou Ahidjo, a northerner.

The Cameroun revolt began in 1955 around the port region of Douala, which had had most contact with European education. From there it spread quickly northward to the hilly, Swiss canton-like tribal regions of the Bamileke. Here there was already considerable discontent caused by land shortage and the breakdown of old tribal systems.

The French Army set out to suppress the revolt, in which a number of French nationals, particularly on remote coffee and banana plantations, were killed. Two years later the revolt was still going on. The casualty figures for September, 1957 to September, 1958, show that 75 civilians and 400 rebels were killed.

By this time the Cameroun already had an autonomous Government under Prime Minister André Mbida, a southerner. However, Mbida's suppression of the revolt was making him unpopular in the National Assembly,

The Post Office at Douala, Cameroun's main port

which wanted increased efforts to negotiate with the party at the head of the revolt, the Union of Cameroun Peoples (UPC).

Mbida fell and his place was taken by Ahidjo, his Vice-Premier. As head of the most unified bloc in the Assembly, the 28 northerners, Ahidjo was able to form a coalition. His party, the Cameroun Union, was originally a northern party but was eventually to expand to cover the whole country.

Ahidjo offered an amnesty to the rebels and a number of influential figures abandoned terrorism and came over to his side. Despite this, the most militant sections of the UPC, led by Rueben Um Nyobe in the forests and Dr Felix Moumie abroad, continued to hold out.

The year 1958 saw a dramatic change in the fortunes of the revolt. Nyobe was killed in September and 2,000 rebels surrendered. Moumie was later to die of poisoning in Geneva in mysterious circumstances.

When the Cameroun became independent on January 1, 1960, there was considerable nervousness for its future, but the revolt was already dying down to isolated incidents of violence.

Ahidjo has preferred 'kid glove' tactics for ruling the many different peoples of the Republic, but he has not hesitated to expose a mailed fist when he thought the country needed it. In 1962 he made the former French Cameroun into a one-party state and arrested the leaders

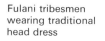

Fulani tribesmen wearing traditional head dress

of other parties who disagreed, including Mbida himself. A softly-spoken and self-effacing man, he has set his face resolutely against nepotism and tribalism. Although a northerner, his presidential offices are staffed largely by southerners.

One of the successes of his Government was the integration of the former British Southern Cameroon into the Republic. The people voted to join the Cameroun rather than Nigeria in a United Nations-sponsored referendum in 1961. This was a complex process involving changes in currency, customs regulations and even the side of the road to be used by motorists (the whole country now drives on the right-hand side).

The Cameroun's preoccupation with internal affairs since independence has prevented it from making the same spectacular economic expansion as the Ivory Coast, a country with which it has many geographic similarities.

Yet the country remains a vital transit area for goods coming to and from the landlocked territories of Chad and the Central African Republic. Its importance has been greatly increased with plans to extend the Trans-Cameroun railway to both these countries.

Ahmadou Ahidjo

AHMADOU AHIDJO

President Ahmadou Ahidjo's career took shape around a firm belief in the feasibility of uniting Cameroun's feuding tribal factions into a single nation.

He has been known above all for his calm – attributed to his upbringing as a member of the northern Moslem Fulani tribe – even in the face of tribal strife, widespread terrorism and threatened assassination.

When he signed the independence agreement with France in 1960 for Eastern Cameroun, the hitherto French-ruled land was torn by internecine warfare and terrorism.

Few people then believed that a new nation could be built round the warring factions. But by the time he came up for re-election to a second presidential term in 1965, Cameroun had achieved what became known to many as the 'Ahidjo miracle'.

Following unification with the formerly British-administered Western Cameroon in 1961, the Federal Republic grew steadily to achieve recognition as a politically and economically viable nation.

During that period, all political movements were drawn together in a single party, the Cameroun National Union – a far cry from the immediate pre-independence days when Ahidjo's life was menaced by extremists opposing the terms for self-rule.

Ahidjo was born in August, 1924 at Garoua, northern Cam-

Benoit Bindzi

eroun. He became a radio operator at the age of 18, moving later into politics.

Elected to the first Assembly of the French trust territory of Eastern Cameroun in 1947, he remained closely associated with plans for its future constitutional progress.

In 1953 he became a councillor in the Assembly of the French Union, and its secretary the following year.

Meanwhile, he kept moving upwards in prestige and power on the domestic political scene, and in 1957 was elected President (Chairman) of the Cameroun Assembly.

He was appointed Deputy Prime Minister of the first pre-independence Government.

On February 18, 1958, when André-Marie Mbida resigned after a cabinet crisis, he succeeded him as Prime Minister and head of government.

In this post, he took Eastern Cameroun into independence on January 1, 1960.

He was re-elected head of government in the general elections of April, 1960, and the National Assembly proclaimed him President of the Republic of Cameroun on May 5 that year.

When Cameroun and the ex-British-administered territory of Western Cameroon were united as the Federal Republic of Cameroun in 1961, M. Ahidjo remained President, and was re-elected for a second term in general elections on March 20, 1965.

His stated aims are cooperation with all nations, and self-reliance for Cameroun.

He has travelled widely, exchanging views with other national leaders, and signing agreements with the USSR and with Western countries.

In 1966 he made a pilgrimage to Mecca, and later the same year discussed world events with Pope Paul in Rome.

His international views and aims can be summed up in his own words, delivered at a press conference during a state visit to Britain in 1953: 'All Africans believe passionately in the final liberation of the whole African continent from the aftermath of colonialism.'

BENOIT BINDZI

Benoit Bindzi, Minister of Foreign Affairs, has spent all his working life in government service and has had wide diplomatic experience at home and abroad.

He headed his country's delegation to the United Nations from 1961–64 and again in 1966. In 1963 he was Vice-President of the General Assembly's 18th session.

M. Bindzi, born in 1924 at Ekok, went to school in Mbalmayo, Yaoundé, and to a Catholic college in Akono before joining the Customs department in 1944.

He held senior posts, including deputy controller at Douala, the main port, and was appointed Principal Secretary to the Minister of Economic Affairs in 1958.

After being attached to the French Foreign Office in Paris for special training, and later to the French Embassy in Bonn, he returned home in 1960 as Principal Secretary to the Foreign Minister.

He took up the United Nations post following a period as head of protocol at the Foreign Office in 1960–61.

On his return from New York he was given his first appointment as Minister of Information. He took over the Foreign Ministry in July, 1966.

Dr Emmanuel Endeley

John Ngu Foncha

SADOU DAOUDOU

Sadou Daoudou, Minister of Defence and acting Minister of Information, entered the Civil Service straight from college in 1948.

For ten years he served as a regional administrative official in various outlying areas.

He moved to the Prime Minister's department in 1958 as Principal Secretary and two years later won a seat in the Cameroun National Assembly in the first post-independence elections (1960).

He was appointed Minister of Defence in 1961. He became acting Information Minister in December, 1966, following the dismissal and imprisonment of former Information Minister, Victor Kanga.

DR EMMANUEL ENDELEY

Dr Emmanuel Mbela Lifaffe Endeley led the Government of Southern Cameroons for its first four years as a separate region in the Nigerian Federation.

He was leader of Government Business until he was formally installed as first Prime Minister in 1958. He narrowly lost office in elections in January, 1959, to M. Foncha's Kamerun National Democratic Party.

Dr Endeley, born in 1916, has played a major part throughout the constitutional development of Cameroun. He remained leader of the Opposition in West Cameroun until he took his Cameroons People's National Congress into the four-party merger in 1966.

He was educated at a government school at Buea and later studied science in Nigeria. After dropping plans to study agricultural methods, he qualified as a doctor in 1942.

Five years later he became a trade union leader on being asked urgently to reorganise the workers of the one year-old Cameroons Development Corporation – and from that time emerged as an important political leader.

In 1951 he was elected to the Nigerian Eastern Region's Assembly, where British Cameroons was represented.

Dr Endeley was among the group who worked to have the territory made a separate region and, when this was done, unsuccessfully threw his weight behind keeping it as a separate region in the Nigerian Federation.

The people finally rejected this view in 1961 by voting overwhelmingly in a plebiscite for unification with the Republic of Cameroun.

JOHN NGU FONCHA

Vice-President John Ngu Foncha, known as a man of tireless energy, has been from the start of his political career a single-minded campaigner for unification of the two Cameroons – formerly British and French.

Typical of his determined approach was the 1959 election campaign when he defeated Dr Emmanuel Endeley in the premiership race in Western Cameroun, despite having to campaign with both collar-bones strapped up and in plaster following a car accident.

Born in 1916 in the Bamenda area of Western Cameroun, he studied and later taught in Catholic schools under the British Administration.

He was active in organising teacher groups, and this interest led gradually to politics.

In 1951, he founded the National Congress of United Cameroun, arguing vigorously

Augustin Ngom Jua

before a visiting United Nations mission in favour of a return to the geographical entity of pre-1914, the German Kamerun.

But a split developed within his party, with several colleagues – including Dr Endeley – preferring straight inclusion of Western Cameroun into the Federation of Nigeria.

In 1955, M. Foncha quit his own party to found another – the Kamerun National Democratic Party (KNDP).

After success in the 1959 elections, he and the party devoted themselves wholeheartedly to a campaign for unification of the two Cameroons. When this merger was achieved in 1961, M. Foncha became Vice-President of the new Federal Republic of Cameroun.

In 1965, running with President Ahidjo, he was elected for a second five-year term.

Throughout his political life, he has been an advocate of a single strong party grouping all political movements within the country, as achieved in the present Cameroun National Union.

He is a devout Roman Catholic.

DR JEAN-CLAUDE HAPPI

Dr Jean-Claude Happi, Federal General Commissioner for Public Health, (appointed in May, 1965) is an eminent medical practitioner who has held many senior posts since leaving Paris University in 1957.

He was born in Bana, French Cameroons, in 1927. He started his education locally but went to France where he completed his schooling in Cannes.

He gained a scholarship to study medicine at Paris University and presented a doctoral thesis in 1957.

In 1958 Dr Happi became medical superintendent of Yaoundé Hospital and then served in the Ministry of Public Health before being appointed Director of Public Health for Cameroun in 1963.

Dr Happi has served a term on the executive council of the United Nations World Health Organisation.

AUGUSTIN NGOM JUA

Augustin Ngom Jua, Prime Minister of West Cameroun, was a teacher for 16 years before turning to politics.

Together with Vice-President Foncha he is a founder-member of the Kamerun National Democratic Party.

Prior to his present appointment in 1965 he was Secretary of State for Finance in West Cameroun. He was born in 1924 at Bamenda, West Cameroun.

DR VICTOR KANGA

Dr Victor Kanga, a law graduate of Paris University, held several important ministerial posts before being dismissed from the Cabinet and then imprisoned in 1966.

He was the Federation's first Minister of National Economy. Later appointments were as Finance Minister and then as Minister of Information and Tourism.

In December, 1966, a court sentenced him to four years' imprisonment and stripped him of his political rights for five years, having found him guilty of publishing anti-Government rumours – pamphlets alleging misuse of funds by high officials.

He was born at Banka, French Cameroons, in 1931, and finished his higher education in France. He took the degree of doctor of law at Paris University.

André-Marie Mbida

Marcel Mboua

Salomon Tandeng
Muna

After working in the Civil Service he was elected to the French Cameroons House of Representatives in 1958.

Soon afterwards he became a senior secretary to the Minister of Education, becoming Minister of Justice in the Cameroun Cabinet in 1960.

Following unification, Dr Kanga was appointed Minister of National Economy in the new Federal Cabinet.

He was later appointed Minister of Finance and then he became Minister of Information and Tourism in July, 1966.

ANDRE-MARIE MBIDA

André-Marie Mbida, leader of the first African Government in the French Cameroons, has featured little in public life since his release from prison.

In 1962 he was one of four prominent politicians convicted on charges of threatening internal security. They served two and a half years.

M. Mbida, a dynamic man who became an eloquent speaker through wide experience as defending counsel in the law courts, was born about 1917 at Endinding.

He was elected to the Territorial Assembly in 1952 as leader of the 'Bloc Démocratique Camerounais'.

Urging close links with France and independence by progressive stages, he won the elections in 1957 for the first Legislative Assembly and became Prime Minister.

His Government fell early in 1958 amid criticism that he was too authoritarian and making too little progress towards independence.

He went into self-imposed exile in Conakry and supported the banned Cameroun People's Union, against whom he had used strong measures while in office.

He broke this association and returned home when his successor as premier, M. Ahmadou Ahidjo, offered a general political amnesty to mark independence.

He founded a new party, 'Démocrates Camerounais', which won 10 seats in the 1960 elections. He joined a Government coalition, although refused a Ministry for himself.

His party's three Ministers resigned some months later over a policy dispute. The party has never been dissolved, but is not among the four that merged in 1960 to form a single national party.

Since his release from prison M. Mbida has spent much time in Paris having eye treatment for an old complaint.

MARCEL MBOUA

Marcel Marigoh Mboua has been President of the Federal National Assembly since 1962.

He was a member of the Territorial Assembly of French Cameroons and held office as Minister of Labour and Social Affairs in 1957–58.

The newly-formed Cameroun National Union elected him at its first meeting in August, 1966, as president of its executive committee.

He was born in 1921 at Batouri and is a teacher by profession.

SALOMON TANDENG MUNA

Salomon Tandeng Muna, Federal Minister of Posts and Telecommunications, ranked high among the main figures in the campaign for unification.

He was born in 1912 in

Lt-Col Pierre Semengue

Dr Simon-Pierre
Tchoungui

Bamenda district, attended local schools, then between teaching jobs studied at a local teachers' college and at London University's Institute of Education.

Abandoning teaching after 20 years, he campaigned for the Kamerun National Congress party, winning a seat in Nigeria's Eastern Region Assembly, where Southern Cameroons was represented.

He became Public Works Minister but resigned in 1953, afterwards devoting himself to recognition for Southern Cameroons as a separate region. After separation from Nigeria he was re-elected and made Executive Council Member for Natural Resources in 1954.

He broke from this Government in 1957 because he advocated early independence followed by unification with the French-administered Cameroons. His party leader, Dr Emmanuel Endeley, favoured remaining in the Nigerian Federation.

He joined M. Foncha's Kamerun National Democratic Party, which favoured unification, and regained office when the party defeated Dr Endeley in 1959.

M. Muna became Minister of Public Works, then Minister of Trade and Industry and in mid-1961 took over from the British administrators as the territory's first African Finance Minister.

In October, 1961, he became Minister for Transport, Mining and Communications in the first Federal Cabinet.

Later he formed a new party, Cameroun United Congress, and led it into the 1966 merger of the Cameroun Federation's four political parties.

LT-COL PIERRE SEMENGUE

Lieutenant-Colonel Pierre Semengue, youthful Commander of the Cameroun Army, is a product of military training establishments in France.

He was born in French Cameroons in 1935 and studied at the French Military Academy of St Cyr and later at the General Staff College in Paris.

DR SIMON-PIERRE TCHOUNGUI

Dr Simon-Pierre Tchoungui, Premier of East Cameroun, was a World War II Free French fighter and is one of his country's best-known medical men.

He has held top posts in the Ministry of Public Health, in hospitals and in several areas as a regional medical officer.

Born in 1916 at Nkolmending, French Cameroons, he started his education at a Catholic mission school and went for higher schooling to Yaoundé.

After various medical jobs he enlisted with the Free French in 1942 and took part in their campaign until the war ended.

Further studies followed at Dakar Medical School. He was deputy head of surgery at Yaoundé Hospital before attending Paris University where he spent five years working on a thesis on 'Tuberculosis in the Cameroons' with which he gained his doctorate.

On returning he served for two years in the Ministries of Public Health and Public Administration.

He was appointed medical superintendent of Yaoundé Hospital in 1960 and became the country's Director of Public Health. He was made Minister of Public Health later the same year.

Dr Tchoungui is president of the Cameroun Red Cross and president of the National League for Ex-Servicemen.

In an area of 240,000 square miles live about 1,320,000 people (United Nations estimate in 1964). The country is land-locked, set back from the Atlantic behind Cameroun and Gabon, with the Sudan and Congo Kinshasa on the eastern and southern sides. The capital is Bangui.

The main products of the Central African Republic are, with the exception of the diamond industry, agricultural. They include cotton and cotton seed, millet, sorghum, maize, groundnuts and coffee.

42

Central African Republic

The Central African Republic became independent on
August 13, 1960. It had been one of the four territories
of French Equatorial Africa and was then known as
Oubangui-Chari.
From December 1, 1958, it was a member-state of the
French Community. In January, 1959, the four Republics-
Oubangui-Chari, Gabon, Congo Brazzaville and Chad-
formed an economic, technical and customs union.

The Central African Republic, once at the forefront
of moves to create a Federation with its three Equatorial
African neighbours, has seen this dream retreat with
sovereignties hardening in former French Equatorial
Africa and from preoccupations within its own national
borders.
The founder of the nation was Barthélemy Boganda,
a former priest. Boganda died in an air crash on the
eve of his country's independence.
Oubangui-Chari, named after the two main rivers
which water the territory, is a bush-covered plateau in
the heart of Africa to which a number of African tribes,
harassed by repressions nearer the coast, retreated over
the centuries. The country is thinly populated.
Its difficult landlocked situation was undoubtedly one
of the factors that inspired Barthélemy Boganda to
press for a Federation of the four territories of
Equatorial Africa – Gabon, Congo Brazzaville, Chad
and Oubangui-Chari – when they achieved
independence.
The French had ruled the region part of the time as
four separate colonies and later as a single colony,
with the former colonies divided as separate
administrative regions.
The area's administrative past thus favoured Boganda's
project. But the richest territory, Gabon, with its
hardwoods and mineral deposits, already considered in
colonial times that it was being exploited to pay for
federation.
When, in May, 1960, the heads of government of the four
countries met in Fort Lamy, capital of Chad, to reach
agreement on forming a union, Gabon opted out.
The other three countries agreed to unite as the Union

Hill-top view of Bangui,
the capital, situated on
the Oubangui River

of Central African Republics, the Union to be responsible
for foreign policy and external defence, each Republic
retaining its internal authority.

A draft constitution was prepared, but before it could be
ratified there was another defection, this time by Abbé
Fulbert Youlou of Congo Brazzaville.

The four States became independent separately. In the
place of the Federation a number of joint services have
been administered by the four. More important, the
Customs and Economic Union for Central Africa
(UDEAC) has been forged between them and
Cameroun, formerly a United Nation's trust territory
administered by France.

Boganda's tragic death put into power a cousin, David
Dacko, who, aged 30 when his country became
independent, was one of the youngest heads of state in
the world.

Dacko had political ability and a strong social conscience,
but he lacked the prestige of Boganda and had to resort
to threats against the Assembly and to jailing Opposition
members.

The country's unpromising economic situation – it relies
on relatively small quantities of groundnuts, cotton
and coffee for its foreign revenues – presented him with a
major problem.

Some of his diplomatic initiatives worried his French
advisers. One was his decision to join Congo Brazzaville
in recognising the People's Republic of China in 1964.

French advisers and Western diplomatic representatives thought the young President had bitten off too much. On New Year's Day, 1966, after growing threats of violence, Lieutenant-Colonel Jean-Bedel Bokassa, 23 years a soldier in the service of the French and head of the Central African Army, stepped in to take over from Dacko, who is also his cousin.

One of Bokassa's first acts was to close the Chinese Embassy, revealing at the same time that the Army had reports of a plot to set up a National Popular Army and to arrest and execute the existing Army leaders.

In a Government reshuffle in January, 1967, Bokassa remained President and head of government.

Jean-Arthur Bandio

Lt-Col Alexandre Banza

JEAN-ARTHUR BANDIO

Born in Brazzaville in June, 1923, of Central African parents, Jean-Arthur Bandio became Foreign Minister in January, 1967. He had occupied the key post of Minister of the Interior both under President Dacko and President Bokassa, who took over from Dacko in a military *coup*.

M. Bandio studied as a teacher at the Edouard-Renard College in Brazzaville and taught until 1953 in Congo Brazzaville.

In 1953 he took up advanced studies in France, returning later to Congo Brazzaville where he was named Assistant District Chief for Sibiti.

Put at the disposition of the Government of Oubangui-Chari he gained a wide experience of the country through serving in a number of districts as District Officer.

He went to the capital, Bangui, in 1959 as Director of Administrative Affairs.

He became a *directeur de cabinet* in July, 1959, and in August, 1960, immediately after independence, became Minister of the Interior in the Government of President David Dacko.

LT-COL ALEXANDRE BANZA

Lieutenant-Colonel Alexandre Banza, a rifleman at 18 and a lieutenant-colonel 15 years later, is a close friend of President Bokassa.

He was commander of an Infantry battalion at the time of the military *coup* in which President Bokassa came to power on New Year's Day, 1966, and afterwards he became Minister of State in charge of Finance and Ex-servicemen in the revolutionary Government. In a reshuffle in January, 1967, he was named Minister of State for Finance and National Economy.

Lieut-Col Banza was born at Carnot in the west of the country in October, 1932, the oldest of nine children. He studied in the French Cameroun and Congo Brazzaville and began his Army career in the First Battalion of the Congo-Gabon Rifles.

He gained a commission and in 1962 was transferred to the Central African Republic Army. He was promoted to lieutenant in 1963, captain in 1964, lieutenant-colonel in 1966 and is now commander of the country's para-commandos.

Col Jean-Bedel
Bokassa

COL JEAN-BEDEL BOKASSA

President of the Central African Republic since a New Year's Day Army takeover which he headed in 1966, Colonel Jean-Bedel Bokassa is a cousin of the man he put out of office.

One of his first acts was to break relations with the People's Republic of China, saying he had evidence of a plot to set up a National Popular Army, disband the Regular Army and execute its leaders.

His cousin, ex-President Dacko, said later that he owed his life to Colonel Bokassa's prompt action in taking over.

A short, jovial and much-decorated officer who served 23 years in the French Army, Colonel Bokassa is one of the more colourful of the French African heads of state.

He is a nephew of the founder of the Central African Republic, Barthélemy Boganda, and was born in the same village – Bobangui, 50 miles from the capital, on February 22, 1921.

Son of a village chief, Bokassa's father was assassinated at the local prefect's office when the boy was only six. His mother committed suicide, leaving orphaned the family of twelve brothers and sisters.

He studied at mission schools in the Central African Republic (then the territory of Oubangui-Chari) and in Brazzaville. Immediately after leaving school in 1939 he joined the French Army and fought with the Free French forces.

Bokassa took part in the arrest of General Husson, Commander-in-Chief of the Brazzaville forces, who had remained loyal to the Vichy Government.

Bokassa also served in the Indo-China campaign. Beside his experience in the field, which won him no less than twelve decorations, Bokassa also studied communications.

He received his commission in 1949 and left the French Army twelve years later with the rank of captain.

In 1960 he was asked by President Dacko to set up the Central African Army, and in 1964 was named Central African Chief of General Staff.

In this capacity he attended the Defence Councils of the Afro-Malagasy Union, which grouped the moderate French-speaking African states, and presided in February, 1965, over the Defence Committee of the Organisation of African Unity.

Colonel Bokassa's *coup* on New Year's Day of 1966 was one of four in quick succession which spread through French-speaking Africa in less than two months. General Joseph Mobutu was the first to act when he took over in Congo Kinshasa (Bokassa was later to pay an official visit to Mobutu). After the Congo came Dahomey, then the Central African Republic and Upper Volta.

Dissension in the Dacko Government, the budgetary crisis and 'foreign factors' – taken as a reference to the activities of the Chinese embassy – were the reasons Colonel Bokassa gave for taking over the Government.

Relations between Colonel Bokassa and the man he ousted remained friendly. The two appeared together within a month at a public reception, at which Dacko stated that he had received a number of anonymous threats against his life just before the *coup*, and that he felt Colonel Bokassa's action had 'saved his head'.

Passionately pro-French since his army days, Colonel Bokassa has sought to strengthen relations

David Dacko

within the regional groupings of moderate French-speaking African states; these include the Central African Customs and Economic Union (UDEAC) grouping Congo Brazzaville, Gabon, Chad, Cameroun and Central African Republic, and the wider Common Afro-Malagasy Organisation (OCAM).

In the new, extensively re-shuffled Government announced in January, 1967, Colonel Bokassa remained President and head of Government. He retained the Ministry of Defence and took over the Interior portfolio but relinquished those of Information and Justice.

DAVID DACKO

David Dacko, President of the Central African Republic for five and a half years until he was ousted in a New Year's Day military *coup* in 1966, was one of the world's youngest heads of state.

A nephew of the Central African pre-independence hero, Barthélemy Boganda, he succeeded him as head of government when Boganda was killed in an air crash.

Dacko was only 28 at the time and 30 when he became President of the Central African Republic, formed from the old French Equatorial African territory of Oubangui-Chari.

He was born on March 24, 1930, into a family of peasant farmers in the village of Bouchia, in Lobaye province. He went to a teachers' training college at Mouyoundzi in Congo Brazzaville and became a teacher and later a headmaster.

His political career began in 1957 when he was elected deputy for Lobaye in the Territorial Assembly with a comfortable majority.

He became successively Minister of Agriculture, Public Works and the Interior.

In April, 1959, after the death of his uncle, the Legislative Assembly named Dacko as head of the Government.

Six months later a motion of no confidence against his Government was introduced into the Assembly but Dacko won the vote by threatening to dissolve the Assembly.

Dacko was also experiencing troubles within the MESAN party founded by Boganda and which he now headed. Part of it broke away to form the Movement for Democratic Evolution in Central Africa (MEDAC). In December, 1960, Dacko dissolved the Opposition party and arrested its leader, Abel Goumba, a former Minister of Finance, and other deputies.

A shy man with a strong social conscience, he constantly castigated his Ministers for not working hard enough or for living too well.

Just before he was overthrown he told a budgetary session of the Assembly which was considering austerity measures: 'Christmas gifts and parties are part of the colonial heritage which insolently opposes the living standards of 50,000 salaried workers like ourselves and the two million rural workers we represent.'

In 1964 Dacko was proclaimed President for a further seven-year term.

Towards the end of his term of office he appeared to be having increasing difficulty in coping with the country's budgetary deficit and the irregularities of some of his Ministers. Prone to taking unexpected diplomatic initiatives his decision to adopt diplomatic relations with Communist China in 1964 caused uneasiness, particularly in the

Dominique Gueret

Antoine Guimali

Antoine Kezza

Republican Army hierarchy.

He was placed under technical house arrest during the *coup* but relations between him and the new chief of state were reported to be good.

MAURICE-THEOPHILE GAMANA-LEGGOS

Having held a number of Civil Service posts, throughout the Central African Republic, Maurice-Théophile Gamana-Leggos was the first Central African to be named a prefect when the Africanisation of high administrative posts began, following independence.

Born at Bamoungue in December, 1925, he was a close confidant of Barthélemy Boganda, the first head of government of the country and the hero of Central African independence.

He was prefect of the Upper Sangha district at Berberati in the west of the country when the military *coup* took place and he was called to the capital to become Minister of Public Works, Posts and Telecommunications.

In January, 1967, he became Minister for Information, Posts and Telecommunications.

DOMINIQUE GUERET

Dominique Gueret, Minister of Education, Youth and Sport, was dropped from the Cabinet in January, 1967. He was born at Mobaye in the south of the country about 1926. He qualified as a teacher in his own country and taught from 1948-59 in Chad.

In 1960 he took charge of education in his own district of Mobaye in the Central African Republic.

From 1961-62 he took advanced studies at the Ecole Normale d'Instituteur in Paris.

On his return to the Central

African Republic he was appointed almost at once to the Education Ministry in the Government of David Dacko, a post which he continued to hold along with Youth and Sport in the succeeding Cabinet of Colonel Bokassa.

ANTOINE GUIMALI

Foreign Minister in the Dacko Government, Antoine Guimali retained this post after the military *coup* of New Year's Day, 1966. He became Minister of Justice in January, 1967.

Born in 1918 at Yetomane in the Central African Republic, M. Guimali spent 28 years in the administration, for much of the time as a court clerk, before becoming a Minister.

He served in the French Equatorial African administration in Gabon, Congo Brazzaville and his home territory, then known as Oubangui-Chari.

Returning to Bangui, his home capital, to spend a long leave of six months, he found himself called upon at the end of that period to take up a post in the new Central African Government as Secretary of State for Justice.

He became Minister of Justice in 1963 and, soon after, Minister of Foreign Affairs, a post in which he represented his country at major African and world conferences.

ANTOINE KEZZA

Born in 1933 at Limassa in the Central African Republic, Antoine Kezza was one of the senior civil servants promoted to a ministerial post in the military Government of Colonel Bokassa.

After a successful early school career in the Central African Republic, he was chosen to continue his education in France.

Timothée Malendoma

Ange Patasse

He obtained his baccalaureate in 1958 and chose to study veterinary medicine, but his home Government asked him to take up legal studies.

Back in the Central African Republic, he was appointed head of Establishment in the Civil Service in 1963. He became Director of the Civil Service in 1964 after this Ministry was re-created by the Government.

Colonel Bokassa made him Minister of the Civil Service and Labour in January, 1966.

ANDRE DIEUDONNE MAGALE

Named by Colonel Bokassa as Minister of Health and Social Affairs after the Army *coup* (January, 1966), André Dieudonné Magale was born in May, 1929, at Mbaiki in the extreme south of the country.

Early in his career he organised youth movements while working as a teacher. As a youth leader he travelled to the United States, Europe and Asia and took part in a large number of youth congresses on the African continent.

He entered the Gendarmerie Instruction Centre at Brazzaville in 1955 and went to France four years later to continue his studies as a gendarme.

Back in the Central African Republic in 1960 he was appointed assistant commander of the Gendarmerie Brigade.

He returned to France again the following year for further studies, was briefly back in his own country as head of the gendarmerie of Berberati in the west of the country, and completed his courses in France in 1963 and 1964, emerging as sub-lieutenant in the gendarmerie in August, 1964.

In the Central African Repub-lic he was promoted to lieutenant in December of the same year. Since the *coup* he has been promoted to the rank of captain.

CAPT TIMOTHEE MALENDOMA

Captain Timothée Malendoma was born in 1935 at Dekoa and joined the French Army in 1953, serving two years in Indo-China.

In 1956 he returned to his own country to serve in the French forces stationed there.

He entered the school for officers at Fréjus, southern France, in 1961, going from there at the request of the Central African Government to the military administration school at Montpellier.

He was transferred to the Central African Army in 1956 as a sub-lieutenant, and became head of administrative services in the First Infantry Battalion of the national Army.

He took up legal studies in the hope of becoming a licentiate in law, but these studies were interrupted by the Army *coup* and his own nomination as Minister of Economic Affairs in the new Government.

ANGE PATASSE

Minister of Development and one of the youngest members of the Bokassa Cabinet, Ange Patasse is a qualified agricultural scientist.

Born on January 25, 1937, at Paoua, he received his diploma from the French Equatorial College in 1959.

In the Central African Republic he served as an agricultural inspector and was appointed late in 1965 as Director of Agriculture for the Republic.

He was only a few months in that post when the military *coup* took place and he was named Minister of Development.

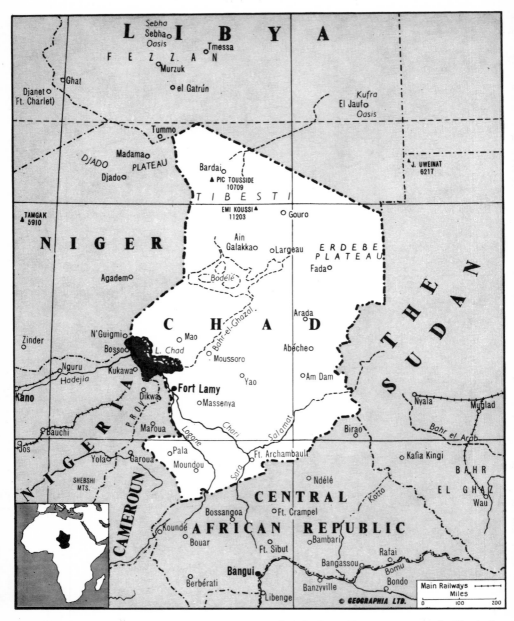

The population of Chad is over 3,300,000 (1965 estimate). The area of the country is about 495,470 square miles, though the figures given range from 485,750 to 534,363 square miles. Chad is surrounded by large neighbours — Libya in the north, Niger to the west (with Nigeria on the other side of Lake Chad), Cameroun and the Central African Republic in the south and the Sudan in the east. The capital is Fort Lamy.

The economy of Chad is founded upon cotton and animal husbandry. Undoubtedly rich in minerals, the country is currently being surveyed for possible future exploitation.

50

Chad

One of the four territories of French Equatorial Africa,
Chad voted in 1958 to become a member-state of the
French Community.
In January, 1959, an economic and technical union was
formed with the three other French territories — Central
African Republic, Congo Brazzaville and Gabon.
On August 11, 1960, the country became the independent
Republic of Chad.

As a colonial territory, Chad played an important role
at a key moment of recent French history. It was from
there, at the beginning of World War II, that the Free
French forces in Africa started their journey across the
Sahara to North Africa, bringing France back into the
fight against Germany.

The man who kept Chad on the side of the Free French
was a Negro, Governor Félix Eboué, who came from the
West Indies.

Eventually the whole of Equatorial Africa swung
over to the Free French and Governor Eboué rose to
become Governor-General for the region, residing in
Brazzaville.

Some students of African history see the fact that
France had appointed a black Governor to one of her
territories, long before African nationalism was in the
air, as putting France in a category by herself among the
African colonisers. They see this as a contributing factor
to the real affection that has survived between France
and many of her former African subjects.

Eboué's prestige created a niche for another West
Indian, Gabriel Lisette, who went to Equatorial Africa
to work in the French Administration at Brazzaville in
1944 and was transferred to Chad in 1946.

Lisette was elected to the French National Assembly as
deputy for Chad and became an active supporter of
Houphouet-Boigny of the Ivory Coast and his party, the
African Democratic Rally. He founded the Chad
Progress Party as the local branch of the Rally and
became its secretary-general.

But some Chadians, particularly Moslem northerners,
objected to Lisette's *émigré* origins, and in 1959 Lisette
handed over the leadership of party and Government to

Carrying pots in the age-old manner

his close associate, François Tombalbaye, a southerner. Tombalbaye, soon to become first President of the Chad Republic (the French spell the country's name Tchad) took over a vast landlocked, half-desert country with no effective all-the-year-round transportation system except by aeroplane. Earth roads covered with choking dust but fairly easy to travel in the months when the Sahara sun beats down on them, become an impassable bog in the rainy season.

Chad's population, divided into a number of tribes, is scattered over a vast territory often inaccessible to the administration.

Relations have never been easy between the proud and often warlike nomads of the north, a mixture of Arab, Berber and Negro, and the more settled population of the south. Once the northerners had invaded and ruled the south. But the period of French occupation and the setting up of a Chad Army largely composed of southern Saras (Tombalbaye's tribe) did much to make matters even.

The known riches of Chad lay in the abundant fish in Lake Chad, the country's cattle and the cotton crop near Moundou in the south. But the remoteness of Chad made it difficult to export these products. The population

A tailor's shop at
Fort Archambault

of southern Chad did not appreciate the economic
importance of export crops like cotton, and Tombalbaye
had to intervene to urge farmers to maintain production.
Mineral riches undoubtedly lie beneath Chad's soil but
surveys of the territory are only just beginning.

Aided by France, which subsidised purchases of Chad's
cotton, Tombalbaye was able to push forward with
development. In 1966 he launched a five-year plan
aimed at boosting animal and crop production, raising
the *per capita* income of Chadians and reducing the
adverse trade balance (9,300 million CFA francs-worth
of exports in 1965, compared with imports of 13,900
million).

To reduce his country's isolation Tombalbaye has joined
wholeheartedly in the regional organisations of former
French Equatorial Africa. Chad is a member of the
Central Africa Customs Union (UDEAC) which
associates Cameroun with the four former Equatorial
territories: Chad, Central African Republic, Congo
Brazzaville and Gabon. Tombalbaye has been a warm
supporter of the extension of the Trans-Cameroun
railway. A branch will travel into the cotton area of
Moundou linking Chad to the key Cameroun port of
Douala.

53

A row of baked-mud houses in Fort Lamy, the capital

Chad is also a member of the Chad Basin Commission set up to study and exploit the resources of the vast desert lake which swells with each year's rains and can flood Fort Lamy thirty miles away. Others on the commission are Niger, Nigeria and Cameroun. Relations have not been consistently good with Chad's eastern neighbour, Sudan. In 1966 there were border incidents between Sudan and Chad but these were ironed out thanks to the good offices of Niger. Politically, Tombalbaye inherited some of Lisette's problems, although in a reduced form. The years of independence have seen a reduction of northern representation in the Government and in the administration but the communal trouble predicted by some has never come about.

Chad has seen plots, clashes between Government and Opposition and a number of ministerial reshuffles, but in his first six years in office Tombalbaye has managed to maintain stability.

Antoine Bangui

TCHERE ADOUM

President of the Chad National Assembly, Tchere Adoum was born in 1925 at Mongo, in the Guera district of Chad. A brilliant student, he joined the French Army and fought in World War II with the Free French forces. He holds the Légion d'Honneur, the Croix de Guerre, the Ex-Servicemen's Merit Medal and the Colonial Medal.

After the war, he turned to politics and in December, 1958, became Minister of Social Affairs and Labour.

Elected a deputy in May, 1959, he was re-elected in March, 1962. He changed ministerial jobs in the meantime, taking over first the Livestock portfolio then the Agricultural Ministry between September, 1960 and January, 1964.

M. Adoum, a member of the national political bureau of the ruling political party, was elected President of the National Assembly in 1964.

ANTOINE BANGUI

Antoine Bangui is Minister of State, with responsibility for Coordination, attached to the Presidency.

Born in 1932, he completed his early studies in what is now the Central African Republic, travelling later to France to study at the École Polytechnique. Returning to the Central African Republic, he taught at the Barthélemy Boganda Secondary School in the capital, then asked to be transferred to his own country where he became a teacher of mathematics and physics at Bongor Modern College.

After Chad gained independence, he became departmental chief at the National Education Ministry, then Minister of Public

55

Dr Jacques Baroum

Georges Diguimbaye

Michel Djidingar

Works; he was also Chad's Ambassador to Bonn.

On April 10, 1966, following a Cabinet reshuffle he was appointed to his present post.

DR JACQUES BAROUM

Foreign Minister of Chad, Dr Jacques Baroum was born on July 13, 1932, at Laye. He was Chad's first African doctor.

After primary school studies in Chad, he went to Brazzaville, capital of French Equatorial Africa, for secondary school studies. From 1953–62 he studied at the Faculty of Medicine in Paris, where he graduated. He also took a diploma in tropical medicine, specialising in paediatrics (diseases of children).

He is a member of the political bureau of the ruling Chadian political party, and his first ministerial post was as Minister of Health and Social Services. He was appointed Minister of Foreign Affairs in 1965.

GEORGES DIGUIMBAYE

Minister of Planning and Co-operation, Georges Diguimbaye was born at Fort Lamy, the capital, on October 16, 1935.

After secondary studies at the Bongor Modern College he went on to take a teaching course and eventually became a headmaster.

In 1961, he went to Paris, where he took a social sciences degree. He took a diploma at the French Institute in cooperative action, and another in community development.

He then returned to Chad, where he became successively between 1961–64 assistant director, director and general commissioner to the Department of Planning. He prepared the interim development plan and Chad's first five-year plan.

After a brief period as Secret-

ary-General to the Presidency, M. Diguimbaye entered the Cabinet on April 19, 1966, as Minister of Planning and Co-operation.

A member of the national political bureau and an Officer of the National Order of Chad, he is also an Officer of Merit for neighbouring Cameroun.

MICHEL DJIDINGAR

Minister of Posts and Public Works, Michel Djidingar was born at Tandjile, Chad, in 1931.

He became Finance and Postal Services Minister in 1963. After a Cabinet reshuffle in 1966 he was given his present job.

COL JACQUES DOUMRO

Colonel Jacques Duomro is Chief of the General Staff of the Chad Army; he was born in 1919 at Fort Lamy.

He entered the French Army in 1938 with the Senegalese Artillery Regiment.

During World War II he served with this regiment, which was one of the first to join the Free French forces.

In 1939, he joined up with the French Sixth Colonial Infantry Regiment, serving three years in Indo-China.

Gazetted sub-lieutenant on April 1, 1955, he was transferred to the Chad Armed Forces in 1961. In 1962 he went to Paris for a general staff college course.

He then became adjutant to the Chief of the Chad General Staff and went on to take over the senior post in January, 1964.

He is president of the Chad Ex-Servicemen's Association, a Commander of the National Order of Chad and also of the Order of Civil Merit; his other awards include the Croix de Guerre and a military medal from the Indo-China campaign.

Rahama Saleh

ADOUM MAURICE HEL-BONGO

Minister of Health and Social Services, Adoum Maurice Hel-Bongo was born at Fort Archambault in the east of Chad on May 30, 1930. He became a senior Government official at the age of 31 and was promoted to Minister at 34.

After primary and secondary studies in Chad, he went to France to complete his education. Later, as a barrister and former student of the Political Sciences Institute of Paris and a graduate of the Overseas School of France, he worked first for the French Government as an adviser in administrative affairs.

On returning to Chad he was named Civil Administrator then Director of the Civil Service from 1960–61.

In quick succession he became Cabinet Director (Permanent Secretary) for the Civil Service, Director of Economic Affairs and interim Counsellor to the Fort Lamy Court of Appeal.

In January, 1964, after a Cabinet reshuffle, he took over the Agriculture and Livestock portfolios. Eleven months later he became Public Health and Social Services Minister. He is a member of the national political bureau of Chad.

ALI KEKE

Minister of Labour, Youth and Sport since January, 1964, Ali Keke was born in August, 1936.

A teacher in Fort Lamy, the capital, he became a professor of physical education after studies in Brazzaville and in France.

He became a municipal councillor in his home town of Bongo in 1961 and was then elected a deputy of the Chad National Assembly in March, 1962.

ABDOULAYE LAMANA

Abdoulaye Lamana, Economy and Transport Minister, was born in 1933 at Massenya.

He went to the Overseas Institute of Higher Studies in Paris after beginning his education in Fort Lamy. From 1962–64 he was Director of Finance in Chad.

In 1964 he was named Minister of Economy and Transport. He is an Officer of the National Order of Chad.

RAYMOND NAIMBAYE

Minister of Agriculture and Animal Production, born in 1936, Raymond Naimbaye studied at Fort Lamy's Félix Eboué Secondary School, then went to Bamako, Mali, studying on a government scholarship at the veterinary college. He graduated from there as a qualified veterinary inspector.

After various changes of office, he became departmental chief at the Livestock Ministry, then switched to a similar post at the Foreign Affairs Ministry, later becoming Chad's Ambassador to Sudan.

He entered the Cabinet on April 19, 1966, as Minister of Agriculture and Animal Production.

MOHAMMED RAHAMA SALEH

The Minister for the Civil Service, Mohammed Rahama Saleh was born in 1940. He became, on his appointment in 1966, one of the youngest men to hold Cabinet rank.

He has a diploma from the Overseas Institute of Higher Studies in Paris, and has served in several capacities as a civil administrator and as a sub-prefect.

Joseph Brahim Seid

Mohammed Talba

François Tombalbaye

JOSEPH BRAHIM SEID

Joseph Brahim Seid, born in 1928, was Chad's first Ambassador to France after independence.

After primary and secondary studies in Chad and Egypt, he went to France, where he took a law degree. He was then appointed a magistrate in Brazzaville, later transferring to Moundou, southern Chad, as a JP.

He was envoy to Paris from 1960 to April, 1966, when he was recalled to Chad to take over the Ministry of Justice.

MOHAMMED TALBA

Mohammed Talba's trade union activities led to a Government post on April 19, 1966, as Secretary of State for Agriculture and Animal Production.

Earlier he was a civil servant; he was for a time a departmental head at the Ministry of Finance.

FRANCOIS TOMBALBAYE

François Tombalbaye, first President of the Republic of Chad after it achieved independence from France on August 11, 1960, was born on June 15, 1918, at Bessada, southern Chad, of a Protestant family. A slim and good-looking man, he is a member of the Sara tribe, which has proved one of the mainstays of French West African armed forces.

He was a teacher for several years, at Fort Lamy and Fort Archambault among other places, before he went into politics. He took part in the founding of the Chad Progressive Party ('Parti Progressiste Tchadien') directed by Gabriel Lisette, a West Indian.

West Indians had enjoyed considerable political prestige in Chad since the days when Governor Félix Eboué, the West

Indian Governor of Chad, had swung Chad behind de Gaulle and the Free French early in the war. This favoured the rise of a foreign-born resident like Lisette to such an important post.

The PPT was founded as the local section of the African Democratic Rally launched by such major West African political figures as Félix Houphouet-Boigny of the Ivory Coast and Ouezzin Coulibaly of Upper Volta.

In March, 1952, Tombalbaye was elected Territorial Councillor for Chad; re-elected in 1957 he became High Councillor for French Equatorial Africa. This Council grouped together all of France's Equatorial African territories with the exception of the Cameroun, which was a League of Nations mandate.

He afterwards became Vice-President of the Grand Council of Equatorial Africa.

In 1957 he was elected member for Middle Chari in the Chad Parliament.

This rapid rise to power brought on an inevitable confrontation between Tombalbaye and Lisette.

Lisette was in 1957 at the height of his power, occupying the two commanding political posts of Prime Minister of Chad and mayor of the capital, Fort Lamy.

But, although Lisette and his lieutenant, Tombalbaye, were close associates, trouble was being stirred up for Lisette in the north by the Moslem leader, Hamad Koullamalah. Tombalbaye was soon to replace Lisette at the head of the political party and in May, 1959, he took over the post of Prime Minister.

In August, 1960, with Lisette on a visit outside the country, Tombalbaye took advantage of a

Ouckar Tourgoudi

Abakar Sanga Traore

political congress at Moundou, in the south, to dismiss Lisette from the Government and exile him. The exile order was later rescinded.

Within the same month independence was declared and Tombalbaye became head of state.

His main problem has been to maintain unity over the vast and underpopulated territory of Chad. Despite occasional Cabinet crises and a crisis between the President and the National Assembly in 1965, Chad has so far escaped the regional strife which has bedevilled the Sudan. The French presence is strongly felt, mainly through the air base in Fort Lamy, although the number of French living in the Chad is not unusually large.

Two plots have been uncovered. The discovery of the 1963 plot led to several Northerners being sentenced to death. In 1965 three Ministers were arrested (Mohamat Baroud, Mohamat El Goni and Robert Delsia Soussia) and the Vice-President of the National Assembly, M. Djellal.

The Chad administration is largely drawn from the educated *élite* of the south – Moslems, Christians and animists – and Tombalbaye has done his best to rectify this and draw more northern support to the Government.

In 1966 a border dispute flared with neighbouring Sudan, which harbours some Chadian political exiles, but this was resolved through the good offices of Chad's western neighbour, Niger.

Tombalbaye's Government has supported the Organisation of African Unity, the Common Afro-Malagasy Organisation – an organisation of generally moderate and pro-Western French-speaking states – as well as more regional groupings such as UDEAC, the Central African Customs and Economic Union. This includes the four former French Equatorial African territories of Congo Brazzaville, Gabon, Central African Republic and Chad, as well as the former mandated territory of the Cameroun.

OUCKAR TOURGOUDI

Ouckar Tourgoudi, Chad's Minister of Information and Tourism and the youngest man ever to hold Cabinet rank in the country, was born in 1942.

A lecturer by profession, he is a member of the national political bureau and entered the Cabinet on April 19, 1966.

ABAKAR SANGA TRAORE

The Finance Minister, Abakar Sanga Traore was born at Fort Lamy in 1932.

He carried out his early studies in Fort Lamy and held several important administrative posts.

Later he went to the Overseas Institute of Higher Studies in Paris, gaining a diploma. He was appointed civil administrator, later becoming director of foreign affairs, secretary-general to the Council of Ministers and finally director-general of fiscal control (auditor-general).

He entered the Cabinet on April 19, 1966, as Finance Minister.

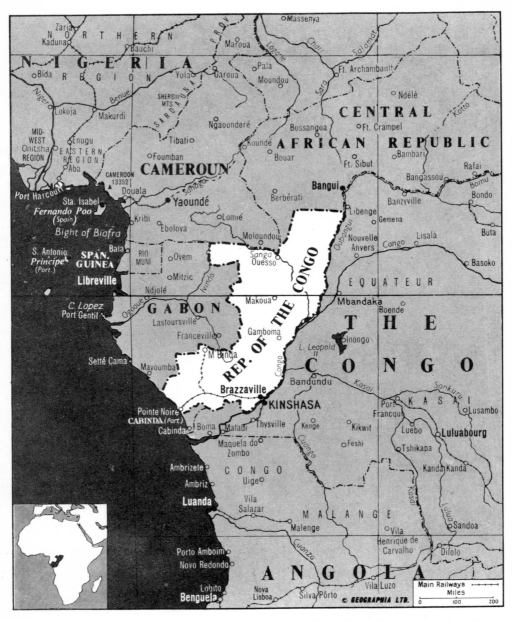

Covering an area of 139,000 square miles, the Congo Republic (Brazzaville) is bounded by Gabon, Cameroun, the Central African Republic, the Congo Democratic Republic (Kinshasa) and the Atlantic Ocean. The population was estimated in 1964 to be 900,000. The capital is Brazzaville.

The chief agricultural products are cocoa, coffee, tobacco and timber. The principal minerals are oil, lead and cassiterite (tin).

Congo Republic (Brazzaville)

The Brazzaville Congo Republic became independent on
August 15, 1960. With Gabon, Oubangui-Chari and Chad
(Tchad) it had formed part of French Equatorial Africa
under the name of Middle Congo.
Three years after independence, to the day, the pro-French
Government of Abbé Fulbert Youlou was overthrown and
replaced by a left-wing Administration headed by
M. Alphonse Massemba-Debat.

The first European contact with the Congo dates back
to the 17th century when Portuguese, English and Dutch
seafarers visited the territory, but civilised life in the
territory is known to have existed for at least 3,000 years.
A Congo empire which extended into present-day Angola
and Congo Kinshasa flourished in the 16th century but
later split into several smaller states.
The first European to explore the interior of the
country was Pierre Savorgnan de Brazza, a French
naval lieutenant, who in 1880 sailed up the Ogowe
River from Port Gentil and then cut inland, reaching the
lake-like expansion of the Congo River on which
Brazzaville now stands. At Mbe, some 100 miles from
the present site of Brazzaville, de Brazza signed a
treaty of protection to the Makoko (king) of the Bateke
people. This treaty opened the door to French influence
in Equatorial Africa.
At the turn of the century the French gained full control
of the territory and turned it into a colony.
The main achievement of the French administration was
probably the building of the artificial harbour and
deep-water port at Pointe-Noire, on the Atlantic coast,
and the 320-mile long railway linking it with the Congo
River at Brazzaville. The line, through tropical forest and
down the Mayombé Escarpment, has involved the
building of 92 bridges and 12 tunnels. Its completion in
1934 marked a turning point in the development of the
hinterland lying to the north and north-east, the
Oubangui River being navigable over a distance of
nearly 1,000 miles upstream from Brazzaville. Another
railway running to the north from Pointe-Noire provides
an outlet for the manganese ore which is mined at

Franceville in the neighbouring Gabon Republic. Brazzaville, already the administrative capital of French Equatorial Africa, became also its main commercial centre following the completion of the Ocean-Congo railway which turned it into a major river port. It was the capital of General de Gaulle's Free France during World War II and the place where he made his major pronouncements on colonial policy.

In 1946 the Middle Congo became the first French possession to elect a majority of African members in the Representative Council, a local government body which later changed its name to Territorial Assembly, and gradually acquired increased powers.

Political parties also began to appear shortly after World War II with the establishment by Félix Tchicaya of the 'Parti Progressiste Congolais' (PPC) in the south of the country. At about the same time a local section of the French Socialist party which later became the 'Mouvement Socialiste Africain' (MSA) was founded in the north with M. Jacques Opangault as its leader.

In 1956, Abbé Fulbert Youlou founded the 'Union Démocratique de la Défense des Intérêts Africains' (UDDIA) as a local section of the African Democratic Rally – the inter-African party led by M. Félix Houphouet-Boigny. This brought about the virtual disintegration of the PPC leaving the MSA and the UDDIA as the main contenders for power. The first round, in 1957, went to the MSA but in the following year Abbé Youlou secured a majority of one in the Territorial Assembly and formed a new Government with himself as Prime Minister. On November 28, 1958, the Assembly proclaimed the Republic of the Congo, later electing Abbé Fulbert Youlou as its first President.

In July, 1960, the Congo Republic initialled agreements with the French Government providing both for the transfer of sovereignty and for continued cooperation in various fields, including defence and foreign affairs. The agreements were signed a month later (August 15), marking the official beginning of independence.

In March, 1961, Abbé Youlou was re-elected President for a five-year term and acquired virtually dictatorial powers. He kept in his own hands the key Ministries of

The Cathedral of
St Anne in Brazzaville

Defence and Internal Affairs. M. Jacques Opangault, the
former head of the Opposition, was appointed Vice-
President in June, 1961, but resigned two years later.
In foreign affairs Abbé Youlou adhered to a policy
of very close collaboration with France. In Africa his
closest friend and ally was M. Moise Tshombe. He
also aimed at a federation of Congolese states on both
banks of the Congo River in preference to an association
with the other countries which had formed part of
French Equatorial Africa.
In the economic field the Youlou administration
attempted ambitious development projects and eventually
secured French and German finance for the projected
Kouilou dam and hydro-electric plant intended to

63

Congo mother
and child

attract an aluminium smelter. Despite these moves,
however, the Youlou administration was unable to
reduce the foreign trade deficit and the level of
unemployment remained high, especially in Brazzaville.
The trade unions became increasingly restless as did the
nationalist and left-wing groups, who resented Youlou's
pro-French policy and alleged that corruption, nepotism
and political oppression had never been so rampant.
In April, 1963, the National Assembly unanimously
passed a bill providing for the creation of a single
party system and the official abolition of an Opposition.
This triggered off a series of minor disturbances which
foreshadowed further trouble.
On August 12, Brazzaville was paralysed by a general
strike and on the following day thousands of
demonstrators attacked the local jail in a Bastille-like
revolt and released its prisoners. French troops, including
units flown in from Chad, were ordered to help
Congolese forces to restore order and protect French
property. An official spokesman in Paris said the Congolese
Government had requested French military assistance,
as was its right under the agreement with France.

On August 15, the third day of the disturbances and the third anniversary of the country's independence, Abbé Youlou resigned after a long meeting with the trade union leaders who had led the demonstrations. French troops were immediately withdrawn from the streets, Abbé Youlou was detained and an eight-man provisional government was set up following talks between the trade unions and the Army – the two bodies which played an important part in the bloodless revolution.

The new Administration, headed by M. Alphonse Massemba-Debat, rested on broad foundations. Its supporters ranged from non-political Army men and moderate Catholic trade unionists to pro-Chinese communists and extreme nationalists. Every group found a champion in the Government and the political bureau of the newly-formed ruling party – the 'Mouvement National Révolutionnaire' (MNR).

But after taking office the new Government began to swing left. The youth group of the party, the JMNR, emerged as the mouthpiece of the left-wing. M. Germain Bicoumat, the Minister of the Interior, and other Ministers and senior officials regarded as moderate were gradually removed from office.

In June, 1966, Army units in Brazzaville attempted a *coup* and gained virtual control of the capital after sacking the MNR headquarters. The Government, including the Prime Minister, had to seek refuge within the concrete walls of a sports stadium on the outskirts of Brazzaville. The mutiny was quelled within three days with the help of some 200 Cuban troops of the Presidential guard. President Massemba-Debat was abroad at the time.

The Government rejected demands to dismiss the Cuban guard and the Prime Minister declared, 'If our Cuban brothers had not swung the people behind them we should perhaps not be here today.'

The country's foreign policy since the August, 1963 revolution has more or less reflected the various changes on the home front as well as economic needs. Relations with France which remained friendly for some time after the revolution, began to deteriorate at the beginning of 1964, whereas Chinese influence increased. In October, 1964, China granted the Congo an interest free loan officially worth 5,000 million CFA francs (about £7.3m sterling) and a number of cooperation agreements were concluded between the two countries.

At the same time relations with neighbouring Congo Leopoldville developed into a state of cold war with each side accusing the other of armed aggression.

In March, 1965, former President Youlou escaped to Leopoldville and tension increased still further. But relations gradually returned to normal after the fall of the Tshombe Government and the Presidents of the two Congos – M. Joseph Kasavubu and M. Alphonse Massemba-Debat – achieved a reconciliation at the 1965 OAU summit conference in Accra.

In August, 1965, the United States broke off diplomatic relations with the Congo after alleged ill-treatment of American diplomats in Brazzaville. Five months later the Congo severed relations with Britain over Rhodesia. Relations with France – which had come close to breaking point following Youlou's escape and the alleged supply, during March, of French arms to counter-revolutionary groups – greatly improved later in the year, a process which continued in 1966.

In October, 1966, Premier Noumazalay singled out three countrues – France, the Soviet Union and the People's Republic of China – as deserving special thanks for aid given to the Congo.

French development projects since the 1963 revolution include a £6.5 million sugar refinery for which the Congolese Government put up one-third of the capital. Chinese projects include a textile mill, and West Germany has granted the Congo a £900,000 loan for the building of a cement factory.

The Congo is an associate member of the European Common Market. The joint European Development Fund has granted about £11 million for projects in the country. It is also a member of UDEAC ('Union Douanière et Economique de l'Afrique Centrale') – a customs union, amounting to a common market, in which its partners are the Cameroun, the Central African Republic, Gabon and Chad.

E. Ebouka-Babakas

David Ganao

André Hombessa

E. EBOUKA-BABAKAS

The man who has had the greatest share of responsibility for the economy of the Congo Republic since the August, 1963 revolution is Edouard Ebouka-Babakas, appointed Minister of Finance, Budget and Mines in December, 1965.

He was no newcomer to these Ministries. A member of the original eight-man team who took over the administration of the country immediately after the revolution and a survivor of the successive reshuffles, he became head of three important economic departments in August, 1963. These were Finance, Mines and Transport. In December, when the provisional Government became permanent, he lost Mines and Transport but acquired two other Ministries – National Economy and Posts and Telecommunications. Although later relieved of both, he retained throughout the Ministry of Finance, for which he has been responsible since he first joined the Government.

He was born on July 14, 1933, at Mossaka, in northern Congo. After a primary education at a mission school he entered the modern secondary school at Dolisie and completed his secondary studies at the Lycée Savorgnan de Brazza. He then went to France to study law and economics at the University of Nancy.

As a civil servant before the revolution he became principal inspector of customs in 1962, at the age of 29. Later he was appointed technical adviser in the Ministry of Finance.

DAVID CHARLES GANAO

David Charles Ganao was appointed Minister of Foreign Affairs on August 15, 1963, the day the Abbé Youlou regime was overthrown and a provisional Government was formed to administer the country.

With President Alphonse Massemba-Debat and Finance Minister Edouard Ebouka-Babakas, he is one of the three members of the original eight-man team who remained in the Government after three and a half years of successive reshuffles.

In May, 1966, he also became Minister of Tourism, Cooperation and Civil Aviation.

He was born on July 20, 1928, at Djambala, central Congo. After completing his secondary education he graduated from a teachers' training college and became first a teacher, then a headmaster and finally an inspector of education. He went to France in 1960 to attend a training course for diplomats at the Quai d'Orsay, the French Foreign Ministry. On returning home he was appointed head of political affairs in the Congolese Foreign Ministry – a post which he kept until the August, 1963 revolution.

As Foreign Minister he has travelled extensively throughout the world, representing his country at African and international conferences.

ANDRE HOMBESSA

André Hombessa became Minister of the Interior in April, 1965, as a result of a Government reshuffle in which three ministers reputed to hold moderate views lost their posts. He acquired at the same time the Ministry of Posts and Telecommunications.

A teacher by profession, he became High Commissioner for Youth and Sport and then began organising young people politically, forming a highly

François-Luc Macosso

militant movement–'La Jeunesse du Mouvement National Révolutionnaire' (JMNR).

He was born in Brazzaville in 1935. In 1956 a Canadian family sent him to the Evangelical Institute in the Cameroun for further studies. He returned to Brazzaville in 1959 and in the following year became President of the National Youth Council.

DR PASCAL LISSOUBA

Dr Pascal Lissouba was a member of the original eight-man administration which ruled the country after the August, 1963 revolution.

In December, 1963, he was appointed Prime Minister, combining these duties with those of Minister of Agriculture, Rural Economy and Forestry.

An intellectual of great integrity, he professed both Marxist and nationalist sympathies. He admired Dr Kwame Nkrumah of Ghana and was successively described as pro-Russian and pro-Chinese.

At the beginning of 1966, when the economic and political situation in the country was deteriorating, he resigned from the Government.

He was born on November 10, 1931 at Mossendjo, in the central region of the country. At the age of 16 he went to France, completing his secondary education in Nice.

In 1953 he was admitted to the Ecole Supérieure d'Agriculture in Tunis from which he graduated three years later at the top of his year. Later he obtained a science degree from the Sorbonne and joined a research team at the French National Centre of Scientific Research. In 1961 he submitted a thesis commended by the University of Paris and became the Congo's first doctor of science. He then returned to his country, after an absence of 14 years, to become head of agricultural services.

FRANCOIS-LUC MACOSSO

François-Luc Macosso was appointed Minister of Justice and of the Civil Service on April 6, 1965, in a Government reshuffle in which younger men who had distinguished themselves as political organisers in the ruling MNR ('Mouvement National Révolutionnaire') were promoted to senior appointments.

He managed so well as head of the two ministries that in the following year a third, Labour, was placed under his control.

A southerner, he was born on October 19, 1938, at Madingo-Kayes, in the Kouilou province, and was educated locally. At the time of the August, 1963 revolution he was manager of the Pointe Noire branch of the Congo National Development Bank. An early supporter of the new regime, he was returned to the National Assembly in the December, 1963 election.

ALPHONSE MASSEMBA-DEBAT

Alphonse Massemba-Debat became President of the Congo Brazzaville Republic on December 19, 1963, four months after the successful revolution which overthrew the administration of Abbé Fulbert Youlou. During these four months he had headed a provisional Government.

From June, 1961 to May, 1963, he had been Minister of Planning and Equipment in the Youlou administration, from which he resigned following differences of opinion with the then President, Abbé Youlou. M. Massemba-Debat was reported in particular

Alphonse
Massemba-Debat

to have opposed the Government's 'bourgeois' tendencies, alleged corruption and what was regarded as an excessively pro-French policy. He was offered the post of Ambassador in Paris but turned it down and retired to his native village of N'Kolo, near Boko. He was still there when the regime was overthrown after three days of disturbances in Brazzaville but was later invited to return to the capital to head the provisional Government.

He was born in 1921 to a Protestant family of the Lari tribe, of which his predecessor, Abbé Youlou, is also a member. After a primary education in his home district he went on to study at a higher primary school in Brazzaville and later at the training college for senior civil servants in French Equatorial Africa.

In 1934 he was posted to Fort Lamy in Chad, at first as a teacher and later as a director of schools. Opposition to the colonial regime induced him to join the 'Parti Progressiste Tchadien' led by Gabriel Lisette– a party which was to become later the local section of the 'Rassemblement Démocratique Africain' (RDA). From 1945-47 he served as general secretary of the 'Association des Evolués du Tchad'.

In 1947 he returned to the Congo to become a headmaster first in Mossendjo and later in Brazzaville. During this period he took an increasing, albeit discreet interest in politics, joining Félix Tchicaya's 'Parti Progessiste Congolais' – the Congolese branch of the RDA. After nine years of active membership, from 1948-56, he joined the 'Union Démocratique pour la Défense des Intérêts Africains' (UDDIA)

which had just been founded by Abbé Youlou to succeed the PPC as the local branch of the RDA.

At the same time he entered full-time into Congolese politics by becoming secretary to Prosper Grandzion, the Minister of Education in the first Congolese Government under the 'framework law' – the regime of local autonomy introduced by the French administration as a first stage towards independence.

Elected in 1959 as an UDDIA deputy to the Legislative Assembly he became President of the Assembly shortly afterwards and was re-elected in the following year. He resigned in 1961 when he was appointed Minister of State, prior to becoming Minister of Planning and Equipment later in that year. As a Minister he often openly criticised Government policy – an attitude which led to his final break with Abbé Youlou in May, 1963.

After becoming President of the country in December, 1963, he devoted himself to the organisation of the political forces which had brought him to power, merging them into a single party, the 'Mouvement National Révolutionnaire' (MNR). The new party, which he described as 'the supreme organ of the nation', was officially constituted on July 2, 1964, and he became its first secretary-general.

As President of the Republic Massemba-Debat has retained from his teaching days an inclination to convince rather than please his audience. He speaks without emphasis and has nothing of the popular orator bent on rousing a crowd. His supporters praise his honesty, his loyalty and his sense of civic duty, which are also recognised by his immediate political opponents.

Aimé Matsika

Throughout his career as President of the country he has had to direct much of his efforts to the reconciliation of divergent interests within the MNR. His colleagues in the all-powerful political bureau have been his main critics, more difficult to please than outside African or world opinion.

More radical members of his party have accused him of being too lenient or too moderate. To some he has appeared to be pro-Western, to others pro-Communist. But it is said of him that he can tackle such situations with the calm of a schoolmaster facing an unruly class.

There is no doubt, however, that as far as domestic policies are concerned he is a declared left-winger, advocating what he describes as 'scientific socialism'. The term has never been clearly defined, but it is generally regarded as meaning a pragmatic form of socialism which allows the leadership to take decisions on merit in the light of a given situation.

While standing for conformism on the domestic front and advocating a monolithic state, including the adherence of all civil servants to the principles of scientific socialism, he has come out strongly against the excesses of extremists.

His personal influence in the ruling party appeared to wane after incidents in February, 1965, but he continued to maintain a balance of power between moderates and extremists in the Party, of which he remained the secretary-general.

In April, 1966, following the resignation of Dr Pascal Lissouba from the premiership, dual leadership effectively ended and Massemba-Debat emerged as the dominant figure both in the party and in national affairs.

In foreign affairs he stands for a policy of non-alignment and friendship with both East and West.

In August, 1965, he paid an official visit to Russia and was described by *Pravda,* the official Party newspaper, as 'an active fighter for the unity of all progressive forces in the struggle against imperialism, colonialism and neo-colonialism'.

In spite of repeated tensions and crises in relations with France he has been consistent in advocating a policy of friendship and collaboration with the former colonial master, often expressing admiration for General de Gaulle.

In December, 1966, he said, 'The Congolese are indebted to France. They need France. But they could not agree with the idea of a France which would not need the Congo.' In the absence of identical political orientations, he added, the two countries could rely on the reciprocal affection which binds them together.

The Congo, he declared, was also 'particularly proud of having among its honorary citizens one of the most illustrious European heads of state of our time, and certainly the most beloved in Africa—General de Gaulle'.

AIME MATSIKA

Aimé Matsika was appointed Minister of Commerce, Industry, Mines and Civil Aviation in December, 1963, at the age of 29.

He had been a trade unionist since the age of 20 and at 21 was elected president of the Union of Congolese Youth. In this capacity he travelled widely, undertaking study tours in such countries as France, Belgium, Germany, Switzerland, Italy, Czechoslovakia, Hungary,

Pierre M'Vouama

Ambroise Noumazalay

Poland, the USSR and China.

He was born at Yétéla in 1934 and received his primary education at the Catholic mission school in his village. From 1943–49 he studied at Brazzaville Technical College.

GEORGES MOUYABI

As President of the Congo National Assembly, Georges Mouyabi is one of the key men in the country. He was elected on May 10, 1966, having been an active back-bencher since December, 1963, when he was returned to the House in the first general election held under the new regime.

His predecessor as President of the Assembly had been the formidable Léon Angor, one of the leaders of the left-wing of the ruling MNR party, whom the House had expelled.

M. Mouyabi was born in 1935 at Madingou, in eastern Congo. After secondary studies in the Congo and Gabon he became a school teacher. In 1960 he started studies at the higher education centre in Brazzaville, following this with a course at Saint Cloud in France.

PIERRE M'VOUAMA

African countries can seldom afford to spare their best technicians for non-technical assignments. But Pierre M'Vouama, a highly-trained telecommunications engineer, was found to be the most suitable person to take charge of the Ministry of Information, Popular Education, Culture and Arts – a post to which he was appointed in May, 1966.

He was born at Kamon, in the district of Kinkala, on May 24, 1934, and went to a primary school in Brazzaville. At the Lycée Savorgnan de Brazza, he took mathematics as his major subject for the baccalaureate. He then went to France, studying physics at the Universities of Bordeaux and Grenoble before entering the Paris École Nationale Supérieure de Télécommunications.

While studying in Paris his fellow countrymen elected him president of the Association of Congolese Students in France. Following the August, 1963 revolution in Brazzaville and the creation of the 'Mouvement National Révolutionnaire' (MNR) a section of the newly-formed ruling party was formed in France. In October, 1964, M'Vouama was elected party vice-president and political secretary.

He completed his studies in July, 1965, becoming a graduate telecommunications engineer, and returned to his country shortly afterwards to become chief of the telecommunications division in the Ministry of Posts and Telegraphs – a post he kept until he became a Minister.

AMBROISE NOUMAZALAY

Ambroise Noumazalay became Prime Minister and Minister of National Planning on May 6, 1966, at a time when the Congo was in the throes of an economic and political crisis. The budget deficit had trebled in a year and Government expenditure was rising as exports declined.

M. Noumazalay succeeded Dr Pascal Lissouba, who had resigned from the premiership a month earlier, apparently unable to cope with the situation and impose his views on the Government and the ruling party. Although a newcomer to the Government, M. Noumazalay was a seasoned organiser and politician, one of the architects of the MNR movement. In July, 1964, he had been elected first secretary of the party and acquired the reputation of being a reliable, hard working backroom boy whose political intransigence was matched only by his undoubted efficiency. Later he combined the duties of party secretary with those of Director of Economic Affairs, a post in which he displayed the same uncompromising attachment to his political views.

His appointment as Prime Minister aroused fears that the regime might become more doctrinaire and take a new turn to the left. These proved totally unjustified. A mathematician by training, M. Noumazalay adopted a scientific approach to current problems, tending to analyse them objectively and to take decisions on merit.

He displayed courage when faced with an Army revolt shortly after assuming the premiership.

With President Massemba-Debat absent from the country, M. Noumazalay and members of his Government had to take refuge behind the concrete walls of the local sports stadium while the mutineers virtually controlled the capital. He rejected an ultimatum from them to dismiss the Cuban troops who were protecting the stadium and used them to quell the rebellion. Later he reinstated a Congolese officer whose discharge had sparked off the mutiny.

M. Noumazalay was born in Brazzaville on September 23, 1933.

ABBE FULBERT YOULOU

One of the most colourful men in African politics, Abbé Fulbert Youlou has also been considered one of the most controversial.

As President of the Congo Republic from November, 1959 to August, 1963, he was probably the most francophile of all African heads of state. Radical and nationalist Africans regarded him as one of the most reactionary. His name became almost a synonym for neo-colonialism. On the African continent his closest friend and ally was Moise Tshombe.

Yet, when a popular uprising overthrew him in August, 1963, the only African head of state who stood by him was Ahmed Sekou Touré, the left-wing, ultra-nationalist President of Guinea. The French Government refused him permission to land when he flew into Paris, although his lawyers claimed that he was technically a French subject – largely as a result of his efforts to keep the Congo in the French Union.

He had been ordained a priest in the Roman Catholic Church but was 'suspended' in 1956. He continued to use the title of Abbé and to wear ecclesiastical clothes – soutanes in different colours – white, black, blue and scarlet.

As President of the Republic, the parties he gave for his friends and guests became famous.

He was born on June 7, 1917, in the village of Madihou, near Brazzaville. The name he was given, *Youlou*, means 'heaven' in the language of his tribe – the Lari branch of the Kongo group to which the Bakongos of Kinshasa also belong.

He was baptised at the age of nine and three years later entered a seminary in Brazzaville. Later he continued his divinity studies in Gabon and the Cameroun, where he also read philosophy.

After working for some years with Catholic organisations, he entered politics as an independent in 1955 and polled some 40,000 votes in a legislative election. In the following year he formed his own party, launched a weekly newspaper to support its propaganda and was elected mayor of Brazzaville. In 1957 his party, the 'Union Démocratique pour la Défense des Intérêts Africains' (UDDIA), won exactly half of the seats in the Territorial Assembly. On November 28, 1958, the Assembly proclaimed the Congo Republic, and he became Prime Minister. In June, 1959, the UDDIA won the general election by a big majority and five months later, on November 21, he was elected President.

He was re-elected in March, 1961, polling 97·5 per cent of the votes. But he did not complete the five-year term for which he was elected. In August, 1963, angry crowds surrounded his palace and he was forced to resign. He had called on French troops to help restore order. They did so but did not put him back in power. He was detained in a military camp which bore his name but escaped in March, 1965, and fled across the Congo River to Kinshasa where his old friend Moise Tshombe gave him asylum. When Tshombe fell he unsuccessfully sought asylum in France. He now lives in Spain.

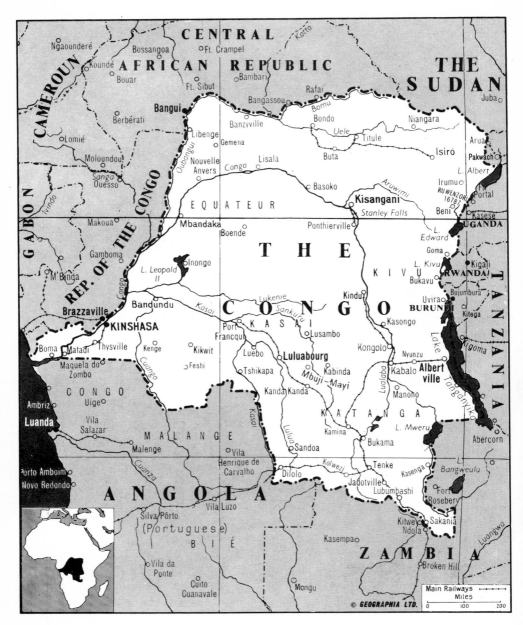

The area of the Congo Democratic Republic (Kinshasa) is 905,582 square miles. Neighbouring countries are Portuguese Cabinda, Congo Brazzaville, the Central African Republic, The Sudan, Uganda, Rwanda, Burundi, Tanzania, Zambia and Portuguese Angola. The population was last estimated in 1964 as 14,150,000. The capital is Kinshasa (renamed from the former Leopoldville).

The Republic's richest exports are copper, diamonds, gold, silver, tin, cobalt, uranium, radium, germanium, zinc and iron. Agricultural exports include timber, cotton, coffee, rubber, bananas and manioc.

74

Congo Democratic Republic (Kinshasa)

The Democratic Republic of the Congo, widely known as Congo Kinshasa, became an independent unitary state on June 30, 1960, under President Joseph Kasavubu and Prime Minister Patrice Lumumba.

The Congo had been under Belgian rule since 1885.

Four days after independence, on July 4, 1960, the Force Publique, the Congo's Army, mutinied against the Belgian officers.

On July 10, Belgian paratroops intervened and Patrice Lumumba called for United Nations intervention. A mixed force was sent in.

Meanwhile, on July 11, M. Moise Tshombe announced the secession of the rich province of Katanga and on August 8, 1960, he was elected President of the Republic of Katanga.

On September 13, 1960, General Joseph Mobutu, the Army's Commander, seized power following a serious conflict between President Kasavubu and M. Lumumba. On December 2, Lumumba was arrested and later sent to Katanga, where he was murdered.

General Mobutu retained power until February 8, 1961, when President Kasavubu resumed as head of state and appointed Joseph Ileo as Prime Minister. M. Ileo remained Prime Minister until August 1, 1961, when M. Cyrille Adoula took over. He in turn was Premier until June, 1964.

Katanga's secession was crushed by the United Nations in 1963 and M. Tshombe went into exile, returning in July, 1964, to become Prime Minister of the Congo in succession to Adoula.

General Mobutu again seized power in a military *coup* on November 25, 1965, becoming President.

The Congo Republic has a president, and a cabinet which was presided over by a prime minister until General Mobutu abolished the premiership on October 26, 1966.

Since independence, followed almost immediately by an Army mutiny, the Congo has been consistently in the world news columns.

Belgium pulled out of its former colonial empire in the heart of Africa leaving few people equipped to run the country. The Congolese inherited a tempest of mutiny, tribal warfare, secession, political assassination, civil war and anarchy. President Joseph Kasavubu in a letter to African heads of state in 1964 estimated that 80,000 had been killed during the 1964 Stanleyville uprising alone.

The upheavals were eventually to end in a takeover by the reorganised Congolese Army late in 1965. The chances of progressing in the Congo seemed brighter although troubles still threatened.

To the outside world the history of the Congo has seemed appalling. To the Congolese it has not always seemed so bad. If independence brought disorders at least they had got independence. Despite the appearance of constant upheaval, a close-knit *élite* known as the Binza group after the Kinshasa suburb where most of them live, has been in power almost continuously since independence. The group includes the present military leader, General Joseph Mobutu. There are even African pessimists in other countries who feel that if their own country is to become fully united it must one day go through the same ordeal by fire that the Congo has experienced.

The Congo's history since independence forms roughly three phases.

The first runs from independence to the end of Katanga's secession: June, 1960 to June, 1963 – three years of turmoil and political anarchy. Patrice Lumumba, the Congo's first Prime Minister, was murdered during this phase, and Katanga's secession was crushed by the United Nations.

The second phase, from June, 1963 to November, 1965, saw the return to power of Moise Tshombe, President of the breakaway Republic of Katanga. He came back from exile to become Prime Minister of the whole of the country. During this phase, there was the bloody revolt in the north-east and east of rebels who became known as the Simbas, and the setting up of a People's Republic of the Congo in Stanleyville (now Kisangani). Belgium intervened to save the lives of hostages held by the rebels. The phase ended with General Mobutu sweeping aside the bickering politicians in a *coup* on November 25, 1965.

The third phase has so far seen the gradual tightening of control by General Mobutu and his concentration of

A tree-lined avenue in the centre of Kinshasa

military and political power in his own hands. When Belgian rule ended after 75 years the Congo did not have the trained men necessary to run a country.

There were only 247 Congolese students at Lovanium, the university near Leopoldville established in 1954. In a country with a population of over 14 million, there were less than 25,000 Africans with any kind of secondary training at all.

Belgium no doubt believed she would remain in the Congo for many years after independence, mothering the young country to maturity. This belief was shattered in the very first days of independence.

Two Congolese clamoured loudest for independence: Joseph Kasavubu, who became the first President, and Patrice Lumumba, the first Prime Minister.

The Mussonoi copper mine in Katanga, the Congo's richest province

Kasavubu, short, rotund, retiring, was educated in a Catholic mission school and at one time was training for the priesthood. In 1955, he founded Abako, a cultural body which slowly turned into the Congo's first political movement. At the time, Kasavubu was a clerk in the Finance Department of the Colonial Government.

Patrice Lumumba, tall, bony, slightly stooping, was a brewery salesman with unusually persuasive oratorical ability. He joined the newly-formed 'Mouvement National Congolais' (MNC), another cultural-turned-political movement, in 1958 and rapidly assumed a position of dominance.

The Congo's demand for independence reached a crescendo in January, 1959, when the Abako staged furious demonstrations against a Belgian ban on a planned meeting. Rioting broke out in Leopoldville and in two days, the authorities said, they had counted 50 dead and 300 injured.

Independence was in the air throughout dependent Black Africa. Ghana had already achieved it; vast Nigeria had won self-rule and was moving quickly towards complete freedom. President de Gaulle had launched the fundamental changes in the structure of the French African Empire which were to lead eventually to independence. Soon Belgium gave way.

A round-table conference of Congolese leaders opening in Brussels on January 20, 1960, and ending a month later, set a date for independence: June 30.

In provincial and parliamentary elections just before independence, Lumumba's MNC, the only party with more or less national following, won by a big majority, and he was nominated Premier. Kasavubu became President.

Lumumba killed Belgium's hopes of long and close cooperation with independent Congo on Independence Day itself.

At the Brussels Conference, he had called for continued Belgo-Congolese cooperation. But with King Baudouin listening, dark-faced, Lumumba bitterly criticised Belgian rule in an Independence Day speech, asking: 'Who could forget the hangings and shootings in which perished so many of our brethren?'

He went on: 'While independence was proclaimed in

agreement with Belgium, no Congolese worthy of the name will ever be able to forget that this independence has been won through a struggle . . .

'We have experienced contempt, insults and blows . . . we knew the law was never the same for the whites and blacks.'

Four days after independence, on July 4, 1960, the *Force Publique*, the Congo's 23,000-man Army, began to mutiny throughout the country. They attacked, and in some cases killed, their white officers, raped white and black women, assaulted, pillaged, burnt and destroyed. Europeans began to flee the country. Leopoldville airport became a battleground as the soldiers tried to stop them getting away. Bullet-holes high up in the main reception hall can still be seen today.

In Elisabethville, capital of Katanga province, mutinous troops shot two of their Belgian officers and four white civilians. After three days of nightmare, Belgian troops intervened.

The Belgian intervention certainly saved many lives, but it buried any lingering hopes there might have been of Belgo-Congolese cooperation.

Lumumba cabled the Security Council asking for UN intervention. On July 13, the Security Council gave the Secretary-General Dag Hammarskjold a mandate to provide the Government with such military assistance as might be necessary until the Congo's own national security forces could function effectively again.

Two days later, the first UN troops, from Ghana and Tunisia, arrived by air in American and British transports. Mr Hammarskjold worked fast to avert the strong possibility of Big Power or direct African interference. Furious at the Belgian intervention, several African states were threatening direct action and Dr Kwame Nkrumah had already announced in Accra that he planned to send in Ghanaian troops.

The Belgian troops began to withdraw as the blue-helmeted UN troops moved in. By July 23, the Belgians had evacuated the whole country except Katanga, where they remained at Tshombe's request.

In the meantime, however, the young nation had suffered another shattering blow. Moise Tshombe had taken Katanga into secession on July 11, proclaiming the Congo's richest province an independent nation.

The Republic of Katanga was Africa's most controversial
State and its leader, Moise Tshombe, the continent's
most controversial figure.

Radical African states alleged that Tshombe and his
Government were puppets of the Union Minière du Haut
Katanga, the gigantic Belgian-controlled mineral
company. Some observers were convinced that long-
standing local tribal conflicts and the chaos in the
rest of the country pushed Katanga to secession and
helped to keep it afloat thereafter.

Katanga's two principal tribes, the Lundas and the
Balubas, both of which had large empires in mediaeval
times, have always been bitter enemies.

Even before independence, the two tribes had powerful,
implacably antagonistic groupings. The Lundas and
allied tribes had Conakat headed by Moise Tshombe,
eldest son of a wealthy merchant and both by blood and
by marriage a member of the Lunda royal family. The
Balubas had the Balubakat Cartel, led by Jason Sendwe,
a 49 year-old medical assistant turned politician.

Katanga's mines produce about eight per cent of the
world's copper, making it the world's fifth largest
producer after the United States, Chile, Zambia and
Canada. They also supply 60 per cent of the world's
supply of strategic cobalt. Until 1960, Katanga also
produced uranium. All the uranium that went into the
atom bombs dropped on Hiroshima and Nagasaki came
from the now historically famous Shinkolobwe mine,
near Jadotville. The mine, said to be exhausted, has
been closed down.

Since the turn of the century, Katanga's wealth had been
in the hands of Union Minière du Haut Katanga which not
only worked the mines, but had extensive other interests
throughout the province. The company was created in
1906 specifically to exploit Katanga's mineral resources.
It was the issue of an economic union between the vast
Société Générale de Belgique and the British Tanganyika
Concessions (generally known as Tanks) which held
15 per cent of Union Minière shares. The controlling
shares, however, were and remained in Belgian hands.

Tshombe's chief lieutenants were Godefroid Munongo, a
35 year-old Bayeke tribesman of royal blood, and Jean
Baptiste Kibwe, who represented another tribe, the
Batabwa. Munongo had the crucial Interior portfolio

in Tshombe's Government and Kibwe, a canny 37 year-old lawyer and judge before independence, was Vice-President and Finance Minister.

Tshombe's first preoccupation after secession was to build up a Katangese Army. Initially trained by Belgian officers loaned by the Belgian Government, and later stiffened by British, French, Rhodesian, South African, Italian and miscellaneous other white mercenaries, the 10,000-man Katangese Army became the best-trained and disciplined fighting force in the country. Eventually, it took an all-out effort by the United Nations, supported by jets, to defeat it.

Territorially, the Tshombe party controlled the southern half of Katanga (including most of the mining areas) while the northern half was controlled by Jason Sendwe's Balubakat Cartel.

Katanga's secession was the Central Government's biggest worry, but by no means the only one. Starvation was widespread, with an estimated 200 people dying every day.

There had been another secession. Barely a month after the Congo's independence, Albert Kalonji, once associated with Lumumba in the MNC and later leader of a splinter MNC (Kalonji) group, declared the Baluba part of South Kasai province, just north of the Katanga provincial border, an independent state. He called it the 'Mining State' and crowned himself King. Kalonji's Balubas were pro-Tshombe and there was vicious civil war between them and Jason Sendwe's Balubakat Cartel.

The Mining State's foundation was the rich local diamond industry. About nine-tenths of the Congo's diamonds come from two areas in Kasai, Bakwanga, which was Kalonji's capital, and Tshikapa.

The Mining State survived a year and a half. On a visit to Leopoldville in December, 1961, Kalonji was imprisoned and finally agreed to end his State's secession.

While Tshombe and Kalonji were breaking away from the rest of the country, the Central Government in Leopoldville was itself showing signs of strain.

The old personal and political antipathies between Patrice Lumumba and President Joseph Kasavubu exploded on September 5, 1960.

Copper ingots, stacked and ready for export, at Lubumbashi

Kasavubu announced in a radio broadcast that he had dismissed Lumumba as prime minister and replaced him by Joseph Ileo, journalist and president of the Senate. Lumumba immediately drove to Leopoldville's radio station, brushed aside the UN guards, took over the microphone and announced that he remained Prime Minister and that he had dismissed Kasavubu.

In the week that followed, Joseph Mobutu, ex-Army sergeant-turned-journalist and post-independence Army Commander, shouldered both men aside and took over the Government. He set up a 15-member 'College of High Commissioners' drawn from young University graduates to run the country.

One of Mobutu's first acts was to break off relations
with the Soviet Union and Czechoslovakia and close
down their embassies. Later, on November 18, his regime
severed diplomatic relations with Ghana on the same
grounds: meddling in the Congo's affairs. On December 1,
relations were also broken off with the United Arab
Republic.(Lumumba had been turning more and more
to these four countries for direct support and advice.)
Lumumba had meanwhile been holding out in the
prime minister's residence in Leopoldville, guarded by
Ghanaian UN troops. In late November, as his support
in Leopoldville was whittled down by Mobutu,
Lumumba apparently tried to join his supporters in
Stanleyville, where his deputy Prime Minister, Antoine
Gizenga, had set up yet another breakaway Government
– a Lumumbist regime which claimed to represent the
whole country.
Lumumba got as far as Port Franqui, a river port in
Kasai, east of Leopoldville. He was arrested and then
was brought back to Leopoldville in chains – showing
signs of having been badly beaten up – and then
imprisoned at Thysville. On January 17, he was sent by
air to Elisabethville and handed over to his worst enemies.
Less than a month later, the Katanga Government
announced that Lumumba had been killed by
unidentified villagers after escaping from Katangese
custody. The two men with him, Joseph Okito, former
Senate deputy Speaker, and Maurice Mpolo, former
Minister of Youth and Sport, were also killed. The
whereabouts of the graves of the three were never disclosed.
Ten months later, a four-nation UN Commission which
had investigated Lumumba's murder found that Tshombe,
Munongo and other members of the Katanga
Government were directly implicated. It also strongly
criticised the Central Government for handing over the
prisoners to 'their bitterest political enemies'.
Lumumba's death sparked widespread and furious
Afro-Asian reaction. He was certainly the best known
of the Congo's leaders. Even his critics were shocked by
the merciless way he had been eliminated from the
Congolese political scene.
Kasavubu named Ileo's Interior Minister, Cyrille
Adoula, as the new Prime Minister on August 1, 1961.
Adoula, 40 year-old son of a dockworker, entered

politics from the trade unions. He was left-wing in his political thinking without being a Communist. He had been on good terms with the UN since the beginning of the UN intervention.

UN troops in Katanga were reinforced by a battalion of Indian (Gurkha and Sikh) troops, bringing the total strength to about 10,000. They comprised mainly Irish, Swedish and Ethiopian troops as well as the Indians, and later they were supported by Indian, Ethiopian and Swedish jets.

Tshombe's 11,600 troops were well-armed and disciplined and largely officered by white mercenaries. In addition, there were separate all-white mercenary units.

These tough soldiers of fortune were the cause of particularly bitter criticism from both Afro-Asian states and from the UN leadership in the Congo itself. Everybody was convinced that without them, the Katanga Government would quickly collapse. They drank hard and fought hard. They were known in Katanga – affectionately or disparagingly – as *Les Affreux*, the Frightful Ones.

They were paid between £100 and £150 a month, plus living costs.

Head of the UN in Elisabethville at the time was Connor Cruise O'Brien, the eloquent, erudite Irish diplomat who played a key role in the events leading to the end of Katanga's secession. Later, he resigned from the UN.

UN hostilities against Tshombe began in August and ended in December, 1961, with Tshombe's defeat. He and a good part of his forces withdrew to Kipushi, on the Rhodesian border, and Katanga's secession eventually ended in June, 1963.

The bloody confrontation between the UN and Katanga led to one of the greatest tragedies directly connected with the Congo – the death of Dag Hammarskjold.

The 56 year-old Swedish Secretary-General of the UN was flying to Ndola, across the Katanga border in Northern Rhodesia (now Zambia), to discuss a cease fire in Katanga with Moise Tshombe. The date was September 17, 1961.

The Ndola meeting had been arranged with British help and Tshombe was already in the small Rhodesian

copperbelt town when the news came through:
Hammarskjold's Swedish UN charter plane, the
Albertina, had crashed near Ndola's airfield. The
wreckage was scattered about a 12-foot high ant-hill.
The UN Secretary-General, the plane's crew of five and
nine of the ten members of Hammarskjold's party were
dead. The tenth member of the party, an American
security officer, died six days later, unconscious most of
the time.

The crash remains a mystery. Exhaustive investigations
failed to find any evidence of sabotage or aerial or
ground attack.

By the middle of 1963, when Katanga's secession
formally ended, the Congo became for the first time
since independence one nation, at least in theory.
Despite all the difficulties, the UN had saved the
country from disintegration. The cost in men and money
had been high and there was the additional major
obstacle of the steady refusal of Russia and other
Eastern European countries and of France to contribute
to the cost of the UN operation in the Congo.

In 1964, the UN began to withdraw. In June, 1964,
Cyrille Adoula's comparatively long and eventful
premiership came to an end. But there were already
ominous new signs of rebellion.

The danger of yet another Baluba bloodbath in
north-east Katanga suddenly became dramatically
serious when Jason Sendwe, the Balubakat leader, was
found murdered in his palace at Albertville that June.
So far as is known, the murderers were never found.
Finally, in an attempt at national reconciliation,
Kasavubu recalled Tshombe from exile and asked him
to form a Government.

On July 10, just over a year after he had been forced
into exile by the UN, Tshombe was sworn in as the
Congo's fourth Prime Minister. He also took control of
foreign affairs, information and foreign trade. The key
Interior Ministry he gave to his old and faithful ally
Godefroid Munongo; he also brought in Kalonji,
erstwhile King of Kasai, as Minister of Agriculture.
Radical Africa made no secret of its deep displeasure at
this development and at least some African states gave
moral or active support to the rebellion which inevitably
broke out in the north-east and slowly spread south.

The leaders were two of Lumumba's old friends, Christophe Gbenye, tough and ruthless Minister of the Interior in Lumumba's first Government, and Pierre Mulele, another Lumumba minister. At the time of Antoine Gizenga's breakaway Republic in Stanleyville, Mulele had been his Cairo representative. When the Gizenga regime fell, Mulele went to Peking.

At first, the Gbenye-Mulele forces were a rabble of some 2,000 men armed with spears, bows and arrows, ancient shot-guns and home-made petrol bombs, but soon they acquired modern guns and learned to use them.

On September 7, 1964, Gbenye announced the formation of a 'People's Republic of the Congo' based in Stanleyville, which his men had captured early in August. Mulele remained his right-hand man and Gaston Soumialot, who had been leading the rebellion in eastern Kivu, became Defence Minister.

The People's Republic lasted nearly four months. Belgian military intervention, supported by the United States, while carried out basically to save the lives of hundreds of European hostages held by the Republic, undoubtedly played an important part in its downfall.

Over 1,500 Europeans were trapped in Stanleyville and other parts of the eastern areas by rebel forces, and their fate became increasingly problematic as Tshombe's forces, led by white mercenaries, penetrated deeper into rebel territory. The majority of the whites were Belgian and there were at least fifty Americans, and scores from Britain and various other nations.

In mid-November, Belgium decided on military action. The UN was told of the operation, which was supported by the United States and authorised in advance by Tshombe's Government and, on November 24, Belgian paratroops dropped on Stanleyville airport. By noon that day the city was taken.

Early in the afternoon, Central Government forces, spearheaded by the mercenaries led by Major 'Mad Mike' Hoare, a stocky, fair-haired Irishman, had also stormed into Stanleyville. Fighting went on both in Stanleyville and in other parts of the east for long afterwards (pockets of rebellion still existed at the end of 1966), but the People's Republic was finished. In all, it

Opposite: A Congolese
mother, transporting
her youngest in
traditional style; under
her arm she carries a
long-bladed knife

is estimated to have cost at least 8,600 Congolese and
500 European lives.

According to the Central Government, about 6,000
people were killed by the rebels – who became known as
the Simbas. After the capture of Stanleyville, about
2,000 Simbas were killed in battle and another 600
executed after summary public trials.

Belgium's intervention caused demonstrations in various
parts of Africa and at the UN there was violent Afro-
Asian and Communist reaction. But the fact was that
with the end of the People's Republic of Stanleyville,
the Congo was once again, if largely in theory, one
country.

Internal opposition to Tshombe, long suppressed,
gradually hardened. Finally, Kasavubu forced Tshombe
to resign on October 13, 1965 and appointed Evariste
Kimba, Tshombe's Foreign Minister in the days of
Katanga's secession, as the new Prime Minister.

Kimba was considered sufficiently close to Tshombe to
cushion any effects of Tshombe's dismissal. Tshombe
then left for Europe.

The Kimba Government lasted barely three weeks. As
he had done in the chaotic days of the Kasavubu-
Lumumba political conflict in September, 1960,
Mobutu, now a General, stepped in.

His *coup* on November 25, 1965, was a swift, painless
one. Mobutu's troops had been in effective command in
Leopoldville, and when he and his generals decided the
politicians had gone too far in their political wrangling,
they merely stepped in and said, 'Enough!'

Kasavubu was put under house arrest. Soon after,
Mobutu declared himself President and announced he
intended to rule for five years. After assuming full
powers, Mobutu gradually tightened his control. The
perpetually quarrelling Parliament was stripped of much
of its authority and the police force, normally under the
Minister of the Interior, became directly responsible to
the Presidency.

On May 20, 1966, Parliament, at Mobutu's instigation,
ousted Tshombe, who despite his absence from the
country had up to then kept his Parliamentary seat.

In October, Mobutu concentrated power still further in
his hands by sacking Prime Minister General Léonard
Mulamba – a member of the original group of Army

The riches of the Congo depend on its copper mines and foundries, like this one at Lubumbashi

officers who helped Mobutu take power in November, 1965 – and assuming the premiership himself.

Many independent observers believed Mobutu's firm, and at times perhaps harsh rule might well be the medicine the country needed to recover from its long sickness. Indiscipline, greed, corruption, political ambitions and immaturity, as well as tribal hatred caused the Congo tragedy; General Mobutu promised to eradicate these evils.

Some of his methods were ruthless and have been widely criticised in Africa. On June 2, 1966, four Congolese politicians were publicly hanged in a central square of Leopoldville for allegedly plotting to murder Mobutu. They were Evariste Kimba, the Prime Minister between Tshombe's dismissal and Mobutu's *coup* the previous year; Jérôme Ananay, Defence Minister in Adoula's Government; Emmanuel Bamba, a Senator and former Finance Minister in the Adoula Government, and Alexandre Mahamba, a Minister in Lumumba's first Government and again in Adoula's Cabinet.

They were tried on the afternoon of May 30 before a crowd of some 200,000 people on the grass in front of the officer's mess at the Camp Kokolo military camp outside Leopoldville. Nothing of what was said at that extraordinary trial was audible. The crowd chatted. At times there were shouts and screams. The accused appeared in chains, dirty, barefooted and dishevelled.

Some 300,000 people saw their execution on June 2, a torridly hot day which had been declared a public holiday. At the foot of the gallows lay four white coffins, the lid of the first open and waiting. All four went to their deaths without a sound, probably gagged under the black hoods that covered their heads.

The executions and the summary trial which preceded them were followed by a wave of horror and indignation throughout Africa and most other parts of the world. But in the Congo itself, the people remained largely indifferent. The country had gone through too much bloodshed and savagery to be affected by four more deaths.

Mobutu had gone ahead with the executions despite appeals from all over the world to reprieve the four men. There is no doubt he intended their hanging as a grim warning to other politicians that the time for plotting and treachery had ended.

Late in 1966, President Mobutu began moves to acquire greater Congolese control of the mainly Belgian-controlled companies which had enjoyed monopolistic rights in the country since early this century. He decreed that all such companies should have their headquarters in the Congo itself and, while most of the companies appeared to agree, the biggest, the Union Minière du Haut Katanga, refused to comply. European directors appointed to the board of a new Congo-based company, the Société Générale Congolaise des Minerais–five Belgians and one Briton–declined their seats. As 1966 ended and 1967 began, copper and ore exports had been suspended and the assets had been taken over in what the Congolese Ambassador in Brussels, M. Mungul-Diaka said was not nationalisation but 'congolisation'. By February, 1967, all but a handful of the 1,650 white technicians had applied for repatriation.

CYRILLE ADOULA

Cyrille Adoula, trade unionist and son of a dockworker, was Prime Minister of the Congo from August, 1961 to June, 1964– a crucial period which saw the final crushing of three separate secessions in the country.

Under Adoula's leadership, the Central Government broke the Lumumbist Government of Antoine Gizenga in Stanleyville, the Mining State of Albert Kalonji in South Kasai and, finally, with UN support, the breakaway Republic of Moise Tshombe in Katanga.

Adoula was born in Leopold-ville on September 13, 1921. His father was a Bangala tribesman from Equateur province and his mother a Baluba from Kasai; as a 'neutral', he later won wide general support at a time when the Congo was torn by political divisions of tribalistic origin.

Adoula was educated at the Catholic Missionary School of St Joseph in Leopoldville and later became a clerk at the Congo Central Bank. He entered politics as a Socialist and became secretary of the General Federation of Congolese Workers, the first real trade union movement allowed by the Belgians to emerge in the Congo.

In 1958, he was a founder member of the 'Mouvement National Congolais' (MNC) which, with Joseph Kasavubu's Abako, was the first organised political group in the Congo.

Another member of the MNC, Patrice Lumumba, later to become the Congo's first Prime Minister, quickly became a dominant figure in the party and in July, 1959, the group split. Patrice Lumumba became the leader of the larger part, the MNC, and Adoula aligned himself with the moderates who formed a splinter group, the MNC (Kalonji) headed by Albert Kalonji.

Adoula became Minister of the Interior in the Government formed by Joseph Ileo, in September, 1960, after President Kasavubu had dismissed Lumumba.

This Cabinet was, however, short-lived. Colonel Mobutu, Chief of Staff of the Congolese Army, seized power on September 13, 1960, peremptorily dismissing the civilian Government and announcing that the Army had decided to neutralise all political activities.

In November, 1960, Adoula became a member of the Congo's delegation to the United Nations.

On August 1, 1961, he was appointed by Kasavubu as the Congo's third Prime Minister.

His Government represented virtually all factions in the country, except that of M. Tshombe, who boycotted it. Gizenga was named one of three deputy Premiers (though he remained at his stronghold, Stanleyville, until his arrest by the Central Government four months later).

Adoula showed himself implacably opposed to any kind of compromise with Tshombe's breakaway Katanga Republic. The United Nations agreed that the Congo's richest province could not be allowed to remain a separate entity and in a series of military actions, bitterly opposed by Tshombe's white mercenary-led forces, the Katanga secession was crushed.

When Adoula resigned the premiership at the end of his mandate in June, 1964, the Congo was, for the first time since independence, one country. A new rebellion was to break out in the eastern areas later, but

Michel Colin

while he was Prime Minister, Adoula worked tirelessly for the unification of his tortured country.

Since his resignation, Adoula has spent most of his time abroad.

JEAN BOLIKANGO

Jean Bolikango is a Congolese politician with considerable support in his north-west Equateur province. Able and moderate, he has held a number of Cabinet posts in successive Governments in the Congo, including a vice-premiership. His portfolios have included Information, Defence and Public Works.

In the crisis which broke out after independence, he was active in attempts to achieve a rapprochement between Antoine Gizenga's Lumumbist breakaway Government in Stanleyville and the Central Government of M. Adoula.

M. Bolikango was also one of the Congolese leaders who went to the Tananarive round-table Conference in March, 1961. The Conference decided to create a Community of Congolese States, a loose confederation of near-sovereign states, but its decisions came to nothing.

After the Army *coup* in November, 1965, which ousted President Kasavubu and Premier Evariste Kimba, M. Bolikango was made Minister of Public Works. He was removed from office in April, 1966, by President Mobutu for disobeying a presidential order.

MICHEL COLIN

Highly respected as another of the Congo's elder statesmen, Michel Colin has held a wide variety of Cabinet posts, including those of Education and Information, and was appointed Minister of the Civil Service on November 28, 1965.

Born on October 15, 1918, in Boma in the Lower Congo, he has long been a power in the Kinshasa area, having been easily elected to Parliament from that constituency both in 1960 and 1965.

A former school teacher and journalist, he served in the information service of the Colonial Government before independence.

ALBERT DELVAUX

One of the Congo's elder statesmen, Albert Delvaux is the personable leader of the people from the Kwango area in south-western Congo.

He has held numerous Cabinet positions, including those of Labour and Justice.

He helped in the unsuccessful negotiations between the Central Government and Moise Tshombe in 1960 aimed at ending the Katanga secession.

In the 1965 elections he gained massive support from the Kwango people living in Kinshasa and held a cabinet position in the government of Evariste Kimba which failed to gain the necessary Parliamentary approval.

LEON ENGULU

Born on April 1, 1934, Léon Engulu became on April 25, 1966, Governor of the large Equateur Province comprising the Congo's north-west region.

An associate of Foreign Affairs Minister, Justin Bomboko, M. Engulu has always devoted himself to provincial affairs.

He was first Minister of the Interior and then Governor of Equateur before it was joined together early in 1966 to form a larger, more viable economic unit.

93

CHRISTOPHE GBENYE

Christophe Gbenye, born in 1927, was President of the People's Republic of the Congo, based at Stanleyville, which survived for nearly three months after its proclamation on September 10, 1964.

An old friend and supporter of Patrice Lumumba, Gbenye was a member of Lumumba's MNC party and became Minister of the Interior in Lumumba's first Government.

After Lumumba's murder in February, 1961, Gbenye joined Antoine Gizenga's Lumumbist regime in Stanleyville, but hurriedly moved to the Central Government's side when Gizenga was arrested and his regime swept away.

Late in 1963, Gbenye again switched sides, joining the rebel National Liberation Committee which was then being formed in Brazzaville, across the Congo River, and which was to sponsor and lead the rebellion in the north-east and eastern areas the following year.

Gbenye gained control of the Liberation Committee, won support from a number of African and non-African States and after his forces captured Stanleyville in August, 1964, he proclaimed himself the heir of Lumumba and President of the People's Republic.

He and most of his top leaders escaped from the Congo when Belgian paratroops and Central Government forces captured Stanleyville and other rebel-held towns in the east towards the end of November, 1964. Since then Gbenye has pursued his political ambitions outside the borders of the Congo, travelling in East and Arab Africa seeking support for another Liberation movement.

ANTOINE GIZENGA

Antoine Gizenga, self-declared political heir of Patrice Lumumba, was always more of a political symbol than a real power in Congolese affairs.

An old ally of Lumumba, he became Deputy Prime Minister in Lumumba's first Government and strongly supported the Premier in the struggle for power which broke out with President Kasavubu in September, 1960, and which was to end when the Army under Mobutu swept both Kasavubu and Lumumba out of office.

Gizenga was born in 1925 in a village near Kitwit, 250 miles east of Leopoldville. He attended a Roman Catholic seminary and served on the teaching staff of a Catholic Mission in Leopoldville before turning to politics.

In 1959, he became one of the founders and the first president-general of the 'Parti Solidaire African' (PSA), a movement of rural workers and peasants from the 25 tribes of the Kwango-Kwilu region in the south-west.

After Lumumba's dismissal from office, Gizenga fled to Stanleyville and established a pro-Lumumba breakaway regime.

Gizenga's regime was recognised later by the Communist bloc and many Afro-Asian states as the Congo's legitimate Government.

In August, 1961, however, Gizenga agreed to resume his post of Deputy Prime Minister in the Central Government and that year represented the Congo with Prime Minister Cyrille Adoula at the Belgrade Conference of Non-aligned States.

On his return, he withdrew from the Central Government and, although he never formally broke with it, refused all requests to return to Leopoldville.

Albert Kalonji

His attempt to maintain his separatist regime in Stanleyville was finally crushed by Central Government troops and Gizenga himself was arrested and imprisoned on the island of Bula Bemba in the Congo estuary.

He was released in July, 1964, by the then Prime Minister, Moise Tshombe, but the following month he announced the formation of a new political party, the United Lumumbist Party which, he said, would be 'animated by the principles of the national hero, Patrice Lumumba'.

Two months later, Gizenga was again arrested and placed under house arrest in Leopoldville, allegedly for aiding unspecified subversive elements.

He was again set free in November, 1965, after Mobutu's second *coup* and later elected national senator from his home province of Kwilu.

In February, 1966, he slipped across the Congo River with his wife and children to Brazzaville and turned up later in Moscow, declaring his safety was in danger in Leopoldville.

Towards the end of 1966, he was still in Moscow.

ALBERT KALONJI

Albert Kalonji achieved world notoriety in August, 1960 – a month after the Congo's independence – when he took his diamond-rich area of South Kasai into secession, declared it an independent Mining State, and crowned himself Emperor Albert I, God-King of the Kasai Balubas.

Born on June 8, 1919, in Kasai, Kalonji was one of the early Congolese leaders.

He became a member of the MNC and later led a splinter group, the MNC (Kalonji) which broke away after Patrice

Lumumba manoeuvred himself into the leadership of the parent body.

The Mining State formed by Kalonji after independence lasted until the end of 1962 when Kalonji, still a member of the National Assembly in Leopoldville, ill-advisedly decided to visit Leopoldville and was promptly arrested by Cyrille Adoula's Central Government.

Kalonji spent some time in prison, then went into exile in 1963, returning the following year to become Minister of Agriculture in the Government of his former fellow secessionist and ally, Moise Tshombe.

In 1965 he became a vice-president and head of the political bureau of Tshombe's Congolese National Convention Party.

Elected a senator for the Kasai region in 1965, M. Kalonji still enjoys strong regional support as a Mulopwe, a Baluba traditional chief.

CLEOPHAS KAMITATU

A special tribunal sentenced former Foreign Minister, Cléophas Kamitatu to five years' imprisonment (June 18, 1966) for alleged complicity in a plot in the previous month to kill President Mobutu. The public and press were excluded from the 45-minute trial conducted by three Army officers. No defence was allowed.

Afterwards, Army Chief of Staff, Colonel Ferdinand Malila, one of the judges, told reporters that M. Kamitatu admitted having given more than 500,000 francs (about £1,200) to one of four former ministers publicly hanged in Leopoldville's main square a fortnight previously for their part in the plot.

The ministers hanged included former Prime Minister Evariste

Jean-Jacques Kande

Joseph Kasavubu

Kimba, under whom Kamitatu served as Foreign Minister until the Government was overthrown by General Mobutu in November, 1965.

Kamitatu gave himself up on June 1, 1966, after his name was listed among those due for government posts if the alleged plot was successful. Colonel Malila said that on May 29, the night the plot was broken, Kamitatu had a meeting with Kimba. On a trip to Europe he also had contact with a number of Congolese politicians.

Kamitatu was at one time Governor of the former Southwestern province and was Interior Minister, later Planning and Coordination Minister, in the Cyrille Adoula Government.

On the day he was sentenced, Government undercover agents who discovered the plot were either promoted or decorated in public. One was Lieutenant-Colonel Pierre Efomi, who first reported the plot in the middle of March.

Among those barred from the military tribunal was M. Jules Wolf, a Belgian lawyer and President of the Judicial Commission of the International Human Rights Commission, which is affiliated to the United Nations. He said afterwards that Kamitatu should have been tried in public and allowed a defence counsel.

JEAN-JACQUES KANDE

Jean-Jacques Kande was appointed High Commissioner for Information immediately after the *coup* in which President Kasavubu was overthrown.

He had been a colleague of the new President, Mobutu, when both men worked on a Congolese weekly newspaper before independence.

Kande is regarded in political circles as a close confidant of M. Mobutu, exerting considerable influence as controller of the country's mass media.

A member of the Baluba tribe, M. Kande was born in Leopoldville on April 23, 1930.

In 1957, when he had become well-known as a writer, he wrote a series of articles on hemp addiction in the Congo, which led the Belgians to imprison him for a short period.

On his release he studied at the University of Elisabethville and in 1960 visited East and West Europe, returning later for two years' study in Prague. He also studied journalism in France, qualifying from the leading French school of journalism, and later worked in the United States as a senior staff member in a press and public relations firm.

In 1963 he was named by the then Prime Minister Cyrille Adoula to head the Government-run Congolese News Agency, a post he held despite opposition from the new Prime Minister, M. Tshombe.

JOSEPH KASAVUBU

Joseph Kasavubu was President of the Congo from independence, on June 30, 1960, until September 13, 1960, when General Mobutu seized power, and again from shortly afterwards until Mobutu's second *coup*, in November, 1965.

Joseph Kasavubu fathered the Congo's independence. He has had the longest leading role yet in the country's turbulent story.

He was often in the centre of the stage, but as often stood in the background, waiting patiently, suggesting the lines to lesser actors or manipulating the plot.

In appearance, he is anything but the hero type. He is small and plump, with a rotund face and thick glasses which distort the oriental slant of his eyes. He speaks softly, is inclined to ramble when launched on one of his pet subjects – such as the language and history of his tribe, the Bakongo–and is shy, retiring, and often indecisive.

Yet he proved for five and a half years to be the most astute and durable of the Congo's politicians. He gave the Presidency enough prestige to make it the one stable element in his storm-tossed country.

Kasavubu was born at Tshela, a village south of Leopoldville, near the Congo's Atlantic coast. The year of his birth is not known precisely, but was probably 1917.

His early education was at Catholic mission schools and for three years he trained for the priesthood at Catholic seminaries. He changed his mind in his last year at the Seminary at Kabwe, in Kasai province, and enrolled at a teacher training college. He became a teacher and then went into the Belgian administration as a clerk.

His drift into politics began in 1955, when he became President of Abako, at that time a non-political organisation created to 'unify, expand and defend' Kikongo, the language of Kasavubu's tribe, the Bakongo.

The Bakongo had a powerful and relatively sophisticated empire in the south-western Congo from the early 14th century to the latter part of the 17th, and at one time were one of the very few African empires with active diplomatic relations with Europe. There were Bakongo ambassadors in Portugal, Spain and the Vatican and a Papal Nuncio at Mbanza, the Bakongo capital.

Kasavubu's great passion was not so much for Congolese independence as for at least some form of autonomy for the one million members of the Bakongo tribe. Like Moise Tshombe, who became President of secessionist Katanga, Kasavubu envisaged a loose Congolese federation with wide tribal self-government.

Whatever Kasavubu's political feelings were, it was the agitation of his party for independence which led the way to the end of Belgian rule.

Abako riots broke out in Leopoldville in January, 1959, after the Belgians banned a party meeting. Official estimates spoke of 50 dead; party sources said there were five times as many. Kasavubu was imprisoned for two months, then sent to Brussels for secret talks with the Government.

By the end of 1959, Belgium gave in to pressure from Abako and from Patrice Lumumba's MNC party, a conference of Congolese leaders was called in Brussels in January, 1960, and Independence Day was fixed for June 30 that year.

Kasavubu had been manoeuvring for the premiership, but in general elections in May, 1960, Lumumba's party emerged victorious. Lumumba became the Congo's first Prime Minister and Kasavubu its first President.

Conservative, anti-Communist and at heart a federalist, Kasavubu was soon in conflict with his mercurial, left-wing Prime Minister who sought to forge a unitary state which ignored the country's tribal realities.

On September 5, 1960, after barely two months of joint rule, Kasavubu sacked Lumumba, who announced in turn that he had dismissed Kasavubu. Before there could be a head-on collision,

General Joseph Mobutu dismissed both Kasavubu and Lumumba and assumed power.

For Lumumba it was the end. He was arrested by Mobutu's troops two months later, sent to Elisabethville in January and murdered shortly after.

For Kasavubu, it was a brief interlude. Mobutu soon found he needed the political skill and prestige of Kasavubu. The President was reinstated and remained head of state until Mobutu's second *coup* in November, 1965.

Throughout Kasavubu's Presidency, the situation in his country would have severely tested the most consummate politician.

Parts of the country were in secession, politicians quarrelled, the Army could never be fully trusted, the administrative machine was in chaos.

There was almost continuous external interference of one kind or another—ranging from discreet pressure to direct intervention. Even Cuba broke in on the act and during the short-lived People's Republic of Stanleyville, there were Castroist Army instructors with the insurgent regime and Cuban exiles flying in Central Government planes.

Then, there was the United Nations. Kasavubu's relations with the UN force in the Congo fluctuated. At one time, in the first months of 1961, he was calling for the UN's withdrawal; later, he apparently came round to the UN's firm objective of a unitary state.

One of Kasavubu's skills was to know precisely when to step back and let others play the leading roles.

He did this when the United Nations decided in the middle of 1961 to crush Katanga's secession. It was Kasavubu's Prime Minister, Cyrille Adoula, who gave the Central Government's blessing to the UN military action.

A year later, when Adoula's premiership ended, Kasavubu could, without too great a loss of face, recall Moise Tshombe from exile and ask him to become Prime Minister of the whole country.

Kasavubu's relations with Tshombe were anything but cordial. They shared much in common, politically: but it soon became apparent that they also shared a common desire for the Presidency. Kasavubu wanted to keep it and Tshombe was very obviously aiming to take it.

On October 13, 1965, Kasavubu – as he had done back in September, 1960 – moved quickly, and won, though his victory this time was brief.

He used his constitutional powers to force Tshombe to resign as Premier and appointed a new Prime Minister, Evariste Kimba, who had been Tshombe's foreign minister during Katanga's secession. Kasavubu probably hoped that the appointment of a man still fairly close to Tshombe would avert a direct confrontation with Tshombe himself.

But this was averted anyway. On November 25, 1965, General Mobutu stepped in, swept civilian government aside, declared himself President and announced he planned to rule for at least five years.

Kasavubu was kept under house arrest in a military camp outside Leopoldville for a week. Then, after announcing his full support for the new military regime, he went back to his small farm near Boma, 300 miles south-west of Leopoldville.

Kasavubu may have hoped that history would repeat itself

Jean Marie Kikangala

Félicien Kimvay

Gen Joseph Mobutu

and that General Mobutu would again have to turn to him for support. But this time, the General announced that he intended to rule for the next five years. And he specifically decreed that neither Kasavubu nor Tshombe would be allowed to return to Congolese politics, at least for that time.

JEAN MARIE KIKANGALA

Jean Marie Kikangala, Minister for Posts, Telephones and Telegraphs, was born in Lubumbashi on March 10, 1937, his family coming from the Kasai.

After secondary studies in Lubumbashi, he went to Brussels where he became a doctor of law. On his return to the Congo during the summer of 1965 he practised law in Luluabourg, before going to Kinshasa, where he was a barrister in the Court of Appeal until his appointment as Minister on December 17, 1966.

He became involved in politics long before independence and was president of the Lubumbashi branch of the People's Party in 1959–60. Later he was a militant member of the Student's Trade Union – the 'Union Générale des Etudiants Congolais' (UGEC) in Brussels.

Soon after his return to the Congo he was elected Governor of the Lomami Province, but he did not hold office as the province became part of the Eastern Kasai Province in April, 1966. At the election for the governorship of the latter province he was beaten by M. Jonas Mukanda, by 41 votes to 37.

FELICIEN KIMVAY

Félicien Kimvay is Minister for Labour, a post he also held in the Central Government of

Joseph Ileo from February to August, 1961.

Born in 1930 in Kingulu, in the Province of Badundu, he studied in Kinzambi, became a civil servant and then taught from 1956–59.

It was then that he began his political career and became the first vice-president of Antoine Gizenga's 'Parti de la Solidarité Africaine' (PSA) in 1960.

In the same year in May, he was elected a member of the Lower House on the PSA list. In 1965 he was elected Senator for the Kwango Province.

He is President of the Southern Kwilu (Kwilu Méridional), one of the twenty autonomous States recognised by the Coquilhatville Conference (April-May, 1961).

VITAL MOANDA

For a long time leader with former President Kasavubu of the Lower Congo area, Vital Moanda became in 1961 Governor of the strategically important Kongo Central Province, through which the mouth of the Congo River flows.

Born in 1922, he is considered a moderate, conservative leader.

LT-GEN JOSEPH MOBUTU

General Joseph Mobutu declared himself President of the Democratic Republic of the Congo soon after seizing power in a *coup* on November 25, 1965.

Born on October 14, 1930, Mobutu is married and has seven children.

He became Chief of Staff of the Congo's Army immediately after independence, seized power on September 13, 1960, held it for five months, then handed it back to a civilian Government.

He became Commander-in-Chief of the Congo's Armed Forces in January, 1961, being promoted from colonel to major-general. He was promoted to lieutenant-general on November 4, 1965 – three weeks before his *coup d'état*.

In October, 1966, he dismissed his Prime Minister, General Leonard Mulamba, becoming both head of state and head of government.

When General Mobutu seized power, 15 of the country's highest ranking officers – the military High Command – had sat up all night planning their moves. As dawn broke, a group of officers went to the radio station and announced that the Army under General Mobutu had taken over. Another group went to the presidential palace and told Joseph Kasavubu he was no longer President.

There was no bloodshed and no ostentatious show of force. The Army had held effective power, and now it had decided to assume executive power as well.

Later that day, Mobutu announced that he intended to rule for five years. He said he and his officers had acted because the country was 'rent by a political feud' between Kasavubu and former Prime Minister Moise Tshombe. Kasavubu had forced Tshombe to resign on October 13, and there was no doubt that Tshombe intended to challenge Kasavubu for the Presidency.

It was the second time that Mobutu had intervened directly and forcefully in Congolese political conflicts. On the previous occasion, September 13, 1960, the two contestants were Kasavubu and the Congo's first Prime Minister, Lumumba.

Kasavubu had dismissed Lumumba. Lumumba, in turn, announced he had dismissed Kasavubu.

Mobutu seized power and dismissed them both.

Mobutu was born in the town of Lisala, in north-west Congo. His tribe, the Bengala, traditionally supplied more recruits to the Congolese Army than any other, and Mobutu duly enrolled for seven years when he was 19, after a primary and secondary education at missionary schools.

The slim, bespectacled, earnest Mobutu left the Army with the rank of sergeant and turned to journalism.

He worked for a daily newspaper, *L'Avenir*, and a weekly, *Actualités Africaines*, of which he later became editor. At the same time, he made his first probe into politics, joining Patrice Lumumba's MNC. He went with Lumumba to the Brussels round-table conference of Congolese leaders in January, 1960, where Lumumba's ideal of a unitary Congo State was accepted by the Belgians.

Mobutu had developed considerable organisational abilities in the Army and he used them on Lumumba's behalf in Brussels. Later he was to use them to reorganise the Congolese Army.

Immediately after independence, Mobutu became Chief of Staff with the rank of Colonel, under the Commander-in-Chief, General Victor Lundala.

Lundala had been a sergeant-major in the old Congolese Army – one rank higher than Mobutu.

In the first weeks of independence, Mobutu established himself as the country's most outstanding Congolese officer. He travelled about in a light plane, appointing Congolese officers, trying to restore some discipline to an Army which had mutinied and turned into a rabble. Whenever he could, he rescued Europeans, mainly from the hands of mutinous soldiers.

In September, 1960, Kasavubu dismissed Lundula and Mobutu became Commander-in-Chief. And, almost immediately, came his first *coup*.

Mobutu appointed 15 University graduates and Congolese technicians, known as the 'Collège des Commissaires', to run the machinery of government. He himself retained leadership of the Army and was the obvious power behind the College.

Kasavubu was quickly reinstated as President of the Republic.

The Government expelled all Russian and East European diplomats and experts in the country and broke off diplomatic relations. At one press conference, Mobutu alleged that there had been Communist interference in the country's international affairs.

Relations with Ghana and with the United Arab Republic were also broken off on similar grounds.

In February, 1961, the College was disbanded. Power was handed back to a constitutional Government headed by President Kasavubu and Prime Minister Cyrille Adoula and Mobutu turned his talents to rebuilding the Congolese Army, now renamed the ANC ('Armée Nationale Congolaise'). But at the same time he kept a close watch on political events.

By the middle of 1961, he and a small group of politicians and businessmen formed a group, known as the Binza group after the Leopoldville suburb where they all lived, which wielded considerable influence in Leopoldville for the next four years.

Mobutu, now a major-general,

accepted some outside help to train his men. He himself took a parachute course in Israel.

He taught his men courage by example. In May, 1963, he walked alone into a camp of mutinous police on the outskirts of Leopoldville and curtly ordered them to put down their guns. Meekly, they obeyed. Mobutu's troops then moved in, stripped the police down to their underpants and paraded them to the ridicule of the delighted crowd that had gathered.

By the time Mobutu seized power a second time in November, 1965, he had the backing of a 25,000-man force which still had serious limitations but had started to look like an army.

There was no other force in the country to oppose him and he could brush aside the existing executive almost contemptuously.

Soon after taking over, Mobutu began to tighten control on the country and concentrate most of the real power in his own hands.

He declared himself President and gave himself powers to rule by decree. He took away most of Parliament's legislative authority (he restored some of Parliament's powers later), suspended all provincial assemblies, reduced the number of Congolese provinces from 21 to 12 and later from 12 to eight to streamline provincial administration.

He also put Leopoldville under direct military control and decreed that the police force, up to now the responsibility of the Interior Minister, would come under him.

Four former Ministers alleged to have plotted to kill Mobutu were summarily tried and hanged in public.

After the takeover, Mobutu had formed a Cabinet which included both civilians and military

Gen Léonard
Mulamba

men, but in October, 1966, he dismissed his Prime Minister, General Léonard Mulamba, one of the military High Command involved in the 1965 *coup*.

Mobutu assumed the premiership himself and announced that the old 'two-headed' form of Government, which in fact had been the direct cause of much of the Congo's woes in the past, had been abolished. He declared Lumumba a national hero.

MAJ-GEN LEONARD MULAMBA

Major-General Léonard Mulamba gained international fame for his defence of the eastern town of Bukavu and for conducting one of the most decisive battles of the 1964 north-east rebellion. This was the most important and most impressive stand by Government troops and American military attachés nicknamed him 'Leonard the Lion'.

When Kisangani (formerly Stanleyville) was recaptured from rebel forces later in 1964, he was named military governor of the entire north-east region and played a prominent part not only in the pacification of the area but also in the reconstruction programme.

General Mulamba, who had been Chief of Staff since October, 1964, was one of a group of 15 senior officers who staged the bloodless Army *coup* of November 25, 1965, which swept away the Government of President Joseph Kasavubu and installed General Mobutu in his place. Mulamba was named Prime Minister at the head of an all-civilian Cabinet.

He was removed from the premiership on October 26, 1966, following pressure from the Army High Command. He was reported first to have refused nomination and then to have accepted it. Meanwhile President Mobutu became head of Government as well as President.

Over Kinshasa Radio, Colonel Ferdinand Malila, Army High Command spokesman, admitted that the Army had been responsible for the General's removal from the premiership. He accused him of being implicated in the mutiny of 3,000 gendarmes in Kisangani in July, 1966, and said he 'had gone so far as to cast doubt on the authority of the President of the Republic'.

Born in Kasai region in 1930, General Mulamba has been a professional soldier all his life, joining the then Belgian-run Force Publique in 1949.

By independence in 1960 he was a sergeant-major and quickly became an officer. In 1962 he was assigned the difficult task of commanding the Third Army group based in Kisangani, which had earlier supported a breakaway government.

General Mulamba has always enjoyed great popularity with the troops. He is known for his straightforward approach to problems. He has a sizeable farm outside Kinshasa to which, he has said, he would like to retire some day.

GODEFROID MUNONGO

Godefroid Munongo was Tshombe's tough, resourceful and loyal Interior Minister and ally during Katanga's secession.

Born in 1925, Munongo is a grandson of M'Siri, last leader of the great Empire of the Bayeke tribe which ruled most of Katanga until the Belgians took over in the first years of this century.

Munongo was educated at Catholic mission schools in the Bayeke tribal capital of Bunkeya and at Elisabethville. Like

Paul Mushiete

Kasavubu, he spent two years in a seminary, but broke off his studies for the priesthood to enter the Kisantu College near Leopoldville. He studied administration there for four years, then entered the Colonial Government.

He became a founder-member of Conakat in July, 1959, and when Tshombe formed his secessionist Government in July, 1960, Munongo became his Minister of Interior and chief lieutenant.

Throughout the period of secession, Munongo worked closely with Tshombe, deputising for him when he was away, and once when he was arrested at Coquilhatville during a round-table conference. Munongo's behind-the-scene manoeuvres contributed largely to Tshombe's release.

A UN Commission which investigated the murder in Katanga of Lumumba in February, 1961, alleged that Munongo, together with both Tshombe and the Katangese Finance Minister, Jean Baptiste Kibwe, was present at the murder. Munongo himself vehemently denied this charge, as did Tshombe and Kibwe.

After Tshombe returned from exile to form a national Congolese Government in Leopoldville in June, 1964, Munongo became his Interior Minister and held the post until the following year when, largely because of pressure within the Cabinet, Tshombe sent him to Elisabethville to become Governor of the province of South Katanga.

In November, 1966, precisely a year after General Mobutu's *coup*, Munongo was recalled to Leopoldville and put under house arrest. Two other Congolese provincial governors were also arrested, all three allegedly because they maintained links with Moise Tshombe, who was again in exile in Europe.

Munongo continues to enjoy wide authority and power in Katanga, particularly among his own warlike Bayeke tribe. One of his brothers, Antoine Mwenda, is a paramount chief of the Bayekes.

PAUL MUSHIETE

Paul Mushiete, Minister for National Economy, was born in Leopoldville on November 19, 1934.

After schooling in Leopoldville, he went to the University of Louvain in Belgium where he graduated in political and economic sciences in 1959.

In 1960, he joined the Central Bank of Congo and Ruanda-Urundi, and became Deputy Commissioner for Finance later the same year when President Mobutu first took control of the country.

In 1962, he was appointed chargé d'affaires in Paris and remained there until early 1966.

On his return to the Congo he was appointed president of the Development Bank, a post he retained after his nomination as head of the Ministry for Economy on December 17, 1966.

THEODORE MWAMBA

A former soccer player and referee, Théodore Mwamba is High Commissioner for Youth and Sport (December 17, 1966).

He was born on January 15, 1929, at Jadotville. He has played and refereed for the Jadotville Sporting Association.

In 1960 he was appointed President of the Sporting Association of Lubumbashi and in 1965 was elected vice-president of FASCO – 'Fédération des Associations Sportives du Congo'.

He is an ex-judge of the

Victor Nendaka

Victor N'Joli

Lubumbashi District Court, a post to which he was elected in 1963.

He was nominated Joint High Commissioner for Youth and Sport in 1965.

VICTOR NENDAKA

Victor Nendaka was once an ally of the Congo's first prime minister, Patrice Lumumba, serving originally as vice-president of his National Congolese Movement political party before independence.

Claiming that Lumumba was a Communist, however, M. Nendaka later broke away and formed his own party. Before independence he was in commercial undertakings in Leopoldville, including insurance and travel agency work.

He became chief of the 'Sûreté Nationale' after M. Lumumba was dismissed as prime minister and in that post wielded considerable power. Although he supported the return to the Congo of Moise Tshombe in 1964 and even joined Tshombe's Congolese National Convention political party in 1965, he worked with Justin Bomboko and Cléophas Kamitatu to form a rival party around the then president, Joseph Kasavubu, who, using this strength, ousted Tshombe in October that year.

On Kasavubu's insistence, M. Nendaka served briefly as Minister of the Interior under Tshombe and held the same post in the short-lived Government of Evariste Kimba which replaced M. Tshombe.

Although appointed to the seemingly minor position of Minister of Transport and Communications in the Mobutu Government in November, 1965, M. Nendaka is nevertheless considered one of the President's

closest advisers and confidants.

He was born in Buta, northern Congo, on April 14, 1924.

VICTOR N'JOLI

Victor N'Joli, High Commissioner of Cultural Affairs and Tourism, is a member of the Executive Committee of the African Football Association.

He was born on April 1, 1928 at Leopoldville and worked for a commercial company for 15 years until 1965.

He was joint High Commissioner for Youth and Sport from November, 1965-December, 1966.

LT-COL HONORE NKULUFA

As Chief of Staff of the Congolese National Army, Lieut-Colonel Honoré Nkulufa has represented his country at several international conferences, particularly at OAU meetings on defence problems at Addis Ababa (1965) and Nairobi (1966).

Born in Bazafe (Province of Equateur) on February 17, 1930, he joined the Army in 1949 and took a training course in 1961 at the Ecole d'Informations Sociales et Culturelles de l'Armée Belge.

By 1962 he was *chef de cabinet* at the Defence Ministry in the Adoula Government.

He was Deputy Chief of Staff when he succeeded Lieut-Col Ferdinand Malila as Chief of Staff on December 16, 1966.

MOISE TSHOMBE

Moise Tshombe was President of Katanga during the Province's secession from July 11, 1960 to early in 1963.

He spent a year in exile, then returned to become Prime Minister of the Congo. Forced to resign by President Kasavubu on October 13, 1965, M. Tshombe again retired into exile.

Moise Tshombe

Moise-Kapenda Tshombe is one of the most extraordinary figures thrown up by African politics in the past decade.

He took Katanga, the Congo's richest province, into secession shortly after the country's independence on June 30, 1960 – and for two and a half years headed a State which no other country in the world recognised.

He went into exile for a year, from June, 1963 to June, 1964, then returned triumphantly to become Prime Minister of the whole Congo – only to flee into exile again at the end of 1965.

He is Africa's only political leader to have lost his State as a result of direct military action by the United Nations.

He has been Africa's most vilified politician. And even after becoming Prime Minister of the whole Congo, he remained unwelcome at African gatherings. When, uninvited, he tried to attend a summit conference of non-aligned states in Cairo in October, 1964, he was promptly placed under house arrest in a Cairo suburb – the only ruling prime minister of an independent African state to have suffered such an indignity.

Tshombe is nearly six feet tall, burly, with slightly protruding eyes and a huge smile. He is an extrovert, fast-talking and eloquent, shrewd, exceptionally energetic. He has made loyal friends – and bitter enemies. He was an effective leader at times when the Congo needed real leadership, but his personal ambitions were unbounded and certainly contributed to his political downfall.

He is one of Africa's most anti-Communist major politicians – and has probably been the most abused by Communist countries.

Moise (Moses) Tshombe was born at Musumba, in Katanga, on November 10, 1919. Related by blood to the royal Lunda family of Mwatiamvu, he later reinforced his royal ties by marrying a daughter of Chief Bako Ditende, who later became ruler of all the Lundas.

The great, warlike, astute Lunda tribe dominates southern Katanga and spreads into neighbouring Portuguese Angola. The Lundas had an extensive empire in mediaeval times. It disintegrated in the 18th century, but the Lundas remained south Katanga's predominant tribe.

Tshombe was the eldest son of Joseph Kapenda Tshombe, a wealthy businessman who owned a chain of village stores, a sawmill, an hotel, a fleet of trucks and a number of cotton plantations.

Moise had a secondary education at an American mission school, then went into the family business – and proved a failure. Three times, the Tshombe business was declared bankrupt and finally Moise handed all business affairs over to one of his brothers and turned to politics. Here he was much more successful.

He was popular both with the Belgian businessmen and Administration in Katanga and with his Lunda fellow tribesmen. In 1956, he became president of the Confederation of Mutual Associations of the Lunda Empire, a non-political group which, however, formed the basis of a new political movement, the 'Confédération des Associations du Katanga' (known as Conakat) in July, 1959.

Conakat comprised both Tshombe's old Lunda Association and allied tribal bodies and as its President, Tshombe went to the Brussels round-table con-

105

ference called in January, 1960 to decide the Congo's future. Tshombe pressed for a weak federation which took into account the country's tribal divisions, but Patrice Lumumba's demands for a unitary state were accepted by the Belgians.

On July 11, 1960, eleven days after the Congo became independent, Tshombe declared Katanga an Independent Republic. On August 8, he was elected head of state by the Katanga Assembly.

Territorially, his Government controlled the southern part of Katanga while the north remained in the hands of the Lundas' bitter enemies, the Balubas.

Financially, Katanga had the support of the giant, Belgian-controlled Union Minière du Haut Katanga.

Politically, Katanga had the moral backing of what was then Northern Rhodesia and the unofficial sympathies of Belgium and France, and perhaps of Britain.

Diplomatically, Tshombe failed to win any recognition. Radical Africa considered him a traitor, and even the more moderate African States were reluctant to support a secession which could set a dangerous precedent in a continent still divided by tribal loyalties.

The murder in Katanga of Patrice Lumumba, the Congo's first Prime Minister, early in 1961 killed any chance Tshombe might have had of achieving eventual general acceptance.

The UN crushed Katanga's secession in a series of increasingly fierce battles in the second half of 1962 and in January, 1963, Tshombe gave in. He stayed on in Katanga until June that year, then went into exile and the province became an effective part of the Congo again.

After eye treatment in France, Tshombe moved to Madrid and from a luxurious suite of offices plotted his return to the Congo.

The country was now united for the first time since independence, but bitter political conflicts were bringing new threats of secession. Prime Minister Cyrille Adoula's term of office was nearing its end and a fierce political scramble had broken out for the succession.

The UN had gone; rebel activity, dormant for a time, was again reported in the north-east.

President Joseph Kasavubu recalled Tshombe and asked him to form a Government.

The President had never liked Tshombe and probably turned to him reluctantly, but, paradoxically, the Katangese secessionist was at the time the only Congolese politician with any chance of keeping the country comparatively united.

Tshombe was sworn in as the Congo's fourth Prime Minister on July 10, 1964, and formed what he called a Government of National Reconciliation.

Within a month, he was facing his biggest trial. Insurgents headed by former associates of Patrice Lumumba captured Stanleyville, the Congo's third largest city. A month later, they set up a People's Republic of the Congo, headed by Christophe Gbenye, Minister of Interior in Lumumba's Government.

Twice Tshombe provoked the furious reaction of radical African States. First, he recruited white mercenaries (as he had done in the early days of Katanga's secession) to strengthen the Congolese Army. Then, in November, 1964, he formally authorised Belgium to send in paratroops to save the lives of

Ferdinand Tumba

about 1,500 whites, mainly Belgians, held as hostages by the Stanleyville regime. The paratroops and the mercenary-led Army broke the rebellion.

Under Tshombe's driving leadership, the Congo's administrative machine, laboriously rebuilt by the UN after its post-independence collapse, gradually became more effective. But political opposition to Tshombe himself was mounting. It became increasingly clear as 1965 went by that Tshombe was aiming at Joseph Kasavubu's presidency.

Kasavubu used his constitutional powers to force Tshombe to resign the premiership on October 13, 1965 – and the decks appeared to have been cleared for a power struggle between the two.

But General Joseph Mobutu and his top Army officers seized power on November 28, 1965. One of Mobutu's first announcements was that he planned to rule for five years – and that both Kasavubu and Tshombe would have to stay out of Congolese politics at least for that time.

Tshombe went back into exile in Madrid.

Since then, he has lost his seat in the Congolese Parliament. In September, 1966, General Mobutu filed charges of high treason against him, alleging he was behind a mutiny by Katangese units in Stanleyville.

Mobutu's aim appeared to be not so much to bring Tshombe to trial – a dangerous manoeuvre in view of Tshombe's continuing support among the Lundas – as to persuade him to stay out of the country. Those who know the resilient Katangese leader are, however, reluctant to believe he will resign himself quickly to political retirement.

Tshombe is married and has ten children.

FERDINAND TUMBA

Ferdinand Tumba, Minister for Land, Mines and Energy, was born in Lubumbashi on December 5, 1930.

He began his political career in Katanga and became senator for North Katanga in 1965.

He first studied medicine, but for ten years years and until 1960 worked in a lawyer's office.

A former municipal councillor for Lubumbashi, he belonged to the 'Mouvement National Congolaise, Patrice Lumumba's party, before joining Jason Sendwe's Balubakat party and becoming a member of the political executive.

He was a political detainee from February, 1961 to April, 1962, during the Katangese secession.

In 1963 he joined the North Katanga Provincial Government.

He was elected permanent secretary of the Afro-Asian Solidarity Organisation in Cairo in April, 1960.

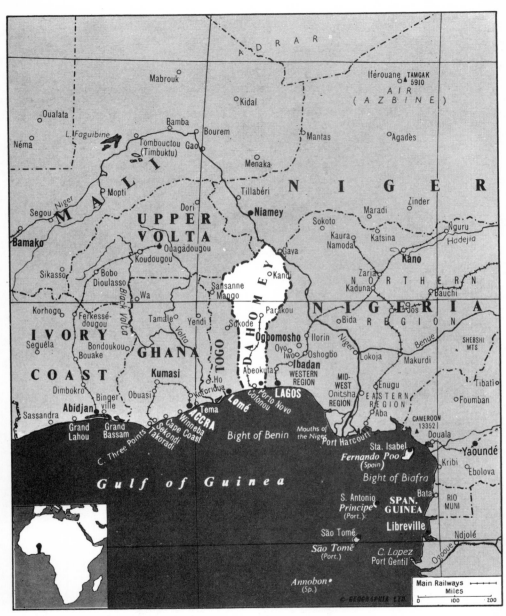

Dahomey's population of about 2,500,000 (1965), is spread over an area of 44–45,000 square miles. It is one of the smallest countries of Africa and lies between giant Nigeria and tiny Togo. In the north are short frontiers with Niger and Upper Volta. The capital is Porto Novo. The economy of Dahomey depends on her principal exports of palm kernels, palm oil and shelled groundnuts. The chief port and business centre is Cotonou.

Dahomey

The Republic of Dahomey became independent on
August 1, 1960. It had been a French territory since
1904.
General Christophe Soglo, Army Chief of Staff, overthrew
the Government on October 27, 1963. President Maga
resigned and the National Assembly was dissolved.
On November 29, 1965, General Soglo forced the
resignations of the President, Sourou Migan Apithy, and
the Prime Minister, Justin Ahomadegbe.
On December 22, 1965, General Soglo sized supreme
power, presiding over a military Government.

Since she became independent of France in 1960,
Dahomey has faced an unchanged basic problem – that of
growing into a modern nation with virtually no natural
resources or economic potential.
A series of civilian governments failed to bring either
economic or political stability, and in December, 1965,
the Dahomey Army, led by its Commander, General
Christophe Soglo, took power in the country.
Since then, Dahomey has been ruled by a military
Government, with General Soglo as President, and has
settled down to the task of husbanding what little wealth
lies within her arbitrary frontiers inherited from the
colonial era.
Dahomey is primarily an agricultural country with
vegetation varying from rain forest along the short
coastline to savannah in the north. Palm produce, fish
and cattle contribute to a gross domestic product of some
£50m sterling, and palm kernels, nuts and oil make up
80 per cent of the country's exports.
There are no mineral resources and no economic wealth
to provide the material needs of a modern nation, such as
roads, schools and communications.
Most of Dahomey's development projects are paid for by
foreign aid mainly from her former colonial ruler, France,
with whom Dahomey has maintained friendly relations
since independence.
France also provides a subsidy to help balance the
country's administration budget, as well as financing
development projects.
Perhaps Dahomey's biggest problem after independence
was that her early leaders paid little attention to the

Digging for the future: one aspect of General Soglo's roadmending and ditchdigging campaign

country's slender resources, and embarked on government spending far out of proportion to the national potential.

The tone was set by the first President, Hubert Maga, whose regime was marked by massive prestige-spending which has still left its elegant mark on Dahomey's picturesque business centre, Cotonou.

Wasteful spending on a luxury sea-front palace and grandiose esplanade, together with other fine but unnecessary public buildings, was a major factor in the discontent which led to President Maga being ousted by popular revolt in 1963.

President Maga's overthrow also brought into the limelight for the first time General Soglo who, as Colonel Soglo of Dahomey's Army, controlled the bloodless end of President Maga's 'first republic' and headed briefly an interim Government until a new constitution was drawn up.

The second republic, born of the revolt, was marred by

A group of women
potters in their village
workshop

intense personal and political rivalry between the two
men chosen as leaders – President Sourou-Migan Apithy
and Prime Minister Justin Ahomadegbe. This, together
with growing financial problems heightened by the
substantial loss of revenue caused by the closure of the
French military base in Dahomey, perpetuated a climate
of political unrest.

In November, 1965, rivalry between President Apithy
and Prime Minister Ahomadegbe reached a climax when
a constitutional deadlock was brought about by their
failure to agree over the appointment of a judge to head
the Supreme Court.

General Soglo again stepped in. He used the Army to
force political arbitration and, in a bloodless *coup*,
dismissed both leaders. This time, General Soglo
appointed as head of state the man next in line under the
constitution – the little-known President of the National
Assembly, Tahirou Congacou – and gave him the task of
organising fresh national elections.

Above: The stilt houses
of Ganevie which may
be reached only by
boat or canoe

Below: A Dahomey
mud-building; the
external walls are
decorated with line
patterns before the
mud sets hard

M. Congacou failed to make any impact on the
complicated political situation, and in December, 1965,
realising that no progress was being made towards
putting the country's affairs in order, General Soglo
stepped in for the third time – this time taking power
himself.

He suspended the constitution, banned political parties
and dissolved municipal councils, instituting a mixed
military and civilian Government, with himself as
President, which lasted through 1966.

The General's policies on assuming office were based on
what he himself described as 'simple military common
sense'. He dealt firmly with any attempt at agitation by
trade unions or political groups, and forced into operation
the country's first austerity budget.

General Soglo has said he recognises that Dahomey's
meagre, largely subsistence economy cannot generate
enough capital for development, and must still rely on
French and other foreign aid, but his aim is to show that
Dahomey is a nation worthy of being helped.

In 1966, General Soglo launched two campaigns – the
'Return to the Fields' and 'Operation Roads and
Bridges' – more for their propaganda and psychological
value than for practical effects.

In the campaigns General Soglo led his Government
personally, first into the harvest fields and then in days of
roadmending and ditchdigging, in an attempt to set an
example of hard work to the nation.

Meanwhile all political activity remained banned, and
the country continued under uneventful military rule.

STANISLAS ADOTEVI

The High Commissioner for
Information, Stanislas Spero
Krokpovi Adotevi was born on
February 3, 1934, at Lomé, Togo.

He received his elementary
education at the Seminary of
Ouidah, Dahomey, before studying in French *lycées* at Dakar and
Caen, France.

Later he read psychology, his-
tory and philosophy at Caen
University, and graduated at the
École Normale Supérieure, Paris.

In 1962 he was appointed
Professor of Philosophy at the
Lycée Behanzin and at the Centre
for Advanced Studies in Porto
Novo.

In 1963 he was technical adviser
to General Soglo, then head of a
provisional Government, and the
following year, was in charge of
research at the Dahomean Institute of Applied Research
(IRAD).

From 1964–65 he was Principal
Private Secretary to the Finance

Stanislas Adotevi

Lt-Col Philippe Aho

Minister, before assuming his present post.

LT-COL PHILIPPE AHO

Lieutenant-Colonel Philippe Aho, Minister of the Interior, Security and Defence, was born at Oumbegame, Zou Department, on July 17, 1914.

From his earliest years, he wanted to be a soldier. In 1931 he gave up his studies to enlist in the French Army, and became a company sergeant-major during World War II, when he fought in France and was taken prisoner in June, 1940. Released in 1941, he was repatriated and promoted regimental sergeant-major.

He then joined the resistance movement, and his brilliant conduct under fire in the French Forces of the Interior, earned him promotion to second-lieutenant in 1944, and lieutenant in 1945. He became a captain after distinguishing himself in the Indo-Chinese campaign of 1953–55, during which he was seriously wounded and mentioned twice in despatches.

When Dahomey achieved independence in 1960, he returned to his native country. In 1964 he became a lieutenant-colonel and Assistant Chief of Staff of the Dahomean Armed Forces, before being appointed to his Government post when General Soglo assumed power in December, 1965.

He was retained in the Government reshuffle of December, 1966.

DR JUSTIN AHOMADEGBE

A former Prime Minister of Dahomey and, for a short time, President, Dr Justin Ahomadegbe was born at Abomey in 1917.

He studied medicine and was called up for war service in 1941. He was demobilised with the rank of sergeant in 1942.

Elected a member of Dahomey's General Council in 1947, he founded the Dahomey Democratic Union (UDD) in 1956, and in the same year, became mayor of Abomey.

In 1959 he was elected deputy to the Dahomey National Assembly, and became its President the same year. After his party was defeated in the November, 1960 elections he retired temporarily from politics to practise dentistry.

He was arrested in May, 1961, following an alleged anti-government plot. But the trial caused a sufficient stir for the Government to free him in November, 1962, after 18 months in jail. He returned to dentistry.

After the Government of President Hubert Maga was overthrown in October, 1963, he accepted a post with Maga in the three-man provisional Government set up by Colonel Christophe Soglo, Army Chief of Staff.

In January, 1964, he was elected Vice-President and Prime Minister under President Sourou-Migan Apithy.

In November, 1965, Ahomadegbe briefly replaced Apithy as President, after leading a move to oust him by the People's Assembly.

This climaxed long-standing disagreement between the two leaders, which came to a head when M. Apithy refused to accept a Government decision, backed by the National Assembly, that the Supreme Court should be headed by a judge appointed by the government and not by a politician appointed by the president.

Two days later, Soglo – now a general and Army commander-in-chief – forced the resignations of both men and installed the President of the National Assembly, M. Tahirou Congacou, in their place, as President.

Sourou-Migan Apithy

HONORE AHOUANSOU

Honoré Ahouansou, Public Prosecutor at the Dahomean Supreme Court since 1964, was born in Grand-Popo, Dahomey, on December 13, 1933, and received a French secondary education in Porto Novo.

For several years he was a clerk in a Dakar court before studying law, first at the Dakar Faculty, and later in Paris, where he graduated in 1957.

He became a magistrate in 1959, and has been presiding judge of the Natitingou and Cotonou labour tribunals. He was in addition legal adviser to the head of the Government from 1964–65.

MAJOR ALPHONSE ALLEY

'Paratrooper' Alphonse Alley, Chief of Staff of the Dahomean Armed Forces since 1965, was born at Bassila, Dahomey, on April 9, 1930.

After completing his secondary studies at Dakar, he enlisted for five years with the Senegalese Fusiliers as an officer, and distinguished himself in the Indochinese and Moroccan campaigns between 1953 and 1956. He later fought in the Algerian campaign, and returned to Dahomey as a lieutenant in 1961.

Following his transfer to the Dahomean Forces, he was promoted captain in 1962, and major in 1964, following General Soglo's military *coup* of October, 1963, in which he played a leading role. He was appointed chief of staff when General Soglo became head of state, after a second *coup*, in December, 1965.

SOUROU-MIGAN APITHY

Sourou-Migan Apithy was born on April 8, 1913 at Porto Novo. He became an accountant, and gained a diploma from the Paris Institute of Political Science.

In 1945 he entered politics, and was a deputy for Dahomey in the French National Assembly from 1946–58, when he became a deputy in Dahomey's Constituent Assembly. He was Minister of State in President Hubert Maga's first Government, and Minister of Economy, Finance and Planning in the second.

When Maga's Government was overthrown in October, 1963, he joined him in a short-lived provisional Government set up by Army chief Christophe Soglo. In January, 1964, Apithy was elected to become President and Prime Minister.

On November 27, 1965, he was deposed by the People's Assembly following a move by his Vice-President Dr Justin Ahomadegbe.

This was the culmination of a long-standing disagreement between the two men. It came to a head when Apithy refused to accept a Government decision, backed by the Assembly, that the Supreme Court should be headed by a government-appointed judge rather than by a politician named by the president.

Two days later, both Apithy and Ahomadegbe were forced to resign by Soglo, who stepped in to end the dispute.

DR DAOUDA BADAROU

The Minister of Public Health and Social Affairs, Dr Daouda Badarou was born on January 7, 1929, at Porto Novo.

He went to school in Senegal and Dakar, where he graduated and began his medical studies before going on to the University of Paris.

In 1957 he obtained his degree of doctor of medicine in Paris after presenting a brilliant thesis at the Faculty of Medicine. He qualified as surgeon in 1961.

Eugène Bocco

Arsène Kinde

Hubert Maga

EUGENE BOCCO

Eugène Bocco, Minister of National Education, was born on September 6, 1927, at Ouidah, Dahomey. He first graduated at the Teachers' Training College of Dabou, Ivory Coast.

After teaching at the Teachers' Training College in Parakou and at the Technical School in Cotonou, he obtained a scholarship for the Paris School of Oriental Languages, and graduated as a professor in science.

He taught natural science at the Lycée Behanzin at Porto Novo, of which he was headmaster from 1961–64.

MARCEL DADJO

Marcel Dadjo, Minister of Post, Transport and Communications, retained this post in the Government re-shuffle of December, 1966.

He was born on January 4, 1925, at Save, and graduated as a public works engineer in 1952.

His Government career started in 1958, when he was made Minister of Public Works. In 1959 he became Minister of Transport. Simultaneously, his political career made him first a member of the Legislative Assembly (April, 1959 to October, 1963) and General Councillor for the Central Department (April, 1960 to September, 1964).

After a two-month spell as Minister of Transport, Communications and Public Works (November-December, 1960) he served in Dahomey's Diplomatic Corps (January, 1961 to August, 1964) as Ambassador to West Germany.

During the first part of his tour of duty in Europe, from January, 1961 to December, 1962, M. Dadjo was also Ambassador to the European Economic Community.

ARSENE KINDE

After holding many important Government posts, Arsène Kinde became director-general of the National Oilworks Company in the Government reshuffle of December, 1966.

Born on April 2, 1920, in Ouidah, M. Kinde received his primary schooling in his home town, and joined the Civil Service as a clerk in 1936. After vainly attempting to take an examination which would have established him in the Public Works administration, he applied in 1946 to the Financial Services of the former French West Africa and was appointed to Dakar in 1948.

He then decided to attend night classes, and took his baccalaureate in 1954. After studying law for a year in Dakar, he registered at the French National School of Overseas Studies in 1956, from which he graduated in 1958 as a civil servant in the French Overseas Services. He was then posted in Dahomey. Since then he has held various offices: Technical adviser to the Finance Ministry (1958); Head of Cabinet at the Ministry of Labour and Social Affairs (1959); Head of the Prime Minister's Cabinet (1959–60); Secretary-General of the National Assembly (1961–62); Head of National Security (1962–63); Secretary of State for African and Malagasy Affairs (1963); Head of Cabinet of the Chief of the Provisional Government (1963–64); Delegate to the Ministers' Council (1964); Counsellor, then President of the Administrative Committee of the Supreme Court (1964–65), and Minister of Justice (1965).

HUBERT MAGA

Dahomey's first President after independence was Hubert Maga.

Chabi Kao Pascal

Gen Christophe Soglo

Born in 1916, he was trained as a schoolmaster, and was head of a school when he was elected to the French National Assembly as deputy for Dahomey in 1951. He held this post for seven years until he became Dahomey's Labour Minister in 1958, and Premier in 1959.

When he became President in 1960, he also held the post of Prime Minister. He continued in these twin posts until October, 1963, when military chief Colonel Christophe Soglo announced he was taking over from Maga.

Maga continued for a short while as member of a provisional Government under Soglo, but in December, 1963, he resigned and was ordered into 'enforced residence' at Bohicon in the south of the country.

This followed a week after charges by Soglo that plotters had planned to re-establish the former regime. In September, 1965, Maga's sister was acquitted of charges arising from riots in northern Dahomey in March, 1964.

In November, 1965, he was freed from restrictions by the Government.

MOISE MENSAH

Moise Mensah became Minister for Rural Development and Co-operation in 1965. He resigned the portfolio, however, on December 31, 1966, after a former Minister in ex-President Hubert Maga's Government, M. Bertin Borna, was brought back into the Cabinet as Finance Minister.

M. Mensah was born in the Ivory Coast, at Sassandra, on March 22, 1934. He attended school in Dahomey and in Dakar, where he took his baccalaureate in 1954.

To complete his education, he went to Grignon in France, where

he received a degree as an agricultural engineer in 1960, and then to the Netherlands, where he qualified in 1962 in economic planning. In 1963 he was awarded a degree in financial studies by the French Caisse Centrale de Coopération Economique.

After working his way into the hierarchy of Dahomey's National Rural Development Board, he became Minister in 1965.

CHABI KAO PASCAL

Born on March 10, 1935 at Parakou, Chabi Kao Pascal studied at the Teachers' Training College at Dabou, Ivory Coast, and then went for advanced studies to France, where he graduated in law and economics at Aix-en-Provence.

He also holds a diploma from the Paris Centre of Financial, Economic and Banking Studies.

He was secretary-general of the Banque Dahoméenne de Développement before his appointment as Minister of Labour.

GEN CHRISTOPHE SOGLO

President Christophe Soglo was born at Abomey in 1909, and joined the French Army as a volunteer in 1931. He distinguished himself during World War II in France and in Morocco, notably when, as a sub-lieutenant in the Senegalese Fusiliers, he took part in Allied landings in Corsica, Elba and the south of France.

After the war he was appointed to the Colonial Forces general staff, and in 1947, held the post of military adviser to the Minister for Overseas France.

As a captain, he took part in the Indochina war, during which he was awarded the Croix de Guerre (1956). After being promoted major he went to Senegal, where he remained until

Nicéphore Soglo

1960, when he was appointed military adviser to the President of the newly-established Dahomey Republic. He became Chief of Staff of the Dahomean Army the following year after opting for Dahomean nationality.

In October, 1963, Colonel Soglo, as he was then, led an Army *coup* when the country was in the throes of a general strike and widespread popular disorder. Parliament was dissolved, President Hubert Maga resigned, and Colonel Soglo became an interim chief of state until a new constitution was approved by popular vote in January, 1964. He resumed his former military functions after M. Sorou-Migan Apithy was elected President, and Dr Justin Ahomadegbe Vice-President and head of the Government.

Promoted general in February, 1964, he returned to the political scene in November, 1965, when he staged his second *coup* in 25 months to end a political crisis arising out of a long-standing disagreement between the President and his deputy, Dr Ahomadegbe.

Dismissing both, he appointed the President of the National Assembly, M. Tahirou Congacou, as head of a provisional Government. But at the end of December he seized power and became head of state and government when politicians failed to agree on a modified constitution for Dahomey.

He declared he had acted to save the country from inter-regional strife and personal politics. The leaders of three political parties recently formed, had shown themselves, he said, 'incapable of rising above their personal quarrels'; his Government's aim was to establish 'a new style of politics under which men will unite around a programme, not around a group of personalities'.

In June, 1966, he announced in a broadcast that he planned to keep his regime in power at least until completion of Dahomey's current five-year plan launched at the beginning of 1966. In November he set up a Superior Council of the Republic to advise him on political, economic and social matters.

During 1966, Soglo and his youthful Cabinet were often to be seen out in the fields alongside peasants, in a move to draw attention to the need to increase the agricultural production on which Dahomey depends.

They were also helping with repair work on roads and bridges to improve distribution in the crucial groundnut and cotton industries.

President Soglo is married to a Frenchwoman. They have adopted four Vietnamese children.

NICÉPHORE DIEUDONNE SOGLO

Nicéphore Dieudonné Soglo, Minister of Finance and Economic Affairs, is a French-educated lawyer who was born in Lomé, Togo, on November 29, 1934.

After studying at Cannes and Nice, he graduated in law in Paris.

He was a technical adviser at the Dahomean Finance Ministry from 1963–64. He represents his country at the International Monetary Fund, and is on the administration of the Banque Centrale des Etats de l'Afrique de l'Ouest.

He was appointed Minister of Economic Affairs and Planning in a Cabinet reshuffle on December 30, 1966, but resigned next day. His resignation followed the appointment of M. Bertin Borna –

Dr Emile-Derlin Zinsou

a Minister in the Government of former President Hubert Maga – as Finance Minister.

CHRISTIAN VIEYRA

Christian Vieyra was made Dahomey's permanent delegate to the United Nations in New York in December, 1966.

He was born on March 30, 1930 at Porto Novo, and studied in France, at Aix, Marseilles and Paris, where he graduated in law and economics. He is also a graduate of the Paris School of Economics.

M. Vieyra has been an assistant judge, a government delegate to the Dahomean Assembly, and a legal adviser to the prime minister and the president. He has also been Public Prosecutor.

After being appointed secretary-general of the African and Malagasy Union by the Tananarive Conference of Heads of States in 1961, he became director of the African Institute for Economic Development and Planning (IDEP) at the United Nations, and head of the Unesco planning mission in South Vietnam.

He was appointed to the Cabinet as High Commissioner for Planning and Tourism in December, 1965.

DR EMILE-DERLIN ZINSOU

Born on March 23, 1918 at Ouidah, the son of a teacher, Dr Emile-Derlin Zinsou studied first at Porto Novo, then at the William Ponty School and the Medical College in Dakar.

He later qualified as a doctor in France. In 1945, he went to France as secretary to Sourou-Migan Apithy, then Dahomey deputy to the French National Assembly, and later to become President of Dahomey.

He was a councillor of the Assembly of the French Union from 1947–53, eventually becoming vice-president. In 1948 he headed the Assembly's first inquiry mission, probing the causes of bloodshed in Madagascar.

He was a founder-member of the inter-territorial African Democratic Rally, and also of Dahomey's first organised political mass movement, the Dahomey Progressive Union (UPD).

An enthusiastic supporter of African unity, he was prominent in the ranks of the African Federation Party (PFA) before becoming secretary-general of the Dahomey National Party, which merged with other Dahomey political movements into the Dahomey Unity Party in 1960.

In 1955, when he was elected a member of the French Senate, he joined the Overseas Independents Party (IOM) led by Léopold Senghor. He had retired briefly from politics after his defeat at the 1953 elections, to practice as a private doctor in the Ivory Coast.

Close to M. Apithy, he became Minister of Commerce in Apithy's pre-independence Government from July, 1958 to April, 1959.

After the fall of President Hubert Maga's Government in October, 1963, in which he was Minister of State for Foreign Affairs, Zinsou retired from political life.

He returned to the scene as Foreign Secretary in General Soglo's new Government of December, 1965.

In the reshuffle of December, 1966, he took on the additional portfolio of Tourism and Planning.

He has been President of the Supreme Court, and Ambassador to Paris.

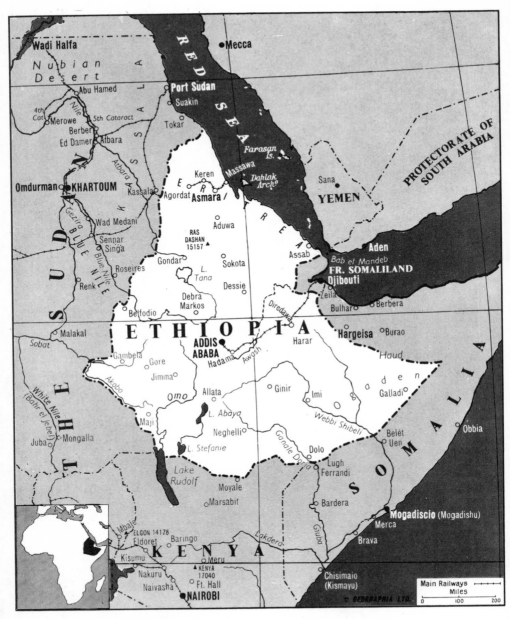

The area of Ethiopia is 395,000 square miles. It has a coastline on the Red Sea and long borders with the Sudan, Kenya and Somalia. It surrounds the small Gulf of Aden enclave of French Somaliland. The population was officially estimated in 1962 to be 21,461,700 (but no census has ever been taken). The capital is Addis Ababa. Coffee is by far the most important source of income in Ethiopia's agrarian economy, which also relies on subsistence farming and animal husbandry.

120

Ethiopia

The Empire of Ethiopia is governed by a Council of
Ministers responsible to the Emperor, with a Senate and
a Chamber of Deputies.
Haile Selassie I was crowned Emperor in 1930. A revolt
during his absence from the country in December, 1960,
was crushed as he returned.

The history of Ethiopia since 1930 can be written in
terms of the achievements of one man – Emperor Haile
Selassie I, who was crowned on November 2 of that year.
He has devoted his life to introducing 20th century
reforms and innovations into his ancient isolated kingdom,
one of the most primitive in Africa, with a tradition
of conservatism that brings change very slowly.
Ethiopia is a land of great contrasts and of great beauty.
The capital, Addis Ababa, is set on the central highlands
at an altitude of about 8,000 feet. From this central
plateau, the country descends in great steps to the burning
heat of the Danakil desert on the Red Sea in the east,
and the Sudanese frontier in the west.
The highlands are slashed by tremendous gorges with
precipitous drops of 3,000 feet or more. The most
spectacular of these is the gorge of the Blue Nile, which
rises in Lake Tana, some 200 miles north-west of the
capital.
Ethiopia's population is generally set at about 20 millions
but as there has never been a census an exact figure
is not known.
The country's existence is virtually based on agriculture,
but the whole system of land ownership and land tenure
does little to help development on any modern scale. The
potential for such development, however, is enormous and
the land is extremely rich.
Industrially, some steps forward have been taken in the last
five or six years with the building of factories and the
production of hydro-electric power.
Coffee is the country's main cash crop and accounts for
some 60 per cent of the exports. The bean is of the
arabica variety and is of high quality.
The overall task of modernisation before Ethiopia is
considerable. There is practically no sector of the
national economy that cannot be developed, but perhaps
the most important are those of agriculture and animal

Above: Young Guji herdboys driving their charges across a river in southern Ethiopia

Below: Addis Ababa's impressive City Hall

A social worker gives advice to a rural family on child welfare

husbandry, for here is a vast potential that could make Ethiopia a prime producer for Africa and the Middle East.

Ethiopia adopted Christianity in the monophysite form of the Church of Alexandria early in the 4th century about the year 330 AD, when the Emperor Azana was converted by Frumentius, Ethiopia's first bishop. The strength of the Christian church in Ethiopia has been one of the dominant factors in the country's history. Many Islamic invasions have been resisted and Ethiopia has remained an island of Christianity amidst a sea of Moslem neighbours.

The history of the Ethiopian royal family dates back for 3,000 years to the legendary visit of the Queen of Sheba, identified in Ethiopia as Queen Makeda, to the court of King Solomon in Jerusalem. From this union was born Menelik, Ethiopia's first king. The 1955 constitution specifically mentions Emperor Haile Selassie's direct descent from Menelik.

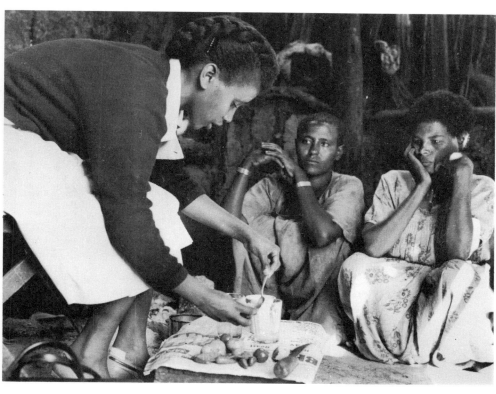

Emperor Haile Selassie

EMPEROR HAILE SELASSIE

Emperor Haile Selassie, King of Kings and Conquering Lion of Judah (these are only two of his archaic titles) was born on July 23, 1892. He was crowned Emperor on November 2, 1930.

In 1931 he gave the oldest Christian nation its first written constitution in 3,000 years. The first Abyssinian Parliament met the following year.

He carried out gradual administrative reforms and reorganised the country's finances. He improved the road network and set up the first radio station.

In 1935 Mussolini invaded his country without declaration of war after the Emperor had appealed in vain to the great Powers and the League of Nations to preserve peace. The Emperor took command of the Ethiopian Army, but they could not prevent the Italians entering Addis Ababa in May, 1936. Haile Selassie escaped with his family and then found refuge in Britain, where he led a quiet and studious life. In vain he continued to plead his country's cause before the League of Nations in Geneva. By 1939 Britain, France and the other big powers, excepting the United States, China and Russia, had formally recognised King Victor Emmanuel III of Italy as Emperor of Ethiopia.

The dispossessed, exiled Emperor had to wait until May 5, 1941 for his triumphal re-entry into his capital. This was made possible by World War II, when Italy entered on the side of Germany (1940). Britain recognised Haile Selassie as an ally and he organised the cooperation of Ethiopian partisans with British forces, successfully fighting the Italians in East Africa.

In 1942 Britain formally acknowledged the autonomy of Ethiopia and the authority of Haile Selassie as Emperor. After the war, in 1950, the United Nations voted to federate an autonomous Eritrea with Ethiopia under the Ethiopian crown, a step which the Emperor had advocated since 1946, stressing, among other factors, Ethiopia's vital need for access to the sea.

His Silver Jubilee came in 1955. With a background of great new pageantry, he promulgated a new constitution which provided for direct elections of deputies by secret ballot and guaranteeing freedom of speech and of the press. He retained, however, certain important powers such as the supreme direction of foreign relations and supreme authority over all affairs inside Ethiopia as head of state.

In December, 1960, while he was on a state visit to Brazil, 6,000 men of his imperial bodyguard rebelled under the leadership of their commander, Brigadier Mengistu Neway.

The Army remained loyal and the Emperor, returning swiftly to Addis Ababa, arrived in time for the final crushing of the revolt. Many thousands died.

The future of the African continent as a whole became the Emperor's interest more and more as time went on. In May, 1963, he convoked in Addis Ababa the first conference of African heads of state at which the charter of the Organisation of African Unity (OAU) was worked out and adopted.

In the following year the OAU established its headquarters there, and observers talked of the Emperor's dream to make his city the capital of a free Africa.

The Empress Menen, to whom Haile Selassie had been married for 50 years, died in 1962. His youngest son, Prince Sahle

Crown Prince
Asfa Wossen

Aklilu Habtewold

Selassie died shortly afterwards. Only two of his six children then survived – Crown Prince Asfa Wossen and Princess Tenagne Worq.

CROWN PRINCE ASFA WOSSEN

Crown Prince Asfa Wossen was born in Harar, near the birthplace of his father, Emperor Haile Selassie I, on July 27, 1916.

He was educated in Addis Ababa and also studied abroad. During the Italian occupation of Ethiopia from 1936–41, he accompanied the emperor into exile in England.

The Crown Prince has been married twice. His first marriage, at the age of 16, was to Princess Wolete Israel, grand-daughter of Emperor Yohannes, and took place in 1932. The only issue was a daughter, Princess Ijigayehu, who died while still very young. This marriage was dissolved in the early 1950s.

Crown Prince Asfa Wossen soon married again, it is believed about 1952, and this time to Medferiyash Worq, daughter of General Abebe Damtchew, who was killed during the Italian occupation.

They have four children, Prince Zere-Yakob, who is second in line to the throne after his father, and three daughters.

During the attempted military *coup* by the Imperial Bodyguard during the Emperor's absence in South America in December, 1960, Crown Prince Wossen made a tape recording – it is said he was forced to do this at pistol point by the rebels – which was broadcast and in which he spoke of a more liberal regime.

AKLILU HABTEWOLD

Aklilu Habtewold was appointed Prime Minister of Ethiopia in 1961. Born on March 12, 1912, in Addis Ababa, he received almost all of his education in France.

After studying at the French Lycée in Alexandria (Egypt), he went to the Sorbonne in Paris where he studied for 16 years, obtaining a number of degrees. Later he attended the School of Political Science at the University of Paris.

Aklilu joined the Government as a Vice-Minister in 1941 and for the next 17 years represented his country in many posts. He was the first African to be elected Vice-Chairman, at the tenth session of the United Nations General Assembly.

At the time of the attempted *coup* by the Imperial Bodyguard in December, 1960, Aklilu was Foreign Minister and Deputy Prime Minister. His brother, Makonnen Habtewold, then Minister of Commerce and Industry, was one of the Government ministers killed by the rebels in the Massacre of the Green Salon at the Palace.

In April, 1966, Emperor Haile Selassie announced a widening of the powers of the Government and Aklilu was given the task of forming a new Cabinet.

COMMANDER ISKENDER DESTA

Commander Iskender Desta, grandson of Emperor Haile Selassie and Deputy Commander-in-Chief of the Imperial Ethiopian Navy, was born in the royal palace in Addis Ababa on July 7, 1935.

Commander Iskender is the youngest of six children born to Ras Desta and Princess Tegne Worq, the emperor's daughter. His father was killed during the Italian occupation of Ethiopia.

His elder brother, Amha Desta, died in Abbis Ababa shortly after

125

Ketema Yifru

Dr Menassie Haile

the royal family returned to Ethiopia following the Emperor's triumphal entry into the capital at the head of the victorious Anglo-Ethiopian army in 1941.

Commander Iskender received his education mainly in England.

In 1960, he was appointed by his grandfather to be Deputy Commander-in-Chief of the Imperial Ethiopian Navy and has his headquarters at Massawa, Ethiopia's main naval base situated in the northern province of Eritrea.

KETEMA YIFRU

Ketema Yifru was appointed Minister of Foreign Affirs in April, 1966, and became one of the youngest members of the Ethiopian Government. He was born at Gara Muleta, in the province of Harar, on December 11, 1929.

During the Italian occupation of Ethiopia in 1936–41, Ketema was taken by his family into what was then British Somaliland.

Returning after the country's liberation, he was educated in Addis Ababa and at the University of Boston (USA) where he studied international relations and political science.

In August, 1952, Ketema returned to Addis Ababa and joined the Italian Department of the Foreign Ministry. For two years, 1958–60, he served as private secretary to the Emperor and in 1961 was appointed Minister of State for Foreign Affairs.

He has travelled widely, accompanying the Emperor on most of his state visits as well as representing Ethiopia at meetings of the Organisation of African Unity.

DR MENASSIE HAILE

Dr Menassie Haile, Minister of Information and Tourism (1966) is also Political Adviser to the

Emperor, Haile Selassie. He is a comparative newcomer to the Government.

Born on March 12, 1930, in Harar, he was educated in Addis Ababa and later went to the University of Wisconsin (USA), where he obtained his degree in economics. He also studied at Columbia University, New York, obtaining LLB, MA and PhD degrees in international law.

Returning to Ethiopia in 1958, he became Chief of Political Affairs in the Emperor's Private Cabinet in 1962 and *de facto* Chairman of the Imperial Cabinet since that date.

In 1965 he was appointed to the rank of Vice-Minister and in the same year he took over the portfolio of Information, continuing his post as political adviser at the palace.

When the new Government was formed in April, 1966, Dr Menassie was made Minister of State of Information and Tourism.

While in the United States, Dr Menassie married an American.

MENASSIE LEMMA

Menassie Lemma, Governor of the National Bank of Ethiopia, was born in Cairo in 1913. He was educated in both Egypt and Ethiopia.

After the liberation of Ethiopia from the Italian occupation in 1941, Menassie Lemma first worked as secretary to the Governor of the Province of Harar.

In 1942, he joined the Ministry of Finance as chief of the Contraband Section and three years later took over the post of head of the Income Tax Department.

Emperor Haile Selassie appointed him Vice-Minister of Finance in 1949. Ten years later, he was

Yilma Deressa

again promoted to the rank of Minister of State at the Ministry of Finance and then became Governor of the National Bank.

RAS MESFIN SELESHI

Ras Mesfin Seleshi, appointed Governor-General in 1959 of the province of Shoa, in which Addis Ababa is situated, was born in Gara-Muleta, Harar province, on July 6, 1905.

Of comparatively humble origin – Emporer Haile Selassie made him a 'Ras', a title roughly equivalent to 'duke', in 1959 – he joined the Imperial Bodyguard and at the time of the Italian invasion in 1936 had reached the rank of major.

He fought ceaselessly during the five years of the Italian occupation and was wounded seven times. Just avoiding capture on several occasions, he managed to escape to the Sudan, from where he was active in organising the patriotic uprising to coincide with the Emperor's return.

He was with Haile Selassie on his victorious return in 1941, and the same year was appointed Governor of Diredawa in eastern Ethiopia. Later he became Governor-General of Wollega and Illubabor provinces.

YILMA DERESSA

Yilma Deressa, who became Minister of Finance in 1960, was born in 1907 at Chuta in the province of Wollega. He is the oldest minister in the Government and is also the only full-blooded member of the Galla tribe in the Cabinet.

After an early education in Addis Ababa, Yilma went to the Victoria College in Alexandria and then to the London School of Economics, where he obtained his degree in 1933. Later, he studied international law in Geneva, Switzerland.

During the Italian invasion of Ethiopia in 1936, he was an active underground fighter and helped found the Black Lion guerilla movement. He was captured and imprisoned in Italy.

On Ethiopia's liberation in 1941, he became Secretary-General at the Ministry of Foreign Affirs but left that ministry the following year to become Vice-Minister of Finance.

Since then he has headed numerous financial and foreign missions until he was appointed Minister of Finance in 1960. This appointment was confirmed once again in the new Government which was formed in April, 1966.

The area of Gabon is 103,317 square miles; its population is over 450,000. The country is bounded on the north by Spanish Guinea and Cameroun and on the west and south by Congo Brazzaville. It has a long Atlantic coastline. The capital is Libreville. Gabon's considerable economic potential derives from rich deposits of iron and manganese ore, oil, natural gas, uranium concentrates and, to a lesser extent, gold. The main agricultural products are cocoa and coffee, in the north, and palm oil, groundnuts and rice in the south.

Gabon

Gabon, a former province of French Equatorial Africa, gained internal autonomy in 1957 and joined the French Community in 1958. Independence was declared on August 17, 1960.

Gabon, the smallest and one of the richest of the former French African states, was proclaimed an independent republic within the French Community under the leadership of President Léon M'ba – a veteran campaigner for African emancipation and staunchly pro-French. He ruled his country for the next six years in almost Gaullist style. Only for two days was he out of power. In February, 1964, he was forced to resign but was promptly reinstated by French troops.

The name 'Gabon' was given by 15th century Portuguese navigators to the inlet on which Libreville, the capital, now stands. The country, staked out by colonial France, and since endorsed as a member-state of the United Nations, forms a rough rectangle stretching inland from the west coast of central Africa.

Over two-thirds of the country is forest, and the other third elephant grass. Until the middle of the 20th century, the main means of communication inland was the Ogowe River and its tributaries, which fan across most of the country. Road-building was discouraged by dense jungle and by a climate consisting of two very hot rainy seasons and two hot cloudy seasons. In 1966, Gabon still lacked a single railway.

When a census was taken in 1960, about 15 per cent of the people lived in three main towns – Libreville, Port Gentil and Lambarene.

Libreville is a curious blend of modern administrative and public buildings, 'old colonial' verandahs, and African townships. It faces the sea across a boulevard lined with palms.

Port Gentil is an expanding oil and timber port at the mouth of the Ogowe River. Lambarene, an Ogowe River port about 150 miles inland, which marks the upstream limit of all-year navigation, was made internationally famous by Dr Albert Schweitzer, who died there in 1965 at the ramshackle hospital he built some 50 years earlier. The census also revealed that there were about 5,000

The famous hospital founded by Dr Albert Schweitzer on the banks of the Ogowe River at Lambarene

Europeans in Gabon. The country's main African tribal grouping is the Fang, numbering about 180,000 and concentrated in the north. They form a single ethnic bloc with the neighbouring peoples of Cameroun and Spanish Guinea. The rest of the country is divided between several dozen scattered tribes, among them the Pygmies (Babinga). The pygmies are said to be the original inhabitants of the country, but they have dwindled to a few thousands in the remoter forests.

A significant and well established mixed-race group in Libreville testifies to relatively easy relations between races.

In 1903, Gabon became a French administrative zone, and in 1910 it was organised as part of French Equatorial Africa (AEF), together with Oubangui-Chari (now the Central African Republic), French Congo (Brazzaville), and Chad. In 1946, under France's post-war constitution, Gabon became an overseas territory with its own Territorial Assembly, deputies in the French National Assembly, and a degree of internal autonomy.

As European missionaries, traders and administrators transformed Gabonese tribal life, so big commercial companies exploiting the country's forest resources, transformed the traditional economy. Hunters and subsistence farmers were drawn away from their tribes by lumber camps offering cash wages.

In 1950, one of the world's largest plywood factories was completed at Port Gentil. By the late 1950s, the most accessible forests had been felled and the timber companies were forced inland. Replanting became urgent. In 1957, when French troops were massively engaged in keeping Algeria part of France, the French territories of Black Africa achieved a new degree of independence. Gabon's Territorial Assembly was opened to election by universal suffrage, and Léon M'ba was appointed vice-president of a governing council under the French Governor.

On September 28, Gabon was one of the dozen French-speaking African states which voted 'yes' for President de Gaulle's 5th Republic constitution, which gave overseas territories a choice of future status.

In November, the Gabon Territorial Assembly voted itself the National Assembly of an autonomous republic within the French Community. On August 17, 1960, after a modification of the Fifth Republic constitution, Gabon became a sovereign independent republic with Premier Léon M'ba its head of state. Strong treaty ties with France remained.

Gabon was admitted to the United Nations and, through France, to associate membership of the European Common Market. Loose economic ties with other states formerly part of the AEF were formalised in a grouping that became the Central African Customs and Economic Union (UDEAC). In 1966, President M'ba signed the charter inaugurating an enlarged grouping of more than a dozen French-speaking African states, the Common Afro-Malagasy Organisation (OCAM). This organisation has tended to counterweight the other more radical group of African states in the Organisation of African Unity (OAU).

Two personalities, Léon M'ba and Jean-Hilaire Aubame, at the head of two political parties, dominated the internal political life of Gabon from the end of World War II until 1964 – when M. Aubame was imprisoned for complicity in the short-lived February *coup*.

Both began by trying to stop what they saw as the corruption of tribal life under the impact of colonial rule and European economic penetration. Neither was a political ideologist nor anti-French, and both opted in the end for political stability and economic development. Yet their continuing personal and political rivalry belied the apparent political stability of the first post-independence years. That stability was in part the result of economic development, rising living standards and relatively full employment.

Though 75 per cent of the population remained employed in agriculture through the mid-1960s, the wealth of the country still lay in its forests – and increasingly in the mineral resources beneath them. Agriculture was little developed: cocoa and coffee had a small place in the north; palm oil, groundnuts and, more recently, rice – in the south. But most of the agricultural population were still occupied with subsistence farming.

Oil was the first big mineral discovery. The first oil strikes in the Port Gentil region raised exaggerated hopes in 1956, but by 1965 oil was the country's third export earner with production steadily increasing. A refinery was to be completed in Port Gentil during 1967 to supply Gabon and its neighbours in UDEAC.

Since 1962, with some of the largest known deposits in the world, Gabon has become a major manganese producer. Highly mechanised mines at Moanda, near the Congo-Brazzaville border in the south-east, produced 1,290,000 tons of high grade ore in 1965. For lack of road or rail links with the sea, the ore was carried by cable-car for 47 miles to the Mbinda railhead across the Congo border. From there it was shipped out, much of it to the United States, through Pointe Noire. The American United Steel Company has a minority share in the French controlled mining company, and takes 50 per cent of the output.

Mounana, a few miles north of the Moanda manganese field, has been producing uranium in significant quantities since 1961 – when the deposits were the largest known in the French-speaking world. The 1965 output was 1,600 tons.

Huge iron deposits, with reserves estimated at over 500 million tons, await exploitation in the Belinga-Mekambo region of north-eastern Gabon. Among the main tasks outlined for the 1966–70 five-year development plan, were the building of a 350-mile rail outlet to Owendo, up the coast of Libreville, and the deepening of Owendo port to take ore boats. The combined project was to cost about 270 million dollars (nearly £100 million sterling) and the first ore trains were expected to reach the coast in 1973–74. US Bethlehem Steel has a 50 per cent share in the future mining company, French companies 34 per cent, and the EEC countries 16 per cent.

France retained a dominant role in the Gabonese economy after independence, and was the main source of foreign investment in development projects – many of which concerned improvements in communications and the economic infrastructure neglected before independence. The EEC, the United States and the UN development fund played a part.

Increased US influence brought French rumours that Americans were behind the 1964 *coup* plot – rumours publicly denied by the State Department.

Political stability under the strong presidential regime of M. M'ba, combined with Gabon's natural wealth and a liberal investments code, attracted heavy private investment. Increasing prosperity and the absence of a large urban proletariat deadened demand for a more radical nationalist or socialist regime. But dependence on France and the dominance of foreign capital was reflected in a continued economic imbalance as well as a lack of agricultural and industrial development to put the country's abundant raw materials to best use.

Despite this, Gabon's economic prospects are bright. The trade balance has been favourable nearly every year: in 1965 exports were worth £37 million against imports of £23 million. Average per capita income was put at about £80 sterling in the same year – relatively high for Black Africa – and an estimated 90 per cent of children reaching school age were being found places. The 1967 budget of £21 million was three million up on the previous year.

By late 1966, the country was on the verge of 'economic take-off', with a five-year plan calculated to see it through the first phase. But doubts had arisen over the political future.

President M'ba, after prolonged stays in Paris earlier in the year, left again for the French capital in August. He entered hospital for treatment of an undisclosed ailment and remained there for the rest of the year. M. Albert Bongo, an able young presidential aide with ministerial status and control of defence, was named Vice-President in November and tipped as heir-apparent.

André-Gustave Anguile

MICHEL ABESSOLO

Michel Abessolo, appointed Minister for Economy, Planning and Mines in October, 1965, was one of the young technocrats brought into the Government by President M'ba in the wake of the 1964 *coup*.

A northerner, born in Oyem in 1933, he went on from the Lycée Léon M'ba in Libreville to university at Poitiers and Lille in France, where he graduated in law and political science.

From university, he joined the Gabonese Embassy in West Germany in 1961. The following year he returned to Gabon, where for two years he was attached to the Ministry of Labour and made responsible for Pensions and Social Security.

In 1964 he entered the Government as Minister of Labour and the Civil Service, to which was added responsibility for Social Affairs and Technical Co-operation.

The following year M. Abessolo assumed the key role of Economy Minister with the task of opening up Gabon's enormous mineral wealth.

EUGENE AMOGHO

Eugène Amogho took over the Forestry and Water Resources portfolio in the Cabinet reshuffle of August, 1966.

Born in the south-eastern town of Franceville in 1918, Eugène Amogho was trained as an administrator. Between 1952 and 1957, he was elected to successive pre-independence Territorial Assemblies and to the Grand Council of the French Equatorial African territories. He was secretary of the Grand Council's standing committee and president of its planning commission.

After the formation of Gabon's first autonomous Government in 1957, M. Amogho was rarely out of the Cabinet. He held various portfolios: Education, Youth and Sports (1957); Planning and Rural Economy (1958); Agriculture, Livestock and Rural Economy (1958–60); Youth, Sports and Social and Cultural Affairs (1960–61); Information, Tourism, Post and Telecommunications (1961–62); Public Works and Transport (1964–65); Public Health and Population (1965–66) and Forest and Water Resources (from 1966).

In the elections that followed the 1964 February *coup*, Eugène Amogho was elected to represent his Upper-Ogowe home region in the National Assembly.

ANDRE-GUSTAVE ANGUILE

André-Gustave Anguile, who resigned as Minister of State in November, 1966, was a French-educated forestry expert who became successively Minister of Finance, Economy and Foreign Affairs.

In 1960 he headed the first Gabonese delegation to the United Nations.

M. Anguile was born in 1920 and educated at Bordeaux and Sens in France. He joined the French forces in 1940.

After the war, he worked in youth camps, saving money to continue his studies until he was able to enter a forestry school in Paris. After graduating, he worked for a year in the forestry section of the French Ministry of Industrial Production.

In 1946, M. Anguile returned to Gabon, which he had hardly known in his childhood, and took over a forest estate left him by his father. In 1952 he was appointed Secretary-General of the Territorial Assembly.

He became Forestry Minister in the first Gabonese Government

(1957) and the following year, was appointed Minister of Finance, Economy and National Planning.

In 1961 he was freed of responsibility for Finance and, as Minister of Economy and Planning, he represented his country at a series of international conferences.

A firm believer in regional co-operation among African neighbour states, André-Gustave Anguile worked hard in the formation of the Central African Customs and Economic Union (UDEAC) in 1964.

JEAN-HILAIRE AUBAME

Jean-Hilaire Aubame, for nearly 20 years Léon M'ba's chief rival for Gabon's political leadership, was sentenced in 1964 to ten years' hard labour for his alleged part in the February *coup*, which would have made him head of state.

Ten years younger than his rival, M. Aubame was born in Libreville on November 10, 1912. He received primary education in the capital, and later entered the AEF Administration, in which he became a chief clerk.

Like M'ba, M. Aubame spent a period working in the interior, and resented what he saw as the perversion of tribal institutions by colonial authority. But his approach to the problems involved was more radical and more influenced by European socialism than that of Léon M'ba.

After World War II, M. Aubame founded his Gabonese Democratic and Social Union (UDSG) in opposition to M'ba's BDG. Just as the BDG was affiliated to the inter-territorial RDA, Aubame's party was linked with the African Regroupment Party (PRA), inspired by future President Léopold Senghor of

Senegal. Of the two inter-territorial movements, the PRA was more influenced by socialism and also more concerned with African unity and freedom from French rule.

M. Aubame's political backing came from the Fang people of Northern Gabon, the most cohesive tribal bloc in the country. This solid support was sufficient to elect him in 1946, and again in subsequent elections, to the National Assembly in Paris, where he sat from 1947–59. But it was no substitute for the broader political base being built up by M. M'ba; and it made the USDG an easier target for hostile colonial authorities than the nebulous political web of the BDG.

M. Aubame's absences in Paris weakened his party management, but despite this his UDSG was only narrowly defeated by the BDG in the 1957 elections. M. M'ba picked three of his Ministers from the minority party, and all three subsequently defected to the majority.

Despite their earlier differences and continuing personal rivalry, M. M'ba and M. Aubame agreed in their approach to the 1958 referendum and their choice of self-government preparatory to independence for Gabon. M. Aubame's weakness in Opposition may have been partly due to his lacking any clearly defined alternative policy to that of his established rival.

For Gabon's first post-independence elections in February, 1961, Aubame merged his UDSG with the BDG in a national front with a single list. He was elected to the Gabon National Assembly and appointed Foreign Minister.

The compromise was uneasy from the start. M. Aubame was first demoted to Minister of State,

Pierre-Auguste Avaro

then dropped from the Cabinet in early 1962. Though he subsequently became President of the Supreme Court, M. Aubame moved back to form a fresh Opposition. By early 1964, his followers were accusing the Government of suppressing democratic Opposition and of making arbitrary arrests.

The President introduced a bill which would in effect have dislodged Aubame from his Supreme Court post and, when the National Assembly failed to endorse it wholeheartedly, called for new elections in February. The UDSG called for a boycott of the elections.

The young officers who engineered the February 18 *coup* said they had done so to forestall election violence in opposition to the Government's repressive measures. They named Jean-Hilaire Aubame to replace President M'ba as head of state.

The French paratroops moved in, M. Aubame was detained along with a few dozen others accused of complicity, and the UDSG was banned. When the elections, delayed by the *coup*, were set for April, 1964, the Opposition was hastily reformed under a new name. It won 16 seats in the 47-seat Assembly but, faced with a Government of National Unity cutting across party lines, the 16 dwindled to three. By 1966, Gabon was a *de facto* one-party state.

In August, 1964, Jean-Hilaire Aubame was one of 26 tried for complicity in the February *coup*. His sentence of ten years' hard labour was to be followed by ten years in exile. Two lieutenants held chiefly responsible, were sentenced to 20 years each, and nine people were acquitted. Since then no new Opposition leader has emerged.

PIERRE-AUGUSTE AVARO

Pierre-Auguste Avaro, who resigned as Minister of the Civil Service in December, 1966, was a founder-member of the ruling BDG party. He had previously served as Minister of Education, Defence, Foreign Affairs and Forest and Water Resources.

He was born in 1911 at Port Gentil, and made his name as president of the labour union grouping Gabon's lumber and plantation workers. A keen educationist, he organised a national association of parents of students and school-children, and joined the committee of the International Federation of Schools, Parents and Educators.

From 1960–63 he was assistant secretary-general of the BDG party, which he had helped secretary-general Léon M'ba to organise. In the 1961 and 1964 elections, he was returned to the National Assembly.

Between 1960 and 1966, M. Avaro held six different Ministries: Education (1960–61); Labour (1961–62); Forest and Water Resources (1963 and 1965); Defence (1963–64); Foreign Affairs (1964–65); and Civil Service and Technical Co-operation (1965–66).

M. Avaro was also chairman of a national company dealing in okoumé (the country's chief timber).

JEAN-REMY AYOUNE

Jean-Rémy Ayoune, appointed Civil Service Minister in December, 1966, had a long career as an administrator and diplomat behind him. He was at one time Ambassador to Bonn.

Born in 1914 at Assewe, in coastal Ogowe, he was educated at a Catholic mission and at seminaries in Libreville and Brazzaville. At 20, he entered the

Albert-Bernard Bongo

French Equatorial African Administration, working first in Libreville and later in Brazzaville. He rose to hold senior administrative posts in the financial and personnel departments, and in 1946, was appointed Press and Information Officer to the Governor-General.

In 1960 M. M'ba, then Prime Minister, sent him to represent pre-independence Gabon in France. After brief courses at the Quai d'Orsay and at the French National School of Administration, he became Gabon's Ambassador to West Germany in 1961.

In March, 1964, he was appointed Secretary-General to the Government, and in 1966, at the age of 52, Minister of the Civil Service.

LEONARD-ANTOINE BADINGA

Léonard-Antoine Badinga was appointed Minister of Finance and the Budget in March, 1965.

In a Government reshuffle on January 25, 1967, he was replaced as Finance Minister by Pierre Mebaley and given a new post— Director of the Gabonese State Insurance Fund.

Son of a trader in Moabi, southern Gabon, Léonard-Antoine Badinga was born in 1923. After Catholic mission school at Mayumba, on the coast of southern Gabon, he went to Brazzaville, where he attended first a technical school, and then a special training centre for local administrators.

From 1947–53, he taught at a technical training school, and from 1954–60 he was head of a vocational training centre.

In 1960 he was appointed a sub-prefect, administering a district. A year later he became Minister of Agriculture, Livestock and Forests, a post he held until January, 1963, when he took over the Public Health and Social Affairs portfolio.

ALBERT-BERNARD BONGO

Albert-Bernard Bongo, named Vice-President in November, 1966, by an absent and ailing President M'ba, was seen as the rising star in Gabonese politics.

Aged 30 on his appointment, M. Bongo was acknowledged by many as heir-apparent to the Presidency a mere six years after leaving the French Air Force to enter political life.

M. Bongo was born on December 30, 1935, in a village near Franceville in south-eastern Gabon. He was educated in Brazzaville, in the French Congo; after primary school he went on in 1952, to the Brazzaville Technical College where he specialised in commerce.

In July, 1958, after a year as a civil servant, M. Bongo was conscripted for military service in the French forces, and joined the Air Force. Demobilised in October, 1960, he was employed in the Gabon Foreign Office.

Less than six months later, in March, 1962, he was appointed deputy to the Director of the President's Office. By October, he was Director, and in that position he established himself in the confidence of President M'ba. From February, 1963 to April, 1964, M. Bongo had special responsibility for Information and Tourism, though still without ministerial status.

After the February, 1964 *coup*, engineered from within the Army, M. M'ba needed a man he could trust to supervise the Armed Forces. He chose Albert Bongo, with whom he had worked closely for two years of changing governments.

Georges Damas

In April, 1964, while still nominally Director of the President's Office, M. Bongo was given charge of National Defence.

On September 24, the following year, he entered the Cabinet for the first time as Minister attached to the Presidency, charged with National Defence and Co-ordination – thus combining supervision of the forces with a wide range of executive powers he had assumed as the President's principal aide.

From November, 1964, to November, 1965, M. Bongo was also the Government's special commissioner to the State Security Court, set up to try the 1964 *coup* suspects.

The Cabinet reshuffle which preceded the President's departure in August, 1966, for medical treatment in Paris, left M. Bongo as Minister charged with Defence, Information and Tourism.

In September, he flew to Paris for talks with the President, who was still in hospital. And on November 13, Albert-Bernard Bongo was made Vice-President 'to ensure the efficient functioning of the Government' through the President's prolonged absence.

Another Minister of State, M. André-Gustave Anguile, asked to be released from his functions. M. Paul-Marie Yembit, displaced by M. Bongo's promotion to the vice-presidency, took over his successor's Information and Tourism portfolio.

At the end of 1966, the President was still convalescing in Paris, while Albert-Bernard Bongo held the reins of government at home.

AUGUSTIN BOUMAH

Augustin Boumah was appointed Gabon's Minister of Youth, Sport and Cultural Affairs following a reshuffle on January 25, 1967.

He was born in Libreville on November 7, 1927, and is a graduate of the French Institute of Overseas Studies.

Before becoming a Minister in the Government he was head of the Gabon College of Administration.

His previous posts included those of Chief Clerk of the Court under the colonial Administration, and Director of Labour and Manpower from 1961–65.

GEORGES DAMAS

Georges Damas, National Assembly President from 1964, and a contemporary of President M'ba, was for 15 years a bank clerk. After World War II, he combined public office with business activities, and at independence composed the Gabon National Anthem, *La Concorde*. From 1961–63 he served as Ambassor to the European Common Market countries.

M. Damas was born in 1902 in Libreville, where he attended the same Catholic mission school as the young Léon M'ba. Some 40 years later, he made a break in his public life to take a diplomatic training course at the Quai d'Orsay (1960).

He was a bank clerk from 1924–39, and accountant to a shipping company for the following 20 years. During that time, he served as adviser to the Privy Council of the French Governor, and in 1956, was elected to the Libreville City Council.

From 1959 until Gabon became independent the following year, M. Damas represented the territory at meetings of the French Economic and Social Council in Paris.

He was appointed Ambassador to the Common Market countries in 1961, and to West Germany in

Léon M'ba

1963. The following year, he was elected to the Gabon National Assembly, and became its President.

JOSEPH ETOUGHE

Joseph Etoughe was appointed Minister of Agriculture in April, 1966, having been recalled from the Gabonese Embassy in Paris only two months earlier, to become Secretary-General to the Cabinet.

Born in northern Gabon in 1932, M. Etoughe was educated at Protestant schools. For ten years after leaving school, he worked as a teacher, then took a secretarial post in the Administration.

In 1960, he was appointed deputy to a local sub-prefect, and spent the next two years in local administration. Since 1956, he had been an active member of the ruling BDG party.

In 1963 he went to the Institute of Advanced Overseas Studies in Paris, to study civil administration. On graduating, he stayed in Paris as commercial attaché.

After the 1964 *coup* he organised the Association of Gabonese Students, supporting the recently reinstated President M'ba. In June that year, he was elected president of the Association.

PAUL MALEKOU

Paul Malekou was the youngest and academically the most highly qualified member of the Cabinet at the time of his appointment to the post of Minister of Labour and Social Affairs in April, 1964. He left the Government in November, 1966.

Brought into a 'new look' Government after the February *coup*, M. Malekou represented the younger generation of Gabonese intellectuals eager for a say in their country's political life. In March, 1965, he was appointed Minister of Education.

Born in 1938, Paul Malekou was educated first in Libreville, then at a *lycée* in Brazzaville, where he passed his baccalaureate. His home town is Fougamou, in western Gabon.

In 1959, he entered Lille University in France, where he took a degree in law and political science. He went on to a diploma course at the Higher Institute of Overseas Studies in Paris.

In 1963, M. Malekou returned to Gabon, where he was made Inspector of Labour and Supervisor of the National Labour and Handicrafts Organisation.

From April, 1964, he held successively the Ministries of Labour and Social Affairs and Education, before leaving the Cabinet in November, 1966.

KASSA MAPSI

Kassa Mapsi, was appointed acting Minister for National Planning, Tourism and the National Organisation of Gabonese Women, in the January, 1967 Government reshuffle.

He was born on November 6, 1932, at Koulamoutou and is a graduate of the French Institute of Political Studies of the University of Paris and of the Centre of Finance, Economic and Banking Research of the French Government Department for Economic Cooperation.

LEON M'BA

Born on February 9, 1902, Léon M'ba became Gabon's head of state on independence in 1960. He was confirmed as President by a sweeping majority in elections the following year.

For ten years after his appointment in 1956 as Vice-President under a French Governor, Léon M'ba dominated his country's

139

political life. His age and political experience made him the elder statesman among French-speaking African leaders. His influence was one of empirical conservatism, despising what he saw as socialist and nationalist extremes.

Léon M'ba was born in Libreville. Educated in a Catholic mission school there, he went on to specialise in tribal customary law. He stood out as one of a new class of French-speaking African – proud both of his French culture and his African heritage, but increasingly aware of a contradiction between the principles of *liberté, égalité, fraternité* and current colonial practice.

Through the 1930s the young M'ba rose through several Civil Service jobs, to be appointed by the French authorities to administer a canton in lower Gabon. During this time, he extended his contacts both among the detribalised townsmen, and through the dispersed rural tribes outside the main Fang centres in the north. He was concerned at the breakdown of tribal life and law, and at the decline in the quality of chiefs nominated by the colonial authorities.

To foster a sense of identity and solidarity among the scattered tribes, Léon M'ba joined and encouraged a new tribal cult known as the 'Bwiti' – a ritualised religion which grew up in reaction to foreign missionary impact, borrowing both Christian and traditional tribal beliefs. Before World War II, M'ba was exiled for his supposedly subversive activities to Oubangui-Chari, the future Central African Republic.

There he was again employed by the Administration, and played a part in recruiting for the Free French forces. Allowed to return to Gabon in 1946, Léon M'ba took a post with a British trading firm, and concentrated his spare time on political action.

M'ba was in touch with other French-speaking African leaders, many of whom were looking for a new deal under a post-war French Government; they were encouraged by plans for social and political progress laid down for the colonial territories at a Free French meeting in Brazzaville in 1944.

The Gabonese Mixed Committee, founded by M'ba in 1946, and later renamed the Gabon Democratic Bloc (BDG), was affiliated to the African Democratic Rally (RDA), an inter-territorial movement launched by M. Félix Houphouet-Boigny (later President of Ivory Coast). The movement sought autonomy for its member territories and opposed the federalist ideas of the Senegal leader, Léopold Senghor.

Léon M'ba, whose political backing at home was never confined to one tribal bloc or interest group, came to the political forefront at a 1947 congress called by the Gabon Colonial Administration, to look into Fang tribal problems. Then, as in the future, he succeeded in establishing contact with apparently opposing groups. His political strength lay in his ability to rally a variety of interests and personalities behind a minimum political programme. In 1952, Léon M'ba was elected to the Gabonese Territorial Assembly, and in 1956 he became mayor of Libreville.

The following year, with the increased territorial autonomy provided for under France's 1956 'framework law', M'ba was Vice-President of the Government Council under the French Governor. His post amounted to the premiership.

In the 1957 territorial elections,

M'ba's BDG narrowly defeated Aubame's Gabon Democratic and Social Union (UDSG). Léon M'ba picked several Ministers from his rival's party, and all subsequently joined him in the BDG.

At an RDA conference in Bamako that year, Léon M'ba was shocked by the left-wing nationalism of men like Sekou Touré, later President of Guinea, and sided firmly with M. Houphouet-Boigny's moderate leadership.

M'ba became Prime Minister of Gabon in July, 1958, when plans were being made for the September referendum and subsequent choice of Gabon's future status. He rejected the idea of a federation of AEF territories, and called for direct links between Gabon and France: 'We are not betraying our African brothers ... but we can no longer consent to our money being used to help Brazzaville mushroom, while we have neither roads nor infrastructure.' (It had been Gabon's constant complaint that it was being milked to help its poorer AEF neighbours.)

The referendum complete, and Gabon's choice of transitional self-government confirmed, M'ba agreed in January, 1959 to join what later became the Central African Customs and Economic Union (UDEAC). Gabon's full independence was proclaimed on August 17 the following year.

In November, 1960, M. M'ba, as de facto head of state, declared a state of emergency for six months. He warned against disorders in the north, stronghold of the Opposition, and a number of prominent figures were arrested.

These included the President and Vice-President of the National Assembly, both members of M'ba's own BDG, and various Opposition leaders. (The arrested Assembly president, Paul Gondjout, had for several years been one of Gabon's representatives in the French National Assembly. He was detained again, but then acquitted, after the 1964 coup.)

In February, 1961, Léon M'ba was confirmed as president in general elections which gave him 95 per cent of the poll. He brought his rival Jean-Hilaire Aubame into the Government and, though the coalition broke down, the country had three years of apparent stability. Only towards the end of that period was there any serious opposition, when the Government was accused of infringing democratic rights.

By January, 1964, political tensions were hard to contain. The President dissolved the National Assembly after it failed to give wholehearted backing to a bill aimed at excluding M. Aubame.

Elections planned for the following month were forestalled by the coup of February 18-20. Troops headed by Army lieutenant Jean Essone and Gendarmerie lieutenant Jacques Monbo, quietly seized key points in the capital on the night of February 17-18, and captured the President in his palace.

No bloodshed was reported and the life of the city appeared normal next day. President M'ba was persuaded to broadcast the announcement of his own resignation. The young officers behind the coup promised to end the 'police regime' and release political prisoners. They appealed to the French not to intervene and named Jean-Hilaire Aubame as new head of state.

On February 19 – apparently in response to an appeal from the Gabon Vice-President, who took refuge in the French Embassy – French paratroopers landed outside Libreville. They retook the city and reinstated President M'ba, who had been taken from the capital by the plotters. Unofficial French accounts put the number killed in the French intervention at 20 Gabonese and one French soldier.

The US State Department denied French rumours that Americans – whose economic stake in Gabon was increasing – had encouraged the *coup*. M'ba and the French Government referred African and other critics of the paratroop action to the terms of treaty agreements between France and Gabon.

Once reinstated, President M'ba said the *coup* had been as short-lived 'as a rose', the work of embittered nonentities. They would get no mercy and no forgiveness. M. Aubame and a number of other civilian and military suspects were detained, and the UDSG party was disqualified from standing in the elections – forestalled by the *coup* and now rescheduled for April, 1964. M. M'ba promised Gabon a new start on a new footing.

In March, French troops intervened again in Libreville to help quell demonstrators, who shouted 'M'ba resign!' An unknown number of people were arrested, and the President threatened firm treatment for future trouble-makers.

The April elections gave the President's BDG 31 seats in the National Assembly, and the Opposition, hastily renamed and reorganised, 16. But over the next two years, all but three of the Opposition members joined the Government, leaving Gabon a virtual one-party state.

On the fifth anniversary of Independence, on August 17, 1965, President M'ba gave a glowing account of the country's economic and social progress. The figures he gave for average income and number of children receiving education were unusually high for Black Africa. Incomes, he said, had risen by 50 per cent in five years. While men were earning more, women were now their equals in society and before the law.

In 1966, when he was not receiving medical treatment in Paris, the President seemed increasingly preoccupied with African international affairs. In June he went to Tananarive to sign the charter of the Common Afro-Malagasy Organisation (OCAM). He described it enthusiastically as a little African common market. In July he was in Paris discussing with General de Gaulle the possibility of a French-speaking Commonwealth, based on an African group bridging the Sahara.

In August, after a brief return to Libreville and a Cabinet reshuffle, President M'ba went into hospital in the French capital for treatment of an undisclosed ailment. M. Georges Rawiri, who in August left the Gabon Government but remained Ambassador to Paris, said the President was paying in fatigue the price of a lifetime's hard work.

On November 13, the President appointed 30 year-old M. Albert Bongo, a trusted Minister of State, already in charge of Defence, as Vice-President of Gabon 'to ensure the efficient functioning of the Government'.

M. M'ba was still in hospital in Paris when he reshuffled the Government on January 25, 1967.

PIERRE MEBALEY
Named Finance Minister in a Government reshuffle on

Stanislas-Jean Migolet

Vincent-de-Paul
Nyonda

January 25, 1967, Pierre Mebaley is a graduate of the Paris Institute of Advanced Overseas Studies.

Born at Port Gentil in 1936, he was educated at the now Lycée Léon M'ba, and at a college in Mitzic in northern Gabon. He went to the Paris Institute of Advanced Overseas Studies on a scholarship.

After holding several other administrative posts, he became sub-prefect of Ndende in the south-west, and then Secretary-General at the Foreign Affairs Ministry.

In 1966, at the age of 30, he was appointed Minister of Labour and Social Affairs.

STANISLAS-JEAN MIGOLET

Stanislas-Jean Migolet, appointed Minister of Health in 1966, has been three times Minister of the Interior and a member of the Gabon Assembly from its earliest days.

He was born in Koula-Moutou in central Gabon in 1920, and received primary education at a Catholic mission school at Mbigou in the south.

In 1941 he became a clerk in the Administration, and from 1947–52, served in the General Council – the elected advisory body to the pre-independence Administration.

In 1957, after a period as Vice-President of the Territorial Assembly, he became Minister of the Interior in Gabon's first autonomous Government.

Re-elected to each successive Assembly from 1958–64, he was appointed Minister of Labour and Social Affairs (1958–60), Minister of the Interior and National Security (1960–61), President of the National Budgetary and Finance Commission (1961–64) and, for a third term,

Minister of the Interior in 1964.

Stanislas-Jean Migolet represented Gabon from 1959–61 in the Senate of the French Community and later on the board of the Equatorial African Posts and Telecommunications Office.

DR BENJAMIN NGOUBOU

Dr Benjamin Ngoubou was appointed Minister of Labour and Social Affairs on January 25, 1967. He was born on July 23, 1925, and studied medicine at the University of Lyons in France. Before his appointment he was head of the maternity and gynaecology department at Libreville hospital.

Dr Ngoubou is an Officer of the Equatorial Star.

VINCENT-DE-PAUL NYONDA

Vincent-de-Paul Nyonda became Minister of State in September, 1965, and held the post through two Cabinet reshuffles in 1966. He was charged with special responsibility for Cultural Affairs, Youth and Sport, and relations with Parliament and the national women's organisation.

He was dropped in a reshuffle on January 25, 1967, and his portfolios divided among several Ministries.

Born in 1918, he did not enter the Catholic mission school in Mouila, south-west Gabon, until 1937. From there he went on to the Catholic seminary in Brazzaville, and by 1957 had qualified as a teacher in Catholic private schools.

Elected to the pre-independence Territorial Council in 1957, M. Nyonda became successively Minister of Public Works and a member of the inter-territorial council for French Equatorial Africa.

In 1963, he was appointed Minister of Youth and Sport in

the independent Gabon Government. He lost his post with the dissolution of the Government early in 1964, but was re-elected to the National Assembly that April. In September, 1965, he re-entered the Government as Minister of State.

LUBIN NTOUTOUME OBAME

Lubin Obame, from 1965 the Minister of Works, Transport, Post and Telecommunications, had previously served as Finance Minister and in the administration of the ruling BDG party.

Born near Libreville in 1931, he was educated at the capital's Collège Moderne. After leaving school, he was an active trade unionist, and became local secretary of the General African Workers' Federation in 1955.

The same year he left for Paris to attend the Institut Normal de Sciences Commerciales. He spent four years there and, from 1959–60, took courses in labour, social administration, and accountancy.

In the first post-independence elections of 1961, Lubin Obame won a seat in the Gabon National Assembly, and from 1961–63 was vice-president of the National Finance Commission.

In February, 1963, he was appointed Finance Minister, and held the post for one year, then becoming secretary-general of the Forestry Office National Committee.

From 1963 he was also a member of the Libreville City Council, and on the boards of the internationally-owned Air-Afrique Company and the national Posts and Telecommunications Office.

He received the portfolio for Works, Transport, Post and Telecommunications in March, 1965, and was made Minister of State in January, 1967.

PIERRE-MARIE ONDO

Pierre-Marie Ondo was one of the youngest men in the Cabinet when he held the Agriculture portfolio from April, 1964 to August, 1966. He resigned on health grounds.

He was born in 1936 at Bitam, in northern Gabon, not far from the Cameroun border. He studied at the St Jean Seminary in Libreville until ill-health forced him to leave school and enter hospital at Ebolowa in Cameroun.

After his recovery, M. Ondo trained at a Catholic teachers' training college before returning to teach at his old primary school, a Catholic mission at Bitam. He became headmaster, then director of the regional education authority.

In April, 1964, when President M'ba was looking round for younger men to bring into his Cabinet after the abortive February *coup*, Pierre-Marie Ondo was appointed Minister of Agriculture.

GEORGES RAWIRI

For a year beginning in April, 1965, Georges Rawiri was simultaneously Minister of Information and Tourism, and Ambassador to France, Israel, Italy, Spain, the United Kingdom and Malta.

A radio expert, M. Rawiri directed the national broadcasting network from 1960–63 and introduced television into Gabon.

In August, 1966, he gave up the Information and Tourism portfolio he had gained on the strength of his radio work. But as Ambassador in Paris, M. Rawiri was in a key position, and played an important linking role between the Government in Libreville and the ailing President M'ba, then in a Paris hospital.

He was born in Lambarene in

Paul-Maurice Tomo

Paul-Marie Yembit

1932. After primary schooling at a Protestant mission, he left in 1946 for France, where he went to a *lycée* in the southern town of Alès.

After matriculating, he spent a year in Paris studying radio techniques and the cooperation between French-speaking radio networks. In July, 1957, he played a major part in setting up the Garoua radio station in North Cameroun, and in 1960 he was appointed director of Gabon's national radio.

In 1963 he was elected to the Lambarene City Council and entered the Government the following year as Minister of Information, Tourism, Post and Telecommunications. In March, 1965, he gave up the Post and Telecommunications portfolio, but was named the following month as Ambassador to half a dozen countries at once.

PAUL-MAURICE TOMO

Paul-Maurice Tomo became Minister of the Interior after holding a series of senior Civil Service posts, including a period in the President's Office.

He was born in 1922 at Ozakong, a village in the Bitam area of Northern Gabon, and educated at the Protestant High School in Brazzaville. In 1944 he became headmaster of the main school at the northern regional centre of Oyem.

A prominent member of the local BDG party organisation, based on Bitam near the Cameroun border, M. Tomo became president of the Civil Service trade union in 1938, and held the post until 1945.

Before independence, he was Permanent Secretary in the Ministry of Forestry and Agriculture. From 1961–66, he held a corresponding post in the Presi-

dent's Office, and during part of that time, had special responsibility for Youth and Sports.

Before his appointment as Minister of the Interior, he exercised wide control over the Civil Service as Secretary to the Administration.

PAUL-MARIE YEMBIT

Paul-Marie Yembit ceded the vice-presidency to Albert-Bernard Bongo in November, 1966. He remained Minister of Justice and took over M. Bongo's Information and Tourism portfolio.

As Vice-President at the time of the 1964 *coup*, it was reported to have been M. Yembit who took the initiative in calling in French troops to restore the legal Government.

Born in 1917 in the south-western township of Ndende, Paul-Marie Yembit was educated at a Catholic mission school, and at the secondary school in the regional centre of Lambarene. With a large family to support, he went into business on leaving school. For 11 years before entering politics, he ran a business in Mouila, not far from his home region.

In March, 1952, M. Yembit entered Gabon's pre-independence Territorial Council, on which he served until 1957. In 1957 he became Minister of Agriculture and Livestock in the Council, by then upgraded to effective Government status. Next year he was Minister of Labour and the Civil Service.

At independence, M. Yembit was deputy secretary-general of the BDG party, second in command to M. M'ba. After the 1961 post-independence elections, he entered the National Assembly and was appointed Vice-President and Minister of Justice.

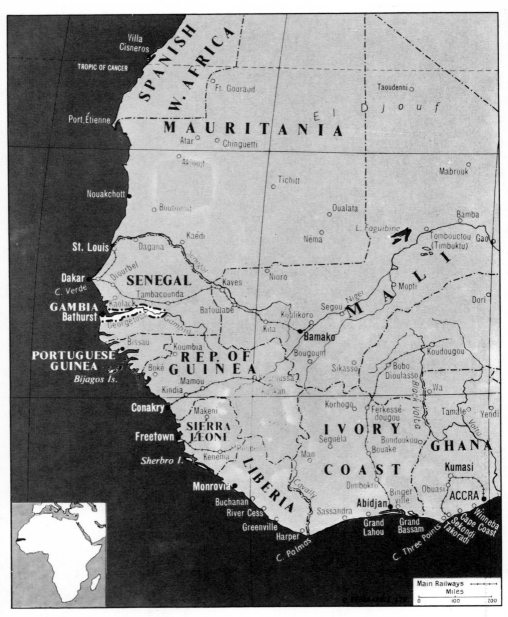

Gambia is a narrow tongue of land lying from between six and ten miles on either side of the Gambia River and extending for about 300 miles into Senegal, which surrounds it on three sides, with the Atlantic Ocean to the west. A total area of 4,132 square miles supports a population of well over 300,000 (1963 census: 315,486). The capital is Bathurst.

Gambia's chief export, groundnuts, is the mainstay of the national economy and the focus of commercial activity. Rice is of growing importance as a local food.

146

Gambia

Gambia, linked with Britain since 1588, became a Crown Colony with a basis of modern constitutional development in 1888. The country retained its economic, ethnic and African language links with Senegal, the French territory surrounding it.

It became self-governing on October 4, 1963, and an independent member of the British Commonwealth on February 18, 1965.

Parliament consists of a Governor-General and a House of Representatives, over which a Speaker presides. The Cabinet is composed of the Prime Minister and six Ministers.

Gambia, discovered by early Portuguese navigators, was Britain's first colony in Africa and still receives £1,500,000 a year from Britain to help with her budget, though this arrangement was to be reviewed in 1967. Having gained full independence, the Prime Minister, Sir Dauda Jawara, held a national referendum in the same year (November, 1965) to decide whether the country should become a republic. A total of 61,568 people voted in favour and 31,921 against. This was less than the two-thirds majority required to change the constitution and the status of Gambia remained unaltered.

The ruling People's Progressive Party had campaigned in favour of a republic and the main Opposition United Party against it.

The minority Congress Party, led by Mr Ibrahima Muhammadu Garba-Jahumpa, and the Gambia Workers' Union, under the secretary-generalship of Momadou Jallow, were also opposed to a change.

The referendum bill had passed through the House of Assembly without any opposition from the UP, but the insistance of the PPP on an executive president altered the situation. The UP saw their hopes of participating in a coalition government becoming increasingly remote under a head of state with increased powers.

Senegal was understood to be opposed to the idea of a republic because it would make the desired closer association more difficult to achieve. The Gambian Opposition parties were well aware of this.

When the Government of Gambia announced that new

elections would be held in the middle of 1966, they raised fears that having failed in the referendum they might ask for a mandate if they won. But the appointment of a leading PPP member, Alhaji Farimang Mamadi Singhateh as acting Governor-General, later Governor-General, to replace British-born Sir John Paul convinced the Opposition that the Republican issue had been shelved for the foreseeable future.

This was confirmed by Sir Dauda Jawara after the elections in May, 1966, which he won with an increased majority. He said he would not attempt another referendum on the Republican issue for five years. The association between Gambia and Senegal goes back to the 18th century when Britain and France were fighting for mastery of this part of the West African coast. In 1779 the French recaptured Senegal. Britain managed to hold the Gambia River but had to accept the break-up of what had been known as Senegambia. It was not until 1854 that the idea of reunifying Gambia and Senegal was revived. In 1863 France proposed to surrender her posts in the Ivory Coast and elsewhere if Britain would cede Gambia, placed right in the middle of her colony and monopolising the best part of the river on both sides. A formal proposal came three years later. But strong opposition to union with a French-speaking colony came from 500 people in Bathurst, the capital; they were Akus, mainly clerks and teachers whose main business value was their command of the English language. Eleven members of the British Parliament accordingly objected to any cession of Gambia to France. Franco-British negotiations on Gambia and Senegal were dropped and in 1889 a frontier between the two colonies was drawn and agreed upon by the two European powers.

Such an artificial boundary and the general lay of the land made customs evasion easy in both directions. The Gambian income on smuggled goods into Senegal has been estimated at about £500,000 a year.

The last attempt between Britain and France to exchange Gambia for another French territory in West Africa was made in 1911 but without any success. Since then the 'wind of change' has blown through both countries.

Two lines of men load groundnuts on board a cargo ship

In 1961 a joint Senegalese-Gambian ministerial committee was formed to help contacts between the two countries. It failed to achieve any concrete results. Regular meetings were held in both countries – though none took place in 1966.

A United Nations Commission set up in 1964 recommended that if the two countries could agree on some form of association, the basin of the Gambia River, which has its source in Guinea, should be developed in consultation with that country 'as a project of paramount importance'. But the majority of Gambians are not too keen on association, refusing to believe that much economic improvement will result from the alliance of two countries both of which are dependent on the same crop, groundnuts.

The UN experts considered complete integration of the two countries unrealistic and recommended instead closer association in easy stages.

No trade agreement has been signed between Senegal and Gambia – a vital first step to really close association. However, on Independence Day, Gambia and Senegal signed three agreements on defence, common representation in foreign countries and cooperation in the development of the Gambia River, which is one of the finest waterways in West Africa.

149

The agreements are nevertheless proving to be a mere statement of intent. Gambia has no army, only a police force, and has not delegated Senegal to look after her interests in any country, even at the United Nations in New York, where she has not yet opened a permanent embassy office.

Senegal, Mauritania, Guinea and Mali have secured United Nations aid to develop the Senegal River Basin, excluding Gambia from the agreement. Even though plans for developing the Gambia River Basin have not been abandoned, it seems likely that negotiations will be held up once work on the Senegal River Basin begins. And with a one-cash-crop economy based on groundnuts, Gambia's economic prospects are not encouraging. Uncertainty about Gambia's future relations with Senegal long inhibited both public and private investment in the country. There are no major industries, except plants for decorticating groundnuts.

The main tribes in Gambia are the Mandingoes (one-third of the population), Fullas (one-fifth) and Wollofs (one-tenth). Mandingoes and Fullas also live in Senegal and Guinea while the majority of Wollofs are to be found in Senegal and southern Mauritania. The Wollofs also form the majority in Bathurst and stand to gain much in the event of any form of association with Senegal. The Bathurst Wollofs occupy over 80 per cent of Civil Service posts and are also employed as clerks in commerce. Minorities include Mauritanians, Guineans, Senegalese, refugees from Portuguese Guinea, Malians and Akus – detribalised Africans whose ancestors were liberated slaves or refugees from other areas at the time of the slave trade. They are mostly civil servants.

The few Europeans are mostly Britons, either Government civil servants or employees of commercial firms. Syrians and Lebanese, who handle the bulk of the retail trade, number around 200; some have been integrated into the community and there are families which can trace back their relations with the country for four generations. But there are no European settlers in the country as in east, central and southern Africa. Over 90 per cent of the population are Moslems and the remaining ten per cent are Roman Catholics, Protestants and Methodists.

ALIEU SULAYMAN JACK

Alhaji Alieu Sulayman Jack, Speaker (President) of the Gambia House of Assembly, is a Moslem Wollof highly thought of by the ruling, Mandingo-dominated People's Progressive Party.

Of medium height and well-built, Alhaji Alieu, who is a company director, began his political career in 1950 when first elected a member of Bathurst Town Council. He was born in Bathurst in 1922, his father being a goldsmith.

Alhaji Alieu was educated at a Roman Catholic mission school and joined the Gambia Civil Service at the beginning of World War II.

PAUL LOUIS BALDEH

The former Education Minister, Paul Louis Baldeh has been described as the most skilful debater in the House of Assembly.

He is a member of the Fulla tribe, who form one-fifth of the population. The only child of a wealthy Moslem farmer, he was born in 1937 at Sare N'Gai, a village about 250 miles from Bathurst, and began his education at a Roman Catholic mission school near his home. His father asked a Catholic priest, who later became Bishop Michael Maloney, to look after him. In 1947 the boy arrived at Bathurst to continue his schooling and was shortly afterwards converted from the Islamic faith to Roman Catholicism. He changed his first name from Mamadou to Paul Louis.

In 1954 he went to Dublin to read for a BA degree. He graduated in economics, history and English in 1960 and returned home to teach at the Catholic Mission Secondary School in Bathurst.

Resigning from his teaching post to enter politics, he aligned himself with the People's Progressive Party, which helped the standing of the party in areas where Fullas are in the majority. He was elected in the 1962 elections and became Education Minister. He could not work in agreement with the Government, however, and was dismissed about a year later. Before Gambia achieved independence (1965), Mr Baldeh returned to his former Ministry. In the 1966 elections he was again returned but was not given a ministerial appointment.

PHILIP RODNEY BRIDGES

Gambia's Attorney-General (appointed in 1964), Philip Rodney Bridges, is the only European member of the Cabinet. Born in England in 1922, he went to Gambia in 1954 to serve the Government as solicitor of the Supreme Court. He is the eldest son of the late Commodore Sir Ernest Bridges.

Mr Bridges studied at Aberdeen University and was commissioned in the Royal Artillery during World War II. He reached the rank of major and served in Burma with the Royal West African Frontier Force. He returned to England at the end of the war and in 1951 qualified as a solicitor.

ANDREW DAVID CAMARA

The Minister of Education in Gambia, Andrew David Camara is a member of the Fulla tribe and the only Anglican member of the Government.

He first entered the House of Assembly as an Independent in 1960. He aligned with the United Party but changed to the ruling People's Progressive Party after the 1962 elections.

Born in 1923 at Mansajang

Sir Dauda Jawara

village, about 240 miles from Bathurst, he has served in the Cabinet since he replaced the dismissed Education Minister, Mr Paul Baldeh, in 1963.

About six feet tall, he is generally regarded as a good administrator. He was born a Moslem but was converted to the Anglican Church at an early age when he started school.

Mr Camara first served as a Minister under Pierre N'Jie, leader of the United Party, when the latter was Chief Minister in 1961. He himself did not become an active party man, preferring to be considered neutral. During the election campaign in 1962, however, he openly aligned himself with the United Party and was returned with a big majority.

He entered politics in 1958 after ten years of teaching at government and mission schools.

SHERIFF MUSTAPHA DIBBA

Sheriff Mustapha Dibba, Minister of Works and Communications, is the son of a chief and one of the young Mandingoes who helped to form the ruling People's Progressive Party. He was Minister for Local Government until the 1966 elections. A skilled debater, he was regarded as No 3 in the Government before he moved to his present post.

Born in 1937, of Moslem parents, he was educated at government and mission schools and worked as a clerk for the United Africa Company until 1959, when he resigned to go into politics.

He was elected to the House of Assembly in 1960 and has since been returned in two elections. Besides his Government post, he is also very active in his party, occupying the vice-presidency of the youth wing.

SIR DAUDA KAIRABA JAWARA

The first Prime Minister of Gambia, Sir Dauda Kairaba Jawara began his working life as a veterinary surgeon. The only university-educated man in the Government and senior in age to most of his Ministers, he has a masterly way of handling them. It is even said that since he formed his first government in 1962 there has never been a problem which has really threatened his control. He does not claim to be a great orator, but his administrative abilities are beyond question.

He was knighted by Queen Elizabeth in 1966.

A member of the Mandingo tribe, he was one of six children born to a Moslem trader and farmer in 1924 at Barajally, a village about 150 miles from Bathurst. A Wollof trader in the capital, who was a friend of the family, was asked to look after him while he attended school there. Thus at the age of ten he went to live among the Wollofs of Bathurst.

On leaving school in 1945, he joined the Gambia Medical Department as a trainee nurse, went to Achimota College in Ghana with a veterinary scholarship, passed his intermediate BSc examination and qualified as a veterinary surgeon after six years at the University of Glasgow, Scotland. He returned home the first Gambian 'vet'.

In 1955 he became a Christian, took the Christian name David and married Augusta Mahoney, a daughter of the late Sir John Mahoney—a member of the Aku tribe and Speaker of the House of Assembly. Miss Mahoney, who had been trained as a nurse in the United Kingdom, became a great political asset to her husband and accompanied him on tours in the provinces, during which she urged women to become interested in politics.

In 1960 Sir Dauda was elected a member of the House of Representatives and became Minister of Education. Ministerial appointments were then the responsibility of the British Governor and there was at the time no provision in the constitution for a Chief Minister. A year later the Governor decided there should be a Chief Minister and his choice fell upon Pierre Saar N'Jie, leader of the United Party, who was to head a coalition Government. Sir Dauda refused to serve under N'Jie and resigned from the Government, taking with him members of his party.

This was the beginning of party politics in Gambia. In the 1962 elections, under a new constitution, Sir Dauda's party just managed to gain a majority in the House. He was the first Gambian to be called upon to form a Government and a year later, with self-government, he became the first Premier, and led Gambia to full independence on February 18, 1965.

Nine months after independence, his party failed to obtain the necessary two-thirds majority in a referendum held to decide whether Gambia should become a republic under an executive president – a post he would have automatically occupied.

He announced that elections would be held in the middle of 1966, and won these in a landslide.

Although he has lived most of his life in Gambia with the Wollofs of Bathurst, except for a brief period when he worked as a 'vet' up country, Sir Dauda never lost contact with his own people, the Mandingoes. From the introduction of modern politics the Wollofs, who form one tenth of the population, dominated the political scene together with the minority Akus.

When the Mandingoes became politically active, they naturally turned to Sir Dauda as a leader. They formed a party, calling it the Protectorate People's Party. As soon as he took control, however, he changed its name to the People's Progressive Party and this helped to allay fears of minorities becoming a problem in Gambia.

In 1965 Sir Dauda returned to his old religion and ceased to be known as David.

KEBBA CHERNO AMAAT KAH

The childhood of Kebba Cherno Amaat Kah, a Wollof and Gambian Minister of Health, was spent in the atmosphere of his father's Koranic school at Medina Mas Kah, a village about 100 miles from Bathurst. To this little centre of learning came Islamic scholars as well as pupils not only from Gambia but also from neighbouring Senegal, Guinea, Mali and Mauritania.

Born in 1934, he went from his father's school to a Catholic mission, then to the Gambia Teachers' Training College. He taught at a number of Government schools until he resigned to become a full-time politician in 1959.

He entered the House of Assembly in 1960 as a member of the Opposition United Party. When Mr Pierre N'Jie, the leader of the party, became Chief Minister, Mr Kah was appointed Parliamentary Secretary to the Ministry of Health.

After the 1962 elections he defected to the ruling People's Progressive Party and became

Pierre Saar N'Jie

Parliamentary Secretary to the Ministry of Finance and later to the Ministry of Works and Communications.

He was appointed Health Minister in 1965.

AMANG SOLI KANYI

Appointed Minister of Agriculture in 1963, Amang Soli Kanyi is a Mandingo and, like Sir Dauda Jawara, was raised in Bathurst by a Wollof family.

He was the son of a prosperous Moslem farmer, born in 1925. He attended Anglican and Methodist schools before returning to his native village of Jassong to set up in business.

He joined the People's Progressive Party and was elected to Parliament in 1960. He was Parliamentary Secretary to the Prime Minister's Office for a short period before he was appointed to the post of Minister of Agriculture.

ALIEU BADARA N'JIE

Alhaji Alieu Badara N'Jie, the Minister of State for Foreign Affairs, is also the Resident Minister in Dakar, Senegal. He is the only Wollof in the Government, has travelled widely and has led his country's delegation to the United Nations for several years in succession.

Tall, slim and hardworking, he has been described as the best administrator in the Government. Behind him are 33 years in the Civil Service.

He is a devout Moslem who has made the pilgrimage to Mecca. He was among those who fought against the introduction of religion into Gambian politics when the Moslem Congress Party was formed in 1951. As a countermove he helped to organise the now defunct Democratic Party.

Born in Bathurst in 1904, he spent most of his youth among the minority Akus. He attended Methodist mission schools and entered the Civil Service in 1925. When he retired from the Government service in 1958 he was Registrar of the Supreme Court. He was the first Gambian to hold this position and the first Moslem to head a Government department.

He forms a bridge between Wollofs and Mandingoes by cooperating as a Wollof with the ruling People's Progressive Party (supported by the majority of Mandingoes) without joining as a member.

He is not related to Pierre N'Jie, the Opposition leader.

PIERRE SAAR N'JIE

The leader of the Opposition and chairman of the United Party, Pierre Saar N'Jie confidently looks forward to the time when he will wrest the leadership of Gambia from his old rival, Sir Dauda Jawara.

He lost the opportunity when he was the country's first Chief Minister. He might have led his people to self-government, but unwisely agreed to further elections half-way through the five year term of the House of Assembly.

The elections (1962) were under a new constitution. The PPP just managed to win the majority of votes. The result was discouraging to his party, and half its members joined the PPP by crossing the floor after the House opened. Consequently it was Sir Dauda who led the country to self-rule and eventually to full independence.

A Wollof and a lawyer trained at Lincoln's Inn, London, Mr N'Jie was born in 1909. He was educated at a Catholic mission school and later became converted from Islam to Roman Catholicism.

He had a successful law practice when he turned to full-time politics in 1954. As Minister of Education and Social Welfare he was dismissed following a clash with the British Governor over allegations he had made concerning the conduct of the Gambian police. A commission of inquiry set up to investigate the charges commended the police instead.

In the 1960 elections Mr N'Jie was elected, but only four other candidates of his party were successful against the PPP's nine (out of 19 seats contested). He declined a Ministry without Portfolio, but in 1961 the Governor offered him the post of Chief Minister in a broad-based Government.

Mr N'Jie has two brothers, both lawyers, and a sister who has been the main drive behind his political success. One of his brothers, Ebrima, is a member of the House of Assembly and has served in the Government.

Many Gambians feel that had Mr N'Jie been prime minister of independent Gambia, he would have succeeded in negotiating some form of association between Gambia and Senegal.

FARIMANG MAMADI SINGHATEH

Alhaji Farimang Mamadi Singhateh was appointed the first Gambian Governor-General at the end of 1966. His appointment was generally regarded with surprise.

Although a leading member of the ruling People's Progressive Party, he always kept himself in the background. A Moslem and a member of the Mandingo tribe, he was best known for the successful drug store he used to

own, known as 'Farimang's Hospital'.

His appointment came after the People's Progressive Party had failed in its bid to turn the country into a republic. It convinced Gambians that the question of changing the constitution was dead, at least for the time being.

Over six feet tall, Alhaji Farimang was born in Georgetown, about 150 miles from Bathurst, in 1912. He was educated at Catholic and Methodist mission schools, and later worked in the Gambia Medical Department.

After qualifying as a druggist, Alhaji Farimang then opened his drug store.

SHERIFF SEKUBA SISAY

The Finance Minister, Sheriff Sekuba Sisay was one of the young Mandingoes who led the move to form the ruling People's Progressive Party. They were motivated in this by the lack of interest in politics among their own tribe, about a third of the population.

The prominent part he played led to unjust accusations that he was fostering tribalism.

Mr Sisay was born in 1935, of Moslem parents, at Kudang village, about 160 miles from Bathurst.

He was elected to the House of Assembly in 1960 and became a Minister without Portfolio. He resigned this post when the leader of the United Party, Mr Pierre N'Jie was made Chief Minister by the Governor. He returned to the Government after his re-election in 1962 and became Gambia's first Finance Minister.

He has been unaffected by two Government reshuffles during his term of office. Many feel he has established himself as the No 2 man in the Cabinet.

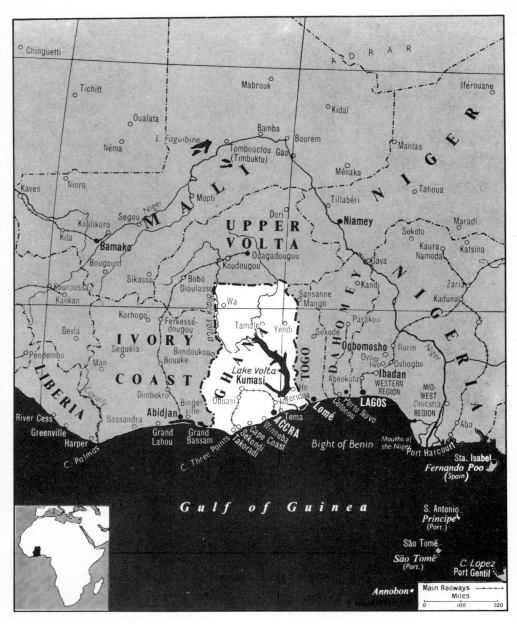

Ghana covers an area of 92,100 square miles. The population was estimated in 1966 to be 7,840,000. Ghana has a coastline on the Gulf of Guinea (Atlantic) and is bordered on the west by the Ivory Coast, with Togo and Dahomey in the east. To the north lies Upper Volta. Accra is the capital.

Ghana is the world's leading producer of cocoa.

The Government has launched a nation-wide literacy drive and a scheme of self-help projects to increase social facilities and boost the standard of living.

Ghana

The Gold Coast, led by Dr Kwame Nkrumah, was the
first British colony in Africa to become independent, as
Ghana, on March 6, 1957.
Ghana was declared a republic within the Commonwealth,
with Dr Nkrumah as President, on July 1, 1960.
Dr Nkrumah was overthrown by Army and police officers
on February 24, 1966. They formed a National Liberation
Council ruling by decree, advised by several committees.
They promised to return Ghana to civilian government
as soon as practicable—a pledge reiterated by
Lieutenant-General J. A. Ankrah, the Chairman, in a
New Year's broadcast on January 1, 1967.
On the *coup's* first anniversary General Ankrah said
their main objective was to 'rebuild the shattered
economy and remove the gross maladministration
characteristic of the ousted regime'.

Ghana first appeared on the world maps on March 6,
1957, when the Gold Coast, with Dr Kwame Nkrumah
at its head, became independent and took the name of an
ancient Sudanic empire that flourished between the fourth
and tenth centuries.
Almost the entire population of Ghana are Sudanese
Negroes. They were the first British colonial people in
Africa to win their freedom. They wanted to get rid of
the name 'Gold Coast' and its unhappy association with
the days of the slave trade, in which the Portuguese,
English, French, Danes, Swedes and Germans all
participated.
Dr Nkrumah was in a colonial jail for sedition in
February, 1951, following his year of 'positive action'
(non-cooperation) against the British, when his
Convention People's Party swept the polls in a general
election which could hardly have had any other result.
The British Government, with great diplomacy, restored
him to his excited people and he at once became the
Leader of Government Business in Parliament and the
most outstanding African nationalist leader on the
continent.
For several years the jubilant Ghanaians represented the
spearhead of political advancement in Colonial Africa,
with many millions of black people and hundreds of
thousands of white in other territories – British, South
African, French, Belgian, Spanish and Portuguese – all

157

watching intently, with every kind of emotion from
respect, admiration and envy to embarrassment, anger
and dismay.

The Ghanaians were a model of African freedom for
other races to emulate. They had inherited from Britain a
sound civil service. They had the immense good fortune
to possess a country so rich in cocoa that it had
become and was fairly certain to remain the world's
biggest producer. Of the ample funds and other assets
worth £200m bequeathed by the Colonial power, £80m
was from cocoa.

With extraordinary energy and drive, Dr Nkrumah went
on from success to success, and from power to still
greater power. By means of legislation passed by his
acquiescing, one-party General Assembly, the members
of which he himself eventually chose, he gained complete
control over his country.

A Deportation Act in 1957 permitted banishment of any
persons whose presence was not conducive to the public
good. In July, 1958, only 16 months after Ghana became
independent, he put through the Preventive Detention
Act. This allowed imprisonment without trial up to five
years, a term which could be extended at the
Government's discretion. At one time or another most of
the leaders of the Opposition United Party were detained
under the Act. They included two lawyers who had
become politicians – Mr Joe Appiah, married to a
daughter of a former British Chancellor of the Exchequer,
Sir Stafford Cripps, and Dr Joseph B. Danquah, who
died in prison on February 4, 1965. (The total number
of men arrested and kept in prison during Nkrumah's
period in power was estimated after the 1966 *coup* to be
2,000.)

When Ghana was declared a sovereign unitary republic
within the Commonwealth on July 1, 1960, Dr Nkrumah's
powers were immense. Parliament consisted only of
himself and the National Assembly. The Constitution
provided for a president who was both head of state and
head of government, and also commander-in-chief of the
armed forces.

In July, 1961, Dr Nkrumah led a Ghanian delegation to
the USSR and a number of East European countries and
China. Discussions there resulted in big trade and
cultural exchanges. Later Russian, Polish, Czech, East

German and Chinese embassies and trade missions in Accra were considerably strengthened and hundreds of technicians and teachers of all kinds arrived.

The Constitution of Ghana included a unique clause which showed Dr Nkrumah's lifelong preoccupation with the idea of a political union of all African countries with a continental government. It declared Ghana's preparedness to surrender its sovereignty, in whole or in part, to bring about a union of African states and territories as soon as that should become practicable. Dr Nkrumah threw himself wholeheartedly into the promotion of the Organisation of African Unity and built at great speed as a top priority his £8m State House to accommodate the 'Summit' of heads of state in Accra in October, 1965.

Several attempts had been made on Dr Nkrumah's life, but he was at the pinnacle of his power when he opened on January 22, 1966, the £150m Volta River hydro-electric scheme at Akosombo, one of the largest in the world. It was expected to revolutionise the standard of living in Ghana, flood the remote dark north with an illumination it had never known before, provide cheap power for old and many new industries and end the country's dependence on the cultivation and export of cocoa. For Dr Nkrumah it was a dream come true. But only a month away was his end as President of Ghana.

As day was breaking on February 24, 1966, a group of Army and police officers took over the country when he was far away in Peking on a self-appointed peace mission to Vietnam.

They suspended the constitution that made him an absolute ruler, dissolved what they called his 'sycophant, rubber stamp Parliament', proscribed his Convention People's Party and rounded up and placed in prison under 'protective custody' all his ministers, advisers, MPs, regional and district commissioners and party 'activists'.

The *coup* coincided with the annual military manoeuvres which had been taking place at Tamale, in the north, on the day before. Since November, 1965, the Ghanaian Army had been in 'a high state of preparedness', on Dr Nkrumah's orders and in support of his plan, since described as 'wild' and one of the causes of the *coup*, to intervene in Rhodesia and topple 'the white settler

Young recruits for
the Ghanaian Army

racist regime' of Mr Ian Smith and his fellow
supporters.

To deceive Nkrumah's military intelligence system, it was
pretended that the first troop movements on February 23
were just another test exercise. But at 4 am on
February 24 the manoeuvres of peace became an
operation of war.

The operation was in fact planned as a full-scale military
movement prepared for the worst. It leaders allowed
for a possible division in the Armed Forces, which in
the event did not materialise, and they were ready to
fight a civil war if the need arose.

Mr J. W. K. Harlley, Commissioner of Police (later
Inspector General) told his men afterwards that while
investigating corruption among Cabinet ministers at Dr
Nkrumah's own request, he discovered that Dr Nkrumah

was also involved. As he was surrounded by a private
army and his own personal security forces, however, the
only way to overthrow him was to wait until he was out
of the country. He therefore consulted various officers
of the regular armed forces and police and they drew
up a plan.

The Army officers leading the *coup* were two brigade
commanders of experience – Major-General E. K. Kotoka
and Brigadier A. K. Ocran – and Colonel A. A. Afrifa,
a 30 year-old Sandhurst-trained officer of dash and
brilliance.

At 5 am troops arriving outside Flagstaff House, the
strongly-guarded residence in Accra of Dr Nkrumah,
where his Soviet-trained bodyguard was stationed, came
under long bursts of heavy machine-gun fire. Colonel
Afrifa has since stated that the fire came from a
Russian-made armoured car. At 5.25 am the Colonel's
men had captured the Ghana Broadcasting Corporation's
transmitters 'without much incident' and awakened
Ghanaians were told to stand by for an important
announcement. By 6 am the Accra police had rounded
up most of the Cabinet.

Christiansborg Castle at Osu, the seat of Government,
a dazzling white former slave stronghold on the shores of
the Gulf of Guinea, fell without a shot being fired.
Flagstaff House was captured later in the day. There
appeared to have been few casualties but no figures were
given. The operation ended as smoothly as it had
begun. It was described as a textbook *coup*.

Kotoka and Harlley had declined to head the
Revolutionary Council in favour of Major-General J. A.
Ankrah, an older man and a father figure much
respected by the Army, who had been brought back from
the retirement to which he had been relegated only a few
months previously by Nkrumah.

There was wild excitement in the streets. The women
traders of Makola Market, accustomed to cheering
Nkrumah, danced and sang derisively, calling him
'Africa's No 1 Dictator' and 'bushman' – the worst
insult they could think of.

The new National Liberation Council lost no time in
announcing that they had no political ambitions and
were anxious to hand over power to a civilian government
as quickly as possible. They said they had seized power

to save the country from economic collapse and famine.
From Conakry, Guinea, where he had sought sanctuary,
the deposed President denied over the radio that
Ghana was on the brink of bankruptcy. He claimed that
the big international agreements he had signed were the
basis of economic stability for generations to come; his
huge development schemes an investment for a bright
future.

Insisting he was still the constitutional head of Ghana,
he denounced the men behind the revolt as 'a clique of
adventurers and stooges of colonialism'. He appealed
especially to the members of his favourite political
organisations – the United Ghana Farmers' Council of
Cooperatives, the National Council of Ghana Women,
the Workers' Brigade and the Young Pioneers – to rise
against their new masters.

The National Liberation Council introduced drastic cuts
in Government expenditure. They appointed economic,
political, legal, constitutional and other committees,
composed of leading academics, civil servants and political
and customary leaders.

They reduced the number of ministries from 32 to 18,
cut the total of Ghanaian embassies by 40 per cent,
reconstructed wasteful, profitless State enterprises and
reorganised and limited the fleets of Ghana Airways and
the Black Star Line.

Ghana was estimated to have a national debt of £400m.
Later she reached agreement with a dozen Western
creditor nations on a repayment schedule for a total of
£155m medium-term loans–part of the total external
debt of about £280m run up by the ousted regime.

The NLC set up many commissions to investigate alleged
irregularities and malpractices by Nkrumah, his party and
his Government. One commission, under Judge Azu
Crabbe, found (October 10, 1966) that the State-owned
National Development Company (Nadeco), set up
ostensibly to finance the CPP, became in reality 'a
clearing house for bribes', paid either to the party or to
Nkrumah personally. It accused him of extorting at least
£1,210,000 from companies dealing with his former
Government and recommended that he and twelve of his
associates be prosecuted 'for their criminal involvement
in the affairs of Nadeco'.

Judge F. K. Apaloo's Commission, inquiring into the

extent of Dr Nkrumah's properties and how he acquired them, reported (January 16, 1967) that although he had arrived in Ghana without means he was worth £2,322,000 at the time of the *coup*.

They said that between February 8, 1951, when he became leader of Government Business, and his overthrow as President on February 24, 1966, his lawful earnings from salary and other sources, including his £10,000 Lenin Peace Prize, had been £134,000, out of which he could only have saved £45,000.

When deposed he had £402,294 in cash, land and property in Ghana, a villa near Cairo, property at Rabat, Morocco, £170,862 in a Swiss bank and other money in London.

The Commission caustically recalled the Socialist President's famous 'Dawn Broadcast' (April 8, 1961) in which he said that people 'must not use their party membership or official position for personal gain or for the amassing of wealth'.

There was no one at any of the commissions to speak for the deposed president and answer the allegations. He was never legally represented. When his ministers were brought from prison to give evidence they blamed him for everything and swore they only carried out his orders, fearing what would happen to them if they did not. No Western correspondents were allowed in Guinea at the time of the *coup* or subsequently. It was therefore impossible for them to obtain Nkrumah's side of the story.

Despite the upheaval, life continued in Ghana with surprising normality. The new regime continued the national policy of diversifying agriculture as much as possible so as to get away from absolute dependence on cocoa, the price of which had fallen so disastrously on the world markets. Farmers were encouraged to grow their own food and produce more palm oil, rubber, citrus fruits and other lucrative crops.

As the country providing nearly a third of the world's requirements of cocoa, Ghana's anxiety was to get the five major consumer countries (the United States of America, Germany, the Netherlands, Britain and France) to agree to an assured price in London and New York so that she would always know how much revenue she was going to have for her national planning schemes. While talks

The £8m State House, which dominates Accra's skyline, was built as a top priority by Dr Nkrumah to accommodate the 'Summit' of the Organisation of African Unity held in Ghana in October, 1965

on this all-important topic went on abroad, at home the emphasis was on teaching the smallholders, also the bigger farmers how to produce as much cocoa as usual – but on less land. They were, in fact, being shown how to obtain 12, 13 and 14 loads of 60 lb from an acre which in the past had yielded only ten.

With political interference withdrawn and a better price being offered, the growers no longer felt they were being swindled and were in a better mood to work harder. Prospects were thought to be very bright for maintaining the production of cocoa at 420,000 tons a year. This was the average for the previous four to five years, excepting the peak (or freak) year of 1964–65 when production reached 571,000 tons—a phenomenon that could happen at any time.

The revolution seemed to give a fillip to everything, rather than slow things down. After a momentary pause, the literacy and self-help campaigns went on as before. Ghana has a large-scale illiteracy problem which it cannot lightly neglect. It was officially recognised that out of a total population of seven million, about three million can neither read nor write in any of the dozen or so natural African languages.

Dr Nkrumah's Government planned to wipe out most of the illiteracy by 1970 and put the drive in the hands of Mrs Susanna Al-Hassan. As Minister of Social Welfare, Mrs Al-Hassan had many responsibilities. They included trying to produce 400,000 new literates each year, encouraging hundreds of towns and villages to initiate their own self-help construction projects, developing welfare activities among women and children and leading a national crusade, launched in the summer of 1965, against prostitution and immorality generally.

Officials suggested that professional prostitutes were not so much a problem in Ghana as the good-time girls – often fresh and attractive school leavers from the villages, who came into the big towns looking for a good job, and wandered into cafes, bars and nightclubs in search of boy friends, adventure, easy money and pretty clothes.

In 1965, about 60,000 people were enrolled in literacy classes in ten different Ghanaian languages and English. More than 29,000 women in 851 groups were being trained in home economics, child care, health and sanitation.

The Volta River hydro-electric scheme, expected to revolutionise Ghana economically, was inaugurated by Dr Kwame Nkrumah on January 22, 1966, a month before his overthrow. The three essentials of the project are the £56,200,000 dam and power station shown here and its 500-mile transmission network, the £35m artificial seaport at Tema specially created to serve it, and a £60m aluminium smelter

When the *coup* came Mrs Al-Hassan, with all the
other ministers, was taken into protective custody and
remained in prison some time.

The new regime discovered, as the old one no doubt had
done, that it was impossible to get 400,000 people
attending reading and writing classes.

Among uneducated people literacy classes had become
vaguely associated with the Convention People's
Party. Each ministry, public service or corporation was
made responsible for its own staff illiteracy problem.
Departmental chiefs were asked to organise classes in
office hours. Messengers, cleaners and other employees
went unwillingly, perhaps suspiciously. Here and there the
atmosphere of compulsion caused resentment. There was
propaganda in the lessons. Even the first primer
contained sentences like, 'The woman has a party card
and always takes the card to party meetings'. These
offending references to the banned party were deleted and
members of the National Liberation Council made
speeches encouraging illiterates to join the classes.

Meanwhile people all over Ghana were showing
magnificently what could be done by communal labour
and voluntary contributions to improve amenities in the
areas in which they lived. They changed the face of rural
Ghana by building schoolrooms, community centres,
markets, bridges, roads, post offices, churches, chapels
and football fields. Drinking water was now piped
straight into villages and the women folk no longer had
to walk to and from distant streams and wells balancing
buckets on their heads. Boreholes were being drilled
everywhere. At least one police station was being built.
The Government gave constructional, architectural and
other advice, and supplied materials and money.
Villagers up country, in the scrub and forest, subscribed
as much as £5 per man and £2 10s. per woman to
cut and build an essential five-mile feeder road – the hard,
back-breaking work being done by themselves.

In 1965 work was either in progress or completed on
731 projects, including over 400 schools and about 75
post offices.

The total value of the 300 self-help projects scheduled to
be completed by the end of 1966 was estimated by the
Department of Social Welfare and Community Development at nearly £895,000. To this the Government

contributed about £125,000. The remaining £770,000 came from the country people in contributions amounting to £471,700, and voluntary labour, officially estimated to be worth about £298,300.

The self-help system in Ghana was considered an example that many other countries in Africa might wish to follow.

Albert Adomako

Col A. A. Afrifa

ALBERT ADOMAKO

To give them expert advice on Ghana's financial difficulties following the 1966 *coup*, the revolutionary Government of Army and police officers set up a National Economic Committee composed of Mr E. N. Omaboe (chairman), Mr R. S. Amagashie and Mr Albert Adomako.

Mr Adomako is Governor of the Bank of Ghana and a banker of 20 years' experience. He went to Cambridge University and was called to the Bar in London.

COL A. A. AFRIFA

Colonel Akwasi Amankwa Afrifa, who played a prominent part in the military operations of the 1966 *coup*, became immediately a member of the National Liberation Council, presided over by General Ankrah.

When the members of the NLC decided to divide among themselves responsibility for the various ministries (all Nkrumah's ministers were in protective custody), Colonel Afrifa was allocated finance, economic affairs and trade. In his indictment of the ousted Nkrumah regime he said it had bequeathed to the country 'an empty treasury and huge debts'. State farms everywhere, he said, were 'eloquent monuments to folly and waste, with thousands of people producing nothing'.

Colonel Afrifa comes of a long line of chiefs who served in positions of command in the Ashanti Army. He was born at Mampong, near Kumasi. The date was not known as neither of his parents had ever been to school. But 'from calculations normal in our tradition', he deduces that it was 'a Sunday in the late sowing season of 1936'.

He received training at the Royal Military Academy, Sandhurst, where he was commissioned as a second lieutenant in July, 1960, coming third in order of merit at the final examination for all Commonwealth cadets. In his book, *The Ghana Coup*, he expresses regret that he was 'always in trouble for breach of discipline' and was 'a thoroughly bad shot, third class'.

But he was 'thrilled with Sandhurst . . . It gave us independent thinking . . . It is one of the greatest institutions in the world'.

After returning to Ghana he was sent to the Congo in command of a rifle platoon. He served first in Leopoldville and later in Luluaborg and Bakwanga Provinces. Early in 1961 he was promoted lieutenant and back in Ghana was posted to the 5th Battalion of Infantry, Tamale, as platoon commander.

He returned to the United Kingdom in August, 1961, to undergo infantry courses in the schools at Hythe and Warminster. As captain in command of a rifle company he went again to the Congo and served at the Kamina base in Katanga.

In 1962, in Ghana, he was posted first to 1st Brigade Headquarters and then to the 2nd

Judge Akufo-Addo

Brigade at Kumasi, in each case as General Staff Officer. He was promoted major in August, 1965.

In his book Colonel Afrifa declared that between 1961 and 1966 the Nkrumah regime 'had instilled fear into every Ghanaian. There were security men and women everywhere, and no one trusted his friend. Fathers did not trust their sons who had been indoctrinated with Young Pioneer ideas, neither did husbands their wives. It was a reign of terror.'

CHIEF JUSTICE
EDWARD AKUFO-ADDO

Mr Edward Akufo-Addo, a former Supreme Court Judge, was chairman of the Political Committee of the NLC and chairman of Ghana Commercial Bank until appointed as from September 26, 1966, at the age of 60, Chief Justice of Ghana.

He succeeded Mr Justice Julius Sarkodee-Adoo. His appointment came ten days after the Government announced that it was reorganising the judiciary to fight corruption and incompetence caused by political appointments by ex-President Nkrumah.

Judge Akufo-Addo, three other judges and Chief Justice Sir Arku Korsah were removed by Dr Nkrumah in March, 1964. In the previous December they had acquitted three men, including two former cabinet ministers, Tawia Adamafio (Information) and Ako Adjei (Foreign Affairs), on charges of treason and conspiracy. Two other accused were found guilty and sentenced to death.

Amendments to Ghana's constitution, approved by the people in a national referendum and later formally accepted by Parliament, had given the President the power to dismiss judges of the

Supreme Court 'for reasons which appear to him sufficient'.

All five accused were kept in prison under the Preventive Detention Act until October 2, 1964, when a second trial on the same charges opened before the Special Criminal Division of the High Court, presided over by a new Chief Justice, Julius Sarkodee-Adoo. Four of the men complained they had been unable to obtain counsel to represent them. The fifth said he had no means to employ a lawyer.

The trial proceeded with all five prisoners undefended and lasted until February 9, 1965, part of the proceedings being in camera. All five were found guilty and sentenced to death. Six weeks later Dr Nkrumah decided to commute the sentences to 20 years' imprisonment.

Judge Akufo-Addo was educated at the Presbyterian Middle School, the Presbyterian Training College and the Theological Seminary at Akropong. After passing in 1932 his intermediate BA at Achimota, where so many West African leaders were trained, he won a scholarship to St Peter's Hall, Oxford University, where he was awarded a BA in mathematics, politics and philosophy. In November, 1940, he was called to the Bar at the Middle Temple, London.

Entering politics on his return home, he was one of the founders of the United Gold Coast Convention and among the six leaders arrested and detained by the British Colonial Government in February, 1948, for political agitation.

He was a member of the Legislative Council for the Eastern Provincial Council of Chiefs from 1950–51. In 1962 he was appointed a judge of the Supreme Court.

Lt-Gen J. A. Ankrah

R. S. AMAGASHIE

Raphael Sylvanus Amagashie, who is a member of the National Economic Committee, is director of the School of Administration at the University of Ghana as well as a director of the Ghana Commercial Bank.

He recekved his education at Achimota and Durham University and became a chartered accountant and company secretary. He began his commercial career with Unilever in London.

LT-GEN J. A. ANKRAH

When the Army and police officers overthrew President Nkrumah they were unanimous in bringing back from retirement Lieutenant-General Joseph Arthur Ankrah as a well-trusted father figure to lead the Army and preside over the new National Liberation Council.

General Ankrah had been dismissed by Dr Nkrumah in July, 1965. (There had been rumours that a *coup d'état* was mooted among high-ranking army officers.) On Republic Day (July 1) only 25 days earlier, Dr Nkrumah had decorated him with the Distinguished Order of the Volta. The sacking of so popular a man as General Ankrah caused much indignation among the public and great resentment in the Army. Colonel Afrifa has called it 'one of the major factors that led to the *coup*'.

General Ankrah was replaced as Deputy Chief of Defence Staff by Major-General C. M. Barwah, who was shot dead at his home on the day of the *coup*. Officers of the new regime have since alleged that General Barwah knew of plans which Dr Nkrumah had to make his private army and security force so strong, with the most up-to-date arms and ammunition landed secretly at night in Ghana from the USSR and China, that he could take control of the country whenever he wished over the heads of the national Army and police force.

General Ankrah is six feet tall and heavily built. He looks a picture of fatherly benevolence, and his self-evident kindliness and twinkling eyes behind large round spectacles have endeared him to the public. But British Major-General Henry Templer Alexander, former Ghanaian Chief of Defence Staff, dismissed by Dr Nkrumah in September, 1961, has said that General Ankrah, while an extremely gentle, kindly man, is 'incredibly ruthless in situations which demand violent action'.

He served in the old Gold Coast Regiment from the start of World War II. He had become a colonel when he served with the United Nations Force in the Congo. In January, 1961, Dr Nkrumah awarded him the Ghana Military Cross for 'saving the life of Patrice Lumumba', the first Congo Prime Minister, who was subsequently murdered.

Born on August 18, 1915, in Accra, a member of the nearly one million-strong Ga tribe who have made their home there for centuries, General Ankrah was educated at a Wesleyan school and was a mission school teacher for some time. He is a prominent Wesleyan, and since the *coup* has made many references to the 'moral degradation' to which the children of Ghana were, he considers, exposed in the Young Pioneers by teachers of 'the fraudulent ideology of Nkrumaism'.

Similar references to the proscribed youth movement, denounced as godless and anti-Christian by other members of the National Liberation Council, have drawn attention to the fact

S. E. Arthur

that all of them have a religious background – Wesleyan, Presbyterian, Roman Catholic and, in one case, Moslem (Mr B. A. Yakubu, the Deputy Commissioner of Police).

As the head of the new regime, making most of the more important pronouncements, General Ankrah made it clear from the beginning that the Army and police officers comprising the National Liberation Council, assisted by constitutional, political and economic advisory committees, were only a caretaker government until they could hand over to a civilian administration, equipped with a new constitution, approved by both chiefs and people, which would 'prevent the recurrence of a one-party dictatorship'.

JOE APPIAH

Joe Appiah, once Dr Nkrumah's confidant but later jailed as a top political opponent, was appointed a member of the new regime's Political Committee on July 1, 1966. In the previous March he had been sent with a mission to various African countries to explain 'Why a *coup* was necessary'. In September, 1966, he went with a goodwill mission to the United States and Britain under the leadership of Dr K. A. Busia.

A lawyer turned politician and a fiery speaker, Appiah shared rooms with Dr Nkrumah in London during the early days of the Gold Coast independence campaign.

He eventually quit Dr Nkrumah's party to form the Opposition National Liberation Movement in Ashanti in February, 1955. At this time Ghana was still a colony ruled by Britain. Appiah accused Nkrumah of illegal attempts to usurp the power, functions and privileges of Queen Elizabeth. He said these constituted an act of sedition and treason and his Opposition would 'rise up in arms, if necessary, against a Government which proved itself disloyal to the Queen'.

Referring to the decision by Dr Nkrumah to set up a 20 ft bronze statue of himself in Accra (this was knocked down, smashed up and taken away on February 24, 1966, the day of the *coup*), Appiah said he was reminded of what happened in Communist countries when they tried to develop with a leader of the party 'the cult of personality'.

Appiah was detained in October, 1961, for alleged activities endangering the security of the state. About 50 people were arrested at the same time, including Dr J. B. Danquah, lawyer and veteran politician, who was released but later was sent back to prison where he died. Appiah was freed from Ussher Fort Prison, Accra, on December 22, 1962, after 15 months under preventive detention.

He is married to Peggy, daughter of the late Sir Stafford Cripps, post-war British Chancellor of the Exchequer.

S. E. ARTHUR

A member of Ghana's National Economic Committee, Mr S. E. Arthur is Principal Secretary of the Budget division of Finance and a career civil servant.

He took an economics degree at the Universities of Ghana and London and during the Nkrumah regime was closely concerned in the production of budgets.

THE ASANTEHENE

The Asantehene (King of the Ashantis), Otumfuo ('the Most Mighty') Sir Osei Agyeman,

The Asantehene

Prempeh II was shorn of all his political powers when independence came, but his influence remains immense and incalculable.

It extends far beyond Ashanti (9,700 square miles), the fourth largest of the nine regions of Ghana, since Brong Ahafo (14,900 square miles and the second largest) was joined to it until independence.

Described as 'a dignified old gentleman' (he was born in 1892), the Asantehene has a strong, rugged, deeply-lined face with a broad forehead. His self-command is perfect, as is his command of English, which he first acquired in a Wesleyan mission school.

Though he was only a store-keeper in Kumasi, the Ashanti capital, when chosen as the most morally suitable nephew to succeed Prempeh I (the succession is from uncle to nephew), he is spoken of with awe. A level-headed man in himself, he is surrounded by an aura of divinity as the Custodian of the Golden Stool, believed by thousands to have come down from Heaven following the incantations of Okomfo Anokye, the chief fetish priest of his 17th century ancestor, Osei Tutu, the founder of the Ashanti Empire.

The religion of Ashanti, as elsewhere in Ghana, is largely the worship of ancestors, and the Golden Stool is their most sacred shrine. People are not allowed to see it except when it is carried in procession on intensely emotional festive occasions. It is a mass of solid gold, about 18 inches high, 24 inches long and 12 inches wide. Attached to it are gold effigies of conquered enemies, illustrating the saying, *In life, someone sits on someone else.*

The other chiefs of Ashanti, all of whom have to swear an oath of loyalty to him, are forbidden to decorate their stools with gold. One who was found to have done so at a durbar in 1941 was reminded that in earlier times this would have led to war. He apologised and was forgiven, but had to slaughter twelve sheep to appease the wrath of the gods.

The Golden Stool is never allowed to touch the ground. It is placed on another stool, which in turn rests on a solid slab of cured elephant hide. When the Asantehene is enstooled (enthroned) he is merely lowered and raised three times over the stool without touching it.

Prempeh I, who died in 1931, was the last ruler of the age in which an Asantehene had innumerable wives, three execution grounds and 100 executioners, and wholesale ritual murders were necessary when one of them died – so that he should not journey into the next world alone.

When the British Army took Kumasi in 1896 and formed a protectorate they found a large grave full of bones and skulls of hundreds of victims. Four years later the Governor of the Gold Coast, as it then was, Sir Frederic Hodgson, completely misunderstanding the significance and sanctity of the Golden Stool, declared that as the representative of Queen Victoria he must take possession of it and sit on it. The horrified Ashantis rose against him, led by one of the Queen Mothers, and besieged his fort. There were nine months of bitter fighting before the British were again in control and Ashanti was declared a British colony (1901).

Thereafter the person and palace of the Asantehene became sacrosanct and untouchable. To-day Prempeh II, as the earthly

Dr K. A. Busia

representative of the myriad hosts of Ashanti dead, is the most venerated and powerful chief in Ghana.

Few of the taboos of his ancestors worry him now. He may cross the River Pra. He has toured Europe and been to Britain for medical treatment. But though he walks through the streets of Kumasi in shorts he is still 'the Most High' to 300 paramount chiefs, well over 3,000 chiefs and an army of sub-chiefs possibly ten times as great.

Over the future of the chiefs of Ghana hangs a big question mark. Colonel Afrifa says they are the 'natural rulers' of the country and 'the rallying point of our national endeavours', but that Dr Nkrumah turned them into 'mere political stooges and imbeciles' among their own people. Since the *coup* there have been signs that some of their ancient glory is returning.

The Houses of Chiefs, joining in solemn conference, have suggested that they should supply two-thirds of an Upper House in a bi-cameral legislature when Ghana returns to civilian government.

Every Ghanaian owes allegiance to a chief and his stool, but some contend that the chieftainship is obsolete and played out. They prophesy that the system will fade and even disappear during the next few decades. They have difficulty, however, in imagining a Ghana without an Asantehene.

DR K. A. BUSIA

Dr Kofi Busia, leader of the defunct United Party and arch-opponent of Dr Nkrumah, returned to Ghana within a month of the 1966 *coup* after almost seven years' voluntary exile, and was carried shoulder high by a

crowd at Accra Airport. Later he was appointed vice-chairman of the Political Committee set up to advise the Army and police officers comprising the National Liberation Council. When Judge Akufo-Addo became Chief Justice, Dr Busia succeeded him as chairman.

Dr Busia estimated that 1,000 members of his party had been in constant detention during the Nkrumah regime.

At the time of his return in 1966, Dr Busia was still a senior member of St Anthony's College, Oxford, in the Department of Sociology.

Just over a year earlier the Nkrumah Government had suggested that Dr Busia and two other Opposition leaders in exile, Dr Kobina Taylor and Mr. K. A. Gbedemah should appear before a court of international jurists sitting in Ghana to contest charges that they were accomplices of men condemned to death for plotting to kill the President. Dr Busia replied that he was prepared to appear before a court of international jurists in Geneva, New York or The Hague. He added, however, that, recollecting what had happened to others, including Dr Joseph B. Danquah, 'I shall not foolishly sign my death warrant by agreeing to go to Ghana'.

Born in 1913 of the Royal House of Wenchi in north-west Ashanti, Dr Busia is an academic who entered politics in Ghana at first because he felt that too few of the educated were active. His political life in Ghana was a fight in and outside Parliament against what he believed were the growing dictatorial tendencies of Dr Nkrumah and his Convention People's Party.

Dr Busia was on the teaching staff at the noted Achimota

A. K. Deku

College when, in 1939, he took an external degree in history at London University and won a scholarship to Oxford. While a lecturer in African studies at the new University College of the Gold Coast, he published in 1951 his standard work, *The Position of the Chief in the Modern Political System of the Ashanti.*

When the Ghana Congress Party (GCP) was formed in 1952 out of the rump of the United Gold Coast Convention in Opposition to Nkrumah's CPP, he was made leader.

In October, 1957 the National Liberation Movement and other Opposition parties merged to form the United Party (UP), of which he became leader. The Nkrumah regime now started arresting the leaders under the Preventive Detention Act, two being accused of plotting to assassinate Nkrumah. The UP was weakened and lost its effectiveness. In April, 1959, legislation was passed disqualifying any member of the Assembly who missed 20 sittings in any one session without the permission of the Speaker (Chairman). Busia, who was lecturing in Holland, was disqualified and chose exile in preference to returning to Ghana.

A. K. DEKU

As Deputy Commissioner of Police, in control of the Criminal Investigation Department, Mr Anthony Kwashie Deku, an officer of 26 years' experience, was responsible for the intelligence side of the preparations for the 1966 *coup.*

Later, when he was Commissioner of Police, 'top secret' documents of the Nkrumah regime made public showed that the deposed president planned a network of spies in African countries to help in his dream of achieving African liberation and the union of the continent under one political government, presumably with himself as president.

According to his view, the French-speaking countries constituted the main danger to the union government. He therefore set up a special department to ascertain by secret means the plans of these countries and how best they could be counteracted.

The special department was concerned with 13 countries – Cameroun, Ivory Coast, Upper Volta, Togo, Congo Kinshasa, Niger, Chad, Central African Republic, Dahomey, Senegal, Rwanda, Malagasy and Gabon. Secret agents sent to these countries were expected to find helpful sources close to the presidents and leaders of opposition parties and any underground movements.

There was a further report that the Ghana police had unmasked a number of Russian, Chinese and East German diplomats and technicians who were working as intelligence agents in Accra. Twenty Russians and three Chinese were immediately deported. The nerve centre was said to have been the Bureau of African Affairs, ostensibly diplomatic but actually responsible for espionage, ideological training and guerilla camps with Chinese instructors.

For the Organisation of African Unity Summit in Accra, the two best known hotels, the Ambassador and the Star, were alleged to have been 'honeycombed' with bedroom listening devices imported from Moscow and Peking.

Mr Deku, who worked for 16 years in the Special Branch, rising to be deputy head, was born at Hedzranao, near Denu, in 1923. He was educated at the Roman Catholic Mission School at Denu.

J. W. K. Harlley

Enlisting in the Ghana Police in 1940 he had become an inspector by 1953. Within a year he was sent to Britain for the police officers' course at the Metropolitan Police College, Hendon, following which he was promoted to the rank of assistant superintendent. His rise then became rapid and on January 1, 1965, he was made Deputy Commissioner.

K. A. GBEDEMAH

Komla Agbeli Gbedemah, one of Dr Nkrumah's principal lieutenants when he was rising to power, visited Accra after the 1966 *coup* following nearly five years of self-exile.

He told a press conference that it was his first appearance since October 16, 1961, when he vainly exhorted the National Assembly to reject a Government Bill setting up a special division of the High Court to try offences against the security of the State.

He explained how two days later, even before the Bill became law, and having already been dismissed by Dr Nkrumah, he 'decided to make discretion the better part of valour' and went into exile.

While abroad, he bitterly criticised his former close friend and accused him of bringing economic disaster and humiliation on the country. Nkrumah's one-party ideology, he said, developed after visiting Russia and other East European countries and China (July-September, 1961).

In November, 1964, Dr Nkrumah's publicity secretariat published a brochure, *The Truth about Komla Gbedemah*. This alleged that Mr Gbedemah, who was Ghana's first Finance Minister, had embezzled £10m in public money. Another charge was that,

'acting as an agent of the American Intelligence Agency (CIA), he planned a *coup* with Dr K. A. Busia's United Party against the Ghana Government'.

The booklet was quoted in Ghana's two national newspapers. In May, 1966, having received letters from Mr Gbedemah's solicitors, they published long front-page apologies on three successive days. The solicitors asked for token compensation of £2,000 in each case.

The newspapers, now under a new Government, management and editorship, said they had no option at the time but to print the article in full.

KWAKU GYASI-TWUM

Principal Secretary to the Ministry of Finance, Kwaku Gyasi-Twum was appointed a member of the National Economic Committee at the age of 38. He was concerned in the drawing up of some of the budgets under the Nkrumah Government.

After taking an economics degree at Fourah Bay and at King's College, Durham, he returned to Fourah Bay to lecture before accepting a post at the Bank of Ghana as chief research economist.

J. W. K. HARLLEY

The *coup* in Ghana was initiated by John Willie Kofi Harlley, Commissioner of Police, later Inspector-General of Police, according to a speech he made to a grand muster of the force just over a fortnight afterwards on March 10, 1966.

He told the assembled policemen that while head of the Special Branch (National Intelligence Service) President Nkrumah gave him a mandate to investigate corruption among his ministers, parliamentarians

Maj-Gen E. K. Kotoka

and functionaries inside the party.

At great risk, he said, to himself and the future of his family, he prepared reports on the 'criminal transactions' of some of the ministers and submitted them to Dr Nkrumah.

Mr Harlley added that later to his horror he discovered that Dr Nkrumah was himself involved in several corrupt practices, the proceeds of which he had been saving abroad. His first consideration as constitutional Commissioner of Police was how to effect Dr Nkrumah's arrest. But the security the President had built up around himself was such that 'it would have been madness' to have contemplated an arrest in the normal way. There was no alternative but to use the regular armed forces. He consulted various officers and to save shedding 'a lot of innocent blood', it was decided to wait until Dr Nkrumah was out of the country before launching a plan of action.

Mr Harlley in this speech called Dr Nkrumah 'an arch criminal' and declared that if he sought refuge in a civilised country he would be extradited and tried in the courts of Ghana.

Born at Akagla in the Volta Region on May 9, 1919, Mr Harlley attended Presbyterian schools before going to Accra Academy. Before entering the Ghana Police Service on May 1, 1940, he was an interpreter in Ewe and Twi, two languages in Ghana, in the District Magistrate's Court and later in the Supreme Court, Accra.

When an inspector of police, which he became on November 1, 1952, he was selected for training at the Metropolitan Police College, Hendon, England. On his return to Ghana he passed quickly through the senior ranks of the Police Service until he became Assistant Commissioner on August 1, 1960 and Commissioner of Police on January 1, 1965.

MAJ-GEN E. K. KOTOKA

It was the cool and confident voice of Major-General (then Colonel) Emmanuel Kwasi Kotoka which at 6 am on February 24, 1966 announced over Radio Ghana, seized only a few minutes earlier, that the Army, in cooperation with the Ghana Police, had taken over the government of Ghana and that 'the myth surrounding Nkrumah has been broken'.

'Parliament is dissolved,' he added, 'and Kwame Nkrumah is dismissed from office. All ministers are also dismissed. The Convention People's Party is disbanded with effect from now. It will be illegal for any person to belong to it.'

Kotoka was in command of the 2nd Infantry Brigade based in Kumasi, the capital of Ashanti, which has always been most opposed to the Nkrumah Government, with its strong centralisation in Accra.

Kotoka at once became a popular figurehead in the revolution and shared the glory of the brief but successful military operations with Ocran and Afrifa. He is widely regarded as a fine soldier, tough, disciplined, and determined.

When responsibility for the ministries and other government departments was divided among the members of the National Liberation Council, Major-General Kotoka, who had been allocated Defence and Health, .gathered the officials together. He told them that he would not tolerate any more of the 'immeasurable inefficiency', with its

Prof A. A. Kwapong

attendant evils of bribery and corruption, into which the Government had drifted during the Nkrumah regime. He said he would pay them surprise visits and would not sit idly by if he saw lack of discipline.

From the moment he enlisted in the then Royal West African Frontier Force in July, 1947, Kotoka showed that as a soldier he was a 'natural'. His qualities were such that he became a company sergeant-major in four years.

After officer cadet training at what is now the Ghana Military Academy at Teshie, he went to Eaton Hall, Chester, England, and was commissioned as a lieutenant on November 20, 1954. After experience in Germany and Ghana, he returned to the United Kingdom for a mortar course at Nether Avon, near Salisbury.

Promoted captain, then major, in the same year (1958), he continued with his original battalion, the 2nd, and went with them (1960) to the Congo as part of the United Nations Peace Keeping Force. He saw service in Leopoldville and Luluaborg, Kasai, and was mentioned in despatches for an act of exceptional bravery.

When he was promoted lieutenant-colonel in September, 1961, and appointed to command the 2nd Battalion, it was noted as of significance that he had been with the 2nd Battalion during his entire military career.

In 1962 he took his men to the Congo for the third time and saw action in the Katanga Province. For his part in the battle in Katanga he was awarded the Ghana Service Order.

Back in Ghana, he was given the command of the 2nd Infantry Brigade Group with the rank of colonel. Colonel Afrifa, who was his second in command then, has described him as 'an infantry officer of the highest calibre . . . a dedicated soldier and a man of transparent honesty. The Army is his life.'

PROF A. A. KWAPONG

Appointed a member of the Political Committee and chairman of the Education Review Committee to advise the new regime after the 1966 *coup*, Professor Alex Kwapong, then aged 39, is Vice-Chancellor of the University of Ghana.

A much respected academic, he received his early education at the Presbyterian junior and middle schools at Akropong and at Achimota College.

He took a BA degree in classics at King's College, Cambridge, with Summa cum Laude, 1948–53. He took his MA and PhD degrees externally from the same university. He became a visiting professor at Princeton University, 1962–62. Before being appointed Vice-Chancellor at the University of Ghana he was Pro Vice-Chancellor and head of the Classics department.

NENE AZZU MATE KOLE

Nene Azzu Mate Kole, Paramount Chief of the Manya Krobos, sometimes referred to as the King of the Krobos, was 56 when appointed a member of the Political Committee of the National Liberation Council (July 1, 1966).

He also was made a member of the Constitutional Commission (November 4, 1966) which was given the important task of drafting a new constitution for Ghana – the first major step towards the re-establishment of civilian rule. He later became chairman of the Political Committee.

The Krobos number about

Dr Kwame Nkrumah

180,000 and live between the sea and the huge new artificial lake being created behind the Volta River dam so that Ghana shall have cheap electricity. Odumase Krobo is their capital and nearby is their sacred Krobo Mountain.

Beneath the lake, according to Nene Mate Kole, lie 75 square miles of Krobo land. They were offered cash as compensation but refused it. The Krobos are keen on possessing land and during the past century have acquired more than 600 square miles. They hang on to this very tenaciously. They seldom sell any, believing that once they own it they must hold it in trust for their descendants.

Nene Mate Kole says, 'They are religiously afraid of betraying this trust, being convinced that if they do their ancestors will visit them with all sorts of disasters like famine, plague and deformed children.'

Nene Azzu Mate Kole is a member of the Volta River Authority, the Government Corporation concerned with the dam. As a paramount chief he has no political power, but is venerated and his moral influence is great. He is a well-educated man. He believes that puberty rites for girls, proscribed generally by Queen Victoria in 1892 but some of which have survived to this day, are good for his people.

When a Krobo girl becomes adolescent, she is taken to the home of a recognised 'wise woman'. Here she finds other adolescent girls. They are taught cleanliness, how to keep house, cook, look after children, make palm oil, yarn and pottery, produce medicine from herbs and other domestic arts. It is considered that a girl should know all these things before she thinks of marrying and having a baby.

A girl who has successfully passed a year's course is presented to the tribe, during a festival known as *Dipo*, as a newly-arrived woman who is known to be chaste and fit to be a wife and mother. She is made up with pigments and bedecked with beads.

On her right hand between thumb and index finger are nine tiny incisions to show that she has been initiated.

Many of the Krobos are pagans, although Nene Mate Kole is a Christian. With modern education, many of the girls have little time for the course. But their Paramount Chief would like to see it perpetuated in a girls' college.

Girls who undergo *Dipo* as pagans are afterwards accepted by Christian priests as candidates for confirmation. Some priests do not discourage them from taking the course.

Sir Emmanuel Mate Kole, the father of the present King of the Krobos, was knighted by Queen Victoria. In 1892 he persuaded his people to come down peacefully from their mountain, where they had been for about four centuries, defending themselves against the Ashantis and other races.

DR KWAME NKRUMAH

The above portrait, of Osagyefo ('The Redeemer') Dr Kwame Nkrumah, was to be seen in every public building when he was President of Ghana and its absolute ruler.

Ironically, it was used in a warrant for his arrest when he was overthrown on February 24, 1966, and all his Ministers, advisers, MPs and party leaders were put in prison in protective custody. The warrant, sent to 60 member countries of Interpol,

177

specified conspiracy to extort, extortion and stealing in connection with the vast assets he was alleged to have accumulated.

Born on an unknown date in September, 1909 (officially the 21st), Francis Nwia Kofie (Kwame) Nkrumah began his career in Ghana in a blaze of idealism and patriotism. Good-looking, with a broad forehead that sloped back and the expression of a visionary, he was a magnetic and fascinating person to talk to.

In search of education he had been to the United States and Britain. The prominence he gained in London as a leader of West African organisations led in 1947 to an invitation to return to his native land as general secretary of the United Gold Coast Convention, formed by Dr Joseph Danquah. Later he quarrelled with Dr Danquah and put him in prison, where eventually he died.

Nkrumah formed his Convention People's Party with the slogan 'Self-Government Now'. He quickly became a national hero. Many people seemed to think he would be another Nehru or a 'modern Moses'. In February, 1951, when he had been imprisoned by the British colonial government for fomenting an illegal strike, his party swept the polls under a new constitution and the British Governor released him to lead the first African government of the country.

On July 1, 1960, following a plebiscite, he became first President of the new Republic of Ghana. He quickly gained complete control over his party and all the organs of state and could at will dismiss Army generals, police chiefs and even judges whose judgments he would not accept. There was a propaganda line that people, party and state were all one, symbolised by Dr Kwame Nkrumah, 'the Keeper of the Nation's Conscience and Fount of Honour'. He had some good advisers and many bad ones, who were inefficient and corrupt.

He launched many elaborate and costly construction schemes, each of which in turn was claimed by the party press as his 'brain child'. The planners, technicians and contractors were from Britain and other European countries and the United States of America. The £150m Volta River hydro-electric scheme was confidently expected in due course to revolutionise the entire economy of Ghana. Others, however, were condemned after his downfall as sheer prestige projects.

These included the magnificent, but usually deserted, £3m Accra-Tema motor road and the grandiose £8m State House ('Job 600') built in great haste to accommodate the short Summit conference of African leaders in Accra in October, 1965, and of no apparent use for anything else.

The realisation of his life's ambition – a socialist Africa of politically unified states under a continental government and president, presumably himself, was still a long, unpromising way off when he flew to China, with a large entourage, including many security men, to find what he called a solution to the Vietnam War.

He was in Peking when he heard that he had been deposed and had lost all in one lightning stroke by a group of Army and police officers.

Everything in Ghana was now changed. Editors of newspapers were arrested and their places taken by journalists who had been imprisoned for years. Editorial praise gave way to abuse. Ghana Radio no longer started each news bulletin with the words, 'Osagyefo the President . . .' Instead there were vitriolic comments about 'Africa's No 1 Dictator'.

His political creed was ridiculed as a hotch-potch of half-digested Marx. The million Young Pioneers, who had been taught 'Nkrumah will live for ever', rejected him as 'a false Messiah'. There was no more singing of old familiar hymn tunes with strange words about a saviour who was not Jesus Christ but, by implication, Kwame Nkrumah.

Among the rough and ready women traders of the crowded Makola Market, whose enthusiastic and noisy support of him had been one of his earliest successes, and very useful on big public occasions, the singing, drumming and dancing stopped. The cheering turned to jeering and fawning to fury as they tore in shreds and stamped underfoot pictures of the man they had affectionately called 'Show Boy'.

Meanwhile Nkrumah had been given asylum in Guinea by President Sekou Touré, and co-opted as joint-president. Over Conakry Radio he denied the allegations of maladministration being made against him by the new government. He said he intended to return.

The number of political opponents incarcerated at different times during his regime was officially estimated to be 2,000. Many commissions were set up to inquire publicly into alleged irregularities and malpractices.

Several attempts had been made on the life of Dr Nkrumah. The one which probably upset him most was the throwing of a grenade at the village of Kulungugu, in northern Ghana (August 1, 1962) when he had stopped during his drive back from meeting President Maurice Yameogo of Upper Volta. Four people were killed and 56 injured, the majority seriously. Nkrumah escaped unhurt – attributed by the Party to divine intervention – but he saw everything that happened. A cheering crowd, in his own words, became 'a screaming mass of people, blood-stained, limping, disfigured'. The incident was followed by others. Explosives were thrown among his supporters when they held mass rallies to demonstrate their loyalty to him. It was said that Kulungugu broke Dr Nkrumah's heart and that he was never the same man again.

Dr Nkrumah appeared to have lost confidence in the Ghana Police Force and began organising his private army and security force, with Russian help, after January 2, 1964. On that date a constable named Ametewee, on guard at Flagstaff House, chased the President, firing five shots at him, missing, but killing the chief presidential guard, Salifu Dagarti. The trial of Ametewee, ending with a death sentence, was followed by a purge and the detention of ten of the most senior officers of the police force, including the Commissioner Mr E. R. T. Madjitey and the Deputy Commissioner, Mr. S. D. Amaning (the latter was alleged to have moved the constable to Flagstaff House).

Dr Danquah, who had opposed Dr Nkrumah in the 1960 presidential elections, was accused of complicity in the plot, and passed the rest of his days in prison. Allegations were also made against other members of the defunct Opposition party and even against men close to the President.

Major-General Henry Templer Alexander, last British Chief of Defence Staff in Ghana, said in his book, *African Tightrope* (banned in Ghana, January, 1966) that Nkrumah, who had dismissed him, 'rules by fear a docile people and has few scruples. He is not a brave man . . . nowadays he keeps himself very much confined. Frightened men, egged on by other frightened but single-minded men, carry out extreme acts.'

Colonel Afrifa, who helped to overthrow Dr Nkrumah, wrote in *The Ghana Coup:* 'Nkrumah could have been a great man. He started well, led the independence movement and became, on behalf of Ghana, the symbol of emergent Africa. Somewhere down the line, however, he became ambitious, built a cult of personality and ruthlessly used the powers invested in him by his own constitution. He developed a strange love for absolute power.'

After the *coup* a series of lectures was given in Accra on the subject 'What went wrong in Ghana between 1957 and 1966'.

It is likely that historians will be asking that question for many years to come.

J. E. O. NUNOO

A member of the National Liberation Council, John Edward Okoe Nunoo, Deputy Commissioner of Police, first attracted attention through his brilliant career in the inspectorate.

He attended a course at the Metropolitan Police Training School, Hendon, England, in 1955 and on his return to Ghana was almost immediately promoted assistant superintendent. By March 1, 1961, he was a chief superintendent.

He was seconded to the Tanganyika Police Force from May 7, 1962 to May 18, 1963. He became Assistant Commissioner of the Ghana Police on March 1, 1964, and took charge of training and welfare.

Born in Accra on May 8, 1917, he was educated at St John's School in Nsawam for six years and then became a clerk in the employ of Messrs. J. Lyons & Company in the same town.

BRIGADIER A. K. OCRAN

Commander of the 1st Brigade, which covered Accra and southern Ghana at the time of the 1966 *coup* against Nkrumah, Brigadier (then Colonel) Albert Kwesi Ocran had seen service in the Congo in 1961 in the United Nations Observer Group and then as Company Commander of the 4th Battalion. He followed this up with a company commander's course at the British Staff College at Camberley, his third army course in Britain.

The first was at Eaton Hall (1954) and was followed by his being commissioned lieutenant. In 1956 he completed two courses suitable for platoon commanders. In between he had been back in Ghana and also was attached for a short time to the British Army in Germany.

In October, 1962, he was appointed Adjutant General, Ghanaian Ministry of Defence, promoted lieutenant-colonel and appointed Commander of the 1st Brigade. This enabled him to play a key role in the *coup*, because the brigade included the Saladin armoured cars of the Recce Regiment, a battalion at Accra, two in Takoradi and the engineers. His armoured cars led the assault on Flagstaff House, the President's residence, office and general stronghold.

After the *coup* he became commander of Ghana's military

E. N. Omaboe

academy. As a member of the ruling National Liberation Council he was given overall responsibility for the Ministries of Works, Housing and Communications, the latter including Ghana Airways and the Black Star Line.

He was born at Brakwa, Central Region, the son of a cocoa farmer and buyer, on July 21, 1929. After attending Accra Roman Catholic Boy's School he joined the Army Education Service in 1947.

E. N. OMABOE

Emmanuel N. Omaboe was 35, and the youngest member of the team, when appointed chairman of the seven-man National Economic Committee immediately after the 1966 *coup*. (The oldest member of this task force charged with the responsibility of leading Ghana back to solvency was only 41.)

Mr Omaboe was the Government statistician under Dr Nkrumah. His annual economic reviews were illuminating and also very blunt and critical. He regularly drew attention to their disastrous economic policy, especially high expenditures and the inefficient and illogical operation of import currency controls.

After the *coup* he said that all the facts in 'the chaotic situation' in the Ghana economy were made known to the old regime. An independent observer commented on one occasion, 'Nobody in the Nkrumah Government took any notice of Mr Omaboe's reviews. The surprising thing is that they were ever published.'

It was said that many men had been detained for lesser 'offences' than Mr Omaboe had committed. The National Liberation Council gave him almost *carte blanche* to put into operation

the advice which had for so long fallen on deaf ears.

When appointed to the National Economic Committee, Mr Omaboe estimated that Ghana, with a national debt of over £400m sterling, needed £15m short-term aid to help overcome her economic difficulties. His immediate problem was to work out a payment schedule by which Ghana hoped to wipe out the great external debt left by the former regime.

Born the son of an Accra goldsmith, he was educated at Legon University before going to the London School of Economics to take a first. He returned to the University of Ghana for a brief period of research and joined the Civil Service in 1959. Besides his statistical work he is also responsible for Ghana's census.

B. A. YAKUBU

Bawa Andani Yakubu was another of Ghana's police inspectors sent to take a course at the Metropolitan Police College, Hendon, England, and who rose rapidly in the service once back in Accra. He was Deputy Commissioner when he took part in the 1966 *coup*.

He was born at Gushiegu in the Northern Region in 1926. Following the pattern of education in that part of Ghana, he started at a Tamale kindergarten school, was sent to the Native Authority School at Yendi and then went back to Tamale, where he was enrolled at the Government senior school.

He joined the Ghana Police Service on February 8, 1945, and reached inspector rank on November 1, 1955. He received his promotion to the rank of Deputy Commissioner on January 1, 1965.

Lying on the west coast of Africa, between Portuguese Guinea and Sierra Leone, Guinea covers an area of 95,000 square miles. The estimated population is approaching 3,500,000. The capital and commercial centre is Conakry. The chief agricultural products of Guinea are rice, palm nuts, bananas, coffee, pineapples, oranges, groundnuts and millet. Coffee is grown in the forest districts. Diamonds are found in the Macenta district and bauxite is found in several areas. The exports are chiefly iron ore, bauxite, alumina, bananas, palm kernels and pineapples.

182

Guinea

Guinea became an independent republic on October 2, 1958, after voting in a referendum on September 28 to leave the French Community.

The constitution provides for the limitation or renunciation of sovereignty in favour of African unity.

The President is elected for a seven-year term and can be re-elected. M. Sekou Touré, who is both President and Prime Minister, was elected in January, 1961.

When Dr Kwame Nkrumah, the President of Ghana, deposed in the *coup* of February 24, 1966, sought refuge in Guinea, President Sekou Touré declared him to be the joint head of state in Guinea (March 2, 1966).

Guinea's voice has always been loud and assertive on the international front, particularly against the twin evils of colonialism and neo-colonialism. At home the Government struggles with a difficult economic situation in which it cannot hope for quick results.

President Sekou Touré's firm insistence on absolute political and economic independence has prevented Guinea from accepting the sort of economic aid which binds other African countries close to their former colonial masters. As a result this potentially prosperous country is likely to remain fairly poor at least in the immediate future.

Guinea's independence in 1958 started unhappily, and there are still signs of this today. Inspired by their then Prime Minister and former trades union leader, Ahmed Sekou Touré, the Guinean people voted against membership of General de Gaulle's proposed French African Community in favour of total independence, when offered the choice in a French referendum on September 28, 1958.

France cut all aid at a moment's notice. Within a month fewer than 20 of the 4,000 French colonial administrators – including doctors, teachers, judges and technicians – were left in the country.

Administrative records were removed or destroyed and embittered French officials left the telephone system in chaos. Untrained Guinean clerks suddenly had to fill responsible posts and try to keep the country running. The lack of trained personnel is still one of Guinea's major

Mobile policewomen
in Conakry

problems. It is being remedied gradually by the training
of administrators and technicians in the 20 or more
countries, from Communist China to the United States,
which give Guinea a kaleidoscopic variety of aid.
On independence Sekou Touré had to look for aid
where he could get it. One of the first to his side was
Ghana's President, Kwame Nkrumah, who offered him a
ten million sterling loan and suggested a union of states.
The union was never fully implemented and the loan
never repaid but the gesture expressed a spirit of African
unity which had an inspiring ideological significance at a
time when Africa was still finding its feet among the
established giants of world politics. For Nkrumah it has
since provided a haven in Guinea to which he was
welcomed and symbolically named co-president when
overthrown by his own countrymen in 1966.

The first non-African states to Sekou Touré's rescue were members of the Communist bloc, but much of early Soviet aid – such as a giant sports stadium, the longest runway in West Africa, bulldozers and combine harvesters for which there was no use – was unproductive.

Since then Guinea has been more critical in its choice of aid offers, and after Sekou Touré's visit to Moscow in August, 1965, the Soviet Union promised a huge new aid programme, including the construction of the Konkoure hydro-electric dam project in the Fouta Djallon Mountains, first studied by the French, which could export power to the whole of West Africa. Work had not started at the end of 1966.

Since 1963 the United States have provided by far the largest slice of foreign aid, mainly in rice, wheat and edible oils which have given the Guineans something better than their traditional subsistence diet of millet. Guinea's relations with both the Soviet Union and the United States have looked dangerously near collapse at times. In 1966 Guinea expelled the Soviet ambassador for a time after Soviet propaganda leaflets were distributed among school teachers and pupils.

In October, 1966, Sekou Touré expelled the US Peace Corps and put the American ambassador under house arrest for a few hours. He considered the US partly responsible for Ghana's arrest of a Guinean Government delegation, including Foreign Minister Louis-Lansana Beavogui, at Accra airport while on a Pan American Airways flight to Addis Ababa.

Rivalry between the ideological camps had kept Guinea well supplied with aid offers. The Communists saw Sekou Touré's Marxism as a sign that he was one of them – until he expelled the Soviet ambassador. American officials have always eagerly interpreted the slightest anti-communist move as a sign that Sekou Touré will remain at least neutral.

Apart from Sekou Touré's emphatic condition that aid must be without strings, Guinea is paradoxically not always able to afford as many loans as it would like. For many years it has been caught in a vicious circle in which hard-earned foreign currency income from exports has been completely swallowed up by credit repayments and interest, leaving nothing over to service more than a handful of new loans.

Modern flats in the
capital rise over a
huddle of tin roofs

To right a crippling adverse trade balance the Guinea
Government cut imports in 1962, particularly of
non-essential foods and textiles now produced by Guinea's
own textile factory. Simultaneously there has been a rise in
exports, mainly in bauxite.

The Fria international consortium, which specialises in
mining bauxite, has been Guinea's largest single enterprise
and best foreign currency earner ever since independence.
Its output provides roughly half of Guinea's exports in value.

Even greater mineral riches are still unexploited in the Boke region of north-western Guinea, which holds what is claimed to be some of the world's purest bauxite. The Guinea Government formed a joint company with the American Harvey Aluminium Company to mine the ore, and the World Bank has accorded a ten-year loan for studies for a railway and port to ship the mineral out of the country.

Although Guinea has been one of the foremost critics of surviving colonialism in Africa, Guinean troops have never fought in the nationalist causes of other countries.

Guinea has long given passive assistance to nationalist fighters in neighbouring Portuguese Guinea, mainly by allowing Amilcar Cabral, head of the Portuguese Guinean guerilla force – the 'Partido Africano da Independencia da Guinee Cabo Verde' – to have his headquarters in Guinea.

Guinea's 4,800-strong Army, trained and equipped mainly by West Germany and the Soviet Union, concentrates on economic development – building small factories, resurfacing roads and organising model farm projects. It includes a few hundred highly-trained paratroopers who have only seen active service as part of the United Nations force in the Congo, until Sekou Touré withdrew them abruptly because he disagreed with United Nations policy there.

The Russian-built Patrice Lumumba printing works at Conakry

An aerial view of Conakry's harbour, with palm trees and a spacious apartment block in the foreground

President Sekou Touré is the uncontested national leader, and his Cabinet, appointed by himself, has undergone little more than periodic reshuffling in the eight years of the country's independence. As well as national President, Sekou Touré is chairman of the only political party, the 'Parti Démocratique de Guinée', whose highly-organised structure covers every village. Local party members not only urge increased national consciousness, universal literacy and increased productivity, but keep a close watch on Guinea's very restricted internal trade for profiteering and black market activities.

Government policy is directed by the Party's political bureau, of which Sekou Touré is also chairman, or, in instances of supreme national importance, by the 'Conseil National de la Révolution', grouping top party officials from all parts of the country. In practice it is Sekou Touré's personality which dominates the Party's ideas and decisions.

Several plots against the Government have been revealed by the President. But none of them appeared to put his Administration in real danger. The French and Ivory Coast Governments were both accused of a part in one which resulted in a total break in diplomatic relations with France.

After its initial displeasure at Guinea's independence vote, France hoped the country would return to the fold of French-speaking states working in close cooperation with it. But Sekou Touré has always condemned the close economic links between France and other former colonies as totally unacceptable neo-colonialism.

Guinea's subsoil is rich, its rivers could supply much of West Africa with hydro-electric power and it has the unique advantage in West Africa of the cool and picturesque Fouta Djallon Hills to give its administrators a break from the humid heat of the tropical plains.

But like other French West African colonies Guinea was little developed before independence compared with France's much nearer North African territories.

Prevented by tight travel restrictions from comparing their own situation with the subsidised prosperity of some of their neighbours, Guineans are now experiencing the first part of Sekou Touré's independence slogan: 'We prefer poverty in freedom to riches in slavery'.

Marof Achkar

Louis-Lansana
Beavogui

MAROF ACHKAR

Guinea's Ambassador to the United Nations, Marof Achkar spent several years with the *Ballets Africains* before entering government service.

Born in Coyah in 1930, he spent five years at school in France before joining the ballet troupe, of which he became deputy director in 1954, and director for two years from 1957.

He served as a member of the Guinean delegation to the United Nations before being promoted to Ambassador in 1962. In the same year he became vice-president of the UN Committee on *Apartheid.*

Marof Achkar is well-known in the United Nations General Assembly for his violently anti-colonialist speeches.

LOUIS-LANSANA BEAVOGUI

One of the most versatile figures in the Guinean Government is Louis-Lansana Beavogui, whose career has taken him from a medical practice through a variety of Guinean economics ministries to the Foreign Ministry.

Born in Macenta in 1923, Beavogui qualified at the West African Medical School in Dakar and first served as assistant medical officer in Gueckedou in southern Guinea before being appointed chief medical officer in the large town of Kissidougou. There he began his political career as town councillor, later becoming mayor.

In the 1956 legislative elections he appeared third on the electoral list of the Guinean Democratic Party, behind Sekou Touré and El-Hadj Saifoulaye Diallo.

Appointed Minister of Trade, Industry and Mining in 1957, he became Minister of Economic Affairs and Planning on independence in 1958, a post he held until he was transferred to the

Foreign Affairs Ministry in 1961.

At the Belgrade Conference of Non-aligned Nations in September, 1961, Beavogui drew attention to Guinea by calling for the admission of Communist China to the United Nations, the elimination of military bases on foreign territory throughout the world, and the setting up of a triumvirate to replace the United Nations Secretary-General.

EL-HADJ
SAIFOULAYE DIALLO

El-Hadj Saifoulaye Diallo, one of the most ardent left-wingers in the Guinea Government, frequently deputises for President Sekou Touré and is considered the most likely immediate successor to the President.

His appointment as Minister of State in 1963 made him the overall watchdog of the Guinean Treasury and economy at a time when Guinea was obliged to take careful stock of its economic situation as credit repayments fell due after extensive foreign borrowing during five years of independence.

Although born of a Foulah chieftain family, in 1916, El-Hadj Saifoulaye Diallo is believed to be more Left than the President. He helped Sekou Touré rid Guinean tribal chiefs of the vestiges of their political power to create a single nation of the distinct and previously rival ethnic groups.

Like many other Guinean Cabinet members he completed his education at the William Ponty School in Dakar before becoming a clerk in the French colonial Administration.

Because of his left-wing activities in the RDA ('Rassemblement Démocratique Africain') he was shifted from post to post in West Africa until he gave up his job to devote himself entirely to

Fodeba Keita

a career in politics in 1955.

He was elected to a seat in the French National Assembly in 1956 and the following year was voted into the Guinean Territorial Assembly of which he became President, a position he held when Guinea became independent.

Himself a member of the Foulah people inhabiting the Foutah Djallon, he played an active part in persuading them to vote for independence from France in the 1958 referendum.

The outward appearance of this tall, silent and aloof Foulah gives no clue to his political acumen, which has earned him the key post of political secretary in the national political bureau, the policy-making body within the Guinean Democratic Party.

FODEBA KEITA

Poet and dancer, Fodeba Keita was for many years Guinea's Minister of Security and Defence before being given his present portfolio of Development, Rural Economy and Working Classes in 1965.

The change followed shortly on the discovery of an anti-government plot allegedly involving the French and Ivory Coast Governments, and was read as a sign that Fodeba Keita, formerly considered one of the strong men of the Cabinet, was in disgrace.

Outside Guinea he is best known as founder of the *Ballets Africains,* the Guinean traditional dance troupe whose appearances in over 30 countries have earned it an international reputation.

Born in 1921 at Siguiri, Fodeba Keita is the son of a male nurse. Like many of his government colleagues he attended the French William Ponty School in Dakar.

He later studied law at the Sorbonne in Paris and for a time augmented his student income by writing poetry and short stories.

He was reportedly strongly influenced by contact with French Communist and left-wing circles in Paris and became a strong supporter of Marxist policies. His poems were so nationalist and anti-colonialist that they were banned in West Africa in 1951.

A talented dancer, singer and banjo player, Fodeba Keita, while still a student, organised West African singers, dancers and instrumentalists into a touring troupe which became the Guinean National Ballet on independence in 1958.

His many recorded musical compositions helped to make him a popular figure in Guinea, particularly among young people.

He was named Minister of the Interior and Security in the first post-independence Cabinet, and was given additional control over the Army in 1960. He was regarded as one of the powerful men in the Cabinet because of President Sekou Touré's trust in placing both the Police and Army in his hands, all the more surprising since Fodeba Keita played little part in pre-independence politics. He is one of the few Cabinet Ministers who is not a member of the National Political Bureau of the Guinean Democratic Party.

Fodeba Keita has published a number of works, including *Poèmes Africains, Le Théâtre Africain, Le Maître d'Ecole* and *Les Hommes de la Danse.*

GENERAL DIANE LANSANA

The Military Minister, General Diane Lansana, a veterinarian and politician by profession, holds the highest military rank ever awarded in Guinea.

191

Diallo Telli

He was named Major-General by the Government to command the Guinean Battalion during its short attachment to United Nations Forces in the Congo, to put him on a par with other nations' commanders.

The highest ranking officer in the Guinean Army is Chief of the General Staff, Lieutenant-Colonel Noumandiane Keita. Lack of higher ranks is consistent with the Government's policy of keeping the military firmly under civilian control and employed mainly on economic projects.

General Diane is the first man with military connections to have occupied the Defence Ministry. He replaced Fodeba Keita after the 1965 anti-government plot in which France and the Ivory Coast Governments were implicated. But unlike his predecessor, he was not given the additional title of Minister of Security, a role filled separately by Secretary of State for Security Magassouba Moriba. Although a prominent member of the Guinean Democratic Party's National Political Bureau, it was the first time Diane Lansana had received a Cabinet portfolio.

Before going to the Congo he was Governor of the provincial Kankan and N'Zerekore regions. On his return he was named Governor of the Labe region in the Fouta Djallon Mountains, an area from which there were periodic reports of unrest among the proud and independent-minded Foulahs who inhabit the region.

DIALLO TELLI

Alhaji Boubakar Diallo Telli, Guinea's representative at the United Nations, was selected as the first secretary-general of the Organisation of African Unity on July 21, 1964, 14 months after the Organisation was founded.

The delay was caused by stiff competition for the post and some opposition to Telli who, as a Guinean, was considered too left-wing by some French-speaking states (although Telli's nomination was also reported to have been opposed by his own country).

Telli, who speaks both French and English, was supported for the post by most of the English-speaking countries.

Born in Guinea in 1925, he belongs to the Foulah tribe whose members, thinly scattered across West Africa, are mainly warriors and nomadic cattle-breeders. They are noted for being oblivious to African frontiers.

A series of 'firsts' marked his academic, administrative and diplomatic career. He was first in the primary school in his native village of Poredaka, first in his class at the Dakar Lycée and first at the Paris Faculty of Law. He took his degree at the unusually early age of 20 and followed it with a doctorate.

In 1951 he was the first black African to enter the École de la France d'Outre-mer – training ground of senior colonial administrators. He worked his way up through successive legal and administrative posts in the colonial administration to become in 1957 secretary-general of the Grand Council of French West Africa.

The Grand Council, consisting of representatives of eight territories – Senegal, Soudan (Mali), Guinea, Mauritania, Ivory Coast, Niger, Upper Volta and Dahomey – was a Federal-like government with a large measure of internal autonomy under French control.

When Guinea seceded from the French Community to become an independent country in Septem-

Ismael Touré

Sekou Touré

ber, 1958, M. Telli immediately transferred his allegiance to his native country and was appointed ambassador-at-large.

His task was to prepare Guinea's entry on the international scene and secure both African and world support for her regime, then boycotted by the offended French Government.

The following year Guinea was accepted as a member of the United Nations and Diallo Telli became his country's first representative to the United Nations as well as Ambassador to the United States.

In 1963 he was elected Vice-President of the General Assembly and also served for a time as president of the special committee on *apartheid*.

His private life reflects to some extent the international nature of his career. His children were born in France, the United States and Ethiopia. He alternates between a smart western suit with a black homburg and the flowing West African robe, the *boubou*, with brimless fur hat. He is a Moslem and has been on the pilgrimage to Mecca.

A socialist by inclination, he is one of the highest paid men in Africa, his salary and emoluments totalling US $40,000 a year.

With the fall of his close friend, Kwame Nkrumah, and with some criticism continuing from moderate French-speaking states, there have been signs, particularly at the 1966 Conference, that Diallo Telli's star may be on wane. Nevertheless, buoyed aloft by his charm and ability, Diallo Telli may ride out this opposition, although his fate as secretary-general will depend on the political trends in African countries which at the beginning of 1967 were not entirely in his favour.

ISMAEL TOURE

Ismael Touré, half-brother of President Sekou Touré, is considered the economic expert in the Government.

He is president of the Economic Committee of the policy-making National Political Bureau of the Guinean Democratic Party, and since 1963 – when Guinea took careful stock of its difficult economic situation – has been responsible for economic development.

A strong nationalist and indefatigable party worker, he is one of the most influential men in the Government.

A few years younger than the President and considered more left-wing in his views, Ismael Touré is seen by many as an eventual political heir to his half-brother.

Born in 1925, Ismael Touré qualified as an electrician in France. He joined the French Meteorological Service in Guinea and was soon named Chief Meteorological Officer in the provincial capital, Kankan.

There he launched into a political career and was first elected to the Kankan Municipal Council in 1956. The following year he won a seat in the Guinean Territorial Assembly and two months later was appointed Minister of Public Works in the Territorial Cabinet.

In the months before independence he was editor of the Guinean Democratic Party's organ, *Liberté*.

SEKOU TOURE

President Sekou Touré, 'the man who said no to de Gaulle', has been head of state of Guinea since October 2, 1958, following his decision to take Guinea out of the French Community in favour of independence.

Handsome, eloquent, and a fearless advocate of direct action, he became a powerful trade union leader and then a leading figure in African nationalism.

His was the only French territory to vote 'no' in the 1958 referendum on France's proposed new constitution and Guinea left the French Union.

'Guinea prefers poverty in freedom to riches in slavery,' he told a mass meeting before the referendum.

Sekou Touré was born on January 9, 1922, in the village of Faranah on the Niger, deep in Guinea's interior. He was the son of a peasant farming family but claims descent from the native hero, Samory Touré, who fought the French until his capture in 1898.

He was raised as a Moslem, although his political thought was strongly influenced by Marxism. He has nevertheless remained a devout Moslem and leads worshippers at main religious festivals.

His career as a rebel began at the age of 15, when he was expelled from a technical college for leading a strike. He became a post office clerk and made up for his lost lessons by reading and by getting his school friends to pass on to him in the evenings what they had learnt each day.

But union organisation was his main passion. He made connections with the 'Confédération Générale du Travail' (CGT), the Communist-dominated French Labour Union and became Guinean secretary-general of the CGT's co-ordinating committee for French West Africa in 1950.

Even in these days Sekou Touré showed his ability to make dramatic breaks. In 1957 he broke with the French Communist Party and helped to set up the General Union of Workers of Black Africa (UGTAN) of which he became secretary-general. He was widely criticised by Communists both in France and Guinea for this.

From militant unionism to politics – the step was a short one. He was a founder member of the African Democratic Rally (RDA) launched by Houphouet-Boigny of the neighbouring Ivory Coast in 1946.

Sekou Touré in 1952 became secretary-general of the Guinean Democratic Party (PDG), the local branch of the RDA. At this time Sekou was vice-president of the RDA and one of Houphouet-Boigny's closest lieutenants although the two men were to fall out later.

Elected mayor of Conakry in 1955, he became a deputy of the French National Assembly from 1956–58.

The rush towards independence was gathering pace in Guinea. The Guinean Democratic Party had become extremely strong by 1956 with organisations in almost every village. Opposition was suppressed and homes of opponents sometimes burned. Some of Sekou Touré's aides were proving more left-wing than he was.

In 1957, Sekou Touré was advanced to the post of Vice-President of the Government Council of Guinea, which was tantamount to being prime minister under the French Governor.

The idea of France's colonies and trust territories being politically independent and economically interdependent within the French Community won general favour in Africa, but Sekou Touré opposed it saying it was just the old French Union in another guise. Sekou split over this with his political mentor, Houphouet-Boigny. The 'no' vote in Guinea for the de Gaulle referendum was ninety-five per cent.

The reaction from France was violent and immediate. Ties between Paris and Guinea were cut and aid stopped. Sekou Touré called in help from the Eastern bloc and West Germany. He travelled almost immediately to Ghana to confer with Kwame Nkrumah and an announcement was made that the two countries would unite as the nucleus of a United States of Africa. Ghana lent Guinea £10 million.

From the early days of independence, when a fervour reigned among Guineans at the thought of 'going it alone' in building their own economy, Guinea's relations with the countries that have helped her seem to have been a constant succession of 'ups and downs'.

Guinea's relations with Ghana turned sour after the assassination of President Olympio of Togo in 1963. Sekou Touré suspected Ghanaians were responsible for the assassination. Later, on an East African tour, he announced that the Ghana-Guinea-Mali union was off. (Ghana has since complained that Guinea never repaid the £10 million loan.) Yet when Nkrumah was overthrown, Sekou Touré was happy to welcome him on Guinean territory and appoint him Co-President.

The United States had been worried about Guinea turning Communist, but in 1961 Sekou accused the Soviet ambassador of being involved in the 'Teachers Plot' and expelled him.

The United States gave the most aid of any country to Guinea, particularly in food, yet in November, 1966, Guinea held America responsible for the arrest of Guinea's foreign minister on a transit air stop in Accra, and temporarily arrested the American ambassador and expelled the Peace Corps.

After the clash with France at independence, relations were patched up a little with the signing of agreements for technical and administrative co-operation and cultural exchanges in 1959.

Negotiations opened on diplomatic recognition in November, 1962, were broken off again, resumed and finally reached a successful conclusion in May, 1963. Again relations were broken in November, 1965, when Sekou Touré implicated France and the Ivory Coast in a plot.

Houphouet-Boigny made an airport stopover in Conakry in August, 1962, to try to mend relations, but particularly since the 1965 plot the Ivory Coast has been a constant butt of Guinean tirades.

Political opposition inside Guinea has been swiftly and effectively dealt with. A number of arrests followed the 'Teachers Plot' of 1961 and the alleged French-inspired plot of 1965. After the latter the popular Minister of the Interior and Army, Fodeba Keita, was downgraded to Minister of Rural Economy.

Guinean exile organisations exist in France and the Ivory Coast.

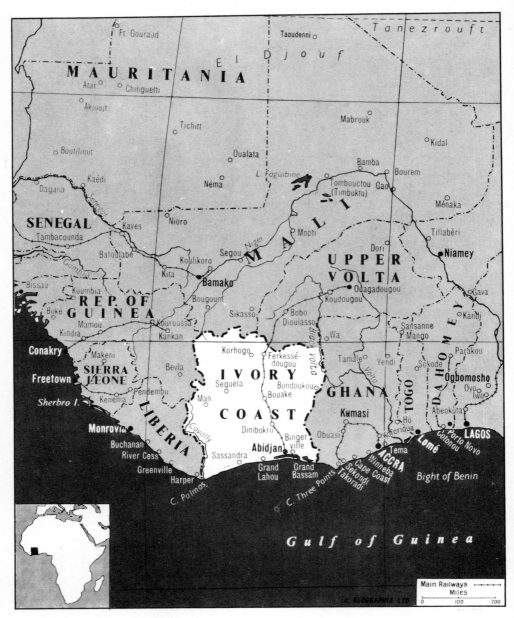

The Ivory Coast covers 124,500 square miles on the north coast of the Gulf of Guinea. It has borders with Ghana, Liberia, Guinea, Mali and Upper Volta. Its population in 1964 was put at 3,850,000.

The capital is Abidjan.
The Ivory Coast's economy is based almost entirely on agriculture. Coffee is the main export and the country ranks third in the world, after Brazil and Colombia, as a coffee producer.

It is the fourth biggest cocoa source after Ghana, Brazil and Nigeria. The Ivory Coast also exports bananas, timber, diamonds, manganese and pineapples.

Ivory Coast

The Ivory Coast, a former French colony, became
independent on August 7, 1960.
Under the 1960 Constitution, executive power is held by the
President of the Republic, head of state, who is elected
by direct universal suffrage for a period of five years.
Legislative power is exercised by a single chamber, the
National Assembly, whose members are elected by direct
universal suffrage.
The Ivory Coast is a member of the *Entente,* an
association of five independent West African states.

The Ivory Coast's post-independence prosperity forms one
of the few economic success stories in Africa.
Endowed with a President of long administrative
experience in Félix Houphouet-Boigny, the country was
steered through the tricky shoals of rapid economic
expansion by Houphouet's able financial advisers,
including his West Indian Finance Minister, Raphael
Saller.
Saller's success in obtaining foreign investment to develop
the natural wealth of the Ivory Coast's rain forests and
savannahs was spectacularly demonstrated by the heady
growth of the capital, Abidjan, from a sleepy lagoon
town of about 20,000 inhabitants just after World War II
to a luxurious metropolis of pastel-shaded skyscrapers,
air-conditioned shopping arcades and ribboned super-
highways of 330,000 inhabitants in the middle '6os.
Abidjan's sudden boom was due to two factors, the passing
of the 'framework law' (*loi cadre*) in Paris in 1957, which
had the effect of splitting up France's former giant
West African territory and drawing investment away from
its capital, Dakar, and the cutting of the Vridi canal from
the rolling Gulf of Guinea into the tranquil waters of
the lagoon some hundred yards inland, which turned
Abidjan into a port for ocean-going shipping.
Abidjan is not a relaxing city. African visitors who
admire its tall buildings and architectural glitter are
ill-at-ease when faced with its roaring traffic and wide
roads with clover-leaf junctions from which – unthinkable
in most of the rest of the continent – the strolling market
mammies with bundles on their heads and the thin-
legged goatherders are rigorously excluded.
A European visitor is also left with the impression that

Turf fans crowd the
rails at an Ivory Coast
meeting

the amiable and easy-going Ivory Coast population is
also slightly uncomfortable in the hurly burly of
metropolitan living, but most Ivory Coasters have a
natural retreat in hospitable and neatly laid out
villages and small towns which dot the rain forests round
the capital. There they can strip off stiff European suits
and don a *pagne* or sarong made of a length of printed
cloth and relax over a dish of *fou fou*, made up of
pounded yam or plantain (the outsized, green banana)
with a mouth-burning chili pepper sauce.

It was in one such forest town, the town of Yamoussoukro,
110 miles to the north of Abidjan, that Félix Houphouet-
Boigny was born into a prosperous planting family round

about the turn of the century. His upbringing moulded
his political outlook. Coffee and cocoa holdings were almost
exclusively in the hands of the local Ivory Coast
population and it was through his efforts to get them fair
prices that Houphouet-Boigny came into politics. From
these early activities grew the giant African Democratic
Rally ('Rassemblement Démocratique Africain'–RDA)
which by 1958 had captured five of the eight French
West African territories.

The Ivory Coast did not have an economy markedly
different from that of some of its neighbours, but from the
outset its path was set firmly on cooperation with the
former colonising Power of France. Other leaders caught
up in the idealistic pan-African movements of post-
independence Africa had some rude things to say about
the Ivory Coast leader. To these critics Houphouet-
Boigny's retort was more disinterested than angry:
'What are we supposed to share – each other's poverty?'
The Ivory Coast, along with most of the other former
French African territories, became an associated member
of the European Common Market. The French were
encouraged to invest and work in the country. There
were 15,000 Europeans in Abidjan in 1966: 40,000 in the
whole country. The President's aim was to create an
atmosphere of confidence which would encourage investment. The gleaming towers of Abidjan were just part of
it. From there State and private investment radiated into
the interior, into huge, scientifically developed palm oil
plantations, modern ricefields in the northern savannahs,
paved roads and up-to-date telecommunications. Abidjan
in the middle '60s was promising to become the focal
point of communications for the West African hinterland.
From the outset the President had possessed a sense of
international relations which was much more akin to the
diplomacy of Europe than to the idealisms based on
sweeping plans for unity of much of newly independent
Africa. While one part of the population of French West
Africa looked forward to the day of the withdrawal of the
French and dreamed of a Federation of Mali founded
exactly on the former colonial boundaries, President
Houphouet sensed the impracticability of this geographic
leviathan and worked for his own independence and
alliances in the more fertile southern half of it.

The Federation of Mali shrank like a pricked balloon to

Opposite: The new
Central Bank of West
Africa building
dominates a quiet
road

the two states of Senegal and Mali, and endured only two
months before these two split up. The alliances which
President Houphouet then formed endure today in the
Entente, a loosely-knit organisation of five West African
states, Dahomey, Togo, Ivory Coast, Upper Volta and
Niger, whose presidents meet regularly to discuss common
problems.
Faced with the task of welding together the many tribes
of the Ivory Coast into a modern nation, President
Houphouet has preferred that his relationship with his
West African neighbours and allies should be one of
consultation and cooperation on practical matters, but he
did allow himself one dream of African unity when in
1965 he tried to introduce a programme of dual
citizenship within the *Entente.* This foundered on old
jealousies. Elements of the Ivory Coast population had,
before independence, risen up and expelled a number of
Togolese and Dahomians who occupied many Civil Service
and commercial posts. These elements began to murmur
against the President's plans. With considerable political
address, Houphouet cut back his programme but still held
out hope that African unity might one day be realised in
this corner of Africa by all citizens of the *Entente* being
legally 'at home' in the Ivory Coast. In the same
retrenchment Houphouet's financial architect, Raphael
Saller, was replaced as part of an Africanisation policy but
the President made it clear that M. Saller's policies
would continue.
Under President Houphouet's guidance *réalisation* has been
the key word of the Ivory Coast. Dreams have only been
permitted to flourish in so far as they can be reduced
to a working plan with a construction date set.
Abidjan, despite its spectacular expansion, is a long way
yet from the city it is meant to be. Old, distemper-
painted villas in the centre of the city are to be swept
away to make room for a *Champs Elysée,* bounded on
each side with parks and skyscraper apartments, leading
right up to the gates of the Presidential palace.
But this Abidjan of the future is no mythical El Dorado.
A working model of it exists in the downstairs apartments
of the President's palace. And the skyscrapers and office
blocks going up in Abidjan, although they appear to be
scattered and without any city planning logic, in fact all
form part of that final plan.

Konan Bedie

Alphonse Bissouma
Tape

CAMILLE ALLIALI

Camille Alliali, lawyer and diplomat, was appointed Justice Minister in January, 1966.

Born on November 23, 1926, he studied law at Grenoble University after going to school in Dakar. For a time he practised at the Paris Bar.

A representative of the Democratic Party, he was Vice-President of the Ivory Coast Assembly from 1957–59, and from 1959–61 represented his country in the French Community Senate in Paris.

Named Ivory Coast Ambassador to France in 1961, he stayed in Paris until 1963, when he was recalled to serve as Deputy Foreign Minister for three years.

LAMBERT AMON-TANOH

Teacher and trade-unionist, M. Lambert Amon-Tanoh became Education Minister in 1963.

Born on November 26, 1926, he studied at a teachers' training college in Katibougou, Mali, before teaching at a boys' school in Bingerville, near Abidjan.

Lively and indefatigable, M. Amon-Tanoh served as a deputy in the Ivory Coast National Assembly and was secretary-general of the Ivory Coast General Workers' Union before he became a Minister.

NANLO BAMBA

Nanlo Bamba became Interior Minister in January, 1966, after three years as Minister of Justice.

A career magistrate, he served in the French colonial administration in Paris (1947–51), in Dahomey, and then in the Ivory Coast.

In 1958 he became Deputy Public Prosecutor at the Abidjan Court, then examining magistrate. From 1959 until August, 1961 M. Bamba served as director of the staff of M. Félix Houphouet-Boigny, Prime Minister and later President of the Ivory Coast.

He later became Deputy Prosecutor at the State Security Court.

KONAN BEDIE

Konan Bedie was recalled from his post as Ambassador in Washington to become Mininster Delegate for Economic and Financial Affairs in January, 1966.

M. Bedie, who was born in 1934, became his country's *chargé d'affaires* in Washington as soon as the Ivory Coast became independent in August, 1960, and presented his credentials as Ambassador the following year. Meantime he had set up the Ivory Coast Mission to the United Nations.

A trained economist, he studied Law at Poitiers University in France. After his studies he worked as a civil servant, and in January, 1960 he was sent on a course at the French Foreign Ministry in Paris.

Two months later he arrived in Washington as counsellor at the French Embassy.

ALPHONSE BISSOUMA TAPE

Alphonse Bissouma Tape, chemical engineer and former trainer and director of the Ivory Coast national football team, was appointed Minister for Youth, Popular Education and Sports in January, 1966.

Youth and Sports had previously come under the Armed Forces Minister.

M. Bissouma Tape was born on August 27, 1932. He was elected to the Ivory Coast National Assembly in 1960 and became secretary of its economic and financial committee.

Alphonse Boni

Mamadou Coulibaly

Auguste Denise

Mohamed
Tiekoura Diawara

ALPHONSE BONI

Alphonse Boni became President of the Supreme Court in February, 1963, after a distinguished legal career.

Born on January 8, 1909 in Tiassale, Ivory Coast, he launched into a career in the colonial Administration after a period at the public prosecutor's office in Toulouse.

He held legal posts in Togo, Mali and Senegal, serving finally as Public Prosecutor in Brazzaville from 1952–58.

He became Ivory Coast Justice Minister in 1959.

MAMADOU COULIBALY

Mamadou Coulibaly, who became President of the Advisory Economic and Social Council, led his country's delegation to the United Nations in 1960 when the newly independent Ivory Coast was admitted to the world body.

Born on October 10, 1910, M. Coulibaly went to school in Dakar and became head of schools in Bingerville, near Abidjan.

An early member of the Ivory Coast Democratic Party – later the country's ruling party – M. Coulibaly served from 1949–56 on the Social Affairs Committee of the French Union Assembly.

In 1959 he became a Democratic Party representative in the Ivory Coast's first legislative assembly, then, with independence in 1960, a deputy in the National Assembly.

He also represented his country in the Senate of the French Community from 1959–61.

AUGUSTE DENISE

Auguste Denise was one of the first companions of M. Félix Houphouet-Boigny – first President of the Ivory Coast Republic – in the political movement which led to the independence of the former French colony in 1960.

He became the dean of the 'old guard' of Ivory Coast politicians who, with M. Houphouet-Boigny, devoted themselves to African evolution.

A member of the political bureau of the ruling Democratic Party, he became in 1961 Minister of State deputising for the President when M. Houphouet-Boigny was out of the country.

Born on February 3, 1906, M. Denise – like M. Houphouet-Boigny – studied at the Dakar School of Medicine.

For ten years from 1946 he was secretary-general of the Ivory Coast Democratic Party (PDCI), part of the inter-territorial African Democratic Rally (RDA) launched by M. Houphouet-Boigny in 1946.

Elected Vice-President of the Ivory Coast Territorial Assembly in 1957, he became in 1958 the first head of the provisional Government of the Ivory Coast Republic – at a time when M. Houphouet-Boigny was a minister in French governments.

When M. Boigny became Ivory Coast Prime Minister in April, 1959, M. Denise was appointed Minister of State for relations with members of the *Entente*, or 'Council of Understanding' – a loose political association of the Ivory Coast, Niger, Upper Volta, Dahomey and Togo.

MOHAMED TIEKOURA DIAWARA

Mohamed Tiekoura Diawara is a technician. A mathematics graduate, he also studied at the Statistics Institute of Paris University and the Economic Development Institute of the World Bank in Washington.

M. Diawara, who was born on May 23, 1928 at Dori, in Mali,

Mathieu Ekra

served in high administrative posts in the Ivory Coast before he was appointed Deputy Minister for Planning in January, 1966. The President, M. Félix Houphouet-Boigny, headed the Ministry.

A year earlier M. Diawara had become governor of the Ivory Coast Industrial Development Bank.

He was General Director of Planning from 1963–66, and had previously held key posts in the Finance Ministry.

LOUA DIOMANDE

Loua Diomande, who has held several ministerial posts, began his political career while a student in France in 1946.

M. Diomande was born on December 12, 1926. He joined the students' branch of the African Democratic Rally (RDA) launched in 1946 by M. Félix Houphouet-Boigny, later first President of the Ivory Coast Republic.

M. Diomande studied at Aix-en-Provence and completed two years of law at Clermont-Ferrand before entering the French overseas administrative service.

First posted to St Louis, Senegal, he returned to the Ivory Coast in 1952.

M. Diomande was elected to the Ivory Coast Territorial Assembly in 1957 and appointed Public Service Minister in 1959 under the French 'framework law' which gave limited autonomy to overseas territories.

A member of the Ivory Coast legislative, constituent and national Assemblies between May, 1959 and January, 1961, M. Diomande became in 1961 Minister in charge of relations with the 'Council of Understanding'—a loose association of the Ivory Coast, Niger, Upper Volta, Dahomey and Togo.

In October, 1963, he became Deputy Minister for Public Service and Information, and a year later Minister for Public Service.

MATHIEU EKRA

Mathieu Ekra, one of the earliest militants of the African Democratic Rally – the political movement which led to the independence of the Ivory Coast in 1960 – became Minister for Public Affairs and Information in 1961 and Minister for Information in March, 1965.

He spent over three years in preventive detention, imposed by the French authorities of the time, for his activities in 1949 as secretary-general of an Abidjan branch of the African Democratic Rally (RDA) during nation-wide agitation for political reform.

Born on February 27, 1917, M. Ekra trained as an administrator and held several posts in the administration of former French West Africa.

He served in the railways and finance administrations before being sent to Guinea in the road transport department.

At Kankan, Guinea, in December, 1946, he set up the first branch there of the African Democratic Rally (RDA) and was elected its secretary-general.

M. Ekra joined the managing committee of the Ivory Coast Democratic Party in 1948, and in 1959 became the Party Political Bureau's secretary for Mass Education.

M. Ekra was a municipal councillor for Abidjan, the capital, in 1956 and became a member of Parliament in 1959.

He headed his country's delegation to the United Nations before becoming a Minister in the Ivory Coast Government.

Félix
Houphouet-Boigny

MICHEL GOLY KOUASSI

Michel Goly Kouassi became Minister responsible for Construction and Town Planning in January, 1966.

Born on September 25, 1932, he studied architecture in Paris before starting his career in the Construction and Town Planning department.

He became Secretary of State in the Department in 1964.

FELIX HOUPHOUET-BOIGNY

M. Félix Houphouet-Boigny, first President of the Ivory Coast Republic, led his country to independence (August 7, 1960) after a long and distinguished career in French politics.

Short and stocky, he was born on October 18, 1905, the descendant of a line of traditional tribal chiefs originating in the old Ashanti kingdom.

The son of a prosperous planter, he qualified brilliantly as a medical *assistant* after studies at the Medical School in Dakar.

In 1940 he became chief of his home district and a planter in his own right.

M. Houphouet-Boigny – the name 'Boigny' means 'The Ram' – began his political career when he created the Ivory Coast's first Agricultural Union in 1944.

This became the mouthpiece of Ivory Coast planters demanding minimum prices for their coffee and cocoa which were forbidden them by discriminatory laws of the colonial regime.

The Union's work paved the way for the great political movement he launched in 1946, the African Democratic Rally (RDA) which by 1958 had a majority in five of the eight territories in then French West Africa.

In 1945 M. Houphouet-Boigny was elected to the French Constituent Assembly.

While serving as deputy in the French Parliament from 1945 to 1949 he was influential in the adoption of the 'Houphouet-Boigny Bill' which in April, 1946, abolished forced labour in French territories in Africa.

He was re-elected Ivory Coast deputy to the French Parliament in 1951, was president of the Grand Council of French West Africa from 1957–58, and was appointed President of the Ivory Coast Territorial Assembly in 1957.

He became mayor of the lagoon-ringed modern Atlantic port of Abidjan, capital of the Ivory Coast, in 1956. In the same year he was given a ministerial post in the French Government.

As a minister he had a considerable part in the construction of the 'framework law' which in 1957 gave internal autonomy to French overseas territories. He held ministerial posts in various French governments until 1958, when he resigned to become Prime Minister of the Ivory Coast.

He was elected President in November the same year.

In 1965 he was re-elected President for another five years. He was unopposed, and the Interior Ministry said M. Houphouet-Boigny received 99·99 per cent of the votes cast.

But all was not plain sailing for M. Houphouet-Boigny after independence. In 1963 over 100 people, including ministers, were accused of plotting to assassinate him and with attempts against the security of the state.

Three years later, however, to mark the sixth anniversary of independence he released three former ministers and 93 other men accused of plotting against the government. He reduced to six

205

years imprisonment sentences passed on ten others alleged to have been implicated in the plots. Nine of them had been sentenced to death, but the sentences were later commuted to life imprisonment.

Also in 1966, President Houphouet-Boigny pardoned a group of exiles sent back from Ghana, where they were alleged to have been implicated in subversion against the Ivory Coast during the regime of Ghana's President Kwame Nkrumah, overthrown by an army *coup* on February 24, 1966.

Endowed with exceptionally strong will-power M. Houphouet-Boigny practises the strictest self-discipline. He has given up coffee, tobacco and alcohol. He is a Roman Catholic and loves music and sport.

SOULEYMANE IBRAHIM CISSOKO

Souleymane Ibrahim Cissoko became Minister for Post and Telecommunications in January, 1966, after serving as Secretary of State for the Ministry.

Earlier he had been director of the Post and Telecommunications administration.

Born on August 18, 1914, M. Ibrahim Cissoko was secretary-general of the Post and Telecommunications Workers' Union from 1947–51.

At the same time he was political adviser to an Abidjan branch of the Ivory Coast Democratic Party.

ALCIDE KACOU

Alcide Kacou made a career in engineering before joining the first Ivory Coast Government in 1957.

He became Minister for Public Works and Transport in 1961, a post he retained in a Cabinet reshuffle in January, 1966.

Born on March 14, 1919, at Bingerville, Ivory Coast, he began his engineering career in France after studies at Aix-en-Provence, France. After two years as a steelworks engineer, he was attached to the French Railways from 1946–47.

M. Kacou then went back to the Ivory Coast, where he was railway depot chief until 1950. He held a similar post in Conakry, Guinea, until 1952, before returning to the Ivory Coast where he ended up as head of the diesel section in Abidjan.

With the French 'framework law', which in 1957 gave internal autonomy to French overseas territories, he became Minister for Technical Education in the first Ivory Coast Government. M. Kacou retained that post until 1961.

He became a deputy in the Territorial Assembly in 1957 and deputy in the National Assembly in 1959.

From 1961–63 M. Kacou was Minister for Public Works, Transport, Post and Telecommunications in the first Government of the independent Ivory Coast.

In August, 1963, the portfolio for Construction was added to his other duties. In September, 1964, he became Minister for Public Works and Transport alone.

LANCINA KONE

Lancina Kone was appointed Minister for Work and Social Welfare in September, 1963.

He was elected to the National Assembly in November, 1960.

Born in 1916 at Mahale in the northern region of the Ivory Coast, M. Kone served in the French Army from 1937–42.

In 1947 he was elected assistant secretary-general of an Ivory Coast Democratic Party branch at Adjame, near Abidjan.

Two years later he became assistant secretary-general of the African Railwaymen's Trade Union.

KOUADIO M'BAHIA BLE

Kouadio M'Bahia Ble is a former schoolteacher who rose to be Armed Forces Minister at the age of 34.

Born on December 19, 1928, M. M'Bahia Ble studied at the William Ponty School in Sebikhotane, Senegal, and then did one year's military service.

He worked as vice-principal at a school in Bouake, in the centre of the Ivory Coast, for three years, before being appointed Director of Schools in 1953.

In 1956 he was sent to Paris where he was responsible for Ivory Coast students in France, serving as a link between two generations – the leaders of the time, and the Ivory Coast students destined to become the *élite* of the country.

In March, 1957, M. M'Bahia Ble was elected territorial councillor for Bouake, becoming a member of the Constituent Assembly in 1958, until April, 1959, then a member of the Legislative Assembly. He became the Assembly's treasurer in December, 1959.

His first ministerial post was that for Youth and Sports in February, 1963. In September of the same year he assumed responsibility for the Armed Forces Ministry as well.

His mission in these two posts was to inculcate Ivory Coast youth with a sense of civic service and to reorganise the Army, adapting it to the needs of economic development and to social needs.

In February, 1966, following a Cabinet reshuffle, M. M'Bahia Ble gave up the Youth and Sports portfolio, remaining Minister for the Armed Forces and for the Civil Service.

JEAN-BAPTISTE MOCKEY

Jean-Baptiste Mockey, a chemist who became a Government Minister and secretary-general of the Ivory Coast's Democratic Party, was sentenced to death in 1965 for plotting to kill the President.

The sentence was later reduced to life imprisonment, and in August, 1966, President Houphouet-Boigny cut M. Mockey's term to six years' gaol.

M. Mockey, born on April 14, 1915, held various hospital appointments after studying chemistry at Dakar.

He was a founder-member of the Ivory Coast Democratic Party set up in 1946 by M. Houphouet-Boigny, who later became first President of the Ivory Coast Republic.

In 1947 he was elected to the Territorial Assembly, and also became administrative secretary of the Democratic Party.

M. Mockey was imprisoned by the French authorities in 1949 for two years because of his political activities.

When the French 'framework law' in 1957 gave limited autonomy to overseas territories, M. Mockey became Interior Minister in the first Ivory Coast Government. He also became secretary-general of the Democratic Party.

Later M. Mockey served as the Ivory Coast's first Ambassador to Israel, then as Minister for Agriculture.

In 1963 he headed a state court which convicted leaders of a plot against the President.

Eventually he was himself arrested and sentenced to death.

Brig-Gen d'Aquin
Ouattara

Abdoulaye Sawadogo

BLAISE N'DIA KOFFI

Blaise N'Dia Koffi trained at the Dakar School of Medicine and held several medical posts in the Ivory Coast and Upper Volta before being named Minister for Health and Population in 1963.

Born on December 28, 1912, M. N'Dia Koffi was director of Treichville Hospital and the Ivory Coast Nurses' School from 1957–59.

He was elected to the National Assembly in 1959.

BRIGADE-GENERAL
D'AQUIN OUATTARA

Chief of the Ivory Coast General Staff, Brigade-General Thomas d'Aquin Ouattara started his military career as a second class private in the French Army in the mid-1930s.

He served in World War II and in the Indochina campaign, rising to the rank of major. In 1961 he left the French Army to become Chief of General Staff, Ivory Coast. In 1964 he was promoted lieutenant-colonel.

In August, 1966, he became the first general in the Ivory Coast Army (the French rank of brigade-general corresponds to the British rank of major-general).

ABDOULAYE SAWADOGO

Abdoulaye Sawadogo, an expert in tropical agronomy, became Minister Delegate of Agriculture in September, 1966, at the age of 33.

He had been a high official in the Ministry since 1961 and, as such, much concerned with the country's agricultural reforms.

Born on February 17, 1933, in Mali, M. Sawadogo studied at the French National Agriculture School in Montpellier before specialising in tropical agronomy in Paris.

ALEXIS THIERRY LEBBE

Alexis Thierry Lebbe became Ivory Coast Minister for Animal Production in January, 1966, after two years as Secretary of State for the Interior and for Information.

Born on March, 22, 1920, he worked as a teacher before launching into a career in the administration of what was then French West Africa.

In 1958 he headed the staff of the Minister for Public Affairs.

He then went on a course in public affairs in Paris and held several administrative posts, finally becoming a prefect (administrator of a *département*).

ARSENE USHER ASSOUAN

Lawyer, politician and diplomat, M. Arsène Usher Assouan was appointed Foreign Minister in January, 1966, after six years as his country's permanent representative at the United Nations.

Born on October 24, 1930, M. Usher Assouan studied at Bordeaux and Poitiers Universities in France, and returned to the Ivory Coast to practise at the Abidjan Appeal Court.

An early member of the Ivory Coast Democratic Party – later to become the country's ruling party—he was Vice-President of the National Assembly in 1960.

With his country's independence in 1960, M. Usher Assouan became the Ivory Coast's first permanent representative to the United Nations.

PHILIPPE YACE

Philippe Yace, a teacher and World War II hero, became President of the Ivory Coast National Assembly in 1960. A year earlier he had become secretary-general of the ruling party.

Born on January 23, 1920, he

Philippe Yace

taught for two years before serving in the French Forces in World War II.

Returning home in 1946—decorated with the French Croix de Guerre—he soon resumed teaching and launched himself into politics as an active worker of the Ivory Coast Democratic Party founded that year by M. Houphouet-Boigny—later President of the Ivory Coast Republic.

After serving as secretary-general for district groups of the party he was elected in 1952 a member of the Territorial Assembly, a post he held for six years.

In 1958, when the French Community was set up, M. Yace was elected to the Ivory Coast Constituent Assembly and became a Senator of the French Community.

He was elected President of the National Assembly when the Ivory Coast became independent in 1960.

In 1963 he became president of the Ivory Coast High Court of Justice.

The 1965 National Congress of the PDCI confirmed M. Yace as secretary-general of the party while President Houphouet-Boigny became the honorary chairman. Yace thus assumed full responsibility for PDCI affairs and as such ranks as the most important figure after the President in the political hierarchy of the Ivory Coast.

Yace has travelled much to represent President Houphouet-Boigny at international and African heads of state meetings.

He has been decorated by the Republics of Dahomey, Niger, Upper Volta and Malagasy.

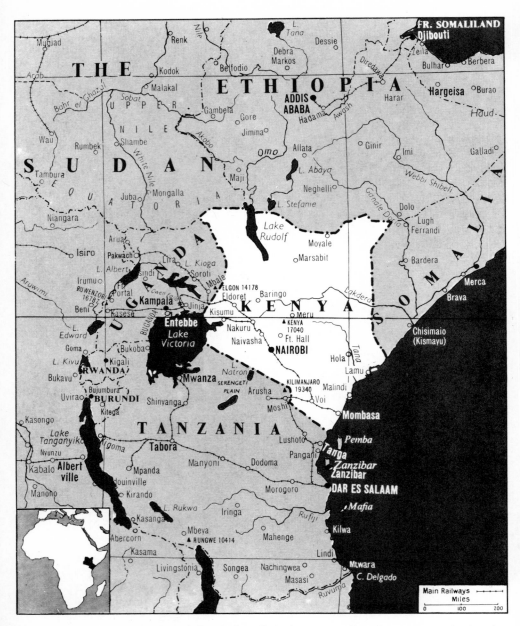

Kenya, bisected by the Equator, has an area of 225,000 square miles and a population officially estimated in mid-1966 to have reached 9,643,000. Kenya has common frontiers with Uganda in the north-west, Ethiopia in the north, Somalia in the north-east and Tanzania in the south. On the east, Kenya faces the Indian Ocean and to the west are the waters of Lake Victoria. The capital is Nairobi.

Kenya's economy is largely dependent on agriculture. The main products are coffee, tea, sisal, wheat, cotton, sugar cane and pyrethrum.

Kenya

The British territory of Kenya became independent on
December 12, 1963, with Jomo Kenyatta as Prime
Minister. One year later, Kenya became a republic and
Kenyatta was chosen to be the first President.
For three years from the date of independence, Kenya's
central legislature consisted of a National Assembly
comprising two Houses — the House of Representatives
and the Senate.
In December, 1966, an amendment to the Constitution was
passed by Parliament providing for the amalgamation of the
Senate and the House of Representatives.
The amendment also allowed for a continuation of the life of
the National Assembly until June, 1970.

A cardinal principle of the constitution of Kenya, with its
many races and tribes, is that there should be no
discrimination whatsoever based on race, tribe, colour,
religion or place of origin. The United Nations were
further assured of this by the Kenya Government in
October, 1966.
Jomo Kenyatta, regarded as Father of the Nation, has
adopted an uncompromising attitude towards inter-racial
bitterness and inter-tribal rivalry, and through his
personal magnetism and his famous slogan of *Harambee*
('Let us all pull together') has led Kenya to the position
of being one of the most envied in Africa for its stability
and tolerance. At the age of 75 he declared that Kenya is
lucky to have people of so many colours and religions
living together in harmony, and he warned non-Africans
to identify themselves with the nation-building efforts of
the Government and the indigenous people, or pack their
bags and leave.
The rapid growth of Kenya's African population creates
enormous problems, such as schooling and housing.
The annual increase is estimated at 300,000. By the time
she has reached the age of 50, the average African woman
in Kenya has given birth to between seven and eight
children, according to official data.
An advisory group which visited Kenya to recommend a
programme of family planning, estimated that with such
a programme Kenya's population would double over
the next 35 instead of the next 18 years, and families
would average four children per woman instead of eight.

The total estimated population of 9,643,000 comprises 9,370,000 Africans, including Somalis, 188,000 Asians, 43,000 Europeans, 38,000 Arabs and 4,000 others.

The African population is sub-divided into some 40 different tribes, the largest being the Kikuyu (over 1,700,000).

The European population is still considerable. A large number of those who decided to remain when the colony became independent under an African government, have taken Kenyan nationality and intend to remain, mostly as farmers.

The Asians, probably more than in any other African country, occupy a significant position in commerce and industry. They control a large sector of the import and export trade, and most of the internal distributive trade. They also provide a substantial number of the country's doctors, dentists, lawyers and other professional men.

A large number of British subjects of Indian and Pakistani origin left Kenya shortly before independence.

Thousands remained and, with their high birthrate, pose a problem which grows rather than diminishes.

The great majority of them were born in Kenya, but a large proportion have not become citizens, or have dual nationality. They have often been much criticised for this, and there are signs at times that their future may be difficult.

The Kenya Indian Congress in November, 1964, suggested a phased five- or ten-year withdrawal of Asians from Kenya's commercial life to facilitate African participation, acknowledging that the African urge for an important place in trade and commerce is a reality which is recognised and must be respected. The problem, it added, 'should not be allowed to fester as racial discord and agitation'.

In August, 1966, a commentary on the Government-controlled 'Voice of Kenya' accused Asians in Kenya of paying only lip-service to integration. It said there were 'daily instances of exploitation and racialist behaviour'.

Looking ahead to 1970, the Kenya Government is occupied with a revised development plan aimed at raising per capita incomes and distributing them equitably.

Among other projects, it will introduce African traders into the main business streets of the major urban areas.

Modern office blocks
and apartments in
Government Road,
Nairobi

Mr Tom Mboya, as Minister for Economic Planning and
Development, has admitted that in such a programme
'take-overs cannot be excluded if found to be necessary'.
But in general, Africanisation will be pursued through a
framework of growth, by enabling Africans to own new
assets.

There is an official campaign urging people back to the
land, but settlement of Africans on sites formerly owned
by Europeans is, according to Mr Mboya, 'very costly'.
Indeed, costs connected with the settling of landless
Africans on the former European farms, providing them
with necessary tools, seed, quality livestock, roads,
buildings, marketing arrangements and, not least,
instruction on how to farm under new conditions,
'amount to much more than the cost of purchasing the
land from the former European owners'.

The progress in agricultural techniques in Kenya is very
noticeable. It has been claimed that with the exception
of South Africa, more is probably being done in Kenya
than in any country south of the Sahara.

213

R. Achieng-Oneko

R. ACHIENG-ONEKO

Ramogi Achieng-Oneko, a Luo born in Central Nyanza, western Kenya, in 1920, started his working life as a meteorological clerk in 1941.

In 1945 he began publishing his own newspaper, and soon joined in the political campaigning for the Kenya African Union.

While secretary-general of the KAU in 1952, he was detained under the Emergency Regulations. His detention lasted up to 1961, and on his release he became personal secretary to President Kenyatta.

He was returned to the House of Representatives as member for Nakuru town, central Kenya, and was appointed Minister for Information, Broadcasting and Tourism.

This portfolio he held – minus Tourism, which was separated in 1965 – until he resigned in April, 1966, in sympathy with Mr Odinga. In a statement, he complained of 'political intrigue' by certain leaders, and said he thought Kenya was no longer non-aligned.

He became publicity secretary of the Opposition Kenya People's Union. During the 'little general elections' which followed Mr Odinga's resignation, he lost his seat to the KANU candidate.

SIR JOHN ALFRED AINLEY

The Chief Justice of Kenya since 1963, Sir John Alfred Ainley has been a magistrate in Ghana (1935), a judge in Uganda (1946), and Chief Justice in Eastern Nigeria (1955) and in Sarawak, North Borneo and Brunei (1959).

The courts of Kenya comprise High Court and Subordinate Courts. There are also Moslem and African Subordinate Courts, with limited jurisdiction. The power of the African courts, of which there are now more than a hundred, is confined to African customary law. The East African Court of Appeal, in Nairobi, is the Supreme Court.

Sir John Ainley was born in 1906 and educated at St Bees School and Corpus Christi College, Oxford, taking an MA degree. He read law and was called to the Bar.

J. H. ANGAINE

Jackson Harvester Angaine, Minister for Lands and Settlement (1963), was born in 1908, the son of an ex-senior Meru chief. He was educated at Alliance High School, Kikuyu, and started as an accountant.

He went into both business and farming, and is now one of the leading farmers in Meru district.

He entered active politics in 1961 and was elected to the Legislative Council.

C. M. G. ARGWINGS-KODHEK

Chiedo More Gem Argwings-Kodhek, Minister of Natural Resources (1966), was born of Luo parents in Nyanza in 1923.

He was educated at St Mary's College, Entebbe and Makerere College Kampala, where he took a teaching diploma.

He went on to take a BA degree at the University of Wales in 1955, and was called to the Bar (Lincoln's Inn) in London in 1951. He returned to Kenya, where he practised as an advocate.

He was elected to the Legislative Council in 1961 and became Parliamentary Secretary to the Minister of Lands, Surveys and Town Planning in 1962. Elected to the House of Representatives in 1963 as KANU candidate for Gem, he held three minor posts in the Government before his appointment as Minister.

Samuel Ayodo

James Gichuru

Jomo Kenyatta

S. O. AYODO

Samuel Onyango Ayodo, Minister for Tourism and Wild Life (1965), was born in 1930 in South Nyanza of Luo parents.

He was educated at Maseno Secondary School, Kenya, Makerere College, Uganda, and Union College, Lincoln, Nebraska, where he obtained a BSc degree in education. He has been a member of the National Advisory Committee on African Education.

He was a teacher until 1959, when he was elected to the Legislative Council. In 1963 he moved to the House of Representatives as KANU member for Kasipul-Kabondo, and was appointed Minister for Local Government.

MUINGA CHOKWE

Muinga Chitasi Chokwe was appointed Speaker of the Kenya Senate in 1963. A Coast man, born at Kilifi in 1921, he served with the police from 1941–46, then went into business.

He became a member of KANU, and was elected to the Legislative Council in 1961. He became Minister for Works in the Coalition Government in 1962.

JAMES SAMUEL GICHURU

James Samuel Gichuru, appointed Finance Minister in 1963, was born in 1914 near Kiambu.

His Kikuyu parents had been among the earliest converts to Christianity in Kenya, and his education was begun at the Church of Scotland Mission School, Kikuyu. It was continued at Alliance High School, and then at Makerere College, Uganda, where he took a teaching diploma.

From 1935–40, he taught at Alliance High School, where Ronald Ngala and Oginga Odinga were among his pupils. In 1951, he was principal of the Church of Scotland Mission School.

In 1944, he became the first president of the Kenya African Union, and held the post until Mr Kenyatta took it over in 1947. In 1950 he was appointed Chief of Dagoretti Location – with his father serving under him. From 1955–60, during the Emergency, he was placed under a restriction order at Githunguri, Kiambu.

In March, 1960, he was appointed first president of the Kenya African National Union (KANU), but relinquished the position as soon as Mr Kenyatta was released and could take over the leadership.

He became Minister of Finance in the Coalition Government, and subsequently Minister of Finance and Economic Planning. Economic Planning was removed from his portfolio in 1965.

JOMO KENYATTA

For 40 years the symbol of African nationalism on the continent, Jomo ('Burning Spear') Kenyatta was born the son of a poor Kikuyu farmer at Ichaweri in the heart of the Kikuyu country, on October 20, 1891.

When he attended a Church of Scotland mission school as a child, he was known as Johnstone Kamau Ngengi.

In 1928, as general-secretary of the Kikuyu Central Association, formed to regain the lands taken by the white settlers, he became the leader of the first nationalist movement in Kenya.

In 1929 he made his first visit to England, then ruling Kenya as a colony, to plead the case of the Africans' lost lands before the Colonial Secretary. He did not gain much ground and returned to Kenya. Next came extensive travels in Europe, during which he visited Russia and studied for a time at Moscow University. Back in London in 1936, he took a post-graduate course in anthropology at the LSE.

Two years later he published *Facing Mount Kenya*, a book in which he tried to demonstrate how tribal life had been disrupted by the coming of Europeans.

During World War II he worked on an English farm and married, as his third wife, an Englishwoman named Edna Clarke.

Campaigning ceaselessly for African rights he joined George Padmore, Kwame Nkrumah and others, in founding the Pan-African Federation (1945), which startled imperial governments with its idea of immediate independence for all.

Returning home in 1946, he became president of the newly formed Kenya African Union. This drew its main support from the Kikuyu, but Kenyatta was careful to put members of other tribes on the executive. Oginga Odinga, for example, destined to become his political antagonist later, organised support from among the Luo tribes, the second largest tribal community in the country, numbering just over a million.

On April 8, 1953, Jomo Kenyatta was sentenced to seven years' imprisonment by the British for 'managing' Mau Mau, described as a terrorist organisation. Five others were sentenced for assisting.

Passing sentence, Mr Ransley Thacker, a retired Supreme Court judge, said he was satisfied Kenyatta was the 'master-mind' behind a plan to drive the Europeans out of Kenya.

'Your Mau Mau,' he added, 'has slaughtered hundreds of men, women and children in circumstances which are revolting.'

Insisting that the Kenya African Union was a domestic body, striving to achieve its aims by constitutional means, Kenyatta replied to the Magistrate: 'None of us would condone the mutilation of human beings. We have families of our own. If you think that in working for African rights we have turned Mau Mau, you have been misled. We feel this case has been so arranged as to bring Mau Mau on us as a scapegoat in order to strangle the Kenya African Union – the only African political organisation which fights for the rights of the African people.' Mr D. N. Pritt, his counsel, acknowledged that Mau Mau existed on a substantial scale and in a terrifying form in Kenya, but contended that the prosecution had failed to prove that the six accused had taken part in it.

Kenyatta was still detained when the Kenya African National Union, today's ruling party, was formed in March, 1960, and he was elected president.

He was released on August 15, 1961, and entered the Legislative Council in January, 1962, as leader of the Opposition against the Kenya African Democratic Union (KADU) Government.

He shepherded his party to victory in the 1963 elections, fought the constitutional battle for independence, and at midnight on December 11, 1963, saw his dream fulfilled: Kenya was at last independent, with himself as Prime Minister. A year later, Kenya became a republic and Kenyatta was its first President. Shortly before this, the KADU Opposition party, headed by Ronald Ngala, voluntarily dissolved itself in the interests of national unity.

In 1966, Kenyatta warned the people of Central Nyanza, home-

Dr Julius Kiano

land of the Luo tribe, where the Opposition Kenya People's Union (KPU) led by ex-Vice-President Oginga Odinga, had had successes in by-elections in June of that year, that anyone who tried to set up a breakaway government 'will suffer the consequences of their folly'.

Heavily-built, with imposing features, a grey beard and a compelling style of oratory, which at one time was drawing as many as 30,000 people to his meetings, Jomo Kenyatta is known to his people as *Mzee* ('Grand Old Man').

His credo for the nation is African socialism: a democratic political philosophy based on African tradition, yet open to the best forces of progress, no matter what their origin, which help the country to nationhood, peace and prosperity.

Kenya's foreign policy is one of strict non-alignment. Technical and financial aid is welcome from both East and West, so long as there is no attempt at the same time to interfere in the country's internal affairs and policies.

His counsel is often sought in Africa. He helped to found the Organisation of African Unity. In April, 1966, he organised and chaired in Nairobi an 11-nation 'Good Neighbours' conference at summit level.

His fourth wife, Mrs Ngina Kenyatta – affectionately known throughout the country as 'Mama Ngina' – was born in 1933, the daughter of a Kikuyu chief.

She was detained for four years during the emergency proclaimed in October, 1952, and in 1959 joined her husband at Lodwar in a remote part of Kenya, while he was kept under house arrest after serving seven years' imprisonment.

They have four children.

DR JULIUS GIKONYO KIANO

Dr Julius Gikonyo Kiano was the first African lecturer at Nairobi's University College, but abandoned an academic life for politics and rose to ministerial rank.

He was born in 1926, of Kikuyu parents, at a small village in the Fort Hall district.

He began his education at the Kagumo Government African School, then went on to Alliance High School, Kikuyu, and to Makerere College, Uganda.

In 1948 he decided to go to the United States, where he attended Antioch College, Ohio, Stanford University, California, and the University of California. When he returned to Kenya eight years later, he held BA, MA and PhD degrees.

He gave up his lectureship at University College, Nairobi, in 1958, when elected to the Legislative Council.

In 1960, he received his first Government appointment, that of Minister for Commerce and Industry, which he held until the General Election the following year. In a Coalition Government, he became Parliamentary Secretary to the Minister of State. In 1963, he again received the Commerce and Industry portfolio, but in 1965 transferred to Labour.

MWAI KIBAKI

Mwai Kibaki, Minister for Commerce and Industry (1966), was born of Kikuyu parents, in Nyeri, in 1931.

Educated at Mangu High School, Kenya, Makerere College, Uganda, and the London School of Economics, he holds the degrees of BA and BSc. After returning from London, he took a lecturing post at Makerere for a year (1959–60).

Mbiyu Koinange

Tom Mboya

In 1961, he became a national executive officer in KANU, and was appointed to the Central Legislative Assembly in 1962. He was elected to the House of Representatives in 1963 as KANU Member for Nairobi Doonholm, and became Parliamentary Secretary to the Treasury.

MBIYU KOINANGE
Mbiyu Koinange, appointed Minister of State responsible for Administration in January, 1967, was born in Kiambu, of Kikuyu parents, in 1907.

His extensive travels abroad for higher education took him first to the USA, where he studied at Hampton University, Virginia, then Ohio Wesleyan University, where he obtained a BA degree, and finally to Columbia University, New York, for his MA.

Next he went to Britain, for a post-graduate education course at St John's College, Cambridge, and a teaching diploma at London University's Institute of Education. Ten years later, in 1947, he returned to Britain to take his PhD at the London School of Economics.

In the intervening years he became principal of the Kenya Teachers' College, Githunguri. From 1951–59 he was the Kenya African Union's representative in Europe. During the last two years he took advantage of his appointment to study trade unionism through the Extra-Mural Department of London University.

On his return to Kenya, he was appointed a director of the Bureau of African Affairs in Accra, where he remained until 1961. In 1963, he was given the portfolio of Minister of State for Pan-African Affairs.

In 1965 he moved over to Education, and became Minister

of State for Foreign Affairs in 1966. He has held the post of secretary-general of the Pan-African Freedom Movement of Eastern, Central and Southern Africa.

MALCOLM MACDONALD
When Malcolm MacDonald was appointed Britain's Special Representative in East and Central Africa based in Nairobi, in October, 1965, he had already had a very distinguished career in the Commonwealth.

He had been British High Commissioner in Canada and India, Governor-General of Malaya and British Borneo, and Commissioner-General for Britain in South East Asia.

He represented Britain in Kenya during its transition from colonial status to independence and finally to a republic.

His connection with Kenya began in 1963, when he was appointed Governor and Commander-in-Chief. After independence in December, 1963, he became Governor-General. When Kenya became a republic, the appointment ceased to exist. He returned early in 1965 as British High Commissioner. Later that year he was made Special Representative, a new diplomatic post.

Malcolm MacDonald was born in 1901, the second son of Ramsay MacDonald, Britain's first Labour Prime Minister.

His book *Treasure of Kenya*, an illustrated record of his observations of wild life in Kenya, was published in 1966.

THOMAS JOSEPH MBOYA
Tom Mboya has played a major role in the labour, political, constitutional and economic life of Kenya. He has held responsible posts on African liberation organi-

Daniel Moi

sations and pan-African bodies, has travelled widely, and represented Kenya at world, Commonwealth and African conferences.

Born of Luo parents on Lusinga island, Lake Victoria, in 1930, he began a course in sanitary inspection in 1948, and three years later, went to work in Nairobi.

He helped to establish the Kenya Local Government Workers Union in 1952, and a year later, was elected secretary of the Kenya Federation of Labour.

In March, 1957, he was elected a member of the Legislative Council, and in the general elections of 1961, was returned for Nairobi South. In the Coalition Government of 1962, he was Minister of Labour. The following year, in the elections for the self-governing regime which preceded independence, he was elected member for Nairobi Central.

On independence, he was Minister for Justice and Constitutional Affairs. When Kenya became a republic in December, 1964, he was made Minister for Economic Planning and Development.

Mboya was appointed secretary-general of the Kenya African National Union on its formation in 1960. He was re-elected at the 1966 party conference.

His wife, Pamela, plays an important role in women's welfare and social activities.

BRUCE ROY McKENZIE

Bruce Roy McKenzie, the only white man in the Kenya Cabinet, arrived in the country in 1946, took some undeveloped land near Nakuru, and built up one of the best farms in the Rift Valley.

Tall, portly, and with a large moustache, he was born at Richmond, Natal, in 1919, and was educated at Hilton College in South Africa, subsequently studying agriculture.

At the outbreak of World War II, he joined the South African Air Force, and was seconded to Britain's Royal Air Force for the duration of hostilities. At the age of 24 he attained the SAAF rank of colonel. He was awarded the DSO and DFC and bar.

He became a member of the Legislative Council in 1957, and was appointed Minister for Agriculture, Animal Husbandry and Water Resources in 1959. He resigned in 1961, however, in order to join KANU.

In the General Election that year, he was elected a national member of the Legislative Council, and later rose to become Minister for Agriculture in the KANU Shadow Cabinet.

He served as Minister for Land Settlement and Water Development in the Coalition Government of 1962. In June, 1963, he was appointed Minister for Agriculture.

DANIEL MOI

Daniel Torotich Arap Moi was appointed Vice-President of Kenya in January, 1967, in succession to Joseph Murumbi, who had resigned to take up a business career.

Moi, who was born at Baringo, north-west Kenya in 1924, was appointed Minister for Home Affairs in 1964, when the then Opposition party KADU was voluntarily dissolved and he joined the ruling party, KANU. Together with the vice-presidency, he continues to hold the Home Affairs portfolio.

He was formerly a teacher. He was appointed Minister of Education in 1962 and later Minister for Local Government. After the

Dr Njoroge Mungai

KANU Government came into power in 1963 he acted as shadow Minister for Agriculture in the Opposition.

DR NJOROGE MUNGAI

Dr Njoroge Mungai, appointed Minister for Defence in 1964, is a Kikuyu, born at Dagoretti, near Nairobi, in 1926.

He took his BSc at Fort Hare University, South Africa, and his BA and MD at Stanford University, California. He completed his studies at Columbia University in 1959.

On his return to Kenya he practised medicine, founding the Riruta Clinic, Nairobi, and the Thika Maternity Hospital.

He was elected to the House of Representatives in 1963 as member for Nairobi West, and was appointed Minister for Health and Housing.

JOSEPH MURUMBI

Joseph Anthony Zuzarte Murumbi, Kenya's Vice-President from May to December, 1966, resigned to join a tobacco enterprise in East Africa.

Son of a Masai woman and a Goan father, Murumbi was born in Kenya in 1911. At the age of six he went to India for his primary and secondary education, and returned to Kenya in 1934 after completing the courses at high schools in Bangalore and Bellary in South India.

In 1941 he joined the British military administration in Somalia, and served in this capacity for ten years. In 1951 he went to England, and was assistant secretary in the Movement for Colonial Freedom until 1957. He returned to Kenya in 1962 and became KANU ruling party treasurer. He was returned as MP for Nairobi South in the 1963 elections, and was Minister of

State in Kenyatta's first Cabinet of independent Kenya.

A year later, he was appointed Foreign Minister. In this capacity Murumbi represented Kenya in a number of Organisations of African Unity (OAU), ministerial and summit sessions, and United Nations' and Commonwealth leaders' conferences.

Following the resignation of Mr Oginga Odinga from the vice-presidency in April, 1966, Murumbi was appointed Vice-President.

Under Kenya law, the post of President is not automatically taken over by the Vice-President.

A keen collector of works of art and antiques, Mr Murumbi is also known to possess a fine collection of books on Africa. His wife Sheila is English.

DAWSON MWANYUMBA

Dawson Mwanyumba was appointed Minister of Works, Communications and Power in 1963; the Ministry was subsequently split, leaving him with the Works portfolio.

A member of the Taita tribe, he was born in 1928, and took a diploma in education at Makerere University, Kampala, in Uganda.

He started his career as a teacher, but abandoned it after a few years in favour of business.

He settled in the Taita District, between Nairobi and the coast, and became chairman of the Taita Cooperative Society and president of the Taita African District Council.

Elected to the Legislative Council in 1961, his first appointment was Parliamentary Secretary to the Ministry of Agriculture in the Coalition Government.

He has visited Britain, the USA, Israel, East and West Europe and the USSR.

Eluid Mwendwa

Ronald Ngala

E. N. MWENDWA

Eluid Ngala Mwendwa, a Mkamba, was made Minister for Power and Communications in 1966.

A teacher by profession, he was born in 1924 in Kitui district, and educated at Alliance High School and Kagumo College.

He was elected to the Legislative Council in 1961, and took over the portfolio of Health and Housing in the Coalition Government. In 1963, he was appointed Minister for Labour and Social Services.

M. K. MWENDWA

Maluki Kitili Mwendwa, Solicitor-General of Kenya (1964), was born in 1929, in Kitui, the son of a senior chief. He was educated at Alliance High School and Makerere College before going to London, Exeter and Oxford Universities for his BA and MA degrees.

He was called to the Bar at Lincoln's Inn in 1960, and appointed an Assistant Secretary in the Ministry of Commerce and Industry in 1962. He filled several senior positions in the Kenya Civil Service before being appointed Solicitor-General.

D. N. NDEGWA

Duncan Nderitu Ndegwa is head of the Kenya Civil Service and holds the appointments of Permanent Secretary, Office of the President, and Secretary to the Cabinet.

Born at Nyeri in 1925, he was educated at Alliance High School and Makerere College, where he received a teaching diploma. After teaching for five years, he was awarded a bursary to St Andrew's University, Scotland, where he received an MA degree.

He has previously acted as Assistant Secretary and Under Secretary in the Treasury, and Permanent Secretary to the Ministry of Finance.

BRIGADIER J. M. L. NDOLO

Brigadier J. M. L. Ndolo, first African Commander of the Kenya Army, was appointed on November 1, 1966, and took over command a month later, with the rank of Brigadier.

He succeeded British Brigadier A. J. Hardy, whose tour of duty was ending. President Kenyatta said Kenya's Army had benefited a great deal from Brigadier Hardy's services. He had maintained a high degree of professional discipline and loyalty within the Army. Since independence, President Kenyatta added, he had been responsible for the expansion and modernisation of the Army.

Brigadier Ndolo began his army career in 1939, and did war service in Burma. He became second-in-command under Brigadier Hardy, with the rank of lieutenant-colonel, in December, 1964.

When he took command, the Navy and Air Force were still under the command of British officers, with President Kenyatta as commander-in-chief of all the Armed Forces.

RONALD GIDEON NGALA

Ronald Gideon Ngala was leader of the Parliamentary Opposition to Kenyatta when he dissolved his party, of which he was the founder, in the interests of national unity.

Born at Kilifi, on the Coast, in 1923, Ngala was educated at the Alliance High School and Makerere College in Uganda. He began teaching in 1949, and became a headmaster in 1955. He served as Supervisor of Schools between 1957–58.

Charles Njonjo

Elected to the Legislative Council in 1958 to represent Coast Rural, he became Minister of Labour, Social Security and Adult Education, and later, Minister for Education and Minister of State for Constitutional Affairs.

He formed and became president of the Kenya African Democratic Union, and was returned as KADU member for Kilifi in the 1963 elections. In the House he was leader of the Opposition against Mr Kenyatta's KANU Government.

During the London Constitutional Conference of September–October, 1963, he defended his thesis of regionalism in a prolonged series of meetings at which Mr Kenyatta led the Government delegation discussing the independence constitution of Kenya.

Mr Ngala continued as leader of the Opposition until November, 1964, when he dissolved his party, crossed the floor amid joyous excitement and joined the ranks of the ruling party.

He was appointed chairman of the Maize Marketing Board, and in May, 1966, was made Minister of Cooperatives and Social Services.

Mr Ngala has shown keen interest in the development of sport in a country which has scored spectacular successes at international meetings.

PAUL NGEI

Paul Ngei was arrested with Jomo Kenyatta in 1952, charged with being associated with Mau Mau, convicted, and imprisoned until 1961.

After a further period of restriction he was released in 1962, and joined the executive of KANU. The same year he founded and became first president of the African People's Party (APP), and was elected to the House of Representatives in 1963 as the APP member for Machakos North.

He subsequently rejoined KANU and was appointed chairman of the Maize Marketing Board in 1963, and Minister for Cooperatives and Marketing in 1964. In 1965 he was given the portfolio of Housing and Social Services, but was suspended in February, 1966, during a Government inquiry into the maize shortage of 1955. He was reinstated as Housing Minister in May, 1966.

A Mkamba, Ngei was born in Machakos in 1923, a grandson of Paramount Chief Masaku. He was educated at Alliance High School, Kikuyu, and Makerere College, Uganda. In the course of his career, he has been a journalist and a film-actor. He had a part in the film *Where No Vultures Fly*.

His chief interest, however, has been politics. He became branch secretary of the Kenya African Union (KAU) in Machakos, in 1945, and was subsequently appointed national deputy general-secretary in 1951.

CHARLES NJONJO

Charles Njonjo became Attorney-General of Kenya in 1963.

A Kikuyu, born in 1920, the son of ex-Senior Chief Josiah Njonjo, he was educated at Alliance High School, Kikuyu, Fort Hare University, South Africa, and the London School of Economics. He holds a BA degree and a diploma in anthropology.

He was called to the Bar (Gray's Inn) in London in 1954 and joined the Kenya Government service in 1955. He acted as Senior Crown Counsel in 1961,

J. J. M. Nyagah

James Nyamweya

Oginga Odinga

and was appointed Deputy Public Prosecutor in 1962.

He is an ex-officio member of the House of Representatives, and a member of the Cabinet.

J. J. M. NYAGAH

Jeremiah Joseph Mwaniki Nyagah became Minister for Education in 1966.

Born in 1920, of Embu parentage, he is a teacher by profession, with an educational background of Alliance High School and Makerere College in Uganda. After twelve years in teaching posts and as an education officer, he was elected to the Legislative Council in 1958, and appointed Deputy Speaker two years later.

In 1963, he entered the House of Representatives as KANU member for Embu South. Prior to being appointed Minister for Education, he held the posts of Parliamentary Secretary to the Ministry of Works, Parliamentary Secretary to the Ministry of Lands and Settlement, and Assistant Minister for Home Affairs.

JAMES NYAMWEYA

James Nyamweya was appointed Minister of State in charge of Foreign Affairs, resposible to President Kenyatta in January, 1967. He belongs to the Kisii tribe and was born in 1927.

He is an LLB of King's College, University of London (1954–58) and a barrister-at-law of Lincoln's Inn. He had been a teacher and was practising law in Kenya when elected to the House of Representatives in 1963.

During the crucial period 1963–64, when Kenya became independent and later a republic, he was Parliamentary Secretary to the Ministry of Justice and Constitutional Affairs.

He then became Parliamentary

Secretary to the Prime Minister (before Kenya became a republic in December, 1964), and Assistant Minister to the President.

He is a leading member of the ruling KANU party.

AJUMA OGINGA ODINGA

Ajuma Oginga Odinga began his political career as a close colleague of Jomo Kenyatta, but became leader of the Opposition in Parliament.

A leading Luo tribesman, it was Odinga who first recruited Luo support for the Kenya African Union when Jomo Kenyatta organised it in 1946, mainly as a Kikuyu movement. At independence in December, 1963, Odinga was one of several Luo Cabinet Ministers; he was given the portfolio of Home Affairs.

When Kenya became a republic a year later, Odinga was made Vice-President. From this office he resigned in April, 1966, accusing his Cabinet colleagues of acting against him. Within a month, he became president of a new political grouping, the Kenya People's Union.

In a policy statement, he denounced what he called the KANU Government's 'capitalistic policies', accusing them of neglecting African traditions and calling for a more equitable distribution of land.

The Government rebutted these accusations, and charged Mr Odinga with association with Communist countries. His 'free land' policy was denounced as impracticable.

Odinga had support from 29 Members of Parliament, who resigned from KANU, leading to a special election in the constituencies concerned. KANU candidates won the majority of these seats, giving KANU 121

223

James Osogo

Joseph Otiende

seats in the House of Representatives against seven KPU, and 39 seats against two in the Senate.

Born in 1912, Odinga was educated at Makerere College, Uganda, where he obtained a diploma in education. He taught for two years then turned to business and politics.

THOMAS OKELO-ODONGO

One of the leaders of the Opposition and a close associate of Mr Odinga, Thomas Okelo-Odongo is a Luo born at Kisumu in 1927.

He was educated in Kisumu and subsequently at Bharati University, India, and Howard University, USA. He obtained the degrees of BA, BEd and MA.

In 1958, he was appointed lecturer in Swahili at Howard University. He then spent two years as research assistant at the School of Oriental and African Studies in London. Returning to Kenya, he founded Lakeside College, Kisumu.

In 1963, he joined the House of Representatives as KANU Member for Kisumu Rural. He was appointed Parliamentary Secretary to the Ministry of Finance and subsequently, Assistant Minister for Finance. He resigned in support of Mr Odinga in April, 1966, and followed the latter across the floor, returning to the House as Kenya People's Union (KPU) member for Kisumu Rural.

DUNSTAN ALFRED OMARI

The East African Common Services Organisation (EASCO), with headquarters in Nairobi, administers 23 services shared by Kenya, Tanzania and Uganda. These include transport, railways, harbours, post offices, income tax, customs, air services, medicine, technology and law.

The Secretary-General, appointed in 1964, is Dunstan Alfred Omari, formerly High Commissioner for Tanganyika in London (1961–62) and Permanent Secretary in the President's Office.

He was born in 1922 at Newala, Tanzania, educated at St Joseph's Secondary School, Masasi, St Andrew's College, Minaki, and Makere College, where he obtained his diploma in education. He went to the University of Wales for his BA in economics.

J. C. OSOGO

James Charles Osogo was appointed Minister for Information and Broadcasting in 1966.

Born in 1932, of Luhya parents, he was educated at St Mary's, Yala, the Railway Training School and Kagumo Teacher Training College.

He taught from 1955–63, during which time he became vice-chairman of the Kenya National Union of Teachers. In 1961 he was elected to the House of Representatives as KANU member for Ruwamba.

He became Parliamentary Secretary to the Ministry of Agriculture and Animal Husbandry in 1963, and Assistant Minister of Agriculture in 1964.

JOSEPH DANIEL OTIENDE

Joseph Daniel Otiende became a member of the Central Legislative Assembly in 1962, and Minister of Health in 1964.

Born at Kegoye village in South Maragoli in 1917, he won a teaching diploma at Makere College. He was a teacher from 1937 until 1948, but all the time his interest in politics was growing.

In 1949, he joined the North Nyanza African District Council, and in 1951, became general

Dr Arthur Porter

secretary to the Kenya African Union. He left this post in 1952, and spent the next three years in comparative obscurity.

He re-emerged in 1955, and became assistant secretary to the North Nyanza African District Council.

From 1963–64 he served as Minister for Education.

SIR EBOO PIRBHAI

Sir Eboo Pirbhai is the representative in Africa of the Aga Khan. Born in 1905, he was educated at the Duke of Gloucester School, Nairobi.

President of the Aga Khan Supreme Council of Africa, and president of the Central Muslim Association, he is one of the most prominent of Kenya's estimated 188,000 Asians.

DR ARTHUR T. PORTER

University College, Nairobi, is a constituent college of the University of East Africa, the others being Makerere University College, Kampala, Uganda, and the University College, Dar es Salaam, Tanzania.

The students – admitted regardless of colour or creed – have increased from about 620 in 1964 to about 1,150 in the 1966–67 academic year.

The Principal is Dr Arthur T. Porter, a Sierra Leonian. He was born in 1924. After secondary education in Sierra Leone, he went to Fourah Bay College, where he obtained the BA of Durham University, England, in 1944. He also holds a BA in history (1950) and an MA (1953) from Cambridge University, a post-graduate certificate in education from the Institute of Education at London University, and a PhD (1959) from Boston University, USA.

He spent a year in the Depart-ment of Social Anthropology at Edinburgh University (1951–52) before returning to Fourah Bay College as a lecturer in history. He did two years (1956–58) of research in African studies at Boston University before being elected to the chair of modern history at Fourah Bay. He was vice-principal there (1960–64), then accepted the post in Nairobi.

LAWRENCE GEORGE SAGINI

Lawrence George Sagini, Minister for Local Government (1965), is from Kisii.

Born in 1926, he was educated at the Holy Ghost College, Mangu, in Kiambu district, and won a teaching diploma at Kagumo Teacher Training College, Nyeri. After several years of teaching, he went to the USA and took a BA in sociology and political science.

On his return, he was appointed Education Officer by the Kenya Government. In 1961, he was elected member for Kisii on the KANU Legislative Council. He became Minister for Education in the Coalition Government. In 1963, he was appointed Minister for Natural Resources, and in 1965, Minister for Local Government.

HUMPHREY SLADE

Humphrey Slade, who became Speaker of the House of Representatives in Nairobi in 1963, was born in London in 1905.

Educated at Eton and Oxford, and a barrister-at-law of Lincoln's Inn, he went to Kenya in 1930. From 1939–41, he was Deputy Judge Advocate General, East Africa.

He is also a farmer, and for several years ran a farm in the North Kinangop. In 1958 he became a member of the Legislative Council, and in 1960, was appointed Speaker.

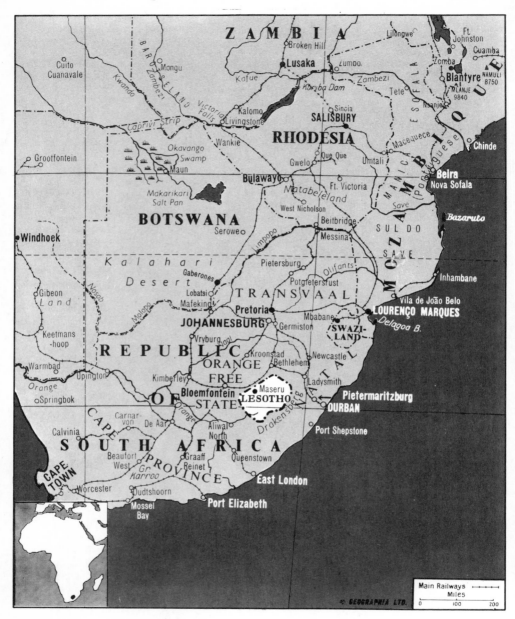

Lesotho, the former Basutoland, covers an area of 11,716 square miles and is wholly surrounded by the Republic of South Africa. The estimated population in 1960 was 888,258. The capital is Maseru.

Lesotho is a pastoral country, without factories or industrial undertakings. Agricultural production is insufficient to feed even the small population. Exports, comprising wool, mohair and cattle, do not bring in enough money to pay for imports. 200,000 men go to work each year in the mines of the South African Republic and the wages they send back are counted part of the national economy.

Lesotho

Basutoland became the independent Kingdom of Lesotho on October 4, 1966, after 82 years of British colonial rule. King Moshoeshoe II, the young hereditary ruler, began a campaign to recover some of the sweeping powers Moshoeshoe I lost during the last century in return for British protection.

What he asked for would have made him virtually an absolute monarch, with control over the armed forces, the police and his country's foreign policy.

Two Opposition parties giving him support were accused by Chief Leabua Jonathan, the Prime Minister, of plotting to overthrow the Government by force.

On January 5, 1967, following riots and ten days under house arrest, Moshoeshoe agreed to be a constitutional monarch.

Chief Jonathan heads Lesotho's Cabinet. There are two Houses of Parliament—a National Assembly of 60 members elected by universal suffrage, and a Senate consisting of 22 principal chiefs and eleven other persons nominated by the King.

Basutoland was the twelfth British dependency to become independent. It followed Ghana, Nigeria, Sierra Leone, Tanganyika, Uganda, Zanzibar (now united with Tanganyika), Kenya, Malawi, Zambia, the Gambia and Botswana (Bechuanaland).

A small, mountainous enclave set in the Republic of South Africa, it is picturesque but impoverished, and economically ill-prepared for viable independence. But its future as a nation may not be quite so gloomy as would appear.

South Africa is the principal customer for Lesotho's exports and its main supplier. It has a customs union with South Africa and uses South African currency. Any Lesotho leader struggling to solve problems of poverty, hunger, lack of industry, trained personnel and equipment always remembers, whatever his views on the racial policy of South Africa, that the kingdom is a dependent black island within a white-dominated country.

Chief Leabua Jonathan, a former tradesman who became the kingdom's first Prime Minister, has already shown a deep awareness of this situation, despite his declared dislike of *apartheid* (separation of races according to colour). 'Everything we have and do,' he declared late in 1966, 'depends on South Africa. Even the water and milk supply for Maseru depends on the republic.' (Maseru lies only a mile from the South African border.) Britain continues to give financial aid to Lesotho and international organisations are assisting with food and technicians. Lesotho's main export are 200,000 of her most able-bodied men who go to South Africa every year to work in the gold mines and elsewhere. The earnings they send back to their families are an important part of the country's economy. There is virtually no industry. There are problems of rail and road transport. There are no tarred roads outside the capital.

A great unexploited asset is the water of the many major rivers of southern Africa which rise in the mountains. Financial support from South Africa is extremely important in the development of this and other potential resources. For several years, ambitious plans have existed to build a dam in a narrow gorge high up in the Maluti. The Basuto name for the gorge means Oxbow – from which the project has taken its name, the Oxbow Scheme. If this project materialises, both water and hydro-electric power could be sold to South Africa, which needs the water. But Lesotho's financial resources are too limited to permit her to develop the scheme alone.

The land in Lesotho is held in trust for the nation by the Paramount Chief and may not be alienated. The main crops are wheat, maize and sorghum. Soil erosion is a problem and a large area has been protected against this by means of terracing, training banks and grass strips. There are large quantities of cattle.

The people of Basutoland were welded into a nation by Chief Moshesh, a minor chief from the north, who in 1818 gathered together the remnants of various tribes who had been scattered by the raids of the Zulu and Matabele. The new nation passed through many troubles, first with the emigrant Boers on the Great Trek, then with the British. Border wars with the burghers of the Orange Free State (1856–68) resulted in a great loss of territory and Moshesh, first to become Paramount Chief, repeatedly appealed to Britain for protection. This was given and in 1868 the people and territory were recognised as British. Remaining unsettled, however, the territory was annexed to Cape Colony in 1871. In 1884, after many disturbances,

Chief Johnathan
greeted by tribesmen
during a tour of
outlying villages
hard-hit by snow and
extreme cold.

it was restored to the direct control of the British
Government and was administered thereafter through the
High Commissioner for South Africa.

South Africa's Act of Union in 1909 included provisions for
the possible inclusion of Basutoland, Bechuanaland and
Swaziland, all administered by the British High
Commissioner for South Africa. But when the South
African constitution was being drawn up, the chiefs in
the three territories objected to any proposals which
would mean coming under the rule of South Africa.
Successive South African Governments, in the years
following 1909, asked for the three countries to be
transferred to them, but successive British Governments
reiterated a pledge that no such transfer could take
place until the wishes of the inhabitants had been
considered.

Unlike Botswana, Lesotho is not blessed with political
stability. Chief Jonathan's Government had an overall
majority of two in the National Assembly (60 seats) in
October, 1966, when the first sitting after independence
was held. He was faced by a vigorous pan-Africanist
Opposition Congress Party, whose main purpose seemed
to be to exploit the innate dislike of many Basuto at being
forced to cooperate with South Africa.

The Congress Party had previously attacked Chief
Jonathan for his readiness to cooperate with South
Africa. The Prime Minister had replied that Lesotho's
geographical position made such cooperation inescapable.

229

Chief Jonathan

CHIEF LEABUA JONATHAN

To many of the people of Lesotho the big, beaming Chief Leabua Jonathan is a kind of saviour who could lead them from desperate poverty to work, comfort and dignity.

He became Prime Minister as a result of the 1965 general elections. His party, given little chance at the start, won with a narrow two-seat majority. While the crowd were cheering he may have recalled that he might never have entered politics but for advice given to him by one of the British administrators when Lesotho was still Basutoland, a British colony.

As the country's most dominating political personality, he has naturally had many foes. Loved by his admirers, he has been reviled by his enemies as a buffoon and a traitor to his race.

He shrugs off the epithets, some of the worst one African could use to another, like a true veteran of 30 years in the rough and tumble of local politics.

Born in 1914, he went to a mission school at Leribe, then off to work, at 17, in the gold mines along the famous 'reef' in South Africa, just as thousands of young Basuto do today.

He was the son of a chief, and after he had been only four years in the gold mines he was recalled to help an uncle, also a chief, with his administrative duties. He had a long and arduous training which is the heritage of many African 'royals'. Any skill in the art of government which he possesses today he attributes in large measure to those early days.

He makes no secret about his lack of formal education, thus disarming his critics in the Opposition Basutoland Congress Party to which most of Lesotho's intelli-

gentsia belong. After winning the pre-independence elections last year, Chief Jonathan told a press conference, 'I haven't got degrees like those fellows in the Opposition. I only made standard six – but I became Prime Minister.'

The English advice to enter politics was in 1951. About eight years had rolled by before he formed his own Basutoland National Party—the first Opposition to the previously all-powerful Basutoland Congress Party. His slogan for combating their pan-Africanist line was, 'Bread and butter politics and a good neighbour policy towards South Africa.'

He lost the local government elections seven months later, but he persevered with his slogan. The 'good neighbour' part began to find favour with the Basuto men who worked in the South African mines, and to women who did not understand the pan-Africanist ideology his bread and butter cry made good sense.

The general election result spoke for itself. The Basuto boy from the South African gold mines had finally succeeded.

The task before him as Prime Minister was enough to daunt anyone – to lead to nationhood a country about as poor as a country could be. In an independence broadcast to his people he said simply, 'Let us go to work immediately to build a more prosperous country. Let us face the future with courage.'

DR SETH MAKOTOKO

Dr Seth Peete Makotoko, leader of Lesotho's royalist Marematlou Freedom Party (MFP), is a tall, suave, soft-spoken medical practicioner who has diverted his talents from medicine to politics.

Generally regarded as a political 'babe-in-the-wood', his venture out of the medical world had brought him to the brink of political annihilation by the latter part of 1966.

He saw his party, which enjoys the support of King Moshoeshoe II, relegated from the position of leading contender in the ruling stakes to that of a minority in the country's new National Assembly.

A political murder in 1965, which was laid at the door of the MFP, led to the defection of thousands of supporters at a time when the party was strong favourite to win the pre-independence general elections.

Dr Makotoko regained some of his prestige after the elections by being chosen first President of the Senate. But, a year later, he drew upon himself the wrath of most members of the Upper House during a constitutional wrangle, and was voted out of office.

Dr Makotoko was born in a northern Lesotho village on August 6, 1925. He received his elementary education at Roman Catholic missions there and went to the South African non-white University College of Fort Hare to study science. In 1948 he enrolled at the University of the Witwatersrand, Johannesburg, to study medicine.

While in South Africa he became disturbed at the inferior position of the black man and the seeds of his political interest were sown.

By 1955 the newly-qualified doctor was back in Lesotho, then the British colony of Basutoland, as a government medical officer. He left the service in 1962 to enter politics and gather support for his newly-formed movement, the Marematlou Freedom Party.

CHIEF SEKHONYANE MASERIBANE

Lesotho's Deputy Prime Minister, Chief Sekhonyane Maseribane, a descendant of the legendary King Moshesh, who founded the Basotho nation, is the third member of a triumvirate of royal sons who rule the Kingdom of Lesotho.

The traditional head of the triumvirate is King Moshoeshoe II, constitutional monarch. The Prime Minister, Chief Leabua Jonathan, is a cousin of both the King and of Chief Maseribane.

A forceful, stocky man, Chief Maseribane is Minister of Home Affairs in the Jonathan administration.

He had the distinction of being the country's first Prime Minister, a post he held briefly in a caretaker capacity after the April, 1965 general elections when Chief Jonathan was defeated at the polls. After Chief Jonathan won a by-election, Chief Maseribane stepped down and was named Deputy Prime Minister.

Chief Maseribane is a stern defender of the system of chieftainship. In the struggle between the Prime Minister and the King over the monarch's constitutional position, he sided with the Premier on the grounds that the King was endangering the system in the long term.

He has a powerful presence in Parliament and dominates debates with his deep bass voice.

A well-travelled man, he has extensive business interests and is devoted to charitable work.

Chief Maseribane was born on May 4, 1918, of the Lesotho royal family at Mount Moorosi in the southern lowlands.

He received his secondary education at Roman Catholic schools and went to work in South Africa as a medical assistant at a labourers' compound.

231

Ntsu Mokhehle

In 1946 he succeeded to the chieftainship of the Maseribanes and a year later was appointed president of the Tribal Court. Later he was named an Assessor of the High Court.

Chief Maseribane is married and his wife – herself the daughter of a chief – has helped him build up a small business empire consisting of a group of general trading stores and a bus service.

NTSU MOKHEHLE

The leader of the Parliamentary Opposition in Lesotho, Ntsu Mokhehle is an ardent disciple of pan-Africanism who propagates his beliefs in the heart of that doctrine's greatest enemy – the Republic of South Africa.

A fervent admirer of the former President of Ghana, Dr Kwame Nkrumah, Mr Mokhehle has organised his Basutoland Congress Party along classic pan-Africanist lines, complete with a militant youth wing.

In a party which has attracted the cream of the country's intelligentsia, Mokhehle – himself a talented scientist – is perhaps the hardest-hitting and most penetrating debater.

Physically imposing, the burly, bespectacled Mokhehle is invariably the cynosure of all eyes when he is in Parliament, whether speaking or merely sitting in his bench, where he glowers at the Government benches and the public gallery alike with what has been called a Mephistophelean air.

Born in December, 1918, he is the son of a sheep farmer. After receiving primary education, he went to a secondary school in the Eastern Cape Province of South Africa.

During this time he showed considerable aptitude for writing articles for a now defunct Basutoland newspaper, *The Comet*, about the hardships Africans endured.

In 1942, while studying for a science degree, he was expelled from Fort Hare University College, South Africa, for political activities and joined the first Basuto national movement, known as the League of the Common Man. Two years later he returned to Fort Hare and obtained the degree of Master of Science in zoology.

By now he had become an active member of the since banned African National Congress Youth League in South Africa. In 1949 he obtained his education diploma and in the following year returned to Basutoland to take up a teaching post. Six years later he was named principal of the Maseru Higher Primary School.

Mokhehle's political activities increased in tempo during the next five years and, heading a strong Opposition, he has become a thorn in the side of the ruling Basutoland National Party.

Should he come one day to power, Mokhehle might be a thorn in the side of the South African Government with his violently anti-*apartheid* views, for which the Pretoria Government has declared him a banned person, in an effort to limit his field of influence.

KING MOSHOESHOE II

Paramount Chief Motlotlehi Moshoeshoe, who became King Moshoeshoe II, was born Prince Constantine Bereng Seeiso on May 2, 1938.

A descendant of Moshesh, 19th century founder of the Basuto nation, he is a tall, aristocratic-looking, Oxford-educated Roman Catholic. He is shy and reserved and dislikes public ceremonial.

He succeeded to the throne at

King Moshoeshoe II

the age of two, on the death of his father, Chief Simeon Seeiso Griffith. He was brought up by his royal uncles and went to a preparatory school with boys who would one day be his subjects. Then, in anticipation of his future role as king, he was sent to be educated in England. He spent two years, from 1954–56, at Ampleforth–a British public school run by Benedictine monks –then went to Oxford University to study politics and economics.

He cut short his studies to take over, in 1960, the throne which had been waiting for him. His stepmother, Princess Mantsebo Seeiso, aged 56, had ruled as regent for 20 years. In vain she tried to persuade him to postpone his enthronement until he had taken his degree and married. But Moshoeshoe was anxious to get into the saddle and regain some of the powers which Moshoeshoe I had relinquished during the 19th century in return for British protection.

When colonial rule ended (October 4, 1966) the new king took an oath to govern according to the constitutional instruments handed to him by Princess Marina, aunt of Queen Elizabeth of England. He had earlier expressed strong displeasure with the constitution and demanded sweeping executive powers for himself instead of his role as a rubber stamp monarch.

He agreed with Princess Marina that there would be stresses and strains in the future, but promised they should do their best 'in all humility and honesty' to solve them.

King Moshoeshoe ignored warnings from Chief Jonathan to keep out of politics. On December 27, 1966, eight people died in riots at the scene of a rally organised by two Opposition parties which Chief Jonathan had accused of plotting with the monarch to overthrow the Government by violence.

Moshoeshoe was kept under house arrest for ten days at his little red brick palace. On January 5, 1967, he agreed to rule constitutionally in future. He signed an agreement providing for automatic abdication if he failed to so so. A government statement said the young king's actions and movements would be controlled. Among the signatories of the document were 22 principal chiefs who have the power to dethrone the king under tribal law.

King Moshoeshoe is married to a Basuto princess, Tabitha Masentle, who studied domestic science in England. Following Basuto tradition he paid for her a bridal price of 40 head of cattle and the tribesmen feasted for three whole days on 100 roasted oxen and large quantities of home-brewed beer.

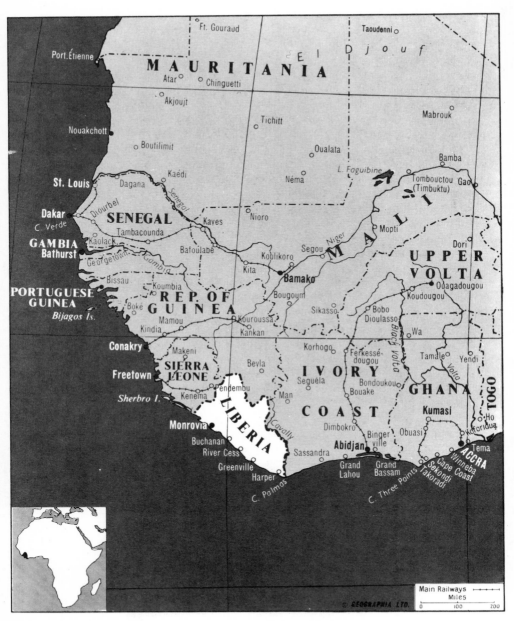

Main Railways +—+—+
Miles
0   100   200

© GEOGRAPHIA LTD.

Liberia's 350-mile coastline
connects Sierra Leone on the
west and the Ivory Coast on
the east. Guinea lies to the
north. The total area is about
43,000 square miles; the population approximately 1,000,000.

The capital is Monrovia.
The opening of the Free Port
of Monrovia in 1948 brought
great economic improvement
to the country.
Liberia's main exports are iron
ore and rubber, which account

for a substantial proportion of
the national revenue. Other
exports include rough diamonds
(about $20m worth a year),
coffee, palm kernels, piassava
fibre, cocoa and cola nuts.

234

Liberia

The Republic of Liberia was originated by American
philanthropists wishing to evangelise West Africa and
find a permanent home for free American Negroes. The
first settlement was formed near where Monrovia now
stands in 1818.
Independence as a republic came on July 26, 1847.
Under the constitution, modelled on that of the USA,
executive power is vested in a President and Cabinet and
legislative power in two Houses, the Senate and the
House of Representatives.
President William V. S. Tubman has been President since
May 6, 1943, re-elected in 1951, 1955, 1959 and 1963.

Few countries in the world can claim greater stability and
continuity of government than the small West African
state of Liberia – the first independent Republic in Africa.
Founded by Negro immigrants from the United States
and the West Indies, who began re-settling on the
continent of their ancestors from 1818 onwards, Liberia
declared its independence in 1847, and its Republican
constitution has been in force for 120 years. The ruling
True Whig party has been continuously in power for over
90 years, although a number of challengers have appeared
on the political scene from time to time and have fought
elections.
The only successful *coup* in the history of the country
occurred in October, 1871, when President Edward
James Roye was ousted and arrested by revolutionaries
after returning from a visit to Britain. But his party, the
True Whigs, returned to power a few years later.
The descendants of the early immigrants from the New
World have now mixed to a large extent with the
indigenous population of over a million, and nearly all
the leading families are of mixed ancestry. The newcomers,
however, imparted to the majority of the tribal
population their Christian faith and ways of life.
The capital city of Monrovia (named after President
James Monroe of the United States) has a population of
about 80,000 with some 100 churches of all Christian
denominations as well as a mosque.
The official language is English, but as many as
20 vernacular dialects are spoken, mainly in the
countryside. A large proportion of the educated class was
trained in the United States or Britain, although the

Graduation ceremony
at the University of
Liberia

University of Liberia, which has been in existence for
about 30 years, turns out growing numbers of graduates.
The Government is divided into three distinct branches –
Legislative, Executive and Judicial.

The members of the Senate and the House of
Representatives are elected directly by universal suffrage.
Each of the nine administrative counties returns two
senators for a term of six years, while members of the
House of Representatives are elected for a term of four
years on the basis of one representative for every
10,000 voters.

Until 1964, the country was divided into five counties, all
situated along the Atlantic coast, and three inland
provinces inhabited predominantly by indigenous tribes
and administered by appointed district commissioners in
cooperation with tribal authorities. During President
Tubman's first term of office, however, the provinces
began to be represented in the Legislature, and in 1964
they were turned into four counties, thus acquiring equal
status with the five coastal counties.

The President is elected by popular vote for an initial
period of eight years and can be re-elected for terms of
four years. He appoints the members of his Cabinet
(Secretaries) and senior Government officials. He is also
commander-in-chief of the armed forces. Under

Anti-malaria sprays being used on village houses

President Tubman's 22 year-old Administration, the office of the Chief Executive acquired an unprecedented prestige, becoming the nerve centre of the country.
The Judiciary consists of a five-member Supreme Court, headed by a Chief Justice, as well as Circuit Courts, Probate Courts and various subordinate courts with limited jurisdiction.
Economically, the country is firmly attached to the principles of liberalism and free enterprise. The official currency is the US dollar, and the country has never known any form of foreign exchange or trade controls. Imports from all countries are subject to identical duty and there are no preferential tariffs.
The value of Liberia's foreign trade increased from US $15 million in 1945 to over $250 million in 1966, while Government revenue rocketed during the same period from about $2m to some $50m. The balance of trade has been almost consistently favourable until 1962, with a surplus reaching $35m in 1951. In 1962 a sharp drop in world rubber and ore prices, combined with heavy investments in the mining industry and in building schemes, resulted in a deficit of $64.8m as against a surplus of $28.8m in the previous year. The gap was narrowed to $27m in 1963, $25m in 1964, and was expected to be closed in 1966.

237

An aerial view of
Monrovia

In spite of drastic austerity measures, the Liberian
Government found itself in financial difficulty at the
beginning of 1964, when it had to request a re-scheduling
of payments on medium term credits and to seek the
assistance of the International Monetary Fund.

In the '60s the rate of growth of the economy has been of
the order of five per cent per annum – one of the highest
in the world.

The opening of the Free Port of Monrovia in July, 1948,
was a turning point in the development of the country.
Until then, ships had to anchor offshore and goods were
landed by surf boats. This ruled out the import of heavy
machinery and commodities could not be economically
exported.

When the port was built with American lend-lease funds
at a cost of over $20m, it was not expected to operate at
full capacity until 1975. Largely as a result of this wrong
forecast, a road linking Monrovia to the Guinea border
was built in the hope of serving the needs of the south-
eastern part of the then French colony, thus enabling the
port to operate more economically. In the event, the port
began to work at full capacity in 1955 – 20 years ahead
of the anticipated time. By 1963, after being considerably
enlarged, it was handling imports and exports at the rate
of 600,000 tons a month, or nearly 100 times the tonnage
recorded during the first year of its existence. In 1964,
the iron ore port of Buchanan began to operate at full
capacity, while the Free Port of Monrovia was further
enlarged.

Another gauge to the spectacular development of the
country is provided by the consumption of electric power
which increased from some 3,000 kilowatts in 1952 to
nearly 70,000 in 1966. Here again, long-term estimates
published by the American Bureau of Reclamation were
exceeded 25 years ahead of schedule.

The country's main exports are iron ore and rubber,
which account for a substantial proportion of the
national revenue.

Iron ore exports rose from just under three million tons in
1960 to over 15 million tons in 1966. The quality of the
ore is regarded as among the highest in the world.

The principal mine, at Mount Nimba, near the Guinea
and Ivory Coast borders is operated by Lamco – a
Swedish-American concern in which the Liberian

Government holds some 37 per cent of the shares. It has involved an investment of nearly $250m, including the building of a deep-sea port and a 65-mile railway line. Other mines are at Bomi Hills, some 54 miles from Monrovia, and at Mano River, near the Sierra Leone border, both operated by American companies, the latter with a substantial Liberian capital participation. A fourth mine at Bong, east of Monrovia, is operated by a German company. It began production in 1965, and is expected to make a further substantial contribution to Liberia's exports when it comes into full operation.

Rubber, which has now taken second place in the country's economy, is exported mainly by the American Firestone Company which operates a 100,000 acre plantation under a 99-year lease agreement concluded with the Government in 1927. Before and during World War II, Firestone played an important part in Liberia's economy, accounting for a large proportion of both exports and imports. It is still the largest single employer of labour with some 25,000 workers on its payroll, including over 15,000 skilled tappers.

After the war, leases for planting rubber were granted to several other foreign concessionaires. The most important was the B. F. Goodrich Company. There are also nearly 3,000 Liberian-owned rubber farms totalling around 68,000 acres.

Liberia exports also, coffee, palm kernels and some piassava fibre, cocoa and kola nuts. Exports of rough diamonds average one million carats a year, worth about $20m.

Imports consist mainly of capital goods for the mining industry, manufactured products, including motor vehicles and foodstuffs. They reached a peak of $131.6m in 1962, mainly due to increased investments in the mining industry, dropping to $108m in the following year, and averaging some $120m in subsequent years. Foodstuffs, beverages and tobacco have to be imported at the rate of about $15m a year.

Government revenue is derived mainly from dividends, royalties and concession fees paid by foreign companies (the Government holds large blocks of shares in some companies), income tax and customs duty. Further revenue is derived from various licence fees, public utilities and the registration of ships.

Foreign private investments exceed $700m, with American investors accounting for more than half of the total. But the rate of investment has fallen from an average of $75m per annum in 1961, 1962 and 1963 to about $25m in 1964 and 1965. This was due partly to the completion of development work in the iron ore industry.

The rate of investment is expected to increase again in 1967 and 1968, following the negotiation of agreement for the establishment of new industries, including an oil refinery, a cement plant, the expansion of forestry, and the possible development of other iron ore deposits.

The retail trade is mainly in the hands of Lebanese nationals, as are a number of smaller industries.

Dr Edwin Barclay

Brig Robert Brewer

DR EDWIN M. BARCLAY

Dr Edwin M. Barclay, Director-General of Liberia's Public Health Service, is responsible for the administration of Government medical facilities and the supervision and coordination of private practices.

He was appointed in 1960, and in the following six years medical facilities in Liberia more than doubled, totalling in 1966 some 150 clinics distributed throughout the country and nearly 2,000 hospital beds. A new 250-bed teaching hospital and medical centre, named after John F. Kennedy, was under construction in 1966.

Dr Barclay was born in Monrovia on May 13, 1922, the son of Anthony Barclay, an Associate Justice of the Supreme Court, and the grandson of Arthur Barclay, a former President of Liberia. His cousin, Edwin James Barclay, had also been President of Liberia.

After graduating from Liberia College in 1944, he studied medicine at Howard University in the USA, obtaining his MD in 1951, and later did post-graduate work in public health at Yale University, Connecticut. In 1959,

he was appointed medical director of the maternal and child welfare centre in Monrovia.

BRIG ROBERT A. BREWER

A professional soldier, appointed in January, 1964, as Secretary of National Defence – a post traditionally held by civilians – Brigadier Robert Alexander Brewer is regarded as one of the most able officers in Liberia.

He was born in Cape Palmas, in southern Liberia, on May 19, 1903, was educated at Liberia College, and entered the Department of National Defence (then War Department) in 1926, as a civilian employee in the accounting branch of the Liberian Frontier Force. Two years later he became a first lieutenant, and was made Finance Officer and Depot Quartermaster. Later he was promoted to the rank of captain in the Frontier Force.

In 1944, after President Tubmin had taken over as Chief-of-Staff, he was appointed commander of the Executive Mansion (Presidential Palace) guard. He was eventually promoted to brigadier-general, and served successively as junior and senior

241

Angie Brooks

Augustus Caine

aide-de-camp to the President.

In 1960 he was appointed Under-Secretary of State for Defence, and was largely responsible for the organisation of the Liberian contingent which took part in peace-keeping operations in the Congo, at the request of the United Nations.

Later, Brigadier Brewer served for a year as Secretary of Defence.

ANGIE BROOKS

One of Liberia's most popular and experienced diplomats, Miss Angie Brooks was appointed Assistant Secretary of State (Foreign Minister) in 1956.

In the preceding two years, as well as in the following ten years, she regularly represented her country at the United Nations where she took the chair of the Fourth (Trusteeship) Committee and of the Ruanda-Urundi Commission (1962). Her speeches at the General Assembly and her uninhibited comments in the Trusteeship Committee and other international gatherings, have made her name famous throughout the world.

A charming and cheerful hostess, she has a large circle of friends among the world's well known diplomats, politicians and socialites. She finds relaxation in reading and dancing.

The daughter of a Liberian Baptist preacher, she is a lawyer by profession – counsellor-at-law at the Supreme Court of Liberia – and served as Assistant Attorney-General of Liberia from August, 1953 to March, 1958, combining for two years important responsibilities for both foreign affairs and for law and order. In 1958, when both the President and the Secretary of State were absent from the country, she acted for a time as Chief Executive of Liberia.

Her impressive academic record includes a BA in social science from Shaw University, Raleigh, USA, an MSc in political science and international relations as well as an LLB from the University of Wisconsin, USA, an LLD from London University, and a law degree from the University of Liberia.

She has also served as a vice-president of the International Federation of Women Lawyers (1956–60) and part-time professor of law at the University of Liberia (1954–58). She has been awarded decoration by the Governments of Liberia, China, Cameroun, Yugoslavia, West Germany and Burundi.

AUGUSTUS CAINE

Augustus Feweh Caine was appointed Secretary (Minister) of Education in July, 1965, at the age of 34, one of the youngest men to have been entrusted with this key post in the Liberian Government.

Born on December 7, 1930, of tribal parents, he received elementary education at St John's Mission School in his home country of Cape Mount. Later, after taking a BA degree at Liberia College, he began to earn his living as a Parliamentary stenographer. In 1953, he won a United Nations International essay contest and travelled to the United States, where he spent 12 years establishing a distinguished academic reputation both as a student and as a teacher.

After taking an MA in anthropology at the Northwestern University, Evanston, Illinois, he went on to obtain a PhD in sociology and anthropology at East Lansing, Michigan. While reading for his doctorate, he worked as a graduate teaching assistant at Michigan State

University, and later as a technical consultant to the American Peace Corps and the University of Pittsburgh, Pennsylvania. In December, 1964, he was appointed Professor of Social Science at the Alcorn Agricultural and Mechanical College (USA) and a year later returned to Liberia to become Associate Professor of Sociology at the University of Liberia.

A tall, affable and highly cultured man, he has shown understanding for the problems of both teachers and students, and has attempted to give a new impetus to education in Liberia.

JOHN W. COOPER

An agricultural expert with a life-long experience in his chosen field, John Wesley Cooper was appointed Secretary (Minister) of Agriculture in 1964, thus returning to a post of which he was the first holder in the 'fifties.

A specialist in animal husbandry, he began his career as a Government agricultural agent, leaving to become food production manager of the Firestone plantations. Later he returned to Government service as Director of the Bureau of Agriculture, becoming the first Secretary (Minister) of Agriculture when the Bureau was made a Department, in 1948.

He has headed several Liberian delegations to world agricultural and trade conferences, including GATT meetings, and was chairman of the special Liberian trade mission to Europe in 1953.

He was educated at the College (now University) of Liberia and in the USA. His policy, as expressed in an article published in 1966, is to develop Liberia's agriculture according to a 'master plan', the primary emphasis of which is the expansion of rice production, improvement and expansion of livestock and livestock feed production, fruit and vegetable development, forestry exploitation, and tree crop production.

McKINLEY A. DESHIELD

As Postmaster-General for some 15 years, McKinley A. Deshield is one of the most senior members of the Liberian Cabinet, and has played a key role in the Tubman Administrations.

He has played an equally important role as secretary-general of the True Whig party, of which he is a life-long member.

Born in Monrovia on February 23, 1909, he was educated at the College of West Africa and the College (now University) of Liberia; he is a lawyer by profession. His first post as a young man was that of secretary at the General Post Office – a department to which he returned later in life, as Postmaster-General, after holding senior positions in the Treasury and the Bureau of Mines. He has also served as a major in the Liberian Army.

As Postmaster-General, he has overall responsibility for internal and external telecommunications and public utilities – which were greatly developed in the late 'fifties and early 'sixties.

A heavily built giant, 'Mac', as he is known to his friends and political supporters, is also one of Liberia's most popular orators.

JOSEPH R. GRIMES

Appointed Secretary of State (Foreign Minister) in 1960, Joseph Rudolph Grimes became one of the four senior politicians in Liberia. Under the constitution, the Secretary of State acts as President in the absence of the Chief Executive.

Rudolph Grimes, as he is

Richard Henries

Alexander Horton

known in Liberia and abroad, was born in Monrovia on October 31, 1928. His father had been an Attorney-General of Liberia, whose ancestors included both early settlers from the United States and indigenous inhabitants of the Vai tribe. After graduating from Liberia College (now University of Liberia) he read law at Howard University in the USA, where he obtained an LLB, and later studied international affairs at Columbia University.

He has worked with patience and perseverance for a realistic approach to African unity and world problems. The present Charter of the OAU (Organisation of African Unity) is still largely based on the draft which he prepared for the Lagos Conference of African Heads of State in 1962.

RICHARD A. HENRIES

As Speaker (Chairman) of the House of Representatives, Richard Abrom Henries is one of Liberia's most senior political personalities.

He entered the House in 1943 as a member of the ruling True Whig party, and soon became leader of the party organisation in Montserrado, his home county. In 1951 he was elected Speaker of the House, and in subsequent years played an increasingly important part in Liberia's political life.

He was born on September 16, 1908 in Monrovia, took his BA and LLD degrees at what is now Liberia University, and was teaching mathematics at Liberia College by the time he was 24.

Two years later, he became chief clerk to the Commonwealth district of Monrovia (Monrovia City Council) and later to the Treasury Department (1936–38). This was followed by a five year

spell as Supervisor of Schools for Sinoe and Maryland counties. After World War II, he was appointed president of the Board of Trustees of the University of Liberia.

A lawyer by profession, he is senior partner in a law firm, whose clients include the Firestone Corporation, one of the largest firms operating in Liberia.

As Speaker of the House of Representatives, Mr Henries has travelled widely in Africa, the USA and Europe, and has represented Liberia at the Washington DC conference (1945) on the reorganisation of the International Court of Justice.

His American-born wife, the former Miss Doris Banks, is a well known author and educationist in Liberia.

ALEXANDER R. HORTON

Many of Africa's successful businessmen began their careers as politicians or civil servants, often achieving ministerial rank before 'retiring' to free enterprise. Alexander Romeo Horton established a distinguished reputation in business, especially banking, before being invited by President Tubman to head Liberia's Department (Ministry) of Commerce and Industry in 1964.

At the time of his appointment, he was president of the Bank of Liberia, one of the country's leading commercial banks, president of the Liberia Realty Corporation, and a director of several other big companies. He was also a successful rubber farmer and chairman of the YMCA Hungry Club (a businessmen's luncheon club).

Born in Monrovia on August 20, 1923, to a distinguished and well-to-do family, he was educated at the Booker T. Washington Institute and later at the

College of West Africa in Monrovia. His higher studies were completed in the USA, where he took a BA in economics at Morehouse College, Atlanta, and an MBA at the Wharton School of Finance and Commerce, University of Pennsylvania.

A believer in free enterprise, he feels African businessmen can play a major part in the development of their continent. He organised the first conference of African businessmen in 1960, and became chairman of its steering committee. Later he sponsored the idea of an African Development Bank, and was elected first chairman of the committee of nine, set up by the UN Economic Commission for Africa, to establish the bank. From 1955–63, he also served as assistant economic adviser to the President of Liberia.

He attended the International Industrial and Development Conference in 1957, was chairman of the Liberian delegation to the UN Geneva conference on Trade and Development in 1964, and represented Liberia at several sessions of the Economic Commission for Africa.

TAYLOR E. MAJOR

Appointed Commissioner of Communications in 1962, Mr Taylor E. Major is also Chairman of the Liberian Public Utilities Authority. He thus has overall responsibility for a vast and growing field which developed out of all recognition in the six years between 1960 and 1966. It includes telecommunications, power, water and sewage – four key utilities on which the development of the country largely depends.

He was born in Greenville, Sinoe County, on November 24, 1918, the second of six children.

After a basic education at the College of Liberia, he matriculated in the United States, and obtained a BSc degree (Magna cum Laude) in electrical engineering at Howard University. Later he did post-graduate work in electrical engineering at Cornell University and an intensive course in telephony with the Automatic Electric Company of Chicago.

He returned to Liberia in 1952, and was appointed Chief Telephone Engineer and Assistant Commissioner of Communications. The telephone system in Liberia at the time was practically non-existent. By 1964, automatic exchanges were installed in Monrovia, with facilities for connecting 4,000 subscribers, and a microwave telephone network linking 31 provincial centres, was commissioned.

In 1961 he also took on the chairmanship of the Power Authority. He told electricity users that he had as yet neither the power not the authority to satisfy their constantly growing demand. Yet consumption doubled within two years, and 3,200 new customers were acquired in the Monrovia area alone. A $30m hydro-electric project, on St Paul River, 13 miles from Monrovia, was expected to be completed by mid-1967, providing ultimately an additional capacity of 102,000 Kw to the national grid.

JAMES PIERRE

As Attorney-General, James Alexander Adolphus Pierre combines (as in the USA) the functions of Minister of Justice and Chief Prosecutor for the State.

He is also the official head of the police force and responsible for internal security.

He has had a long legal career,

Charles Sherman

William Tolbert

first as counsel, then as judge. Prior to his appointment as Attorney-General, he was a member of Liberia's Supreme Court.

He was born at Harford, Grand Bassa County, on July 18, 1908. He was educated at the Bible Industrial Academy in Grand Bassa County and later graduated from Cuttington College and Divinity School.

CHARLES D. SHERMAN

Charles Dunbar Sherman became the head of Liberia's Treasury in 1958, and resigned on medical grounds in October, 1966, after making a significant contribution to his country's financial success.

During the six years he headed the Treasury, revenue nearly trebled from under $18m per annum to over $50m.

He began to earn his living at the age of 12 as a post office messenger. In the following 28 years, until his appointment as Secretary of the Treasury (Minister of Finance) he graduated from the College of West Africa in Monrovia and the Albert Academy in Freetown. Then he went to the United States, obtained a Magna cum Laude certificate in economics at Howard University, a BSc in economics at the University of Pennsylvania, and an MA in public finance, also in the United States. In addition, he acquired a practical experience of financial affairs on the New York Stock Exchange.

He returned to Liberia to become professor of economics at the University of Liberia and, later, economic adviser to the President.

He was born in the county of Cape Mount on September 27, 1918. His father's ancestors had come from the United States. His mother belonged to the Vai tribe,

and he was brought up largely in the tradition of the indigenous people.

He is president of the World Alliance Council of the YMCA.

CLARENCE L. SIMPSON

One of Liberia's most prominent statesmen and diplomats, Clarence L. Simpson has played an important part in the affairs of Liberia for over three decades.

Born in 1896 at Royesville, near Monrovia, he was educated at the College of West Africa, and later read law at Liberia College. After a successful legal career, first as a barrister and then as a county attorney, he entered politics, becoming acting Postmaster-General.

In 1930 he was elected secretary-general of the ruling True Whig party, a post he kept for 14 years. From 1931–34 he was Speaker of the House of Representatives. During the following nine years (1934–43), he was Secretary of State (Foreign Minister), and represented Liberia at the League of Nations.

In 1943, running with Mr Tubman, he was elected Vice-President of Liberia for an eight-year term. Two years later he headed the Liberian delegation to the San Francisco Conference which gave birth to the United Nations. He signed the Charter on behalf of his country.

In 1952, on the expiration of his term, he retired from active politics, serving successively as Liberian Ambassador to Washington and London. In 1960 he returned to Liberia – a respected elder statesman – and resumed his legal practice after an interruption of 35 years.

WILLIAM R. TOLBERT

William Richard Tolbert was elected Vice-President during the

Edison Townsend

William Tubman

re-election of President Tubman in 1951, becoming one of the youngest in the history of Liberia to hold that office.

Standing as second to President Tubman, he was re-elected three times to the second highest office in the land, in 1955, 1959 and 1963.

He was born in Bensonville, Liberia, on May 13, 1913, to a well-known family of early settlers. From an elementary school in his home town, he went to Crummell Hall, a Protestant Episcopal high school in Clay Ashland on the St Paul River, and then to Liberia College (now the University of Liberia) where he took his degree in 1934. In 1952 the University conferred on him the degree of Doctor of Civil Law. He also belongs to the French Institute of Humanities.

Known as an active churchman who is sympathetic towards all denominations, he is a Baptist, an ordained elder, president of the Liberia Baptist Missionary and Educational Convention, and world president of the Baptist World Alliance, having been world vice-president in 1960.

He began his career as a typist in the Treasury in 1935, and worked up to higher posts, including that of Government Disbursing Officer. Later he entered politics, and in 1943 was elected to the Legislature as a representative from Montserrado County, where he was born.

As Vice-President of Liberia, Mr Tolbert is ex-officio President of the Senate and next in line of succession to the President. But under the Liberian Constitution, he cannot act for the President while the latter holds office.

He represented President Tubman at the inauguration of Harry S. Truman as President of the United States of America, and at the Coronation of Queen Elizabeth II.

EDISON R. TOWNSEND

The information services of Liberia may be said to have grown with Edison Reginald Townsend, a journalist who became Press Secretary to President Tubman in 1954 and later Chief of the Bureau of Information.

The office developed first into the Liberian Information Service and later into the Department of Information and Cultural Affairs after Mr Townsend had been made a full Cabinet member.

In the years that he has been largely responsible for informing the public about national affairs and projecting the country's image to the rest of the world, Liberia has acquired a broadcasting station, and television and local newspapers have been developed throughout the land.

An industrious man, who works up to 16 hours a day, 'Reggie' Townsend was born in the settlement of Schieffelin, Marshall Territory, on July 23, 1920. He was educated at the Lott Carey Mission School in Brewerville and the Liberia College High School, before taking a BA in Washington DC, and an MA at Michigan State College.

WILLIAM V. S. TUBMAN

The history of Liberia from the end of World War II has been inseparably linked with the name of William Vacanarat Shadrach Tubman, President since 1943, and often referred to as 'the maker of modern Liberia'.

The main task of his life has been developing Liberia's resources, and welding into one homogeneous nation the many different racial groups inhabiting the country – descendants of freed

247

slaves from 27 American states, the Congo and various British transatlantic possessions, and members of 28 indigenous tribes.

He gave the aboriginal people of the hinterland equal status with the Americo-Liberians who came to found the country, and granted tribal representation in the Legislature.

He has prevailed over xenophobic feeling, secured American aid, and practised an 'open door' policy which has attracted foreign, mostly American, enterprise. During his administration, foreign investments have totalled some US $700m and Government revenue has risen from under two million dollars in 1944 to over $56m in 1966. The rate of growth of Liberia's production has been the highest in the world. This applies in particular to iron ore, the production of which rose from three million tons in 1960 to over 15 million in 1966.

President Tubman's 'open door' policy includes as a rule attractive tax concessions for newly-established enterprises, exemption of import duty on capital goods, and freedom of restrictions on the repatriation of capital and profits.

The Free Port of Monrovia, Liberia's first deep water port, the iron ore port of Bechanan, a network of macadamised roads, a nation-wide power grid, state-supported schools and hospitals, and modern telecommunications have all been constructed during his long period of office.

Dynamic, ebullient, easily accessible and affable in private, Mr Tubman is a stickler for the greatest dignity in public administration and etiquette in official functions. He rises every morning at 5am and dictates to two secretaries for three hours. His official day begins at 9am and

continues uninterruptedly until 3 pm. During this time he receives dozens of visitors. In the lobbies and ante-chambers of the Executive Mansion, his official residence, Cabinet Ministers, Government officials, ambassadors and businessmen from foreign countries mingle with a crowd of tribal chiefs and ordinary citizens, waiting to submit their particular problem to the President. Familialy known as the 'Old Man', he tries to see them all.

He personally appoints and commissions every senior civil servant, and has to approve all payments of over $25 made by the Liberian Treasury.

He likes to spend weekends at his Totota farm, some 80 miles from Monrovia, where he owns a country house and a small private zoo. But even there he spends a good deal of his time conferring with officials of every kind. The atmosphere in Totota, however, is much less formal than in Monrovia.

President Tubman was born in the county of Maryland, in the south of Liberia, on November 29, 1895, to Elizabeth Rebecca Barnes, who had emigrated from Atlanta, Georgia, in 1872, and the Revd Alexander Tubman, a former Speaker of the Liberian House of Representatives, who was a descendant of early settlers from Augusta, Georgia.

Educated at Cape Palmas Methodist Seminary and Cutting-ton College Divinity School, he is a devout Christian and a lay preacher of the Methodist Church. His speeches abound with biblical quotations. He has supported legislation to ensure observance of the Sabbath, and has opposed measures which appeared to conflict with Christian ideals. For some years he even argued against a proposal to hold the first census in Liberia's history on the ground that God had punished David for counting his men.

He granted a free pardon to a man sentenced to death for attempting to assassinate him.

He could probably have become a bishop, but gave up his divinity studies at the age of 18 to earn his living as a high school teacher. He taught for several years while reading for the Bar under a private tutor. He practised law for some time in his home town of Harper, becoming known as the 'poor man's friend' because of the many cases he pleaded on behalf of people with little or no money. Later he entered Government service as Recorder in the Probate Court, and in 1919, at the age of 24, became a county attorney. Four years later, he entered politics and was elected to the Legislature – the youngest senator in Liberia's history. He represented his home county in the Senate for nearly 15 years until 1937 when, at the request of President Edwin Barclay, he resumed his legal career to become an Associate Justice of the Supreme Court.

He also served in the Army, rising through the ranks to become a colonel, and taking part in two expeditions against rebel tribes.

In 1943 he was elected President of the Republic for a term of eight years. He was the 18th President of the country, and the first 'provincial' to head its Executive. He was re-elected for several four-year terms under a constitutional amendment passed in 1949, and soon became the 'doyen' of African heads of state.

He never left Liberia before his election to the presidency, but he has travelled extensively since, paying several state visits to the United States and European countries as well as to most of the newly independent African states.

He was associated with Dr Kwame Nkrumah, then President of Ghana, and President Sekou Touré of Guinea, in the holding of the Accra Conference in 1958, and the Sanniquellie (Liberia) Conference in July, 1959, at which cooperation between independent African states was discussed for the first time. In 1961, he sponsored and organised in Monrovia the first broad conference of African heads of state to promote unity and cooperation in Africa. The Conference was attended by 21 out of 28 heads of state, forming the so-called 'Monrovia group'. Two years later he took part in the Addis Ababa conference which gave birth to the Organisation of African Unity.

He has attended all the OAU 'summits' since then. He has often expressed the view that a union of African states on the American model would be a mistake because of their different systems of Government and non-African affiliations, and that the way to an eventual unity is through cooperation in practical fields and coordination of policies. At the OAU summit in Accra in October, 1965, he said that keeping 28 tribes together in Liberia had been difficult enough; to put hundreds of tribes all over Africa under one continental government would prove an impossible task.

In 1964, President Tubman suggested a free trade zone consisting of the Ivory Coast, Guinea, Sierra Leone and Liberia.

In foreign affairs, President Tubman stands for a strict observance of the accepted principles of international law and conduct, and has consistently criticised attacks on foreign embassies, the use of force as a means of settling disputes, and the unilateral denunciation of agreements. To an American millionaire who offered to make a big industrial investment in Liberia, provided an agreement with a certain individual could be rescinded, he replied, 'No, an agreement is an agreement'.

Following the unilateral declaration of independence in Rhodesia by Mr Ian Smith, President Tubman was probably the only African head of state to have condemned immediately as 'wrong' the December, 1965 resolution of the OAU Ministerial Council, calling for the severance of diplomatic relations with Britain. He said African states should have supported Britain in her stand against the Smith regime, rather than condemned her.

He has repeatedly refuted the assumption that African states are entitled to aid as a matter of course and has put forward the idea of 'trade, not aid'.

In his younger days he used to play cricket in a country where the game was virtually unknown. He now enjoys fishing and sailing. He chain-smokes Havana cigars and has a lively, sometimes self-deprecatory sense of humour which disarms his critics.

An American journalist once asked him how the Liberian authorities defined persons of Negro descent – who alone qualify for citizenship in Liberia. He replied, 'We check the record, and if we cannot find the record we look at his face.'

At a press conference, Liberian journalists asked him a series of questions about what the Government proposed to do to improve the state of the country's roads, education and health services. After listening patiently to each question and answering it, Mr Tubman asked, 'And now, gentlemen, what are *you* doing to improve the standard of the Liberian press?'

It is said that one of the reasons why there has never been a serious challenge to President Tubman at elections is that the various Opposition groups which have emerged from time to time have failed to find a leader of sufficient standing.

There have been three plots to assassinate him – in 1955, 1961 and 1963. The 1963 plot preceded a Presidential election campaign. Huge demonstrations were being held throughout the country, calling on Mr Tubman to stand for re-election. Addressing a crowd in Monrovia, he said he could not agree he was the only man fit to lead the country. 'I am sure,' he declared, 'there are other people in Liberia who could make a good President . . . and who appear to be more anxious than I am to have the job.'

On his 71st birthday (November 29, 1966) he said he would like to give up the presidency after 22 years in office, and would be happy if his party would nominate a successor. Subsequently great pressure was put upon him to continue.

Mr Tubman is married to Antoinette Padmore, granddaughter of the late Arthur Barclay, an immigrant from Barbados, who became President of Liberia in 1904 and served until 1912. Her uncle, Edwin Barclay, was President from 1930–43. She was married to Mr Tubman in 1948, four years after the death of his previous wife, Mrs Martha Aletha Tubman.

After completing her secondary education in Liberia, Mrs Antoinette Tubman studied fashion in France, and returned to Liberia to open the first design and fashion school in the country. Liberia's First Lady devotes much of her time to charitable and social welfare activities. She is also a collector of Liberian historical relics and a keen gardener.

Mr and Mrs Tubman have one daughter; Mr Tubman has four other children by his previous marriage. His elder son, William (Shad) Jr, is a former president of the Liberian Trade Union Movement and a successful businessman.

JAMES MILTON WEEKS

James Milton Weeks was appointed Secretary of the Treasury (Minister of Finance) in February, 1967, following the resignation on medical grounds of Mr Charles D. Sherman. He had already been in charge of the Treasury, as acting Secretary, at the beginning of 1965, during Mr Sherman's prolonged absence on sick leave.

Mr Weeks established a reputation as a brilliant economist when he was given the task of introducing planning into the framework of a liberal free enterprise economy. In May, 1962, he was appointed Director of the new National Planning Agency becoming also a *de facto* member of the Cabinet. He remained in charge of economic planning for nearly five years becoming Liberia's First Secretary of Planning and Economic Affairs in August, 1966, when the National Planning Agency became a full department.

Mr Weeks was probably ideally qualified to head the newly established department. Born in Croizerville, near Monrovia, on November 15, 1921, and educated at Liberia College, he was the first Liberian to have studied at the London School of Economics, where he took a BSc in economics in 1955, followed by an MSc in 1957. Before travelling to Britain to complete his training in economics, he obtained a BA from Liberia College, and spent eight years working in Liberia – four teaching mathematics, and another four helping to run a bank.

Shortly after returning to Liberia in 1956, he joined the Bank of Liberia as a senior executive, and later was assigned for short periods to the Treasury, the National Production Council and the Budget Bureau. In October, 1959, he became the first director of the newly established Bureau of Economic Research and Statistics. In May, 1962, the direction of the National Planning Agency was added to his responsibilities.

While fully supporting the principles of free enterprise and President Tubman's 'open door' policy, Mr Weeks also believed in a planned development with the voluntary participation of both the private and public sectors of the economy. He has expressed the view that 'with appropriate public policy instruments, such as taxation, credit, commercial policies and general regulatory measures, the Government can influence the tempo of private activity and guide it in desired directions, complementing public programmes and policies designed to increase the rate of social and economic development'.

His wife, Monroette, became the first nurse in 13 years to be awarded a gold medal by the British hospital in Uxbridge, London, where she completed her training in 1958.

251

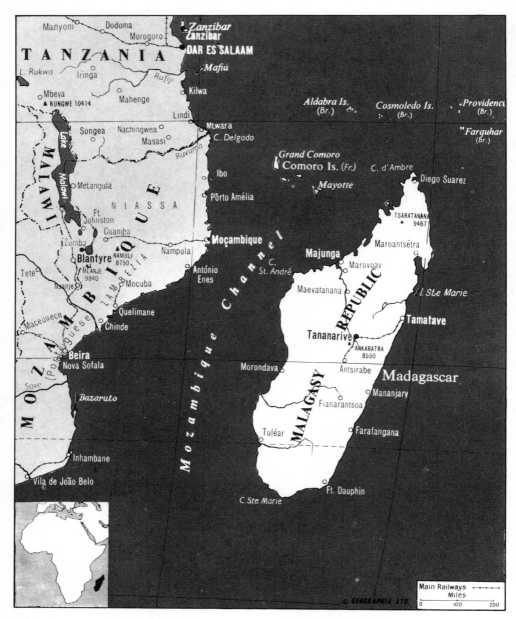

Madagascar, with an area of 228,000 square miles, is the fourth largest island in the world after Greenland, New Guinea and Borneo. It lies in the Indian Ocean 300 miles off the south-east coast of Africa.

The population of the Malagasy Republic was officially estimated in August, 1966, at 6,300,000. The capital is Tananarive.
The Malagasy economy is mainly founded on agriculture.

The chief exports are coffee, vanilla, rice, sugar and tobacco. The island is rich in minerals which include graphite, uranium, mica and precious stones.

Malagasy Republic

The Malagasy Republic, formerly the French colony of Madagascar, was proclaimed an internally self-governing republic within the French Community on October 14, 1958.

The country became a fully independent member of the Community on June 26, 1960.

The French Community began in 1958, grouping with France a number of internally self-governing states, formerly French colonies in Africa. In 1960, as the states became fully independent, it was transformed into a loose association of free and equal partners.

The President, who is also head of government, is elected by a college which includes the members of Parliament and of the General Councils of the provinces as well as delegates from the municipal and rural assemblies.

There are two Chambers — the National Assembly (elected members) and the Senate.

Madagascar, *la Grand Ile*, lay across the historic European trade routes to India, and was visited in turn by Portuguese, French, Dutch and British colonisers. Despite these incursions by Europeans the island remained independent until the end of the 19th century when its last ruler, Queen Ranavalona III, fell victim to Anglo-French colonial rivalries, saw her island taken over by the French in 1895 and was exiled.

In 1947 the island was the scene of one of the most tragic independence uprisings. It was sternly suppressed. Nevertheless France granted independence to Madagascar 13 years later and relations between the two republics have been excellent.

The ancestors of the majority of the Malagasy people came from the East—Melanesians, Malays and Indonesians. Their Eastern origins are apparent in the language which, spoken by all groups with only differences of dialect, belongs to the Malay-Polynesian group of tongues.

Later migrations included Arab, Persian and Bantu. Africans also came to the island as slaves.

Roughly two-fifths of the Malagasy are Protestant and Roman Catholic Christians, many of whose ancestors were converted by Christian missionaries.

Most of the remainder practise a form of ancestor

Military march-past in
Tananarive, the capital

worship. One feature of this religion is the ritual
feasting with the dead. On special occasions the family
tomb is opened and the dead are brought out and given
new winding sheets to the accompaniment of dancing
and singing.

Madagascar was already a well-organised country when
it was taken over by the French and immediately
after World War II strong nationalist tendencies began
to be felt.

Two parties were formed, the moderate Malagasy
Democratic Party, which drew largely on the bourgeoisie
for its support, and the Party for the Restoration of
Malagasy Independence, which by means of its electoral
organisations had a strong influence thoughout the
country.

The two leaders of the latter party, Joseph Ravoahangy
Andrianavalona and Joseph Raseta, were elected to the
French Constituent Assembly. There they put forward a
motion for Malagasy independence, but to no avail.
Their party, reconstituted under the less aggressive
name of the Democratic Movement of Malagasy
Revival, won the territorial elections in 1946 and
asked the French Government for a referendum on

A group of Malagasy women whose features reveal their mixed African, Arab and Malayo-Polynesian origins

independence. Their demands were not met.
Relations were by now becoming strained between the local population and the French settlers.
On November 10, 1946, Ravoahangy, Raseta and Jacques Rabemananjara were elected to the French National Assembly. Still thwarted in their efforts to secure independence by constitutional means the nationalists took the offensive.
On the night of March 29, 1947, rebellion broke out in different points of the island and spread rapidly on the east coast. At Moramanga, north-east of Tananarive, the military camp was attacked by 2,000 men armed with spears, axes and machetes. A part of the garrison was massacred.
The Senegalese Rifles at the post who survived the initial attack pushed back the rebels and the death toll was heavy.
In other parts of the island the revolt failed. Reprisals were harsh: an estimated 20,000 people were killed. Members of Parliament and the leaders of the Democratic Movement of Malagasy Revival were put on trial from July 2 to October 4, 1948, accused of responsibility for launching the rebellion. Six were

255

condemned to death, including Ravoahangy and
Raseta. Eight were sentenced to hard labour, including
Rabemananjara. Those sentenced to death were later
reprieved and others were amnestied from 1954
onwards.

From then on Madagascar, like other French territories,
was set on the road to internal self-government and
eventual independence. In December, 1956, Philibert
Tsiranana launched the Social Democratic Party and
the island found a good-humoured and effective leader
capable of bridging its internal divisions and making it
turn away from the bitterness of the past.

Tsiranana fostered good relations with France, which
has generously aided the Republic's development. At
home the President maintained a relaxed political
atmosphere and the Malagasy Republic is one of the few
independent African territories where Opposition parties
are legal.

RICHARD ANDRIAMANJATO

Richard Andriamanjato, a Protestant pastor and mayor of
Tananarive at the age of 29,
became leader of the left-wing
nationalist AKFM Party from its
foundation in 1959.

The AKFM (Congress for
Independence Party) was formed
by a number of Malagasy parties
opposed to the ruling Social
Democratic Party.

It called for a more socialist
programme by the Government.

Born on July 31, 1930, M.
Andriamanjato studied theology
at Montpellier in France, and did
an arts course at Strasbourg,
obtaining his degrees in 1957.

He was elected to the Malagasy
National Assembly as deputy for
Tananarive City in 1960 and was
re-elected in 1965.

M. Andriamanjato, pastor of
Ambohitantely Church in Tananarive, became mayor of Tananarive, the capital, in 1959.

A lover of music, especially the
piano, and painting, M. Andriamanjato was, when in France,
president of the Association of
Malagasy Students from 1956–57.

CELESTIN ARIDY

Célestin Aridy, a founder member
of the Malagasy Social Democratic Party, was named Secretary
of State for Social Affairs and
Public Health in August, 1965.

He was born on January 5,
1919, and worked as a teacher,
becoming a headmaster and head
of the Majunga Provincial Teaching Service.

The Social Democratic Party,
formed in 1956 by M. Philibert
Tsiranana, later first President of
the Malagasy Republic, was set
up in M. Aridy's house in
Majunga. M. Aridy became a
member of the party's managing
committee.

He was elected to the Malagasy
National Assembly in September,
1960, and was also appointed
Secretary of State for Diego
Suarez Province in the same
year.

Siméon Japhet

LAURENT BOTOKEKY

Laurent Botokeky was appointed Minister for Cultural Affairs in August, 1965.

He had been Minister for Education since May, 1959.

Treasurer of the managing committee of the ruling Social Democratic Party, and a teacher by training, M. Botokeky was born on December 5, 1919.

He was elected a member of the Provincial Assembly of Tulear in 1957, and became a member of the Malagasy National Assembly in 1958.

A year later, in February, 1959, he received his first senior posting as Secretary of State for the Interior.

XAVIER DELMOTTE

Xavier Delmotte, a farmer's son, became Secretary of State for the Development of the High Plateaux in September, 1965.

Mayor of Ambositra, his home-town in Eastern Central Madagascar, since 1960, M. Delmotte was nominated a member of the Malagasy Senate in 1961.

He has served as reporter for the Senate's Legislation Committee and in various Senate missions, including a study mission which visited West Germany in 1962.

Born on January 6, 1918, M. Delmotte began his career in industry and served many years as an industrial manager.

In World War II he served as a non-commissioned officer in the French Army.

SIMEON JAPHET

Siméon Japhet was elected President of the Malagasy Senate in December, 1964.

A doctor of medicine, he had been a member of the Upper House since October, 1960.

Born in Tamatave Province on February 17, 1906, he studied medicine at the Tamatave School of Medicine, and served as a doctor in the Medical Assistance Service in various parts of the island.

He was active in the Social Democratic Party – formed in 1956, and later to become the ruling party – and became a municipal councillor in Tamatave in 1959.

As a senator, he was member of a number of commissions and took part in missions abroad, in particular to the Parliamentary Commission of the Common Market.

M. Japhet was nominated Vice-President of the Senate in May, 1964, and became President following the resignation of M. Jules Ravony, appointed Malagasy Ambassador to Bonn.

JEAN-FRANCOIS JARISON

Jean-François Jarison became Minister of Labour and Social Affairs in October, 1960. He was not named in a new Malagasy Government formed in August, 1965.

M. Jarison served as Secretary of State for Tamatave Province from June, 1959 until 1960.

He was born in 1914 in Tamatave Province, and entered the administration as a translator in 1933. He was elected to the Tamatave Provincial Assembly in 1948, becoming its President in May, 1957. He joined the Malagasy National Assembly in October, 1958.

BARTHELEMY JOHASY

Barthélemy Johasy was appointed Secretary of State for the Budget, Trade and Finances in August, 1965.

An administrator, born on September 10, 1927, he attended courses on planning and banking

Alfred Nany

in Israel and France, and was named director of the Malagasy National Development Bank in January, 1964.

He was top of his year (1958–60) at the French Institute for Overseas Higher Studies.

From 1960 onwards he has occupied senior posts in the administration.

EUGENE LECHAT

Eugène Lechat, a French farrier's son, who went to Madagascar as a teacher in 1952, was appointed Malagasy Minister for Equipment and Communications in August, 1965.

He had been Minister for Public Works, Transport, Construction, Post and Telecommunications since 1960. Before that, from May, 1959, he was Minister for Public Works, Equipment and Transport.

M. Lechat was born in the village of Mesloup in the Orne Department of France on May 21, 1919.

After training as a teacher he served as an officer-cadet in the French Army at the beginning of World War II, and was captured by the Germans. He escaped in July, 1940, went underground and made contact with a resistance group.

When Allied Forces drove the Germans from France in 1944, M. Lechat joined the Youth and Sports administration. Between 1948 and 1950 he left the administration and worked as head of a professional training school for a leading shoe firm.

In 1956 he was elected a municipal councillor for Mananjary.

M. Lechat, who had been a member of the French Socialist party since 1945, became a provincial councillor a year later, and a member of the Representative Assembly.

In 1959 he became a member of the Senate of the French Community. He was elected to the Malagasy National Assembly in September, 1960.

ALBERT LEDA

Albert Leda was named Secretary of State for Social Affairs and the Civil Service in August, 1965. He had been Secretary of State for the Province of Tulear since 1960.

A provincial councillor in 1957, he was elected to the Malagasy National Assembly in September, 1960.

He is a member of the Social Democratic Party and was born in 1925.

VICTOR MIADANA

Victor Miadana first reached Cabinet rank when he was appointed Malagasy Finance Minister in January, 1963. He became Minister for Finance and Trade when a new Malagasy Government was formed in August, 1965.

He was Secretary of State for the Budget from 1960 63.

A teacher, born in 1920, M. Miadana was elected to the Majunga Provincial Assembly in 1957.

In 1958 he became president of the Diego-Suarez Federation of the Social Democratic Party. He was elected to the National Assembly in the same year.

ALFRED NANY

Alfred Nany was elected President of the Malagasy National Assembly in November, 1960, and by August, 1966, had been re-elected six times to the post.

He entered the administrative and financial services in 1934. He became a provincial councillor for Majunga in 1952, and a deputy in the Malagasy Assembly in 1958.

A member of the ruling Social Democratic Party, M. Nany was born in 1916.

He was named vice-president of the Malagasy National Assembly in October, 1960, becoming its President in the following month, when M. Calvin Tsiebo resigned to become Deputy Prime Minister.

JEAN-JACQUES NATAI

Jean-Jacques Natai became Secretary of State for Agriculture concerned with the development of West Madagascar in August, 1965. He had been Secretary of State for the Province of Majunga, in the north-west, since June, 1959.

M. Natai, who was born on March 16, 1917, studied at the medical and dentistry schools of Tananarive. He became a municipal councillor in Majunga and provincial councillor for Majunga in 1957.

A member of the Social Democratic Party, he was elected to the Malagasy National Assembly in 1958.

JACQUES RABEMANANJARA

Jacques Rabemananjara, one of the leading Malagasy poets of modern times, was appointed Minister for Agriculture, Land and Food in August, 1965, after five years as Economics Minister.

An early campaigner for self-government for the then French colony of Madagascar, he was detained in France after the nationalist uprising in Madagascar in 1947, which was put down by French troops.

M. Rabemananjara returned to Madagascar in 1960, when the country became a fully independent republic, and was elected to the National Assembly.

Born on June 23, 1913, in the Tamatave province of Madagas-car, M. Rabemananjara joined the French administration in 1939 after his schooling, and went on a course at the Ministry of Colonies in Paris.

Unable to leave France during World War II, M. Rabemananjara took an arts degree and became well-known in French literary circles as a poet and writer. He returned to Madagascar after the war, and in 1946 was elected deputy for Madagascar in the French National Assembly.

M. Rabemananjara joined the Democratic Movement for Malagasy Revival (MDRM), became its first secretary-general and campaigned for self-government for the island.

After the nationalist uprising of 1947 – in which an estimated 20,000 people were killed – he was sentenced to forced labour for life, but was finally detained in France.

M. Rabemananjara has published collections of poems, dramas and political works.

ALFRED RAJAONARIVELO

Alfred Rajaonarivelo was appointed Malagasy Secretary of State for Information and Tourism in October, 1960.

Born in 1908, he studied medicine at the Tananarive School of Medicine, and worked as a doctor in the Medical Assistance service before continuing his studies at the Medical Faculty in Bordeaux, France, and the French Dental School in Paris,

He returned to Madagascar as a dental surgeon, and set up practice in Tananarive.

M. Rajaonarivelo was first elected to the Malagasy National Assembly in September, 1960, as a candidate on the list of the ruling Social Democratic Party.

EMILE RAKOTO

Emile Rakoto was appointed Reforestry Minister in September, 1963, after four years as Secretary of State for Fianarantsoa Province. He was dropped from the Government in August, 1965.

Born on May 27, 1915, M. Rakoto first worked as a clerk in the administration.

He was elected to the Fianarantsoa Provincial Assembly in 1950, and joined the Malagasy National Assembly in 1958.

In May, 1959, he became head of the Fianarantsoa Provincial Council.

ALBERT RAKOTO RATSIMAMANGA

Dr Albert Rakoto Ratsimamanga, a distinguished scientist, was appointed Malagasy Ambassador to France in 1960.

Founder-director of the Malagasy Institute for Applied Research, Dr Rakoto Ratsimamanga's major works include writings on the anthropology of Madagascar, bio-chemistry and physiology. He is especially interested in nutrition.

Born in Tananarive on December 28, 1907, Dr Rakoto Ratsimamanga studied medicine and science at Paris University.

He headed research at the French National Centre for Scientific Research, and in 1958 represented France at a meeting of the World Health Organisation.

In 1960 he was a member of the Executive Council of the United Nations Educational Scientific and Cultural Organisation, becoming its vice-chairman in 1962.

During World War II, Dr Rakoto Ratsimamanga served as a volunteer in the French Army.

HENRI RAKOTOBE

Henri René Alfred Rakotobe, a distinguished lawyer, parliamentarian and sportsman, became President of the Malagasy High Council of Institutions in December, 1960. This body is responsible for seeing that all laws and regulations are constitutional.

The son of a master tailor, M. Rakotobe was born on July 8, 1918, in Tananarive. He went to schools in Hanoi, Paris and Tananarive and studied law at universities in Algiers and Paris, becoming a lawyer in the Madagascar Appeal Court in 1946.

M. Rakotobe served as a municipal councillor and deputy mayor of Tananarive from 1956–59. He also became vice-president of the country's Provincial Constituent Assembly and, in 1959, President of the National Assembly.

M. Rakotobe was Justice Minister in 1960 before becoming President of the High Council of Institutions.

He has a bronze medal from the French Lawn Tennis Federation and is a keen player of golf and bridge. He was president of the Malagasy Bridge and Judo Federations, and president of the Malagasy Olympic Committee.

GABRIEL RAMANANTSOA

General Gabriel Ramanantsoa became chief-of-staff of the Malagasy Armed Forces in 1960 as a colonel, after a distinguished career in the French Army. He was promoted general in July, 1961.

General Ramanantsoa went to high school in Tananarive and then Marseilles, France, where he studied for entry to the French Military Academy at Saint-Cyr.

He passed the Saint-Cyr examination, and left there as a second-lieutenant in the Colonial Forces in October, 1931.

After three years as assistant to the head of the Military Preparatory School for Boys at Tananarive, the future general, by then a lieutenant, was posted in 1935 to the Moroccan Colonial Infantry Regiment, then in garrison at Aix-en-Provence, France.

He served in Tunisia from 1936–40, when he went to France with an African battalion and took part in battles against German forces. At one stage he took command of his battalion following the death of his commander.

After the defeat of the French and the Armistice of May, 1940, M. Ramanantsoa was posted to Madagascar, where he organised at Fianarantsoa a school for boy soldiers.

Returning to France in 1946, he served at the headquarters of Colonial Forces in Paris until 1948, when he went to Tananarive, attached to the French High Commissioner's staff.

After three more years at Colonial Forces headquarters in Paris as a major, the future Malagasy chief-of-staff went in 1953 to Indochina, where he commanded an African battalion in North Vietnam.

He later served in the French headquarters at Hanoi and Haiphong before returning in 1955 to France where he was promoted to lieutenant-colonel.

A full colonel in 1959, he studied at the French Institute for Higher Studies in National Defence before returning to Madagascar in June, 1960.

ALFRED RAMANGASOAVINA

Alfred Ramangasoavina was appointed Malagasy Minister of Justice in October, 1960.

A lawyer, he had earlier served as Finance Minister (1957), Minister for Equipment (1958), and Minister for Industry and Planning (1959).

He was elected to the Malagasy National Assembly as Social Democratic Party deputy for Tananarive Province in September, 1960.

M. Ramangasoavina was born on November 2, 1917. He served in the administration in Madagascar from 1939–47, when he went to France to complete his studies in law and political science.

Later a lawyer in the Tananarive Appeal Court, he worked in the Paris Appeal Court from 1952–54.

In 1954 he served at the Central Treasury for Overseas France for two years, and was then posted to the Madagascar Exchange Office.

M. Ramangasoavina began his political career in 1956, when he was elected a municipal councillor for Tananarive, the capital.

SAMUEL RAMILAMANANA

Samuel Ramilamanana was appointed Secretary of State for Local Government and Works in August, 1965. He had been Secretary of State for the Province of Tamatave since October, 1960.

A doctor by profession, he was elected municipal councillor for Tamatave in 1956, and entered the National Assembly in 1958.

From February–March, 1960, he was a member of the Malagasy delegation which went to France for negotiations on Malagasy independence.

NORBERT RANOHAVIMANANA

Norbert Ranohavimanana, a mathematician and teacher, was named Secretary of State for Tamatave Province in 1965.

Born on September 23, 1926, he studied mathematics, teaching and astronomy in Paris, and returned home in 1956 after two years' teaching in France. He continued teaching in Madagascar, and was a high school headmaster when he became Secretary of State.

RENE RASIDY

René Rasidy was named Minister for Mines and Industry on August 28, 1965, after five years as Minister for Agriculture and Farming.

Born on July 5, 1927, M. Rasidy studied at the Teachers' Training College in Caen, France, and in 1956 was a founder-member of the Madagascar Social Democratic Party, which later became the country's ruling party.

In 1957 he was elected a provincial councillor for Majunga – his home province – and a year later he became a deputy in the Malagasy Assembly. In June, 1959, he was made Secretary of State for Farming.

GILBERT RATSITOHARA

Gilbert Ratsitohara was appointed Secretary of State for Cultural Affairs, Youth and Sports in August, 1965.

A teacher, who trained at the International Institute for Pedagogical Studies at Sèvres, France, he taught in various parts of Madagascar, and was for many years secretary of the Teachers' Trade Union.

He became a municipal councillor in Tananarive in 1959, and was elected to the National Assembly a year later.

National secretary of the Malagasy Red Cross and assistant secretary-general for Youth, of the ruling Social Democratic Party, M. Ratsitohara was born on March 31, 1914.

JOSEPH RAVOAHANGY ANDRIANAVALONA

Doctor, journalist and trade unionist, Joseph Ravoahangy Andrianavalona started fighting for self-rule for Madagascar in 1916, and was deported to the Comores Islands by the French colonial authorities for seven years. He was exiled after the 1947 nationalist uprising which was put down by French troops.

He returned home in 1960, became a member of the National Assembly, and was appointed Minister for Public Health and Population. In August, 1965, he was made a Minister without Portfolio attached to the Presidency.

M. Ravoahangy Andrianavalona was born on October 28, 1893. He went to school at a Norwegian Protestant mission, and studied at the Tananarive Medical School.

His medical studies were interrupted when the French authorities exiled him to the Comores for his activities as a founder-member of the VVS, an opposition movement campaigning for self-rule.

On his first return from exile, M. Ravoahangy Andrianavalona finished his medical studies and served as a doctor in Tulear Province's medical service from 1924–27.

On leaving the service he went to Diego Suarez, where he wrote in several nationalist newspapers.

He was active in trade unionism and set up medical and dental trade unions and the Franco-Malagasy Press Trade Union.

In 1945 he was elected deputy for Madagascar to the French National Assembly, and set up the Democratic Movement for National Revival ('Mouvement Démocratique de la Rénovation Malgache' – MDRM), whose leaders were arrested after the 1947 uprising.

DR JULES RAVONY

Dr Jules Ravony was named Malagasy Ambassador to West Germany in December, 1964. He had been President of the Malagasy Senate (Upper House) since October, 1960.

Before entering the Senate he served as President of the National Assembly from 1959.

Born on December 22, 1905, M. Ravony studied at the Tananarive School of Medicine and worked in the Medical Assistance Service from 1930–56. He was in the French Armed Forces between 1939 and 1942.

He began his political career in 1957, when he became a provincial councillor, and was elected to the Malagasy Assembly the following year.

In February and March, 1960, he was a member of the delegation which went to France for negotiations on Malagasy independence.

JULES ALPHONSE RAZAFIMBAHINY

Jules Alphonse Razafimbahiny became Director-General of the Malagasy Foreign Ministry in October, 1964.

Born on April 19, 1923, he trained as a lawyer and economist.

In 1960 he was in Brussels as President of the Committee of Overseas Countries associated with the European Common Market. He then returned to Madagascar and served for a year as technical adviser to the Economics Ministry. The Government also made him Chairman of the Madagascar Power Company.

From 1962–64 M. Razafimbahiny served as secretary-general of the Afro-Malagasy Organisation for Economic Cooperation (OAMCE), based in Yaoundé, Cameroun.

ANDRE RESAMPA

André Resampa, a founder-member of the Malagasy Social Democratic Party, became

Minister of the Interior in 1959.

Three years earlier he had joined Philibert Tsiranana–later first President of the Malagasy Republic – in setting up the party which was to rule the country.

M. Resampa, an able administrator, became secretary-general of the party in 1958, succeeding M. Tsiranana.

A Roman Catholic, he was born on June 24, 1924. M. Resampa joined the administration as a secretary-interpreter, then became a clerk in the Department of Justice.

He was elected to the Provincial Assembly of Tulear in 1952. Five years later he was elected to the Representative Assembly of Madagascar.

In October, 1958, when Madagascar was proclaimed an internally self-governing republic within the French Community, he became a deputy in the National Assembly.

The same year he became Minister for Social Affairs, Education and Health.

In 1960, he headed the Malagasy delegation negotiating the transfer of power from France to the Republic.

M. Resampa remained Interior Minister when a new Government was formed in 1965.

DR ALBERT SYLLA

Dr Albert Sylla, who began his political career in 1952, was named Malagasy Foreign Minister in October, 1960.

He had earlier held the posts of Deputy Prime Minister concerned with Agriculture (from May, 1959) and Minister for Planning, Farming and Tourism (from January, 1959).

Dr Sylla, born on February 18, 1909, at Tulear, studied at the Tananarive Medical School, and joined the Medical Service.

Philibert Tsiranana

In 1953 he became Councillor of the then French Union, and a provincial councillor of Tamatave.

In 1958 he entered the National Assembly.

CALVIN TSIEBO

Calvin Tsiebo, a former teacher and administrator, was named Deputy Prime Minister of the Malagasy Republic in October, 1960.

In 1965 he added to his other duties the task of Minister for Social Affairs charged with Administrative Coordination.

Born on July 12, 1902, near Betioky in south-west Madagascar, M. Tsiebo received his education at an American Protestant mission and at several private schools.

From 1923 he taught for two years at a Protestant mission school before being appointed a deputy chief in the local administration.

M. Tsiebo advanced in the administrative field, becoming in 1956 an administrative secretary for Madagascar – then a French colony.

In 1957 he was elected provincial councillor for his home province, and a year later became a deputy in the constituent National Assembly. He was elected President of the National Assembly in October, 1960, by 101 votes out of 107, but resigned this post on his appointment as Deputy Prime Minister.

PHILIBERT TSIRANANA

Philibert Tsiranana, who once tended his father's flocks in the mountains of northern Madagascar, was the chief architect of his country's independence, and first President of the Malagasy Republic.

Known as the 'Father of Independence', this stocky, energetic man was returned to power for a second seven-year term as President in 1965.

He received over ninety per cent of the votes cast in a three-cornered election – Madagascar's first presidential election by popular vote.

M. Tsiranana, who was born in 1912 and is a Roman Catholic, was elected first President of the Malagasy Republic by Parliament in congress in May, 1959. There were 114 voters, and 113 voted for him.

M. Tsiranana, who has a lively sense of humour, favours colourful sports shirts and usually wears a white panama hat, has retained the practical outlook of his peasant background.

He was twelve before he went to school, but proved a brilliant student, becoming a teacher and later a professor. After a period of teaching in Madagascar he went in 1946 to Montpellier, France, returning to Madagascar as a technical teacher after four years' study.

In 1952, he was returned unopposed as councillor on the Madagascar Representative Assembly.

In 1956, he was elected deputy to the French National Assembly in Paris, representing the West Coast constituency of Madagascar.

In the same year, M. Tsiranana founded his own party – the Social Democratic Party (PSD) – and became its secretary-general in December, 1957.

In 1957 he served as deputy head of the Madagascar Government under the French governor, and in October, 1958, when Madagascar was proclaimed an internally self-governing republic, he became head of the provisional Government.

Voted first President of the Malagasy Republic in May, 1959, he proclaimed the Republic's full independence in June the following year. Under the constitution M. Tsiranana, as President, is also head of government.

An outspoken supporter of democracy, he allowed the Opposition to campaign and run a number of newspapers critical of Government policies.

In 1965, he complained that the Opposition was too weak to be constructive. He said he wished it were stronger.

At the time his Social Democratic Party had 98 seats in the 107-seat Lower House of Parliament, the Movement for National Revival six, the Congress Party two – and one seat was vacant.

The Opposition parties in general called for greater independence from France, particularly in the commercial field, and a more radically socialist policy, with more nationalisation at home and more contacts with the Communist world.

M. Tsiranana adopted a policy of close cooperation with France and encouragement of foreign investment. Despite the close commercial ties with France, however, he insisted on aid and cooperation without strings.

He has said he is '100 per cent socialist', but he has warned against widespread nationalism simply for the sake of ideology.

M. Tsiranana has been outspoken about what he considers dangerous Communist activities in Africa. This concern overrode even his usual agreement with French foreign policy, and he refused to follow France's example in recognising the People's Republic of China.

In November, 1966, he stated:

'I have denounced on several occasions the actions of the Communist Chinese in the "Third World" and in Africa in general.

'A people essentially peaceful, whose golden rule is not to encourage subversion, we will not accept the admission of Communist China to the United Nations, even if we should be the only country left to oppose them.'

M. Tsiranana was a major champion of the union of the majority of French-speaking African states, which eventually (in 1965) became the Common Afro-Malagasy Organisation (OCAM) – a loose political association.

Unassuming – he once told a man who had not recognised him, 'I work for the Government' – and informal, M. Tsiranana is well known for his habit of taking pictures of photographers taking pictures of him.

PIERRE ZAKA

Pierre Zaka was the youngest minister in the Malagasy Republic when in August, 1965, he was appointed Secretary of State for Agriculture concerned with the development of the eastern regions.

M. Zaka, who was born in 1929, had been Secretary of State for Transport since 1963.

He began his political career in 1956 as a municipal councillor, became a provincial councillor a year later, and was elected to the National Assembly in September, 1960, as deputy for Tamatave Province.

He became deputy-mayor of the east-coast port of Tamatave in 1959.

M. Zaka, a sport-lover, is especially keen on football, volleyball and basketball.

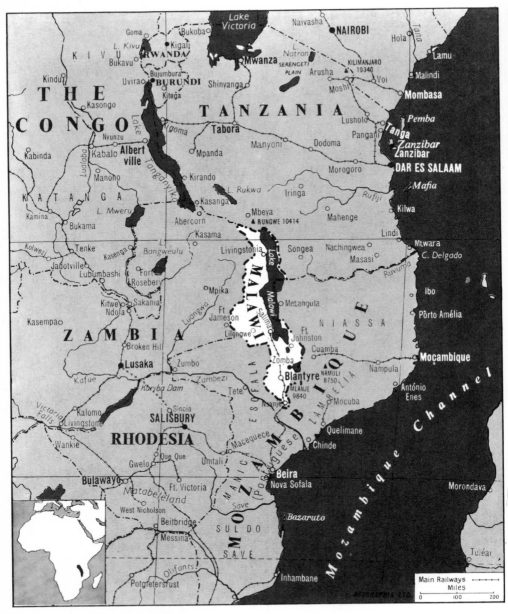

Malawi is a landlocked territory of 45,747 square miles (9,266 being water) bounded by Tanzania to the north, Zambia to the west and Portuguese Mozambique to the east and south. The population in 1963 was estimated at 4,042,412. A new city at Lilongwe will replace Zomba as the capital. Malawi's purely agrarian economy, based on exports of tea, cotton and tobacco, is dependent upon the Mozambique port of Beira for egress to the Indian Ocean. Another Mozambique port, Nacala, will be available to Malawi when the railway line from Mpimbe, Malawi, to Nove Freixa and Nacala is completed.

Malawi

Malawi, formerly the British Protectorate of Nyasaland, constituted on May 15, 1891, became independent on July 6, 1964, and a republic exactly two years later.

The first President was Dr Hastings Kamuzu Banda. He had led his people in the struggle to free themselves from the Federation of Rhodesia and Nyasaland, established by the British Government in 1953 and dissolved in 1963.

Dr Banda had returned to Nyasaland in 1958 to take direct control of the African National Congress. During unrest, the British Governor, Sir Robert Armitage declared a state of emergency on March 3, 1959. Congress was outlawed and rioting followed. Dr Banda and nearly 1,500 of his followers were arrested in 'Operation Sunrise'. It was alleged that there was a 'plot' to massacre leading white officials including the Governor himself and assassinate certain African chiefs who were collaborating with the Protectorate Government.

The Devlin Commission (July, 1959) accepted that there had been 'talk of beating and killing Europeans but not of cold-blooded assassination or massacre'. It did not accept the Government's claim that there was a widespread murder plot and absolved Dr Banda.

Malawi aims one day to become financially, as well as politically, independent of Britain. This is one of the objects of the Five Year Plan.

But Dr Hastings Banda, the President – who is also head of government – told delegates of the ruling Malawi Congress Party towards the end of 1966: 'This country does not pay for its keep. It costs more to run the country than we earn. If Britain stopped helping us, we could not stand and function for a single day.'

Britain is committed for three years (1966–68) to subsidise the budget by some £5,250,000 annually and has advanced a £7m development loan over the same period.

During the Federation of Rhodesia and Nyasaland, set up in 1953, the country received between £3m and £4m annually from the Federal Government.

One of the great tasks of development is the construction of the Great Lake Shore Road, running along the western shores of Lake Malawi, to open up the hitherto unexploited agricultural potential of the northern and central regions.

Mlanje Mountain, seen
from a tea plantation

The £3 Nkula Falls Hydro-Electric Scheme, regarded
as the key to the country's future, is a joint effort
between the British and Malawi Governments, with the
Commonwealth Development Corporation as the major
financier. With more plentiful electricity, it is expected
to transform the southern region, which is rapidly
becoming the industrial centre of the country.

Most development in Malawi is channelled through the
Malawi Development Corporation, started in 1964 with
a grant from the British Government. Dr Banda gave it
wide investment powers and freedom to do everything
possible to develop the commercial, industrial and
agricultural possibilities of the country. It has acquired
an interest in everything from cold storage plants to
quarries. It runs cattle ranches and a distillery. It works
in close association with the Commonwealth
Development Corporation and similar organisations
in countries like Denmark, France, West Germany and
the USA.

The two mainstays of Malawi's economy, tea and
tobacco, account for 45–55 per cent of the country's
exports. The tea industry is largely under the control
of British business interests, the crop being sold in
Mincing Lane, London. Tobacco, apart from a small
European-grown flue-cured crop, is peasant-grown, but
bought and processed by British firms in Limbe. They
export about 55 per cent of it to the United Kingdom,
the rest going chiefly to West Africa and Continental
Europe.

Malawi's other exports are cotton, coffee, tung oil and
maize. Sugar may soon be added. The largest single
agricultural development in recent years is the £3m
Lonrho sugar project in the Lower Shire River area.
It went into production in the middle of 1966. By 1970
Malawi hopes not only to be self-supporting in sugar
but also to have an exportable surplus.

The capital of Malawi is Zomba, but work on a new
£11m capital about 200 miles to the north and about
four miles north-east of the Central Region capital of
Lilongwe, was started late in 1966.

Zomba, which will become the home of the University –
at present accommodated in a secondary school at
Blantyre – is not suited to meet the needs of a functional
centre of government. Five Ministries are based

Women tea pickers on
the Lujeri estate

elsewhere because of lack of space in what is a mountainous area of the country. Many of the buildings are old and due for replacement, and the ultimate cost of attempting to rehabilitate, pull down and rebuild Zomba would, it is calculated, be greater than creating comparable facilities elsewhere.

Aleke Banda

Dr Hastings Banda

ALEKE BANDA

Aleke Kadonaphani Banda, appointed Minister of Development and Planning in 1966, has played a prominent part in building the Malawi Congress Party into one of the most powerful political movements in Central Africa. He was appointed secretary-general when it started on September 30, 1959. He also became chairman of the League of Malawi Youth which includes the Malawi Young Pioneers.

The opportunity to figure in the African struggle for independence, something he had always wanted, came when the Southern Rhodesian Government deported him and he says he was 'just dumped in Blantyre', where he knew no one.

Banda is short, slight, soft-spoken, modest and polite. Born on September 19, 1939, in Livingstone, Northern Rhodesia, of a family from Nyasaland, he went to the United Missionary School at Que Que, Southern Rhodesia, where his father had a job at Moss Mine.

Encouraged at home to read and study all he could, he was recognised at school as a boy with unusual ability. While at Inyati School (London Missionary Society) in Bulawayo, he was prefect, Sunday school teacher and editor of the school magazine. He received and built the Southern Rhodesia African Students Association into such a political force that eventually it was banned by the Government.

At 15 he was secretary of the Que Que branch of the Nyasaland African National Congress, already an ardent nationalist, writing articles breathing fire on the imposed Federation of Rhodesia and Nyasaland.

When a state of emergency was suddenly declared in Southern Rhodesia, Banda says he was picked up by policemen from his school desk on March 10, 1959, and taken to Khami prison. He was then doing the fourth year of the Cambridge Overseas Certificate. The police also took away a sackful of papers.

At Khami, Banda met many leading politicians from Nyasaland.

He has since been the first editor of *Malawi News*, personal secretary to Dr Banda, and has taken part in three constitutional delegations to London in 1960 and 1962. He became Director-General of the Malawi Broadcasting Corporation in 1964, and a director of the Reserve Bank of Malawi (1965). He relinquished both appointments when he became Minister of Development and Planning, controlling the Department of Information.

DR. HASTINGS KAMUZU BANDA

Ngwazi (Chief of Chiefs) Dr Hastings Kamuzu Banda was the first Prime Minister when the former British Protectorate

271

of Nyasaland became the independent State of Malawi, still owing allegiance to Queen Elizabeth, on July 6, 1964. He was the sole nominee for President when Malawi became a republic on July 6, 1966.

A medical practitioner who has lived most of his life among white men, he was hailed as a messiah when he returned home on July 5, 1958, after an absence of over 40 years. He led the four million people of Nyasaland, as undisputed spokesman, in their struggle for independence from the Federation of Rhodesia and Nyasaland.

Born in 1906 to a family of the Chewa tribe in the Kasungu district of Nyasaland, he later adopted as his first name the surname of a missionary friend, John Hastings.

Having become proficient in English at the Livingstonia mission of the Church of Scotland and exhausted all the education available in the land of his birth, he set out when only 13 years old to walk about 1,000 miles to the Union of South Africa, without money, spare clothes or identification papers. On his way he got a job as orderly at an African hospital at Hartley, near Salisbury, Southern Rhodesia. What he saw there decided him to become a doctor.

In Johannesburg he worked as a clerk and interpreter in the Rand Goldfields, He remained there eight years, continuing his education at night schools. After hearing a lecture by a noted Negro political leader, Dr J. E. Kwegyir Aggrey, of Accra, he resolved to go to the United States: he was helped financially in this by an American Methodist bishop.

At Indiana University he passed in history and political science; at the University of Chicago, where he was the only Negro student, he received his PhB degree in 1931. His dream of becoming a doctor was realised in 1937, when he qualified for his MD degree at Mcharay Medical College, Nashville, Tennessee. He studied medicine further at the Universities of Glasgow and Edinburgh, where he became an elder of the Church of Scotland. Then followed years of practice as a doctor in Liverpool, North Shields and in Kilburn (1953), a populous district of London where he served about 4,000 patients.

To his home came African nationalist leaders like Kwame Nkrumah of the Gold Coast (as it then was) and Jomo Kenyatta, of Kenya. As a result of voluminous correspondence with African leaders in Nyasaland, the Nyasaland African Congress was established in 1950, with himself as the obvious and unchallenged leader.

When the British Government in London drew up their plans for a Federation of the two Rhodesias and Nyasaland, Dr Banda led the opposition from his surgery in London. When the Federation was established in 1953 he accused the British Government of betraying his people. He said the country would have to become a concentration camp before federation could suceed.

To be nearer his native land, he moved to the Gold Coast and practised in Kumasi, the Ashanti capital.

In 1958, when there was unrest among the people of Nyasaland, he returned to take over the direct leadership of the Congress and was elected President-General. With a background of passive resistance, but determined to get government by elected representatives and ultimate freedom from the deeply resented Federation, he called for friendly negotiations between Africans and Europeans. He expressed a desire to keep Nyasaland within the British Commonwealth.

Congress was banned on March 3, 1959, and there was rioting amid allegations that there had been a 'plot' to massacre white officials.

While Dr Banda was in prison at Gwelo, Southern Rhodesia, following 'Operation Sunrise', his followers, under the leadership of Orton Chirwa, formed the Malawi Congress Party (September 30, 1959), with a programme dedicated to democracy, socialism, nationalism and pan-Africanism. In England an agitation for the release of Dr Banda was increasing, supported in Labour and Liberal circles. In Central Africa, the Federal Prime Minister, Sir Roy Welensky, an architect of federation, and other officials were strongly opposed to his release.

On April 1, 1960, during a visit by the British Colonial Secretary Mr Iain McLeod, he was unconditionally set free. There was great jubilation among his followers but before he left to attend the Nyasaland Constitutional Conference in London, he told them: 'Do not spoil my work. If you listen to me, you will have your own government. I want everybody to keep quiet while I am in London.'

Various London conferences frustrated Dr Banda, but in August, 1960, Nyasaland achieved a constitution under which 100,000 Africans (out of four million) were able to vote because they met the necessary income, property and literacy qualifications. The Africans were guaranteed a solid majority on the Nyasaland Legislative Council.

Elections on August 15, 1961, took on the atmosphere of a personal contest between Dr Banda and Sir Roy Welensky and were an opportunity to answer the question whether Nyasaland should remain in the Federation.

Eighty thousand Africans took part. The Malawi Congress Party secured all 20 of the legislative seats on the lower roll with three of the eight seats on the upper roll, the remaining five being won by Welensky's United Federal Party.

Very soon afterwards the Malawi Congress Party gained control of the Executive Council as well as of the Legislature.

Two months after independence, an internal crisis developed. Dr Banda dismissed three of his Cabinet and three others resigned. After an eleventh-hour sitting of Parliament, Dr Banda won an overwhelming vote of confidence. His chief opponent, Henry Chipembere, then Minister of Education, was placed under house arrest but got away. Dr Banda announced new security measures to stop armed rebellion. In May, 1965, he said 400 men had been captured.

Dr Banda is of medium build, grey-haired, dynamic, tempestuous, with searching, analytical eyes, a gift of oratory and a sense of humour which can become caustic.

He believes in a realistic approach to resolutions on the situation in Rhodesia or South West Africa by the United Nations, the Commonwealth Conference or the Organisation of African Unity. He ridiculed the OAU's idea of African states using armed force to topple the Ian Smith regime in Rhodesia, following its unilateral declaration of independence. He said it

G. C. Chakuamba

Qabaniso Chibambo

was not realistic and could not be implemented. 'Where is the African country,' he asked, 'which has the army or economy to conquer Smith?'

He laughed at the notion of the United Nations taking over and administering South West Africa. If the South African Government refused to move out, he demanded, who was going to eject them? Was a British, American, Russian or African army going to do it? 'Let us face reality,' he said.

AUGUSTINE BWANAUSI

Augustine Bwanausi was Minister of Development and Housing when Dr Banda dismissed him and other dissident members of the Cabinet in 1964.

Since Malawi became self-governing he held various portfolios.

Born in 1930, he was educated at Makerere College, Uganda, and took a Bachelor of Science degree in London and a diploma in education at Bristol. He became a schoolmaster in Nyasaland, teaching science, and later went to Tanganyika, where he was soon caught up in politics, becoming a senior member of Dr Nyerere's Tanganyika African National Union.

When Dr Banda returned to Malawi, Bwanausi went home and joined the new leader.

He was detained, along with Dr Banda and other leading nationalists, during the 1959 Emergency.

G. C. CHAKUAMBA

Confinement in cells and long interrogations were the experience of Gwandanguluwe Chikanzi Chakuamba during the grim period in 1959 when Congress leaders were accused of being implicated in a 'massacre plot' and there were wholesale detentions.

Chakuamba was born on April 4, 1935 at Nsanje (then Port Herald). At Solusi College near Bulawayo, where he matriculated, he worked hard and did well, winning two first class diplomas in essay writing.

In 1958 he won a scholarship for study in the United States of America, but like a lot of other young Nyasalanders, decided to abandon the pursuit of higher education in order to do something for the future of his country. He devoted all his time and energy to the Nyasaland African Congress, leaders of which were quick to recognise his frankness, courage and dedication. He was soon appointed organising secretary for Nsanje but before four months had elapsed he and more than a thousand other Congressmen had been detained. He was one of those who gave evidence before the Devlin Commission.

He was elected to the Legislative Council for Lower River in 1961 and returned for Nsanje North in 1964; in that year he became Minister of Community and Social Development.

Q. Y. CHIBAMBO

One of the many consistent foes of Federation was Qabaniso Yesaya Chibambo, who became Minister of Works in 1964 and of Health in 1966.

He was born in 1917, the first son of the late Revd Yesaya Chibambo, one of the first African ministers in the Presbyterian Church of Central Africa, a man of great repute who made sure that all his children (three sons and three daughters) went to and completed school at an early age.

After leaving school in 1936,

Richard Chidzanja

the future Congress leader went to Livingstonia for a commercial course. As a trained man he got a job with the Nyasaland Tobacco Board and exerted strong influence on the farmers. He joined the District Commissioner's Office at Lilongwe, served at several places in the Northern and Central Regions and was finally head clerk at Fort Manning, where he became popular with both chiefs and people and helped to organise branches of the Nyasaland African Congress. In 1948 he was retransferred to Lilongwe.

He was relentless in his opposition to Federation. In 1953, while in the Government service, he was arrested and sentenced to 15 months for Congress activities, then restricted to Nsanje (Port Herald).

One profile of him recalls that he lived in 'a small world' for eight years, reporting to the police twice a day, at 6 am and 6 pm. He was prohibited from seeking employment with the Native Authorities anywhere, the Nyasaland Railways or the Education Department. His only freedom was to write letters or memoranda 'that were later torn in his presence by the District Commissioner'. He could, of course, 'lie on his bed and do some endless thinking'. He made great use of his long detention.

He was at Khami, Marandellas and Kanjedza. He knew everybody, officials and detainees, as camp leader and chief spokesman. He was released as a 'camp finalist' in 1960.

He was returned as MP for Mzimba North in 1961 and again in 1964.

RICHARD B. CHIDZANJA

A Chewa of the Central Region, Richard B. Chidzanja became Minister of Home Affairs, then Local Government (1964).

Born on May 5, 1921, he was a vernacular teacher when he started on his adventures in Southern Rhodesia and South Africa.

At home he went into active politics in 1950. He visited the chiefs in the Central Region advising them not to accept federation with Southern Rhodesia. He was active during the Congress boycott of the coronation of Queen Elizabeth in 1953 and when federation celebrations were being organised.

He served on local councils and was one of the Congressmen who in 1957, from Blantyre, sent a telegram to Dr Banda calling upon him to return home and lead his countrymen to independence and away from federation.

He was among the many arrested after 'Operation Sunrise' (1959) and was described as 'one of the most jovial personalities in detention'.

HENRY CHIPEMBERE

Henry Masauko Chipembere was one of the Malawians chiefly responsible for getting Dr Banda to return to lead the country to independence in 1959. But by September, 1964, when he was Minister of Education, he had taken to the forests in rebellion. By October, 1966, Dr Banda was acusing him of organising in exile a Malawi underground movement, with the sympathy of Tanzania. He forbade the people of Malawi to mention his name and said anyone found reading his circulars would be jailed.

Chipembere was the most powerful African politician in Malawi next to Dr Banda. The dissident faction which he led in the Cabinet revolt said they wanted the leader to be less autocratic and give the ministers more say in the day to day running of the country.

They also wanted him to accept an alleged £18m loan from the Communist Chinese Government. But Dr Banda's comment was that there was no need for China to dangle a loan 'like a carrot before a donkey's nose'. 'I am an elder of the Church of Scotland. I do not understand the language of bribery,' he said.

The Cabinet 'revolt' was brought into the open by Kanyama Chiume, External Affairs Minister, but Chipembere, returning from Canada, made a speech in Parliament during a debate which preceded a vote of confidence in Dr Banda, and emerged as the leader of the Opposition. Six Ministers were dismissed (September, 1964) or resigned, among the latter Chipembere.

In October, 1964, Dr Banda, who had been calling Chipembere 'my favourite son', restricted his movements to within a three mile radius of his home at Malindi, Fort Johnston, on the shores of Lake Malawi.

Not long afterwards, Chipembere, refusing to accept his confinement, slipped away into the hills along the Mozambique-Malawi borders, and, with what appeared to be a considerable following, ran a series of running battles with security forces led by British officers.

Dr Banda put a *Wanted – Dead or Alive* notice on his head and offered a reward of £500. The money was never collected.

During February, 1965, Chipembere struck back at the Government and personally led an armed raid on the town of Fort Johnston, capturing the police post, destroying telecommunications and capturing a large quantity of arms, ammunition and transport. The rebels set out to march on Zomba, the capital, some 150 miles to the south, but were confronted by security forces on the banks of the Shire River at Liwonde, 30 miles from their goal. They fled in disorder.

Harried by the security forces, Chipembere fled from Malawi and later appeared in the United States. He left behind his leading lieutenant, Medson Evans Silombela, to carry on the fight. Silombela was eventually captured, admitted in court to eight cold-blooded killings and was hanged for the murder of a party official.

Four hundred ruling party members and relatives of the people he was said to have killed were admitted to Zomba prison to see him die.

In his writings, Chipembere has said that Malawi, in practice, is a one-party State, the party having a life chairman who selects the Central Executive. 'The practical result is that the party is an instrument for suppressing all criticism and ensuring the perpetuation in power of an individual or clique.'

In one of his broadcasts, Dr Banda said Chipembere was not a brave man – 'not a lion, a leopard or even a wild cat, but a coward, a hyena'.

Born in 1930, Chipembere was educated at Blantyre Secondary School and Goromonzi Secondary School, and graduated with a BA degree from Fort Hare University College.

He was the secretary-general of the former African National Congress in Malawi, and retained this post in the subsequent Malawi Congress Party until his suspension in 1964 after opposing Dr Banda. He was elected a member of the Legislative Assembly in 1955 under the British Colonial Government.

During the March, 1959 'Massacre Plot' he was arrested by the British and imprisoned for the duration of the Emergency. Later, leading a vitriolic campaign against the Federation, he was jailed for a further two years for urging violence. Released in 1963, Dr Banda appointed him Minister of Local Government. In a subsequent Cabinet reshuffle, Chipembere became the Minister of Education.

ORTON CHIRWA

Orton Chingoli Chirwa was Minister of Justice in the Malawi Government until the Cabinet 'revolt' of September, 1964, when he was dismissed.

Along with the five other dissident Ministers, he objected to what they called the authoritarian rule of Dr Banda, especially in the field of Africanisation, which they claimed was not going fast enough.

Born in 1919, Chirwa was the first Malawian to be called to the English bar after he had obtained his BA at Fort Hare University College.

In 1957 he returned home to practice as a barrister in partnership with an Indian barrister and defended many of the African nationalists charged with offences by the British Colonial Government. Gravel-voiced, he displayed the mannerisms and wore the dress of an English barrister.

On March 3, 1959, Chirwa was arrested for alleged complicity in the 'Massacre Plot', which was alleged in a British White Paper (official report) to be a conspiracy to assassinate the British Governor, leading members of the Colonial Administration and other prominent Europeans.

Chirwa was released early in 1960, long before Dr Banda or any other nationalist, and at once formed the Malawi Congress Party with himself as president, declaring that this position would be Dr Banda's as soon as he was free.

Chirwa kept his word, handed over the leadership to Dr Banda in due course and himself became legal adviser.

Chirwa's premature release caused speculation and controversy. It has been alleged by leading British administrators that Chirwa was in fact a go-between for the British Government and Dr Banda during the contacts made before the break-up of the Federation of Rhodesia and Nyasaland, which was being imposed by the British Government under the premiership of Sir Roy Welensky.

Chirwa obtained the portfolio of Justice when Malawi became self-governing in 1964. When dismissed by Dr Banda, he returned to his home constituency of Nkata Bay on the eastern shores of Lake Malawi, then went to Zambia and later Tanzania.

YATUTA CHISIZA

Yatuta Chisiza, Home Affairs Minister involved in the Cabinet crisis of September, 1964, left the country and later went to Dar es Salaam.

Dr Banda has accused him of organising rebels against the Malawi Government.

Born in 1926, Chisiza was educated at Livingstonia, the first Scottish missionary school in Nyasaland. He joined the Tanganyika Police and rose to the rank of inspector, unprecedented for an African in those days.

When Tanganyika attained self-government he was offered

A. B. J. Chiwanda

the post of Chief of Police. He declined the offer and returned home to help in the campaign for independence.

A large man physically, he was Dr Banda's bodyguard for some time and was jailed with him in Gwelo prison during the 1959 Emergency.

M. W. KANYAMA CHIUME

Kanyama Chiume, Malawi's former External Affairs Minister, was a prime mover in the Cabinet 'revolt' against Dr Banda in September, 1964.

Six Ministers left the Government. Chiume, Chirwa and Bwanausi were said to have been sacked, while Chisiza, Chipembere and Chokani resigned in sympathy.

Small, dapper and fond of bow-ties, Chiume is a forceful speaker.

Born in 1929, Chiume won a diploma of education at Makerere College and was elected a member of the Legislative Council under the British Colonial Administration, along with his colleague Chipembere, in 1955. With other leading Nyasaland nationalists he was responsible for the recall of Dr Banda from London to lead the campaign for independence.

During the State of Emergency declared in March, 1959, following the alleged 'Massacre Plot', Chiume was on the high seas returning home after a tour of Britain. He promptly left the ship and flew back to England, where he agitated for the release of Dr Banda and other nationalists on British television and at public meetings in London and Manchester.

On Dr Banda's release Chiume returned to Nyasaland and became publicity secretary of the newly formed Malawi Congress Party.

Chiume was the first Minister of Information in self-governing Malawi and in 1964 was Minister in charge of the independence celebrations. On Independence Day (July 6, 1964) Dr Banda made Chiume Minister of External Affairs and took over the Ministry of Information himself.

After the Cabinet crisis and the motion of confidence which Dr Banda won overwhelmingly, Chiume went to his home constituency of Rumpi in the northern region. A few weeks later he moved to Dar es Salaam from where he worked in active opposition to Dr Banda.

A. B. J. CHIWANDA

Appointed Minister of Labour after the independence celebrations, Albert B. J. Chiwanda had become MP for Mwanza-Neno in 1964.

He was born on March 14, 1933, at Mlanje and educated at the Henry Henderson Institute and Malamulo Mission, where he reached standard six.

He worked as a carpenter at home and in Southern Rhodesia, became organising secretary of the Msasa branch of the Nyasaland African Congress, then in 1959 went to Southern Rhodesia for a second time, threw himself into political activities and was dismissed by his employers for that reason.

In 1960 he was chairman of the Mapanga branch of the Malawi Congress Party. In July, 1962, he was appointed to the Blantyre District Council and was elected chairman in the following January. In the same year he became chairman of the Malawi Congress Party.

WILLIE CHOKANI

Willie Chokani was Minister of Labour until the Cabinet crisis

J. T. Kumbweza

John Msonthi

of September, 1964, in which he supported Chipembere in disagreement with Dr Banda's manner of ruling the country. He was later reported to have gone to Zambia, working as a schoolteacher.

A quiet, soft-spoken man, firm in his principles and ideals, Chokani aligned himself with the nationalist movement to attain his country's independence from British colonial rule. He was an active campaigner and solid supporter on behalf of the Malawi Congress Party and Dr Banda.

Along with others prominent in the movement, he was detained by the Colonial Government during the 1959 Emergency.

Born in 1930 and educated at Blantyre Secondary School, he won a scholarship to India and obtained a BA at St Stephen's College, Delhi, with a diploma in education.

J. T. KUMBWEZA

Jeremia T. Kumbweza, who reached the Malawi Cabinet as Minister of Trade and Industry, was born at Mlongoti village near Mitundu Market in 1925.

His interest in politics began in 1951 when he became a member of the Nyasaland African Congress. While selling timber he studied privately by correspondence, passed book-keeping and accountancy examinations and in 1959 was elected vice-treasurer of the Malawi Congress Party.

In 1961 Dr Banda chose him for the Legislative Assembly and three years later he had the parliamentary secretaryship to the ministry over which he was soon to preside.

JOHN MSONTHI

'Kaka' – which means 'brother of everyone' – is a nickname which John Dunstan Msonthi was given during his 14 months in prison after 'Operation Sunrise' in March, 1959. He had been arrested during disturbances when a campaign by the Nyasaland African Congress for immediate self-government led to a state of emergency being declared by the Colonial Government.

At Zomba Central Prison and other places of detention his efforts to cheer up all the other prisoners made him very popular. He served on the Detainees Committee, a sort of liaison between prison officials and the inmates, and was among those who helped to pass the time 'inside' by running a school.

When Dr Banda took over government he was appointed Minister of Trade and Industry (1962) and later became Minister of Transport and Communications.

Msonthi was born on January 12, 1928 at Kayoyo, near Visanza in Nkhota Kota district, the eldest son of the local schoolmaster, the Revd B. C. Msonthi.

His parentage made it possible for him to start school at the age of five. He has humorously recalled that he always hesitated to play truant lest his father should use him as 'a guinea pig' for an exercise in the administering of discipline. As a result he passed all his examinations at the top of the class.

From Likuni White Father School he went in January, 1945, to Zomba Secondary School, where he says he was much influenced by two Roman Catholic priests. At the Government standard eight examinations he came out second in the whole country. He persevered with the school course right through to standard nine. In December, 1948, he and

A. A. Muwalo

another student were the first candidates from their country to appear for the Cambridge School Certificate in Nyasaland.

He went to India with a Government of India cultural scholarship, studied at the University of Bombay at St Xavier's College under Jesuit fathers and learned from them something of their simple detachment from world affairs.

As chairman of the African Students' Association of Bombay he helped to secure the banning in India and also in Britain and the USA of films which portrayed African people and their problems in a wrong, prejudiced and even derogatory manner.

During the Suez Crisis of 1956 he was one of eight students who staged a march of protest towards the British High Commissioner's Office to hand in a memorandum. As there was a state of emergency in Bombay, he was arrested and detained, though only for seven hours.

After five years at St Xavier's he obtained a BA degree in sociology, with philosophy as a subsidiary subject, and a Bachelor of Education degree.

Returning home in 1958 he started teaching at Zomba Catholic Secondary School. It has been said that he never allowed anything to interfere with 'his greatest hobby – politics'. He was seen at all meetings addressed by Dr Banda.

After 'Operation Sunrise' and imprisonment, he taught for a time at St John's Teacher Training College at Lilongwe.

A. A. MUWALO

Albert Andrew Muwalo had already been Minister of Information when he became Minister of State in the Prime Minister's Office.

Born on June 23, 1927, he was educated at a primary school at Gowa and at Blantyre Secondary School. He began as a teacher then was an assistant at a medical training school for 13 years. In 1956 he was elected secretary-general of the Nyasaland African Medical Association and was the organisation's chief spokesman during the struggle against the imposition of federation.

When the State of Emergency was declared in March, 1959, he was dismissed from his job, arrested and taken to Zomba Prison, then Kanjedza Detention Camp and lastly to Lilongwe.

On release, though restricted to his area, he was appointed district chairman of the Malawi Congress Party in Ncheu.

He was the first chairman of the district council in Ncheu, when district councils were reconstituted in 1962, and Dr Banda made him a member of the Central Executive Committee of the Malawi Congress Party in Limbe. He became administrative secretary of the party after a three month visit to Ghana to study party administration and press management.

ALEC NYASULU

Alec Mjuma Nyasulu was the first African Speaker of the Malawi National Assembly (1963); then he became Minister of Natural Resources (1964), Health (1965) and Education (1966).

During World War II he served with the King's Africa Rifles in India and East Africa.

After the war he joined the Nyasaland Education Department as an inspector of schools and during this time began correspondence with Dr Banda, whom he had never met.

During the 1959 Emergency he

John Tembo

played a major role in preparing memoranda for the Devlin Commission.

He was born in the Mzimba district in 1920. He was returned an MP for this part of Malawi in 1961 and again in 1964.

JOHN TEMBO

First Malawi Minister of Finance in July, 1964, when the country attained its independence, John Zenas Ungapake Tembo was born in September, 1932.

The son of a prominent Presbyterian minister, the Revd Zenas Tembo, and a nephew of Chief Mpheza in Dedza district, he began his education at local mission schools. In 1947 he went to a senior primary school at Kongwe but while in standard five he was involved in a school strike and as a result was not admitted to standard six the following year.

He then entered Mlanda School in Ncheu district where he distinguished himself as the best pupil in standard six in 1949. Joining Blantyre Secondary School he passed the Cambridge School Certificate examinations four years later.

He worked for the Colonial Audit Department in Zomba until March, 1955, when he was awarded a Nyasaland Government scholarship to Roma University College, Basutoland. Here he became a keen student of political philosophy and threw himself enthusiastically into student activities.

While in Basutoland he met national leaders like Mokhehle and prominent members of the African National Congress in the Transvaal.

Unlike other students from the northern territories, John Tembo frequently elected not to return home for holidays but spent them with relatives in Benoni.

It was there, it is said, that his hatred of Afrikaner nationalism was most intensified. Returning to college, he became actively interested in South African liberation movements, declaring that the only hope for the non-Europeans was a united front against the Government. Since the African Students' Representative Council at Roma, of which he was a member, was affiliated to the National Union of South African Students (NUSAS), an organisation for students of all races, Tembo questioned its usefulness and began to campaign against it in the campus; for this he was labelled anti-white. An article he wrote in 1957 for a student paper caused a sensation among African students in many places and at Roma a more militant student organisation for Basutos was formed.

Tembo graduated at Roma in December, 1958, and returned to Nyasaland, where Dr Banda had already been back several months. He went to Salisbury for his educational diploma course, but had hardly been there a fortnight when a state of emergency was declared in Nyasaland.

He completed his course in November, 1959, obtaining a diploma of the University of London and in the following January he joined the staff of Kongwe Secondary School.

He was elected to the Legislative Council for Dedza in 1961 and a year later was Parliamentary Secretary for Finance. He became MP for Dedza North in 1964, took over the portfolio of Finance on Independence Day and added Trade and Industry, Development and Planning later the same year.

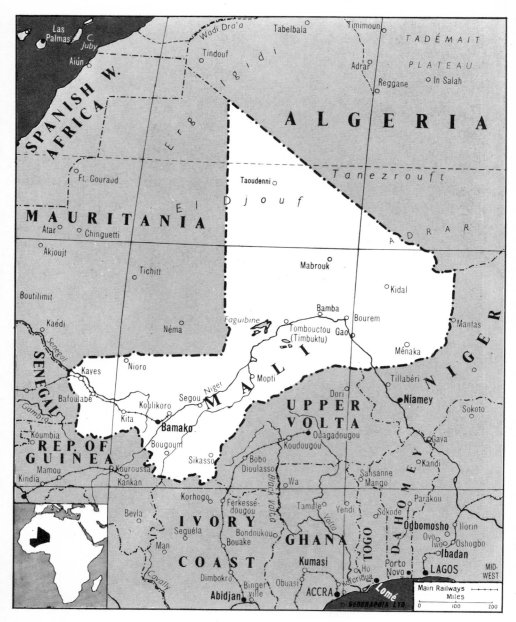

Nearly five million people (1965 estimate: 4,900,000) inhabit an area of 584,942 square miles. Mali is bounded by Mauritania and Senegal in the west, Algeria in the north and Niger in the east. The Republic has southern frontiers with Guinea, the Ivory Coast and Upper Volta, and depends for outlets to the sea on routes through Senegal and the Ivory Coast. The capital is Bamako.

Mali's economy, based on agricultural produce, is organised on the Israeli pattern of collectives and State buying organisations. Chief products are millet, sorghum, rice, maize and groundnuts.

Mali

The Republic of Mali, formerly French Soudan, became
independent on September 22, 1960.
For roughly two months from January, 1959, the country
was a partner with Senegal in the Federation of Mali,
which was then abandoned.

Cradle of the great civilisations of the West African
hinterland, Mali has, since independence, provided one
of the few constant experiments in modern socialism on
the continent.
The Empire of Ghana is supposed to have existed in the
present territory of Mali, along the banks of the broad
Niger River, from the 4th century onwards. (In 1957,
Kwame Nkrumah, with his passion for emphasising the
glories of Africa's past, decided to give his own country
the name of Ghana when it became independent.)
After the decline of the Empire of Ghana, the Empire
of Mali rose to prominence between the 13th and 15th
centuries. One of its trading cities was the fabled outpost
of Timbuctoo (Tombouctou) on the Niger River. This
civilisation provided the name for the ill-fated Federation
of Mali founded in 1959 to link the former territories of
French West Africa, and which broke up after about two
months of independence. Finally, Mali was the name
given to the Republic of Mali—formerly known as the
French Soudan.
In launching itself upon a policy of socialism at home
and of active and outspoken anti-colonialism in foreign
affairs, Mali has in many ways paralleled the
development of its neighbour, Guinea. There have been
important differences, however, as when Sekou Touré
of Guinea decided to advise his countrymen to vote 'no'
in de Gaulle's referendum in 1958 on future association
with France. Mali's ruling party decided on a 'yes' vote,
and thus ensured French help and goodwill for the
change-over of the administration to independence.
Mali's Government has, in addition, a more collective
leadership than that of Guinea, which is angled heavily
on the personality of the leader, Sekou Touré.
Lacking her own seaports, Mali (then the French
Soudan) was one of the countries which hoped to
see French West Africa transformed into a federation of
West African states. But support for the idea was

Opposite: The
market-square at
Bamako, the capital

disappointing. At independence only two of the West
African territories were members of the Federation of
Mali – Senegal and the Soudan.

Modibo Keita, a Soudanese, was head of the Federal
Government. He and his Soudanese colleagues were
supporters of a centralist form of government. The
Senegalese disagreed, and when troubles started Keita
declared a state of emergency. Parts of the Army,
which was largely Senegalese, revolted and the
Soudanese leaders were arrested and forced to return to
their own capital of Bamako. Soudan then became the
Republic of Mali and Modibo Keita its President.

The Malians are a proud race and did not take kindly
to this turn of events. As they returned to their large
inland republic the door was firmly slammed behind
them. The Dakar-Bamako railway link was closed with
the result that Mali had to look mainly to the Ivory
Coast for outlets to the sea. Since those days relations
between Mali and Senegal have steadily improved and
the railway line was later re-opened.

In 1960, Mali joined the Guinea-Ghana-Mali union.
This was intended to be the foundation of an eventual
federation of West African states like the United States
of America. Mali was also a member of the Casablanca
group of socialist African states. Both organisations
were subsequently wound up with the founding of the
Organisation of African Unity in 1963.

In 1962 Mali withdrew from the West African Monetary
Union which circulated a single currency, the CFA franc,
throughout the whole of former French West Africa,
and launched their own currency.

In February, 1967, however, Mali signed with France
a bilateral agreement to help her to rejoin the Union
after a transitional period.

Mali has not had an easy existence in independence.
The break with Senegal and the need to transport by
road raised export costs and import prices. Export
earnings were too heavily centred on the single crop of
groundnuts and the Mali Five-year Plan has sought to
diversify and expand agricultural production.

Apart from an initial setback at the time of the break-up
of the Mali Federation, Mali has generally maintained
good relations with France although they have not been
as close as those of other former French colonies.

MAMADOU AW

Mamadou Aw became Minister of Public Works, Telecommunications, Housing and Transport on September 17, 1966.

He was born on December 5, 1924 at Segou in the west of Mali. After primary and secondary school, he studied as a public works engineer in Dakar and Paris and took a diploma from the College of French West Africa and the Special School for Public Works and Building in Paris (1951).

Founder of the Union of Public Works Employees in French West Africa in 1945, he became chairman of the Association of African Engineers and Technicians (AITA). He was elected municipal councillor of Koulikoro near the capital, Bamako, at the same time he was head of the service of topographical studies, city planning and housing in the Housing Service in Dakar from 1951–57.

With the founding of the Federal Government of Mali in Dakar in May, 1957, M. Aw was appointed Minister of Public Works, Transport and Communications until August, 1960.

On January 20, 1961, he became Minister of Public Works, Telecommunications, Housing and Power Resources, and Minister of Transport in May, 1961. In the Cabinet reshuffle of September, 1966, he dropped the Power Resources portfolio.

OUSMANE BA

Ousmane Ba is Mali's Minister of Foreign Affairs. He was appointed to the full post of Minister in September, 1966, after having been Minister Delegate to the Presidency in charge of External Affairs, from September, 1964.

He was born in 1919 at Bafoulabe in the extreme west of the country. He graduated as a doctor after studying at the African School of Medicine and Pharmacy at Dakar.

A militant unionist, he quickly turned to politics and became a member of the coordinating committee of the African Democratic Rally (RDA), the West African political organisation which was founded in the Mali capital in 1947.

His political career began in neighbouring Upper Volta, where, from May, 1957 to December, 1958, he was Minister of the Civil Service in the Government Council.

Returning to his own country of Soudan, soon to become the Republic of Mali, he was Minister Delegate to the Presidency in the provisional Government of the Soudan from December, 1958 to April, 1959.

Since then M. Ba has occupied posts continuously both in the Federation of Mali Government and in the various Governments of the Republic of Mali after the Mali-Senegal union broke up. He was successively Minister of Labour, Civil Service and Social Affairs (April, 1959 to September, 1962) and Minister of the Interior, Information and Tourism (September, 1959 to September, 1964) before becoming Minister in charge of Foreign Affairs in 1964.

OUMAR BABA DIARRA

The first African to be elected chairman of the board of the International Labour Organisation, a specialised agency of the United Nations, Oumar Baba Diarra has held a number of Government posts in Mali.

Born on December 30, 1929, at Bamako, he went to France for advanced studies in the Faculty

Mahamane Alassane
Haidara

of Law at Montpellier, where he took a degree in law and a diploma in political economy.

He was at first an economist in the French Office of Overseas Scientific Research before turning to politics.

Successively Secretary of State for Labour and Social Services, Animal Husbandry and then for the Civil Service and Labour, he was appointed Minister of the Civil Service and Labour in September, 1966.

SOMINE DOLO

Minister for Public Health and Social Affairs in Mali since September 17, 1962, Somine Dolo is a doctor by profession.

Born in 1924 at Sangha-Bandiagara, he studied medicine at Bordeaux and took a doctor's diploma.

Back in his own country he went into practice, beginning at the same time his involvement in politics. He represented the Dogon people of central Mali as territorial councillor for Bandiagara.

He was elected a deputy in March, 1957.

MAMADOU GOLOGO

Mamadou Gologo has been a leading figure in Information in Mali since pre-independence.

He was chief of Information Services in October, 1958, Commissioner of Information from 1959–61, Secretary of State from 1961 to 1964 and since that year has been Minister of Information and Tourism.

M. Gologo is also president of the Union of Journalists of Mali and vice-president of the International Organisation of Journalists, the headquarters of which are in Prague.

He was born in 1924 at Koulikoro near the capital,

Bamako, and studied in the William Ponty School in Dakar, then entered the School of Medicine and Pharmacy in Dakar where he qualified as a doctor. He was later attached to the health service of French West Africa.

His political career began in 1957 when he became secretary to the Minister of Health.

In October, 1958, he entered the Information Ministry as head of the Information Service. He is a member of the political bureau of the Soudanese Union, the ruling party.

MAHAMANE HAIDARA

President of the National Assembly of Mali, Mahamane Alassane Haidara was born in 1910 in the historic town of Timbuctoo (Tombouctou) on the River Niger.

A teacher, with a diploma from the William Ponty School in Dakar, he was a senator of the French Republic from 1942–59, as well as a councillor of the Territorial Assembly of Soudan from 1952–57.

He is a member of the political bureau of the Soudanese Union and was a member of the co-ordinating committee of the regional political body, the African Democratic Rally (RDA) from 1948-57.

He has been Speaker of the National Assembly since August, 1960.

MADEIRA KEITA

Minister of Justice in the Mali Government since 1962, Madeira Keita has played a leading political role both in his own country and in neighbouring Guinea.

Born in 1917 at Kita in western Mali, he studied at the William Ponty School in Dakar,

Modibo Keita

taking up politics almost immediately on leaving.

He was a founder of the Guinea Democratic Party (PDG) and that party's secretary-general before this job was taken over by Sekou Touré in 1952.

He was arrested nine times for political activities and suspended from his job at the French Institute of Black Africa. Forced by the colonial administrators of French West Africa to keep constantly on the move, he finally came back to Mali (then the Soudan) and was made a member of the political bureau of the Soudanese Union which, like the PDG of Guinea, was then linked with Houphouet-Boigny's African Democratic Rally.

In April, 1959, he was named Minister of the Interior in Soudan's pre-independence Government and kept this key post in the short-lived Federation of Mali which linked Mali and Senegal.

When the Mali Federation broke up in 1960, he retained the Interior Ministry in the Government of the new Republic of Mali.

A strong supporter of the need for the single party system in Africa and particularly in Mali, he has played a considerable role in the organisation of Mali's ruling party.

MODIBO KEITA

Physically a giant among African statesmen, Modibo Keita is a socialist President who has acquired a reputation as a successful mediator.

About 6ft 3in tall and of an imposing build, dressed usually in a flowing white gown – the boubou–a white hat, and Moorish slippers, the Malian President towers head and shoulders above his colleagues at meetings.

A member of the now-disbanded Casablanca group of African socialist states, he came into world prominence as the mediator in the 1963 Algerian-Moroccan border war. At home he is noted for ruling carefully by consensus among the members of his Cabinet. The Mali Government is a tough one, governing firmly through a single party which is organised down into every village. It struggles with a lack of foreign exchange and imposes high and strict taxes. But President Modibo has not used this power to impose government by textbook theories.

Of his own job as President he says: 'He must be of the people, so that he can know their real aspirations and help them to realise them. He must mould himself in the image of his people and not make his people according to his own image of them.'

The President is a holder of the Lenin Peace Prize.

He was born on June 4, 1915 at Bamako, into the Malinke race, and studied first in Koranic schools and primary and secondary schools in his own country. He then went to the William Ponty School in Dakar, where he passed with honours, and later served as a teacher from 1936.

With the end of World War II, the Malians launched themselves into politics and the fight for independence. In 1945 Modibo joined with Mamadou Konate, who died 12 years later, to found the 'Bloc Soudanais' (Mali was then known as the French Soudan). The next year was to see the launching of the African Democratic Rally, the French African political grouping, in the Soudan capital, Bamako.

The 'Bloc Soudanais' merged with the Rally (RDA), and

became known as the 'Union Soudanaise-RDA'.

Modibo Keita became one of the closest lieutenants of the rally's leader, Félix Houphouet-Boigny of the Ivory Coast, a collaboration which was to persist until the eve of independence, when the two men split over the issue of federalism in the former French West African territories.

Politics soon landed the future Malian President in trouble with the colonial authorities. In 1946 he was accused of contempt of the authorities and his friend Mamadou Konate, just elected a deputy of the French Assembly, brought him to Paris to try to settle the accusation. This move did not help and he was arrested and imprisoned for 20 days in Paris.

In 1950 he was again in trouble. The RDA was then linked with the French Communist party in the merry-go-round of political alliances which prevailed in the Fourth Republic. The Soudan authorities branded Modibo an 'unrepentant Communist' and he was sent as a teacher to a remote Saharan school.

Two years later he was elected to the Territorial Assembly which the French authorities had set up in the Soudan and their other territories as a move towards eventual self-government. The break between RDA and the Communists led to an improvement in his relations with the authorities.

He was elected a deputy for the French Soudan in the French National Assembly in 1956 and while in France he gained valuable parliamentary experience.

He was in 1956 the first African to be elected Vice-President of the French National Assembly. He resigned this appointment to become Secretary of State for France Overseas in Maurice Bourges-Manoury's Cabinet and, when that Government fell, served more than a year in the Félix Gaillard Cabinet as Secretary of State to the Presidency of the Council.

On June 1, 1958, General de Gaulle came to power and a new era opened in French African politics. The radical Sekou Touré of Guinea wanted African states to vote 'no' to a French constitutional amendment which would set up the French Community. Modibo Keita and his Soudan political associates, considering especially the economic aspects of association with France and the possibility of transforming French West Africa into a federation, decided to recommend their countrymen to vote 'yes'.

In December, 1958, a number of French West African states had met in Bamako to discuss the question of Federation. The following month four countries – Senegal, Soudan, Upper Volta and Dahomey – agreed to join and proclaimed the Federation of Mali.

But by the time independence came in 1960, Upper Volta and Dahomey had withdrawn and the Federation consisted of only Soudan and Senegal.

It lasted no more than two months. The two countries interpreted federalism differently. Modibo Keita, Prime Minister of the Federation, wanted a strong central government; the Senegalese wanted a loose grouping.

The Federation was broken up and the Republic of Mali established. Modibo Keita, who occupied the key post of secretary-general in Mali's only and ruling party, became the first President.

Negotiating the end of French bases in Mali, the Republic then entered into association with the socialist states of Africa.

Ghana and Guinea had already formed a loose union which it was hoped might one day become the basis of a West African federation like the United States of America. Mali joined with the other two in this new Union of West African States.

Mali also signed the Casablanca Charter linking the Arab states of North Africa and the socialist states of Black Africa. This was dissolved with the founding of the Organisation of African Unity, as was the Ghana-Guinea-Mali union, but Modibo Keita's experience within this organisation enabled him to be an effective mediator to end the Algeria-Morocco border dispute in 1964.

His split with Senegal forced him to keep up his friendship with the pro-Western Houphouet Boigny of the Ivory Coast, a long-standing opponent of federalism in West Africa. Mali needed the Ivory Coast's road system to export its groundnut crop and bring in its imports—at least until an agreement could be reached with Senegal to reopen the Bamako-Dakar railway.

Modibo Keita and the Senegal President, Léopold Sedar Senghor, staged a public reconciliation at Addis Ababa in 1963, embracing before cheering delegates at the founding session of the Organisation of African Unity. In December, 1966, Modibo Keita made a state visit to Senegal.

On the economic side, Keita's Government has had to keep up a constant austerity campaign. Mali is self-sufficient in food but poor in exports, relying principally on groundnuts, and a hard road undoubtedly still lies ahead of the young Republic. The decision to withdraw from the West African Monetary Union in 1962 gave Mali an independent currency but added to the difficulties of regional trade.

The President is a devout Moslem but sees no need for a clash between Islam and socialism. He told a reporter in 1965: 'Many people—including priests—have tried to create an artificial conflict between religion and socialism. The basis of religion is brotherhood between men. Religion indeed constitutes the true base of socialism... A good Moslem or a good Catholic must have a socialist soul.'

MOUSSA KEITA

Moussa Keita became High Commissioner for Youth and Sport in the Cabinet reshuffle of September 17, 1966.

A keen athlete, he was a champion sprinter during his university career in France, since when he has devoted his entire career to youth and sport in his own country.

A brother of President Modibo Keita, he was born in September, 1925 at Bamako, the capital. He took his advanced studies in France, where he became a licentiate in natural science.

He was a science teacher before becoming administrative director of the Boys' College of Bamako.

He began his political career in April, 1959, when he was named Commissioner for Youth. He became High Commissioner in January, 1961, and three years later he was appointed to the rank of Secretary of State, in May, 1964.

Jean-Marie Kone

JEAN-MARIE KONE

A former head of the Soudan Government in pre-independence days, Jean-Marie Kone conceded his position to Modibo Keita when the short-lived Federation of Mali, uniting Senegal and Mali, broke up and former French Soudan became the Republic of Mali.

He has served President Modibo Keita as a Minister of State ever since, and is a member of the political bureau of the ruling party.

Since September, 1962, his post has been Minister of State charged with Planning and Co-ordination of Economic Affairs and Finance.

He was born in October, 1913, at Sikasso in the south of Mali, and studied at the William Ponty School in Dakar where he became a teacher.

His political career began in 1957 when he was elected deputy for the Territorial Assembly of the Soudan, then Vice-President of the Soudan Government in May, 1957 – which amounted to being Prime Minister under the French governor.

In the short-lived Government of the Federation of Mali he was Vice-President in charge of Justice and the Civil Service.

ATTAHER MAIGA

Attaher Maiga was appointed Minister of Commerce of Mali on September 17, 1966.

He was born in 1924 at Baria and, like many future politicians in Africa, took his diploma at the William Ponty School in Dakar.

He worked for a while as a civil servant before turning to politics. He was a territorial councillor for Mali and a deputy from March, 1957. He entered the Government in 1959 as Minister of Finance, was Minister of Finance and Commerce from 1964–66, and Minister of Commerce from September, 1966.

SALIF N'DIAYE

Salif N'Diaye was appointed Secretary of State to the Presidency in charge of Power and Industry on September 17, 1966. It was his first ministerial post.

He was born on April 6, 1934, at Kati near Bamako, the capital. An engineer by profession, he studied at the School of Public Works at Bamako and took a diploma at the Special School of Public Works and Building in Paris as an engineer-surveyor.

He was assistant director of the Topographical Service and director of the National Institute of Topography of Mali before becoming, in June, 1961, secretary to Mamadou Aw, Minister of Public Works. He retained this post until September, 1966, when he joined the Government.

LAMINE SOW

Lamine Sow is the Minister concerned with the control of state societies and enterprises. He was appointed to this, his first ministerial post, on September 17, 1966.

Born in Bandiagara in central Mali, he was a militant unionist and became secretary to the Minister of Finance in 1958–59 when the country was still the Soudan.

His career as a politician began when he was elected in March, 1959, to the Legislative Assembly of the Soudan which afterwards became the National Assembly of Mali.

He was governor of the Bank of Mali from July, 1962 to June, 1964.

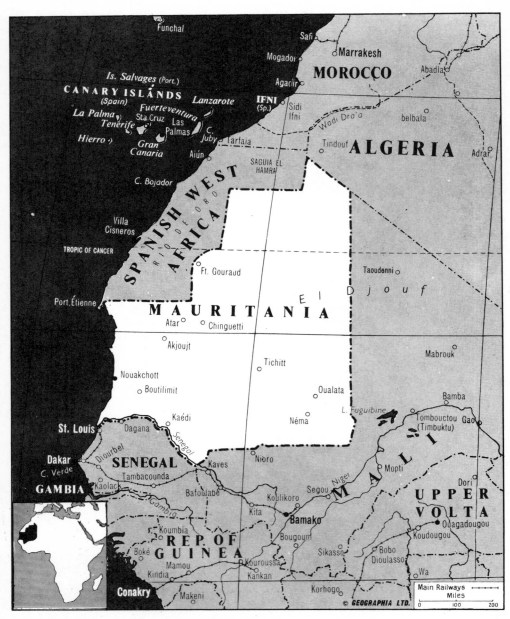

The area is 418,810 square
miles, the population about one
million (1963 estimate:
770,000). Mauritania's
neighbour in the south is
Senegal. Mali lies to the south
and east and there is a short
frontier in the north with
Algeria. The Spanish Sahara
(Rio de Oro) occupies more
than half the Atlantic coastline,
to the north and north-west. The
capital is Nouakchott.
Mauritania's chief sources of
income are cattle, camels, gum,
salt and a variety of haricot
bean. There is a growing
fishing industry and large
deposits of iron ore and copper
are currently being exploited.

292

Mauritania

Mauritania became independent on November 28, 1960, having been a French protectorate (1903 onwards) and colony (from 1920).
The Republic is administered by a Government Council of eight Ministers. The National Assembly consists of 34 members, elected by universal suffrage.

Mauritania has a population of about one million, divided among the Moors (the name generally given to the nomadic Berbers and Arabs) and the negroid people of the south who are outnumbered by the Moors by about five to one.

The Moors are the descendants of the all-conquering race who overran the whole of North Africa, Spain and a large portion of France until defeated at the battle of Poitiers (France) in 732.

In modern times Mauritania belonged to France.

It is predominantly desert and the Moors possess little save their camels, their cattle and their tents with which they wander the terrain in an endless search for pasture, as they have done for centuries.

Despite this bleak demographic picture, Mauritania is one of those rare African countries which can look to the future with what President Moktar Ould Daddah has described as 'some serenity'.

By 1966 Mauritania had achieved a balanced budget and a favourable balance of foreign trade. In addition the medium-term outlook for the economy appeared modestly promising. Already an important iron ore exporter, the country's copper production was due to get under way in the 1970s.

The Mauritanians are also fortunate in that their Atlantic coastline is an extremely rich fishing ground; at the end of 1966, mixed government and private capital schemes to develop this resource were already showing satisfactory progress. Other exports are camels and cattle which are mainly sold to Senegal, her southern neighbour, and Mali, which lies on her eastern frontier.

Most of the country's agricultural crops, such as millet for local consumption, are grown in the south of the country where the Senegal River marks the frontier with the country of the same name. Mauritania is a member with Senegal,

Opposite: Nomadic
tent-dwellers on the
fringes of Nouakchott,
the rapidly growing
capital

Below: A camel
parade during the
independence
celebrations in
Nouakchott

Mali and Guinea of the Senegal River States Organisation,
a body whose aim is to develop the agricultural and other
resources of the Senegal River basin. Though not as yet of
great economic importance, mention should also be made
of Mauritania's traditional silver and leatherwork which is
amongst the finest in Africa.

Mauritania gained independence in 1960 together with the
majority of the rest of French West Africa. Her constitution
is somewhat similar to that of France's Fifth Republic,
in that executive power is centralised on the President
who can appoint, reshuffle, and dismiss his ministers at
will. Legislative power belongs to a single House, the
National Assembly.

A one-party state (Mauritanian People's Party), the
official title of the state is 'The Islamic Republic of
Mauritania'. Though religious freedom is guaranteed by
the constitution, virtually the whole population is Moslem.
An example of the orthodoxy of their religious belief can
be seen in a notice displayed in every hotel and bar in
the country, which states that it is an offence to serve a
Mauritanian citizen with any alcoholic beverage.

In sharp contrast to their abhorrence for alcohol is their
respect for water, a commodity which is scarce almost
throughout the land and on which the future of the
country will almost certainly depend. Mauritania must be
one of the few countries where a visitor to a country family
can give as a much-appreciated gift a couple of bottles of
mineral water.

As a people, the Mauritanians show a hospitality to
strangers characteristic of desert peoples and their cuisine
can be excellent. Whole roast sheep, eaten with various
grains and herbs, and dates, are characteristic dishes.

As drinkers of tea the Mauritanians leave even the
British standing. Any visit to a Mauritanian's tent or house
is incomplete without a lengthy tea-drinking session.

Apart from the immense task of developing the country's
economy, the main problem that has shown itself since
independence on the internal political scene has been a
racial one.

The African minority are not in general nomadic and
because of this they were more influenced by the French
in the colonial era. In particular they took more readily
to the educational facilities provided by the colonial
authorities. In consequence they secured more adminis-

trative and other work than the majority of the Moors, who preferred to preserve their nomadic life, their traditional ways, and their Arabic language.

Since independence a clash of black African and Moorish interests has shown itself in the Government itself, the Civil Service, and in the schools, where the compulsory teaching of Arabic has been an issue. Early in 1966 there were clashes between Black African and Moorish students which led to bloodshed and the closing for the rest of the year of a number of secondary schools. These events led to dissension within the Government and Civil Service and 26 people were put under house arrest. However, by the end of the year the schools had reopened and the 26 people had been released and 'reintegrated into national life', as President Moktar Ould Daddah put it.

In foreign policy Mauritania has pursued an independent and radical line. A supporter of the admission of China to the United Nations, the President announced in 1966 that he had accepted invitations to visit not only Peking but North Korea and North Vietnam as well. Mauritania was one of the African states which severed diplomatic relations with Britain following the 1965 meeting of the Organisation of African Unity which recommended such a course because of British policy over the unilateral declaration of independence in Rhodesia.

However, the Mauritanian Government has maintained cordial relations with most of the Western Powers, including the United States and, more particularly, France. As for the latter, President Daddah has never hesitated to express in public frank recognition and gratitude for French aid to his country. In 1966, France remained by far the most important supplier of foreign aid. The only country with which Mauritania has actively bad relations is Morocco. This discord has an elementary cause: the Moroccan Government claims that what is now Mauritania is historically part of Morocco. It is not surprising that in recent years relations between Mauritania and Algeria (which has also had border disputes with Morocco) have become especially close. Mauritania's relations with her eastern and southern neighbours, Mali and Senegal, have been consistently good. Her only other immediate neighbour is the Spanish Sahara. This is another cause of friction with Morocco, as both countries claim the area.

Despite her radical foreign policy which some foreign observers have gone so far as to describe as 'leftist', Mauritania's internal and external economic policies belie any extreme form of socialism. Internally the favoured method for mounting new enterprises is to set them up with a mixture of governmental and private (foreign and local) capital. Foreign capital also comes mainly from the Western countries. A striking example of this came in 1966 when the Mauritanian Government announced it had chosen a London-based firm, Chartered Consolidated, to exploit her copper deposits. The announcement came less than a year after Mauritania had severed relations with Britain over the Rhodesian question.

Abdallahi Ould Daddah

ABDALLAHI OULD DADDAH
Formerly Mauritanian Ambassador to London, Abdallahi Ould Daddah was transferred to Washington in August, 1966.

As delegate to the United Nations, he figured in a debate in October, 1966, in which the Morrocan Foreign Minister, Mohamed Cherkaoui, accused Spain of seeking to continue its domination of Spanish West Africa (Rio de Oro) and Ifni.

He declared that while Spain had told the United Nations it was prepared to let the inhabitants determine their own future, it was building up military bases and encouraging Spaniards to migrate with the aim of maintaining its domination.

For Mauretania, Abdallahi Ould Daddah said that Spanish West Africa was an integral part of his country. Mauritania regarded Ifni and Spanish West Africa as one, whereas Morroco looked on them as two separate territories. (This was, in fact, the central issue in a long-standing territorial dispute with Morocco.)

The Spanish delegate, Senor Manuel Aznar, said his country's policy was in complete conformity with UN resolutions calling for self-determination.

M. Cherkaoui called for the withdrawal of all Spanish troops from the territories, retention of police forces considered necessary by the UN, withdrawal of the Spanish Administration and permission for refugees to return to the territories.

Once these conditions had been realised, M. Cherkaoui added, a referendum could be under UN auspices or under the joint supervision of Moroccan and Spanish authorities.

ABDELLAHI OULD SIDYA
Abdellahi Ould Sidya was appointed High Commissioner for Information, Handicrafts and Tourism in October, 1966.

Born in 1938, he was an official of Radio Mauritania (1957–58) when he went to France for a course with OCORA, the organisation which helps to train officials and technicians for overseas radio stations.

In January, 1966, he was named Director of Radio.

Baham Mohamed
Laghdaf

AHMED BAZEID OULD AHMED MISKE

Minister of Defence (appointed February, 1966), Ahmed Bazeid Ould Ahmed Miske was born in 1933.

He completed his secondary education at the Lycée in St Louis, Senegal, in 1954 and then entered the Civil Service in the Public Works department. In 1955, he took part in the creation of the Mauritanian Youth Organisation, of which he was a central committee member until 1958. In 1956 the French colonial authorities dismissed him from the Civil Service owing to his political activities in the Youth Organisation. He then went to Dakar, Senegal, where he worked as a teacher at a secondary school.

In May, 1957, when the first Mauritanian Government (internal self-government) was formed, Moktar Ould Daddah recalled him and he became a high official in his office. The following year he went to France where he studied at the Institute of Higher Overseas Studies. In 1960, he returned to Mauritania and became a top official in the regional administration.

In June, 1961, he was appointed director of the Sûreté Nationale (criminal investigation department). In July, 1963, he was elected a municipal councillor in the capital and was then named Assistant Secretary-General for Defence and the Armed Forces (at this time the department was part of the Presidency).

In October, 1964, he again returned to President Moktar Ould Daddah's office as one of his main officials.

In May of the following year he was elected to the National Assembly and in February, 1966, became Minister of Defence.

AHMED KILLY

Ahmed Killy, appointed High Commissioner for the Civil Service in October, 1966, has a law degree awarded him by the Faculty of Law and Economic Science in Paris.

He worked for a time as an official in the President's office in Mauritania.

He was born in 1942.

BAHAM MOHAMED LAGHDAF

Baham Mohamed Laghdaf was named Minister of Health and Labour in October, 1966.

He has worked as a civil servant, interpreter, and regional administrator and is a former director of Radio Mauritania (1962).

In July, 1963, he was appointed Minister of Justice and Legislation and in January, 1965, became Minister of Education, Youth Affairs, and Information.

In February, 1966, he was nominated Minister of Health, Labour and Social Affairs but in the following October the Social Affairs part of his portfolio was transferred to a High Commissioner.

He was born in 1934.

ELY OULD ALLAF

Ely Ould Allaf is a highly qualified technologist. As a scientist he studied at Dakar University from 1957–62, and continued his education in Paris from 1962–64. He studied telecommunications at the Ecole Nationale Supérieure and won a diploma as a civil engineer.

Returning to Mauritania, he entered the Posts and Telecommunications department, and became the director.

From December, 1965 to February, 1966, he was Minister of Youth Affairs, Information and Telecommunications, thereafter

Moktar Ould Daddah

being appointed Minister for Education and Culture.

He was born in 1937.

HAMDI OULD MOUKNAS

Hamdi Ould Mouknas is a lawyer by profession.

He was named High Commissioner for Youth Affairs and Sports in February, 1966.

The following June he was elected to the ruling party's political committee and, in October, Social Affairs was added to his portfolio.

He was born in 1935.

MALOUM OULD BRAHAM

Born in 1930, Maloum Ould Braham was named Minister for Rural Economy in October, 1966.

Educated in Mauritania and in Senegal, he worked as a teacher and teaching inspector.

He was made Minister for Foreign Affairs in February, 1966.

In the following October he was transferred to his present Ministry.

MOHAMED LEMINE OULD HAMONI

Mohamed Lemine Ould Hamoni was appointed Minister for Justice and the Interior in February, 1966. From November, 1965 until then, he was President of the Supreme Court.

Born in 1923 and educated in Mauritania, he served as an interpreter from 1944–48, then worked in the administration until 1958. In 1962 he returned to Mauritania after a course at the Institute for Higher Overseas Studies in Paris.

From 1963–65 he was a High Commissioner. In Mauritania the number of ministries is limited under the constitution. Because of this certain departments are administered by high commissioners who, though civil servants, have powers similar to the ministers.

MOHAMED SALEM OULD M'KHAITIRAT

Mohamed Salem Ould M'Khaitirat entered the Government as Minister for Finance and Commerce in October, 1966. He was born in 1923.

Educated locally and in France, where he studied at the Institute for Higher Overseas Studies, he worked as an interpreter and as a civil servant in several parts of Mauritania.

From 1962–64 he was Permanent Secretary at the Ministry of Commerce and Industry. In 1965, he became Permanent Secretary at the Interior Ministry.

MOKTAR OULD DADDAH

The President of Mauritania, Moktar Ould Daddah is a lawyer by training. He is regarded as the master of Mauritanian politics.

A quiet-spoken, modest man, he has shown throughout his political career a preference for practicality and attention to detail rather than for the political *tour de force*. He reflects the traditional spirit of his people. Master of the sole political party, he was re-elected President for a further five years in a massive turnout of the Mauritanian electorate in August, 1966.

Met personally, Moktar Ould Daddah gives the impression of a courteous, modest, almost shy man. He must be one of Africa's least flamboyant heads of state. He lives simply. Despite this impression, however, he has shown himself a determined and tough politician who is not prepared to take any nonsense from his subordinates.

By the end of 1966 he had in effect taken the politics out of his Cabinet by removing the most outspoken political figures and replacing them with young civil servants and technocrats.

An able administrator, he has on several occasions run individual departments concurrently with leading the Government. The tenor of his major political speeches gives a good clue to the man. Whereas a major speech by a head of state (particularly in French-speaking Africa) is often the occasion for a series of ringing, elegantly phrased generalities, President Daddah's discourses are apt to be crammed with statistics and administrative detail. He is also frank with the press and his public, not hesitating to point to governmental shortcomings or to admit the existence of serious problems.

Born on December 25, 1924, he was educated at the School for the Sons of Chiefs at St Louis, Senegal. He then worked as an interpreter. In 1948 he went to France for secondary education.

He took his baccalaureate at Nice and proceeded to the Paris Law Faculty where he obtained a law degree.

In 1957 he was back in Africa serving a lawyer's apprenticeship in Dakar, Senegal, at the office of M. Léon Boissier-Pallun.

In 1957 he was elected Vice-President of the Government of Mauritania, which was not yet an independent state. At the same time he had responsibility for the Ministry of Youth Affairs and Education. In July of that year he made the decision to build the capital of Mauritania at Nouakchott and set out the construction programme for the future city. Until then the administrative headquarters for Mauritania were still at the old French Government offices at St Louis, Senegal.

The following year he was elected secretary-general of the 'Parti du Regroupement Mauritanien' (PRM), which represented a fusion of several parties.

On November 28, 1958, the Islamic Republic of Mauritania was proclaimed a member state of the French Community with internal self-government. The constitution was adopted in March of 1959 and, in May, Moktar Ould Daddah was elected a member of the National Assembly. On June 23, 1959, he was named by the Assembly as Prime Minister retaining until November of the following year the Ministry of the Interior. In November, 1960, Mauritania became a fully independent state, full powers having been transferred from France.

After independence the Prime Minister exercised the prerogatives of head of state and assumed responsibility for National Defence and Foreign Affairs. In May, 1961, the National Assembly adopted a new presidential-type constitution and in the following August Moktar Ould Daddah was elected by universal suffrage as first President of the Republic, an election for which he was the only candidate.

In December, 1961, a 'Unity Congress' meeting in Nouakchott elected him secretary-general of the Mauritanian People's Party following the dissolution of all former political organisations.

PAPA DAOUDA FALL
Born at St Louis, Senegal, in 1931, Papa Daouda Fall was appointed High Commissioner for Industry and Mines in October, 1966.

After studying veterinary science in France he worked in the Civil Service in Mauritania in agricultural departments until his present appointment.

SAMBA GANDEGA
Samba Gandega, High Commissioner for Technical Education,

was born in 1919 and is a health and hospital worker by profession.

He worked in this capacity in Senegal for 22 years before returning to Mauritania in 1958. He has been an active trades unionist and has held several posts in the Mauritanian Civil Service since independence in 1960. In June, 1963, he was elected a municipal councillor of Nouakchott.

He was named High Commissioner for Technical Education in October, 1966.

SIDI MOHAMED DIAGANA

Sidi Mohamed Diagana was appointed Minister for Construction, Public Works, Transport and Telecommunications in February, 1966.

Born in 1929, he was educated in Mauritania and in Senegal and is a teacher by profession.

Municipal councillor and assistant mayor of Kaedi from 1960–66, he was made Minister of Health, Labour and Social Affairs in January, 1965.

WANE MAMADOU BIRANE

Wane Mamadou Birane, born in 1929, was appointed Minister for Foreign Affairs and Planning in October, 1966. Coming immediately after the President on the government list, he is the most highly placed black African personality in Mauritania.

After completing his secondary education at St Louis, Senegal, he was appointed in 1946 an agent of the Meteorological Services at Atar in Mauritania. He was subsequently admitted to the Federal School for Posts and Telecommunications at Dakar in Senegal. By 1955 he was a high grade civil servant in the French colonial administration and went to Niger, where he studied telecommunications at the Institute for Higher Studies.

After continuing his Civil Service career in Senegal he returned to Mauritania in 1960 and was appointed director of Posts and Telecommunications. The following year he became *directeur de cabinet* (the equivalent of permanent secretary) at the Ministry of Transport, Posts and Telecommunications.

In 1963, he was named Director-General of Transportation and the following year was elected a member of the political committee of the ruling party.

In February, 1966, he became Minister for the Plan, a post he held until the following October when he was named Minister for Foreign Affairs and Planning.

President Moktar Ould Daddah has explained that the rather unusual grouping of these two portfolios was 'for the very simple reason that the biggest part of our plan is and will be financed by bilateral and multilateral overseas cooperation'.

Mauritania's second four-year Plan was due to start in 1968.

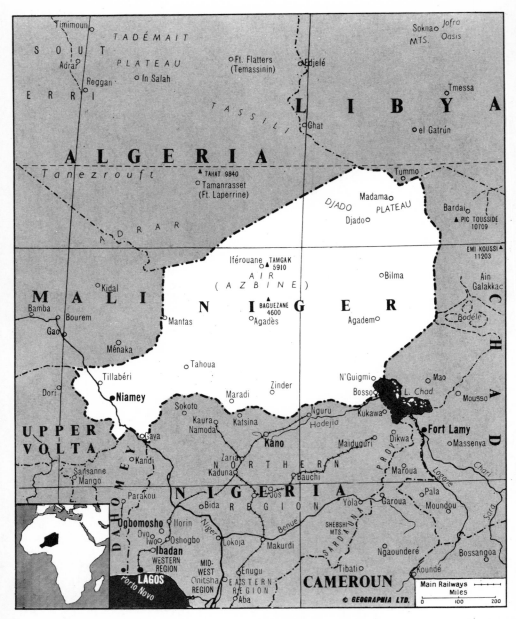

The landlocked Niger Republic covers an area of 484,000 square miles. The population is about 4,034,000. It is bordered by the Sahara and Libya in the north, Chad to the east, Nigeria to the south and Upper Volta and Mali to the west. The capital is Niamey.

The economy of Niger is largely founded on her agricultural products of millet, groundnuts, beans, manioc and, in the river districts, cotton and rice. Mineral riches, still largely unexploited because of transport problems, include uranium, tin, copper, iron ore, wolfram, colombite, molybdenum, lead sulphates and manganese ore.

Niger

A territory of French West Africa from 1904, the Republic of the Niger became independent on August 3, 1960. The Republic is administered by a Government of 13 Ministers. The National Assembly consists of 60 Members.

Niger is a sprawling country which encroaches deep into the Sahara. Its people, engaged mostly in agricultural and pastoral activities, provide an ethnical and cultural mosaic, ranging from black settled peasants in the south to nomadic white Touaregs and Arabs in the north. The overall density of the population is extremely low, due mainly to the fact that much of the country is virtually desert. Nearly half the inhabitants, including the vast majority of the settled population, live in the southern belt, an area amounting to less than one-twelfth of the national territory. This is about the only area where rainfall, totalling three to four inches a year, is sufficient to raise crops on any scale.

The various racial divisions tend to live in particular regions – the Hausas along the Nigerian border, the Djermas in the west and the small Touareg community in the north – except for the Peuls (Fulani) who live in every part of the region.

The huge distances between relatively small centres render difficult the action of the Central Government in Niamey in the fields of public health, education and professional training.

The nomads in the north cannot be reached except in one month of the year when they gather their cattle in the richer pastoral region of Agades. Less than three per cent of the population live in the four main centres of Niamey, Tahova, Zinder and Maradi. Nearly 70 per cent live in widely scattered secondary centres, with seldom more than a few hundred inhabitants in one place, and over 25 per cent still roam the country.

Despite its seemingly insuperable problems the Niger Government has tackled the development of the country with imagination. It has given priority to a programme of water-prospecting and drilling which has helped to settle thousands of semi-nomadic cattle breeders who, for generations, had been prevented by the vagaries of rainfall from establishing homes.

Livestock breeding is one of the country's main sources

A village woman at
Bouza talks to a
radio interviewer

of income. Between them the people of Niger own
nearly 14,000,000 animals, an average of four per head.
However, most of the animals have to travel thousands
of miles every year in a perpetual search for drinking
water. Shortage of water – one ox needs at least four
gallons of water a day – results in only one calf in four
reaching maturity and large tracts of rich pasture land
remain unused.

Surveys have ascertained that immense reservoirs of
water exist in many areas, deep down under the dry
soil. First drillings, carried out in 1962 by a British
firm from Northern Nigeria, resulted in water splashing
out of the ground at the rate of 10 cubic metres an hour
from a lake 1,000 feet below the surface.

The Government has also encouraged canning and has
helped the State-backed meat cooperative to acquire
improved refrigeration facilities. But a substantial
proportion of the large quantities of meat available for
export has to be dried in the sun, thus greatly
depreciating its value, or else sold 'on the leg' to
foreign customers after exhausting journeys.

Niger's main export crop is groundnuts; production

reaches some 200,000 tons a year, of which only a small proportion is used for local consumption. The staple food of the population is millet with rice supplementing the diet. Although Niger is a great meat producer, the local population consumes an average of only about 20 lbs per head a year.

Cotton and other cash crops, as well as a large variety of vegetables, are grown on a small scale along the banks of the Niger River, the waters of which are thick with natural fertilisers. Shortage of capital has delayed extensive irrigation projects which, according to experts, could render the banks of the Niger as fertile as those of the Nile.

One of the Government's main achievements has been the launching of consumer and producer cooperatives and State-backed trading corporations.

Of the State-owned Groundnut Corporation, President Hamani Diori says: 'We were almost ashamed to announce our profits. We started with a capital of 120,000,000 African francs (just less than £200,000) and by the end of the first season had made a profit almost double our capital.'

Private companies have been invited to join in these mixed enterprises and the Government has invited five of its neighbours to form a joint purchasing corporation to reduce import costs.

Niger undoubtedly has great mineral resources but finding them and, once found, transporting them to the sea, are two stumbling blocks. The hope persists that Niger, lying as it does between Africa's two oil giants of Algeria and Nigeria, has both oil and natural gas in commercially exploitable quantities.

Stored away beneath the vast expanse of barren lands, which stretch over 1,000 miles from east to west, and span the Sahara desert, lie also many other valuable minerals including uranium, tin, copper, iron ore, wolfram, colombite, molybdenum, lead sulphates, gold barytes, fluor, manganese ore, chromite and titanium ore.

Of these only tin is mined in commercial quantities by villagers using primitive methods and by a small local company.

A solid mass of 225,000,000 tons of iron ore, and an additional estimated reserve of 575,000,000 tons, barely camouflaged by sparse vegetation, is known to exist near the Niger River, 30 miles upstream from Niamey. Projects to exploit some of these resources, both agricultural and mineral, have been defeated by transport difficulties. Landlocked as it is, Niger is dependent on costly air transport and a few laterite roads. The nearest railway station is Nguru, terminus of the Lagos-Kano line, in Northern Nigeria. Though not too far from the Niger border, it is over 600 miles from Niamey and the agricultural centres to the south-west. The shortest distance to the sea, on the Dahomey coast, is over 500 miles: from Goya, on the Niger border, to Cotonou. This route involves a 350-mile journey by road from Niamey to the terminal point of the Dahomey railway at Parakou, whence passengers and goods can be moved by rail to the port of Cotonou. Government development projects provide for a new direct road to Ghana through Upper Volta, and for the opening of a route to the Mediterranean, via Algeria. Niger has also pioneered a Unesco-backed programme of closed circuit television for educational purposes. President Diori believes that for a long time to come teachers will not be available in sufficient numbers to tackle the task of education on a massive scale, and that filmed lessons may help to solve the problem.

Prophets of doom predicted communal strife in the vast former French territories which straddle the southern regions of the Sahara, but Niger, in the first seven years of its independence, escaped major unheavals.

President Hamani Diori, a big, pleasant man who takes a keen interest in world events, revealed himself one of the moderate leaders of Africa, both in home politics and continental affairs. But the Republic, which came into being at the end of a fierce struggle for leadership between the moderate, pro-Western Diori, and the pro-Communist Djibo Bakary, has known brief and isolated flare-ups of violence.

In the bitter pre-independence leadership struggle, Djibo Bakary came within an ace of winning the day when, after victory in local elections, he became mayor of Niger's capital. The mayoral post was for many African leaders the last rung before the presidency. But Djibo decided to vote 'no' in the 1958 de Gaulle referendum on association of the African states with

France. He was crushingly defeated and went into exile.
An Army mutiny took place in December, 1963,
but it was abortive and five were condemned to death
for it in 1965.

In 1965, an attempt on the life of President Hamani
Diori in a Niamey mosque, in which the President
escaped unscathed but one man died and four were
injured, was attributed to communist subversion and
Ghanaians were blamed for aiding the plot.

Fortunately these incidents have not unduly upset the
Republic's slow but noticeable attempts to overcome the
crushing drawbacks of geography. President Diori's
policy of trying to balance tribal forces at home and
fostering friendship with his neighbours has secured the
necessary peace to make headway with the major tasks.

BARKIRE ALIDOU

Born in Niamey in 1925, Barkiré
Alidou is the youngest Minister
in the Niger Cabinet.

After graduating from the
Frederic Assomption Teachers'
Training College in Katibougou,
Mali, he became a senior civil
servant at the Ministry of
Defence.

On November 23, 1965, he
was appointed Minister of
Economic Affairs, Commerce
and Industry. He is a member of
the political bureau of the 'Parti
Progressiste Nigérien'.

DJIBO BAKARY

With much the same academic
and political education as the
rest of Niger's leaders, Djibo
Bakary, head of the banned
'Sawaba' (Freedom) party,
advocated a 'no' vote in the
critical question of association
with France in the de Gaulle
referendum of 1958, was heavily
defeated and forced into exile.

In this opposition to association with France, Bakary, a
Communist, took the same stand
as the Guinea President, Sekou
Touré.

Born in 1922, Bakary trained
as a teacher at the William
Ponty School in Dakar. After
several years teaching he entered
politics and in 1946 became
founder secretary-general of the
Niger section of the African
Democratic Rally, the Niger
Progress Party.

From that moment almost
until independence Bakary was
involved in every major political
event in Niger.

A keen trade unionist, Bakary
was active in the Niger section of
the CGT (the French Communist
trade union). When the parent
political organisation, the African
Democratic Rally, after riots in
the Ivory Coast decided to sever
its links with the French Communist Party, Bakary rejected
this decision, thus provoking a
major split in the Niger party.
Breaking away he set up his own
party, the Niger Democratic
Union, which had the bulk of its
support in the western region.

At the 1956 general elections
to the French National Assembly,
Bakary opposed Hamani Diori
and nearly defeated him. This
near success was followed by

Arabe Chawey Balla

Courmo Barcougne

Mahamane Dandobe

Ousman Bassarou
Diallo

victory in local elections and Bakary became mayor of Niamey.

Only at this point did things start to go wrong. The decision to oppose the near mythical figure of de Gaulle in the 1958 referendum undoubtedly told heavily against him. At the elections to the Nigerian National Assembly in the same year as the referendum, Bakary was crushingly defeated. The Niger Progress Party, the party which he had helped to found and had since left, won 54 out of the 60 seats. As a result, Hamani Diori became President.

Bakary's Niger Democratic Union, now renamed the 'Sawaba' (Freedom) party was dissolved by order of the new Government in October, 1959. Several of its leaders were arrested and Bakary went into an exile which according to reports has taken him to Mali and Ghana and probably to Guinea as well as further afield to Communist countries.

ARABE CHAWEY BALLA

Although not the highest ranking officer in the Niger Army, which includes two lieutenant-colonels, Major (Commandant) Arabe Chawey Balla is its Chief of General Staff.

Born on July 25, 1925 at Niamey, he entered a military school in Senegal at the age of 19 and continued his training at a non-commissioned officers' school in France.

In the French Army he rose through the ranks. He served in a number of African countries, including Algeria in 1956–57, after an earlier spell in Madagascar between 1946–49.

His decorations include the National Orders of Niger, the Ivory Coast and Tunisia as well as the Egyptian Order of Merit.

COURMO BARCOUGNE

Born in 1916, the same year as the President, Courmo Barcougne followed the same educational path as many West African leaders, first attending the William Ponty School in Dakar then going on to the French Department of Overseas Studies in Paris.

M. Barcougne's role in the Government has always been that of an economist and until the reshuffle of 1965, he was at the head of the Ministry of Finance and Economic Affairs.

The Ministry was divided into two sections in 1965, when M. Barcougne was given special responsibilty for the Finance department, which in Niger covers a great variety of Government activities.

MAHAMANE DANDOBI

Mahamane Dandobi first attracted attention in 1958, when as director of the Niger National Troupe, he presented a play of his own called *Kabrin Kabra*. The play retraced the history of a tribe called the Maori and their totem, a jackal, and it enjoyed an enormous public success.

M. Dandobi has been Minister of Justice since November, 1965. He is also a member of the political bureau of the ruling 'Parti Progressiste Nigérien'.

He was born at Guecheme in 1923 and is still head of that district.

OUSMAN BASSAROU DIALLO

As President of the Supreme Court and President of the Constitutional Council, Ousman Bassarou Diallo is Niger's senior legal figure.

M. Diallo is an old friend of President Hamani Diori, in whom he and some of his friends

Hamani Diori

placed all their hopes when, in 1946, they decided to finance the future President's first election campaign, culminating in the nomination of Hamani Diori as Niger's representative in the French National Assembly.

M. Diallo started his career in the Civil Service as a clerk under French rule in Niger, after having completed his primary schooling and taken the equivalent of an 11-plus.

M. Diallo has received many decorations; he is a Grand Officer of Niger's National Order of Merit, and holds the National Orders of Upper Volta, the Ivory Coast and the French Légion d'Honneur.

HAMANI DIORI

First President of the Niger Republic, Hamani Diori was born on June 1916, not far from the capital, Niamey. After successful studies at Niamey regional school and the Victor Ballot School in the capital of the neighbouring territory of Dahomey, he entered the William Ponty Teachers' Training College at Dakar, where he obtained a diploma.

On leaving school he became a teacher until 1938 when he was called to Paris to teach his own tribal language, Djerma, and the related language of Hausa at the French Institute of Overseas Studies – the training ground for the civil servants that France sent to the former colonies.

The year 1946, which saw General de Gaulle's provisional post-war Government and the creation of France's Fourth Republic, was also M. Diori's starting-point in politics.

In that year he joined forces with the Ivory Coast planter, Félix Houphouet-Boigny, and the Upper Volta political organi-

ser, Ouezzin Coulibaly, and several others to found the African Democratic Rally ('Rassemblement Démocratique Africain'), the party which organised the fight for independence throughout French West Africa. At the same time he founded with Boubou Hama the Niger Progress Party ('Parti Progressiste Nigérien') which is the Niger section of the African Democratic Rally.

In November of the same year he was elected deputy for Niger in the French National Assembly. But luck was against him in the next elections, in 1951, and his mandate was not renewed. Hamani Diori went back to schoolteaching. He became director of a school in Niamey which, to mark the appointment, has since borne his name.

Hamani Diori used his spare time from teaching to improve his political organisation and these activities brought him success when in 1956, in a bitter contest with the now-exiled Opposition leader Djibo Bakary, he regained his seat in the National Assembly. A year and a half later he was promoted to Vice-President (Deputy Speaker) of the Assembly, at the same time serving as a municipal councillor for Niamey after election in November, 1957.

General de Gaulle's return to power in 1958 stepped up the pace of West African politics and Hamani Diori was well organised to take advantage of these events. The referendum of September 28, 1958, whereby the former French Union was to be replaced by the French Community was seen by M. Diori as a way of replacing colonialism by interdependence between France and her African territories. He threw his weight behind the 'yes' vote. His opponent Djibo Bakary joined Sekou Touré of Guinea in favouring a 'no' vote and went down to a crushing three-to-one defeat.

In December 1958, he was elected chairman of the Government Council of Niger, then Prime Minister and finally to the Presidency of the new Republic on November 9, 1960, after just over two years of autonomous rule.

A tall, softly spoken and pleasant man who wears the flowing Saharan *boubou* at home and a lounge suit on most of his visits abroad, President Diori has worked with great vigour towards the goal of securing investments to develop his vast inland state.

Businessmen who travel to Niamey with capital or even ideas find themselves almost immediately shown in to the President's office. There, instead of luxurious furnishings and introductory protocol, they find the President hard at work behind a desk in a simply furnished room, much like the head of any business corporation. President Diori is proud of his tribal associations with the Hausas, the traders of western Africa, and admits he enjoys commercial negotiations.

His eyes sparkle when he talks of the success of some of the State-backed organisations he helped set up in Niger, but he quite frankly admits the losses made by others and speaks of his plans to recover those losses.

In Continental politics the President has always ranked as one of the moderates. Only once has Niger had serious trouble with one of her neighbours. That was when a clash with Dahomey over the disputed island of Lete in the River Niger led to bloodshed, the expulsion of Dahomeians from Niger where they occupied key posts in the Civil Service and commerce, and the temporary blocking of Niger's export and import routes through Dahomey. The argument was finally settled within the *Entente*, a loose association of West African French-speaking states which groups Niger, Dahomey, Togo, Ivory Coast and Upper Volta.

With his record of moderation and desire for conciliation in international disputes President Diori's role has continued to increase in importance, particularly in the councils of French speaking African states, such as the Afro-Malagasy Union, the Common Afro-Malagasy Organisation (OCAM) which later replaced it, and the West African *Entente*.

In August and September of 1966 President Diori played a successful role of conciliator in the border dispute between Chad and the Sudan.

He was appointed by the Common Afro-Malagasy Organisation to investigate the possibility of a Commonwealth of French-speaking states throughout the world, much on the lines of the British Commonwealth. This idea was particularly desired by some members of OCAM but met opposition from the Arab states of North Africa where France plays a less crucial role than it does in Black Africa.

His Moslem faith has led him to take a keen interest in the affairs of the Arab states to the north and the President is a keen follower of world events.

His contacts with the Arab world have nevertheless not ruled out good relations with the Israelis, who provide aid.

Boubou Hama

Noma Kaka

BOUBOU HAMA

The 'number two' personality of a former French African territory is often not a member of the Cabinet but wields power as head of the National Assembly and the local political party.

Such is the case with Boubou Hama, politician, businessman and writer.

M. Hama's favourite subject in the many books, pamphlets and theses he has written is the study of the genesis of the African race. He is a dedicated defender of the theory that humanity had its origins on the African continent.

He is a member of the Association of Negro Writers and his better-known works include: *The Niger* (1955), *Religion and Politics, their role in the evolution of the African black races* (1955), and *Study of the Foundations and Genesis of African Unity* (1966).

He was born in 1906 in the district of Tera, took a teaching diploma at the William Ponty School in Dakar, and was first a teacher and then headmaster of a school. A grand councillor of French West Africa and several times territorial councillor for Niger, he was elected a deputy then President (Speaker) of the first Niger National Assembly in 1958. A senator of the French Community, he has also been vice-president of the Euro-African Assembly in Strasbourg and a member of the permanent committee of this Assembly.

He was a founder-member of the ruling Niger Progress Party ('Parti Progressiste Nigérien') and is the party's president. As only one legal party is permitted in Niger this post gives him considerable political power.

Boubou Hama is also chairman of several State-backed trading corporations.

IBRAHIM ISSA

The Minister of Public Health, Ibrahim Issa was born at Zinder in 1922.

Formerly a company clerk, he was elected member of the Legislative Assembly for Zinder in June, 1959.

He was active in the local branch of the 'Parti Progressiste Nigérien' in Zinder and on November 23, 1965, was appointed Minister of Public Health.

AMADOU ISSAKA

Amadou Issaka was born in 1924 at Kantche and is chief of that district. He rose up through all the levels of public office, being regional councillor in 1946, territorial councillor in 1952, member of the new Niger Assembly in 1958 and senator of the French Community in 1959.

In 1965 he was appointed Minister of the Civil Service and Labour, a post held by an interim appointment since 1963 when the then Minister, M. Diallo Boubacar, was arrested for plotting against the state and sent to prison where he died of fever.

NOMA KAKA

A political figure with a big personal following, Noma Kaka is another Niger leader who came to politics through teaching. He graduated at the William Ponty Teachers' Training College in Dakar. M. Kaka has been Niger's Minister for Defence since November, 1965, after having previously been responsible for the Information and Youth Ministries as well.

He was born in 1920 in Doutchi and entered the political scene on a national level when, in 1958, he was elected member of Parliament. A few months later the landslide swing in

Harou Kouka

Diamballa Maiga

Boukary Sabo

favour of association with France carried M. Kaka into the senate of the French Community.

Before Niger's independence, M. Kaka was grand councillor for French West Africa. He is a member of the political bureau of the ruling party and president of the State Security Court.

LEOPOLD KAZIENDA

Léopold Kazienda, Minister of Public Works, was born in Kaya, Upper Volta, in 1921. After graduating from teachers' training college in Dakar he attended classes at the French teachers' college of Saint Cloud. Thus qualified, he began teaching and rose to a headmastership.

The creation of the RDA (African Democratic Rally) was for him a stepping stone into the world of politics. An active member of the rank and file of the party, he was brought to the notice of the head of state and was appointed Minister of Posts and Telecommunications, and later of Public Works, Mines, Transport and Urban Development.

He was awarded national orders by Niger, France, Tunisia, Upper Volta and Belgium.

HAROU KOUKA

Harou Kouka, Niger's Minister of Education, born in 1922, obtained a degree at the African School of Medicine in Dakar.

He was elected a deputy to the Union of the Franco-African Community and later entered the Legislative Assembly.

He first joined the Government in 1959 as Minister of Labour, soon afterwards becoming Minister of Labour and Social Affairs, until December, 1960.

In a Government reshuffle in 1960 he was given responsibility for Public Health.

MAMOUDOU MAIDAH

Mamoudou Maidah was born in 1924 in Tessoua (District of Maradi).

After his primary schooling, he attended classes at the national school of Frederic Assomption in Katibougou, Mali, from which he graduated with a primary school-teacher's diploma.

When Niger was a member of the French Community, he joined the Government, in 1959, as Minister of Agriculture.

In 1960, when Niger became independent, he became Minister of Education until 1963. He was then made Minister of Rural Affairs and Economy.

DIAMBALLA MAIGA

Born in 1910, in the Niamey district, Diamballa Yansambou Maiga has been Minister of the Interior since 1958; he is the oldest member of the Cabinet.

M. Maiga has a considerable knowledge of Arabic which is fairly rare among politicians in the region south of the Sahara.

He is one of the three cornerstones on which the State rests, the other two being President Hamani Diori and the President of the National Assembly, Boubou Hama.

BOUKARY SABO

Boukary Sabo, Minister of Information and Youth, entered the Government on November 23, 1965.

He was born in 1924 in the district of Maradi. A graduate of the Frederic Assomption Teachers' Training College in Katibougou, Mali, he was elected a member of the Niger Assembly in April, 1959.

MOUDOUR ZAKARA

Niger's nomadic population of the Sahara presented the Govern-

Moudour Zakara

ment with such a special problem that the President believed this justified the existence of a special Ministry.

Ever since independence Moudour Zakara, a Touareg, has been responsible for Saharan and Nomad Affairs in the Cabinet. The reshuffle of 1965 added the job of Postmaster General to his responsibilities.

M. Zakara's job as Minister of Saharan Affairs involves him each year in August in the traditional ceremony of the 'salted cure'. This gathering is attended by all the nomad cattle breeders who drive their herds to the Agades district in the centre of Niger where the pastures are richer in salt. The Minister takes this opportunity to inquire about the nomads' problems and to inform them of the Government's decisions affecting their way of life.

M. Zakara is the same age as President Diori. He was born in 1916 and started out in life as a clerk in the Civil Service.

While in the Civil Service he represented Niger at the 'Organisation Commune des Régions Sahariennes' (Common Organisation for the Sahara).

When, in 1958, Niger was granted the right to have a National Assembly he was elected Member of Parliament for Tahoua, in the west. His election was soon followed by a Cabinet post.

A man of striking appearance, particularly in his Touareg robes, M. Zakara astonished his hosts when on a visit to Egypt he deciphered hieroglyphics of early Egyptian dynasties.

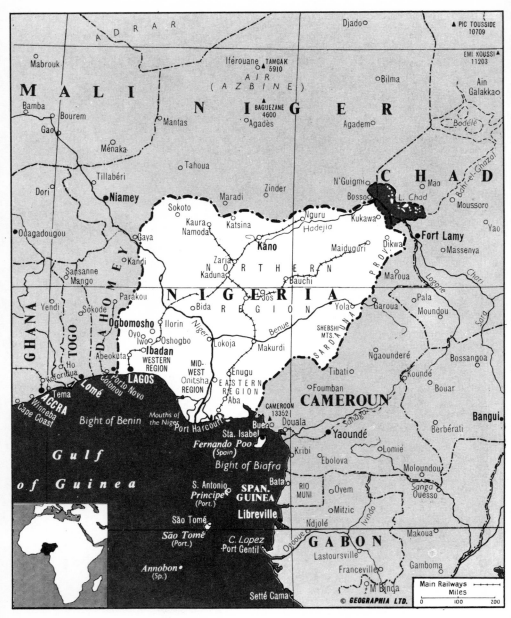

Nigeria covers an area of over 350,000 square miles and has an estimated population of 56,000,000 people. More than half (29 million) live in the Northern Region. Dahomey lies to the west, Niger to the north and Cameroun to the east. In the north-east corner is Lake Chad, across which lies the Republic of Chad. The capital is Lagos.

Rich in natural resources, Nigeria's main economic wealth is derived from agriculture and some minerals, including petroleum, groundnuts, cocoa, palm produce, tin, rubber, and timber.

Nigeria

Nigeria became independent of British rule on October 1, 1960, and a republic on October 1, 1963.

Four main regions, all self-governing (Northern, Western, Mid-Western and Eastern) had been under a Governor General as a federation since October 1, 1954.

There are three great racial groups — Northern Hausas, Western Yorubas and Eastern Ibos.

A Federal Parliament and a largely Northern Government headed by Sir Abubakar Tafawa Balewa ended in a *coup d'état* led mainly by Eastern army officers in January, 1966. Sir Abubakar was assassinated. So were Sir Ahmadu Bello and Chief Akintola, the Northern and Western Premiers.

Major-General J. T. U. Aguiyi Ironsi, head of the Army and an Ibo, suppressed the revolt and assumed supreme power as President. He suspended the constitution.

In July, 1966 Northern officers led a mutiny. General Ironsi was murdered. He was succeeded by a Northern officer, Lieutenant-Colonel Yakubu Gowon who became head of the military Government.

The Federation of Nigeria, Africa's most populous nation, entered 1967 in a state of political stalemate after more than a year of violent and bloody upheaval.

Six years of independence since October 1, 1960, saw the failure of a major experiment in civilian federation, two military *coups d'état*, an abortive attempt to create a unitary state and communal and inter-tribal rioting costing many thousands of lives.

Nigeria's military Government, headed by Lieutenant-Colonel Yakubu Gowon, faced the task of finding a new constitutional formula for keeping the country together amid mounting fears that tribal passions had been inflamed to a point where cooperation was barely possible between the country's many disparate regions.

The military Government was seeking a compromise amid calls for a loose confederation of large regions and a tight federation of small states. As 1966 ended, no solution appeared to be in sight.

Nigeria's 350,000 square miles enclose some of Africa's most important economic riches—petroleum, groundnuts, cocoa, tin, rubber and timber—contributing to a gross domestic product of over £1,000 million.

Aerial view of Kano, with the mosque surrounded by buildings of baked mud in the old, traditional city

Her estimated 56 million population, backed by such wealth, makes Nigeria potentially one of the world's great nations, but right from her emergence from British colonial rule her affairs have been overshadowed by the fear of breaking up into several minor countries based on component regions or tribes.

Nigeria's many tribes and areas, originally grouped by British conquest rather than natural factors, attained nationhood as a federation – first of three regions, North, East and West – with a fourth, the tiny Mid-west, added later, and Lagos as the federal capital.

A constant source of political friction was the imbalance in the size of the regions.

Population figures arrived at after two bitterly controversial censuses showed the largely arid, savannah Northern region to have some 29 million people.

This was more than half the country's population and ensured virtual built-in control of the Federal legislature and institutions.

Up to January, 1966, when a military *coup d'état* swept away civilian rule, Nigeria was governed by a Federal Parliament and a largely Northern Government headed by a Prime Minister, Alhaji Sir Abubakar Tafawa Balewa. The legislature was the scene of shifting alliances, but Northern control of the centre was a constant factor.

Nigeria's first major political crisis after independence came in 1962 in the cocoa-producing, rain-forest Western region, home of the Yoruba tribe, one of Nigeria's three main ethnic groups.

With support from the Northern-dominated Federal Government, Chief S. L. Akintola, the Western Premier, was able to wrest control of the region from his more popular rival, Chief Awolowo.

Chief Awolowo was later jailed for treasonable felony and was only released in 1966 by military government pardon. Northern political domination created growing unrest in the rest of the country, particularly in the oil-bearing Eastern region, home of the industrious and progressive Ibo tribe.

Although the main Eastern political party was at one time in alliance with the ruling Northern party, the East felt it was being frozen out of the nation's affairs. This feeling reached a climax in December, 1964, when the first federal elections since independence were held.

A Kano mother
carries her baby
past a plot of
groundnut pyramids

The country was divided roughly into two main political
alliances, one led by the North (Nigerian National
Alliance – NNA) and the other by the East (United
Progressive Grand Alliance – UPGA).

The UPGA boycotted the elections after repeated allegations of election rigging and intimidation but was politically
out-manoeuvred, and the East was forced to back down
from its first major threat to secede from the Federation.

Allegations of political malpractice added to growing
instances of official corruption and a widening gap
between the haves and have-nots brought the Federal
Government into considerable disrepute, affecting even the
high reputation as a statesman of Sir Abubakar Tafawa
Balewa.

Discontent reached its high point at the end of 1965 when,
with Northern support, Chief Akintola blatantly rigged his
regional elections to retain power in the Yoruba West,
ushering in a period of violent and lawless protest and
setting the stage for the end of civilian rule.

In January, 1966, a *coup*, planned and executed by a
small group of mainly Eastern Nigerian army officers, took
Nigeria and the world by surprise and shattered the
political foundations of the country.

The Prime Minister, Alhaji Sir Abubakar Tafawa Balewa,
the Northern leader, Sir Ahmadu Bello, and Western
Premier Chief Akintola were all assassinated and many,
mainly Northern and Western army officers, were
murdered.

The *coup's* organisers were arrested, but the army remained
in power and the head of the armed forces, Eastern Ibo
Major-General J. T. U. Aguiyi Ironsi, was named
President.

The new military Government announced itself as a source
of national political cleansing to replace the corrupt,
discredited civilian rule.

It also announced plans to move away from federation
towards a unitary state, claiming the federal system had
forced politicians to play on tribal passions to cement their
supporters and thus had driven wedges between the
country's regions.

But this view of the military *coup* as a bid for clean
government was never accepted by the massive Northern
region.

The mainly Moslem Hausas of the North saw the *coup* as an

The Federal House of Representatives building in Lagos

Ibo power-play designed to smash the Northern grip on the country.

Four months after General Ironsi came to power, an announcement of moves towards unitary government sparked off violent protest demonstrations in the North which quickly turned into bloody anti-Ibo tribal rioting. Hostility between North and East continued to grow until, in July, 1966, in a mutiny led by Northern officers, General Ironsi was assassinated and a Northern officer, Colonel Gowon, was put in his place.

Again the country came close to breaking up amid fears either that the North would secede despite its landlocked geographical situation or would push the East towards secession by continued anti-Ibo persecution.

Colonel Gowon, himself a non-Moslem from the less feudally traditionalist middle belt of Northern Nigeria, announced that his military Government would be temporary, and called national constitutional talks to draft a new constitution and save the country from splitting

320

The Library at
Ibadan, Nigeria's
foremost University

into separate and mutually hostile states.
But the talks dragged slowly then halted completely after
more rioting in the North, where Northern soldiers were
reported to have helped civilian mobs in massacring
many thousands of Ibos.

By the end of 1966, the country seemed to have settled on
the very brink of break-up with the East – held back from
the final step only by fears of the economic and
international consequences of secession.

Nigeria's prosperity was not at first badly hit by the
political troubles – mainly because oil production and
revenues continued to rise dramatically and international
market factors hardened the world price of cocoa after a
temporary slump.

But Nigeria's image as a safe haven in Africa for
international investment was severely damaged and small
middle-grade investment showed a marked falling off by
the end of the year. The inter-tribal violence also touched
off a population shakeout as hundreds of thousands of

Nigerians retreated to their tribal homelands in fear of a further worsening of the political situation or possible civil war – a further hamper on economic development.
But the Eastern region, although already severed emotionally from the Federation, did not take the final step of secession – partly braked by fears that the Eastern minority tribes on whose land much of the oil lies would not support an independent Eastern state.
Politically the whole country remained in turmoil – grappling both with old problems and with many new forces released by the upheavals such as the powerful new non-traditionalist voice in the North.
Talks continued to try to bring the representatives of all regions and in particular, Eastern Nigeria's military Governor, Lieutenant-Colonel Odumegwu Ojukwu, to the conference table.
Colonel Gowon announced he would create a new 'constituent assembly' to draft a fresh constitution, replacing earlier conferences, but at the end of 1966 no solution was in sight.

Col Robert Adebayo

COL ROBERT ADEBAYO

Colonel Robert Adeyinka Adebayo, military Governor of Western Nigeria, is the son of a retired Nigerian Railway official.

Born in 1928, he was educated at Christ's School, Ado-Ekiti, eight miles from his home town, Iyin-Ekiti, and at the Eko Boys' High School, Lagos. He left school in 1947 and enlisted in the Army the following year.

In 1951 he attended a course at the School of Infantry, Accra, Ghana, and was commissioned a lieutenant at Eaton Hall, England, in 1953.

He returned to Nigeria the following year and was promoted captain in 1957, major in 1960, lieutenant-colonel in 1962 and full colonel in January, 1964.

Colonel Adebayo, who is the second military Governor of Western Nigeria, has held a number of important positions in the Nigerian Army including ADC to the Governor-General (1957–58), and Chief of Staff of the Nigerian Army (1964–65).

He served in the Congo (Kinshasa) under the United Nations Peace Keeping Force from 1961–63.

Colonel Adebayo attended the Staff College at Camberley, England, and was half way through a course at the Imperial Defence College when he was recalled, in August, 1966, to take up the appointment of Military Governor of Western Nigeria.

He led the Nigerian delegation to the 1966 Conference of the Organisation of African Unity (OAU), and was reported to have saved the formal opening of the conference from being called off over the Ghana-Guinea issue. Opposing moves by certain states to have the conference adjourned indefinitely, Colonel Adebayo

Sir Adetokunbo
Ademola

warned that such a step would bring shame to the Organisation and give it a bad name.

DAUDA SOROYE ADEGBENRO

Alhaji Dauda Soroye Adegbenro was until early in 1966 acting leader of the banned Action Group.

Born in 1909 at Abeokuta in Western Nigeria, he worked first as a clerk in the Nigerian Railways and then as a storekeeper for the United Africa Company.

He entered politics in 1951, when he was elected to the Western Region House of Assembly on the platform of the Action Group.

In 1954 he was successively Parliamentary Secretary to the Minister of Justice, Minister of Lands and Labour and Minister of Local Government.

While Minister of Local Government, Alhaji Adegbenro proved himself an able and impartial administrator, at a time when party politics were at their peak.

After the late Chief Samuel Akintola had been sacked by the Governor in 1962, Alhaji Adegbenro was elected Premier of Western Nigeria; but a fight broke out in the Western House of Assembly (May 25) on the day a vote of confidence was to be passed.

He was unable to officiate in this post as the Government was suspended following the declaration of an emergency in the region.

His movements were restricted in May, 1962, after the disturbances in the Regional House but he was released, and when his leader, Chief Obafemi Awolowo, was detained following the discovery of a plot to overthrow the Federal Government, he be-

came the acting leader of the party.

At the end of the emergency in December, 1962, with Chief Akintola reinstated as Premier, Alhaji Adegbenro became the leader of the Action Group Opposition.

He is a staunch Moslem and widely respected for his administrative ability.

SIR ADETOKUNBO ADEMOLA

Sir Adetokunbo Ademola, Chief Justice of the Federation of Nigeria, is an illustrious son of an illustrious father.

His father was the late Alake (Paramount ruler) of Egbaland in Western Nigeria (1920–62), Sir Ladapo Ademola. Sir Adetokunbo is among the most distinguished and most respected Nigerians. He has had a brilliant career. Over the years, he has built for himself an international reputation, being a member of several world bodies.

Born on September 1, 1906, at Abeokuta, capital of Egbaland, Sir Adetokunbo studied law between 1928–31 at Cambridge University, obtaining a BA degree. He received his MA later.

He was called to the Bar (Middle Temple) in London in 1934, and later became the only African ever appointed a bencher of the Inn.

Back in Nigeria, Sir Adetokunbo worked from 1934–35 as Crown Counsel at the then Attorney-General's Office, then for a year as assistant secretary at the Southern Secretariat in Enugu, Eastern Nigeria.

From 1936, Sir Adetokunbo practised until 1939, when he was appointed Magistrate of the Protectorate Court. In 1949 he became the third Nigerian to be appointed a Puisne Judge.

In 1948 he served as a member of the Commission for the revision of court legislation.

In 1955, a year before Western Nigeria became internally self-governing, Sir Adetokunbo was appointed Chief Justice for Western Nigeria, thus becoming the first Nigerian head of the Judiciary anywhere in Nigeria.

Sir Adetokunbo's string of 'firsts' continued when, three years later, he became the first Nigerian Chief Justice of the entire Federation of Nigeria.

He was knighted in January, 1957, and in 1963 was appointed one of Queen Elizabeth's Privy Councillors. Later that year, the Queen awarded him a KBE.

He is married to Miss Kofo Moore, the first West African woman graduate – she took a BA at Oxford – and daughter of the late Eric Moore, first Lagos member of the Legislative Council of Nigeria.

At the end of 1966, then aged 60, Sir Adetokunbo was serving a second term as member of the United Nations committee of experts advising on labour conventions and regulations.

He is also a member of the United Nations International Public Service Advisory Board, member of the International Commission of Jurists, executive member of World Peace Through Law, vice-president of the World Association of Jurists, president of the Nigerian Red Cross Association, chairman of Nigeria Cheshire Homes, member of the International Olympic Committee, member of the Nigerian Institute of International Affairs and president of the Reformed Ogbonni Fraternity.

Sir Adetokunbo is also one of the founders and the chairman of the Metropolitan Club, a founder member of the Island Club and vice-patron of the Yoruba Club. Sir Adetokunbo has been in the forefront of the several peace moves in Nigeria.

SIR FRANCIS AKANU IBIAM

Sir Francis Akanu Ibiam, Adviser to the military Governor of Eastern Nigeria, was the first civilian Governor of Eastern Nigeria.

Son of a pagan, Sir Francis has become the foremost Christian leader in Nigeria.

An elder of the Presbyterian Church of Nigeria, he is currently one of the four presidents of the All-Africa Conference of Churches and one of the six presidents of the World Council of Churches.

Born on November 29, 1906, at Unwana in the Afrikpo Division of Eastern Nigeria, Sir Francis became a Christian a few years later through the influence of a Christian uncle.

He had his secondary education at the Hope Waddell Institute, Calabar, and King's College, Lagos; later he studied at the University of St Andrew's, Scotland, where he graduated in medicine.

On his return to Nigeria, he worked for many years as a medical missionary with the Church of Scotland Mission in Eastern Nigeria.

Sir Francis was a member of the old Nigerian Legislative Council and of the Executive Council between 1947 and 1952.

He was knighted by the late King George V in 1951 and then in 1962 received the KCMG from Queen Elizabeth II for 'selfless services to Nigeria'.

A Privy Councillor, Sir Francis has held a number of top positions in Nigeria including chairmanship of the Council of the University College, Ibadan – Nigeria's premier university.

Chief Obafemi
Awolowo

Sir Francis is one of the most widely travelled Nigerians. In 1959, he attended the East Asia Christian conference in Kuala Lumpur, Malaya, and the World Council of Churches' conference in Greece.

He was at the third Assembly of the World Council of Churches in New Delhi, India, in 1961; and in 1964 attended the Executive Committee meeting of the Council in Moscow.

He was responsible for the holding in Enugu in 1965 of the conference of the World Council of Churches – the first such meeting in Africa.

Sir Francis was appointed first African civilian Governor of Eastern Nigeria in 1960. He was awarded the GCON (Grand Commander of the Order of the Niger) – Nigeria's highest award – in 1964.

A very active sportsman in his heyday, his time latterly has been almost entirely devoted to Christian and religious work. But he is also one of the senior advisers of the Eastern Nigeria military Government on whom the future of the country depends.

CHIEF OBAFEMI AWOLOWO

Chief Obafemi Awolowo, leader of the banned Action Group and leader of the Yorubas of Western Nigeria, was born on March 6, 1909.

Son of a farmer and a self-made man, Chief Awolowo was educated at Anglican and Methodist schools in Ikenne, his home town, and at the Baptist Boys' High School in Abeokuta, Western Nigeria.

His education being curtailed from lack of money, Chief Awolowo worked as a pupil teacher and then went to Wesley College in Ibadan, capital city of Western Nigeria, to attend a course in teacher training.

Leaving Wesley College, he studied shorthand and typing, and after working for a while in Lagos, returned to Wesley College in 1932 as a clerk.

Two years later, he became a trader and a newspaper reporter. He organised in the late '30s the Nigerian Produce Traders Association and became secretary of the Nigerian Motor Transport Union.

Not satisfied with his education, Chief Awolowo took up spare-time studies and, after matriculating in 1939, went on to obtain a Bachelor of Commerce degree in 1944; in that year he was also editing the now defunct *Nigerian Worker*.

In June, 1940, he became secretary of the Ibadan Branch of the Nigerian Youth Movement (NYM) and, in this position, led the agitation for the reform of the Ibadan Native Authority Advisory Board in 1942.

He was co-founder of the Trade Union Congress of Nigeria in 1943. The following year, he went to London to study law and founded the Egbe Omo Oduduwa, a Yoruba tribal society.

After qualifying in 1947, he returned to Nigeria to set up legal practice and continued to work for the Egbe Omo Oduduwa, becoming general secretary in 1948.

Two years later he was the moving spirit in organising with other Yoruba leaders the Action Group, which won the Western Region elections in 1951.

Chief Awolowo was Leader of Government Business and Minister of Local Government from 1951–54 when, with the introduction of the new Constitution, he became the first Premier of Western Nigeria.

Dr Nnamdi Azikiwe

Chief Awolowo, who is highly competent, full of initiative, original in thought, practical and very often stubborn when he is convinced about something, built the Action Group into what has been described as 'the best political party south of the Sahara'.

With an able and efficient team, both in Government and in party, he succeeded in making the Western Region the cynosure of the rest of the Federation of Nigeria.

He resigned the premiership of Western Nigeria in 1959 to contest the Federal elections but, failing to win, became the Leader of the Opposition in the Federal House of Representatives.

Chief Awolowo led his party's delegation to the London and Lagos Constitutional conferences in 1953 and 1954, and to a later conference in Lagos in 1958.

So excellent was the administration of Western Nigeria during Chief Awolowo's tenure of office as Premier that when in 1953 the British Government announced its intention to grant self-government in 1956 to any Region desiring it, the Action Group Leader asked for and secured it in the same year.

Chief Awolowo is an unyielding advocate of a federal constitution for Nigeria. He is also a strong antagonist of the North's feudal system and its spread to other parts of Nigeria; and an advocate of the creation of more states in Nigeria.

A fight broke out in the Western House of Assembly (May 25, 1962) following an attempt by the Action Group to discipline Chief Awolowo's next in command, the late Chief Samuel Akintola, who was then Premier of the Region.

The Federal Parliament met four days later and decided to declare a state of emergency all over the Region. Chief Awolowo and the main leaders were put under restriction, but later the Action Group Leader and some of his aides were detained following the discovery of a plot to overthrow the Federal Government.

On November 2, 1962, Chief Awolowo and 28 other members of his party were put on trial for treasonable felony. After a hearing lasting eleven months, he was sentenced (September 11, 1963) to ten years imprisonment, and, on appeal to the Federal Supreme Court, the sentence was confirmed.

He spent just over three years in Calabar prison. He was released on August 3, 1966 with a state pardon. Nine days later, amid jubilation, he was unanimously elected leader of 10,500,000 Yorubas and leader of Western Nigeria's delegation to the All-Nigeria Constitutional Conference on the future association of Nigeria.

Chief Awolowo is married and has four children. While he was on trial, his eldest son, a Cambridge law student, died in a car accident near Ibadan.

Chief Awolowo is an author whose publications include *Path to Nigerian Freedom*. In his latest book, *Thoughts on the Nigerian Constitution,* which he wrote while in prison, he advocates that 'a confederal constitution is probably the only way out of the present impasse in Nigeria'.

Chief Awolowo is expected to play a leading role in future moves to settle Nigeria's pressing difficulties.

DR NNAMDI AZIKIWE

Dr Nnamdi Azikiwe, popularly known as 'Zik', is the father of modern Nigerian nationalism and chief architect of the country's independence.

The first Nigerian to be appointed Governor-General and later President of Republican Nigeria, Dr Azikiwe was the founder of the National Convention of Nigeria and the Cameroons (now the National Convention of Nigerian Citizens) – one of the ruling political parties in the country until the military take-over of January, 1966.

A political scientist, author, journalist, educationist and orator, Dr Azikiwe was born on November 16, 1904 at Zungeru, Northern Nigeria, where his father – an Ibo – was working as a clerk in the Nigeria Regiment.

Receiving his education at the Hope Waddell Institute, Calabar, and later at the Methodist Boys' High School, Lagos, Dr Azikiwe worked in the Treasury Department in Lagos from 1921–25 before stowing away on a ship bound for the United States.

With the assistance of public-spirited Americans and wages earned from doing menial jobs, he went through his studies at Storer College, West Virginia, and at Howard and Lincoln Universities, where he read political science.

He later did a post-graduate course at the University of Pennsylvania and lectured at Lincoln University before returning to West Africa to join in the struggle against colonial rule which was sweeping across that part of the continent.

Dr Azikiwe was for three years editor of the *African Morning Post* published in the Gold Coast (Ghana). Following an alleged seditious article in that paper, he was charged and convicted by the then Colonial Administration but was acquitted following a successful appeal.

He returned to Nigeria in 1937 and set up a chain of newspapers, including the *West African Pilot* which he edited himself. With these papers, he intensified the fight against colonialism and championed the cause of the working class.

At the same time he joined the country's only nationalist movement, the Nigerian Youth Movement, and was in the forefront of the agitation for self-rule.

By 1942, Dr Azikiwe had won widespread Nigerian support by his anti-British campaign and fierce editorials which paved the way for the formation of his party – the NCNC.

In 1944, the NCNC fused with the Nigerian National Democratic Party, led by the late Herbert Macaulay (grandson of the first African Bishop, the Reverend Ajayi Crowther), already a prominent political figure in the country.

Herbert Macaulay was president, and Dr Azikiwe secretary of the new party which inherited the name of the NCNC. This was the first real national political party, embracing all tribal groupings, in the country.

When Macaulay died in 1946 during a country-wide political tour, Dr Azikiwe became president of the party.

In 1951 the British decided to grant Nigeria internal self-rule, following sustained agitation spearheaded by the NCNC. Dr Azikiwe was one of his party's candidates who swept the polls in the federal territory of Lagos.

By this time Chief Awolowo's Action Group party had emerged as a strong force in Western Nigeria. And then began the bitter rivalry between the two Southern parties – one pro-Yoruba, the other pro-Ibo.

Meanwhile, Dr Azikiwe's party was returned to power in Eastern Nigeria and his aide, Professor Eyo Ita from the Calabar minority area of the region, was appointed Leader of Government Business. Azikiwe himself remained in the Western Legislature as Leader of the Opposition.

But in the following year his lieutenants, who headed the Eastern Nigeria government, rebelled. With the support of the masses who regarded him as a 'saviour', Dr Azikiwe crushed the rebellion and the Regional Legislature was dissolved. In a subsequent election the NCNC was returned to power and Dr Azikiwe, who contested the elections, left the Western Legislature to become the Leader of Government Business and later Premier of the East.

Dr Azikiwe was Premier of Eastern Nigeria until the 1959 pre-independence federal elections. In the elections, none of the three major political parties – the Northern Peoples' Congress, the NCNC and the Action Group – won an absolute majority.

The Northern Peoples' Congress, which won more seats, and the NCNC, with the second largest number of successful candidates, decided to form a coalition, leaving the Action Group in opposition.

Under an agreement reached between leaders of both parties, Dr Azikiwe was appointed Governor-General of Nigeria and deputy Leader of the NPC, with the late Sir Abubakar Tafawa Balewa, as Prime Minister.

Had the NCNC teamed up with the Action Group, Dr Azikiwe would have been Nigeria's first Prime Minister.

Dr Azikiwe explained then that he turned down offers from the Action Group in order that Britain should grant independence to Nigeria. If the two Southern parties had ganged up against the North, he feared Britain would have withheld independence.

Thus, Dr Azikiwe forsook active politics to become the ceremonial Head of State, handing the leadership of his party in 1960 to Dr Michael Okpara.

When Nigeria became a republic in October, 1963, Dr Azikiwe was unanimously appointed President by the Federal Parliament.

Dr Azikiwe's contribution to education was the founding of the University of Nigeria, Nsukka, of which he was the first Chancellor until his removal after the January, 1966 military takeover.

Immediately after the takeover, Dr Azikiwe, like most former politicians, went into virtual isolation, confining himself in his country home at Nsukka, where he made preparations to return to his old profession, journalism, and to devote time to writing books.

With the second military *coup* in July, 1966, the East was obviously in need of mature advisers and Dr Azikiwe came out of retirement to act as one of the leading advisers to the military Government of Eastern Nigeria.

In a statement towards the end of 1966 which was acclaimed all over the country, Dr Azikiwe suggested a meeting of elder statesmen to mediate 'in the situation facing the nation'.

He said the fate of the nation 'swings like the pendulum of an erratic clock' and that 'commonsense makes it imperative that statesmen and women of this nation should now intercede, because if we do not have peace within ourselves it is vain to seek

Sir Mobolaji
Bank-Anthony

The Oba of Benin

for it from external sources'.

Six feet tall and of stately presence, Dr Azikiwe was appointed a member of the Privy Council by Queen Elizabeth in 1960 when he became Nigeria's Governor-General.

Dr Azikiwe's interests are walking, reading and writing. His works include two studies of modern African affairs, entitled *Liberia in World Politics* and *Renascent Africa*.

SIR MOBOLAJI BANK-ANTHONY

Sir Mobolaji Bank-Anthony is a company director whose many business connections and social standing have placed him in a position of great influence, although he has never become involved in party politics.

Son of Mr Anthony Bank-Anthony of Lagos, one of the country's pioneers in business, Sir Mobolaji was born in Leopoldville (now Kinshasa), Belgian Congo, on June 11, 1907.

After attending kindergarten schools in Calabar, Eastern Nigeria, and Lagos, Sir Mobolaji went to the Methodist Boys' High School and the CMS Grammar School, both in Lagos, and the Ijebu-Ode Grammar School.

He joined the Posts and Telegraphs Department as a clerk in 1924, resigning eight years later to work with his father in Lagos.

Sir Mobolaji set up his own business the following year after a business trip to Germany. 'I started as a hawker of patent medicine and watches,' he once said. 'By the end of World War II, I found myself in a good position and started to expand.'

Within four years, he had floated four enterprises – The Nigerian Marble Industries, M. de Banks Transport (road trans-

port), M. de Banks Brothers (general merchants) and Boroni Prono, Nigeria (builders).

At the end of 1966, Sir Mobolaji was either chairman or director of over a dozen companies. Among them were: Mobil Oil (Exploration) Nigeria, British Insulated Callender Cables, Pressed Metal Works, the Aero Contractors Company of Nigeria and the Tourist Company of Nigeria.

Sir Mobolaji was awarded the OBE in 1958 and knighted by Queen Elizabeth II in 1962 for his public services to Nigeria.

A Christian and philanthropist, Sir Mobolaji is president of the Lagos branch of the Young Men's Christian Association.

He is among the most widely travelled Nigerians, having toured extensively in Europe, the United States and Asia.

OBA OF BENIN

Oba (King) Omonoba Ukuakpolokpolo Akenzua II, one of the most prominent of the traditional rulers in Nigeria, is the monarch of the ancient kingdom of Benin, the seat of the Mid-Western Nigerian Government.

He ascended the throne on April 5, 1933, following the death of his father, Oba Eweka II.

Born in Benin City in 1899, he Entered the Benin Government school (headed by the late W. T. Okai, a Ghanaian) at the age of eight. In 1918 he gained admission to King's College, Lagos – Nigeria's leading secondary grammar school at the time.

Returning to Benin in 1921 at the completion of his secondary education, Oba Akenzua joined the Benin Native Authority as a transport clerk. In 1924, he was a confidential clerk to his father and was sent to Abeokuta, Western Nigeria, to carry out further

329

studies in native administration.

Since ascending the throne in 1933, Oba Akenzua has established himself as a key figure in the country's political evolution.

Fearless and outspoken on national issues, he was nominated a member of the Western House of Assembly in 1947 and later a member of the old Nigerian Legislative Council.

With the introduction of the 1951 constitution, which gave internal self-rule to the regional governments, he became a member of the Western Nigeria House of Chiefs.

In 1955, he was one of the few natural rulers in Western Nigeria appointed Cabinet Minister without Portfolio by the Awolowo Government; he served in the Cabinet until the 1962 Western Nigeria crisis which brought an end to Action Group rule in the region.

Although a Minister in the Western Nigeria Government, Oba Akenzua campaigned for the carving out of the Mid-West region from Western Nigeria. And when the new state was created in 1963, his position as the most influential natural ruler in the region, made him an automatic choice for President of the Mid-Western House of Chiefs – a position he held until the Army takeover in January, 1966.

In March, 1966, the military regime of Major-General Aguiyi-Ironsi appointed Oba Akenzua Chancellor of the Ahmadu Bello University in Zaria, Northern Nigeria.

Oba Akenzua is the first Christian Oba of Benin.

He was awarded the CMG by the late King George VI.

Oba Akenzua has nine wives and his family includes more than eighty children and grandchildren.

DR S. O. BIOBAKU

Dr Saburi Oladeni Biobaku, Vice-Chancellor of the University of Lagos, is one of Nigeria's leading educationists and administrators.

Born in Abeokuta, Western Nigeria, on June 16, 1918, he began his education at Government College, Ibadan, and later went to the Higher College, Yaba – Nigeria's highest institution of learning in the '30s and cradle of most of the country's prominent intellectuals and professionals.

After a brief spell as a teacher at the Government College – his alma mater – Dr Biobaku went to the United Kingdom in 1944 for advanced studies. He graduated with a BA in history at the University of Exeter in 1945 and a BA (English) two years later at Trinity College, Cambridge.

With a double degree in three years, Dr Biobaku returned to Nigeria in 1947 to re-enter his old profession, teaching, at a time when the Civil Service offered tremendous attractions.

He was back in London in 1950 and won a doctorate in history at the London Institute of Historical Research.

Apart from the five-year period from 1957-61 when he worked in the Civil Service as secretary to the Western Nigeria Premier and Executive Council, Dr Biobaku's career has been larely devoted to education.

Between 1951–53, he was assistant liaison officer for Nigerian Students in the United Kingdom and, from 1953–57, he held the post of Registrar of University College, Ibadan – the country's foremost university.

In 1961 he held the dual positions of Professor of History and Pro Vice-Chancellor of the University of Ife, in Western Nigeria.

In December, 1964 he was appointed Vice-Chancellor designate of the University of Zambia, but withdrew three months afterwards to take up his present job as Vice-Chancellor of the University of Lagos. This appointment led to students rioting in the University and the resignation of some of the expatriate academic staff of the institution who felt it was tribally inspired. Dr Biobaku himself was stabbed by one of the rioting students.

Son of Chief S. O. Biobaku, a transporter and produce buyer, Dr Biobaku is vice-president of the Nigerian Society of African Culture, member of the Antiquities Commission, member of the West African Examinations Council, chairman of the Nigerian Society for Public Administration and a member of the board of the 'Encyclopaedia Africana' which the Nkrumah regime were planning to publish in Accra, Ghana.

Regarded as an authority on Yoruba history, his many publications and articles include two books – *The Egba and their Neighbours* and *The Origin of the Yorubas*.

Dr Biobaku is a Moslem and went on a pilgrimage to Mecca in 1959.

He received the CMG from Queen Elizabeth II in 1961 in recognition of his outstanding services to Nigeria.

INCREASE HERBERT COKER

Increase Herbert Ebenezer Olisa-Eloka Coker, Federal Military Government Liaison Officer, is one of the oldest practising journalists in Nigeria.

He has remained with the profession since he joined it in 1943 – soon after leaving college – and has contributed much to its development.

Born on March 10, 1920, Mr Coker joined the *West African Pilot* and Zik's Press Ltd in 1943. In 1946, he was appointed editor of *Defender*, one of Zik's (Dr Nnamdi Azikiwe's) newspapers, and the following year he became editor of the main newspaper, the *West African Pilot*, which he edited until 1951.

Between 1951–54, Mr Coker was Information Officer to the Produce Marketing Boards of Nigeria, and Senior Information Officer, Federal Ministry of Information, from 1954–61.

In 1961, he was seconded to the Federal Government-owned Nigerian National Press, where he was appointed editor-in-chief of Periodicals and General Publications.

In 1963 he was promoted commercial manager and deputy general manager of the Nigerian National Press, and remained in this post until he left in July, 1966 to take up the post of Federal Military Government Liaison Officer.

Mr Coker, whose father was a civil servant in the old Calabar (Eastern Nigeria) Consulate (later Residency), has several publications to his credit. These include a number of Nigerian social and historical studies, such as *The Surplus Women* (1949), *Grammar of African Names* (1964) and *Seventy Years of the Nigerian Press* (1953).

ZANA BUKAR SULOMA DIPCHARIMA

Zana Alhaji Bukar Suloma Dipcharima, District Head of Yerwa in Maiduguri, Northern Nigeria, was Minister of Transport in the suspended Federal Government.

A member of the Kanuri tribe, Zana Dipcharima was born in 1917, and was educated at the Maiduguri Middle School and at Katsina Higher Training

331

College, where he qualified as a teacher.

From 1938–46, he taught at various schools and was on the delegation of the National Council of Nigeria and the Cameroons (NCNC), sent to London in 1947.

Zana Dipcharima worked as a manager for John Holt from 1948–54, taking no further part in NCNC politics; but from 1954–56 he served as a member of the Native Authority in Borny with special responsibility for police and prisons.

He became district head of Yerwa in 1956, and took on the title of Zana.

He was elected to the Nigerian Federal House of Representatives in 1954 on the platform of the NPC and served from 1956–57 as Parliamentary Secretary to the Minister of Transport.

In 1957 he was appointed Minister of State without Portfolio and then Minister of Commerce and Industry. He was Minister of Transport from 1964 until the military *coup* of January, 1966.

Zana Dipcharima is a prominent member of the banned Northern Peoples' Congress (NPC), and occupies an extremely influential position in the political affairs of Borny Province.

CHIEF SHAFI LAWAL EDU

Alhaji Chief Shafi Lawal Edu, the son of a Paramount Chief of Epe, Western Nigeria, rose from ship's chandler to become one of the big names in business and commerce not only in Nigeria but in the Commonwealth also.

President of the Commonwealth Chamber of Commerce for the year 1966, Chief Edu was the first African to hold this post, which he was elected to at the age of 53.

After attending the Epe Government School and a private school owned by his father, Chief Briamoh Edu, he taught for a while before taking up an appointment in Epe in 1936 as a clerk with the African Oilnut Company, a subsidiary of the United Africa Company.

Chief Edu was soon seconded to the Holland West Africa Lines and became the local manager of the company in Epe.

He resigned from Holland West Africa Lines in 1945 and set up in private business; starting as a ship's chandler, he later became a food contractor for the Army in Lagos.

In 1951, Chief Edu was elected to the Western House of Assembly and subsequently nominated by the Action Group Government to represent the West in the then House of Representatives.

When the House was dissolved in 1954, Chief Edu did not seek re-election, deciding to devote all his time to the expansion of his business interests. He concentrated his efforts on the timber trade and in transport and insurance.

By 1958, Chief Edu had made such an impact in business and commercial circles that he was elected vice-president of the Lagos Chamber of Commerce. He became president in 1963.

When, in 1962, the Balewa government declared a state of emergency in Western Nigeria following disturbances in the Western Legislature, Chief Edu was one of the leading Western Nigerians appointed to administer the region for a six-month period. He served as Commissioner in charge of Health.

Chief Edu was elected vice-president of the Commonwealth Chamber of Commerce in 1965 and president in 1966.

As president of the Nigerian Association of Chambers of Commerce, Industry and Mines, Chief Edu is on the board of directors of over a dozen companies in Nigeria, including British Petroleum (Nigeria), the Nigerian Oil Refinery Company, the Palm Lines and the Nigerian Ports Authority.

Chief Edu is a practising Moslem and has made the pilgrimage to Mecca.

Lt-Col David Ejoor

Dr T. O. Elias

LT-COL D. A. EJOOR

Lieutenant-Colonel David Akpode Ejoor, Military Governor of Mid-Eastern Nigeria, rose to that position from humble beginnings.

Born to a Roman Catholic peasant family on January 10, 1934, he began his elementary education six years later.

He combined his studies with periodic work on his father's farm, concluding his elementary education in record time.

After a brief spell as clerical assistant at the Customs and Excise Department, he resigned to join the Army.

He went through the training for regular officers in Accra, Ghana, and followed this with a course at the Royal Military Academy, Sandhurst, in 1954.

He was gazetted second-lieutenant in 1956 and while holding this rank served Nigeria in various capacities. Eight years later he was appointed General Staff Officer (Grade One).

Lieutenant-Colonel Ejoor's assignments outside Nigeria have included peace operations in the Republics of Cameroun and Congo Leopoldville – now Kinshasa.

DR T. O. ELIAS

Dr Taslim Olawale Elias, Attorney-General of the Federation of Nigeria, is a constitutional expert and an outstanding scholar and author.

He came into the limelight of Nigerian politics when, at independence in October, 1960, he was the first Nigerian to be appointed Attorney-General and Minister of Justice of the Federation.

After the January military *coup* he was the only Minister in the former civilian Government retained by the military Administration, although he was later dropped following a newspaper attack.

Before his appointment in 1960, Dr Elias was a governor of the School of Oriental and African Studies, University of London.

As Attorney-General, he modernised and extensively revised the laws of Nigeria. They are now widely agreed to be among the most original and up-to-date laws in Africa.

On October 1, 1963, when Nigeria was declared a Republic, Dr Elias was one of the first five Nigerians awarded Nigerian honours, including that of Commander of the Federal Republic (CFR).

Dr Elias was born in Lagos on November 11, 1914, and began school twelve years later.

After a secondary education in two grammar schools in Lagos, he worked for nine years for the Audit Department and Nigeria Railways in Lagos before travelling to the United Kingdom to read law.

He entered University College, London, in 1944, but because of the war was for some time at Trinity College, Cambridge.

He graduated with a BA the year he entered the university, having already, at home, passed the intermediate BA and intermediate LLB examination.

Two years later, Dr Elias graduated with an LLB(London) and in April the following year he was called to the Bar.

In September, 1947, he became the first and only Nigerian to be awarded a scholarship for the study of law by both his university (London) and his Inn of Court (Inner Temple). In 1949 he became the first Nigerian to obtain the PhD degree in law of the University of London.

In 1951, he was awarded a UNESCO Fellowship to do research in aspects of the legal, social and economic problems of Africa. In October of that year, he was appointed the Simon Senior Research Fellow by the University of Manchester and in that capacity taught law and social anthropology.

In 1955, the University of Oxford appointed him Oppenheimer Research Fellow at the Institute of Commonwealth Studies and Queen Elizabeth House, Oxford. He was later appointed a Research Fellow of Nuffield College, Oxford.

In the same year, he was invited to India as visiting professor of political science at the University of Delhi and, besides helping in the reorganisation of the courses and the establishment of the Department of African Studies, he lectured on law, government, politics and social anthropology at Delhi, Bombay, Calcutta, Allahabad and Aligath Universities.

Back in London in 1957, after the visit to India, he was appointed a governor of the School of Oriental and African Studies, University of London, as Nigeria's representative. He held this position until 1960, when he was invited to take up the post of Attorney-General and Minister of Justice in the Federal Government, and returned to Nigeria.

As Constitutional and Legal Adviser to the National Council of Nigeria and the Cameroons (later the banned National Convention of Nigerian Citizens), he attended the 1958 London Conference and helped to found the Constitution under which Nigeria has been governed since October 1, 1960.

In 1963, he became the first and only African to be awarded, by examination, the LLD degree of the University of London for his work in the field of African Law, Constitutional Law of the Commonwealth and Colonial Law.

After he was dropped in 1966 from the former military Administration, he was appointed Dean of the Faculty of Law at the University of Lagos, but was recalled by the succeeding Federal Military Government to take up the post of Attorney-General.

Regarded as one of Nigeria's most distinguished scholars, Dr Elias has written a number of books which are prescribed texts for the university of London LLM Degree examination. They are *Nigerian Land Law and Custom* (1951); *Groundwork of Nigerian Law* (1954), revised as *Nigerian Legal System* (1963); *Nature of African Customary Law* (1956); *British Colonial Law—a Comparative Study* (1962); *Ghana and Sierra Leone: Development of Their Laws and Constitutions* (1962) and *Government and Politics in Africa* (1961).

CHIEF ANTHONY ENAHORO

Chief Anthony Eronsele Enaharo, Deputy Leader of the banned Action Group and Leader of the Mid-Western Nigeria delegation to the All-Nigeria Constitutional Conference in Lagos, late in 1966, has had a chequered career in both journalism and politics.

Chief Enaharo, who comes of a long line of chiefs who persistently fought the British Government, was born at Uromi, in Mid-Western Nigeria, on July 25, 1923.

He is the son of Chief Okotako Enaharo, a government headmaster and customary court judge. His father wanted him to study law but he decided instead to start work on newspapers owned by Dr Nnamdi Azikiwe (1942), and two years later became editor of the *Southern Nigeria Defender*.

He edited the *Daily Comet* from 1945–47. During this period he was jailed for a seditious article, released and jailed again for delivering a seditious speech.

When released, Chief Enaharo became the assistant editor of the *West African Pilot* and editor of the *Nigerian Star*.

Early in 1951, he accepted an invitation to convene a meeting of leaders in Benin and Warri Provinces to form the Mid-Western Action Group, which merged with the Action Group of Yorubaland of Western Nigeria in April, 1951.

The Action Group of the entire region of Western Nigeria, including the Mid-West, contested the election of that year, and in August, Chief Enaharo was elected First Member for Ishan Division in the Western House of Assembly.

An attempt to unseat him by the British District Officer because of his previous convictions failed when an action in the High Court was dismisssed.

In 1953, Chief Enaharo moved in the Federal House of Representatives the since famous independence motion in which he asked 'that this House accepts as a primary political objective the attainment of self-government for Nigeria in 1956'.

After giving up his double membership of both the Federal House and the Western House, retaining the latter, Chief Enahoro was in 1954 appointed the first Minister of Home Affairs in the Western Region Government, adding Mid-West Affairs to his portfolio in 1957.

An able parliamentarian and keen debater, Chief Enahoro became in 1958 Chairman of the Mid-West Advisory Council, set up to represent minority interests in the area. He was also Leader of the House in the West.

He was, in addition, a member of the Action Group delegations to the first and second All-African Peoples' Conference – at Accra in 1958, and Tunis in 1960 – being elected to the AAPC Steering Committee.

Tired of purely regional politics, Chief Enahoro was elected to the Federal Parliament in 1959 and became shadow Minister of Foreign Affairs in the Action Group Opposition. He was also Opposition spokesman on the Legislature and Internal Affairs.

After a fight in the Western House of Assembly on May 25, 1962, Chief Enahoro, although a Member of the Federal Parliament was, along with top members of the Action Group, including its Leader, Chief Awolowo, first restricted, then detained.

Chief Enahoro broke detention and fled the country in September, 1962, two months before he was due to appear in court to answer charges of treasonable felony.

He was arrested in London and detained for six months in Brixton Prison, during which he faced the sensational extradition trial which rocked the British Government.

Lt-Col Yakubu Gowon

Chief Enahoro was deported to Nigeria on June 24. The following day, his trial began on a three-count charge. He was sentenced to 15 years imprisonment, which was later reduced to seven years on appeal to the Federal Supreme Court.

On August 2, 1966, he was granted a state pardon.

Two months later, praised as a reliable, practical, competent and honest politician, he was elected leader of the Mid-Western Nigeria delegation to the All-Nigeria Constitutional Conference in Lagos.

Chief Enahoro once prophesied he would one day become the prime minister of Nigeria. He is expected to play a leading role in the future development of his country.

EFFIONG OKON EYO

Effiong Okon Eyo, former Opposition Action Group member of the suspended Eastern Nigeria House of Assembly, was born in April, 1918.

A member of the Ibibio tribe, a minority group in Eastern Nigeria, he was educated at Government College in Umuahia between 1932 and 1936.

He joined the banned National Convention of Nigerian Citizens (formerly the National Council of Nigeria and the Cameroons) in 1951.

He was elected to the Eastern House of Assembly that year and nominated as one of the Region's representatives in the Federal House of Representatives in Lagos.

He gave up his double membership in 1954, remaining in the Eastern Region Assembly, and became Chief Whip of the NCNC-controlled Assembly. He also served as Deputy Speaker from 1954–55.

From 1955–56, Mr Eyo was Chairman of the Eastern Region Development Corporation (ERDC). He was the main accuser of Dr Nnamdi Azikiwe, then Premier of Eastern Nigeria, of improper conduct in the handling of the Region's funds.

In April, 1956, Mr Eyo moved a resolution in the House calling for a public inquiry. This led to the appointment of the Foster-Sutton Tribunal by Lennox-Boyd, then British Secretary for Colonial Affairs.

He resigned as Chief Whip and also his membership of the NCNC, and in 1957 joined the Action Group and won election to the new House of Assembly.

He was Opposition Chief Whip in the House until 1962, when the House was dissolved. During the campaigns that followed he was arrested, tried and jailed for attempted murder. He was released in August, 1966 when he was granted a state pardon by the Federal Military Government.

Mr Eyo is a strong and uncompromising advocate of the creation of more states in the country, particularly in his home region, Eastern Nigeria, to solve the present difficulties.

LT-COL YAKUBU GOWON

Lieutenant-Colonel Yakubu Gowon became head of the Federal Military Government and Supreme Commander of the Armed Forces in August, 1966. At 32 he was Africa's youngest head of state.

This followed a brilliant Army career which began in 1954, a year after he left college.

Before his assumption of office, Lieut-Col Gowon was Chief of Staff, Nigerian Army and, as such, a member of the first Supreme Military Council.

Sir Kashim Ibrahim

Born on October 19, 1934, he received his secondary education in Zaria, Northern Nigeria where, in 1953, he obtained the senior Cambridge school leaving certificate.

The following year, he enrolled in the Nigerian Army and was sent to the Regular Officers' Special Training School at Teshie in Ghana.

In 1955, he went to Britain for further military training, and was at Eaton Hall, Cheshire, until May, 1955, before entering the RMAS Anzio Company, Sandhurst, where he remained until the end of 1956.

For the first half of 1957, Lieut-Col Gowon attended the young officers' course at Hythe and Warminster, England. Returning to Nigeria, he was posted as second-lieutenant to the 4th Battalion of the Nigerian Army at Ibadan, Western Nigeria's capital city.

In 1960, he served as platoon commander in operations at the Nigeria-Cameroun border. Later he became the first Nigerian to be appointed Adjutant of the 4th Battalion.

Lieut-Col Gowon also served in Congo (Kinshasa) under the United Nations Peace Keeping Force until 1961 when, on his return to Nigeria, he was posted to Army Headquarters as staff officer.

He attended a course at the Staff College, Camberley, Surrey, in 1962, and, soon after his return to Nigeria, was again sent to the Congo.

In 1963 he was promoted lieutenant-colonel and appointed Adjutant-General of the Nigerian Army.

He was given command of the 2nd Battalion in January, 1966. With the transfer of power to the Armed Forces by the civilian Federal Government, following the military *coup* of January 15, he was appointed Chief of Staff at Army Headquarters.

The son of a missionary, Lieut-Col Gowon is a keen hockey player and has taken part in competitive athletics, football and boxing. His other hobbies include cinematography and bird-watching.

ABUBAKAR GUMI

Alhaji Abubakar Gumi, Northern Nigeria's Grand Kadi (head of the Muslim Sharia Court), was born in 1922 and educated at the Sokoto Middle School, Kano Law School and Bakht-er Ruda, Sudan.

He was chief Alkali court scribe from 1947–48, and taught between 1947 and 1953.

He was Assistant Secretary, External Affairs Ministry, in Lagos from 1957–58 and Deputy Grand Kadi from 1960–62.

He was appointed Grand Kadi in 1962. He is a member of the Constituent Council of the World Islamic League in Mecca, and member of the Academy of Research, Al-azhur University, Cairo, United Arab Republic.

He was also a member of the Judicial Service Commission from 1962–65 and member of the Judicial Advisory Council of the Supreme Military Council.

SIR KASHIM IBRAHIM

Alhaji Sir Kashim Ibrahim, Adviser to the military Governor of Northern Nigeria and Leader of the Region's delegation to the All-Nigeria Constitutional Conference in Lagos in 1966, was born in 1910 at Maiduguri.

Educated at the Bornu Provincial School and at the Katsina Training College, he was appointed Native Authority Visiting Teacher in 1933.

When the Richards constitution came into force in 1946, Sir Kashim was nominated special member of the North's Consultative House of Assembly.

In 1951, he led an educational delegation to Bakhda-Ruda Institute of Education in Sudan.

He was a founder member of the Northern Peoples' Congress (NPC) in 1951; was elected member of the Northern House of Assembly and nominated to represent the Region in the Federal House of Representatives, where he became the first Nigerian to be appointed Central Minister of Social Services.

In 1954, by not contesting the Federal election, he remained in the Northern House and was appointed Regional Minister of Social Development and Survey.

He led a goodwill mission to Pakistan in 1954, and two years later was appointed Waziri (chief councillor) of Bornu. In 1958 he led a legal delegation to the Sudan in connection with Northern Nigerian law reforms.

Sir Kashim served on the Ashby Commission on higher education from 1959–60 and was appointed chairman of the provisional council of the Ahmadu Bello University in 1961.

In 1962, he became the first indigenous Governor of the North, and was knighted the same year.

When the Armed Forces took over the Government in January, 1966, Sir Kashim was appointed Adviser to the Regional Military Governor.

ONI OF IFE

Sir Aderemi Adesoji II, The Oni (Paramount Ruler) of Ife, and spiritual head of all the Yorubas of Western Nigeria, was born in 1889.

Sir Aderemi, whose crown is the oldest among the Yoruba-speaking people, sits on the throne of Oduduwa, the 'ancestral father' of all Yorubas.

Sir Aderemi, a member of the Akin Royal House of Ile-Ife, went to St Phillip's Church Missionary Society Day School, Ife, and with no hope of paying his way through a secondary education, embarked on private studies.

In 1910, he took a job in the Traffic Section of the Nigerian Railways and later filled the post of chief signaller, then station master and, finally, traffic inspector.

He left in 1919 to embark on trading, but when this did not prove profitable he returned to the railways only to leave again in 1921 to resume trading once more. This time, with the aid of his past experience, he soon became one of the leading produce and merchandise traders at Ile-Ife and in other parts of the Western Region.

Sir Aderemi was elected to the throne of Ile-Ife in September, 1930. Once on the throne, he reorganised the administration of schools, built new roads and improved old ones, and soon his kingdom became the most progressive in Nigeria. He also founded the Oduduwa College.

In 1952, Sir Aderemi was appointed Minister without Portfolio in the Central (now Federal) Government, resigning during the constitutional crisis of 1953, but returning afterwards. He was knighted in 1955.

He was elected President of the Western House of Chiefs in 1954, and on July 8, 1960, was appointed Governor of Western Nigeria, thus becoming the first African to be appointed to the post.

He was suspended as Governor, along with the regional government, as a result of the pro-

Aminu Kano

clamation of emergency rule in the region, following a fight in the Western House of Assembly (May 25, 1962).

LATEEF KAYODE JAKANDE

Lateef Kayode Jakande, a journalist, became known through his strong and fearless criticism of the suspended Federal Government.

He entered journalism as a reporter in 1949, when he left college, and within eleven years he had become managing director and editor-in-chief of a chain of Action Group party newspapers.

He was jailed for seven years in September, 1963, for his part in an alleged plot to overthrow the Federal Government.

Born in Lagos on July 23, 1929, Mr Jakande joined the now defunct *Daily Service* as a reporter in 1949, and in three years was an associate editor.

In 1953 he took over the editorship of the *Nigerian Tribune* at Ibadan, capital of Western Nigeria, and in 1954 became managing editor (until 1956).

In that year too, he became general manager of the Amalgamated Press, Lagos, also taking on the post of editor-in-chief until he relinquished it in 1960 to become the managing director and editor-in-chief of the succeeding company, Allied Newspapers, Lagos.

He was still in the post when, on May 30, 1962, he and some prominent members of the banned Opposition Action Group, including its leader, Chief Obafemi Awolowo, were detained after a fight in the Western House of Assembly (May 25, 1962), and charged with treasonable felony.

Mr Jakande was among those jailed at the end of the trial in Lagos High Court. He was released on August 3, 1966, by the new Federal military Govern-

ment after serving part of his seven-year sentence.

Mr Jakande is a member of the executive Board of the International Press Institute, member of the International Association of Mass Communication Research, first president of the Newspaper Proprietors Association of Nigeria and president of the Nigerian Guild of Newspaper Editors. He is the author of the *West Africa Directory* – a reference book on West Africa.

Mr Jakande's new role in 1966 was that of leader of the Lagos delegation attending the All-Nigeria Constitutional Conference.

AMINU KANO

Alhaji Aminu Kano, Leader of the banned Northern Elements Progressive Union (NEPU) was born in 1920.

He was educated at Katsina College, gaining his diploma in education in 1942 before going to Bauchi for teacher training.

In 1946 he took a one-year course at the Institute of Education in London and, while there, helped to found the Northern Teachers' Association.

In 1947, Alhaji Kano returned to Nigeria to teach at the Bauchi Training College. He was a founder member, with the late Prime Minister, Sir Abubakar Tafawa Balewa, of the Bauchi General Improvement Union. In 1948, after refusing a job in the Kaduna Secretariat, he became head of the Teacher Training Centre in Maru, Sokoto.

In 1949, he was made president of the Maru Branch of Jam'iyyar Mutanen Arewa, a cultural organisation which later developed into the Northern Peoples' Congress (NPC). In July, 1950 he helped to found the Northern Element Progressive

The Emir of Kano

Lt-Col Hassan Katsina

Union, becoming leader in 1953.

Alhaji Kano led the NEPU delegation to the London and Lagos Constitutional Conferences of 1953 and 1954. In 1959 he was elected to the Federal House of Representatives after two previous failures and was appointed Government Chief Whip.

A convinced modernist, Alhaji Kano found it difficult to reconcile his post of Chief Whip with his opposition to the Northern Peoples' Congress – the ruling party both in the Federal and Northern Regional Governments. He is largely responsible for the existence of an Opposition in the Northern House of Assembly.

Just before the 1964 Federal elections, he was secretary-general of the Northern Progressive Front, which grouped together Opposition parties in the North.

EMIR OF KANO

Alhaji Ado Bayero, Emir of Kano, the richest emirate in Northern Nigeria, was born in 1930.

He was educated at the Kano Middle School and, on leaving, worked as a clerk in the Bank of West Africa.

He entered the Northern House of Assembly in 1955, but resigned in 1957, when he was appointed Chief of Kano Native Authority Police.

Alhaji Bayero was appointed Nigeria's Ambassador to Senegal in 1962, until his appointment as Emir of Kano in 1963.

He became Chancellor of the University of Nigeria, Nsukka, Eastern Nigeria, in April, 1966.

LT-COL HASSAN KATSINA

Lieutenant-Colonel Hassan Usman Katsina, Military Governor of Northern Nigeria, was born in Katsina on March 31, 1933.

Son of the present Emir of Katsina, Alhaji Usman Nagogo, he was educated at Kankiya Elementary School, the Katsina Middle School and the Kaduna College, Zaria, where he stayed four years before going to the Institute of Administration, also in Zaria.

Lt-Col Katsina transferred from the Institute of Administration to the Nigerian College of Arts, Science and Technology, Zaria, before he joined the Nigerian Army in 1956.

After six months in Ghana, where he underwent cadet training, Lt-Col Katsina received further military training in Britain. He was at the Cadet School, Aldershot and the Royal Military Academy, Sandhurst for two years.

He was also at the Small Arms School in Kent for three months in 1959, and at the School of Infantry, Warminster.

On his return to Nigeria in July, 1959, he became platoon commander in the 2nd Battalion, and in 1960 he was demonstration platoon commander attached to Kaduna.

In 1961, Lt-Col Katsina served in the United Nations Peace-Keeping Force in the Congo (Kinshasa). He was in the Intelligence Headquarters of the 3rd Brigade. In 1962, he received further training in infantry manoeuvres in the United States, following which he was appointed company commander in the 5th Battalion of the Nigerian Army.

Lt-Col Katsina was squadron leader in January, 1965, and six months later, regimental commander.

Soon after the military takeover on January 16, 1966, he was appointed the Military Governor of Northern Nigeria and promoted to lieutenant-colonel.

The Oba of Lagos

OBA OF LAGOS

His Highness Adeyinka Oyekan II, Oba of Lagos, the Federal capital of Nigeria, ascended the throne of his ancestors at the climax of a struggle which had been long and sometimes bitter.

In February, 1965, 15 years after the trouble began, Oba Oyekan was able to fulfil his principal ambition in life when his candidature for the throne was approved.

Son of Prince Kushanu Abiola Oyekan and grandson of Oba Oyekan I, who reigned from 1885–1900, Oba Oyekan II was born on June 30, 1911.

He was educated at the Methodist Boys' High School, Lagos; the Eko Boys' High School and finally at King's College, Lagos. He entered the School of Pharmacy, where he qualified as a pharmacist in 1933. He was a practising pharmacist until appointed Oba of Lagos.

In 1957, Oba Oyekan entered Edinburgh University for a few months to take a course in agriculture. This was the year when his hope of becoming Oba of Lagos seemed to be shattered. The Privy Council dismissed his appeal against the judgment of the then West African Court of Appeal which had favoured his rival, the late Oba Adele II.

He returned to Nigeria in 1958 to re-establish his pharmacy business.

As Oba of Lagos, Oyekan II was, by right, a member of the suspended Senate (Nigeria's Upper House) and president of the suspended Lagos City Council.

He has travelled extensively and is a firm advocate of the unity of Nigeria.

Oba Oyekan has five wives and twelve children. His grandfather had 20 wives.

Unlike most Obas before him, Oba Oyekan II is a devout Christian and a member of the Methodist Church.

CHIEF SAMUEL MARIERE

Chief Samuel Jereton Mariere, Adviser to the Military Governor of Mid-Western Nigeria, was first civilian Governor of the Region (February 7, 1964) until the Army takeover (January, 1966).

As a member of the Nigerian Federal Parliament, it was he who in 1960 tabled the historic motion praying the Nigerian Government to create the Mid-West State, which was then part of Western Nigeria.

With the army still in control and political parties banned, Chief Mariere is the rallying point for politicians in quest of power after military rule.

Chief Mariere was born at Evwrenri in Central Urhobo in the Delta Province in 1907.

Educated at St Andrew's School, Warri, he became a teacher at the African School, Okpari, but gave up the profession after two years.

In 1939, he joined the firm of John Holt and was in charge at Agbor – an Ibo-speaking town in the Mid-West. He retired after 22 years' service.

Chief Mariere's early contacts with Chief Dennis Osadebay, who was later to become the first Premier of the Mid-West, excited his latent interest in the nationalist movement in the early 'forties.

Like Chief Osadebay, he joined the National Convention of Nigeria and the Cameroons (NCNC) – Dr Azikiwe's party – and with the consent of his employers in 1954 was elected to Nigeria's Federal Parliament as an NCNC member for Urhobo East.

Chief Mariere represented his constituency in the Federal Par-

341

Matthew Mbu

liament until his appointment as Governor of the Mid-West.

When the battle for the creation of the Mid-West was eventually won in 1963, he was appointed Deputy Administrator and Commissioner for Chieftancy Affairs in the interim administration which paved the way for an elected Government. His old-time associate, Chief Osadebay, was the Administrator.

He holds two chieftancy titles – the Lorogun of Evwreni and the Onisogene of Agbor.

As a reward for his services to Nigeria, Chief Mariere was awarded the GCON (Grand Commander of the Order of the Niger) in 1964.

SIR LOUIS MBANEFO

Sir Louis Nwachukwu Mbanefo, Chief Justice of Eastern Nigeria, Chairman of Ibadan University Council and Chancellor of Niger Diocese of the Anglican Mission in Nigeria, was the first Ibo tribesman to qualify as a lawyer.

His brilliant career on the bench was climaxed by his appointment in 1962 as a judge of the International Court in The Hague which heard the final phase of the South-West Africa case.

Born in May, 1911, Sir Louis belongs to a noble family in Onitsha, Eastern Nigeria.

He went to the United Kingdom in 1932, graduated with an LLB at London University in 1935 and was called to the Bar (Middle Temple) on November 18 of the same year.

Returning to Nigeria, Sir Louis had a lucrative private practice for many years.

He was a member of the old Nigerian Legislative Council from 1949–51; in 1952 he was appointed a judge of the Supreme Court of Nigeria. He became the first indigenous Chief Justice of Eastern Nigeria in 1959.

Sir Louis has served Nigeria in various capacities. He was a member of the Board of Education, member of the Nigerian Coal Board and of the Eastern Nigeria Development Board.

He was chairman of a commission appointed by the Nigerian Federal Government in 1959 to review the salaries and wages of government servants throughout the country.

Sir Louis was knighted by Queen Elizabeth II in 1961.

He is a member of the Nigerian Olympic Committee and the British Empire and Commonwealth Games Committee.

MATTHEW TAWO MBU

Matthew Tawo Mbu, Chairman of Eastern Nigeria's Public Service Commission, was Minister for the Navy until the military *coup* of January, 1966.

During the civil administration, he distinguished himself as a politician, diplomat, negotiator and Cabinet Minister.

He is held in high esteem by the country's military rulers and this has placed him in a position as one of the builders of the new Nigeria.

One of the first group of Nigerians to experience parliamentary life, Mr Mbu held successive Cabinet posts in the Federal Government, except for the period between 1955–59 when he served as the country's first High Commissioner in the United Kingdom and later as Nigeria's Liaison Officer in Washington.

Son of a local Chieftain, 'M.T.', as he is popularly called, was born on November 20, 1927 at Okundi village in the Ogoja Division of Eastern Nigeria. He is a member of the Osokom Clan.

Completing his primary education at a village Roman Catholic school in 1943, he joined the firm of John Holt at Bansara becoming produce manager.

In 1952 he was elected to the Eastern House of Assembly on the ticket of Dr Azikiwe's National Convention of Nigeria and the Cameroons (NCNC) of which he was a foundation member.

Mbu was one of the 34 Eastern Nigeria legislators selected to represent the region in the House of Representatives in 1952 and from 1953–54 served as the country's Central Minister of Labour.

Before taking up his assignment as Nigeria's first High Commissioner in the United Kingdom later in 1955, Mr Mbu acted as Central Minister of Commerce and Industry and Minister of Works.

He staged a comeback to politics after his five-year diplomatic career and was appointed Minister for the Navy after the pre-independence federal elections in 1959, which he won with a landslide.

A self-made man, Mr Mbu is a lawyer today by sheer dint of hard work and personal effort. With only a primary school education, he matriculated and subsequently earned an LLB degree through private studies and correspondence courses.

As a negotiator, Mr Mbu led Nigeria's delegation to several important international conferences. He was the country's chief negotiator at the Geneva disarmament talks.

Handsome and always well-dressed, he was the deputy leader of Eastern Nigeria's delegation to the All-Nigeria Constitutional Conference; this was subsequently dismissed by Lt-Col Yakubu Gowon because delegates failed to agree on their meeting place.

His appointment as chairman of the Eastern Nigeria Public Service Commission in October, 1966, was evidence of the high trust placed in him at a time when most former politicians had been forced to retire from the Nigerian scene.

Mbu's interests outside politics are farming (he owns a 400-acre cocoa farm in his village) and hunting.

PROFESSOR ENI NJOKU

Professor Eni Njoku, Vice-Chancellor of the University of Nigeria, at Nsukka in Eastern Nigeria, led the Eastern Nigeria delegation to the All-Nigeria Constitutional Conference (November, 1966) dismissed by the country's military ruler, Lt-Col Yakubu Gowon.

An eminent scholar and one of the country's top academicians, Professor Njoku has devoted his time to university work since he returned from Britain, except for the short period he served as a Cabinet Minister in 1952.

A native of Ohafia in Umuahia Province of Eastern Nigeria, Professor Njoku was born in 1918. He received his secondary education at the Hope Waddell Institute, Calabar, before going to the Yaba Higher College, Lagos, and the University of Manchester, where he graduated with first-class honours in botany. He also took a BA degree at London University and returned to Nigeria in 1948 to join the staff of the University College, Ibadan, as a lecturer in botany.

He left academic work for politics after two years and was elected to the Eastern House of Assembly on the Platform of Dr Azikiwe's party – NCNC – in 1952.

He was one of the Eastern Nigeria legislators sent to the

Lt-Col C. O. Ojukwu

House of Representatives in Lagos and became the country's first Central Minister of Mines and Power.

Following the revolt against Dr. Azikiwe by NCNC legislators in Enugu and Lagos, in which he played a leading part, Professor Njoku was forced to resign his Cabinet post and returned to academic life in 1953.

Back in Ibadan University, he rose to the post of senior lecturer then Professor of Botany and from 1959–62 he was Dean of the Faculty of Science.

Between 1959–62, he combined his academic duties with the part-time chairmanship of the Electricity Corporation of Nigeria and was also a member of the Senate – Nigeria's Upper House.

Professor Njoku was appointed first Vice-Chancellor of the University of Lagos in June, 1962 – a post he held until the middle of 1964.

Until he went over to the University of Nigeria in June, 1966, Dr Njoku worked with the Michigan State University as a visiting professor.

He was the first president of the Science Association of Nigeria and a member of the provisional council of the University of Zambia.

Professor Njoku is one of the principal advisers to the Military Government of Eastern Nigeria.

BRIGADIER BABAFEMI OGUNDIPE

Brigadier Babafemi Olatunde Ogundipe, Nigeria's High Commissioner in the United Kingdom, was born on September 6, 1924.

Before his diplomatic posting in August, 1966, soon after the July military *coup*, he was the Chief of Staff, Supreme Military Headquarters.

He enlisted in the Army in 1943,

on leaving school in Eastern Nigeria.

He is regarded as the most experienced of all the officers in the Nigerian Army, having seen active service during World War II in India and Burma.

After the war, Brigadier Ogundipe attended several military courses in Britain at the Officer Cadet School, Chester, the School of Infantry, Warminster, the Staff College, Camberley, and the Imperial Defence College, London.

He was commissioned in 1953, and became one of the very few indigenous officers in the then British-controlled Nigerian Army.

Brigadier Ogundipe was one of the Nigerian officers who served with the United Nations Peace-Keeping Force in the Congo (Kinshasa) from 1960 to 1963.

He commanded the 2nd Brigade of the Nigerian Army before he was appointed Chief of Staff, at Supreme Military Headquarters, following the January military *coup*.

In this position, Brigadier Ogundipe was a member of the first Supreme Military Council of Nigeria.

LT-COL C. O. OJUKWU

Lieutenant-Colonel Chukwuemeka Odumegwu Ojukwu became Military Governor of Eastern Nigeria after the military *coup* of January 15, 1966, which overthrew the Federal Nigerian Government. He was then 32.

Before the *coup*, Lt-Col Ojukwu commanded the 5th Battalion Nigerian Army in Kano, Northern Nigeria. This post, after barely seven years in the Army, highlighted the character and industry he had displayed in his career. This began with employment in the Eastern Nigerian

Dr Michael Okpara

Public Service soon after his return from Britain where he had graduated with a BA degree. (Modern History) in 1955.

After a year's course at two military institutions in Britain and a spell at the Royal West African Frontier Force Training School in Teshie, Ghana, where he taught officer cadets tactics and military law, Lt-Col Ojukwu returned to Nigeria to hold several military posts. These culminated in his promotion to the rank of Major in 1961.

Lt-Col Ojukwu was then posted to Kaduna, Northern Nigeria, where he assumed duty as Deputy Assistant Adjutant and Quartermaster General. Soon afterwards he went to the Congo under the United Nations peace-keeping programme and served in Luluaburg in Kasai Province. He was selected to attend the joint Services Staff College in England in 1962. Returning to Nigeria at the end of that year, he was promoted lieutenant-colonel in January, 1963 and appointed Quartermaster-General. A year later he was appointed to command the 5th Battalion in Kano.

Lt-Col Ojukwu, who was born at Zungeru, Northern Nigeria on November 4, 1933, is of rich parentage. When his father, Sir Odumegwu-Ojukwu, died in 1966, he was one of the wealthiest men in Nigeria. His mother is also a well-to-do business woman. Young Ojukwu attended the best schools in Lagos before travelling to England, where he entered Epsom College, Surrey. In 1952 he gained admission to Lincoln College, Oxford, where he graduated three years later.

DR. MICHAEL OKPARA

Dr Michael Iheonukara Okpara was the Premier of Eastern Nigeria and leader of the National Convention of Nigerian Citizens (NCNC), known at its birth as the National Council of Nigeria and the Cameroun.

He and Chief Dennis Osadebay of the Mid-West were the only Regional Premiers who survived the army revolt of January, 1966, in which two other premiers were killed.

An Ibo from Ohuhu, near Umuahia-Ibeku in Eastern Nigeria – Nigeria's first military ruler, Major-General J. T. U. Aguiyi-Ironsi, also came from Umuahia – Dr Okpara was at 46 the country's youngest Premier.

The son of a labourer, he was born in December, 1920. After attending mission schools, he went to the Uzuakoli Methodist College, near his village, and won a scholarship to the then Yaba Higher College, Lagos, to study medicine. Completing his medical studies at the Nigerian School of Medicine, Dr Okpara worked briefly as a government medical officer before setting up private practice in Umuahia.

While carrying on his practice, Dr Okpara showed great interest in the Zikist Movement (named after Dr Azikiwe), the militant wing of Dr Azikiwe's NCNC which brought the independence struggle to a head in the late 'forties.

After the shooting of rioting workers at the Enugu coal mines (1949), Dr Okpara was one of the Zikists arrested by the government for allegedly organising the workers for political ends. He was later released.

Following the granting of internal self-rule by Britain, Dr Okpara was elected to the Eastern House of Assembly in 1952 on an NCNC ticket.

Between then and 1959, when he took over from Dr Azikiwe

as Premier of the East, he held various Cabinet posts from Minister of Health to Agriculture and Production.

When, in 1953, NCNC legislators in the Eastern House of Assembly and the Central Government in Lagos revolted against the party leadership, Dr Okpara was among party loyalists who joined forces with Dr Azikiwe.

It was not until November, 1960, when Dr Azikiwe finally left active politics to become Nigeria's first African Governor-General, that Dr Okpara was elected leader of the NCNC.

Very forceful and outspoken, Dr Okpara is uncompromising on vital national issues.

This in 1963 led to severe strain in relations with the ruling Northern Peoples' Congress of the late Prime Minister Abubakar Tafawa Balewa, with which the NCNC formed the country's first post-independence Government.

A strong advocate of what he calls 'pragmatic socialism', Dr Okpara believes the country's salvation lies in agricultural revolution.

He owns a large farm in his hometown and thus inspired many Eastern Nigerian leaders to take an interest in farming.

Dr Okpara was one of the politicians detained soon after the military *coup* of January, 1966, which brought to an end civilian rule. He was released in July after a second *coup* swept General Ironsi out of power.

Dr Okpara's fine record as Premier of Eastern Nigeria and his dynamic leadership have combined to make him a good candidate for leadership in the region when military rule comes to an end.

He received the award of GCON (Grand Commander of the Order of the Niger), the country's highest decoration, in 1964 in recognition of his services to the country.

CHIEF VICTOR ONABANJO

Chief Victor Olabisi Onabanjo, one of Nigeria's foremost journalists, has in recent years played a leading role in politics.

His career in journalism began soon after his return in 1951 from London, where he had done a year's course at the Polytechnic.

For two years, Chief Onabanjo edited the *Nigerian Citizen*, switching over to the editorship of the *Daily Service* for another year.

In 1955 he became the first editor of the *Radio Times*, then deputy editor-in-chief of the Nigerian Broadcasting Corporation, until 1958.

From 1960–63, he was editorial director of the *Daily Express*, one of Lord Thomson's group of newspapers which also had a local partnership.

He was still in this post when, following the suspension of the Action Group Government of Western Nigeria he, along with all important members of that party, was restricted, then detained (after release from restriction) together with a lesser number of party members.

In October of that year he was among members of the Action Group, including its leader, Chief Obafemi Awolowo, who were tried for their part in the alleged plot to overthrow the Federal Government.

At the end of trial at the Lagos High Court the following year, he was among those discharged and acquitted for want of sufficient evidence.

By this time, Chief Onabanjo had turned his attention more

Chief Dennis Osadebay

and more to politics, unlike his earlier role as a critic of the coalition Federal Government through his widely-read column, *Aiyekoto* (the parrot).

In December, 1964, he won a seat in the Federal House of of the Action Group.

In 1966 he was director of a printing and publishing company, Modern Publications, and combined this with running a poultry farm.

Chief Onabanjo was born in Lagos on February 12, 1927, and attended the Baptist Academy.

CHIEF DENNIS OSADEBAY

Chief Dennis Chukude Osadebay, lawyer, politician, poet and first Premier of Mid-Western Nigeria, was born at Asaba on June 29, 1911.

In a country where most of the tribally-divided politicians were uncompromising, ruthless and held fast to the Mosaic law of 'a tooth for a tooth', Chief Osadebay has been considered the most temperate. He has been described as 'harmless and as pious as a saint'.

If his political formula for Nigeria had been put into effect, Nigeria might not have witnessed the series of army revolts which marred the country's reputation as the most stable Black African country.

A strong believer in an all-party government for Nigeria, Chief Osadebay argues that such a system of government leaves no room for political victimisation and persecution.

Chief Osadebay comes from the Ibo-speaking area of the Mid-West. He had his early education at the Government School, Asaba, before attending the Sacred Heart School and the Hope Waddell Institute, both in Calabar, Eastern Nigeria.

In 1929 he joined the Customs and Excise Department as a customs officer, retiring in 1946 after 16 years' service.

In July the same year he went to the United Kingdom to read law at Lincoln's Inn and London University. He graduated Bachelor of Law (London) in July, 1949 and returned to set up private practice in Eastern Nigeria.

At this time, the agitation against colonial rule was already gathering increasing momentum. Chief Osadebay immediately identified himself with the movement.

When, in 1951, the country's self-government constitution was put into effect, he was one of the candidates of Dr Azikiwe's National Convention of Nigeria and the Cameroons (NCNC), who won the first parliamentary election for the Western House of Assembly. (The Mid-West was then administered as part of Western Nigeria.)

Thus began his political career. As national legal adviser of the NCNC, Chief Osadebay became the leader of the NCNC Opposition in the Wetern House of Assembly, controlled by Chief Obafemi Awolowo's Action Group – a post he held from 1954–56.

In spite of the bitter struggle and antagonism between the governing Action Group and the NCNC Opposition, Chief Osadebay was appointed Deputy Speaker of the Western House of Assembly in 1958.

When the campaign for the creation of the Mid-West Region from the Yoruba West started in the mid-'50s, Chief Osadebay was in the forefront and naturally became the leader of the Mid-West Movement.

On the attainment of indepen-

Kam Selem

dence in October, 1960, he was appointed President of the Senate, the country's Upper House, in succession to Dr Azikiwe, who had been made Nigeria's first Governor-General. Between June and August, 1961, Chief Osadebay acted as Governor-General.

He gave up the post of President of the Senate to become the Administrator and later Premier of the Mid-West when the new region was eventually proclaimed in 1963.

An outstanding African poet, Chief Osadebay has written a great deal of poetry; one collection, entitled *Africa Sings*, contains 100 of his poems.

The only surviving son of the late Mr Adigwe Osadebay, Chief Osadebay is, like his parents, a devout Christian and philanthropist.

Chief Osadebay was awarded Nigeria's highest honour, the GCON (Grand Commander of the Order of the Niger) in October, 1965, for outstanding services to his country.

KAM SELEM

Kam Selem became Inspector-General of the Nigeria Police on September 1, 1966, at the age of 42, after the former holder of the post had resigned for health reasons.

He is the second Nigerian to be appointed to that post.

Mr Selem decided as early as 1941, when he left college, to make a career in the Nigeria Police Force. Since enrolling on April 24, 1942, he made steady, consistent progress, becoming Deputy Inspector-General in July, 1965.

After the basic training and various postings in parts of Northern Nigeria, Mr Selem was promoted sub-inspector in April,

1950, the year he attended the British Industries Fair in the United Kingdon, together with another Nigerian police officer.

In 1953, he was promoted assistant superintendent, and three years later attended an officers' course at Ryton-on-Dunsmore, England. After some brilliant investigation work, he was promoted deputy superintendent in 1955, superintendent in 1959 and senior superintendent (now chief superintendent) in 1960.

Mr Selem will always be remembered for his part in the investigation of a sensational counterfeiting case in 1958, in the course of which he visited the Middle East.

He was promoted Assistant Commissioner in December, 1961 and Deputy Commissioner in March, 1962. Six months later, he was the third Nigerian to attain the rank of Commissioner of Police.

Mr Selem is president of the Nigeria Branch of the International Police Association and a member of the International Association of Chiefs of Police. He has received many awards and decorations.

As head of the Nigerian Police Force, Kam Selem is an *ex officio* member of Nigeria's Federal (Military) Executive Council.

SULTAN OF SOKOTO

Sir Abubakar, Sultan of Sokoto and Sakin Musulmi (spiritual leader of the Moslems) has been Minister without Portfolio in all successive governments of Northern Nigeria. He was born in 1901.

He was given a traditional Islamic education and in 1931 became Sokoto Native Authority Councillor with the title of

Sardauna (heir apparent to the Sultanate).

An Islamic scholar, Sir Abubakar was appointed District Head of Talato Mafara from 1931–38 when he became Sultan of Sokoto.

He was first appointed Regional Minister without Portfolio in 1952 and has held this post until January, 1966, when the Army took over.

He was knighted in 1954.

As spiritual leader, Sir Abubakar wields tremendous influence in the religious circles of the Northern Region, but only late in 1966 did he begin to play a key role in national affairs.

YUSUF MAITAMA SULE

Alhaji Yusuf Maitama Sule, Minister of Mines and Power in the suspended Federal Government, was born in 1927.

He was educated at Kano Middle School and Kaduna College. In 1947 he took a special teachers' training course at Zaria and was a teacher between 1947–53.

After working as an information officer in Kano, Alhaji Sule successfully stood as a candidate of the Northern Peoples' Congress (NPC) for election to the Federal House of Representatives.

Re-elected in December, 1959, he became Federal Minister of Mines and Power and NPC Chief Whip. He represented the Nigerian Government at the second Conference of Independent African States in June, 1960.

An efficient administrator and very popular in the Kano area, Alhaji Sule was re-elected to the Federal House and re-appointed Minister of Mines and Power in 1964, a post he held until the Army took over in January, 1966.

He loves debate and is a keen actor.

JOSEPH TARKA

Joseph Tarka is President-General of the banned Opposition United Middle Belt Congress (UMBC) in Northern Nigeria, and a member of the Federal House of Representatives, which was suspended. He was born on July 10, 1932.

He was educated at Gboko Senior Primary School, Benue Middle School, Bauchi Teacher Training College, and at the Science Centre, Bauchi (1952–53).

He was senior science master at the Benue Provincial Secondary School from 1953–56, when he resigned to work at the Tiv Native Authority. He entered politics in 1957.

He was a member of the Federal Parliament from 1954–59, and a member of the Public Accounts Committee of the House in 1958.

Mr Tarka led the UMBC delegates to the 1957–58 Nigerian Constitutional Conference held in Lagos. He was also a member of the Parliamentary delegation to Britain, Canada and the United States and on the delegation to the Pan-African Conference at Accra in 1959.

Generally known as the 'strong man' of the Tiv Division, he was elected to the Federal House of Representatives in 1959 and became the Opposition Action Group's shadow Minister of Commerce and Industry.

When his party, the UMBC, formed an alliance with the Action Group he was made a federal vice-president of the Action Group (1962).

He has always been an uncompromising advocate of the creation of a Middle Belt State. It was this that led him to form his party in 1957.

Mr Tarka was arrested in 1962 and charged with plotting to

Commodore
J. E. A. Wey

overthrow of the Federal Government along with some members of the Action Group, but was discharged and acquitted for want of sufficient evidence.

In the Northern Region, where his party provided a strong Opposition to the Government, he faced a series of court actions for political offences, but, on each occasion, was freed.

He was chosen one of the four delegates to represent the Northern Region at the All-Nigeria Constitutional Conference late in 1966.

INUA WADA

Alhaji Inua Wada, Defence Minister in the Federal Government, which was suspended, was born in 1917.

He is a grandson of the man who was Chief Alkali of Kano when Lord Lugard invaded the Emirate.

After attending the Katsina Higher College (1933–38), he worked as teacher in the Kano Emirate for nine years.

He was travelling Scout Commissioner, chief clerk of Kano Native Authority Electricity Board in 1949 and Native Authority Information Officer in 1951.

He also became Native Authority chief scribe in 1953, Native Authority staff officer in 1954 and a foundation member of the Northern Peoples' Congress in 1954.

Alhaji Wada was elected to the Northern House of Assembly in 1951 and to the Federal House of Representatives in 1954. He was also general secretary of the NPC and later became its national organiser.

On various occasions he was a member of the Boards of Governors of the Nigerian College of Arts, Science and Technology,

the Nigerian Coal Corporation and Nigerian Groundnut Marketing Board before becoming Federal Minister without Portfolio in 1954.

From 1955–57, Alhaji Wada was Federal Minister of Works and from 1957 to May, 1965, Federal Minister of Works and Survey. Then, on the death of Alhaji Muhammadu Ribadu, he was appointed Federal Minister of Defence, a post he held until the Army takeover in January, 1966.

COMMODORE J. E. A. WEY

Commodore Joseph Edet Akinwale Wey, O.F.R. Commodore Commanding the Nigerian Navy and member of the Supreme Military Council, Nigeria's highest executive body, was born on March 7, 1918.

He is the oldest member of the Supreme Military Council and took over the command of the Navy in 1964.

Commodore Wey joined the former Marine Department as a trainee Junior Technical Apprentice in 1939, becoming a junior engineer at the end of his training.

From 1945–49 he served on board several ships, and in 1949 attended the London County School of Technology for Marine Engineers.

After working as engineer from 1950–56, he was transferred to the Nigerian Naval Forces as a Senior Engineer and, in 1958, sub-lieutenant (Engineering).

He was promoted lieut-commander in 1960 and full commander in 1962. The same year he was appointed Fleet Engineer Officer as well as naval officer in charge of the Apapa Naval Base.

Promotion to captain came in June, 1963. He led a deputation that year to India. The following year, he went out with the India Fleet during the Commonwealth Naval exercises in the Bay of Bengal, which lasted three months.

On his return to Nigeria in March, 1964, he was promoted commodore and appointed head of the Nigerian Navy. He is an associate member of the Institute of Marine Engineers and chairman of the Lagos branch of the Institute.

CHIEF FREDERICK WILLIAMS

Chief Frederick Rotibi Alade Williams, Queen's Counsel and former Minister of Justice, was born in December, 1920.

He began practising as a barrister at the age of 23 – a rare feat in these days – and today he is widely regarded as a legal luminary.

Son of a barrister, Chief Williams was educated at Olowogbowo Methodist School and at the CMS Grammar School, Lagos.

From 1939–42, he read law at Selwyn College, Cambridge, and in 1943 was called to the Bar at Gray's Inn.

While in Britain, Chief Williams headed a West African Students Union study group; returning to Lagos in 1943, he began to build up a legal practice, and served as general secretary of the Nigerian Youth Movement.

In 1950, he won a municipal election to the Lagos Town Council, but lost the election to the Federal House of Representatives in 1951.

He was made a Chief in 1952 by the Alake (Paramount Ruler) of Abeokuta, his home town. That year he was nominated to the Western House of Chiefs.

He was chairman of the Lagos Town Council in 1953 and 1954, and following the introduction of a new constitution, became the first Minister of Justice in the Western Region Government. He was also Minister of Local Government.

Chief Williams was a member of the Western Region delegation to London, Australia and the USA in 1954.

In 1958 he became the first Attorney-General of Western Nigeria, and in December of that year led the Action Group delegation to the first All-African Peoples' Conference at Accra.

In 1960, Chief Williams, who had acted as Premier in Western Nigeria during Chief Obafemi Awolowo's absence, resigned from the Government and returned to private practice when Chief Samuel Akintola took over the premiership. He retained his post of legal adviser to the Action Group.

After the fight in the Western House of Assembly on May 25, 1962, and the subsequent proclamation of an emergency in the Region, Chief Williams had his movements restricted along with top members of the Action Group, including Chief Obafemi Awolowo, the party leader.

He was the only restricted person who, after making representation to the regional administrator of Western Nigeria, and failing, successfully instituted a Federal Supreme Court action against the order.

He was also among the first few Nigerian lawyers to be made Queen's Counsel.

He was chairman of the Constitution Review Committee appointed by the former Federal Military Government.

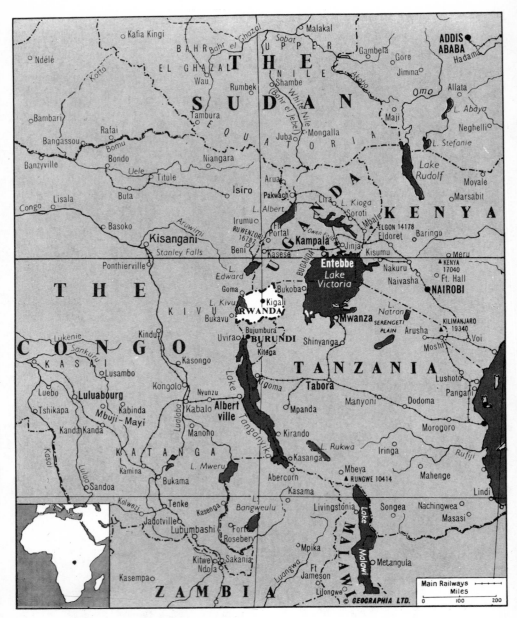

The population of Rwanda is the densest in Africa outside the Nile Delta: 3,069,000 (January 1, 1965) living in an area of 10,166 square miles. Rwanda is bounded in the south by Burundi, in the west by Lake Kivu and Congo Kinshasa, in the north by Uganda and in the east by Tanzania. The capital is Kigali.

Rwanda depends for its day-to-day livelihood on subsistence agriculture, the staple food crops being beans, cassava, maize, sweet potatoes, peas, groundnuts and sorghum. The main crops are arabica coffee and tea, and there are plans to produce pyrethrum, cotton and rice.

Rwanda

The Republic of Rwanda became an independent state on July 1, 1962.

With the neighbouring Kingdom of Burundi it used to form the Belgian mandate and trusteeship territory of Ruanda-Urundi (1920-62). Earlier it had been part of German East Africa, but was ceded to Belgium by the League of Nations after World War I. Subsequently Belgium governed Ruanda-Urundi under a United Nations trusteeship agreement.

An uprising of the Hutu race in Rwanda in 1959 destroyed the Tutsi feudal monarchy of the Mwami (King) Kigeri V, who left the country.

The republican party of emancipation, the Parmehutu ('Parti du Mouvement de l'Emancipation du Bahutu'), won an overwhelming majority in elections and a referendum held under United Nations auspices in September, 1961.

The Parmehutu proclaimed a republic on January 28, 1961. This was recognised by the Belgian administration in the following October but not by the United Nations.

Internal self-government was granted on January 1, 1962 and Rwanda became independent by a decision of the General Assembly on July 1, 1962.

As a republic, Rwanda has an executive President as head of state assisted by a Council of twelve Ministers. The National Assembly consists of 47 Members elected by universal suffrage for four years.

Elections on October 3, 1965 returned President Kayibanda, first elected on October 26, 1961, for a further four years of office. His Parmehutu party won all seats in the National Assembly.

Rwanda is difficult of access and fundamentally poor. There are no proper roads, and the wagon is the only means of transport with neighbouring countries. There are no hotels or big buildings. Its capital, Kigali, is only a village with a recently acquired airfield. There is no general industrial development apart from the mining of cassiterite, two or three hydro-electric installations, and a brewery. The Government is making urgent appeals for foreign investment.

Despite its remoteness, buried in the heart of Africa between the Congo, Uganda and Tanzania, a surprisingly large amount is known about the early history of this former German and Belgian territory.

The ancient Banyarwanda called it 'The Land of a

Thousand Hills'. The first known inhabitants of the region were the Twa, a pigmy race under five feet tall, who hunted, used poisoned darts and made pottery. They were never very numerous, and today number only 50,000, or less than two per cent of the population. From the west came a Bantu farming folk, the Hutu. They cleared forest land for the cultivation of crops, but often in so doing laid bare the tops and sides of hills, causing soil erosion which is the main problem of agriculture to this day. They were unskilled and had no cattle.

The Hutu remained farmers, and now constitute 85 per cent of the population.

Around the 15th century, it is believed, came the Tutsi, giant, slim nomadic shepherds, many of them up to seven feet tall, from the Nile or Somalia. They brought with them many head of lyre-horned cattle. They conquered the Hutu and the Twa, making them their labourers and slaves. They became the undisputed feudal lords of the territory, giving the impression with their immense height of being a master race of divine descent. These movements and clashes of primitive peoples occurred in a most difficult terrain. The Nile-Congo mountain divide, 9,000 ft high in places, and the Birunga volcanoes (Mount Karisimbi is over 14,000 ft high) rise sheerly from Lake Kivu in the west. They form part of the northern frontier, then gradually drop down to a central plateau (5–7,000 ft) in the east and finally to a wide range of marshy lakes in the upper reaches of the Akagera River, which separate the animal reserve of the Mutara Plain from Tanzania.

To the south another river, the Akanyaru, forms a border against Burundi. Rwanda has always been a difficult country for migratory peoples to penetrate, but once inside they were offered the safety of comparative isolation.

The Tutsi, who in the 1960s form 14 per cent of the population, set up a very remarkable feudal system, with the Mwami (King) at the apex of the pyramid. It lasted, in fact, until 1959. The Hutu contend that the Belgians, when they were the guardians of the country, supported the Tutsi for their own ends, while doing much to moderate abuses which have been described as inhuman. It was during the Belgian mandate that domestic slavery was finally abolished in the territory, in 1923.

All the land belonged to the Mwami, and there were no opportunities for foreign settlers.

Instruction of the serfs was forbidden, but the Hutu were able to study in Roman Catholic seminaries, priests from Rome having converted a large part of the population. From 1956, some of the Hutu had been organising social movements and, despite the efforts of the Mwami and the feudal chiefs, proclaimed a 'Manifesto of the Bahutu' which had a profound effect.

The death of old Mwami Mutara in July, 1959, was the signal for a social revolution. Unprepared for his future role and with little natural ability, his young brother Kigeri allowed himself to be ruled by Tutsi extremists, now grouped in a new party called the UNR ('Union Nationale Rwandaise').

Attempts to exterminate the Hutu intellectuals and nullify their influence was a spark to the gunpowder. The revolution began in the north, reached the capital in a few days, then spread like wildfire all over the south, the Twa pygmies supporting the Hutu.

Kigeri and many of the Tutsi were chased out of Rwanda. It is estimated that as a result of the troubles of 1959–61, over 140,000 Tutsi took refuge in neighbouring countries. In January, 1964, several thousand Tutsi were massacred by the Hutu, and there was an exodus of about 12,000 more of the once ruling caste.

Belgium recognised the Hutu regime in 1960, appointed Hutu chiefs, and later accepted the proclamation of the republic.

The United Nations, however, asked for elections. These took place under their control and confirmed the Hutu victory: 87 per cent against the Mwami and in favour of a republic.

Grégoire Kayibanda, founder of the Muhutu Social Movement, which had been renamed the Parmehutu, as a party for the emancipation of the Hutu, was made Prime Minister and then, at independence on July 1, 1962, President of the Republic. The Parmehutu became stronger and stronger, and in the 1965 elections obtained 97 per cent of the votes.

The old Tutsi chiefs did not remain idle. Using refugees who had remained at the frontier, mainly that of Burundi, they planned reconquest. But only once was the peace of

A view across the
quiet waters of Lake
Bulera

the country seriously disturbed. This was early in 1965,
when the Tutsi chiefs still inside Rwanda tried a *coup
d'état* with the help of invaders. This provoked severe
reprisals in several frontier villages. Those responsible for
the plot were tried and executed. Altogether between
500 and 1,000 Tutsi died.

There are still about 100,000 Tutsi refugees outside the
country. An estimated 500,000 remain within. They have
accepted the regime, and large numbers serve in
administrative posts.

Feelings in the interior at the end of 1966 were very
difficult to gauge. The leaders in exile left behind many
sympathisers who could again become active and cause·
trouble. Men on the borders, once in prominent places,
keep alive the thought of reconquest with the aid of Tutsi
intellectuals, gradually returning from studies in Europe.
Armed refugee groups have been reported to be fairly

With their children
looking on, these
women prepare the
ground for cultivation

numerous in the north of Burundi and less numerous in
the southern part of Uganda. There was a small-scale
attempt at armed intervention on the Uganda frontier at
the beginning of September, 1966. According to the
Belgian Ministry of Foreign Affairs, commandos, trained
and armed by Chinese, continued to make preparations
in Burundi. The Rwanda national guards were reported
to be watching the southern frontiers very closely.
Despite these distractions, Parliament gave the impression
of functioning in an orderly way. Apart from racial
division, the country's main difficulties are poverty,
malnutrition and problems of an economic kind. Many of
the areas devoted to agriculture suffer from erosion, but
they still produce results. Belgium and Common Market
countries are helping to improve the situation. While the
main crops are coffee and tea, there are plans to produce
pyrethrum, cotton and rice, and to increase the banana

357

crop. Efforts are also being made to increase the
production of long-horned Ankole cattle, which play an
important traditional role though their economic value
has been allowed to become negligible.

A few mines producing tin ore and wolfram and a little
gold are being worked to the maximum. Methane gas
under Lake Kivu is abundant and there are plans to
exploit it.

The country is sadly handicapped by the lack of buildings.
There is little accommodation to offer foreign technicians,
and the complete lack of motor roads and hotels prevents
the country from engaging in the tourist trade, which
might in time provide a lucrative source of revenue.

President Kayibanda's regime is one of severe austerity,
with low salaries for ministers and others in high places.
The whole policy of the country is concentrated on the
national development plan, with which the prefectures
and the communes, and indeed all movements, are
expected to associate themselves.

Great efforts are being made to instruct the masses, using
up 50 per cent of the national budget. Primary
school education is obligatory for all. The social services
are principally directed at the promotion of mothercraft.
A university is being founded with American aid, while a
school, administered by Belgium, is specialising in the
training of people for administrative and agricultural work.
The finances of the country are said to be sound, but a
greater effort will be needed to fight under-development,
especially in view of the growing population, which
increases by three per cent per annum, and could double
itself (to over six million) in 24 years.

THADDEE BAGARAGAZA

Minister of International Co-operation and National Planning, Thaddée Bagaragaza was born on June 6, 1936, at Muvumo, Biumba.

He holds a high place as a Hutu intellectual on the national committee of the Parmehutu, the emancipation movement, and is closely associated with other leaders who took part in the uprising.

He began his education at the mission school at Rulindo (1945–51), then went to the Petit Séminaire at Kabgayi, and the Grand Séminaire at Nyakibanda, before proceeding to the University of Lovanium at Leopoldville.

In January, 1961, he became chief of the Department of Social Affairs, and secretary-general in the following May.

In October the same year, he was made Minister of Social

Balthazar Bicamumpaka

Gaspard Cyimana

Affairs and Information, and in 1963 became Minister of National Planning, International Co-operation and Technical Assistance.

BALTHAZAR BICAMUMPAKA

Balthazar Bicamumpaka, who became President of the Legislative Assembly after the 1965 elections, is one of the principal leaders of the Parmehutu (the party for the emancipation of the Hutu race) and exercises a great influence.

He is an original member of the Assembly and of the national committee of the Parmehutu.

Born in 1920 at Mukono in the prefecture of Ruhengeri, he came of a Hutu peasant family and went to a village mission school for his early education. He received his secondary studies from the Josephite Brothers. His companions were aborigines. He devoted himself to teaching in this region until 1957. He was one of the few Hutu scholars to come under the influence of the Belgian missionaries, who recognised his intelligence and hard work by giving him a post as under-chief in the feudal regime.

He was also one of the first militants of the Muhutu Social Movement, and took part in the revolutionary uprising of 1959–60. His district was one of the least subject to serfdom in the country and was the first to be liberated from the Tutsi chiefs.

At the beginning of 1960, the Belgians made him an intermediary chief during the transition period before the elections and the advent of the Republic.

M. Bicamumpaka, whose family continue as farmers at Rwasa in the Mulera area, was Minister of Agriculture in the first Republican Government and in succeeding Governments.

BISHOP BIGIRUMWAMI

Monsignor Aloysius Bigirumwami, Bishop of Nyundo, a man of great personal charm and dignity, is linked in the popular mind, as a Tutsi, with the old regime.

It is thought by many that the secret aspirations of the former rulers and their sons to return to power are fostered to some extent by priests.

Bishop Bigirumwami was the first African bishop in Rwanda.

GASPARD CYIMANA

As Minister of Finance since 1960, Gaspard Cyimana has been a member of all the delegations which in Belgium, at United Nations, and in the Common Market countries have discussed financial and technical assistance for his country.

He plays an important part at the centre of the Parmehutu movement which has done so much for his fellow Hutu tribesmen.

He was born at Rulindo in the Kigali region on May 31, 1930, and was one of the first Hutu to obtain a study grant after completing his classical studies at Kabgayi and three years in philosophy at the Grand Seminary of Nyakibanda.

He did his administrative studies at Kisantu (Lovanium in the then Belgian Congo). After four years there he obtained a second grant to take a commercial and financial science course at the St Ignace Institute at Antwerp.

While abroad he kept in close contact with the Hutu scholars at home, and wrote many articles for Belgian newspapers and magazines about the abuses of the feudal regime in Rwanda.

He returned to Rwanda in July, 1960, as a licentiate and with a Belgian wife. He was im-

Bishop Gahamanyi

Grégoire Kayibanda

mediately appointed Minister of Finance and Overseas Commerce in the first Government. His wife became a social worker, attached to the Rwanda Ministry for Social Affairs to work on the promotion of women's interests.

BISHOP GAHAMANYI

Monsignor Jean-Baptiste Gaha-manyi, Bishop of Butare from November 11, 1963, is a Tutsi prince related to the old royal family. His brother Kayhura is in exile and has been in close touch with ex-Mwami Kigeri.

Mgr Gahamanyi is respected by the masses as one who has defended the lowly as priest and bishop. His attitude remained unchanged during the revolt. He has been criticised by his tribe.

He was born at Kaduha in the archdiocese of Kabgayi in 1920, ordained in 1951, elected a bishop in 1961 and consecrated in 1962.

GREGOIRE KAYIBANDA

Grégoire Kayibanda was first elected President of Rwanda and Prime Minister on October 26, 1961. He was re-elected for a further four years on October 3, 1965.

Born on May 1, 1924, he dedicated himself to the emanci-pation of the Hutu from the overlordship of the Tutsi. He came of a Hutu family at Tare, in the commune of Musambira in the prefecture of Gitarama. He married a Hutu.

He received his primary and secondary education at the Kab-gayi Mission, now the head-quarters of the Roman Catholic archdiocese. Entering the Grand Seminary of Nyakibanda in 1943 he completed his phisophical studies in brilliant style.

He then left the seminary to devote himself to the welfare of the Hutu masses, whose servitude under the feudal Tutsi regime both distressed and obsessed him.

In 1949 he became a teacher and adviser at the Léon Classe Institute at Kigali, and in 1953 was named inspector of schools in the Kabgayi diocese.

During this period, he had founded with some friends the Muhutu Social Movement, which denounced the abuses of the Tutsi administration and demanded justice and respect for 'the Hutu serfs and the Twa slaves'. He founded a small review and became editor-in-chief of a dio-cesan organ with which he continued his struggle for social justice.

He was the first member of the Popular Catholic Action youth movement, and as such was sent to Belgium and Rome for several months by the Archbishop of Kabgayi, Monsignor Perraudin. He worked for periods in factories and among farmers. From these experiences he took the idea of creating in Rwanda a cell of the Muhutu movement on every hill.

He went back to Belgium again in 1958 to take a course in journalism. At the Brussels Inter-national Fair, he was an *attaché* at the missionary press centre. He returned to Rwanda in 1959, when the Tutsi chiefs were becoming alarmed at the spec-tacle of even Hutu intellectuals coming under the influence of a mass movement. Some Hutu under-chiefs were dismissed and there were some assassinations.

These events did more than anything else to turn the Muhutu Social Movement into a political force, supported by the Hutu masses. For a time M. Kayibanda was receiving Belgian protection against the Tutsi.

As President of the Parmehutu, his main object was to build up

Fulgence Seminega

the organisation in all its sections and make it thoroughly national. He did not participate in the provisional bodies set up by Belgium, nor in the discussions that preceded the granting of independence to his country at the United Nations.

His energies were rewarded because he was a good organiser, knew the needs and aspirations of his people, and set an example of asceticism, impartiality, disinterestedness and simplicity. As he entered the last three years of the 1960s, his prestige in the country was high. He had demonstrated his belief in enduring democratic institutions. He had shown that he did not want dictatorial power.

Although he has a residence at Kigali, the President continues to live in his house at Kabayi, where his children attend the missionary school.

ARCHBISHOP PERRAUDIN

Monsignor André Perraudin, Roman Catholic Archbishop of Kabgayi, exercises great influence over the affairs of Rwanda because of his concern from the beginning for the welfare of the people.

As the Hutu were excluded from the secondary schools during the Tutsi regime, they entered the Catholic seminary in large numbers. Many left with a fine education including philosophy, and these young men were prominent in the task of emancipating their race.

Archbishop Perraudin declined various feudal titles and property, and his prestige in the spiritual world became comparable with that of President Kayibanda in the secular sphere.

There is a perfect understanding between Church and State in Rwanda, but their powers are clearly divided, teaching being the responsibility of the State.

Archbishop Perraudin's father was Swiss.

ETIENNE RWIGEMERA

One of the brothers of the Mwamis (Kings) Mutara and Kigeri, Etienne Rwigemera lives quietly in Kigali, working as a transport contractor.

But as the Tutsi chief in the Biumba region, he was once president of the Rwanda Democratic Party founded by some Tutsi intellectuals who saw the regime tottering and wanted Mutara to save the situation.

This party was prepared to support some Hutu democratic aims and participated with the Parmehutu at conferences. But it could not agree to the assumption of power by the Hutu majority, and in 1960 allied itself to the conservative party, the UNAR.

M. Rwigemera had visited Belgium on many occasions, when he was opposing his brothers. After the republic came into being, he retired from the political scene and concentrated on earning his living as a transport contractor.

FULGENCE SEMINEGA

The President of the Supreme Court, Fulgence Seminega is a Doctor of Law.

A Hutu born at Kibande in the Biumba region on November 21, 1936, he received a secondary education, including Greek and Latin, at the St Esprit College at Bujumbura (Burundi).

University studies followed in Belgium – at Namur and Louvain. On his return to Rwanda in 1963, he was at once appointed President of the Supreme Court. He is a quiet, jovial man.

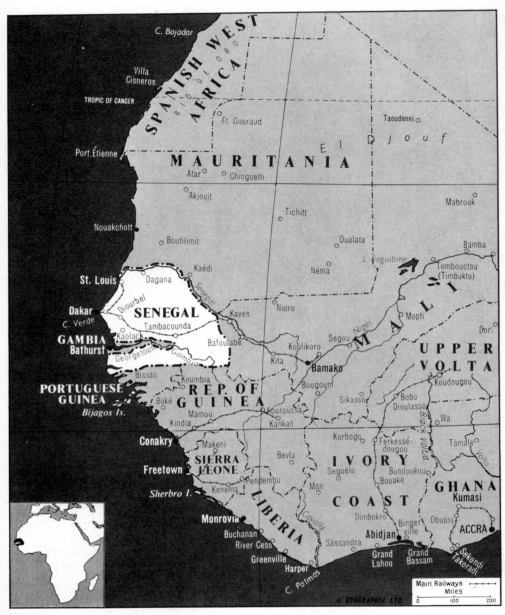

C. Bojador

SPANISH WEST AFRICA

RIO DE ORO

Villa Cisneros

TROPIC OF CANCER

Ft. Gouraud

Taoudenni

Port.Étienne

MAURITANIA

El Djouf

Atar   Chinguetti

Akjoujt

Mabrouk

Nouakchott

Tichitt

Boutilimit

Oualata

Bamba

L. Faguibine

Tombouctou (Timbuktu)

Kaédi

Néma

St. Louis   Dagana

Senegal

Dakar
C. Verde   Diourbel   SENEGAL   Kayes   Nioro

Tambacounda

Mopti

MALI

Dori

GAMBIA   Kaolack
Bathurst   Bafoulabé   Koulikoro   Segou

Georgetown   Kita   Niger

Gambia   Bamako   Bougouni

UPPER VOLTA

PORTUGUESE GUINEA   Bissau   Koumbia   REP. OF GUINEA   Koudougou

Boké   Sikasso   Bobo Dioulasso

Bijagos Is.   Mamou   Kouroussa   Wa

Kindia   Kankan   Black Volta

Conakry   Makeni   Korhogo   Tamale

Bévla   Ferkesse-dougou   Volta

Freetown   SIERRA LEONE   IVORY   GHANA

Séguéla   Bundoukou
Pendembu   Bouaké   Kumasi

Sherbro I.   Kenema   Man   COAST

LIBERIA   Dimbokro   Binger ville   Obuasi   ACCRA

Monrovia   Cavally   Abidjan   Sekondi
Takoradi
Buchanan   Sassandra   Grand   Grand
River Cess   Lahou   Bassam
Greenville
Harper
C. Palmas

Main Railways
Miles
0   100   200

© GEOGRAPHIA LTD.

Senegal's area is over 76,000 square miles, with a population of under 3,500,000. It has borders with Mauritania, Mali, Guinea and Portuguese Guinea, with Gambia as an enclave penetrating inland on both sides of the Gambia River. The capital is Dakar.

The country's economy is based for the most part on the groundnut crop, which is either processed locally in large oil mills or exported. Other developments include phosphate mining and prospecting for off-shore oil. With Mali, Guinea and Mauritania, Senegal is a member of the Senegal River States Organisation.

362

Senegal

Senegal, a former French territory, became independent on August 20, 1960.

It had been a member of the French Community from November, 1958. From January, 1959, it was a partner, together with the Soudanese Republic, of the Federation of Mali. It withdrew because of serious disagreement on the implementation of the federal constitution.

As an independent republic, Senegal had a President and a Prime Minister. In December, 1962, the Prime Minister, Mamadou Dia, unsuccessfully attempted a *coup d'état* against President Léopold Senghor. In May, 1963, he was sentenced to life detention.

A new constitution gave the President complete executive control. The constitution describes Senegal as secular, democratic and social, organised on the principal of government of, by and for the people. The one-chamber National Assembly is elected for four years.

The Republic of Senegal acceded to independence in the year which saw nearly all the countries of former French West Africa reach nationhood.

Dakar, the capital, was the headquarters for the whole of this vast colonial region, and the city's size and elegance recalls its former unchallenged pre-eminence. Senegal, or rather the small area round Dakar, was the first French colony in Africa (1659) and it is here that French culture and ways of thought have penetrated deepest. Over 76,000 square miles in area, the country is thinly peopled, particularly in the east, by a multi-tribal population which numbers under three and a half million. Its greatest riches are its people. Because of its long colonial history Senegal, unlike the majority of African countries, is comparatively rich in trained men, particularly in the professions and administrative fields. During the colonial era Senegalese were used in the administration throughout French West Africa, and since independence more than one African country has requested technical assistance from Senegal.

Despite this, the economic outlook for Senegal does not seem brilliant. Heavily dependent on one crop, groundnuts, which make up over 80 per cent of the value of her exports, agricultural development is likely to be slow, largely because of the very long dry season which lasts from November to May. The only important mineral

exploited is phosphates, though searches for oil off-shore,
and for gold and diamonds in the desolate Eastern
Province, are under way.

While Senegal is by African standards fairly heavily
industrialised, it is difficult to envisage any rapid growth
because of the country's small market and population,
which has a very limited purchasing power.

Had the majority of the countries of French West Africa
reached independence as a close-knit federation (as many
Senegalese hoped) Dakar, with its excellent port facilities
and communications, might have become a boom town.
In the event only Senegal and what is now Mali (former
French Soudan) federated, and even this experiment

Dakar, a sophisticated capital, offers its housewives a variety of ways to shop: in the bustle of the market, *above left,* or in the more ordered calm of a supermarket

lasted only a few months before it was abandoned. Immediately after independence, Senegal had a 'two-headed' government – a President and a Prime Minister. However, in December, 1962, the then Prime Minister, Mamadou Dia, attempted a *coup d'état* against President Léopold Senghor. He failed and was sentenced to life imprisonment.

At his trial, Mamadou Dia was accused of having ordered the armed forces to expel deputies from the National Assembly, to prevent them passing a censure motion which would have put him out of office. A further charge was that he had ordered the arrest of deputies and cut the telephone lines of President Senghor's residence.

A view of Dakar's
impressive University

Four former ministers were sentenced with him – Ibrahim
Sarr, Valdodio Ndiaye and Joseph Mbaye, who received
20 years, and Alioune Tall (Minister of Information),
who was jailed for five years.

For the defence, Maître Baudet, of the Paris Bar, termed
the December events 'a clash between two able men',
Dia and President Senghor. 'Each was mistaken,' he said,
'about the other's intentions.' M. Dia, he contended,
acted according to his rights as Prime Minister, in
opposing moves by another political group which he
believed to be illegal.

A new constitution was adopted which centred all
executive power on the President. Under this constitution
Ministers can be appointed and dismissed at will by the
President. The National Assembly is elected on the
nation-wide single-list system. The party which gains the
majority of the votes in the nation as a whole, wins all
the seats in the National Assembly. Ministers are not
allowed to be members of the National Assembly, and as
President Senghor is secretary-general of the ruling
Senegalese Progressive Union (UPS), his control over
national affairs is complete.

Because of this, any understanding of Senegalese affairs
in the years immediately following independence centres
round the figure of Léopold Sedar Senghor.

Amadou Cisse Dia

LEON BOISSIER-PALLUN

Léon Boissier-Pallun became in 1964 President of Senegal's Economic and Social Council.

This body has no real equivalent in the English-speaking countries, but in French-speaking states it is of considerable importance. It is separate from both the executive and legislature, and is named in the constitution. Basically, it is a consultative body which is at the government's disposal to make studies of specific problems, mainly of an economic nature. It will be asked, for example, to study the practical implications of planning legislation. Through it the private sectors of the economy have, from their representation on it, a useful communications channel to the executive.

The son of a lawyer, Boissier-Pallun was himself successful in his legal career. He was born at Djougou, in what is now Dahomey, on June 29, 1916, and is of mixed African and European descent.

His advanced education was at the University of Bordeaux in France. He has a degree in law, and was a defending advocate at the Court of Appeal in Dakar. From 1958–64 he was a deputy in Senegal's National Assembly. Even before independence he was a prominent figure in public life, being President of the Grand Council of French West Africa, a body which had wide responsibilities under the French authorities for the internal administration of the area.

During the short-lived Mali Federation, Léon Boissier-Pallun was also a member of the Federal Assembly.

After the Federation broke up he was named Senegal's first ambassador to Britain, a post he held until June, 1966, when he was transferred to France. How-ever, he resigned this post after only a few months, to return to Senegal.

He is a rich man. An urbane, polished figure with great knowledge of business affairs, he is said to be a man whose advice President Senghor does not lightly disregard.

DANIEL CABOU

Reputed to be one of the abler departmental administrators of President Senghor's team, Daniel Cabou, the Minister for Commerce and Industry, was born on July 16, 1919, at Ziguinchor, capital of the southernmost province.

He is a bachelor of law, and his studies in France were completed by his achieving the full qualifications of an administrator for the French Overseas Territories.

He is regarded as an approachable, friendly man.

From March, 1960 to November, 1962, he served in the administration as Governor of the Fleuve region. With headquarters in St Louis, he acted as the Government's chief representative in this important region of Senegal.

In December, 1962, he entered the Government itself, following Mamadou Dia's unsuccessful *coup d'état*, as Secretary of State for Finance and Economic Affairs. He held this post until December, 1963, when he was appointed Minister of Commerce and Industry.

AMADOU CISSE DIA

Amadou Cisse Dia is one of President Senghor's most trusted lieutenants. In the Government list of Ministers he ranks immediately after Doudou Thiam, the Foreign Minister. If both the President and Thiam are out of

Abdoulaye Fofana

Amadou Karim Gaye

the country, he acts for Senghor in his absence. Since January, 1966, he and Thiam have been joint assistant secretary-generals of the ruling UPS party.

He has extremely wide experience in government, having held no fewer than five different portfolios since 1960. At independence he was Minister of Commerce and Industry. On May 13, 1961, he was appointed Minister of Health and Social Affairs. Later he became Minister of Technical Cooperation.

On December 19, 1962 (following Mamadou Dia's attempted *coup*) President Senghor named him Minister for the Armed Forces, a post he held until March 18, 1965, when he became Minister of the Interior.

Born on June 2, 1915, he is a medical man by profession. He received his diploma at the Dakar School of Medicine in 1940.

DIAKHA DIENG

Diakha Dieng was named secretary-general of the African and Malagasy Union for Economic Cooperation (UAMCE) in 1964 and then of the Common African and Malagasy Organisation (OCAM).

He was born August 16, 1933 at St Louis, Senegal. He studied law in Dakar and Paris, where he obtained a degree in political law and political science.

In 1962 he was appointed Counsellor at the Senegalese Embassy in Brussels and in 1963 First Counsellor at the Embassy in Paris.

ABDOULAYE FOFANA

Abdoulaye Fofana is a politician with a sharp and ready wit, who became Minister of Information and Tourism in 1965.

Born on July 15, 1917, he is a teacher by profession, and administrative secretary of the ruling party.

From April, 1959 to August, 1960, when it broke up, he was Minister for Health and Education in the Government of the Mali Federation. After Senegal broke away from the Federation, Fofana became Minister for Posts, Telecommunications and Transport, but the following month (September, 1960) was appointed Minister for Commerce and Industry.

In the *coup* crisis of 1962, Fofana played a leading role in the National Assembly in organising the opposition to Mamadou Dia.

Following the failure of Mamadou Dia's *coup*, Senghor appointed Fofana Minister of the Interior, a post he held until being appointed to his present job in March, 1965.

HENRY-CHARLES GALLENCA

Probably the most important business and financial figure in Senegal is Henry-Charles Gallenca, president of the Dakar Chamber of Commerce, Agriculture and Industry.

Born on April 8, 1906 at Marseilles, he is a director of several companies. His other appointments include: president of the Dakar Port Authority and member of the Monetary Committee of Senegal, the Board of the Senegal Railways, the Board of the Posts and Telecommunications Administration and Dakar University Council.

In addition, he is a member of several international organisations in the financial and economic field as well as a member of the International Chamber of Commerce.

AMADOU KARIM GAYE

The Minister for the Armed Forces in Senegal is Amadou

Lamine Gueye

Amadou Moctar M'Bow

Léopold Sedar Senghor

he broke with Senghor over the referendum held throughout French West Africa by France, in which the issue was a choice between immediate independence or continued membership of the French Community.

M'Bow and many others favoured a 'no' vote (that is, in favour of immediate independence) but Senghor carried the majority with him.

M'Bow and others broke away and remained opponents of Senghor until June, 1966, when their party, the PRA-Senegal, merged with the ruling party, and M'Bow and two other PRA leaders entered Senghor's Government.

M'Bow is a dynamic figure with a high reputation as an administrator.

A teacher by profession, he was born on March 21, 1921.

LEOPOLD SEDAR SENGHOR

Léopold Sedar Senghor is almost certainly Africa's most scholarly and erudite head of state. Known in the French-speaking world as much as a poet and man of letters as a politician, his personal bibliography covers six closely-typed pages. In 1962 he was a strong contender for the Nobel prize for literature.

Born on October 9, 1906, and educated mainly in France, he is a member of the select club of *Agrégés de Grammaire* – the highest French academic qualification. Because of his French literary background and easy-going manner some commentators have dismissed him as a black French poet with his head in the clouds.

That this was not the case, Mamadou Dia, his Prime Minister, discovered to his cost, when he attempted a *coup* against him in 1962, two years after independence. Apprised of the

danger, the President organised his political forces, and despite the fact that some of the Army were acting for Mamadou Dia, snuffed out the *coup* without great difficulty.

Léopold Sedar Senghor was a student at the Sorbonne in Paris, and has spent much of his life in France, either as a student or as a politician. Before World War II, from 1935–38 he taught at the Descartes Lycée at Tours, and from 1938–44 at the Marcellin Berthelot Lycée in Paris.

After the war he was a member of the two constituent assemblies in France from October, 1945 to June, 1946 and from June to October, 1946. He then served from November, 1946 until November, 1958 as a deputy representing Senegal in France's National Assembly. Senghor, despite his long involvement in French academic and political life, was one of the first Africans to state clearly that eventual political self-determination for the Africans was necessary.

However, like many other future leaders from the French African colonies, he profited from his participation in French metropolitan politics by gaining useful experience in the arts of government – an experience not shared by the future leaders of English-speaking Africa.

Twice he represented France at UNESCO. From March, 1955 to February, 1956 he served as Secretary of State at the Presidency of the Council (Prime Minister's Office) in the French Government of M. Edgar Faure, and played an important part in the negotiations which led to Tunisia's independence. From July, 1959 to July, 1960 he was Minister-Counsellor for Cultural Affairs, Education, and Justice in the French Government.

Despite his active participation in French metropolitan affairs, he was already an active and leading member of the series of African-based political parties which increasingly pressed for self-rule for the African territories. Around 20 made their appearance at one time or another. Senghor emerged as the leading figure in Senegalese politics mainly because:

1. Though a leading member of the French-influenced *élite*, he realised at an early stage that political success would depend on active campaigning throughout the rural areas of Senegal to produce a party or coalition with a broad base and without an unduly rigid political doctrine.

2. He possessed the necessary personal qualities to achieve this: particularly a talent for resolving differences among his followers.

Senegalese political policies and the general character of political life in the country in the years following independence reflected very closely the character and beliefs of President Senghor. This was particularly true following the abortive *coup* in 1962, after which executive power became so centralised in the person of the President.

Such terms as 'leftist', 'rightist', 'moderate' and 'conservative' have their dangers when used to oversimplify African politics; but 'gradualist' is probably a fair word to describe Senghor's general political character. He describes himself as a socialist, but he has done what he could to encourage private enterprise.

Talking to him one does not receive the impression of a man who thinks it possible to transform his country politically or economically overnight. A striking example of his caution, or, put another way, his preference to manipulate existing political and economic forces rather than to overcome them, has been his attitude towards the religious leaders in Senegal.

Senegal is over three-quarters Moslem, and the leaders of the Moslem sects are extremely powerful. In the countryside their followers regard them with great awe and listen to their pronouncements as having divine sanction. They are also extremely rich, as their peasant followers are quite happy to donate to them an astonishingly high percentage of their meagre cash earnings.

Similar conditions have existed in many African countries, but elsewhere nationalist governments have often taken strong measures to clip the wings of religious leaders whom they regarded as divisive influences and as brakes on their desire to create modern states. In Senegal the leaders of the big Moslem sects are rivals and are certainly potentially divisive influences.

In this sense they far over-shadow any tribal differences. Senegal is, in fact, a country surprisingly free of tribalism. Rivalry between the majority Wollofs and the other tribes has been, since independence, a factor of no great significance in Senegalese politics. However, the rival religious leaders have remained powerful factors to be reckoned with by any government wishing to preserve its power and influence throughout the country. In this situation, paradoxically, one of Senghor's strongest cards has been the fact that he is not a Moslem but a member of the small Roman Catholic minority.

Though a Catholic, he pays a great deal of attention to the Moslem religious leaders, attending their festivals, receiving them and their envoys in his office and so on. He is also a member of a

371

minority tribe in a country dominated by large tribal units. Being both a religious and a tribal 'outsider' the rival sects are able to trust him, which might not have been the case had he been, for example, a member of the Mouride or Tidjani Moslem sects, or of the Wollof or Toucouleur tribes. Similarly in the political in-fighting his great strength has been his flexibility and, so far, his success in preserving a national consensus.

There is no legal bar in Senegal to Opposition parties, but time and again he has succeeded in absorbing opposition elements into his ruling Senegalese Progressive Union (UPS). In June, 1966, he succeeded in persuading the sole existing legal Opposition party, the PRA-Senegal, to dissolve and join the UPS. Part of the deal was that three prominent PRA leaders became cabinet ministers. This was not the first time Senghor had succeeded in such a manoeuvre and it may well not be the last. His domestic political tactics might well be summarised as: 'If you can't beat them, get them to join you'.

Another example of how Senegalese life following independence was strongly marked by Senghor's personal predelictions, has been the very great emphasis laid on cultural activity in this country. Here again the paradoxical nature of the man has had its effect.

There is probably no single African head of state who expresses such unqualified and unstinting admiration for French culture. This is quite understandable in view of the fact that he is a poet who has passed much of his life in literary and academic circles in France.

Yet it was Senghor together with Aime Cesaire, the West Indian poet, who were the first exponents before World War II of the concept of *négritude*. The idea of 'negritude' was to express the values of the black man's culture and to explain its contribution to universal culture. Thus Senghor, though a thorough admirer of French culture, has been a champion of African culture and its contribution to the cultures of other peoples. Culmination of Senghor's policy came in 1966 when the First World Festival of Negro Arts was held in Dakar. This brought together artists, sculptors, musicians, poets, playwrights, art historians, and cultural experts from all over the world.

Senegal's foreign policy in the years following independence has also been very much a reflection of Senghor. From the beginning, Senghor was sceptical of an early attempt to create African unity by simply forming a central government for the whole of Africa, as was suggested by ex-President Kwame Nkrumah of Ghana. Instead he pressed for a gradual policy based on regional cooperation within Africa.

Thus Senegal is one of the four states making up the Senegal River States Organisation – the others are Mali, Guinea, and Mauritania. The aim is modest – to develop the resources of the Senegal River basin by the construction of dams and other works. However, it is hoped that the four states will be able to develop more general economic links and co-operation. A believer in 'dialogue' as the only effective way to conduct foreign or domestic politics, Senghor has preserved cordial relations with both the Soviet Union and the United States, as well as with both Israel and the Arab states. Another example of his desire to preserve

Doudou Thiam

Habib Thiam

his ties with French culture has been his constant championing of the series of organisations set up to link the French-speaking countries of Africa. He was one of the main moving forces in the attempt to set up an organisation to link France and French-speaking countries throughout the world. This idea, known as *francophonie,* aims to produce some sort of French-speaking equivalent of the Commonwealth.

But Senghor's attitude towards French or African culture is not exclusive or defensive. For example, he has recognised the need in Africa of bilingualism in French and English.

English is a compulsory subject for all Senegalese advanced secondary students. One reason for this is the problem of The Gambia. Now an independent country, this was a former British territory. However, it is very small and is surrounded on all its land frontiers by Senegal. Senghor hopes as a long-term aim that will form a federation with Senegal while still preserving some degree of autonomy.

DOUDOU THIAM

Doudou Thiam has the distinction of having risen to high office in spite of belonging to one of the lower tribes in the traditional social hierarchy of Senegal.

Born on February 3, 1926, he has been Foreign Minister of Senegal since independence in 1960.

Because of his long tenure of office, this dapper ex-lawyer, who possesses great personal charm, is one of the best known figures in African diplomacy. The author of a book on the foreign policies of African states, he has shown himself on occasions to be in favour of a more radical line in foreign policy than President Senghor.

Prior to independence he had a distinguished legal career. A doctor of law, he was a defence counsellor of the Court of Appeal of former French West Africa in Dakar. He was laureate of the Paris law faculty and the Poitiers law faculty, and an *administrateur* of the Assembly of the French Union from 1949–51.

Secretary-General of the UPS from April, 1958 to February, 1959, he was elected mayor of M'Backe on August 3, 1960. In 1958 he was elected a deputy to the Senegalese Constituent Assembly. He was subsequently elected a member of the National Assembly. He also served as a Grand Councillor of French West Africa from 1957–59.

During the short-lived Federation linking Senegal and Mali, he served as Minister of Economic Affairs and Planning in the Federal Government.

Apart from being Senegal's Foreign Minister, he is in addition the Minister who most usually stands in for President Senghor when he is out of the country.

HABIB THIAM

The Minister for Planning and Development (appointed 1963), Habib Thiam is one of the youngest of Senghor's Ministers. He was born on January 21, 1933.

Like Daniel Cabou he enjoys a good reputation as a departmental administrator. Like Cabou he won his diploma at France's special school for overseas administrators. He managed to combine athletic with academic success.

To date one of Senegal's most successful athletes, he was twice champion of France for the 200-metres between 1954 and 1956.

From 1960–62 he was Permanent Secretary at the Foreign Ministry.

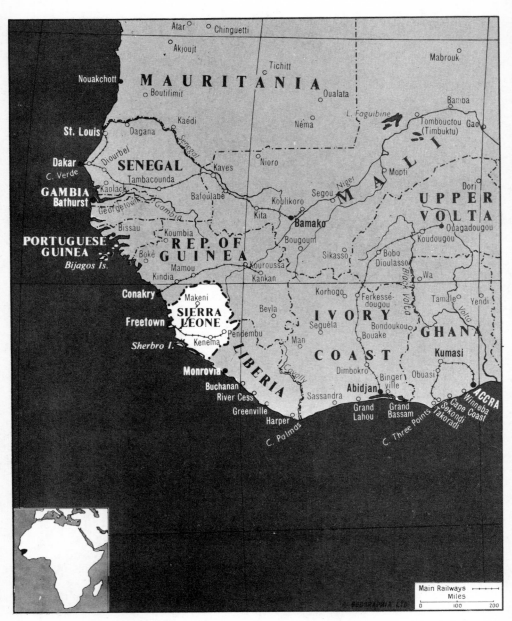

Sierra Leone, with a population of 2,180,355 (1960 census), covers an area of 27,925 square miles. It has common inland frontiers with the Republics of Guinea and Liberia, and a sea border on the Atlantic Ocean. The capital is Freetown.

About 80 per cent of the Sierra Leonean people live on the land. Diamonds are a main source of revenue and with iron ore they account for some 80 per cent of the nation's exports. Other products include palm kernels, cocoa, ginger plassava and coffee. Rice is the country's staple food.

Sierra Leone

Sierra Leone, an independent nation within the Commonwealth since April 27, 1961, took the first step towards becoming a republic on January 25, 1967. A draft constitution introduced in Parliament by the Prime Minister, Sir Albert Margai, was approved with the necessary two-thirds majority. To become law the Bill required a similar vote by the new Parliament set up after the 1967 elections.

Anti-Government demonstrations broke out, the Opposition party claiming that the Bill gave the Prime Minister excessive powers.

On February 8, 1967, Sir Albert said that a controversial proposal to make Sierra Leone a one-party state would be dropped and not raised again. Later the same day he announced there had been a plot by Army officers to murder him and others and overthrow the Government. This had been crushed with the help of President Sekou Touré of Guinea, who had moved troops to the border.

The West African country of Sierra Leone derived its name from the rumble of thunder among its mountain peaks and the imagination of an adventurous 15th-century Portuguese sea captain. To Pedro da Cintra, exploring this coast in 1460, the distant thunder resembled a lion's roar. In recording his voyage he named the mountainous area 'Serra Lyoa' – mountain of the lion. More than three centuries later the country became a home for Africans freed from slavery, symbolised by the apt name of its capital, Freetown.

Some researchers suggest that about 2,000 years before the arrival of the first Portuguese, Hanno the Carthaginian watered his ships in Freetown harbour, one of the largest natural harbours in the world. During World War II this harbour was an assembly point for Allied convoys with more than 300 ships anchored there at one time.

The charts prepared by the Portuguese explorers opened up the country to merchants and adventurers from many lands – and with them came the notorious slave-traders.

Probably the first Englishman to land there (1562) was Sir John Hawkins, a sea captain raiding the West African coast for slaves. He was followed by the traders

and in 1663 the first Royal Charter was granted to
'The Company of Royal Adventurers in Africa'.

The profitable slave trade received its death blow when
the British Parliament outlawed it in 1807 and the Navy
operating from Sierra Leone suppressed it.

Catholic and Protestant missionaries were active in the
colony's early years building schools and churches. In
1827 the Church Missionary Society founded Fourah
Bay College to train teachers and clergymen. For more
than a century it was the only institute of higher
learning in British West Africa, producing a long line of
distinguished African judges, lawyers and educationists.
To many West Africans this college is what Oxford and
Cambridge are to the British and Harvard and Yale to
the Americans.

Meanwhile, with company rule replaced by direct
British Government rule through a governor, the colonist
Creoles were gradually participating in the running
of the peninsula colony.

Sierra Leone's present frontiers were finally fixed in
1911, after the hinterland country with its 13 indigenous
tribes, each with their own language, was made a
British Protectorate. The jurisdiction of the nominated
legislative and executive councils established in the
colony in 1863 was extended to the Protectorate, thus
paving the way for a united country.

But it was not until 1951 when the first political party,
the Sierra Leone People's Party (SLPP), was formed
by an Edinburgh-trained doctor, Milton Margai,
knighted in 1959, that Britain opened the door to
internal self-government with a new constitution.

The SLPP had resulted from the merger of the People's
Party, a colony group standing for unity with the
peoples of the Protectorate, and the Sierra Leone
Organisation Society, a Protectorate party founded by
Dr Milton Margai in 1946 to further the interests of the
hinterland people and emancipation within a
constitutional framework.

A limited franchise was extended to the Protectorate
where the overwhelming majority of the people lived,
the legislative and executive councils were controlled by
elected representatives instead of by British civil servants
and six government departments were headed by African
ministers.

Three years later, Sir Milton Margai was the chief
Minister. Since its formation, his People's Party has
been the majority party in the legislature, which in
1957 became the House of Representatives. All the
British officials holding seats were removed and Sir
Milton became the Premier.

Earlier in that year the SLPP won the election with a
substantial majority and then split into two factions: a
moderate group led by Dr Milton Margai, and a more
radical one led by his half-brother, Albert Margai. In
1958 the radical faction broke away from the SLPP to
form a new party – the People's National Party (PNP)
with Mr Albert Margai as its leader and Mr Siaka
Stevens as deputy leader.

In 1960 the SLPP, the PNP and other groups formed a
national front with a view to speaking with a single
voice at the Constitutional Conference due to be held
in London in April. The Sierra Leone delegation
demanded independence by April, 1961.

Meanwhile, full self-government, the prelude to
independence, was achieved with British agreement that
year and a Cabinet system of government was introduced.
On April 27, 1961, Sierra Leone emerged as an
independent nation within the Commonwealth. Mr
Albert Margai remained in the united front after the
London talks and later became Minister of Natural
Resources in the first coalition Government formed after
independence. Mr Siaka Stevens, however, broke away
from the united front to join the All People's Congress
(APC) which remained the leading Opposition party.

Sierra Leone's House of Representatives comprises 62
constituency elected members and 12 paramount
chiefs elected by district councils. There are 15 Ministers
in the Cabinet.

General elections in 1962 firmly established Sir Milton's
People's Party, which draws its main support from the
former Protectorate, in the Government of the new nation.
It controls 47 of the constituency seats and has the
support of all 12 chiefs. The Opposition All People's
Congress, led by Mr Siaka Stevens, a former mayor of
Freetown and a trade union leader, has 14 seats and
there is one allied independent.

Sir Milton, who died in 1964, was affectionately known
as 'The Doctor'. He consistently opposed proposals

Opposite:
Diamond-washers
at work in a stream
near the diamond
town of Kenema

intended to curtail the rights of the Opposition, ensured
an equitable representation of all ethnic groups both in
the ruling party and the Government, africanised the
Civil Service, and encouraged foreign investments.
Under his administration further efforts were made to
develop the hinterland, both socially and economically,
and to unify the nation.

His work for women's social services was immense. He
also supported the idea of closer regional links, leading
to a possible free trade zone covering Sierra Leone,
Guinea, Liberia and the Ivory Coast.

Sir Milton could be caustic over the pretensions of the
great 'African personalities' contemporary with himself.
His attitude towards African unity was to prefer a loose
association of African states. He hated ideological
regimentation as not conducive to the flowering of
native genius.

When he died, his half-brother Albert (later Sir
Albert), who had served in the Cabinet as Minister of
Natural Resources and as Finance Minister, succeeded
him as Prime Minister and party leader.

Sir Albert Margai proposed early in 1966 the
introduction of a democratic one-party system of
government and set up a committee to study the
implications and problems involved. There was adverse
comment in Sierra Leone on the one-party system
following the downfall of Dr Nkrumah and his one-
party regime in Ghana.

Sierra Leone's economic structure has been transformed
since 1930, when diamonds were discovered in the
Sewa River area. About the same time large deposits
of high-grade iron ore were found. In the next 30 years
surveys uncovered new mineral resources, the chief ones
being rutile, which contains heat-resisting titanium, and
bauxite.

When big new deposits of diamonds were found in
many river beds in the early 1950s, tens of thousands of
African prospectors swarmed into the country. A private
company had a mining monopoly, but illegal digging and
smuggling was widespread. By 1957 the Government
had brought most of the illegal digging and smuggling
under control.

The diamond boom and the new mineral exports gave
a much needed boost to living standards and particularly

Above: Houses on the fringe of Freetown, with Mount Aureol in the background

Below: Street market in Freetown

to the social services. The post-war years saw a big spurt in agricultural and industrial development. New roads were built, the country's main airport near Freetown was brought up to international standards and harbours and railways were extended. There were more schools and hospitals and work started on a new university.

Britain has been Sierra Leone's main source of external aid but in recent years the country has attracted government loans or capital investment from the United States, France and West Germany.

In 1962, the Government launched an ambitious £125m sterling ten-year development plan but in 1965 it was decided to reduce its scope and adapt it to a more realistic five-year plan formulated with United Nations help.

In 1966, the country experienced difficulties in servicing debts totalling some £35m, much of it resulting from short and medium term credits extended by suppliers and contractors. Like many other African and European countries it had to resort to the assistance of the International Monetary Fund whose experts requested a drastic limitation of further commitments and other economy measures. At the same time the Government made some attempts to increase revenue through diamond and other mineral exports.

The staple food of Sierra Leone is rice, quantities of which have had to be imported since independence. To remedy this situation the Government set up a Rice Corporation under the Ministry of Trade and Industry and launched a four-year programme aimed at bringing 70,000 acres under rice cultivation and eventually making the country self-sufficient in this staple food.

Britain is Sierra Leone's biggest single trading partner. It took in 1964 more than 66 per cent of its exports and provided about 38 per cent of its imports.

Sierra Leone has a prodigious coastal rainfall. In the rainy season from May to October the Freetown area has about 150 inches.

The Mende and Temne tribes make up about 60 per cent of the population. There are only a few hundred Europeans and about 2,500 Lebano-Syrians. It is estimated there are about 500,000 Moslems in the country and 100,000 Christians, chiefly Creoles. The remainder follow traditional local beliefs.

JUSTICE SAMUEL BANKOLE-JONES

Justice Samuel Bankole-Jones was appointed President of the Sierra Leone Court of Appeal in October, 1965. He is chairman of the Fourah Bay College Council.

Born on August 23, 1911, he was educated at the Methodist Boys' High School in Freetown, where he was head boy in 1928.

He entered Fourah Bay College in 1929, was prizeman during his second and third years and graduated as a Bachelor of Arts in 1932.

For two years he was a teacher at his old school before going to Britain to study law at the Middle Temple. He was called to the Bar in 1938.

Justice Bankole-Jones, who also won a civil law degree and a diploma in education from Durham University, returned to private practice in Sierra Leone; there he taught as a part-time lecturer in law and public administration at Fourah Bay College.

Appointed a police magistrate in 1949 he became a puisne judge ten years later. He was promoted Chief Justice of Sierra Leone in 1963. He represented Sierra Leone in Britain and France at the 1960 centenary celebrations of the maritime laws of England and France.

Justice Bankole-Jones was a member of the United Nations Commission which investigated the death of Secretary-General Dag Hammarskjold in a plane crash near Ndola in Northern Rhodesia (Zambia) in 1961, on his way to cease-fire talks with the Katangese leader, Moise Tshombe.

SIR HENRY BOSTON

Sir Henry Lightfoot Boston was appointed Governor-General and Commander-in-Chief in July, 1962.

He was the first Sierra Leonean to be appointed to the post; before this he had served five years as Speaker of the House of Representatives.

Born on August 19, 1898, he was the youngest of nine children of the Revd N. H. Boston, pastor of St Charles' Church, Regent; he was educated at the Cathedral Boys' School, the Church Missionary Society Grammar School and Fourah Bay College. He graduated as a Bachelor of Arts of Durham University in 1919, won his Master of Arts degree the following year and took a Treasury post in the Sierra Leone Civil Service.

He resigned in 1922 to study law at Lincoln's Inn, London, after passing the intermediate law examination of London University as an external student. He passed his final law examinations with honours and was called to the Bar in January, 1926. Returning home he opened a private law practice and was later appointed City Solicitor in Freetown.

In 1946 Sir Henry was appointed a police magistrate. Eleven years later he became a puisne judge of the Supreme Court.

Queen Elizabeth made him a Commander of the Order of St Michael and St George in 1959 and three years later he was made a Grand Commander of the Order.

As the Deputy Visitor of Fourah Bay College by Royal appointment he confers degrees when the Queen, who is Visitor, is unable to attend convocations.

BISHOP BROSNAHAN

Rt Reverend Dr Thomas Joseph Brosnahan became the Roman

Ella Koblo Gulama

Catholic Bishop of Freetown and Bo in 1952.

He was born in 1905 and ordained a priest in Dublin in 1929.

He became a missionary in Eastern Nigeria in the following year and was the Vicar-General in the archdiocese of Onitsha from 1950–52.

KANDE BUREH

Kande Bureh is known for his work in bringing about a closer relationship between tribes in Sierra Leone. He was appointed Minister of Transport and Communications in 1964.

Born at Mange Bure in the Port Loko district in 1908, he received his education at the local primary school before entering the Methodist Boys' High School in 1921. He became a teacher but left this profession in 1945 and was elected tribal chief of the Temne community in Freetown.

It was in this capacity that he began reorganising various sections of the tribes. His public service included membership of the Government's Town Planning Committee, and membership of a committee on constitutional proposals for the new House of Representatives.

He managed the Wellington Village Approved School in the Freetown rural area and organised the Temne Scholarship Scheme. He was Minister of Works and Housing until 1964.

GERSHON COLLIER

Gershon Beresford Onesimus Collier, Sierra Leone's chief delegate to the United Nations, was appointed Chief Justice in January, 1967.

A close associate of the Prime Minister, Sir Albert Margai, he was elected chairman of the

General Assembly's special committee on colonialism in 1966. He was formerly Ambassador in Washington.

ELLA KOBLO GULAMA

The first woman Cabinet Minister in West Africa, Ella Koblo Gulama, who is a Paramount Chief, became Sierra Leone's Minister of State in May, 1962, and subsequently Minister without Portfolio.

She was born on January 26, 1921 in Moyamba, Kaiyamba chiefdom, Moyamba district.

She was educated at the Harford School for Girls in Moyamba from 1928–38 and at the women's teachers' training college in Freetown from 1938–41. She was the first supervising teacher to be appointed in the province.

A member of the Kaiyamba ruling family, her father and grandfather were also Paramount Chiefs. She was elected Paramount Chief of the Kaiyamba chiefdom in 1953 and four years later became the only woman member of the House of Representatives.

She led Sierra Leone's delegation to the conference of the Council of West African Women held in Conakry in July, 1961, after selection as president of the Sierra Leone Women's Federation.

She was re-elected to Parliament in 1962 and two years later took the Sierra Leone dancing troupe to the United States for the New York World Fair.

Queen Elizabeth made her a Member of the British Empire (MBE) in 1959 and later awarded her the Order of the British Empire (OBE).

She is married to Paramount Chief Bai Koblo.

Salia Jusu-Sheriff

Kutubu Kai-Samba

Maigore Kallon

ADESANYA KWAMINA HYDE

Adesanya Kwamina Hyde, Secretary to the Cabinet (1965) won the DFC (Distinguished Flying Cross) during World War II after taking part in the Allied D-Day invasion of Normandy and 31 bomber raids. He was wounded over France in 1944. He enlisted in the Royal Air Force in 1941 and became a navigator in Bomber Command. He was demobilised in 1947.

Born on September 4, 1915, in Murray Town, he was educated at the Church Missionary Society Grammar School and the Methodist Boys' High School.

He was appointed to the Colonial Administrative Service and in 1962 was made Permanent Secretary to the Ministry of Health.

His hobbies are cricket and shooting.

SALIA JUSU-SHERIFF

Salia Jusu-Sheriff was appointed Minister of Education in 1965.

Born on June 1, 1929, he was educated at Bunumba Central School, Fourah Bay College and King's College, Durham University, England, where he graduated as a BComm in 1954. He later qualified as a chartered accountant.

He practised as a chartered accountant in Sierra Leone until elected to Parliament in 1962, becoming Minister of Natural Resources. In August, 1963, he was given the portfolio of the Trade and Industry Ministry and later became Minister of Health.

Mr Jusu-Sheriff led Sierra Leone's delegation to the United Nations conference on trade and development in Geneva in 1964 and the following year headed a delegation to the Cambridge conference on health.

KUTUBU KAI-SAMBA

A barrister by profession, Katubu Ibrahim Kai-Samba was appointed Minister of Agriculture and Natural Resources in September, 1964.

He was born on March 6, 1931 in Pendumbu, in the Eastern Province of Sierra Leone, and was educated at the Bo Government School and later at Fourah Bay College, the university college of Sierra Leone.

He left for Britain in 1954 to continue his studies at King's College, Durham University, with which the Fourah Bay College is affiliated. Afterwards he read law at Gray's Inn and was called to the Bar in 1960.

In the following year he returned to Sierra Leone and established a legal practice.

He was elected to Parliament in 1962 and two years later received his Cabinet post.

MAIGORE KALLON

Maigore Kallon, made Minister of External Affairs in a Cabinet reshuffle in November, 1965, is also Leader of the House.

Son of the late Section Chief A. J. M. Kallon, of Jawe chiefdom, Kailahun district, he was born on February 1, 1929, at Karlu, in the Jawe chiefdom.

He was educated at the Methodist Central School, Bunumbu, the Bo Government School, and in 1949 entered the University of Pennsylvania in the United States, where he obtained a BA Honours degree in economics and political science and an MA in public finance. From 1955–56 he undertook research in public finance.

Mr Kallon returned home in January, 1957, and was elected to Parliament in that year.

After his re-election to the House of Representatives in the general elections in 1962, he was appointed Government Chief Whip and Leader of the House.

He became Minister of State in 1963.

In the Cabinet reshuffle in May, 1964, following the death of the late Prime Minister, Sir Milton Margai, Mr Kallon was appointed Minister of the Interior and once more was made Leader of the House.

During his tenure of office as Minister of the Interior, he travelled widely throughout the country establishing closer links between the tribal population of the former Protectorate and the more sophisticated society of the former colony. As a hinterland man who spent some of his formative years in Freetown, he feels equally at home in both communities. In his work he is regarded as a leading example of the younger generation of politicians who bridge the gap between the two sections of the population.

Affable, unassuming and highly cultured he has a large number of friends both at home and abroad.

Good-looking and athletic, he is a keen tennis player. His other hobby is his farm and a small but efficient palm tree plantation.

JOE KAMANDA-BONGAY

Mohamed Joe Kamanda-Bongay was appointed Minister of Trade and Industry in November, 1965.

Born on March 15, 1919, the eldest son of the Honourable P. C. Kamanda-Bongay, a noted hereditary chief in the Bo area, he attended the Bo Government School where he was senior prefect.

' He became a sanitary inspector in the Health Department and served in the provinces but resigned in 1951 to enter private business. He was a Bo District councillor and was elected to the town council in 1955, becoming its chairman.

His entry into national politics came with his election to the House of Representatives in 1957 and he was appointed a ministerial secretary

After attending a Commonwealth Parliamentary course in Britain he was appointed Government Chief Whip from 1958–62.

In 1965 he attended the London conference of Commonwealth Ministers of Trade and negotiated agreements for the establishment of new industries in Sierra Leone.

As Minister of Trade and Industry, Mr Kamanda-Bongay has also overall responsibility for the Sierra Leone Rice Corporation established by the Government to make the country self-sufficient in its staple food.

R. G. O. KING

Robert Granville Ojumeri King was appointed Minister of Finance in May, 1964.

Born on November 11, 1906, at Campbell Town, Waterloo Rural District, he was educated at the Free Church School, the Government Model School and the Church Missionary Society School in Freetown.

He took up teaching as a career and became headmaster of Newton Rural School and a member of the Board of Education.

He was also a member of a housing committee and of the local education authority in the Colony rural area.

His parliamentary life began when he was elected as a member for British Koya in 1957. This was followed by appointments as ministerial secretary in the Ministries of Education and Welfare and of Communications.

His first ministerial post was in 1961 when he became Minister of Development; he held this appointment until 1964.

Mr King is a Commander of the Order of the British Empire.

CHIEF RAYMOND KOKER

Paramount Chief Raymond Brima Sese Koker was appointed chairman of Sierra Leone External Communications in 1964. He played a leading role in the constitutional negotiations with Britain that led to independence.

Born on January 17, 1912, he was educated at the Jimmi Rural School, the Zion School in Freetown and the Bo Government School, afterwards working as a draughtsman with the Consolidated African Selection Trust and the Sierra Leone Selection Trust at Yengema.

He was the organising secretary of the Yengema diamond workers' union from 1940–42 and was elected Paramount Chief, Babgo chiefdom in February, 1943. From the Bo District Council, he entered the Protectorate Assembly and was elected to the Legislative Council in 1951.

He was a Minister without Portfolio in 1957 and two years later was appointed leader of Government Business in the House of Representatives. He has also been acting Prime Minister.

He was awarded the Order of the British Empire in 1961.

BRIGADIER DAVID LANSANA

Brigadier David Lansana was appointed Commander of the Royal Sierra Leone military forces on January 1, 1965.

He was the first Sierra Leonean to be commissioned in the Sierra Leone military forces. Born on March 27, 1922, he was educated at the Central School and Union College, Bunumbu. Enlisting in the Army as an officer cadet in August, 1947, he trained with the First Battalion of the Sierra Leone Regiment.

He attended the officer training school at Chester, England, and was commissioned in 1952. Promotion to captain came in 1956 and by July, 1963, he had risen to the rank of lieutenant-colonel. After completing a staff and command course at the British Army Staff College at Camberley, he took command of his old regiment.

He was appointed deputy Force Commander in April, 1964, and promoted to full colonel; shortly afterwards he was awarded the Order of the British Empire.

Brigadier Lansana visited many European countries on military duties and represented Sierra Leone at defence conferences in Africa as well as at a United Nations peace-keeping conference in Canada in 1964.

His wife is the sister of Paramount Chief Madam Ella Koblo Gulama, Minister without Portfolio and only woman member of Parliament. His hobbies are football, tennis, swimming and shooting.

LESLIE W. LEIGH

Leslie William Leigh, first Sierra Leonean Commissioner of Police, was appointed in 1963.

Born on February 23, 1921, of West Indian descent, he was educated at the St Anthony Primary School and the St Edward's Secondary School in Freetown.

He joined the Royal Air Force in 1942 and obtained his pilot's wings in Saskatchewan, Canada, in 1943. The following year he

Sir Albert Margai

was commissioned as a flying officer in Britain and served with the RAF Transport Command in Ghana in 1945.

He joined the Colonial Police service on demobilisation in 1947, returned to Ghana for training and was then appointed assistant superintendent of police in Sierra Leone. He was equerry to President Tubman of Liberia during his state visit to Sierra Leone and was in charge of security arrangements for the visit of Queen Elizabeth and the Duke of Edinburgh in 1961. His father, a Liberian citizen, was a member of the Liberian Legislature.

He was made a member of the Victorian Order (MVO) by the Queen and also won the police medal for distinguished service. He was awarded an OBE in 1965.

His hobbies are shooting fishing, football and cricket.

BERTHAN MACAULAY

Berthan Macaulay, Queen's Counsel, was appointed Attorney-General on November 28, 1963.

Born in Opobo, Nigeria, on November 12, 1929, he was educated at the Government Model School, the Sierra Leone Grammar School in Freetown and the British Universities of Durham and London.

He holds the degrees of Master of Arts (philosophy) from Durham University and Bachelor of Laws, London University, and was the 1952 Lee prizeman of Gray's Inn, London. His legal publications include the 1954 *Questions and Answers on Contracts,* published in London, and he has also contributed to such London publications as *Modern Law Review, Criminal Law Review* and the *Journal of African Law.*

Mr Macaulay returned to Sierra Leone, served on a number of legal bodies and was secretary of the International African Legal Education committee and a member of the executive committee of World Peace Through Law Institute.

He was a member of the Sierra Leone Government delegation to the Commonwealth Prime Ministers Conferences in London and Lagos, Nogeria. He also attended the meetings in Ghana, the United Arab Republic and Ethiopia of the heads of state of the Organisation of African Unity.

His hobbies are writing, gardening and swimming.

SIR ALBERT MARGAI

Sir Albert Michael Margai, Prime Minister of Sierra Leone, and Minister of Defence, succeeded his elder brother, Sir Milton Margai.

The sixth of seven sons of a merchant in the southern province district of Bonthe, Sir Albert is a barrister. Born on October 10, 1910, he was educated at a local Roman Catholic school and at St Edward's School in Freetown.

His first job was as a male nurse in the Government Medical Department in 1931. He later qualified as a druggist. He left the service in November, 1944, to study law in Britain at the Middle Temple. Three years later he was called to the Bar.

He returned home in 1948 to set up in private practice in Freetown – the first barrister from the provinces of Sierra Leone.

He was soon engaged in local politics, became a district councillor and was elected to the Protectorate Assembly. He cooperated with his brother, Sir Milton, in forming the Sierra Leone People's Party in 1951, was elected by the Protectorate Assembly to a seat in the Legisla-

John Nelson-Williams

tive Council in the Colony and was appointed Minister of Local Government and Education. The Council became the House of Representatives under the 1957 constitution.

In the general elections that year he was elected to the House with the biggest majority in the country. The brothers grew apart politically and after a policy clash Sir Albert refused to accept a Ministry in the new Government, left the party in 1958 and formed the People's National Party, opposed to the conservatism of his brother's People's Party.

His political career suffered a temporary set-back when the National Party suffered a crushing defeat in the district council elections in late 1959, winning only 33 out of 324 seats.

The first steps to political reconciliation came with the approach of the Independence conference in London in April, 1960. Sir Albert agreed to bring his new party into an all-party united front organised by his brother for the negotiations with the British Government. The delegates returned with independence assured and Sir Albert and his party rejoined the People's Party. In the ensuing Cabinet reshuffle for a coalition Government, Sir Albert became Minister of Natural Resources. He was Minister of Finance in 1962.

In July of that year, by order of Pope John, he was made a papal knight of the Grand Cross of St Gregory the Great. He was created a Knight Bachelor by Queen Elizabeth in the 1965 New Year's Honours List.

The powerfully-built Prime Minister, who used to be an amateur boxer, showed himself to be one of the most militant of the African leaders in Commonwealth conferences over the Rhodesian independence crisis. A highlight of the January, 1966 Commonwealth Prime Ministers' meeting in Lagos were his sharp clashes with the British Prime Minister, Mr Harold Wilson, over Britain's refusal to use force to topple the white-minority Rhodesian regime.

His hobbies are football, tennis and cricket.

JOHN NELSON-WILLIAMS

John Arnold Nelson-Williams was appointed Minister of Information and Broadcasting for a second time in May, 1964, following a Cabinet reshuffle on the death of Sir Milton Margai.

Born in 1932, he was the son of the late Mr T. E. Nelson-Williams, one of the leading barristers in Sierra Leone.

He was educated at the Methodist Boys' High School, the Prince of Wales School, Freetown, and Igbobi College in Nigeria.

Before and even since he became fully involved in politics, Mr Nelson-Williams has been a prolific writer and regular contributor to the local press.

He took to politics early, and was co-founder of the United Sierra Leone Progressive Party in 1954. He became the first national secretary-general of the party and was elected to the House of Representatives in 1957. He proved himself a forceful debater.

In August 1959, he broke away from the UPP and with four other parliamentarians founded the Independent Progressive Party.

Mr Nelson-Williams was appointed ministerial secretary to the Ministries of Education, Communications and Social Welfare in June, 1960. After the formation of the coalition

Government and for most of the following twelve months he he was acting Minister of these Ministries.

He retained his Parliamentary seat in the 1962 elections.

DR DAVIDSON NICOL

Dr Davidson Nicol was appointed Principal of Fourah Bay College, the University College of Sierra Leone, in 1960.

He was born in 1924 and began his education at the Government Model School and the Prince of Wales School in Freetown. He was a schoolteacher in 1942.

Dr Nicol went to Britain to study at London and Cambridge Universities and had a distinguished academic career, being six times prize-winner and taking degrees in natural sciences, medicine and philosophy.

He held research and resident posts at the London Hospital, went to Nigeria as lecturer in Ibadan University's faculty of medicine and was also an honorary district medical officer in Nigeria.

Dr Nicol has also toured abroad as a guest lecturer in universities in the United States, Germany and Ghana.

His appointments include those of consultant pathologist to the Sierra Leone Government, member of the Public Service Commission and director of the National Bank of Sierra Leone.

Dr Nicol has been chairman of various educational conferences and associations. Four years after his appointment as Principal of Fourah Bay College he was made a Companion of the Order of St Michael and St George by Queen Elizabeth.

DR MOSES SCOTT

The Rt Revd Dr Moses Christopher Omobiala Scott was consecrated Anglican Bishop of Sierra Leone in 1961.

He was born on August 18, 1911 at Calabar, in Nigeria, and was educated at the Sierra Leone Grammar School and Fourah Bay College. He became a school teacher and a missionary in 1943, was ordained as a deacon and later as a priest but continued to teach until 1946.

He was appointed pastor of Bo and a provincial superintendent of church work in 1950. In that year he entered the London College of Divinity in England and read for the diploma in theology. From 1952–54 he served as a curate at Grappenhall, near Warrington, England, and then returned to Bo.

He was a town councillor at Bo and a member of the local education authority.

He became Archdeacon of Bo in 1958 and was consecrated bishop three years later.

CHIEF BAI SHERBO YUMKELLA

Paramount Chief Bai Sherbo Yumkella II was named Minister of State in June, 1962.

Born in 1922 in Kychom, Samu chiefdom in the Kambia district, he was educated at the Bo Government School and entered the Sierra Leone Civil Service in 1942.

He resigned in 1947 to pursue higher studies and two years later was elected regent chief of the Samu chiefdom. He won the chieftancy in April, 1953.

He has served on various public boards and committees since 1952 and was chairman of the Local Education Authority, Kambia district, from 1957–62.

He was a leading figure in the Kambia District Council before his election to Parliament in May, 1957.

Dr D. L. Sumner

SIAKA PROBYN STEVENS

Siaka Probyn Stevens became leader of the Opposition All People's Congress Party in Parliament following the 1962 general election.

Born in the Moyamba district of the Protectorate on August 24, 1905, he was educated at the Albert Academy in Freetown.

He joined the Sierra Leone police force in 1923, rose to the rank of sergeant and then, in 1930, became a railway construction worker, later station master. His long association with trade unionism began in 1943, when he helped to form the United Mineworkers Union, later becoming its general secretary.

He served as a district and city councillor and in 1945 was appointed to the Protectorate Assembly to represent workers' interests. Two years later he won a British Council scholarship and studied industrial relations at Ruskin College, Oxford.

Elected to the Legislative Council by the Protectorate Assembly in 1951, when he was a member of the Sierra Leone People's Party, led by Dr Milton Margai, he became Minister of Lands, Mines and Labour. He lost his seat, however, in the general election of 1957.

He left the People's Party to join the breakaway People's National Party formed by Dr Margai's brother, Albert, and became its deputy leader.

He was a member of the United National Front delegation formed by all the political parties for the 1960 London conference on an independence constitution.

Mr Stevens disagreed sharply with some of the conference decisions, refused to sign the agreements and was soon after expelled from membership of the People's National Party.

He then formed his own All People's Congress Party in 1960, campaigned forcefully against his political rivals and was soon in trouble with the authorities following demonstrations and street disturbances. He was sentenced to imprisonment in June, 1961 for libel and conspiracy but the conviction was quashed on appeal in July. His party contested the 1962 post-independence elections in alliance with the now-dissolved progressive independence movement.

He is a former mayor of Freetown.

DR D. L. SUMNER

Dr Doyle Leonard Sumner, a Masters of Arts and Bachelor of Science, became Minister of Works in a Cabinet reshuffle in November 1965.

He was born on February 19, 1907 at Shenge in the Moyamba district, received his primary education at schools in Freetown, Bonthe, Pendembu and Shenge and attended Albert Academy school from 1922–25.

Dr Sumner was actively associated with educational development and in the period 1946–57 he was president of the teachers' organisation, a member of the Board of Education and of the students' advisory committee.

He represented Sierra Leone in the United States, where he was a class valedictorian at Lincoln University, Pennsylvania.

He was elected to Sierra Leone's Parliament in 1957, was appointed Minister of Communications and became Minister of Health in 1961.

BANJA TEJAN-SIE

The Speaker in the House of Representatives since 1962 has been Banja Tejan-Sie.

Ahmad Wurie

Born on August 7, 1917, he was educated at the Bo School and the Prince of Wales School in Freetown. He first worked as a railway station clerk, then as a male nurse in the Medical Department from 1940–46. He studied at the London School of Economics and in 1951 was called to the Bar.

Entering politics, he became vice-president of the Sierra Leone People's Party from 1953–56. He served on a commission on electoral reform and was a police magistrate in the Eastern and Northern Provinces until 1958.

He was a Sierra Leone representative at a London conference in 1959 on the future of law in Africa and became a senior police magistrate for the Provinces in 1961.

In 1962, Mr Tejan-Sie led Sierra Leone delegations to the middle-level manpower conference in Puerto Rico and to the Commonwealth Parliamentary Association conference in Nigeria.

PETER LOUIS TUCKER

Appointed Secretary to the Prime Minister on April 18, 1966, Peter Louis Tucker is one of the most important officials in Sierra Leone.

As the Prime Minister's right hand man he is concerned with all aspects of Government activity.

He was born in 1927 at Bonthe Sherbro, Southern Province. Educated locally and at Freetown, he entered Fourah Bay College in 1948. He graduated

with a BA degree three years later and obtained a diploma in education in 1952. He then went into teaching and in 1955 became headmaster of Kenema Secondary School. In 1957 he obtained an MA at Durham University and later became an education officer in Sierra Leone. In 1960 he took a further course at Oxford University, then returned home to take charge of training and recruitment in the Ministry of Education.

In March, 1963, he was appointed Establishment Secretary.

AHMAD WURIE

Ahmad Wurie, Minister of the Interior (1965), began his working life as a teacher.

The son of the late Paramount Chief Bai Sekka Bundu of Gbinti, he was born on August 27, 1898, and educated at the school for the sons of chiefs at Bo.

He was the first African acting principal of the Bo school in 1933 and headmaster of Koyeima school in 1935. Then followed posts as inspector of schools and education officer and provincial education secretary in the Northern Province. By 1953 he was a Port Loko district councillor and chairman of the Port Loko Education Authority.

His work in the educational field was crowned with his appointment as Minister of Education in 1961.

Mr Wurie was made an MBE for his services to education in 1955 and became a Commander of the Order in 1964.

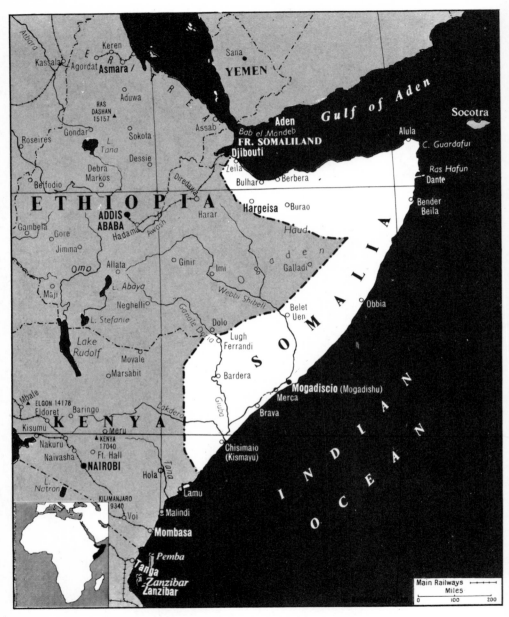

Somalia covers an area of over 246,000 square miles known as the 'Horn of Africa'. It is bounded on the north by French Somaliland and the Gulf of Aden, on the west by Ethiopia, on the south by Kenya and on the east, around the 'Horn', by the Indian Ocean. The Somali population is estimated at three million. There has never been an official census. The capital is Mogadishu (Mogadiscio). Somalia is essentially a pastoral country. Four-fifths of the people depend on the rearing of cattle, sheep, goats and camels. Agricultural produce includes bananas, sugar cane, maize, sesame, groundnuts and cotton.

Somalia

The Somali Republic came into being on July 1, 1960,
as a result of the merger of the British Somaliland
Protectorate, which became independent on June 26, 1960,
and the Italian Trusteeship Territory of Somalia.
The constitution established under the Italian trusteeship,
adopted by the two regions in an Act of Union and
approved by national referendum in June, 1961, provides
for a President and a single Chamber elected by universal
adult suffrage. The executive consists of a Prime Minister
and his Ministers.

The first European foothold in Somalia was in 1840,
when Britain signed treaties with Somali sultans for the
occupation of the strategic coast opposite Aden, on the
route to India.

The northern region of the country became the British
Protectorate of Somaliland in 1887. A year later Britain
and France agreed on the establishment of the enclave
of French Somaliland. In 1894 a tripartite accord
established Italian control of the southern part of the
territory to a point south of Mogadishu.

The Somali Republic is a Moslem state, but one of the
first articles of its constitution stipulates that all citizens
shall have equal rights and responsibilities before the law
without distinction of race, national origin or religion.
Another article declares that the Republic 'shall promote
by legal and peaceful means, the union of Somali
territories'.

The Somali Republic, which broke off relations
with Britain in March, 1963, claims that on six
occasions Britain has 'sacrificed Somali territory for
reasons of political expediency', ceding it to France,
Ethiopia and Kenya.

The five points of the star on the national flag are
symbols of the components of the state as claimed by the
Somalis: British Somaliland, French Somaliland, Italian
Somaliland, land allegedly conceded by Britain to
Ethiopia and the 'Northern Frontier District' in Kenya.
The ruling Somali Youth League which at the end of
1966 held nearly 80 of the 123 seats in Parliament,
stands for peaceful reunion of all Somali territories
and repudiates tribal and religious distinctions.

Somalia is a country with potential resources but remains

Side by side in
Mogadishu stand the
twin towers of the
Roman Catholic
Cathedral and the
gleaming minaret of
the nearby Mosque

as yet underdeveloped. Prime Minister Abdirazak Haji
Hussein said in December, 1966: 'Our country is
not poor, but the fact remains that we have not yet
proved capable of fully developing our national
resources.'

Urging that agriculture should be developed, he said
that only a twelfth of the cultivable land available
had so far been utilised.

Transport facilities in Somalia are inadequate and costs
are high. Of about 7,500 miles of roads, only 625 miles
or so were surfaced with tarmac at the end of 1966.

Above: White buildings forming part of Mogadishu, seen from the carved balustrade of the sea-wall

Below: A ceremonial charge by Somali tribesmen

There are no railways and no adequate sea-port, though Kismayu (Chisimaio) in the south and Berbera in the Gulf of Aden are being developed. Mogadishu is linked by air with East African, Middle Eastern and European capitals.

In the first six years of independence, the Somali Republic made great efforts and achieved some solid progress in the development of agricultural production and the livestock industry. Roads were built and communications improved.

The judiciary was remodelled to some extent, special

attention was given to internal and external security problems and the Armed Forces were substantially strengthened.

The United States, the Soviet Union, West Germany and Italy all helped. So did the European Economic Community, of which Somalia is an associate member. The United Nations, in an advisory capacity, have maintained numerous missions.

In view of the small size of the population and the relatively large area in which they have to live, the country is unlikely to have a population problem in the forseeable future. The birthrate is not known, in the absence of census information, although an official handbook says it is probably high. Due to poor health services, however, the death rate is also likely to be high. The services are being improved and this will lead to an increase in population growth.

There was a budget deficit of about £1,250,000 in 1966 and the Government took special measures to meet the contingency. They cut the pay of civil servants and other government employees and government posts considered redundant were abolished.

ABDIRAZAK HAJI HUSSEIN

Abdirazak Haji Hussein

The Prime Minister of the Somali Republic, Abdirazak Haji Hussein is also secretary-general of the Somali Youth League, the ruling party formed in 1943, which stands for peaceful re-union of all Somali territories.

The programme he presented to the National Assembly makes the cause of national unity the principal motive of Government action, present and future.

Fluent in Arabic, English and Italian, Abdirazak was born in the Galkayo district in 1924. After attending Koranic schools he educated himself up to inter-mediate level.

He joined the Somali Youth League in 1944 and in 1950 spent eight months in prison on political charges.

In June, 1955, the SYL sent him to the United Nations to present a petition and at the end of that year made him their president. He entered Parliament in 1959.

After independence (July 1, 1960) he was appointed Minister of the Interior. Later there came criticism from various parts of the country and in a Cabinet re-shuffle he changed his portfolio to Communications and Public Works.

In the general election of March 31, 1964, he went back to Parliament and was made Prime Minister by the President despite a unanimous recom-mendation by the SYL that Dr Abdulrashid Ali Shermarke should occupy the premiership for a second term.

Abdulkadir Mohamed
Aden

Abdullahi Issa
Mohamud

Abdirazak's first Government failed to obtain a vote of confidence in the House. Nevertheless he was nominated Prime Minister again and a further vote of confidence went in his favour by 91 votes out of 123.

ABDULKADIR MOHAMED ADEN

'A man or iron will who can face any critics' is a description which has been applied to Abdulkadir Mohamed Aden.

When he was made Minister of the Interior in March, 1964, he was fiercely attacked by many members of Parliament. They resented his being placed in such a key position. He was known as a man who favoured regionalism and federalism, whereas his critics wanted a minister who would promote unity and centralisation.

Abdulkadir is from the Baidoa area of the Upper Juba, and it was the support of about 20 MPs from the Upper and Lower Juba that enabled him to keep his seat in the Cabinet.

He joined the Somali Youth League in 1944, the year following its beginning as an underground independence movement, served for some time on its central committee, then became associated in 1950 with the Hisbia Digil wa Mirifleh Somalo (later renamed Hisbia Dastoor Mustaquilla Somalo). Of this important regional-ethnic organisation, based on the southern population, he became secretary-general and twice attended sessions of the United Nations Trusteeship Council in New York where he, along with other representatives of now defunct parties, demanded that Somalia should stay longer under Italian administration.

He served as Vice-President of the Territorial Assembly,

from May, 1959 to July, 1960.

On the eve of independence he returned to the League and became Minister of Finance in Dr Abdulrashid Ali Shermarke's Government. When Abdirazak Haji Hussein succeeded Shermarke, the appointment of Abdulkadir as Minister of the Interior was one reason, among others, why the new Government failed to secure a vote of confidence.

Abdulkadir decided in 1958 to support federation, most probably so that his region could develop and utilise its agricultural and other economic resources by itself.

He was born in November, 1919, studied at Koranic schools, then at Italian schools in Afgoi and Mogadishu. In 1952 he went to Cairo as student at an Egyptian secondary school, later taking the Lower Cambridge Certificate under the auspices of the British Council.

ABDULLAHI ISSA MOHAMUD

One of the 13 who founded the Somali Youth League in 1943, Abdullahi Issa Mohamud, a future prime minister, became its secretary-general in 1947.

The following year he was at the United Nations, then meeting in Paris, as the League's representative, asking for a four-power trusteeship for his country. He failed in his mission, however, and in 1950 the Italians returned.

In 1953, when Haji Mohamed Hussein left for Cairo, he took over the SYL leadership with Aden Abdullah Osman. In 1956, when the SYL won a clear majority in the territorial elections, he became Prime Minister and Minister of Justice, proving himself an enlightened and moderate leader, anxious to

397

Sheikh Abdulle
Mohamoud

Dr Abdulrashid Ali
Shermarke

modernise the country in every way and prepared to cooperate closely with the Italian Government.

In 1959, he was re-elected Prime Minister, but was bitterly attacked by Hussein, on the latter's return from Cairo, for his cooperation with the Italian Administration.

When the British Somaliland Protectorate and Italian Somalia became independent on July 1, 1960, he was named Minister for Foreign Affairs, a portfolio he held until March 30, 1064.

He was made Minister for Health and Labour when Abdirazak Haji Hussein succeeded Dr Abdulrashid Ali Shermarke (Prime Minister from July, 1960 –March, 1964) and formed his first Government. He was transferred to the Ministry of Industry and Commerce in a Cabinet reshuffle in March, 1966, having retained his seat in Parliament since the first Legislative Assembly in 1956.

Abdullahi was born in 1922 at Agfoi on the banks of the Shebelle River near Mogadishu. He was educated at a Koranic school at Mogadishu then at the Italian Government school. In 1937 he entered the Italian Government service as a clerk, but, losing his job when the British military Administration took over, he went into business in Beledwein.

ABDULLE MOHAMOUD

Sheikh Abdulle Mohamoud, the Minister for Public Works, was born at Galkayu in 1923. Starting his primary schooling in his own town, he studied in Mogadishu from 1942–46 acquiring a sound knowledge of Islamic culture.

Receiving a diploma from Mogadishu's Political Administration School in 1954, he went

to Italy for further studies, and took a degree at Rome University.

He was made head of the Economic Affairs Department on his return to Somalia in 1957.

Elected as SYL candidate for Dusa Mareb while still studying in Italy, he became chairman of the committee which drafted the Republic's Constitution.

Dr Abdulrashid Ali Shermarke's first Government in 1960 made him Minister for Industry and Commerce–a post from which he resigned in 1962.

Securing his seat in Parliament in the 1964 general elections, Sheikh Mohamoud was made Minister for Public Works and Telecommunications in Premier Abdirazak Haji Hussein's Government in August, 1964.

This Ministry was divided in two–Public Works, and Transport and Telecommunications–in a major Cabinet reshuffle early in 1966.

DR ABDULRASHID ALI SHERMARKE

Dr Abdulrashid Ali Shermarke was Prime Minister from July, 1960 to June, 1964, during which time he visited Moscow, Peking, Washington and London.

Following a return visit to Somalia by the Chinese Prime Minister, Chou-en-lai, in February, 1964, Dr Shermarke said the Chinese were increasing their aid. In an interview he declared it was 'a great injustice' to suggest Somalia was going over to the Communists. Communism, he added, was against the religion and especially the traditions of the people. The nomadic Somalis were accustomed to the idea of private property and were 'too individualistic' to be Communists.

Born in 1919, Dr Shermarke took his doctor's degree in political science at Rome in 1958.

Adan Issak Ahmed

Aden Abdulla Osman

Ahmed Yusuf Duale

ADAN ISSAK AHMED

Adan Issak Ahmed, appointed Minister for Transport and Tele-communications in 1966, was born at Borama (Northern Region) in 1921. He served in the Army from 1943–45, entered the teaching profession in 1946 and joined the staff of Burao Inter-mediate School in 1957.

A two-year scholarship took him to the United Kingdom in 1960.

He joined the Foreign Ministry in 1961 as Cultural Counsellor at the Somali Embassy in Moscow–a post which he held until he resigned in 1963 to take part in the 1964 (March 30) general election campaign.

He was appointed Defence Minister in Premier Abdirazak Haji Hussein's first Government in August, 1964.

ADEN ABDULLA OSMAN

The President of the Republic, Aden Abdulla Osman was born in 1908 at Beledwein, and spent his childhood in conditions of great poverty. Later, a kindly Italian gave him some education and taught him how to use a typewriter.

He served the Italian Admini-stration from 1929–41, when he left to establish his own business in Beledwein. In 1944 he became an active member of the Somali Youth League, but was one of those most strongly in favour of cooperation with the Italian Administration. He believed it would advance independence, and he showed himself unequivo-cally opposed to the policy of Mohamed Haji Hussein. When Hussein left for Cairo in 1953, Aden took over the leadership of the League with Abdullah Issa Mohamud, and became President of the League from 1954–56. After the 1956 elections, he was

made President of the Somali Legislative Assembly. In 1958, when Hussein left the League altogether in order to form his own party, Aden Abdulla Osman once again became its President.

When British Somaliland and Italian Somalia became inde-pendent, the two Territorial Assemblies merged and Aden Abdulla Osman was elected provisional President of the new Somali Republic for one year.

The United Territorial Assem-blies then adopted a constitution which was accepted by the people in a general referendum, and Aden was re-elected President for a six-year term on July 4, 1961.

AHMED YUSUF DUALE

Widely travelled as Foreign Minister of Somalia, Ahmed Yusuf Duale has represented his country at many important conferences, ranging from small regional African 'summits' to the United Nations General Assembly.

He received the portfolio in August, 1964, and has held office through every Cabinet reshuffle since Abdirazak Haji Hussein came to office.

He was elected a Member of Parliament for Gebileh Hargeisa in March, 1964.

He was born at Hargeisa in 1935. He completed his elemen-tary education there and at Sheikh and in 1951 joined the Bakhta-Rida, the teachers' insti-tute in the Sudan where he successfully completed a two-year course.

Returning to the former British Somaliland, he worked as a teacher until May, 1956. Next month he went to Cairo for a two-year course in journalism. In 1958 when the newspaper *Al-Liwa* (The Flag) appeared,

Ali Omer Shego

Kenadid Ahmed
Yusuf

he was number two on the editorial staff. He became editor-in-chief the following year and remained so until January, 1963, when the newspaper ceased publication.

ALI OMER SHEGO

Ali Omer Shego, Minister for Finance, was born at Mogadishu in July, 1924.

Gaining a diploma from Mogadishu's Political Administration School, he went for advanced studies to Italy.

He was a district commissioner in 1955–56 and was made Benadir's Governor in 1958–60, during which time he was also the president of the Somali Olympic Committee.

As a high official of the Foreign Ministry, Shego was appointed permanent representative to the European Economic Community (EEC) in Brussels.

Successful in the 1964 general elections, he was made Minister for Justice in Premier Abdirazak's first Cabinet in August that year and was transferred to the Finance Ministry early in 1966.

KENADID AHMED YUSUF

The Minister for Education, Kenadid Ahmed Yusuf, was born at Qalaafo (Ogadenia under Ethiopian rule) in 1928. He attended Koranic schools, then went to Italian primary schools in Mogadishu. In 1945 he studied at institutes established by the British Administration.

He joined the Somali Youth League in 1946, and won a competition for a customs officer's post in 1951.

He won a teacher's diploma and was sent to Italy for an advanced course. He graduated in political science in 1958–61.

Returning home, Kenadid worked for a while in the Finance Ministry and was appointed Mayor Extraordinary of Mogadishu. His achievements in that post won him high praise.

He was elected for the Upper Juba region in the 1964 general elections (March 30). He was appointed Minister of Education the following August and kept the portfolio despite numerous student demonstrations demanding more schools. He blamed the Government for not allocating enough money to meet the rapidly increasing needs of education.

GENERAL MOHAMED ABSHIR MUSSE

The Somali Police Force is regarded as one of the best of its kind in Africa. General Mohamed Abshir Musse is recognised as its organiser. He was appointed Commander on July 1, 1960.

He was born in the district of Obbia in 1925. Having completed his Koranic schooling at the age of 18, he joined the Somali Gendarmerie in February, 1943, and, after various promotions, attained the rank of full inspector in 1947.

In April, 1952, he completed four months' intensive training at the Somali Police Training School in a preparatory course for officer cadets which he successfully passed. From August to December, 1952, he went through the first and second phases for officers in training in Florence and Rome, Italy.

From 1954 to 1960 he passed quickly through the ranks, from junior lieutenant to general, and between 1950 and 1958 he had been officer in charge of more than six police divisions at various places in the Somali Republic. He was nominated Commander of the Somali Police Force on the day of independence.

Mohamoud Abdi Nur

Yusuf Adan Boukah

During the academic year 1962–63, General Mohamed Abshir Musse attended the University of Princeton, USA, for a course in general education and in April, 1966, completed a four-month course of higher education in Washington at the International School of Police.

He has participated in various international conferences on the organization of police in the USA, Europe, Africa and the Middle East.

He is fluent in Italian, English and Arabic.

MOHAMOUD ABDI NUR

Mohamoud Abdi Nur, Minister for Agriculture and Animal Husbandry, was born in the Upper Juba region in 1923. He studied first at the Koranic schools and then at government institutions.

He joined the Somali Youth League in 1944 and soon organised several local party branches in the Upper Juba region. A member of the Advisory Council for the region in 1946–47, he was the SYL secretary in Baidao for many years.

In 1951 he was appointed to the Territorial Council, and five years later was elected a member of the Legislative Assembly for the Baidao constituency.

Minister for General Affairs in the first Somali Government from 1956–59, he became Minister for Public Works and Telecommunications in Dr Abdulrashid Ali Shermarke's second Government.

In 1962 he became Minister for the Interior as well as a member of the SYL Central Committee.

After the 1964 general elections he was made Minister of State for the Prime Minister's Office and was transferred to the

Ministry of Agriculture in a major Cabinet reshuffle early in 1966.

MUKHTAR MOHAMED HUSSEIN

Sheikh Mukhtar Mohamed Hussein, elected President of the National Assembly on March 8, 1966, was born in 1912 at Baidoa and studied at Koranic schools.

Son of a businessman, he began to help his father at the age of 14. In 1935 he joined the Higher Islamic Institute, and on completing his education there was appointed consultant in Islamic Jurisdiction at Wajid, Baidoa.

Sheikh Mukhtar joined the Somali Youth League in 1947, was elected secretary of the party's local branch in Huddur (Baidoa) in 1949; he became a regional adviser, then a Sharia Judge, in Mogadishu in 1953.

In the 1959 elections he was elected SYL deputy in Huddur constituency and became Under-Secretary to the Ministry of Justice and Religious Affairs. In the 1964 elections he secured a seat in the Assembly and was elected Vice-President of the National Assembly, later taking over as President.

YUSUF ADAN BOUKAH

Appointed Minister of Information in 1964, Yusuf Adan Boukah was born in Burao in 1930. At the age of 13 he entered elementary school in Hargiesa; completing his intermediate education in Sheikh, near Burao, in 1949, he became a teacher.

He was elected MP in the 1964 elections as a member of the now defunct United Somali Party (USP), from which he resigned.

He has attended many international conferences, including the UN General Assembly.

The Sudan, the largest country in Africa, covers an area of 967,500 square miles, mostly desert. The population is about 14 million, an estimate on January 1, 1964, put it at 13,011,000. About 11 million are thought to be Arab by blood and language and Islamic by faith, tradition and way of life. Three million are thought to be Christian or pagan people of negro origin, inhabiting the three southern provinces of Bahr El Ghazal, Equatoria and the Upper Nile. The capital is Khartoum.

The Sudan's economy is predominantly agricultural. Cotton is by far the most important cash crop.

402

Sudan

The Sudan, ruled by a British-Egyptian Condominium since
1899, became a sovereign independent republic on January
1, 1956.
On November 17, 1958, the Army seized power in a
bloodless *coup* and established a military regime.
A popular revolution deposed the regime on October 21,
1964, and restored civilian rule.

Present-day Sudan is a constitutional republic which, it
might be said, was born out of international conflict.
The country entered a lingering period of internal conflict
even before it became independent.
Geographically, it is the largest country in Africa. It has
also been described as 'Africa in miniature', for its
far-flung territory has infinite variations, from sandy desert
to sub-tropical forest, and its population includes almost
600 tribes comprising 56 tribal groups. Its capital,
Khartoum, is at the confluence of two great life-giving
rivers, the Blue Nile coming from Ethiopia, and the
White Nile flowing from Lake Victoria in the south.
Historically, the area now forming the Sudan was made
up of a number of independent kingdoms, sultanates, and
the like, until Mohammed Ali Pasha, Viceroy of Egypt
under the Turkish Empire, sent forces to conquer it in
1822. He unified the country with its present boundaries
for the first time and established a Turco-Egyptian rule
which continued for several decades. Then in 1881–82
Mohammed Ahmed raised the standard of revolt.
Known as The Mahdi, or The Divinely-Guided One, he
was backed by tens of thousands of Sudanese, who
overthrew the Egyptians in a great religious crusade, and
ran the country until Anglo-Egyptian forces under Lord
Kitchener of Britain reconquered it in 1898. In that year
the modern Sudan was born.
The Mahdi himself died in 1885, but a son was born to
him posthumously and kept alive the banner of Mahdism,
which was to become the most powerful religious sect in
the Sudan under the name of Ansar. In 1899, an
Anglo-Egyptian agreement was signed for the country to
be administered as a Condominium (or co-dominion
under these two Powers) but more trouble developed in
1924 when the British Governor-General, Sir Lee Stack,

was assassinated in Cairo and Egyptian troops in the
Sudan defected and were withdrawn. From then on the
Sudan remained a Condominium, but was fundamentally
administered by the British, although Egyptian troops
returned to the country after the Anglo-Egyptian Treaty
of Friendship of 1936. At that time the Sudan was
administered by a British Governor-General with an
Executive Council, but World War II, in which the
Sudanese fought with the Allies, saw the swift
development of political articulation among educated
Sudanese and their closer association with Government.
Thus, in 1944, an Advisory Council for the Northern
Sudan was set up, with Sudanese among the members
whose task was to advise the Governor-General on various
domestic matters. Then came a Legislative Assembly in
1948, which also included members representing the
more backward negroid Southern Sudan. In 1953 came
a period of internal self-government, with the first
Sudanese Parliament meeting on January 1, 1954, then
self-determination, and finally complete independence
from the Condominium Powers from January 1, 1956.
In the meantime, two major political parties had emerged,
both with powerful religious backing. One was Umma,
which is traditionally supported by the Mahdists, and the
other was the Ashigga, which later developed into the
National Unionist Party, and was supported by another
strong religious sect, the Khatmia under Sayed Ali
Mirghani. Many other political groups have been born
since, but these two parties have always dominated
Sudanese political life, with religion always influential in
the background.
Independence was not to come easily for the Sudan.
In August, 1955, Southern Sudanese troops mutinied
amid rumours that when independence came the country
would be dominated by the Moslem Northerners.
The aftermath of that mutiny was to linger on in the form
of strife and bloodshed in the South for many years, with
some dissidents seeking either complete autonomy or
some kind of federation.
Then, in November, 1958, the Army in the north revolted
against the Government, seized power in a bloodless
coup, and imposed a military regime under General
Ibrahim Abboud, who became President, which was to
last until October, 1964. The Army's declared aim was to

Secondary school girls travelling on the school bus in Omdurman

end the political corruption and a deteriorating economic situation which it said had characterised the first years of independence under the civilian Parliament. Abboud abolished Parliament and political parties, initially banned all trade unions, reaffirmed a foreign policy of strict non-alignment, took steps to increase exports of cotton, the Sudan's major export commodity and its economic life-blood, and introduced a massive 10-year plan of social and economic development, to which many overseas countries and organisations contributed millions of pounds.

Then in October, 1964, Abboud's regime was deposed by a people's revolt and the nation returned to civilian rule. Elections were held in 1965 again for the first time in over six years, Parliament was restored in the shape of a Constituent Assembly, which still has the task of drafting a constitution, the political parties came back and a Supreme State Council was set up. Its elected President was Sayed Ismail El Azhari, the veteran leader of the National Unionists, who was the Sudan's first Prime Minister in 1954. His party, however, failed to win

405

the elections in 1965. Umma gained a majority and a coalition was formed with Sayed Mohamed Ahmed Mahgoub, a veteran Umma politician, as Prime Minister. In July, 1966, Mahgoub was defeated in the Constituent Assembly on a censure motion put forward by members of his own party, and Sayed Sadik el Mahdi, president of Umma and a direct descendant of the Mahdi who revolted against the Egyptians, was elected the new Prime Minister. At 30 he was one of the world's youngest-ever prime ministers. One of his first acts was to announce a new policy for marketing the Sudan's cotton in an effort to stem a drastic decline in the country's foreign exchange reserves, boost exports, and reinvigorate the economy. Then, in October and November, he visited the Southern Sudan, still torn by conflict, and announced that a national committee drawn from all political parties was working on the final stages of a new framework for establishing future political relations between the north and the south, restoring peace and developing the economy. He reaffirmed his Government's pledge to grant an amnesty to all refugees returning to the south – late in 1966 it was estimated there were about 125,000 in neighbouring countries – and said new elections would be held in 1967.

Lt-Gen Ibrahim Abboud

LT-GEN IBRAHIM ABBOUD

When the Sudanese Army took over the country in a bloodless *coup* on November 17, 1958, Lieutenant-General Ibrahim Abboud, widely respected on account of his seniority over all the other officers, was made President of the Supreme Council.

He was in power for six years, until October, 1964, during which time he sought to improve the nation's economy by increasing sales of its major export commodity, cotton, diversifying its crops and extending industrialisation. To this end he accepted foreign aid whether from East or West, but always maintained a declared foreign policy of strict neutrality.

In his six years' rule he probably became the Sudan's most travelled statesman, visiting Moscow and Washington, London and Peking, New Delhi and Karachi, as well as many parts of Europe and many places in Africa. In 1961 a massive 10-year plan of economic and social development was launched, and to this overseas countries and organisations contributed many millions of pounds.

Abboud's regime was strict and determined. He banned political parties, dissolved Parliament, and imposed many of the restrictions usually associated with a state of emergency. He always pledged, however, that he would give the Sudan a form of democracy best suited to it, and half-way through his regime introduced a pyramid type of democratic administration based on part-elected, part-nominated local councils, provincial councils and a central council. Eventually, civil servants, frustrated politicians and the urban population in particular, found some of his restrictions irksome, and his overthrow in a civilian revolt in 1964, when his administration seemed to be a fixture, is sometimes referred to as 'the Popular October Revolution'.

Fifty people were killed. Abboud was under house arrest for a period, but he was soon at liberty and living in an expensive house in Khartoum. During some of the official inquiries after his downfall, he denied that he gained power in a military *coup d'état*. He said he was ordered to take over the country by Brigadier Abdalla Khalil, then Prime Minister and Minister of Defence, but retired from the Army.

General Abboud was born on October 26, 1900 at Mohamed-Gol in the Red Sea, the son of a junior official in the British administration.

Of Shaigi origin, he became a second lieutenant in the Sudanese battalions of the Egyptian Army in July, 1918. For the next seven years he served as a military engineer, and when the Sudan Defence Force was formed in 1925, he transferred to the Sudan Service Corps. In 1949 he was the first Sudanese to be appointed Officer Commanding the Sudan Service Corps. As the force became more Sudanised, he was promoted to major-general, and became assistant to the commander-in-chief (August, 1954).

ABDEL SALAM ABOUL ELA

A millionaire in his fifties and popular for his modesty and sense of humour, Abdel Salam Aboul Ela occupies a key position in his country's economic fortunes.

He is the head of the leading Sudanese business-house of Aboul Ela, which deals in almost everything, but is especially a producer and exporter of cotton.

For many years he has been chairman of the Sudan Chamber of Commerce.

MOHAMED AHMED ABU RANAT

Mohamed Ahmed Abu Ranat, born in 1905, was the first Sudanese Chief Justice. He took over from the last British Legal Secretary when his country attained independence in 1956.

He was regarded as the principal adviser to General Abboud's military regime and the chief architect in the planning of its constitutional and legal structure. For this reason he retired when the regime fell in 1964.

He was chosen by the British Government to be a member of a constitutional committee for South Arabia. He declined this office when asked to do so by the Sudanese Government, following representations by South Arabian national organisations which opposed the setting up of the committee.

A jurist with an international reputation, Abu Ranat is a member of the United Nations Human Rights Committee, and took part in commissions that reshaped the judicial machinery in many African countries.

IBRAHIM AHMED

Ibrahim Ahmed, a leading educationist, was the first Sudanese students' warden at the then Gordon Memorial College, now the University of Khartoum. After independence he became president of the Council.

Leaving the University, Ibrahim Ahmed entered business,

Jamal Mohamed
Ahmed

and as an Umma Party supporter became Finance Minister in the second national Government.

During the military regime Ibrahim Ahmed, who is a Nubian, helped to create the first Sudan Commercial Bank, of which he is managing director.

He was born in 1901.

JAMAL MOHAMED AHMED

One of the leading thinkers and educationists in the Sudan, Jamal Mohamed Ahmed went as ambassador to London in 1965, after being the first Sudanese diplomat in Arab countries and a representative at the United Nations.

He has long been regarded as destined to hold the highest offices in the state.

Born in 1916, he comes from Sudanese Nubia. From Khartoum University, where he was students' warden and a teacher, he went to Oxford and graduated there. He has written several books, including the well-known *Intellectual Origins of Egyptian Nationalism*. He is also noted for his translations.

BABIKER AWADALLA

Babiker Awadalla, the Sudan's Chief Justice, has been in law all his life, since graduating from Khartoum University College and becoming a barrister in London.

Known for his anti-military regime activities, he was a leading figure in the formation of the National Professional Front, which took over from the military regime. But he refused to become its first prime minister, preferring to go back to the judiciary.

Judge Awadalla was the Speaker in the first National Parliament which, when the British left the Sudan, declared the country's independence. He was born in 1915.

HASSAN AWADALLA

A former football star in the Sudan, Hassan Awadalla became the first Minister of Agriculture in the country and a deputy to the secretary-general of the National Unionist Party.

He is the Minister of Education and a leading member of the NUP. He was born in Omdurman in 1918.

PROF EL NAZEER DAFAALLA

Professor El Nazeer Dafaalla has played an important role in the work of round-table conferences held to harmonise relations between Northern and Southern Sudan. He was made chairman in 1965 of one such conference.

He is president of the African Universities Council, vice-chancellor of Khartoum University and a veterinary scientist of international repute.

DAWOUD ABDEL LATIF

Dawoud Abdel Latif was the first Sudanese Governor in Equatoria Province, Southern Sudan, where he performed great work in soothing racial feelings and trying to bring closer the Negro southerners and Arab northerners. He is a Nubian from Wadi Halfa and trusted by southerners.

A leading Umma politician, born in 1914, he was a prominent civil servant under British rule. After independence he became Under Secretary at the Ministry of the Interior, and was responsible in the early stages for the removal of 52,000 Sudanese Nubians from Wadi Halfa to new homes at Khashm El Girba (East Sudan) before their land was submerged by the Aswan Dam.

He became Minister of Information and Labour. He fell out with the military regime over their policy towards the Wadi Halfans from the old Nubia area,

Sayed Santino
Deng Teng

Ismail El Azhari

and returned to business life.

While a political tactician, Dawoud El Latif is also a successful businessman and a social personality; he was responsible for the greater part of the new development in the capital when he was town clerk.

WILLIAM DENG

William Deng is the president of the Sudan African National Union (SANU), a party representing Negroes in Southern Sudan. He believes a federal system is the best solution for the South's problems, which began with an army revolt in 1955, when independence was near and the Sudanese were taking over the country from the withdrawing British.

In 1961, when district commissioner of a border district in the Upper Nile Province, he decided to leave the country. With other southerners living in exile in Uganda and Kenya, he formed SANU and was joint author with Joseph Oduhu of a book, *The Problem of Southern Sudan,* in which they wrote about racial and political differences with the north.

When Khalifa's Government, on the fall of the military regime, called for a round-table conference in Khartoum between the two sides, with an amnesty offer and African observers admitted to the talks, Deng returned to the Sudan to engage in politics openly.

He no longer stands for separation for the south.

SANTINO DENG TENG

Santino Deng Teng is a prominent Southern Sudanese politician, enjoying popularity among the strong Dinka tribe in the Bahr El Ghazal Province.

He holds the position of Presi-

dent of the Sudan Unity Party.

Born in 1922, he became a member of Parliament after independence in 1956, and held ministerial rank throughout the military regime of 1958–64, and the Governments which preceded it.

ISMAIL EL AZHARI

Sometimes called the 'Father of Modern Sudan', Sayed Ismail El Azhari was born in 1898. He founded the National Unionist Party and became President of the Supreme Council of State after being the first Prime Minister, from 1954–57.

He was the leader of the Ashigga Party (later the NUP), formed in 1946. He stood for unity of the Nile Valley (unity with Egypt) and was fully backed by the old Egyptian rulers. After winning the first national elections, however, he came under strong Egyptian criticism for changing his policy in Parliament with a declaration of independence. To Cairo this amounted to betrayal.

Many said he would be the Sudan's first President. He has been twice in prison – during British rule and General Abboud's military regime.

SHERIF HUSSEIN EL HINDI

In the Mahgoub Government, Sherif Hussein El Hindi was Minister of Local Government and also a Minister of Finance and Economics.

Born in 1925, he is the son of the late Sherif El Hindi, head of the Hindi religious sect, considered in Sudan to be third in importance after the Mahdists and the Mirghanis Khatmia.

A prominent NUP member, Sherif Hussein El Hindi's great task in the Cabinet is to liquidate the old Tribal Administration, in

409

El Hadi El Mahdi

Sadik El Mahdi

existence for more than a century, through which certain families and sheiks rule the rural areas, as they did on behalf of the British Government. Possessing judicial powers also, the sheiks have enormous influence over local affairs. It was proposed that civil servants and judges should administrate in their place.

IMAM EL HADI EL MAHDI

El Hadi El Mahdi is the Imam of the Ansari Mahdists, who claim three million followers, mainly in Western and Central Sudan.

Born in 1918, he was educated in Egypt.

He is a grandson of the Great Mahdi, and a brother of the third Mahdi and the fourth Imam.

SERR EL KHATIM EL KHALIFA

The military regime having been overthrown in the October revolution of 1964, Serr El Khatim El Khalifa became Prime Minister.

Prominent in the world of education in Southern Sudan, he had no political background, but was accepted as a compromise by the politicians and Army officers negotiating a new order.

When this Government ended after eight months with parliamentary elections (1965), he preferred, at the age of 47, to go into the diplomatic service, and was appointed ambassador to Rome.

While Premier, he married a great grand-daughter of the Mahdi and became Sadik El Mahdi's brother-in-law.

SADIK EL MAHDI

Sayed Sadik El Mahdi, who became Prime Minister on August 4, 1966, at the age of 30, is widely regarded as the ideal of the rising generation in the Sudan. Educated at Oxford, he has good

looks and a charming manner, and is dignified, gentlemanly, courteous and devout.

In the Sudan's 967,500 square miles, most of it desert, are eleven million Arab Moslems (in the north) and three million Christian or pagan Negroes (in the south). A bitter separatist struggle by the Negroes, begun with an Army revolt and massacre just before independence came to the country on January 1, 1956, after 55 years of British rule, cost thousands of lives and precipitated a severe economic crisis.

Sadik's life has been devoted to unifying the country racially, politically and socially, despite the great differences in origin and in religion.

He is the president of Umma, the Sudan's largest political party. The leadership has come mainly from his own family, one of the richest and most powerful in the Middle East. He believes this to be a disadvantage and has aimed at building up a strong modern political force.

He started his political career during a military regime, by helping his late father, Imam Siddik, to organise the National Opposition Front.

His election as Prime Minister and leader of the party followed what was considered a progressive movement inside the party to liberate it from the domination of his uncle, the Imam of the Mahdists. This caused a split in the party which he has since reunited, with himself as political leader and the Imam as patron.

His Government replaced that of Mohamed Ahmed Mahgoub, a veteran Umma politician, which had resigned ten days before. It is a coalition of Umma, the minority National Unionist Party, two independents from the Negro south and an independent

Sayed Ali El Mirghani

Ibrahim El Mufti

financial expert. It has the support of one of the strongest religious sects in the Sudan, the Ansaris.

A great grandson of the great Mahdi, whose Dervish revolt drove the Egyptians out of the Sudan in 1882, he is a strict Moslem, though against rigid medieval interpretations of Islam.

DR TIGANI EL MAHI

A psychiatrist of international repute, Dr Tigani El Mahi is considered in the Sudan to be the country's most learned man in various fields of knowledge. He also owns the best and richest private library.

During the military regime he resigned his post as the senior Government psychiatrist, joined the WHO regional office at Alexandria, and went on many world lecture tours.

After the October revolution, he became a member of the first Supreme Council of State. He had been nominated by the National Unionist Party from which he later resigned, saying it was not on the right path.

Author of many books, Dr Mahi is an external examiner in medicine at both Khartoum and Cairo Universities.

At the end of 1966, at the age of 55, Dr Mahi had retired and was doing part-time work in his daughter's clinic at Khartoum North.

ALI EL MIRGHANI

Sayed Sir Ali El Mirghani is the spiritual leader of the two million strong Khatmia sect which rivals the Mahdist Ansaris.

One of the richest landowners in the Sudan, he is the patron of the pro-Egyptian Peoples Democratic Party, in opposition to the coalition comprising the Umma Mahdists and National Unionists.

He is supposed to have been born around the year 1869. 'But no one knows,' declare supporters, 'and he does not say.'

His son, Mohamed Osman is being prepared to succeed him.

IBRAHIM EL MUFTI

A lawyer by profession, Ibrahim El Mufti helped to found the old pro-Egyptian National Unity Party of El Ashigga with his relative, President Ismail El Azhari.

He became the first Minister of Commerce after independence, and Minister of Finance following the military regime.

His next Cabinet rank was Deputy Prime Minister and Minister of Foreign Affairs.

NASR EDDIN EL SAYED

Nasr Eddin El Sayed has been deputy secretary-general of the coalition National Unionist Party since its reorganisation after the October (1964) popular revolution.

He became Minister of Communications and Tourism in both Premier Mahgoub's and Sadik El Mahdi's coalition Cabinets.

Educated at Khartoum University and Bristol, England, he first started as a police officer and later became town clerk of Khartoum North. He has represented this constituency in the former Parliament and the present one. Nasr Eddin, who was born in 1921, is strongly anti-left and pro-Islamic.

MOHAMED SALIH EL SHINGITI

One of the oldest politicians in the Sudan–born in 1898–Mohamed Salih el Shingiti is also one of the leading businessmen, dealing in cotton and other materials.

He was one of the first Sudanese civil judges, and became Speaker

411

of the British-created Constituent Assembly in 1948, which was boycotted by almost all the pro-Egyptian parties.

Later he became Speaker of the second Parliament, dissolved when the Army took over the country in 1964.

He is an authority on Sudan's history, and was a close friend of the late Imam Abdel Rahman El Mahdi, son of the Great Mahdi.

DR ABDEL HALIM MOHAMED HALIM

Although he influences the policy of Umma, Dr Abdel Halim Mohamed Halim is chiefly devoted to medicine.

Born in 1907, he is one of the best known medical men in the Sudan, being both an MRCP and FRCP of London (Member and Fellow of the Royal College of Physicians). He was president of the Sudan Medical Association for more than 15 years.

As an Umma man he rose to be a member of the Supreme Council of State. He resigned so as to be free to return to medicine and resume his sporting activities as president of the Football Association and the Khartoum Racing Club. For many years he was chairman (mayor) of Khartoum Municipal Council.

ABDIN ISMAIL

Abdin Ismail, a leading socialist born in 1915, was president of the Sudan Bar Association for over ten years.

After the October revolution he joined the transitional Government as deputy premier to Serr El Khatim Khalifa and was his Minister of Local Government.

He played an important role in the popular movement that brought down the Abboud military regime. He later formed with others the Democratic Socialist

Congress, a party which did not win much support from the public as a whole, but has many members among educated people and the intellectuals.

The party won only one seat in the 1965 elections in the graduates' constituencies. The successful candidate was a journalist, Mahgoub Mohamed Sali, editor of the leading *El Ayam* daily newspaper.

IBRAHIM HASSAN KHALIL

Ibrahim Hassan Khalil, a former Deputy Commissioner of Police, became after the October revolution Director-General of the Ministry of Information and Social Affairs.

He is responsible for the Sudan Radio and Television and the Information Departments of the State.

He was born in 1921.

MOHAMED IBRAHIM KHALIL

Mohamed Ibrahim Khalil, lawyer and prominent Umma Party member, became Foreign Minister in Premier Mahgoub's Cabinet.

He helped Sadik El Mahdi to the premiership against Mahgoub but preferred not to participate in Sadik's Cabinet and practised law instead.

Before the October revolution, Khalil, who was born in 1921, was Dean of the Faculty of Law at the University.

AHMED KHEIR

Ahmed Mohamed Kheir is considered by many to be the father of the Graduates' Congress, the first national political organisation in the Sudan, from which later the Umma and National Unionist Parties were created.

Kheir kept aloof from political parties, but when the Sudan attained independence many of

Mohamed Ahmed
Mahgoub

his friends believed he was bitter because he had not been given any office. This, it is said, was the reason why he cooperated with the military regime, and became its strong man and Foreign Minister throughout its six years in power.

When Abboud was ousted, Kheir was arrested and kept with other Abboud ministers in custody for about six months. Later he resumed practising law in Khartoum.

MAHGOUB ABDEL KHALIQ

Mahgoub Abdel Khaliq, born in 1927, has been described as 'the most important Communist in the Arab world'.

Educated in Cairo, he returned to the Sudan in 1954 and led a split in the Communist Party which resulted in his becoming secretary-general.

He stood for election in 1965 in Omdurman against Ismail El Azhari, the President of the Supreme Council of State, and lost by a few votes.

In November, 1965, when the Communist Party was 20 years old, it was banned and went underground – following nationwide anti-Communist troubles precipitated by a provocation to religious feelings said to have stemmed from a Communist student.

But although the party was proscribed, it continued functioning more or less openly through organisations of students, workers and various professions and newspapers.

MOHAMED MAHGOUB

Former Prime Minister Mohamed Ahmed Mahgoub is a man of many parts: professional lawyer and ex-judge, civil engineer, and among the top poets in the Arab world. He struggled all the time

for independence when Azhari and others were campaigning strongly for unity with Egypt.

He was the Sudan's first Opposition leader, on behalf of the Umma Mahdists, in the first Legislative Assembly created by the British administration in 1948.

He became Minister of Foreign Affairs during Khalil's Government, which was said to have brought about the military *coup* in 1958. He displayed an almost old-fashioned belief in parliamentary democracy and was not prepared to compromise.

After the 'popular October revolution' he became Foreign Minister once more in Serr El Khatim El Khalifa's national Government. After the first general elections he was made Prime Minister in a coalition of the Umma and National Unionist parties.

He was voted out of office on July 25, 1966 in a split in his own party, and was succeeded by its President, Sadik El Mahdi.

Out of office, he returned with greater energy than ever to practising law and writing poetry, which some people think he likes more than politics.

Born in 1908, he stood when 50 for the Presidency of the United Nations. He lost to Dr Charles Habib Malik, of Lebanon.

MAMOUN BIHEIRY

Mamoun Biheiry was Minister of Finance during the last days of General Abboud's military regime. He is regarded by many as a pro-Western economist not interested in politics as such.

Several loan and aid agreements with Britain were negotiated by him when he went to London with General Abboud.

Born in 1925, he took a BA degree in economics at Oxford University.

Clement Mboro

Hamza Mirghani

Abdalla Abdel
Rahman Nugdalla

He founded the Sudan Central Bank and was its first governor. Eventually he became president of the Development Bank of Africa at Abidjan, Ivory Coast.

CLEMENT MBORO

Coming from a small southern tribe, Clement Mboro formed with others the strong Negro Southern Front,· which was generally accepted as going further than the other parties — such as SANU (Sudan African National Union) — towards separation from the predominantly Arab north.

He was the first southerner to become deputy governor of a province.

During the Khalifa October revolution he was selected to represent the south and became Minister of the Interior.

HAMZA MIRGHANI

Hamza Mirghani, an able economist, born on January 1, 1922, and educated at Cambridge University, was appointed Minister of Finance and Economics in the Mahdi Government in 1966.

After independence, he became the first Under Secretary of Finance, but resigned as a result of his strong differences with the military regime. He was appointed Director of the United Nations Department of Administration in New York, but after two years left to become head of the African section of the International Monetary Fund. in Washington. While there he was asked to return to his own country as Finance Minister.

He is believed to be more interested in economics than in politics. His father, Mirghani Hamza, was an NUP minister several times, holding in turn the portfolios of Education, the Interior, and Irrigation before the

military regime. He is now a leading industrialist, and one of the Sudan's finest engineers.

LT-GEN
EL KHAWAD MOHAMED

Lieutenant-General El Khawad Mohamed, commander-in-chief of the Sudanese Armed Forces, was given this post after the overthrow of General Ibrahim Abboud's regime in October, 1964.

When Abboud took over, Mohamed was a Brigadier. He became a member of the then ruling Supreme Council of the Armed Forces, but later, not interested in politics, he resigned and went back to the Army.

During the war he served with the Allied forces in Libya and Ethiopia and won several decorations. He was born in Shendi, Northern Sudan in 1915.

ABDALLA ABDEL
RAHMAN NUGDALLA

Abdalla Abdel Rahman Nugdalla, Minister of the Interior and Defence, has been deputy secretary-general of the Umma Mahdists Party since its creation in 1947 and secretary-general since January, 1965.

Son of one of the great Mahdist Emirs, he was born in 1912.

He played an important part in the Sudanese national movement that led to independence. A strong opponent of unity with Egypt, he led a demonstration of Mahdists on March 1, 1954, during which thousands marched on the Governor General's Palace where General Mohamed Naguib, then President of Egypt, was on a one-day visit.

Over a hundred Mahdists were killed in a clash with the police.

Nugdalla was later tried as the man responsible and was sent to prison for three years. After independence, however, and

Ali Abdel Rahman

Beshir Mohamed
Saeed

before completing the sentence, he was pardoned by the Supreme Council of State.

For his activities against the military regime of General Abboud, he was kept in custody in Juba, Equatoria Province, for six months in 1963 along with a dozen other politicians.

In the 1965 general elections, Nugdalla won a Mahdist constituency. He became Minister of Local Government under Premier Mahgoub but switched to the Ministries of the Interior and Defence in the Government of Prime Minister Sadik El Mahdi.

ALI ABDEL RAHMAN

Sayed Ali Abdel Rahman, a former Sharia judge, was one of the founders of the first 'Union with Egypt' Ashigga Party, and became the first Minister of Education in the Sudan.

Strongly pro-Nasser, he became President of the People's Democratic Party, in opposition, backed by the Khatmia sect.

He boycotted the 1965 elections, held only in the north, claiming that they would lead to a breakaway by the south.

BESHIR MOHAMED SAEED

As the owner of the two best-selling Arabic and English daily newspapers in the Sudan – *Al Ayam* and the *Morning News*– Beshir Mohamed Saeed is thought to be perhaps the most influential voice in the Sudanese press.

His daily column is regarded by many as the best informed and most widely read. He is sympathetic to the West, strongly anti-Communist, and also opposed to the Nasserites.

When his newspaper was suspended by the military regime, he worked for the United Nations in New York, returning later to resume his profession.

He was born in 1921, and has written a book on the Southern Sudan problem. He is president of the Sudan Press Association.

DR MUBARAK SHADDAD

Dr Mubarak El Fadil Shaddad, the Speaker of the Constituent Assembly, originally practised as a gynaecologist and later became director of the Omdurman Civil Hospital.

Noted for his great political independence and active interest in social and local affairs, he was actually selected after the October revolution as the first Prime Minister in the transitional Government but was rejected on the grounds that General Abboud was still to be kept in office. When Abboud was finally deposed, Shaddad became a member of the Supreme Council of State. After the general elections he was elected Speaker of the Constituent Assembly.

He is patron of a national front for the unity of North and South Sudan.

He was born in 1913.

DR HASSAN EL TURABI

Dr Hassan El Turabi is the secretary-general of the Islamic Charter Front (Moslem Brotherhood) which has been gathering strength in the Sudan since the October revolution, in which Turabi played an important role.

Graduating from Khartoum University, he took a doctorate in law at the Sorbonne in Paris. He became Dean of the Faculty of Law in Khartoum University, but after the October upheaval, became a professional Moslem brother and gained the highest votes of the graduates' constituencies in Parliament. Anti-Communist and anti-Nasser, Turabi leads the movements against both in the Sudan.

415

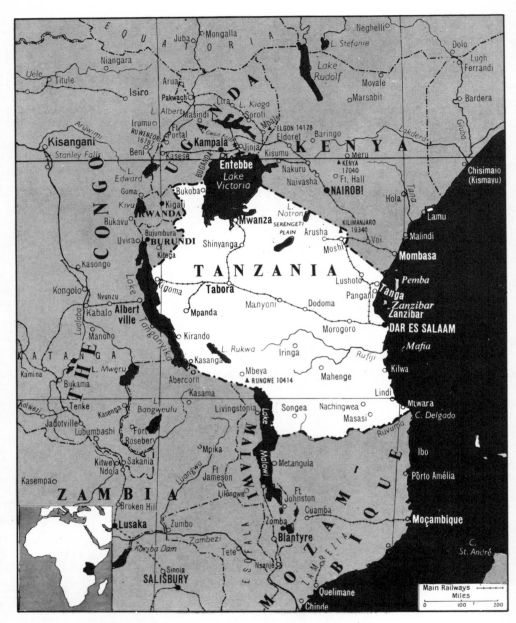

The area of Tanzania (including Zanzibar and Pemba) is 363,708 square miles. Across Lake Tanganyika is Congo Kinshasa. There are land borders with Burundi, Rwanda, Uganda (Lake Victoria lies between the two countries), Kenya, Portuguese Mozambique, Malawi (with part of Lake Malawi between) and Zambia. The population (1964 estimate) is 10,100,000. The capital is Dar es Salaam.

Tanzania is the world's chief producer of sisal. Other major exports are coffee and cotton. Cloves come entirely from the islands—mostly from Pemba.

Tanzania

Tanganyika became independent on December 9, 1961,
and adopted a republican form of government a year later.
Zanzibar became independent on December 9, 1963.
On January 12, 1964, the Sultan of Zanzibar was
overthrown and exiled.
Tanganyika and Zanzibar combined to form the United
Republic of Tanganyika and Zanzibar on April 27, 1964
(named Tanzania on October 29).
Supreme executive power rests with the President, who is
both head of state and head of government. He has
two Vice-Presidents, responsible respectively for Zanzibar's
internal affairs and for internal affairs and defence on the
mainland. He chooses them and his Cabinet from among
the members of the National Assembly.

Tanganyika had a history of both German and British
rule before becoming independent and uniting with the
island of Zanzibar under a new name – Tanzania.
It was part of German East Africa, occupied by German
colonists from 1884 and placed under the protection of
the German Empire in 1891. It was conquered by the
British in the course of World War I, and
subsequently divided between Britain and Belgium, the
latter receiving the territories of Ruanda and Urundi
and the British the remainder, except for the Kionga
triangle, which went to Portugal.
The country was administered by Britain under a
League of Nations mandate, becoming known as
Tanganyika, until 1946, and then as a United Nations
Trusteeship territory until independence was declared
on December 9, 1961.
It has a coastline of some 500 miles and a coastal plain
varying in width from ten to 40 miles. Behind this the
country rises to the great central plateau, about 4,000 ft
above sea level. Kilimanjaro, the highest mountain in
Africa, with a permanent snowcap rising to 19,340 ft,
lies in the north-east, near the Kenya border.
The islands of Zanzibar and Pemba, which lie on the
eastern side of the African continent just south of the
Equator, were placed under British protection by the
Sultan in 1890 and a regular Government was set up
the following year.
The African population of Tanganyika is made up of

Orange-seller in
the market at
Dar es Salaam

members of more than 100 tribes, each with a distinctive
dialect. They are mostly of Bantu origin, although there
are a considerable number of Hamitic and Nilo-Hamitic
people among them.

The languages are Swahili (the most generally spoken
and understood), Arabic, English, Hindi, Gujerati and
the many African vernaculars.

At present two-thirds of the ten million people –
including some 100,000 Asians and 20,000 Europeans –
live in ten per cent of the country, where plentiful
water is assured. Ninety-six per cent of them are farmers

Drying sisal, the country's major product, near Himo

and peasants, and agriculture accounts for more than half of the gross domestic product (£240m in 1965) as well as all important exports – sisal, cotton, coffee and oilseeds.

The rich agricultural highlands are in the north and south, with vast areas of rolling, semi-arid plains between.

With new techniques, and campaigns against the tsetse fly, agriculture is spreading fast. The country's enormous economic potential, though far from realisation, is beginning to be seen.

Above: Offices and apartment blocks in Dar es Salaam

Below: Women wait outside a medical dispensary on the Island of Pemba

President Julius Nyerere's concern for Tanzania's development is matched by his determination that total political independence be preserved. He refused substantial West German aid rather than agree to have no relations with East Germany. He broke relations with Britain over its handling of the Rhodesia crisis in December, 1965, in obedience to an Organisation of African Unity resolution, at the cost of a £7,500,000 loan already committed to vital development projects up and down the country.

When he broke with Britain, he is said to have wept at 'his betrayal by people he thought were his friends'. On non-alignment, Nyerere has said that Tanzania, with its history in the Western sphere, must tend to the East to reach a central position – and be seen to do so. 'But we are not going all the way to Peking,' he added. When he returned from the OAU 'Summit' Conference in Addis Ababa in November, 1966, President Nyerere said that France and Britain had more power in the OAU than the whole of Africa put together. It was up to Africa to decide whether to become truly independent or remain colonies of France and Britain. 'I think African countries will have to make up their minds whether to give priority to Africa or to their associations with former rulers.'

A. M. A. R. Babu

A. M. A. R. BABU

Ahmed Mohammed Abdul Rahman Babu, Minister for Commerce and Cooperatives (1965), was the organising brain of the left-wing anti-Government militancy which set the scene for revolution in Zanzibar in January, 1964.

Born in 1924 of mixed Arab-Comorian descent, Babu went from an island school to Makerere University College, Uganda, then to London University to study English literature, philosophy, social psychology and journalism.

His active participation in Zanzibar politics began in 1957, after six years with the Zanzibar Clove Growers' Association and

another six behind a savings bank counter in Acton, West London.

Rapidly he emerged as leader of a minority Marxist-inspired faction in the Zanzibar National Party (ZNP), which won successive electoral victories by linking the island's Arab, Asian and African communities through the common bond of Islam.

After a two-year battle to turn the essentially conservative, pro-Sultanate ZNP away from Koranic principles towards strict socialism, Babu finally resigned before the July, 1963 elections and founded the Umma (Masses) Party.

Umma took no part in the elections, which brought a ZNP

421

coalition to power despite a 54 per cent popular poll by the Afro-Shirazi Party.

But Babu developed his party in the next six months into a tightly-knit, powerful Marxist organisation providing a meeting-place for all anti-Government groups, a unifying force among long divided trade unions – and a spur to increasingly authoritarian measures by the Government as Zanzibar approached and achieved independence that December.

Babu was in Tanganyika when the Government was overthrown. A week earlier his party had been banned.

He returned to be appointed Minister of Defence and External Affairs in a revolutionary Government formed from leaders of both Umma and Afro-Shirazi Parties. The parties merged as the ASP soon afterwards.

Babu's first post after the Tanganyika-Zanzibar merger in April, 1964 was Minister of State.

MARK BOMANI

Mark Bomani, appointed Attorney-General in 1965, is one of a trio of brothers, sons of a northern Tanganyika Protestant minister, who have risen to prominence in public life. One brother, Paul, became Minister for Economic Affairs; another, Emmanuel, general manager of the vast Victoria Federation of Cooperative Unions which handles a major share of the country's cotton production.

Mark Bomani was born at Musoma, on the eastern shore of Lake Victoria, in 1932. He completed his schooling at the Government Secondary School, Tabora, and went on to Makerere College, Uganda.

From there he went to London to study law. He took London

University BA and LLB degrees, and was called to the Bar at Lincoln's Inn.

Bomani was appointed Deputy Solicitor-General in 1964 and Attorney-General the following year.

PAUL BOMANI

Paul Lazaro Bomani, Minister for Economic Affairs and Development Planning, achieved political prominence and a key role in Tanganyika's progress to independence by way of the cooperative movement, in the cotton country south of Lake Victoria.

Bomani was born in 1925 west of the Lake at Musoma, son of a Protestant minister.

After a period at a Seventh Day Adventist teachers' training college he turned down a teaching career, striking off on his own to take a job as cashier at a diamond mine.

A correspondence course in accountancy qualified him for his first post in the cooperatives, the secretaryship of a Mwanza society, at the age of 22.

Intensive campaigning through lake villages followed. He showed farmers how they could beat exploitation by Asian middlemen, and by 1950 had registered the Lake Province Cotton Cooperative.

By 1955 this had become the Victoria Federation of Cooperative Unions. He was general manager of the largest marketing cooperative in Africa.

Bomani had been provincial chairman of the Tanganyika African Association since 1952, carrying his TAA branches over to TANU when Julius Nyerere formed the new party two years later.

Backed by Nyerere, the British administration in 1954 nominated him to the Legislative Council. For the next three years he was TANU's sole mouthpiece there, and an invaluable asset to Nyerere in his struggle for responsible African government.

In 1959 Bomani returned to the Council as an elected TANU member. In 1960 he became Minister for Agriculture and Cooperative Development, in 1961 Minister for Agriculture, and in 1962 Minister for Finance.

In the all-TANU 1965 elections he was one of two senior and six junior ministers who lost their National Assembly seats.

Nyerere made him Minister for Economic Affairs, with overall responsibility for implementation of the country's all-important Five-Year Development Plan; as a nominated member he was the only Cabinet member without a constituency.

R. G. MacCORMACK BROWN

Roland George MacCormack Brown, Legal Adviser to the Tanzanian Government, was constitutional adviser to the then Chief Minister Julius Nyerere at the March, 1961 conference in Dar es Salaam which brought independence that December.

From independence until 1965 he was Attorney-General.

Brown was born in London in 1924 and was educated at Ampleforth College. Leaving Cambridge University in 1949 with an MA, he became a barrister-at-law at Gray's Inn, London.

Soon after, aged 25, he unsuccessfully stood for Parliament as Labour candidate in the 'safe' Conservative constituency of Stratford.

Long a sympathiser with African independence demands, Brown first came to the continent to take part in Uganda's legal disputes following Britain's banish-

ment of Sir Edward Mutesa (1953).

In 1966, President Nyerere 'lent' him to Zambia's President Kenneth Kaunda to head an inquiry into a wave of strikes hitting production on the Copperbelt.

D. N. M. BRYCESON

Derek Noel MacLean Bryceson, the only remaining European in Tanzania's Cabinet, holds one of its key posts as Minister of Agriculture, Forests and Wildlife. Well over ninety per cent of the country's people are peasants and farmers, and national development is closely tied to their efforts in production for the export market.

Born in China in 1924, Bryceson was educated at St Paul's School, London, and Trinity College, Cambridge. He emigrated to Kenya to farm in 1947, moving south to Tanganyika four years later.

Three years' wartime flying with the Royal Air Force had ended with a crash in the Western Desert which left him tied for life to a walking-stick.

Bryceson's friendship with Julius Nyerere was the indirect result of a newspaper attack he made on the young nationalist in 1957, accusing him of racialism. He later invited Nyerere to lunch. Three days of argument and discussion followed and with them came the basis for a lasting trust and understanding.

Bryceson became Assistant Minister for Social Services the same year, and gave TANU staunch support – returned by the party – in the subsequent movement for responsible government.

His ministerial responsibilities since independence have also included Labour and Health.

At the elections in September,

S. N. Eliufoo

Abdulla Kassim Hanga

Amir Habib Jamal

1965, he polled 37,770 votes in his Dar es Salaam constituency – 30,000 more than his African rival in the one-party poll.

S. N. ELIUFOO

Solomon Nkya Eliufoo, appointed Minister of Education in 1962, came to the post with several years' teaching experience, first at Makerere College, Uganda, later at a teachers' training college and a commercial college in Tanganyika.

Born in 1920 in Kilimanjaro District near the Kenya border – part of which he represents in the National Assembly – Eliufoo was himself educated at Makerere; Bethany College, Kansas, where he obtained his BA, and Bristol University, England.

He was elected to the Legislative Council in 1958. The following year he was one of five 'unofficial ministers' whose appointment marked the end of wholly official executive government in Tanganyika.

The Government places enormous emphasis on the rapid development of education, particularly the expansion of secondary schools, and Eliufoo's Ministry absorbs more than one-sixth of its annual budget.

CHIEF JUSTICE P. T. GEORGES

Philip Telford Georges, Chief Justice of Tanzania, is a West Indian and formerly a judge in the High Court of Trinidad and Tobago.

He was born in Dominica in 1923. From the island grammar school he went to the University of Toronto, Canada, and to the Middle Temple, London.

He was in private practice in Trinidad from 1949–62, when he was appointed a judge, and was seconded to his present office in 1965.

ABDULLA KASSIM HANGA

Abdulla Kassim Hanga, Minister of State (in the President's Office) for Union Affairs, is in effect chief liaison officer between the Central Government in Dar es Salaam and Zanzibar's semi-autonomous administration.

Born in Zanzibar in 1932, Hanga was educated locally and later went to Moscow, where he studied economics. For a time he was married to a Russian woman.

As deputy general secretary of the Afro-Shirazi Party, in opposition to the Government when the island achieved independence, he was one of the ASP's strongest admirers of the more militant Umma Party.

Immediately after the January, 1964 revolution, he was proclaimed Prime Minister. Then, when the post was abolished a few hours later, he became Vice-President of the new Republic.

Hanga was first appointed a Minister of State with the Tanganyika-Zanzibar Union in April, 1964. His present appointment follows a term as Minister of Industries, Mineral Resources and Power.

AMIR HABIB JAMAL

Amir Habib Jamal, born in 1922 into a Dar es Salaam business family, got to know Julius Nyerere in his earliest political days and worked closely with the country's future leader through the formative years of TANU and the independence Government.

Nyerere valued him as one of the very few members of the middle-class Asian community prepared to take an active part in political life.

First elected to Parliament in 1958, Jamal, a quiet spoken, thoughtful, pipe smoker, was appointed the following year, on

Aboud Jumbe

Michael Kamaliza

Nyerere's recommendation, one of Tanganyika's first five 'unofficial ministers'. He held office continuously and became Finance Minister in 1965, the only Asian in the Cabinet.

Jamal originally planned to become a doctor. He turned to politics and economics (at Calcutta University). having failed despite high marks to enter Bombay's crowded medical faculty.

This training and later practical experience in his family's business, combined with a first-class brain, have made him a powerful force in the economic affairs of Tanzania.

ABOUD JUMBE

Mwinyi Aboud Jumbe, Minister of State in the First Vice-President's Office and a key figure in Zanzibar's administration, was for 14 years a schoolmaster before he went into full-time politics in 1961.

Born in 1920, Jumbe was educated in Zanzibar and at Makerere College, Uganda, where he took a diploma in education.

In 1953, he was a leader of the Zanzibar National Union, a short-lived attempt at a multi-racial nationalist movement linking Arabs and Africans in a common struggle for independence.

Jumbe resigned his teaching post in 1960 to join the Afro-Shirazi Party, and was elected an ASP member in both 1961 polls. Subsequently appointed Opposition Whip, he attended constitutional talks in London in 1962 and 1963.

Jumbe was Minister for Home Affairs after the January, 1964 revolution. At the union with Tanganyika later that year he became Minister of State.

MICHAEL KAMALIZA

Michael Marshall Mowbray Kamaliza, Minister for Labour, is also leader of the country's monolithic trade union movement, the National Union of Tanganyika Workers (NUTA).

Kamaliza came to politics through Tanganyika's labour organisations as they developed through the 1950s, first parallel with then as a virtual branch of TANU, the nationalist party which brought the country to independence.

In 1952 he became treasurer of the Tanganyika Federation of Labour, in 1957 general secretary of the Transport and General Workers' Union, and in 1960 president of the TFL with executive powers.

Though Julius Nyerere had insisted on complete separation of the unions from TANU, disputes between their leaderships forced reversal of this policy two years later. Kamaliza was then preaching the message that 'a man is incomplete if he doesn't possess both a trade union card and a TANU card'.

In 1964, when Kamaliza already held the Labour portfolio, every workers' union in the country was absorbed into the single organisation NUTA, which he heads as general secretary.

In 1966, a Presidential Commission was ordered to look into the organisation and activities of NUTA to see if it was performing the function intended – to safeguard the interests of workers in the context of the interests of the country as a whole. One question believed under review was the practicability of Kamaliza's two-hatted job.

Kamaliza is also a vice-president of the All Africa Trade Union Federation (AATUF), the headquarters of which were

O. S. Kambona

Abeid Karume

transferred in December, 1966, from Accra to Dar es Salaam.

He was born in 1929 in Nyasaland, son of a teacher on the small Lake Nyasa island, Likoma. His mission school education there was completed with a diploma in book-keeping and accounting.

O. S. KAMBONA

Oscar Salathiel Kambona, Minister for Regional Administration, an ardent socialist and anti-colonialist often well left of the political mainstream, was one of the pillars of the nationalist movement which brought Tanganyika to independence.

He has been organising secretary and general secretary of TANU since shortly after the party's foundation in 1954. Prominence in the international field came with his appointment in 1963 as Minister for External Affairs and Defence, a post he resigned, ostensibly on health grounds, two years later.

When President Nyerere took over the Foreign Ministry Kambona continued, despite his then domestic responsibilities, as chairman of the Dar es Salaam-based African Liberation Committee of the Organisation of African Unity.

After representing Tanzania in the Addis Ababa OAU Assembly in early 1966 – and leading a delegation walk-out – Kambona spent three months in Holland, undergoing treatment for long-standing circulatory trouble. His absence was accompanied by persistent rumours of policy differences with Nyerere, brought into the open by the President himself with a categorical denial.

Kambona again led Tanzania's team at Addis Ababa at the ministerial council session before the Summit in November, 1966.

Kambona was born in 1928, the son of a Nyasaland Anglican priest who came to live in southern Tanganyika. He was educated at a missionary school, then at the famous Government Secondary School, Tabora, attended by so many of Tanganyika's future leaders.

He taught for a time at a provincial teachers' training college and a secondary school, abandoning this career in 1954 – it is said – when a pupil asked him, 'You've told us what's wrong with our country. Why don't you do something about it?'

He offered his services to Nyerere the same year, and was appointed TANU organising secretary. Fruit of his energetic campaigning was a membership of 10,000 in six months, and 100,000 in a year.

In 1955, Kambona went to Britain and studied at the Middle Temple on a British Government scholarship. Five years later he was Education Minister in Tanganyika's pre-independence Government, and from 1962–63, Home Affairs Minister.

When the Tanganyika Army mutinied in January, 1964, he played a major role in the first critical hours, broadcasting an appeal for calm, as the only effective voice of authority when the Government had temporarily ceased to function.

In popularity among the mass of the people, Kambona is considered second only to Nyerere. Among his fellow leaders he has sometimes appeared a controversial figure.

ABEID A. KARUME

Abeid A. Karume, a powerfully-built former merchant seaman with little formal education, came to power in Zanzibar with the African revolution which in

Rashidi Kawawa

January, 1964, swept out the spice island's centuries-old Arab oligarchy.

For three months, until he negotiated the Union with Tanganyika that April, he was President of the Zanzibar People's Republic.

The aim of Karume's continuing revolution is a wholly egalitarian society. Its toughest problem is achieving self-sufficiency.

While he holds fast to the spirit of the Tanzanian Union, citing it often as an example to the rest of Africa, his Government is retaining considerable autonomy in foreign as well as domestic affairs, at least until its special problems are solved.

The economy of Zanzibar and the twin island Pemba to the north – 1,000 square miles in all with a population over 300,000 – has long been tied to a near world monopoly in cloves.

Economic depression accompanying falling demand for the product, together with the lasting effects of neglecting food crops in its favour, has faced Karume's revolutionary regime with some of its most demanding tasks. Added to this has been the severe economic dislocation involved in de-stratifying island society.

In agriculture, as in military and other development efforts, Zanzibar has found readiest technical and financial aid in Communist countries, particularly China, East Germany and the Soviet Union. Semi-voluntary 'self-help' projects are the other stand-by.

Born in 1905, Karume entered politics only in 1954, after a life at sea. Later he became president of the island's African Association.

This united with the Shirazi (indigenous African) Association three years later, winning elections as the Afro-Shirazi Party (ASP).

In an all-party caretaker Government following elections in 1961, Karume held the Health portfolio.

Elections in 1963, the last before independence from Britain that December, saw the ASP's defeat despite a proportionally majority poll. Karume led it in opposition to a two-party coalition which, though largely African-backed, seemed set to perpetuate Arab political and economic supremacy in independent Zanzibar.

Six months later came the January 12 revolution, spearheaded by young ASP militants, and Karume assumed leadership of the Revolutionary Council and of the new Republic.

RASHIDI MFAUME KAWAWA
Rashidi Mfaume Kawawa, appointed Second Vice-President in 1964, is the President's principal assistant, helping him with his executive functions relating to mainland Tanzania, and leader of the National Assembly.

He is also responsible for defence, the National Youth Service and other youth organisations, and refugees.

Son of a Southern Tanzanian elephant hunter, he is a stocky, five-foot-two, tough and competant administrator to whom idealogical 'isms' are just theories.

'My first thinking,' he said on one occasion, 'was not of politics but of service to my people.'

Born in 1929, Kawawa was already closely involved in workers' organisations and political life in the mid-1950s, becoming president of the Tanganyika Federation of Labour and, in 1957, a nominated member of the Legislative Council.

427

Early in 1962, after terms as Minister of Local Government and Housing and Minister without Portfolio, he succeeded his close friend, Julius Nyerere as Prime Minister when the future President suddenly stepped down to devote himself to the reorganisation of TANU.

Like many other future national leaders, Kawawa completed his education at the Government Secondary School, Tabora.

His early career was more colourful than most, It included highly successful welfare work among Kenyan Kikuyu detained in the Mau Mau emergency, and – unprecedented for a Tanganyikan – star roles in three locally-made comedy feature films.

TAWAKALI KHAMIS
Tawakali Khamis, Parliamentary Secretary of the Ministry for Foreign Affairs, heads the Union Ministry's Zanzibar branch.

Though external affairs became a Union Government responsibility with the April, 1964 merger, the Zanzibar administration has retained considerable freedom of movement in this sphere, especially as regards aid and trade. It regularly sends independent delegations and missions abroad.

Born in the island in 1914 and trained in Tanganyika as a surveyor, Khamis was surveyor in charge of Zanzibar's sister island Pemba; then, from 1962–64, surveyor superintendent.

For a few months from the end of 1964 he was a regional commissioner in Zanzibar.

Khamis has been active in island politics since 1947. In that year he joined the African Association, later to join forces with the Shirazi Association in the single Afro-Shirazi Party.

SHEIKH THABIT KOMBO
Sheikh Thabit Kombo, secretary-general of Zanzibar's monolithic Afro-Shirazi Party (ASP), is considered second only to First Vice-President Abeid Karume in the island Government's little-known political hierarchy.

Born in 1904, Kombo is a Shirazi, a member of the majority (200,000 out of a population of 300,000) indigenous African community which traces connections with voyagers from Shiraz, Persia, in the 10th century.

With little formal education – beyond study of the Koran – he became a leader of the Shirazi Association after working on local ships and as a railroad engineer. For a period he ran a shop for the Shirazi Cooperative in Zanzibar Town.

Kombo was one of two Shirazi Association leaders determined that Zanzibar's independence struggle should be waged on the basis of African, not Arab nationalism. Shirazis as a whole had co-existed well with their Arab overlords, much better than mainland Africans whose forebears arrived in Zanzibar in slavery, and the Association's other wing was content with the *status quo*.

His efforts led to cooperation between his Association and the African Association in the 1957 elections. Soon afterwards, with a joint majority in the Legislature, the two parties merged into the ASP, with Kombo as secretary-general.

The ASP was defeated in the pre-independence elections of 1963. It returned to power after the January, 1964 revolution, merging with the more militant organisation Umma (the masses), and all other political parties were banned.

Job Lusinde

JOB LUSINDE

Job Marecela Lusinde, awarded the portfolio of Minister for Communications and Works in Tanganyika's independence Government in 1961, came to politics from teaching and local government service.

He had had five years' practical experience of local government, first as an executive officer, then as town council chairman at Dodoma, his birthplace in 1930.

Lusinde was educated at Dodoma and the Government Secondary School, Tabora.

At both schools he was a contemporary of the future TANU secretary-general Oscar Kambona, and his politics, like Kambona's, have often appeared degrees further left than the Government's as a whole.

Lusinde went on from Tabora to take a diploma in education at Makerere College, Uganda, where he later began his five-year teaching career at the College School.

He was appointed Minister for Home Affairs in 1962.

H. MAKAME

Hasnu Makame, appointed Minister for Health in 1965 after a period as Minister for Communications and Works, is one of the Zanzibaris in the Union Government.

His first post following the April, 1964 Tanganyika-Zanzibar merger was Minister of State for External Affairs.

During the brief period after the January revolution he served as Zanzibar's Minister for Finance and Development and in New York as the revolutionary Government's ambassador to the United Nations and the United States.

Makame was born in Zanzibar, in 1920. He spent three years

as a teacher, then, after a course in public administration at Exeter University, England, went into government service in 1948.

A labour officer from 1957–60, he became a member of Parliament in 1961, and later treasurer of the Afro-Shirazi Party.

JOHN MALECELA

Cigwiyemisi Samuel John Malecela, permanent representative of Tanzania at the United Nations, is a fiery, uncompromisingly anti-colonialist diplomat whose General Assembly speeches, it has been said occasionally surprise his own Government.

Malecela was educated at a mission school at Dodoma, his hometown, and later at one of East Africa's oldest educational foundations, St Andrew's College, Minaki, outside Dar es Salaam. Between 1953–59 he attended Bombay University, taking a Bachelor of Commerce degree, and then went to Cambridge.

Entering government service in 1960, he was appointed two years later as Tanganyika's Consul to the USA and Third Secretary to the newly independent country's United Nations mission.

He returned to New York as chief of the UN mission after a period from 1963 as regional commissioner of Tanganyika's Lake Region.

SAIDI ALI MASWANYA

Appointed Minister of Lands, Settlement and Water Development in 1965, Saidi Ali Maswanya came to politics after service in the Uganda and Tanganyika Police.

He held several regional posts in TANU during the late 1950s, rising to deputy organising secretary-general at headquar-

Hassan Nassor Moyo

ters in 1959, and becoming a member of the Executive Committee two years later. In 1960 he was also deputy mayor of Dar es Salaam.

Appointed Minister without Portfolio in 1962, he moved to Health, then Agriculture, then Lands, Settlement and Water Development.

He was born in Tabora, and attended the Government Secondary School there which has produced so many of Tanzania's future leaders.

C. Y. MGONJA

Chediel Yohane Mgonja, chosen as Minister of Community Development and National Culture in 1965, was a civil servant and foreign officer before he entered Parliament and received the portfolio.

Youngest member of the Government, he was born in 1934, at Vudee in the northern highlands.

From local Lutheran primary and secondary schools he went on to the famous Government Secondary School at Tabora, then to Makerere College, Uganda, where he took a London University BA.

A brief career in local government – as District Officer at Tanga and Arusha – was sandwiched between two courses at Cambridge University, England, where he studied administration and international relations.

From 1962–64, Mgonja was a member of Tanganyika's United Nations Mission. For the remaining year before he stood for the National Assembly seat in his home district he was Assistant Secretary in the Foriegn Ministry.

Considered a possible future choice for Foreign Minister – a portfolio retained by the President – he was back in New York late in 1966 as leader of Tanzania's UN delegation.

HASSAN NASSOR MOYO

Hassan Nassor Moyo, Zanzibar Minister for Agriculture and Land Reform, is a one-time carpenter and trade union leader with a background of political studies in the Soviet Union.

He has charge of two of the revolutionary Government's most important programmes. One is land redistribution. Eighty per cent of the fertile land was owned by non-Africans before the revolution. His second concern is the basic reorientation of agriculture to feed the people. Just how seriously farmers had over-concentrated on spices, relying on the proceeds to cover food imports, was discovered when the clove market began to fall.

Moyo was born in Zanzibar in 1933.

Equipped with only primary education, he rose in the trade union movement to become secretary-general of the (now defunct) Zanzibar and Pemba Federation of Labour, a post he held six years, and a member of the Afro-Shirazi Party National Executive.

Following the Tanganyika-Zanzibar merger in 1964, he was appointed Justice Minister in the Union Government. This portfolio was later abolished.

E. I. M. MTEI

Edwin Isaac Mbiliewi Mtei, Govenor of the Bank of Tanzania, directed the complex financial operation which brought about the Bank's foundation and Tanzania's break with the 40 year-old East African Currency Board in June, 1966.

Tanzania regarded complete control of her financial resources

Bhoke Munanka

Julius Nyerere

as essential for the success of her development programme. But the Government has pledged readiness to re-merge the monetary system with those of Kenya and Uganda – which established their own Central Banks soon after – if East African federation is ever realised.

Born in 1932 near Moshi, in the northern highlands, Mtei entered the government service in 1959 with a BA Honours degree from Makerere College, Uganda, and after two years' management training in the East African Tobacco Company.

His first important post concerned Africanisation and training in the Civil Service.

Seconded to the East African Common Services Organisation – administering railways, harbours, customs, telecommunications and various other shared services – he held a series of high appointments, mostly financial, until 1964.

While planning, on his return to Dar es Salaam, the new bank and a Tanzanian shilling worthy of world respect, Mtei was a Principal Secretary in the Treasury.

BHOKE MUNANKA

Isaac Muller Bhoke Munanka, Minister of State in the President's Office, heads the Government's Central Establishment Division responsible for Civil Service organisation and training.

A former vice-president of TANU's forerunner, the Tanganyika African Association (TAA), he joined the new party soon after its foundation in 1954 and served from 1958–60 as its National Treasurer.

Bhoke Munanka was born in 1927 in North Mara, near the Kenya border on Lake Victoria, and attended the Government Secondary School at Tabora.

His first employment was as a government clerk.

At TANU's annual conference early in 1958, he was one of Julius Nyerere's principal opponents in the critical decision to take part in Tanganyika's first general elections despite what were regarded as unfair electoral arrangements. Like many other delegates he urged a boycott of the poll and a general strike, but Nyerere's arguments prevailed.

Earlier in his TANU career, public disorders in Lake Province were followed by the British administration banning branches for which he was responsible.

Appointed Minister of State in 1965, Bhoke Munanka previously served as Parliamentary Secretary in the Vice-President's Office.

JULIUS NYERERE

Julius Kambarage Nyerere, President of the United Republic of Tanzania, was born in March, 1922, at Butiama near the eastern shore of Lake Victoria, the son of Nyerere Burito – a chief of the small Zanaki tribe – and his eighteenth wife, Mugaya.

His mother does not know the exact day, but named him after a rain spirit because it was raining. *Nyerere* commemorates a plague of army-worms at the time of his father's birth in 1860.

Zanaki means 'Those who came with what?' Nyerere's early life, despite his royal birth, was spent in poverty as real as any his Government is striving to eradicate today.

His parents sent him to school, it is said, because of his remarkable skill with a complicated African game called *soro*. His education began, and the foundation for his profound Roman Catholic faith was laid, in a boarding school at nearby Musoma.

First signs of Nyerere's political aptitude appeared later at the Government Secondary School in the western town of Tabora, alma mater of many Tanganyikan leaders-to-be. Appointed a prefect, he discovered their privileges included double rations. He agitated against such inequalities, and they were dropped.

In 1943, Nyerere continued to Makerere College, Uganda, another hatchery of political ideas and associations which would later dominate the country's independence struggle. He returned to Tabora two years later with a diploma of education, and taught history and biology until 1949 at St Mary's, a White Fathers' school there.

With the White Fathers' help, he then travelled to Edinburgh on a special scholarship to study British history, English, moral philosophy, political economy, social anthropology, constitutional law and economic history. 'I evolved the whole of my political philosophy while I was there,' he has written.

Back in Tanganyika in 1952, with an MA degree, Nyerere resumed teaching near Dar es Salaam, within reach of fellow enthusiasts for the nationalist cause, and the following year he became president of the Tanganyika African Association.

In 1954, he remodelled the 25 year-old social organisation into the Tanganyika African National Union (TANU), a single political organisation in the present one-party state.

In the ensuing hard-pressed but bloodless independence struggle, Nyerere's agitation and, in 1955, his testimony before the United Nations Trusteeship Council, made him increasingly unpopular with the British administration. He served four months in 1957 as a nominated member of the Legislative Council, then resigned. He was convicted and fined the following year for criminal libel of the Administration in his party newspaper.

In 1958 and 1959, now a full-time party worker, he saw every TANU-supported candidate elected to the Legislative Council, and in 1960 the party won all but one of the 71 elected seats. He became Chief Minister, intensified his campaign for independence, and Tanganyika became a sovereign state within the Commonwealth on December 9, 1961.

One month later, Nyerere startled everyone by resigning the premiership to concentrate on rebuilding TANU for its post-independence role. He was preparing, too, for elections late in 1962, which returned him with a 97 per cent popular poll to become President of the Tanganyika Republic exactly one year after independence.

In January, 1964, an African revolution overthrew the Arab-dominated regime in Zanzibar, the spice island 40 miles from Dar es Salaam granted independence from Britain only a month earlier. One week elapsed and, in a climate of unease which extended throughout East Africa, troops of the Tanganyika Rifles mutinied and an attempt was made to convert the mutiny into a *coup d'état*.

Nyerere called in British troops to uphold his Government.

That April, in another surprise move, Nyerere announced a union agreement with the Zanzibar People's Republic, making him President of the United Republic of Tanganyika and Zanzibar – later to be re-named Tanzania.

Cardinal Rugambwa

From abroad, Zanzibar was widely seen as a bridgehead for Communist penetration into Africa. With the union, Tanzania as a whole was viewed, to a lesser degree, in the same way.

Tanzanian mainlanders, however, feel the union has not so much unbalanced their leaders' non-aligned stand in world affairs as moderated Zanzibar's Eastern leanings. They speak of the union as an example of what could be achieved throughout Africa, given the will, and criticise it most often for the restrained pace of integration.

True independence for Tanzania and all Africa, African strength through unity, and refusal to be drawn into the Cold War are the principal platforms of Nyerere's foreign policy. He expounds his beliefs both frequently and with rare eloquence.

In domestic affairs the President stands for equality of opportunity and reward and his people's fight against 'the three enemies: poverty, ignorance and disease'. Late in 1966 he slashed all middle and high Government salaries including his own £3,000 a year to narrow the yawning salary-basic wage gap.

In tours of the countryside, President Nyerere has constantly preached the need for self-reliance and, in 1966, he said that begging missions by Tanzania abroad could lower the country in world respect.

Married to Maria Gabriel, daughter of an elder in his home district, with eight children, Nyerere lives in a modest beach-side house outside Dar es Salaam built with the aid of a bank loan.

His official sobriquet, and the name by which most Tanzanians speak of him is *Mwalimu*, meaning 'teacher'.

CARDINAL LAURIAN RUGAMBWA

Cardinal Laurian Rugambwa, the first Negro to enter the Roman Catholic College of Cardinals, was received on March 31, 1960.

Born a pagan at Bukongo, north-west Tanganyika, on July 12, 1912, he was converted to Christianity at the age of nine, with his parents and two brothers. He is of noble ancestry on both sides of the family, his father belonging to the Basita tribe, which has given many kings of Kiyanja; his mother, a Bayinga, is also of direct royal lineage.

While attending a mission school run by the White Fathers, Laurian became interested in their work. He entered the junior seminary at Rubya, in Bukoba diocese, then went to the senior seminary at Katigondo in Uganda.

Ordained a priest in 1943, he was sent to Rome in 1948 to study canon law, receiving his doctorate in 1951. His doctoral thesis was on social and educational work in East Africa. In the same year he was created first Bishop of the new diocese of Rutabo.

CHIEF ADAM SAPI

Chief Adam Sapi (Mkwawa), appointed Speaker of the National Assembly in 1962, was one of a handful of hereditary Tanganyika leaders fitted by education and political philosophy, when their chiefdoms were abolished in all but name, to continue playing an important part in the country's public affairs.

Until 1962, Chief Sapi was Paramount Chief of the Hehe, a southern warrior tribe claiming Portuguese blood among its ancestors. His grandfather, Mkwawa, carved a place for

433

himself in national history by leading a series of brilliant harassing actions against the German colonial army in the 1890s.

Born at Iringa, central Tanzania, in 1920, Chief Sapi attended the Government Secondary School at Tabora, and in 1940 (the year he succeeded to the chiefdom), Makerere College, Uganda.

In 1947 he was appointed a member of the Tanganyika Legislative Council, opened to Africans only two years earlier.

Another of his present posts is chairmanship of the Board of Trustees of Tanganyika's National Parks. He holds the Order of the British Empire.

BRIGADIER
M. S. H. SARAKIKYA

Brigadier M. S. H. Sarakikya, Chief of the Tanzania People's Defence Forces, was given the command soon after the Army mutiny of January, 1964, when still a captain.

The Army was then commanded by a British officer. Of two other Tanganyikans who shared Sarakikya's rank, one was detained and dismissed from the service almost immediately. The other was placed in preventive detention a few weeks later and, it was reported, quietly released in 1966.

Sarakikya was born at Meru, in the northern highlands, in 1934. From Tabora Government Secondary School he went to the Military Academy at Sandhurst, England. He entered the Tanganyika King's African Rifles in 1958 as a private.

Self-effacing to the point of shyness but a smart, efficient soldier, the young Brigadier commands some 2,500 men in mainland Tanzania, and an undisclosed number but possibly more in Zanzibar.

Mainland forces are trained with Canadian assistance. Canada is also training crew and presenting several piston-engined aircraft for a small Air Wing.

Zanzibar's only partially integrated forces are trained and equipped, with substantial numbers of anti-aircraft and field guns and armoured troop-carriers as well as light weapons, by the Russians and Chinese.

The commander-in-chief of the People's Defence Force is the President. There is no Defence Minister, but all military affairs are handled by the Second Vice-President.

A. K. E. SHABA

Austin Kapere Edward Shaba entered the Cabinet as Minister of Housing in 1963, after serving with Tanganyika's mission at the United Nations.

His previous portfolios were Local Government, and Local Government and Housing.

Born in 1925 in Tanganyika's extreme south-west, at Sumbawanga, Shaba went to Tabora Government Secondary School and then to Dar es Salaam Medical School to train as a medical assistant.

As assistant in charge of a hospital in the southern highlands, it is related, he once incurred the wrath of a British District Commissioner by taking home Julius Nyerere – 'harbouring an undesirable agitator'– after the DC had found Nyerere sleeping space at the local labour camp.

Shaba's work in colonial Tanganyika's Medical Services earned him the British Empire Medal.

He has made frequent trips abroad, successfully enlisting aid

Lawi Sijaona

Idris-Abdul Wakil

from a number of countries, notably West Germany, in Tanzania's ambitious national housing programme.

LAWI NANGWANDA SIJAONA

As Minister of Home Affairs, Lawi Nangwanda Sijaona is responsible for police, prisons, immigration and citizenship.

Tanzania's rising crime graph requires as firm a hand with the first two as its proudly multiracial ideals demand delicacy with the last, and he has won wide approval for his quiet efficiency in the office.

In the National Assembly Sijaona represents part of Newala District, in the far south-east near the Mozambique border, where he was born in 1928.

Educated to Senior Cambridge Overseas School Certificate level, he began his career on the staff of a local magazine.

Then he moved to local government, becoming Clerk to Newala Local Council in 1955, and six years later joined the Central Government.

Sijaona was given his first ministry – National Culture and Youth – when Tanganyika became a republic in 1962. He has also held the Lands, Settlement and Water Development portfolio.

During 1966 he several times represented Tanzania in contacts with neighbouring states – Malawi and Burundi among them.

NSILO SWAI

A. Z. Nsilo Swai, a former schoolmaster and businessman, became Minister of Industries, Mineral Resources and Power in 1965 – the sixth Government post of his career.

In 1962 he represented Tanganyika at the United Nations.

He was born in 1927 into northern Tanganyika's industrious Chagga tribe and educated at Makerere College, Uganda, and the Universities of Bombay, Delhi, and Pittsburgh, USA.

IDRIS-ABDUL WAKIL

Idris-Abdul Wakil joined the Cabinet from Zanzibar as Minister of Information and Tourism in April, 1964.

Elected to the Zanzibar National Assembly in 1963, on the Afro-Shirazi Party ticket, he emerged from the January, 1964 revolution as a member of the Revolutionary Council and Minister of Education and National Culture in the People's Republic.

Wakil was born in Zanzibar in 1926, had his secondary education in the island and went on to take a diploma of education at Makerere College, Uganda.

He taught in various island schools for ten years, including the teachers' training college, resigning from the headmastership of a primary school to stand in the 1963 elections.

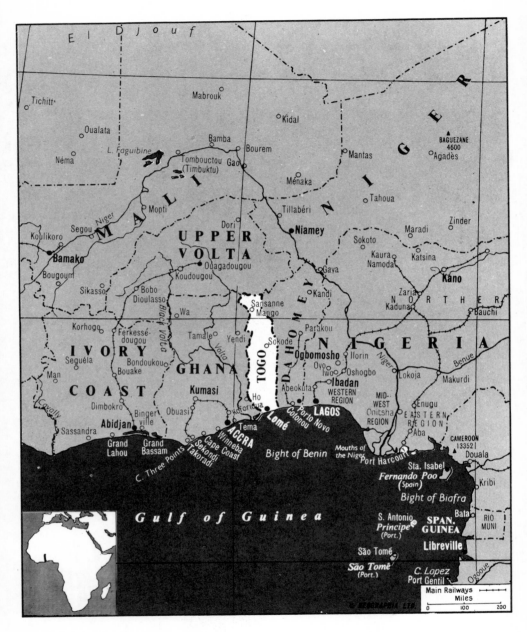

The population of Togo is over 1,603,000 (United Nations estimate, 1964) living in an area of 20,400 square miles. Togo has common frontiers with Upper Volta in the north, Dahomey in the east and Ghana in the west. In the south are the Gulf of Guinea and the Atlantic. The capital is Lomé. Togo's economy is largely dependent on agriculture and the exploitation of mineral resources. Coffee and phosphates are the major exports. Other principal products are palm kernels, cotton, kapok, manioc and groundnuts.

Togo

The Republic of Togo became independent on April 27, 1960. It was a German colony from 1894 to 1914, then at the beginning of World War I it was surrendered to the Allies. The territory was subsequently divided between the British and the French. In October, 1956, the French-administered territory voted for an autonomous republic within the French Union. They retained this status until independence.

In December, 1956, the UN General Assembly approved the termination of the British Administration and the union of the territory with the Gold Coast (now Ghana) when it attained independence in 1957.

in United Nations-supervised elections in French Togoland on April 27, 1958, the party of Sylvanus Olympio was swept into power and M. Olympio became head of the Government. On November 14, 1958, the General Assembly accepted unanimously the French-Togolese proposal that the trusteeship should be abolished on independence.

Togo has a President and a 46-member Legislature. Two Togolese Presidents have been overthrown by the Army since independence.

The first, President Sylvanus Olympio, was assassinated on January 13, 1963. Four years later to the day, on Friday January 13, 1967, his brother-in-law, Nicolas Grunitzky, the exiled Opposition leader who had succeeded him was thrown out by a second *coup*.

Events leading up to independence forced Togo's leaders to take a differing line on relations with the former administering power, France.

Grunitzky was the first to become head of the Government in pre-independence Togo. Olympio was unpopular with the territorial administrators and when he and his political supporters forced the United Nations to police an election in the territory in 1958, he himself was unable to run because his civil rights had been suspended for five years.

The electors judged Grunitzky too pro-French for the nationalistic mood of that time. Olympio's party, the Togolese Unity Party (PUT) – then known as the Togolese Unity Committee (CUT) – swept into power winning 31 seats out of the 46. The ban on Olympio

was lifted and he became Prime Minister, then
President.

Sylvanus Olympio enjoyed an influence stretching far
beyond the border of his little sliver of a country on the
Gulf of Guinea. A former manager of the Unilever
Organisation in West Africa, he had a firm grasp of
economic questions and his fluency in languages – he
spoke faultless English, French and German – impressed
foreign visitors.

He made no less of an impression with African leaders,
including some who were not easily impressed or
influenced, like Sekou Touré of Guinea. He was friendly
at the outset with Kwame Nkrumah of Ghana, but
relations soured when Ghana started talking of making
Togo a 'Ghanaian province'. By the time Togo achieved
independence, three years after Ghana, Olympio had
already dubbed Nkrumah a 'black imperialist'.

One of Olympio's main political aims was to reunite
the Ewe people, the race to which he belonged. The
Ewe, with cultural disciplines laid down in German
times and favoured by the French in colonial days as
clerks and civil servants, are probably one of the most
able and best trained of the West African tribes.

In the division of Germany's colonies after World War I
the Ewe found their territory split. Olympio wanted to
join them up again under the 1956 United Nations
referendum in British Togoland, but Nkrumah won the
referendum and British Togoland became part of
Ghana.

The assassination of Olympio by Togo soldiers
dissatisfied with his army policy, caused violent reaction.
African states refused to recognise the new Government,
and France used her good offices to make sure there
was no take-over by the men directly responsible for
Olympio's death. In the mood of Africa at the time
Togo might have been diplomatically isolated.

Nicolas Grunitzky, Olympio's brother-in-law but a
member of the opposing political camp, was recalled
from exile to head the Government.

One factor overlooked by foreign visitors to Togo,
impressed by Olympio's efficiency, urbane manner and
simple style of living, was that he was ruthless with his
opponents. The Juvento Party (Movement of Togolese
Youth) was originally Olympio's youth group but,

The Presidential Palace in Lomé, seen through the main gateway

displeased with their radical aims, he drove them out of the Government and jailed two of their leaders, Anani Santos and Firmin Abalo. After Olympio's assassination jail conditions for political prisoners were revealed to be particularly harsh.

In contrast, the Grunitzky Government which followed was essentially a 'mild' one. All parties, including Olympio's, were called to a round-table conference to set up a coalition.

Grunitzky's Government did not reject any of the international friendships that Olympio had fostered, although it concentrated most on good relations with France and the moderate group of French-speaking states around Togo. Togo became the fifth member of the *Entente*, a loose grouping of French-speaking West African states which up to then had comprised Dahomey, Ivory Coast, Niger, and Upper Volta.

But despite the tolerance of Grunitzky's regime, opposition came to a head again at the end of four years, particularly among the country's youth.

In November, 1966, sympathisers of Sylvanus's party urged demonstrators out on to the streets to demand Grunitzky's resignation. But the Army, headed by a youthful former fighter in Indochina and Algiers, Lieutenant-Colonel Etienne Eyadema, 29, declared in favour of Grunitzky and the leaders of the demonstration either fled or were arrested.

Grunitzky's fall was not to be long delayed. Discussions about overthrowing his Government and holding elections were going on under his nose and on January

13, 1967 (the anniversary of Olympio's overthrow was probably deliberately chosen) the Army called on him to stand down.

Grunitzky resigned and left the country for France. The Army set up a Committee of Reconciliation headed by Colonel Kléber Dadjo, Chief of Staff under Olympio, which was given the job of organising elections within three months.

On the economic front, Olympio did a great deal to encourage foreign investment to exploit Togo's limited natural resources and at the same time maintained an iron grip on budgeting at home. His economic policies were in general followed by the Grunitzky Government. Phosphate mining in southern Togo began in 1962 and is expanding rapidly. Coffee is the other major export, although it is in oversupply on world markets. Because of this Togo has a continuing trade deficit which in 1965 amounted to about £6.4 million sterling. Nevertheless, foreign aid, from France, West Germany and the United States, has helped erase the effect of this deficit.

JOSEPH FENENOU ABALO

An influential member of the radical Juvento party of which he was secretary-general until 1964, Firmin Joseph Fedenou Abalo was at first an ally of President Sylvanus Olympio and was then imprisoned by him without trial in December, 1961.

He came out of prison in 1963 after the assassination of Olympio and was spokesman for his party at numerous party round-table conferences.

He was born in 1918 at Okou in the plateau region, was educated in Togo and was a Catholic religious instructor from 1934–36 and a customs agent from 1936–52.

PIERRE ADAM ADOSSAMA

Pierre Adam Adossama, a member of the Togolese Unity Party, founded by Sylvanus Olympio, was one of the two Ministers whose resignation triggered off the overthrow of the Grunitzky Government in January, 1967.

He was born in September, 1929 in the capital, Lomé.

From 1949–58, he was a radio operator, telegraphist and meteorologist. He took a course at the School of Meteorology at Saint Cyr in France from 1956–57.

In 1958 he was appointed to the office of the Togolese Minister of Education and in 1959 took his certificate at the Togolese School of Administration. Under the Sylvanus Olympio Government he served in the key post of Chief Administrator of the Ministry of Economic Affairs.

With the assassination of Olympio, Adossama joined in Grunitzky's coalition conferences. He was first appointed Minister of Education before his nomination as Minister of Labour, Civil Service and Social Services in January, 1966.

Georges Apedoh-Amah

On November 19, 1966, Adossama handed his resignation to President Grunitzky, as did Benoit Malou. A few days later demonstrations broke out in the streets demanding the resignation of Grunitzky. On that occasion the Army chiefs backed Grunitzky and the leaders of the demonstration either fled or were jailed.

Adossama was reportedly held in a police camp. Grunitzky charged him with being in liaison with the leaders of the demonstration.

After the Army *coup* of January 13, 1967, Adossama was named chief adviser to the eight-man Committee of National Reconciliation charged with running the country and preparing elections.

At the same time he undertook an important mission for the Committee, representing Togo at the Council of the *Entente,* the grouping of moderate French-speaking West African states, which was then meeting in the Ivory Coast capital, Abidjan.

MAJOR ALBERT ALIDOU

Major Albert Alidou became head of the Togo National Police Force (Gendarmerie Nationale) in September, 1965.

Born on February 3, 1922, he joined the Togo militia in 1942. After serving as troop commander in various parts of the country, he completed a three-month course at the French Police Officers' School at Melun in 1961.

In 1963 he was promoted to captain, commanding the Mobile Police Force; in 1965 he became a major.

GEORGES APEDO-AMAH

Georges Apedo-Amah was a staunch political ally of Nicolas Grunitzky and Foreign Minister in the Grunitzky Governments.

Much admired abroad for his efficiency as an administrator and conciliator, he became unpopular with the younger leaders of the Army and political parties and a target of the 1967 Army *coup.*

Born on August 21, 1914, at Anecho in the south of Togo, he held a variety of Civil Service posts in the colonial Administration and a number of portfolios in M. Grunitzky's pre-independence Cabinet before becoming Foreign Minister in 1963.

Widely respected by both African and non-African diplomats, he made valuable contributions to various regional and continental meetings he attended.

Educated in Togo, M. Apedo-Amah entered the colonial Administration in 1930 and later occupied various important posts including Secretary to the French High Commissioner at Lomé. In 1958 he was named Government Counsellor in charge of Education, Youth and Sport and became Minister of Finance in the country's first Government.

M. Apedo-Amah left Togo when Grunitzky's party was voted out of power in the elections supervised by the United Nations in 1958. He worked first in France and then with the European Economic Community in Brussels.

MAJOR JAMES ASSILA

Major James Assila, Deputy Chief of Staff of the Togolese Armed Forces, was transferred to the Togolese Army in 1962 after eleven years in the French Army.

He was born at Nuatja in 1932. Joining the French Army in 1951 he served in Indochina and Algeria (1956-57).

He became a captain in 1963 and a major in October, 1965.

Col Kléber Dadjo

BENOIT BEDOU

Benoit Bedou, the Minister of Finance and Economy appointed in January, 1967, spent 27 years as a civil servant concerned with financial matters. For 21 years he was at Dakar as head of the Federal Finance Services of the AOF – the former organisation of French West African States.

He was born of Togolese parents at Porto Novo, Dahomey, in 1920. Graduating from the William Ponty School in Senegal in 1940, he occupied various official posts before going to the United States in 1960 for training in economics and finance.

In 1961 under the late President Olympio he became director of the Department of Finance.

COL KLEBER DADJO

A reluctant adherent to the military *putsch* of January, 1963, after the assassination of President Sylvanus Olympio, Colonel Kléber Dadjo was given the job of heading a provisional governing committee when the Army stepped in a second time to overthrow Olympio's successor, Nicolas Grunitzky, in January, 1967.

Colonel Dadjo was born on August 12, 1914, in the central region of Togo. From 1933–38 he served in the Togo Police Force and joined the Free French Army in June 1941. He was sent to Accra where the Free French Forces were training and was later posted to Brazzaville, Dakar and Cotonou.

In August, 1948 he was sent to France where he embarked a few months later for Indochina. He fought with the French Army there until 1955.

He returned to Togo as a Chevalier de la Légion d'Honneur and was stationed in Lomé.

He rose rapidly through the ranks. Promoted captain on April 1, 1957, he became commander of the para-military Garde Togolaise and a major in 1960. He was promoted to lieutenant-colonel in 1963 after the military *putsch* that overthrew Olympio's Government. Late in 1963 Grunitzky, alarmed by a plot by Olympio supporters, promoted Dadjo to the 'safe' post of military attaché to the Presidency. Dadjo was made full colonel in October, 1965.

When the Army seized power again under Colonel Etienne Eyadema in January 1967, Dadjo was called back to head an eight-member National Reunification Committee. They were given the job of running the country temporarily and preparing – within three months – for new elections. On the Committee, Colonel Dadjo was put in charge of Defence and Foreign Affairs.

BOUKARI DJOBO

One of the young 'technocrats' brought into the cabinet in the last months of the Grunitzky Government, Boukari Djobo, a northerner, is likely to play a role of increasing prominence in Togolese affairs.

Born at Sokode in 1936, he went to schools in Togo, Senegal and France.

His law course was divided between the Universities of Dakar, Bordeaux and Paris, with a year in each.

He returned to the Togolese Civil Service in October 1960 and from 1961-62 he took a training course for African economists at the United Nations in New York.

From 1960-63 he was director of the international aid section of the Planning Office under the economics-conscious President, Sylvanus Olympio.

443

Lt-Col Etienne
Eyadema

After the assassination of
Olympio he was named to head
the Togolese delegation at the
18th session of the United Nations
General Assembly.

In June, 1964, he became a
civil administrator at the Planning Office, chairman of the
board of the Union Togolaise de
Banque, and a governor of the
International Bank of Reconstruction and Development.

He was appointed Minister of
Finance and Economic Affairs in
the Grunitzky Cabinet of
January, 1966, and with the
Army *coup* a year later became
one of the eight-member Committee of National Reconciliation charged with running the
country and preparing elections.
On the committee he was charged with running the Civil
Service and social services.

PAULIN EKLOU
Paulin Eklou was released from
the Mango Prison (north Togo)
after the *coup* of January 13, 1967,
to become Minister of Commerce,
Industry and Tourism. With
other intellectuals, he was involved in the attempt in
November, 1966, to overthrow
the Grunitzky regime.

M. Eklou was born in central
Togo on February 13, 1928. He
went to France in 1947 for his
secondary education and entered
Montpellier University in 1950.
Two years later he was at the
National Institute of Economic
and Financial Sciences, graduating in 1957.

For a time he was attached to
the Central Bank in Paris and
did practical training overseas in
Brazzaville and Cotonou. He
went to the United Nations for
further training and in 1962 was
appointed by the late President
Olympio as head of Togo's
Economic Planning Department.

LT-COL ETIENNE EYADEMA
Lieutenant-Colonel Etienne
Gnassingbe Eyadema, Chief of
the General Staff, was born
about 1937 in the Lama-Kara
region of northern Togo.

Joining the French Army in
May, 1953, he was sent to Indochina, where he fought for 18
months.

At the end of the Indochina
war, he was transferred to Algeria
to complete his active service.
Later he was stationed in
Dahomey and Niger.

Eyadema was one of the
principal organisers of the military *putsch* against the regime of
ex-President Olympio.

An adjutant before the *coup,* he
was promoted captain after the
May, 1963 elections and major in
1964.

He was named Chief of the
General Staff of the Togolese
Armed Forces in 1965 after
Major Emmanuel Bodjolle was
dismissed by President Grunitzky,
who accused the former Chief of
Staff of abuse of power and in-
efficiency.

Promoted to the rank of
lieutenant-colonel on October
29, 1965, Eyadema visited France
for a few weeks in July, 1966, and
was received by General de
Gaulle.

When demonstrators massed
in the street in November, 1966,
calling for President Grunitzky
to resign, Eyadema at first
supported the President.

But two months later with
political ferment still continuing
he called on him to resign.

Eyadema, who announced
publicly that he had no political
ambitions, asked another former
Chief of Staff, Colonel Kléber
Dadjo, who occupied this key
Army post under the Government
of President Sylvanus Olympio,
to set up a governing Committee

Dr Emmanuel Gagli

Nicolas Grunitzky

of National Reconciliation to run the country and prepare new elections.

Thus Eyadema followed the lead of a neighbouring military colleague, Colonel Kotoka of Ghana who, after overthrowing President Kwame Nkrumah in an early-morning *coup,* called on his former commander to head the Government.

DR EMMANUEL GAGLI

Dr Emmanuel Gagli practised medicine full-time until he entered the Togo National Assembly in 1963 and began a political career. This brought him the Ministries of Justice and Health after the abortive *coup* of November, 1966, and Health alone when the Cabinet was again reshuffled in less than a month.

Dr Gagli was born at Atakpame in the Plateau Region, in 1915.

He went to primary and secondary schools in his own country, then left for Senegal where he attended the William Ponty School and then medical school in Dakar. He returned to Togo in 1938 and worked in medicine until 1953.

From 1954–56, Dr Gagli was at Dakar Hospital. In 1956 he went to France to complete his medical studies. He spent a year at the Faculty of Medicine at Bordeaux, then on to Paris for his doctor's diploma. At the same time he also qualified as a medical inspector at the National School of Public Health.

Dr Gagli went back to Togo in 1960 to take charge of the administration of the Health Service until December of that year, when he resigned. In July, 1962, he accepted the job of chief medical officer at Dapango in the extreme north of Togo.

After the legislative elections in 1963 he became a deputy in the National Assembly and was elected Deputy Vice-President of the Assembly in 1965 and first Vice-President in 1966.

NICOLAS GRUNITZKY

Nicolas Grunitzky was Togo's second President. He came to power in 1963 after the assassination of his brother-in-law Sylvanus Olympio.

A moderate in political outlook, M. Grunitzky was highly regarded as a hard-working and efficient administrator. Educated in France as an engineer specialising in public works, he has also had a successful business career in transportation and contruction.

M. Grunitzky was born to a Polish father and a Togolese mother in the western Togo town of Atakpame on April 5, 1913, only one year before British and French troops attacked the Germans who had been controlling the area since 1884. The 1919 Franco-British agreement gave the area of Togo where young Grunitzky lived to France, who ruled it under a League of Nations mandate. The future President took his higher education in France, gaining his baccalaureate in mathematics and a diploma in engineering.

On completion of his education in 1937 he returned to Togo. When the territory went under the control of the Vichy Government during World War II, M. Grunitzky, then working in Lomé, became an active Gaullist and member of the underground. In 1946, Togo, although now a French UN Trusteeship, was also integrated into the French Union and became represented in the French Assembly and other French governing bodies as an associate member. M. Grunitzky was elected to the French Assembly as the Togolese representative in 1951 and again in 1956.

Meanwhile, agitation for more self-rule was manifested in southern Togo by members of the Ewe tribe, who also live along the coastal areas of neighbouring Ghana (then the Gold Coast) and Dahomey. The agitation, coupled with a similar, and successful, independence struggle in the Gold Coast, led the French to start Togo on the road to internal self-government. With the Togolese demanding the lifting of the trusteeship, the French on August 26, 1955, gave the territory a new status, the Autonomous Republic of Togo (République Autonome du Togo). Under the scheme a Legislative Assembly and a Council of Ministers was created to manage Togo's internal affairs, while the French remained in charge of defence and foreign affairs. In a national referendum, 72 per cent of the population voted for the new status, although the majority of the Ewes, who were demanding union with the Ewes in Dahomey and the Gold Coast, voted against the proposition.

Meanwhile M. Grunitzky had formed the Togolese Progress Party ('Parti Togolais du Progrès') which won the subsequent national election, thus making its leader the first Prime Minister of Togo. But only two years later, in 1958, M. Olympio's then Togolese Unity Committee ('Comité de l'Unité Togolaise') a more radical and more anti-French party, gained 31 seats to the PTP's three, removing M. Grunitzky from power. On April 27, 1960, Togo gained its full independence under the premier-

ship of M. Sylvanus Olympio.

Following his 1958 defeat, M. Grunitzky the following year combined his party with the Union of Chiefs and Population of the North ('L'Union des Chefs et des Populations du Nord') into a new party called the 'Union Démocratique des Populations Togolaises' (UDPT). But the merger was of no avail and in the 1961 elections, which also approved a change to a presidential system, M. Olympio's party won every seat.

M. Olympio instituted a tight policy of economic and fiscal control which led to his death on January 13, 1963, when a group of soldiers who opposed his plan to trim the Army budget killed him and took temporary control of the country.

Under Army rule a provisional Government was set up with M. Grunitzky, who had gone into exile in Dahomey in 1962, as President. On May 5, 1963, the Togolese population went to the polls to approve a new Constitution and vote for a new Parliament. Four parties won seats in the new Parliament and M. Grunitzky formed a coalition Government. In the new Government, which received backing from the Army, UDPT members also held the office of Vice-President and the Ministries of Foreign Affairs and the Interior. Other parties represented were M. Olympio's UT, the Togolese People's Movement and Juvento.

As President, M. Grunitzky improved relations with the French Government, which had become strained while M. Olympio was in power. Other Western powers have also forged strong links with Togo and are aiding it with its five-year development plan which aims to increase production and agricultural output and improve social conditions.

Although more moderate members of the UT joined the Government, its more extreme wing opposed it and during the following three years various men were arrested and held on subversive charges. Others went into exile. Finally on November 21, 1966, a group of UT supporters temporarily took over the radio station and, claiming they had the backing of the Army, called on the population to come out into the streets to overthrow the Government.

Hundreds of people did demonstrate that morning, but following consultations between Col Eyadema and M. Grunitzky, the Army moved in and broke up the demonstration, arresting a number of ringleaders. Others, including the UT deputy general secretary, Noe Kutuklui, fled.

At the same time a dispute within the ranks of the UDPT, which developed while M. Grunitzky was in Paris for medical reasons earlier in the month, came to a head. Faced by both crises, the President held negotiations with leaders of all four parties and formed an entirely new Government.

In the new Administration M. Grunitzky also assumed the portfolios of Defence, Public Works, Mines, Transport and Post and Telecommunications.

The new Government lasted only two months.

The Army which had come to M. Grunitzky's rescue during the street manifestations called on Grunitzky to resign on January 13, 1967, the fourth anniversary of Sylvanus Olympio's overthrow.

Grunitzky complied and the *coup* was bloodless. He left later for France.

NOE KUTUKLUI

The recognised leader of the extreme wing of the United Togolese Party, Noe Kutuklui has been named both by the Government and his own supporters as the man behind the attempt to oust President Grunitzky in November, 1966.

At the height of the street demonstrations against the President, M. Kutuklui, a fiery, persuasive speaker, addressed a large group of UT supporters, urging them on in their campaign. Later that day as the Army moved in to crush the demonstrators M. Kutuklui went into hiding.

Very close to the murdered President Sylvanus Olympio and acknowledged as his heir-apparent, M. Kutuklui is a staunch socialist and nationalist who repeatedly stated his opposition to the close relations the Grunitzky Government had with France.

He was born into a poor family on December 2, 1923, at Anecho, on the eastern coast of Togo. He went to Dakar for his secondary school education and received his baccalaureate in 1945. Two years later he went to France to study mathematics, but changed his mind and took law at Caen University.

His political activity began with his higher education. He gained prominence in various Togolese and African student groups in France and was president of the Federation of Black African Students in France (FEANF).

Following his return to Lomé in the late 1950s, he joined the United Togolese Movement and at its Congress in October, 1962, became deputy secretary-general.

In the provisional Government which was formed after M.

Olympio's assassination, M. Kutuklui held the post of Minister of Labour and Social Affairs. Following the 1963 general elections he became identified as leader of the extreme wing of the UT and was eventually arrested on the charge of planning a *coup* against President Grunitzky. He was given ten months' imprisonment by a specially constituted court and when released returned to his work as a noted lawyer in Lomé.

After the January, 1967 Army *coup*, it was announced that M. Kutuklui was free to return home if he wished.

BARTHELEMY LAMBONI

Until the bloodless military *coup* of January, 1967, Barthélemy Lamboni was President of the Togo National Assembly. He was given the portfolio of National Education in the new Government set up by the Reunification Council.

He was born on December 16, 1937 in northern Togo. After completing his secondary education, he proceeded to France with a government scholarship and from 1956-60 read law at Bordeaux and Paris Universities. On graduation he did a year's practical course in parliamentary proceedings and returned to Togo, where he became Clerk of the Assembly.

In 1963, following Olympio's assassination, M. Lamboni, who is a member of the Juvento, was given the portfolio of Education in Grunitzky's provisional Government. He was elected to the Togo Assembly two months later and became its Speaker (President) on May 5, 1963.

BENOIT MALOU

Benoit Malou is one of the group of young Togolese 'technocrats' whose intervention resulted in the toppling of the Grunitzky Government.

With M. Pierre Adossama he resigned from the Grunitzky Government on November 19, 1966, thus precipitating the crisis that was to lead to Grunitzky's downfall two months later.

M. Malou was born at Pya in 1932 in the extreme north of Togo. He comes from the Lama-Kara district which produces the largest number of Togolese troops. He is a nephew of Lt-Col Eyadema, Togolese Chief of Staff.

He went first to a missionary school in his own district and then trained to be a teacher in Lomé, taking his certificate in 1953.

From 1953-57 he was a schoolteacher at Farende and Lomé.

In charge of a course at the Protestant seminary at Atakpame in the south in 1958, he entered the police training school of the short-lived Mali Federation in Dakar the following year.

With the break-up of the Federation he returned to Togo where he served with the National Security office in Lomé, Sokode and Atakpame before becoming Assistant Director of National Security in August, 1963.

In March, 1965 M. Malou studied with the Police School in Paris. Having obtained his diploma he returned to serve with the Interior Ministry until his appointment as Minister of Education in the Grunitzky Government in January, 1966.

Malou's action in resigning from the Grunitzky Government in November, 1966 quickly led to the street demonstrations of the same month which failed to bring Grunitzky down.

Malou was reported to be under arrest in a police camp

Fousseni Mama

Antoine Meatchi

and Grunitzky charged him with being in contact with the demonstration leaders.

After the Army *coup* of January 13, 1966, Malou was named as one of the eight members of the Committee of National Reconciliation charged with preparing elections within three months. He was given responsibility for running the Ministries of Information and the Interior.

FOUSSENI MAMA

Born in Sokode in the north of Togo in 1924, Fousseni Mama's political fortunes have been closely associated with those of President Grunitzky's party.

After finishing his studies in Dakar he taught for eight years at a number of centres in Togo.

He was a member of the Territorial Assembly of Togo from 1951–56 and a councillor of the French Union from 1953–56.

From 1956–57 he was Minister of Public Works, Mines, Transport, and Post and Telecommunications in the Government of the Autonomous Republic of Togo. From then until M. Grunitzky's Government fell he was Minister of State in charge of the Interior, Post and Telecommunications.

With the return of the Grunitzky Government, he was Minister delegated to the Presidency in May, 1963, and Minister of the Interior from October, 1964. He was named Minister of Education after the attempt to overthrow Grunitzky in November, 1966, and held the same post when the Cabinet was reshuffled a month later.

ANTOINE MEATCHI

The tall, forceful Antoine Meatchi rose to the highest post ever occupied by a Togolese northerner, that of Vice-President, but lost it in constitutional changes which followed the abortive *coup* of November, 1966, against President Grunitzky.

The reasons for the introduction of a constitutional amendment which abolished the vice-presidency and stripped Meatchi of most of his power were never entirely explained. President Grunitzky himself told the Assembly that he wished to avoid the 'double headed' type of Cabinet which had caused so much trouble in Africa.

An Army spokesman said on January 28, 1967, that a major reason behind the second *coup* was a power struggle going on between Grunitzky and Meatchi.

Meatchi's political career started late – in 1955 – following a long period of study and service in agriculture. Born on September 13, 1925, in the leading northern town of Sokode he attended primary school in Togo before going abroad in 1942, first to Mali and then to France for extensive study which made him an expert both in general and tropical agriculture.

M. Meatchi returned to Togo in 1953 and became deputy chief of agricultural services in Lomé, head of agricultural direction in the south-western town of Klouto and director of the Farm School at Tove.

A member of the Togo Government Council he became Minister of Agriculture in M. Grunitzky's first Government. Following the 1958 elections which ousted the Grunitzky Administration, M. Meatchi was voted into the Togo Assembly where he became the leader of the parliamentary Opposition to the late Sylvanus Olympio's Government.

In the ensuing 1961 general election Meatchi lost his parliamentary seat, then was accused of subversion and arrested. On his release he went into exile in Ghana.

After the 1963 *coup* he returned to become Minister of Finance, Public Works and Post and Telecommunications in the Grunitzky provisional Government.

He assumed the vice-presidency and was responsible for Finance and Economic Planning in the permanent Government formed after the 1963 elections.

In 1965 his Ministries were changed to Finance and Economy.

In the Government formed immediately after the abortive *coup* in November, 1966, he dropped the Finance portfolio but took over the key post of Minister of the Interior.

Subsequent to this reshuffle a number of political moves took place which effectively reduced M. Meatchi's power. On December 14, Parliament voted by 41 votes for and three against to eliminate the vice-presidency from the Government's hierarchy.

In a new reshuffle of Cabinet posts on December 23, M. Meatchi was the Minister mainly affected. He lost the key Interior Ministry and became Minister of Works, Mines and Transport.

ALEX MIVEDOR

One of the leaders of the abortive *coup* of November, 1966, Alex Mivedor was recalled from exile in Mali by the Reunification Council (January, 1967) to take up the portfolio of Public Works, Post and Telecommunications. He had been an influencial member of the late President Olympio's party (CUT).

M. Mivedor was born in southern Togo on March 2, 1927. A government scholarship en-

abled him to study at Toulouse University, France, where he graduated in 1955 as an electrical and hydraulic engineer.

While working in Mali as an engineer he became a member of the Mali Youth Association. Returning home in 1958 he was placed in charge of the electrical and hydraulic services of the Public Works Department.

ALEX OHIN

The only Togolese surgical specialist who has had both French and American training, Alex Ohin is the Minister of Health and Social Welfare. He was appointed by the Togo Reunification Council after the military *putsch* of January 13, 1967. He was involved in the abortive *coup* of November, 1966, and was arrested and imprisoned.

Born on March 18, 1920 in southern Togo, M. Ohin received his medical education in Dakar up to 1943. For ten years he practised as a medical officer in Togo then went overseas for further studies. He attended Vancouver University (Canada), the University of California (USA) and graduated in Missouri. For six years he was in charge of a clinic in Washington.

He returned home in 1961 and was appointed surgeon at Lomé Central Hospital.

M. Ohin is the author of many research books on cancer and surgical metabolism.

MAITRE ANANI IGNACIO SANTOS

Maître Anani Ignacio Santos first came into the political limelight in 1957 when he pleaded before the United Nations General Assembly in New York for Togo's independence from colonial France.

In the 1958 general elections,

Léonard Ywassa

supervised by the UN, he was elected to the Togo Assembly and became Minister of Justice in President Olympio's first Government. His resignation two years later created the first serious crisis in the Government, which was a coalition of the United Front – the 'Comité de l'Union Togolese' – and its left wing, the Juvento. In 1961 Maître Santos was arrested for alleged subversion and imprisoned until the January, 1963 *coup* in which Olympio was overthrown.

Maître Santos has appeared in many famous cases and is regarded as one of the most distinguished lawyers in Africa. He was born in 1915. His father was of Brazilian descent, his mother a Togolese. He graduated a doctor of law at Paris University, returned home from France in 1946 and began practising in Lomé the following year.

DR VALENTIN VOVOR

President of the Supreme Court of Togo, Dr Valentin Mawupe Vovor was born at Agome-Koussountou in the south on October 29, 1925.

After primary studies at a Catholic school in Palime, Togo, he went to Dakar to the William Ponty School then to the School of African Medicine. He took his baccalaureate in France in 1948 and 1949, then went to the Universities of Montpellier and Dijon, becoming a licentiate in sciences at the first and a doctor of medicine at the second, with a prize and honourable mention for his thesis.

Then, at Dijon Hospital, he specialised in surgery and gynaecology, and in 1957 he became a surgeon at the National Central Hospital in Lomé and head of the surgical clinic of the Faculty of Medicine in Dakar (1961).

The following year he was back in his own country as head doctor of the subdivision of Palime in the south and head of the Studies' office at the Ministry of Public Health. In 1962 he added the directorship of the Nursing School of Togo to his other duties.

He has written some 60 scientific papers and books and these won him the decoration of Knight of the Order of Merit of Public Health.

LEONARD YWASSA

Secretary-General of Grunitzky's 'Union Démocratique des Populations du Togo', Léonard Ywassa, a northerner, served in the pre-independence Government of M. Grunitzky and held the post of Minister of Rural Economy after President Grunitzky's return to power.

He was an Opposition deputy when the Grunitzky party was defeated in 1958 and in 1960 he became party secretary-general.

Born on December 1, 1926 at Niamtougou-Koka, M. Ywassa is an agricultural engineer with a diploma from the National Agricultural College at Nancy, France. On his return to Togo in 1953 he became head of the agricultural district of Anecho in 1953 and later head of the district of Mango in the north and of a pilot agricultural station.

In 1956 M. Ywassa entered the first Government of the Autonomous Republic of Togo as Minister of Labour, Civil Service and Social Affairs as well as Minister of Education.

As Minister of Rural Economy after the return of the Grunitzky Government, M. Ywassa has undertaken a number of missions to the United States and Europe.

Uganda is the smallest of the East African countries. Of its 91,076 square miles, 4,694 are swamp and 11,670 open water, mainly the Uganda section of Lake Victoria, from which the Nile starts its 3,000-mile journey to the Near East and the Mediterranean. The population is 7,551,000 (mid-1965 estimate). Uganda has frontiers with Sudan to the north, Kenya to the east and Tanzania to the south. Congo Kinshasa lies to the west. The capital is Kampala. Primarily agricultural, Uganda's economy relies largely on its farms and smallholdings. Coffee and cotton between them account for about three-quarters of the value of all exports.

Uganda

The British Protectorate of Uganda, consisting principally
of tribal districts and four traditional kingdoms joined in
federal relationships with the Central Government,
became a fully independent member of the Commonwealth
on October 9, 1962.
A year later the post of Governor-General was replaced by
that of a President, elected by the National Assembly for a
five-year term.
The first President was Sir Edward Mutesa, Kabaka (King)
of Buganda, the richest of the kingdoms.
Early in 1966 there was political unrest and Opposition
members of Parliament made accusations of corruption
against the Deputy Commander of the Army, Colonel Idi
Amin, and Ministers of the Government.
Dr Milton Obote, the socialist Prime Minister, assumed
full powers of government (February 22) and two days later
suspended the constitution, saying there had been an
attempt by people who held positions in the Government
to overthrow it with the help of foreign troops. Five
Ministers were detained.
In April, 1966, Dr Obote introduced a new constitution
which abolished the federal relationships, ousted the
Kabaka and himself became Executive President.
He declared that the Kabaka had made a request for
foreign troops to be sent to Uganda. Sir Edward denied
this and ordered Dr Obote to withdraw his government
from Buganda.
The Uganda Army besieged the Kabaka's Palace (May 24,
1966) and Sir Edward fled to England. Dr Obote declared
that by fleeing he had abdicated. Sir Edward, however,
contended that he had not.
At the end of 1966 Dr Obote told Parliament that the new
constitution had been introduced after a revolution.
'The revolution', he said, 'is still going on.' Under the
abrogated constitution new elections were due by April,
1967. But Dr Obote said there would be no elections for five
years.

There were strong elements of monarchy in the new
constitution with which Uganda began independence.
It was a cluster of tiny kingdoms. Merged together as five
federal states were Buganda, Ankole, Bunyoro and Toro
(the kingdoms) and the territory of Busoga. Supreme
legislative power was to rest with a single-chamber

Climbers rest during an ascent of Mount Baker, in the range known as the 'Mountains of the Moon'. The spiky outlines of the giant groundsels are a familiar feature of the Uganda landscape

National Assembly, with Buganda, the largest of the kingdoms, enjoying a high degree of autonomy in internal affairs.

Dr Milton Obote, who had led his country to independence after only five months in power, was Prime Minister when, in February, 1966, he suspended the federal constitution in the interests of national stability, public security and peace. Under a new constitution, introduced in April, 1966, he supplanted the Kabaka of Buganda as President and assumed executive powers.

Dr Obote, outwardly a quiet, thoughtful, pipe-smoking man much given to reflection, has shown himself to be a man of action, a revolutionary, tough, courageous, resourceful and strongly opposed to Uganda following stereotyped European ideas. Uganda has, indeed, plenty of traditions and a native genius and inventiveness of her own.

When Speke and Grant, the first European explorers reached the Buganda capital in 1862 they found themselves among an organised and comparatively civilised people whose way of life had been established for a long time.

Dr Obote has reached the top by practising parliamentary arts and by shrewd party management. He has been described as 'a politician's politician'. This is because he has no profession other than politics, although his earlier occupations were extremely varied, from goatherd to labourer and teacher.

He always aims, it is said, at theoretical perfection, but he has demonstrated that he aims mainly at achieving solutions that work.

Uganda is a country of great beauty and varied, even magnificent, scenery. There are large stretches of arid plateau and wide areas of thick, luxurious rain forest. In the 60-mile long Ruwenzori Range in Western Uganda are the perpetually snow-capped peaks of the fabled 'Mountains of the Moon', whose highest peak reaches 16,794 ft.

There is an abundance of wild life, including huge herds of elephants.

The population of 7,551,000 comprises 7,452,000 Africans, 85,900 Asians, mainly engaged in trading activities, 8,800 Europeans, for the most part expatriates doing administrative, professional or technical work and not permanently settled, 2,100 Arabs, and 2,000 others.

The Parliamentary buildings in Kampala, housing the national Legislature and, in the office block to the right, executive departments of the Civil Service

There is no universally spoken language. The most widely understood African language is Luganda, the language of Buganda. There are many other African vernaculars. English is the official language.

Many of the people hold traditional beliefs, but over half of the African population is Christian and there are several hundred thousand Moslems. The people have often been described as among the most advanced in East Africa.

It was at Makerere in Kampala, now a college of the University of East Africa, that the first university-type college in this part of the continent developed in the 1920s.

Visitors to Uganda sometimes gain the impression that it is more prosperous than it really is. The masses of ordinary people seem determined to keep up the best possible appearances on their incomes, however low. The women are very clothes-conscious and know how to make the most of pretty-coloured materials. They take great pride in their huts and their possessions.

Over 50 years ago Sir Winston Churchill said of Uganda, 'The scenery is different, the vegetation is different, the climate is different and, most of all, the people are different from anything elsewhere to be seen in the whole range of Africa'.

Colonel Idi Amin

COLONEL IDI AMIN

Colonel Idi Amin, Chief of the Uganda Army and Air Force Staff and Commander of the Army, was a central figure in the constitutional crisis in Uganda in 1966, which led to the adoption of a new constitution and the flight to England of the former President and Kabaka of Buganda, Sir Edward Mutesa.

Deputy Commander of the Army at the beginning of 1966, Colonel Amin was the subject of a motion tabled in Parliament on February 5, calling for an investigation of his bank account. At a subsequent judicial commission of inquiry into this and allegations of illegal gold dealings by some Ministers, Colonel Amin said he had been paid large sums of money by Congolese revolutionary leaders to purchase non-military supplies, which he did. He also said he had been sent by the Uganda Government to the Congo in 1964 to organise the training of revolutionary forces and as a contact man. Cabinet Ministers gave evidence at the inquiry of the bad relations existing between Colonel Amin and the Commander of the Army, Brigadier Shaban Opolot.

Shortly after February, 1966 – when, it was later claimed by the Government, there had been attempts by certain Army officers and other prominent people to overthrow the Government – Colonel Amin was appointed Chief of the Army and Air Force Staff and, although not immediately stated, became in effect Army Commander. Brigadier Opolot was transferred to the Ministry of Defence as Chief of the Defence Staff until October, 1966, when he was summarily dismissed from the Army and detained under the Emergency regulations which were in force in the territory of Uganda.

Colonel Amin led the Army operations against the Kabaka's palace in May, which crushed the Buganda rebellion, and became the most prominent figure in the Army. On October 9, the day after Opolot's arrest, he led a large Army and Air Force parade in Kampala to mark the fourth anniversary of Uganda's independence.

Colonel Amin, who joined the Army in 1946 as a private in the 4th (Uganda) Battalion of the King's African Rifles, comes from the West Nile district in northern Uganda. He is a large, cheerful man, extremely popular with the ordinary soldier. He served in the KAR with the 11th East African Division in Burma during the World War II and later in Kenya during the Mau Mau Emergency. He is a former Uganda heavyweight boxing champion (1951–60), also an enthusiastic rugby player. In 1959 Amin, who had attained the rank of sergeant-major, was promoted to *effendi* (a new rank at the time for African soldiers). In July, 1961, he was commissioned, and promoted to major in November, 1963. During a course in Israel he gained paratrooper wings. After the departure of British officers from the Uganda Army following the brief mutiny in 1964, he was promoted colonel and became Deputy Commander.

OMUGABE (KING) OF ANKOLE

Sir Charles Godfrey Gasyonga II, Omugabe of Ankole, was born in 1910 and educated in Uganda.

His kingdom covers 6,000 square miles and has a population of 550,000.

He comes of a race of near-giants. He is well over six feet, and the previous king, his uncle, measured six feet eight inches.

He has a ranch in his kingdom where he specialises in breeding pedigree long-horned Ankole cattle.

J. K. BABIIHA

John Kabwimukya Babiiha, the oldest member of the Cabinet, was appointed Vice-President of Uganda in May, 1966, under the constitution introduced following the deposition of Sir Edward Mutesa as President. Mr Babiiha, Minister of Animal Industry, Game and Fisheries from 1962, combines politics with a keen scientific interest in animal life and maintained this portfolio after assuming the Vice-Presidency.

Married with several children, Mr Babiiha was born in Toro, in western Uganda in 1913. In 1933, after education at various schools in Uganda, he gained a Government scholarship to Makerere College, where he took a diploma in veterinary science. Thereafter, from 1939–45, he worked as a veterinary officer in Uganda. In 1946 he joined the Toro Kingdom Government, first as secretary to the Rukurato (Parliament) and later as assistant treasurer. In 1954 he was nominated by the Rukurato as a Toro member of the Uganda Legislative Council. In 1958 he was elected to the Council and re-elected in 1961 prior to the attainment of independence, when the Legislative Council became the Parliament of Uganda.

Mr Babiiha showed a keen interest in the constitutional arrangements being made for Uganda and in 1958 issued a manifesto on constitutional reform. He urged a compromise between a unitary State and a federal one, with the provinces of Uganda having their own provincial assemblies and a two-house Central Parliament. He suggested that the traditional rulers should form a council of state, from which they would be chosen in rotation to serve as head of state for a period of five years. This last proposal was embodied in the 1962 Constitution for Uganda, but in 1966 it was replaced by a new constitution under which the powers of the regions were reduced.

In 1960, with the forming of the Uganda People's Congress by Dr Obote, Mr Babiiha became national chairman of the party and has since been closely connected with party affairs.

He is, *inter alia,* a member of the Uganda Economic Development Council and the Uganda Planning Commission; he is also chairman of the East African Council of Veterinary Education.

Mr Babiiha has travelled widely in Africa and Asia and has also made visits to Britain and Australia.

B. K. BATARINGAYA

Basil Kiiza Bataringaya is the only Minister in Dr Milton Obote's Government who also served as a Minister (of Local Government) in the Democratic Party Government of Mr Benedicto Kiwanuka, which was in power during the internal self-governing stage in Uganda from 1961–62.

Mr Bataringaya, who was also secretary-general of the Democratic Party between 1961 and 1964 and leader of the DP Opposition in Parliament (1962–64), switched in 1965 to the Uganda People's Congress and later became Minister of Internal Affairs in Dr Obote's Government.

After the arrest of five Ministers in February, 1966, for allegedly attempting to over-

Godfrey Binaisa

throw the Government of Dr Obote, Mr Bataringaya held the additional portfolio of Agriculture and Cooperatives until the new constitution was introduced in April of that year.

Mr Bataringaya, who comes from Ankole Kingdom, in western Uganda, was born in 1927 and won a Diploma of Education at Makerere College (1953–56). He worked for several years as a senior secondary schoolteacher in Uganda, later becoming supervisor of schools for the Roman Catholic mission in Ankole. He was elected a Democratic Party Member of Parliament in 1961 and was also chairman of the Ankole Eishengyero, the kingdom's Parliament.

GODFREY BINAISA

Godfrey Lukongwa Binaisa, QC, appointed Attorney-General of Uganda in 1962, was the first African in East and Central Africa to become Queen's Counsel.

Mr Binaisa is a Muganda, born in Kampala in 1920. Educated at King's College, Budo, and Makerere University College, he took his law degree at King's College, London, and was called to the Bar in Lincoln's Inn in February, 1956. He returned to Uganda in May of that year and was in private practice in Kampala until his appointment as Attorney-General in Dr Obote's Government prior to independence in October, 1962. His appointment as Queen's Counsel was made in July, 1962.

After the introduction of a new constitution for Uganda in April, 1966, under which Dr Obote became executive President, replacing Sir Edward Mutesa, the Kabaka of Buganda, as constitutional President of Uganda, Mr Binaisa was sent to London to

explain the constitutional position. He had talks with British Government leaders. He was the first Ugandan Minister to point out publicly that what had happened in Uganda was in fact a revolution.

OMUKAMA (KING) OF BUNYORO

Sir Tito Winyi IV, Omukama of Bunyoro, was born in 1883 and educated in Uganda. His country has an area of 7,700 square miles, with a population of 180,000.

He fought in the last tribal war to be waged against the British at the beginning of this century.

M. L. CHOUDRY

Maximo Lokwang Choudry, a former constitutional head of Karamoja district in northern Uganda, generally considered the most backward area in Uganda, became Minister of Mineral and Water Resources after the Cabinet reshuffle in May, 1966, following the introduction of a new constitution by Dr Obote.

Previously he had been Deputy Minister for Planning and Community Development. After his entry into Parliament in 1961 (he was subsequently re-elected in 1961), he became in turn Parliamentary Secretary, Ministry of Land, Mineral and Water Resources, and Parliamentary Secretary, Internal Affairs.

The son of a sub-county chief, Mr Choudry was born in 1933. After education at various schools and colleges in Uganda he became a clerk and later chief interpreter at the DC's office in Moroto, Karamoja (1955–56), moving in 1958 to a position as High Court interpreter and chief court clerk in the Judicial Department. He was elected MP

John Kakonge

for North Karamoja constituency in 1961.

JOHN KAKONGE

John Byabazaire Tinkasimire Kakonge, although an active politician for several years, entered the Cabinet for the first time in May, 1966, on the introduction of a new constitution with Dr Obote as executive President. As Minister of Planning and Economic Development he was, at 32, Uganda's youngest Cabinet Minister.

Mr Kakonge comes from Hoima, Bunyoro Kingdom, and was born in 1934. He began his political career in 1959, when he returned to Uganda with an MA degree in economics from Delhi University. He joined the Obote wing of the Uganda National Congress, and in 1960, on the formation of the Uganda People's Congress, with Dr Obote as president-general, was elected secretary-general.

The following year he became UPC Member for South Mengo, Buganda, in the National Assembly and was Opposition spokesman on foreign affairs. He played a leading role in his party's victory in the elections prior to independence in 1962. Mr Kakonge did not contest a seat then, and claimed later that he had been wrongly excluded from the party's list for specially-elected Members of Parliament. He thereupon resigned from the party and flew off to Tanganyika. He returned twelve days later, however, reconciled with the party. He was returned unopposed as secretary-general and in 1963 became Director of Planning in the Prime Minister's Office, a new post.

Mr Kakonge was accused by some party elements of being too Left-wing. He was reported as saying, 'Every African nationalist is a Socialist and so are most economists.' In the elections for secretary-general in April, 1965, he was defeated by Mr Grace Ibingira, one of the five Cabinet Ministers who were later arrested (February, 1966) for allegedly trying to overthrow Dr Obote's Government. Mr Kakonge claimed that there had been a deliberate plot in the party to oust him.

He continued as Director of Planning and in May, 1965, was given a vacant (specially-elected) seat in Parliament. When, in February, 1966, the motion by Mr Daudi Ocheng calling for an investigation into the bank account of the Deputy Army Commander, Colonel Idi Amin, was accepted by the Government after allegations that Dr Obote and two other Ministers were involved in illegal gold deals in the Congo, Mr Kakonge was the only MP to vote against the motion. He expressed his suspicions that the motion was being debated during the absence of the Prime Minister. (Dr Obote was later to claim that the motion was all part of the plot to overthrow him.)

After the abrogation of the constitution by Dr Obote and his assumption of the Presidency under a new constitution, Mr Kakonge was brought into the Uganda Cabinet as Minister of Planning and Economic Development.

W. W. KALEMA

William Wilberforce Kalema, a Muganda born in 1926, is Minister for Works and Communications and, since the Cabinet reshuffle in May, 1966, Housing as well.

A graduate from Edinburgh University, he was educated pre-

Laurence
Kalule-Settala

viously at King's College, Budo, and Makerere College (1945–48) where he took a diploma in education. He taught in Uganda from 1948–53, before going to Edinburgh.

On his return to Uganda he became a senior assistant secretary in the Ministry of Education in the Buganda Government, later becoming (1961) Permanent Secretary in that Ministry.

The following year Mr Kalema was nominated by the Lukiko (Parliament) of Buganda as one of the Buganda Members of the Uganda Parliament, and was later appointed Parliamentary Secretary to the Uganda Ministry of Education.

LAURENCE KALULE-SETTALA

Laurence Kalule-Settala, who became Minister of Finance in the Uganda Government in 1964, is a Muganda who was elected a Member of the Buganda Lukiko (Parliament) in 1962. He became a Member of the Uganda National Assembly as one of the members elected indirectly by the Lukiko to represent Buganda.

Mr Kalule-Settala was born in 1924; after education at St Mary's College, Kisubi, and Makerere College (1945–49) he went to the University of Hull (1953–56), where he took a BA Honours degree. Between 1950 and 1953 he was a teacher in Uganda.

He entered Uganda's political life by becoming a member of the Progressive Party, which was one of the smaller parties in Buganda supporting a federal system of Government for Uganda, with the Kabaka (king) of Buganda as symbolic Head of State. In 1963 he became first Minister of Community Development in Dr Obote's Government and later Minister of

Industry and Communications until 1964.

C. B. KATITI

The widely travelled Constantine Baranga Katiti, a former schoolteacher, became Minister of Community Development and Culture when this new portfolio was created in the Cabinet reshuffle in May, 1966.

Mr Katiti, who comes from Ankole Kingdom, western Uganda, where he was born in 1919, was educated at King's College, Budo, and Makerere College (1939–41).

After a spell of teaching in Uganda he went to University College, Exeter, England (1952–53). Returning to Uganda he resumed teaching, but also took an interest in politics and was appointed a Member of Uganda Legislative Council in 1954. He served on the Council until 1961, when he became an elected Member. The following year he was re-elected Member of Parliament for Central Ankole. Eventually he became Parliamentary Secretary in the Ministry of Regional Administrations, and later Deputy Minister.

He visited the USA and Puerto Rico during 1963–64. He was deputy leader of a Uganda goodwill mission which went to Yugoslavia, Russia, China, Japan and India after independence.

Mr Katiti's recreations are Scouting and swimming. He has served on Ankole District Council and was for some time Enganzi (Premier) of the Ankole kingdom's Parliament.

ERISA KIRONDE

Erisa Kironde, chairman of the Uganda Electricity Board since 1962, is a member of the Planning Commission for Uganda. He is a Muganda from Mukono,

Benedicto Kiwanuka

in the east of Buganda kingdom.

He was educated at King's College, Budo (1944–45), Makerere College (1946–49) and Cambridge University (1950–54), where he graduated with a BA Honours degree. He was a teacher at his old school, King's College, from 1954–59 and then until 1962 a lecturer at Makerere College. He is chairman of an insurance firm in Uganda.

BENEDICTO KIWANUKA

Benedicto Kagimu Mugumba Kiwanuka, first Prime Minister of Uganda from February-April, 1962, in the self-governing period before independence (October 1962), is president-general of the Democratic Party, but plays little part otherwise in the political life of the country.

The Democratic Party, which is the main Opposition party in Parliament, was at one time criticised for being a Roman Catholic group, but this has been strenuously denied.

Mr Kiwanuka, a lawyer with a private practice in Kampala, was born in 1922, a Muganda from Buddu, in the west of Buganda Kingdom. He was educated privately, at Pius XII University College, Basutoland (1950–52) and University College, London (1952–56), where he took a law degree. He was called to the Bar at Gray's Inn in February, 1956.

He served in the Army from 1942–46, attaining the rank of sergeant-major, and after the war was for some time a High Court interpreter before going abroad to study.

Mr Kiwanuka, who has travelled extensively both in Europe and the United States, was elected to the Uganda Legislative Council as Member for Masaka and in 1961 became Minister without Portfolio, Leader of the House and Government Business.

Later that year, with the constitutional progress in Uganda, he became Chief Minister and for a brief period in 1962 until Dr Obote's Uganda People's Congress came to power, was Prime Minister. He lost his seat in the April, 1962 elections and since then has not sought re-election.

A. A. LATIM

Alija Alexander Latim, secretary-general of the Uganda Democratic Party and Leader of the Opposition in Parliament, was elected MP for North-West Acholi in 1961.

He served as Parliamentary Secretary to the Ministry of Finance in the Democratic Party Government prior to independence (October, 1962). He was re-elected that year and leads the Opposition in the absence of the president-general of the party, Mr Benedicto Kiwanuka, former prime minister, who failed to obtain re-election.

Mr Latim is a teacher by profession. He was born in Acholi, northern Uganda, in 1924. After teacher-training, including four years at Makerere University College, he taught in various schools before he turned to full-time politics and was elected to Parliament.

LAMECK LUBOWA

Lameck Lubowa was 37 when he became Minister of Labour in May, 1966.

He is a Muganda, born in 1929. After education at Nabumali High School and Makerere College (1948–50), where he took a diploma of education, he taught in Uganda for a short time before going to India to study at the University of Delhi (1951–56).

John Lwamafa

He then switched to law and was called to the Bar at Lincoln's Inn, London, in 1959. He went back to Uganda to practise as an advocate and in 1962 was elected a Member of the Lukiko (Buganda Kingdom Parliament).

The Lukiko nominated him to sit as a Buganda Member in the Uganda Parliament. Later he joined the Uganda People's Congress and became Minister of Agriculture and Cooperatives in Dr Oboto's Government (1962–64). He was Minister of Commerce and Industry from 1964 until 1966, when he took over the Labour portfolio in the Cabinet reshuffle under the new constitution.

JOSHUA LUYAMBAZI-ZAKE

Joshua Luyambazi-Zake, a Muganda from Kampala, became Minister of Education in the Uganda Government after independence in 1962.

He was for some years Legal Adviser to the Lukiko (Buganda Kingdom Parliament), becoming an elected member of the Lukiko in 1962. From the Lukiko he was nominated to the Uganda National Assembly.

Mr Luyambazi-Zake was educated at King's College, Budo, and Makerere College (1938–40). He was a teacher in Uganda and South Africa (1941–44), where he attended Fort Hare University (1945–47). From there he went to London to study law and was called to the Bar at Gray's Inn, London, in 1952. He also attended the University of Chicago (1957–58) and North-Western University (1961). He holds the degrees of BA, LLB, M Comp Law and PhD. Nominated to the National Assembly as a Kabaka Yekka ('The King Only') representative, Mr Luyambazi-Zake decided soon afterwards to cross over to the Uganda People's Congress, which had been in alliance with the Kabaka Yekka party from 1962–64.

JOHN LWAMAFA

John Wycliffe Lwamafa became Minister of Regional Administration in 1964 when he was 46.

He is the son of a farmer in Kigezi, in the south-west corner of Uganda, born in 1918. He received his education at King's College, Budo, and Makerere College (1941–43), and became a teacher, later a headmaster.

In politics, he became an indirectly elected member of the Legislative Council (1954–61), and was Parliamentary Secretary, Education and Labour, from 1958–61. He was also a member of the East African Central Legislative Assembly from 1958.

Mr Lwamafa became an elected Member of Parliament (Uganda People's Congress party) in 1962 and was appointed Minister of Lands and Water Resources in Dr Oboto's independence Government.

R. J. MUKASA

Roger Joseph Mukasa, chairman of the Uganda Coffee Marketing Board since 1963, was born in 1926. After leaving Makerere College (1948–51), he was a teacher in Uganda and in 1955 went to the University of Wales, where he took a degree in economics. For two years he was employed by the Shell Co. in Uganda, then went to the USA. There he graduated in 1961 with a Master's degree from the University of Cincinnati, Ohio.

On his return to Uganda he was appointed assistant secretary of the Coffee Marketing Board and became deputy chairman in 1963. From 1964–65 he was

463

Sir Edward Mutesa,
the exiled Kabaka

president of the Inter-African Coffee Organisation and from 1965–66 he served as chairman of the International Coffee Council.

SIR EDWARD MUTESA

His Highness Kabaka Mutesa II of Buganda (Sir Edward Frederick Mutesa), 35th hereditary ruler of the largest of the four kingdoms of Uganda, fled to Britain after Uganda Government troops attacked his palace (May 24, 1966) on Mengo Hill on the outskirts of Kampala.

The attack followed a political crisis in which he had ordered Uganda's President, Dr Milton Obote, to withdraw his government from the soil of Buganda because Buganda refused to accept changes introduced by him.

One of the changes was the removal of Sir Edward from the post of President, to which he was elected in 1963.

Dr Obote said Sir Edward had abdicated by flying from his kingdom and was no longer Kabaka. But the King, in Burundi and later in London, announced that he had no intention of abdicating and planned to return when circumstances permitted. He maintained, on the advice of Queen's Counsel and an expert in constitutional law, that Uganda's 1962 constitution contained certain 'entrenched provisions' which were intended by the British Protectorate Government 'to safeguard Buganda and the Kabakaship' and any attempt to alter them would be illegal. In the meantime the Uganda Government administered Buganda directly, and the normal kingdom system of government ceased to function as from May, 1966, when the crisis broke.

It was the second time Sir Edward had tasted exile. In 1953 there was serious disagreement between him and the British Government. In November of that year, the British Governor, Sir Andrew Cohen had him escorted aboard an RAF plane at Entebbe and flown to London for failing to fulfil his treaty obligations to cooperate loyally with Britain. The Kabaka had been insisting that his Kingdom Parliament had the right to demand a time limit for independence and an assurance that Uganda would never be linked in a federation with neighbouring Kenya and Tanganyika. In London, where the Kabaka lived in a flat in a fashionable quarter, the newspapers called him 'King Freddie'. After two years' exile he was allowed to return to his country (1955) under a new agreement.

This reaffirmed the status of Buganda as a province of Uganda and defined the Kabakaship as that of a constitutional monarch with no executive powers.

Edward William Frederick David Wagulembe Lawangula Mutebi, Kabaka Mutesa II was born on November 19, 1924, son of the 24th Kabaka, Sir Daudi Chwa II. He succeeded his father in November, 1939, at the age of 15, his coronation taking place in 1942.

He can trace his royal ancestry in an unbroken line back to the 16th century. He was educated at King's College, Budo, and at Makerere College before going to Britain to study at Magdalene College, Cambridge. He served a short course of military training with the Brigade of Guards and is an Honorary Captain of the Grenadier Guards.

In addition to Buganda, the largest of Uganda's kingdoms (2,000,000 people), there are three hereditary kingdoms in the

Western Region – Ankole, Bunyoro and Toro.

ADOKO NEKYON

Adoko Nekyon

Akhbar Adoko Akaki Nekyon, who became Minister of Agriculture and Cooperatives in October, 1966, entered Parliament as elected Member for Lango South East in 1961.

A cousin of President Obote, he was born in 1931 at Lango, in northern Uganda. He was educated at King's College, Budo (1951-53) then went to India where he took a BA Honours degree at the University of Kerala (1955-60). He later worked as a clerk-interpreter in Uganda and was for a period of six months a trainee sales executive with the Uganda Shell-BP Company.

After entering Parliament he became Minister of Information, Broadcasting and Tourism (1962-64), then Minister of Planning and Community Development. In the Cabinet reshuffle of May, 1966, following the introduction of the new Constitution, his portfolio was divided and he was appointed Minister of Agriculture and Cooperatives.

Mr Nekyon was, with the then Prime Minister, Dr Obote, and the Minister of State for Defence, Mr Onama, accused in the Parliamentary debate of February, 1966, of being involved in illegal gold and ivory deals in the Congo. This led to a commission of inquiry under the chairmanship of East African Appeal Court Judge Sir Nageon de Lestang. Mr Nekyon and the other Ministers denied the allegations.

Mr. Nekyon is the author of two books in the Lango language. He is a Moslem and president of the National Association for the Advancement of Moslems in Uganda.

S. K. NKUTU

Shaban Kirunda Nkutu, one of the two Moslems in President Milton Obote's Cabinet, became Minister of Health in May, 1966, when he was 36. He took over the portfolio previously held by Dr E. B. S. Lumu, one of five Ministers detained in February, 1966, for allegedly attempting to overthrow Dr Obote's Government.

Mr Nkutu comes from Busoga District, eastern Uganda. He is the son of a (parish) chief. After attending a teacher-training college at Mbarara (1950-51) and Makerere College (1953-56), where he took a diploma in education, he became a teacher until 1961, when he entered the Uganda Legislative Council as a UPC Member.

He was spokesman on Education for the UPC Opposition and when Dr Obote formed his independence Government in 1962 he became Parliamentary Secretary to the Ministry of Economic Affairs, switching the following year to a similar post in the Prime Minister's Office and becoming Government Whip. In November, 1964, he became Deputy Minister of Education.

ARCHBISHOP EMMANUEL NSUBUGA

The Most Revd Mgr Emmanuel Nsubuga was 50 when appointed Roman Catholic Archbishop of Kampala in August, 1966.

His archdiocese had just been created. It comprises the former archdiocese of Rubaga (Uganda) and the diocese of Kampala.

Mgr Nsubuga succeeded the former Archbishop of Rubaga, Dr Joseph Kiwanuka, who died in February, 1966. He was vicar-capitular of Rubaga at the time of his appointment.

Dr Milton Obote

He trained at seminaries in Buganda and was ordained priest in 1946.

Mgr Nsubuga became Vicar-General of the Rubaga Archdiocese in 1961 and showed ability, efficiency and determination in running the archdiocese during the absence of Archbishop Kiwanuka.

E. K. K. NTENDE

Uganda has been represented at many International Cotton conferences in India, Africa and Europe by Elizaphan Kawangu Kalange Ntende, chairman of the Uganda Lint Marketing Board since 1963.

Born in 1931, and a graduate (BA) of Makerere, he worked first in the Labour Department as a cadet labour officer (1955–56) before joining the Shell Co. in Uganda.

Mr Ntende served with this company until 1963 as salesman, supervisor, sales promotion supervisor and later trade relations officer in various parts of East Africa.

SEMEI NYANZI

The chairman of the Uganda Development Corporation, the organisation which controls much of Uganda's economy, Semei Nyanzi is a former headmaster and university lecturer. He was appointed joint chairman and director of the UDC in January, 1964, and chairman in October, 1964, on the resignation of Mr J. T. Simpson.

Mr Nyanzi, born in 1933, comes from Acholi, in northern Uganda, He went to school in Uganda and the Sudan, became headmaster at Gulu High School (1955–56), then went to Edinburgh University (1957–61), for an Honours MA in economics, a certificate in public administra-

tion and a diploma in education. On his return to Uganda he became a lecturer in economics at Makerere University College, Kampala.

He is a member of the East African Central Legislative Assembly and secretary of the Uganda Economics Society.

In October, 1966, he married Dr Juanita Kagwa, daughter of a former Katikiro (Prime Minister) of Buganda, and one of the first African women in Uganda to qualify as a doctor.

DR MILTON OBOTE

Apollo Milton Obote, elected Executive President of Uganda on April 15, 1966, is a self-declared opponent of hereditary privilege and a champion of the 'common man'. Yet until 1966 he was Prime Minister of a country composed principally of four kingdoms, joined together in a federal relationship, with one of the Kings, the Kabaka of Buganda, its constitutional President.

This anomaly was forced on Obote by the peculiar circumstances of Uganda from its early days as a British protectorate at the end of the last century.

The richest and most populous part of the country is Buganda, whose people had evolved a sophisticated form of government under a Kabaka long before the explorer Speke discovered the Nile source at Lake Victoria, near Jinja, in 1862. The major problem in Uganda's progress towards independence during the 1950s centred on the proudly autonomous status of the Buganda kingdom, and its reluctance to see itself swallowed up into an independent African state, ruled possibly by people who in the past were traditional enemies and 'inferiors'.

It was largely due to the efforts of Dr Obote, himself from northern Uganda, that the Baganda were persuaded to go into the independence experiment. As late as 1961 there were serious doubts whether Buganda would take part in the London conference that decided the terms for independence. But Dr Obote's party, the Uganda People's Congress, won them round and made an alliance with the Buganda party of Kabaka Yekka ('The King Only') by supporting the Buganda claim for federal autonomy.

As a result Dr Obote swept into power in the final elections of April, 1962, with 68 seats in Parliament for the UPC-Kabaka Yekka coalition against the 24 for the Democratic Party, under their leader and former Prime Minister, Mr Benedicto Kiwanuka.

It was perhaps inevitable that a clash would develop between the traditionalist Buganda leaders, wedded through their Kabaka to a system of feudalism, and the forward-looking Prime Minister, determined to create a united nation out of a variety of peoples.

The alliance between the UPC and the KY quickly eroded, but Dr Obote's chance of overthrowing the whole federal structure of the State came in 1966, when he suspended the Constitution, arrested five of his Ministers and claimed that there had been a plot, involving the Kabaka of Buganda (then constitutional President of Uganda) to oust the Government.

After the introduction of a new constitution in April, 1966, under which Dr Obote became executive President and the federal relationships between the kingdoms and the Central Government were scrapped, some people in Buganda attempted an abortive uprising in May. The Kabaka's palace was captured after being stormed by the Uganda Army, and the Kabaka fled to England.

Shortly afterwards Dr Obote declared that Sir Edward Mutesa had abdicated by fleeing from Uganda and was no longer Kabaka, and that Buganda would be administered as four separate districts under the Central Government. Speaking at the independence anniversary celebrations in October, 1966, he hinted that there would be further changes affecting not only Buganda. Observers took this to mean that he intended measures which would affect the positions of the remaining traditional rulers in Uganda, which is regarded as too small a country to afford the complications of a multi-kingdom federation.

Dr Obote (his doctorate is an Hon LLD from Long Island University, USA, 1963) was, like most of Uganda's leaders, a student at Makerere, but he did not complete his course in English, economics and politics. He says simply, 'I was not happy at Makerere.' The third of nine children of a northern chief, he was born at Akokoro village, in Lango in 1925. After leaving Makerere in 1950 the young man who had only a few years previously been herding his father's goats, tried to obtain scholarships to study abroad. There is a note of bitterness when Dr Obote describes this period in his life. He was offered a scholarship to study law in America, but the then colonial Government turned it down on the ground that a knowledge of American law would be useless in Uganda. Subsequent attempts for scholarships to London and to Gordon College, Khartoum, were likewise turned down.

Cuthbert Obwangor

James Ochola

Dr Obote decided to become a labourer and learn about trade unionism from the bottom. He worked first at a sugar works near Kisumu, in Kenya, later joining a construction company in Uganda and moving with it back into Kenya.

The stay in Kenya gave him his first real grounding in politics and he became an active member of Mr Jomo Kenyatta's Kenya African Union, until it was proscribed at the start of the Mau Mau Emergency in 1953.

Before his return to Uganda in 1957 Dr Obote became associated with the African social clubs then being formed in place of the banned political parties. He helped, with Mr Argwings-Kodhek, who later became a junior Minister in Kenya, to found the African District Congress and also a branch of the Capricorn Society.

On his return to Uganda, Lango District Council nominated him as its representative in the Uganda Legislative Council. From there he began his climb to the top political position in Uganda.

In the first elections in October, 1958, Dr Obote was returned as a Uganda National Congress Member.

The UNC was led at the time by Mr Joseph Kiwanuka, but after a split with him Dr Obote formed his own party, the Uganda People's Congress, in 1960, with himself as president-general.

The General Election of that year was boycotted by Buganda. This enabled the Democratic Party under Mr Benedicto Kiwanuka to form the Government. The UPC was the second largest party in the House and Dr Obote became Opposition leader. With great skill he engineered the alliance with the Buganda Party, the Kabaka Yekka, and thereby led the country to independence in October, 1962.

CUTHBERT OBWANGOR

A former trader and railwayman, Cuthbert Joseph Obwangor, born in 1920, was made Minister of Commerce and Industry in May, 1966, after the introduction of the new constitution under Dr Obote. Previously he was Minister of Justice and before that, in 1963, Minister of Regional Administration.

Mr Obwangor, who comes from Teso, in eastern Uganda, first entered the Legislative Council in 1954, after spending many years in Kenya, first at the railway traffic school in Nairobi (1942–46) then working as railway clerk, cashier and traffic instructor. In 1951 he returned to Uganda and opened a business in Teso, becoming a member of Teso District Council in 1952.

He was elected chairman of Teso District Council in 1958 and became elected Member of Parliament for East Teso. He was spokesman on Commerce and Industry for the UPC Opposition in 1961 and the following year became Minister of Regional Administration when Dr Obote formed his 1962 independence Government.

JAMES OCHOLA

James Silas Malilo Ochola was appointed Minister of Public Service, a new portfolio, in May, 1966, after the introduction of the new constitution by Dr Obote.

He was previously a Democratic Party member and became Parliamentary Secretary to the Ministry of Agriculture and Animal Industry (March, 1962) in the pre-independence Government of Mr Benedicto Kiwanuka.

Sam Odaka

A. A. Ojera

After Dr Obote's Uganda People's Congress came to power, Mr Ochola continued as Opposition Chief Whip but, in January, 1965, accompanied by Mr Bataringaya, the leader of the Opposition, crossed the floor and joined the UPC.

He was Deputy Minister for Information, Broadcasting and Tourism, until his appointment in 1966 as Minister of Public Service.

Mr Ochola, the son of a clan leader, was born in 1924 in the Bukedi District, in eastern Uganda, and became an accounts clerk in the Provincial Administration (1946–47), later a labour inspector (1948–53). In 1954 he was made manager of the South Bukedi Cooperative Union, a post he held until 1959. He was a Bukedi District Council member from 1949–51.

SAM ODAKA

Sam Ngude Odaka, Uganda's Minister of Foreign Affairs, was born in 1933. He had several years' apprenticeship in local government in Uganda before being elected in 1961 to the Uganda Legislative Council.

The son of an eastern Uganda fishmonger, he took a BA degree at Makerere College (1952–55). He joined the Standard Vacuum Oil Co. in Uganda and held an executive post until 1962, when he decided to go into politics full-time.

From 1957–59 he was a Kampala municipal councillor and from 1959–62 a member of Jinja Municipal Council. In 1961, as a Member of Parliament, he was spokesman for health and water resources for the Uganda People's Congress Party Opposition, becoming Parliamentary Secretary for Finance in Dr Obote's Government in 1962,

later Deputy Minister for Foreign Affairs.

In 1964 he was made Minister of State and, after the introduction of the new constitution in April, 1966, took over the Foreign Affairs portfolio previously held by the then Prime Minister, Dr Obote. Mr Odaka was a director of the Uganda Electricity Board from 1959 to 1962. He was married in August, 1965, to Miss Margaret Kavuma, daughter of the former Omuwanika (Finance Minister) in the Buganda Kingdom Government, Mr Blasio Kavuma.

As Minister, and Minister of State for Foreign Affairs he has several times addressed the United Nations General Assembly in New York. After the arrest of five Ministers for allegedly attempting to overthrow the Government, Mr Odaka took over the additional portfolio of Minister of State in the Office of the Prime Minister from February to May, 1966.

A. A. OJERA

Alexander Arthur Ojera, appointed Minister of Information, Broadcasting and Tourism in 1964, is a former schoolteacher and the son of a teacher; he was born in 1929. From Makerere College, he went to the University of Exeter, England, then to Lincoln University, Pennsylvania, and Rutgers University, New Brunswick.

Back in Uganda with a BA degree, he accepted a teaching post at the Sir Samuel Baker School, Gulu, the town of his birth.

As secretary of the local Uganda People's Congress branch and a member of the district council he entered the Uganda National Assembly in 1961.

469

Felix Onama

E. W. Oryema

In the first independence Government in 1962, he became Parliamentary Secretary in the Office of the Prime Minister and Government Chief Whip. In 1963-64 he was Minister of Community Development and Labour before becoming Minister of Information.

Mr Ojera held the additional portfolio of Mineral and Water Resources from February to May, 1966, as a result of the arrest in February of the Minister, Mr B. K. Kirya, one of five Ministers accused of attempting to overthrow the Government.

FELIX ONAMA

Felix Kenyi Onama, appointed Defence Minister in April, 1966, at the age of 45, is the son of a county chief in Madi district, northern Uganda. He was a civil servant in the Cooperative Development Department before entering politics.

After attending various schools in Uganda, Mr Onama went to study at Makerere College, then to the Cooperative College, Loughborough, England. He was a cooperative officer in the Uganda Government from 1950–60 and also general manager of the W. Nile Cooperative Union.

He entered the National Assembly as a Uganda People's Congress member in 1961 and became spokesman for the Opposition on Works and Labour. In 1962, when the UPC formed the Government under Dr Obote, he became Minister of Works and Labour, the following year taking over Internal Affairs. In 1965 he was appointed Minister of State for Defence in the Prime Minister's Office and in April, 1966, he became Defence Minister.

Mr Onama also took over as secretary-general in an acting capacity of the UPC after the arrest in February, 1966, of Mr Grace Ibingira, Minister of State, who was alleged to have been involved in an attempt to overthrow the Government.

Mr Onama was accused in February, 1966, in Parliament along with the then Prime Minister, Dr Obote, and another Minister, Mr Adoko Nekyon, of being involved in illegal gold and ivory deals in the Congo. The accusations became the subject of a judicial commission of inquiry. Mr Onama and the other Ministers denied the allegations.

E. W. ORYEMA

Erenayo Wilson Oryema was appointed Inspector-General of Uganda's Police in 1964, when he was 47.

He is an Acholi, from northern Uganda. He joined the Uganda Police Force as a constable in 1939 and shortly afterwards was seconded to the King's African Rifles, where he became a close friend of Idi Amin, now commander of the Uganda Army.

Mr Oryema was made an inspector in 1951 and the following year attended a course at the Hendon Police Training College in Britain. He became an assistant superintendent of police in 1954 and was awarded the Colonial Police Medal in 1958.

While deputy Inspector-General in 1963, he attended a further police course (intelligence and security) in London and a senior officers' course at the Police Academy in Washington.

He is commissioner of the St John Ambulance Brigade, Uganda.

ARCHBISHOP ERICA SABITI

The Most Revd Erica Sabiti was the first African Protestant archbishop elected by the Churches

Omukama of Toro

Joshua Wakholi

of Uganda, Rwanda and Burundi (1966).

He was 65 and had been in the ministry 36 years. Formerly he was Bishop of Ruwenzori diocese, which covers the kingdoms of Toro and Bunyoro (Uganda) and the deanery of Mboga, in the Congo.

Educated at King's College, Budo, and Makerere College (1925–28) and trained as a teacher, he entered the Church in 1930. He was made a deacon in 1933, priest a year later and was consecrated bishop in 1960.

On his appointment as Archbishop, succeeding Dr Leslie Brown, he said, 'I hate politics in the Church. I will discourage my brother bishops and clergy from mingling with politics. We belong to the people.'

OMUKAMA (KING) OF TORO

Omukama Patrick Olimi III, born in 1945, succeeded to the throne of Toro in December, 1965.

He was studying at Sherbourne School in England when his father, Sir George Rukidi died suddenly in his capital, Fort Portal. Sir George's death ended an unbroken 38 years on the throne, a period during which Toro, and the rest of Uganda, made the transition from a part of Britain's colonial empire to a newly independent nation.

The kingdom is 5,233 square miles in extent, and includes the eastern side of the Ruwenzori Mountains (the Mountains of the Moon) bordering on the Congo. The population is 400,000.

The customs of the Toro Kingdom go back far beyond the 100 years of written history in Uganda, which began only in 1862 when the first white men, the explorers Speke and Grant, reached the country in their search for the source of the Nile.

King Patrick's nomination by his father as his heir was regarded as a sign of the determination of the late Omukama to ensure that his kingdom kept pace with the modern world. He passed over his elder sons when he chose the young Prince to succeed him.

JOSHUA WAKHOLI

Joshua Nabusoba Khaluswa Wakholi, who comes from Bugisu District, on the Kenya border, was 40 when appointed Minister of the Cabinet Office in May, 1966.

This was a new Ministry created under the new Constitution. Formerly, from November, 1964, Mr Wakholi had been Deputy Minister of Agriculture and Co-operatives.

Mr Wakholi began his career in the civil service in 1954, as an assistant in the Department of Cooperative Development. As a cotton grower he was a member of the Bugisu Cooperative Union (1955). He was elected to the Bugisu District Council, in eastern Uganda, in 1954 and became chairman of the council in 1958, holding office until 1962, when he was elected to the Uganda Legislative Council as a member of the Uganda People's Congress.

He was deputy spokesman on Works and Labour for the UPC Opposition during the self-governing period under the Democratic Party Government, later becoming Parliamentary Secretary to the Ministry of Health in Dr Obote's Government on independence (October, 1962).

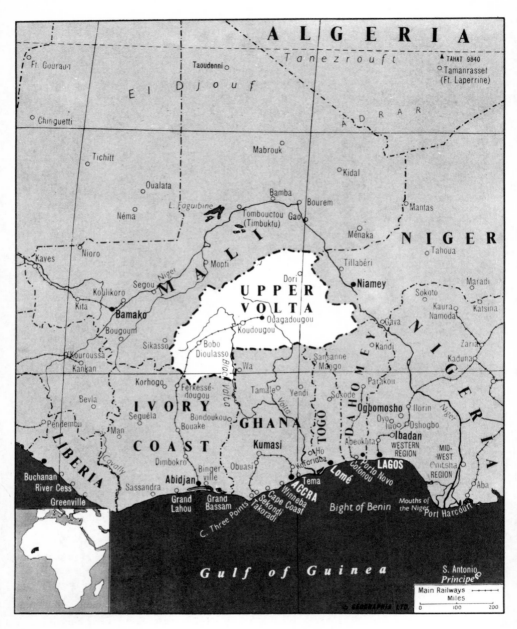

The area is 105,841 square
miles. The population
approaches five million; it was
estimated at 4,860,000 in 1965.
The landlocked Upper Volta is
surrounded by Mali to the north
and west, Niger to the north
and east, and the Ivory Coast,
Ghana, Togo and Dahomey to
the south. The capital is
Ouagadougou.
The Upper Volta produces millet,
sorghum, maize, rice and yams;
cultivation of rice, cotton and
groundnuts is of increasing
importance. Cattle breeding
provides an additional source
of revenue. Deposits of
manganese, gold and
diamonds are currently being
prospected.

Upper Volta

A separate French colony of Upper Volta was carved in
1919 out of the colony of Upper Senegal and Niger, which
had been established in 1904.
In 1932 the territory was divided between the Ivory
Coast, the Soudan (modern Mali) and Niger. On
September 4, 1947, Upper Volta was reconstituted, to
comprise the area of the old colony.
On December 11, 1958, the country became an autonomous
member of the French Community, and was granted
independence on August 5, 1960.
On January 4, 1966, Lieutenant-Colonel Sangoule
Lamizana, the Army Chief of Staff, deposed President
Maurice Yameogo, suspended the constitution and
declared himself the new head of state.

The history of Upper Volta is essentially that of the
country's chief tribe, the two million-strong Mossi,
although the second President of the Republic,
Lieutenant-Colonel Sangoule Lamizana, is not a member
of the tribe.
Under their rulers, the Moro Naba – the present ruler
is the 35th holder of the title – the strongly disciplined
Mossi set up an enduring Empire in the savannah lands
of West Africa. They alone resisted the southward drive
of Islam, and their resistance provided a protective
cover for the present countries of Ghana, Ivory Coast,
Togo and Dahomey, which remain largely Christian or
animist to this day.
The founder of the present Mossi kingdom was the Moro
Naba Ouedraogo. A national hero who lived about the
12th century, his name is the most widespread in the
country. Visitors to Upper Volta can be forgiven for
thinking that half the population of the country is
called either Ouedraogo or Yameogo.
France found the Mossi empire on the point of splitting
up at the end of the 19th century. A protectorate was
established and in 1919 several of the provinces were
merged into a territory called Upper Volta. This was
dismembered in 1932. But under the prodding of the
last Moro Naba before independence, France
reconstituted the territory and eventually this became
the Upper Volta Republic.
The country is not rich. Ninety per cent of the people
live off the land. They are hard-working farmers but

People gather to
buy and sell in
Bobo Dioulasso's
market-square

are hampered by unproductive soil, erosion, primitive
methods of agriculture and lack of water. The main
export crop is groundnuts. Cattle also form an important
export. The European Economic Committee has set up
an agricultural research station to try to deal with
problems of land productivity.

Important sources of revenue for Upper Voltans, who
can often display surprisingly modern fittings inside their
neatly constructed mud huts, are service in the French
Army (now coming to an end) and work in the richer
countries to the south, such as the Ivory Coast.

A Mossi labour force constructed the Vridi canal which
in 1951 opened Abidjan to the ocean and began a new
era of prosperity in the history of the Ivory Coast.
Mossis, their broad faces marked by semi-circular
tribal scars, are to be seen on Ivory Coast plantations,
in road gangs, or as servants in restaurants or houses.

The railway station at Bobo Dioulasso, which stands on the country's key rail link with Abidjan (Ivory Coast) and the sea

They are esteemed both for hard work and loyalty. But working abroad cannot provide a permanent foundation for Upper Volta's economy, and both Presidents since independence have grappled with vast problems of budgeting and economic development. Upper Volta flirted with the Mali Federation, which was to have linked the former territories of French West Africa into a federal state, and also the socialist Ghana-Guinea-Mali union, but in each case was held back by economic considerations affecting her close link with the Ivory Coast to the south.

Ouagadougou has a rail link with Abidjan. The largest expatriate population of Upper Voltans is in the Ivory Coast, and the latter country, as well as France, has provided Upper Volta with important aid.

Although he refused to sign a defence treaty with France, and closed down the once important French

Two young fishermen with their catch of mudfish

military base at Bobo Dioulasso because he did not wish to offend his socialist neighbours, President Maurice Yameogo remained staunchly pro-French and pro-Western. Western aid helped him to balance his budget despite recurrent financial crises.

It was a budgetary crisis which brought Yameogo's rule to an end in January, 1966. He had ordered cuts in civil servants' salaries as an austerity measure, but many of his countrymen thought he handled the issue badly. The measures were introduced while Yameogo was on an expensive honeymoon in Brazil; at the same time his construction of a Presidential house in his home town of Koudougou was being severely criticised.

Unionists demonstrated for four days outside his palace and finally the Army took over at Yameogo's request. The military regime under Colonel Lamizana cancelled Yameogo's unpopular austerity measures but soon found itself forced to introduce others. Political agitation started in Yameogo's home district in September, 1966, and the military Government, while announcing in December that it would stay in office for four years, to repair the country's economy, banned political activities and set up special courts to try cases of subversion. On the first anniversary of the *coup*, in 1967, President Lamizana told his people: 'The honeymoon of our independence is over. The time has come for hard work.'

Lt Bonde Bagnamou

Pierre Damiba

LT BONDE BAGNAMOU

The Minister of Justice, Lieutenant Bonde Bagnamou was born at Boni, in the district of Hounde, in the west of Upper Volta, on September 22, 1934.

He attended a primary school at Hounde from 1943–46 and completed his secondary studies at the western town of Bobo Dioulasso from 1946–50.

He joined the French Army in December, 1950, and took part in the campaigns in Indochina and Algeria.

Gazetted sub-lieutenant on October 1, 1962, he went to the officers' training school at Melun in France from 1962–63.

He was promoted to lieutenant in the para-military security forces, the Gendarmerie, in October, 1964, by the Government of President Yameogo. He was named Minister of Justice in January, 1966, after Yameogo's Government fell and the military took over.

CAPTAIN ROBERT COEFE

Captain Robert Coefe served for 25 years in the French Army before being transferred to the Upper Volta Army.

With the military takeover in January, 1966, he became Secretary of State for National Defence and Ex-Servicemen.

Born about 1912 in Ouagadougou, he joined the French Army in 1932.

LT ANTOINE DAKOURE

Secretary of State for Information, Youth and Sport in the military Government of Colonel Lamizana, Lieutenant Antoine Dakouré was born at Tampoui on November 26, 1936.

He studied at a seminary in Upper Volta and then went to St Louis in Senegal to continue his education.

He was at the Army officers' school in France from 1960–62 and the school for military engineers from 1962–64.

Back in his own country he became an aide-de-camp to ex-President Yameogo.

PIERRE CLAVER DAMIBA

Minister of Development and Tourism in the military Government, Pierre Claver Damiba was born in February, 1937, at Koupela in eastern Upper Volta.

He studied at university in France, obtaining his *licence* in economic studies in 1961, followed by a diploma from the Centre for Economic and Banking Studies. After his return home to Upper Volta he was engaged in development planning. He was Director of the Planning

Lt Marc Garango

Pierre Ilboudo

Dominique Kabore

Bureau from 1962–65 and Director of Industries from 1965, until he entered the Government early in 1966.

LT MARC GARANGO

Lieutenant Tiemoko Marc Garango, Minister of Finance and Commerce,ˎ served with the French Army in both the Indochinese and Algerian campaigns.

He had a distinguished academic career, studying law and economics in the Universities of Dakar, Paris and Aix-en-Provence. He did his military training at Bingerville, near Abidjan, Ivory Coast.

Promoted to lieutenant in 1961, he was raised to the rank of captain in 1963. Serving next as Supply Officer for the Upper Volta Army in 1965, he joined the military Government early in 1966 as Minister of Finance and Commerce.

In this post, the youthful Minister (he was 38) had to deal with some of the country's most pressing problems. Ex-President Maurice Yameogo had been overthrown because of his introduction of cuts in Civil Service salaries. These austerity measures were put off by the new military regime, but within a few months the Government had to start introducing others, including cuts in MPs' salaries and new taxes.

Lieutenant Garango was born on July 27, 1927, at Gaoua in the extreme south of the country.

PIERRE ILBOUDO

Secretary of State for Foreign Affairs in the military Government, Pierre Ilboudo was born on December 24, 1936, at Kombissiri, near the capital, Ouagadougou.

A licentiate in arts of the University of Dakar, he won a diploma for higher studies in Paris in 1964. M. Ilboudo was with the permanent delegation of the Upper Volta at the United Nations from 1961–63 and secretary-general to the Ministry of Foreign Affairs in Ouagadougou, until his nomination to the Cabinet early in 1966.

DOMINIQUE KABORE

Minister of the Civil Service in the military Government which took power in January, 1966, Dominique Kabore was born in 1919 in the Barma district near the capital, Ouagadougou.

He studied in the administrative section of the William Ponty School in Dakar and gained his certificate (*brevet*) at the French Overseas School set up to train administrators for the overseas territories.

In 1958 he joined the French Civil Service and was transferred to the Upper Volta administration in 1964. District Commissioner for Bobo Dioulasso, the key western town of the Upper Volta, from 1959, he was also head of the Bobo Dioulasso commune for three years.

Under President Yameogo he occupied the key post of President of the Economic and Social Council from 1960–62 and was transferred from there to be district commissioner for Fada N'Gourma in eastern Upper Volta. He was occupying that post when called to the Government in January, 1966.

KOUGRI NABA

Thirty-fifth Emperor (Moro Naba) of the nearly two million-strong Mossi tribe, the Moro Naba Kougri belongs to one of the few traditional ruling African families whose power was not sapped by the Republican ideals

Lt-Col
Sangoule Lamizana

and plans of colonial France.

The father of the present Moro Naba was able to bring pressure on France to reconstitute Upper Volta as an administrative region just after World War II. Thus Upper Volta avoided being absorbed into the Ivory Coast and Mali (French Soudan) and became an independent republic in 1960.

What the French had not done to reduce the Moro Naba's power was then achieved by the process of African politics, and the youth and political inexperience of the present Moro Naba when he succeeded to the throne in 1957.

Despite the fact that many Mossi still prostrate themselves before him, the Moro Naba Kougri found himself stripped of power during the term of office of President Maurice Yameogo and a virtual supplicant to the Government for his livelihood.

The Moro Naba lives in a whitewashed villa on the outskirts of the capital. In a dusty courtyard behind the villa the remains of his ancestors are housed in round huts.

The Moro Naba symbolised the sun on earth. Ruling through ministers and dignitaries he maintained a rigid and disciplined society of a sort uncommon in modern Africa. Almost on a war footing, the Mossi resisted the southward drive of the Arabs, forcing them to fan westward towards Guinea and eastward towards Nigeria, which became heavily Moslemised. Ghana, the Ivory Coast, Togo, and Dahomey, sheltered by the Mossi resistance, remained largely animist and Christian. The Mossi tribe is today partly Christian and partly Moslem.

Kougri Naba succeeded to the throne in 1957 at the age of 35. He was chosen to fill the post by the tribe's 'four wise men' – Tansoba Naba, Minister of War, Ouidi Naba, Chief of Cavalry, Gounga Naba, Chief of Riflemen, and Larale Naba, Minister of Defeat. (The last of the four was considered to have the trickiest post as it was his job to explain to the Emperor when things went wrong.)

He rode through the capital on a white charger and Mossi cavalry performed a mounted war dance round the Palace to the beating of drums.

He has a number of wives married to him under Mossi tribal law but in 1958 he married Miss Ouedraogo Diarra, daughter of a transport contractor, at a civil service in Ouagadougou Town Hall.

LT-COL
SANGOULE LAMIZANA

Lieutenant-Colonel Sangoule Lamizana took control of Upper Volta on January 3, 1966, in response to demonstrating unionists and at the request of the beleaguered ex-President, Maurice Yameogo.

At the end of his first year in office Lamizana, a quietly spoken self-effacing man, announced that the Council of the Armed Forces, the governing body, had decided to extend its mandate for a period of four years in order to cure the country's pressing economic ills.

Born in 1916 at Dianra in the north-western district of Tougan near the frontier of Mali, Colonel Lamizana is one of the few leaders in Upper Volta who is not of the important Mossi tribe. Tougan was once part of French Soudan (Mali) until the various sections of neighbouring countries were put together in 1941 to form Upper Volta, at the bidding of the Mossi Emperor.

479

Colonel Lamizana speaks the Mali language, Bambara. He completed his primary schooling in Upper Volta and joined the French Army on January 18, 1936. In December of that year he was transferred as a secretary to the Mauritania Military Command at St Louis, Senegal. While there he continued his secondary school studies.

Transferred to North Africa in 1943, he returned to Upper Volta with the rank of chief adjutant in 1947.

In April 1949 he was promoted to sub-lieutenant, travelling to Paris soon after for a short visit to the Centre of African and Asian Studies in Paris where he was an instructor in the Bambara language.

He completed two tours with the French Armed Forces in Indochina and was promoted to lieutenant in 1951. He is a holder of the Légion d'Honneur.

In October, 1956, he was appointed deputy head of the military staff of the Governor of the Ivory Coast, and was promoted captain in 1957. From 1959–61 he served in North Africa in command of a company.

After Upper Volta became independent he was sent back to his own country to help with the setting up of its army. Soon afterwards he became first Chief of the General Staff of Upper Volta's Armed Forces.

In this post Colonel Lamizana served President Yameogo loyally. But political upheavals late in 1965, brought on by an austerity campaign and the growing unpopularity of Yameogo, forced Lamizana to take a political role.

The unionists who crowded the front of Yameogo's palace demanding his resignation also called on Colonel Lamizana to take over.

Finally President Yameogo saw that this was the only way. He stepped down after asking Lamizana to take control of the country. Upon handing over, Yameogo said, 'Contrary to what may be thought, I am the first to rejoice, and my Ministers with me, at the way things have worked out.'

After taking power Lamizana was forced to come to grips with a difficult economic situation. A number of missions were sent to France to try to secure help with economic projects. Upper Volta is poor in cash crops, relying heavily on groundnuts, and much of its earnings from abroad comes from the Upper Voltans working in neighbouring countries who send money back to their families.

Colonel Lamizana continued the policy of his predecessor. Upper Volta remained a member of the *Entente*, a consultative group joining five pro-Western West African states, although on returning from one of the *Entente* meetings in Abidjan, Upper Volta unionists complained that Colonel Lamizana had not been accorded the treatment due to a head of state. The Ivory Coast Government, which had enjoyed close links with Yameogo, denied that Lamizana had in any way been slighted.

He also maintained his country's links with the Common Afro-Malagasy Organisation (OCAM) of French-speaking states, and the Organisation of African Unity.

Late in 1966, Lamizana quashed recurring rumours of a possible return to civilian rule by announcing that the military Government would continue to rule for four years to restore the country's economic situation.

At the same time he announced the suspension of political and union activities and special courts for people charged with subversion. The action against political parties followed violent incidents in Maurice Yameogo's home district of Koudougou in the east of the country late in September.

As well as being President of the military Government, Lamizana is Prime Minister and Minister of National Defence, Ex-Servicemen, Information, Youth and Sport.

EDOUARD OUEDRAOGO

Minister of Public Works, Posts and Telecommunications in the Military Government, Edouard Ouedraogo was born on February 17, 1919.

He joined the French Army in 1937 and was made a prisoner of war in June, 1940, escaping in August, 1942. He received the Croix de Guerre.

After the independence of Upper Volta he became secretary to the Minister of Public Health and administrative head of the Public Works and National Economy Ministries, before himself advancing to ministerial rank.

MAURICE YAMEOGO

President of Upper Volta from birth of the Republic in 1960 until his overthrow following four days of union demonstrations in January, 1966, Maurice Yameogo was placed under house arrest by the Army after his downfall and attempted suicide in December, 1966.

He was born on December 31, 1921, at Koudougou in the east of the country, and belongs to the Mossi race, the key ethnic group in the history of the region.

After schooling at a seminary he joined the French West African administration as a clerk.

His political career began in 1946 when he became a councillor for the Ivory Coast and then Upper Volta in the Grand Council of French West Africa in Dakar.

He was active in the Christian trade union movement in his own country and took part in the founding of the African Democratic Rally, the giant West African political movement launched by Ouezzin Coulibaly of Upper Volta and Houphouet-Boigny of the Ivory Coast.

However, he subsequently decided to form his own political party, the Voltaic Democratic Movement, and was elected to Parliament on that ticket in 1957. In that election the local branch of the African Democratic Rally headed by Ouezzin Coulibaly won 37 seats and Yameogo's party 26.

Following the elections a coalition was formed between the two parties and Yameogo obtained the post of Minister of Agriculture.

Ten months later the Coalition was in disarray with sections breaking away from both parties. Yameogo took some of his party into the ranks of the African Democratic Rally and was awarded the key post of Minister of the Interior.

When Ouezzin Coulibaly, one of the great figures of West African politics, died late in 1958, Yameogo, after a close intra-party contest, became Prime Minister.

The first political battle Yameogo had to face was over the question of whether Upper Volta should be part of the Mali Federation, which was intended to group all the territories of French

Captain Bila Zagre

Cardinal Zoungrana

West Africa. The Ivory Coast was opposed to it. Yameogo opted out and faced another parliamentary crisis. He went to the country under the banner of a new party, the Voltaic Democratic Union, and won 64 of the 75 seats.

Short, dynamic and impulsive, Yameogo enjoyed a political role somewhat larger than the agricultural economy of his country would normally have permitted because of the lynch-pin geographic situation of Upper Volta. If Yameogo had fallen under Nkrumah's sway, the socialist countries of Mali, Guinea and Ghana would have enjoyed land contacts through Upper Volta.

For a while Yameogo did flirt with Nkrumah and in 1961 signed a Customs agreement with Ghana. But disillusionment set in and finally Yameogo stayed loyal to the *Entente*, the loose grouping of pro-Western, West African States organised by President Houphouet-Boigny of the Ivory Coast.

At the end of his career Yameogo's political touch seemed to desert him. His divorce and the way he sent his wife packing back to her village had an unpopular reception, as did his marriage to 'Miss Ivory Coast' in 1965 and his expensive honeymoon in Brazil – at the same time as he was decreeing cuts in civil servants' salaries as an austerity measure at home.

Unionists demonstrated for four days demanding that Colonel Lamizana, the head of the Army, take over. Finally Yameogo agreed to step down and asked Lamizana to take office. A military Government statement in December, 1966, said Yameogo had attempted to commit suicide in the villa where he lived under house arrest.

CAPTAIN BILA ZAGRE

Secretary of State for the Interior and Security in the military Government, Captain Bila Jean Gérard Zagre was born on July 24, 1925, in the capital, Ouagadougou.

Like many of his brother officers in the Upper Volta Army he performed his military studies at Bingerville in the Ivory Coast. He joined the French Army in November, 1943.

Sub-lieutenant on January 1, 1958, and lieutenant two years later, he was aide-de-camp to President Yameogo in 1960–61.

Transferred to Army HQ from 1962–65, he became a captain in January, 1964, and entered the Government early in 1966.

CARDINAL ZOUNGRANA

Cardinal Paul Zoungrana was the second African to be appointed a Prince of the Roman Catholic Church. He was made a cardinal by Pope Paul VI in February, 1965, after being consecrated Archbishop of Ouagadougou by Pope John XXIII in Rome on May 8, 1960.

Born in the capital of Ouagadougou in 1917 and a member of the important Mossi race, he was ordained a priest in October, 1942, after completing his studies at the seminary of Koumi in the west of the country.

He completed his novitiate in 1948 with the White Fathers at Maison Carrée, Algeria, then went to Rome, where he obtained his doctorate in canon law, and to Paris and the Catholic Institute, where he became a licentiate in social sciences.

He was named professor of canon law and sociology at the Koumi seminary, where he had studied, and also became curate of a parish near the seminary. Later he took charge in Bobo

Dioulasso, the country's main western city, of coordinating catholic social action.

It was while he was baptising the son of President Yameogo (the child incidentally bore the rather grand name of Charlemagne) that a telegram arrived from Rome telling him that he had been appointed Archbishop of Ouagadougou. Five years later he was admitted to the Sacred College of Cardinals, thus becoming the second African cardinal after Mgr Laurian Rugambwa, Bishop of Bukota in Tanzania.

Tall, with twinkling eyes set behind small, gold-framed spectacles, Cardinal Zoungrana is one of the most imposing figures of the African clergy. His personal influence and authority is not confined to Upper Volta but extends to neighbouring states where a number of Presidents are Roman Catholics.

He is known for his frank speaking and some of his statements on the political and social life of his country have caused a considerable stir. In November, 1966, in a sermon entitled 'The Christian in Political Life', he made allusions to the political errors of the past in Upper Volta and attacked leaders who had been neither impartial nor incorruptible.

This was interpreted as a reference to former Catholic President Maurice Yameogo, whose divorce and harsh treatment of his former wife acutely embarrassed the Upper Volta clergy. At the time of the political crisis in Upper Volta which led to the downfall of President Yameogo, Cardinal Zoungrana was away at the Vatican Council in Rome.

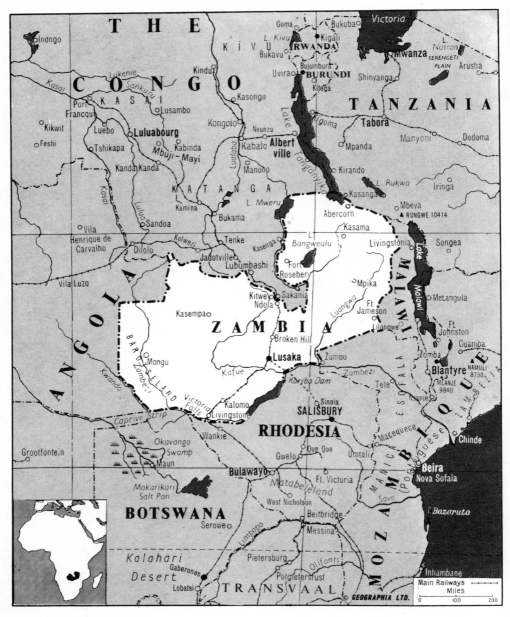

Zambia's area is 290,587 square miles. It is landlocked, surrounded by Portuguese Angola, Congo Kinshasa, Tanzania, Malawi, Portuguese Mozambique and Rhodesia, with a tiny frontier with Botswana and the Caprivi Strip of South West Africa. The population was estimated in December, 1965 to be 3,780,000. The capital is Lusaka.

Copper-mining is the mainstay of the economy, other minerals being zinc, manganese and cobalt. The main crops are maize, tobacco and groundnuts.

Zambia

The British territory of Northern Rhodesia became the
independent Republic of Zambia on October 24, 1964, after
ten months of internal self-government following the
dissolution of the Federation of Rhodesia and Nyasaland.
The Constitution provides for a President, elected in the
first instance by the Legislative Assembly and thereafter at a
general election by the electorate. The Vice-President,
appointed by the President, leads the Government in the
National Assembly.

Most leaders of newly emancipated African states want
to change the face of their country. For Dr Kenneth
Kaunda, 42 years old when he became President of
Zambia on Independence Day, it was an economic and
political necessity.

Dr Kaunda found himself in control of a sprawling,
landlocked country with a population of which half is
under 20 years old. It is one of the richest states in
East or Central Africa. The wealth is drawn almost
entirely from the Copperbelt, a 90-mile long corridor in
the middle of the country which produces more than
£100m worth of copper a year.

At independence in Zambia there were only four
African doctors, half a dozen African lawyers and one
African engineer.

In addition to having to contend with a 'crisis of
expectation' from his people, Dr Kaunda also had to
pay heed to the special problems created by a large
white minority in the country.

Many of the white population of more than 70,000,
particularly those working in the seven copper mines,
are of South African or Rhodesian origin and, at
independence, had little sympathy with African
aspirations. But their continued presence was necessary
if the economy was to keep its strength and supply the
capital for ambitious development schemes.

A great worry for President Kaunda and his Government
was Zambia's dependence on its southern neighbours
for vital communication links. Historical patterns of
development in southern Africa resulted in Zambia
being developed northwards from the south, with
communications running in the same direction. This
process was strengthened and accelerated during the

In the heart of
the Copperbelt—
a mine at Kitwe

Federal era. Nearly half of Zambia's imports came from
Rhodesia or South Africa and virtually all her exports
went on routes traversing Rhodesia.

Politically the new Zambian Government looked north
to the other independent states. Long-range plans called
for the development of links with the north, particularly
with Tanzania, the nearest friendly coast.

On November 11, 1965, came Rhodesia's unilateral
declaration of independence, an action to which the
Zambian Government was bitterly opposed.

The gigantic and often frustrating task of re-gearing the
economy so that dependence on the south was reduced
or eliminated became the Government's first priority.

At the same time Dr Kaunda had to maintain internal
stability which, in practice, meant satisfying the demands
of his followers for action while ensuring there was no
disruption of the racial harmony that had characterised
Zambia's first months of independence.

There was a long-term goal. Dr Kaunda once defined it
as 'putting a pint of milk and an egg on every Zambian
breakfast table and a pair of shoes on every Zambian's
feet'. This promise could not just be pushed aside.
Zambians had to be given a better standard of living.
But the Rhodesia crisis made equal demands. Few people
were better equipped to deal with such a complicated
situation than the brawny schoolteacher-farmer turned
politician, with the shock of prematurely-greying hair,
who found himself squarely in the middle of this
complicated situation.

Justin Chimba

H. D. BANDA

Hyden Dingiswayo Banda, appointed Minister of Transport and Works in January, 1965, was one of the key members of the Zambian Cabinet involved from the start in the crisis caused by Rhodesia's unilateral declaration of independence (November 11, 1965).

Many of the jobs involved in switching the country's communications away from the south fell on his shoulders, and he achieved a reputation as an able and efficient organiser.

His middle name means 'the troubled one' and one newspaper commented that it was singularly appropriate for the man in charge of the country's transport.

He was born in eastern Zambia in 1925 and trained as a book-keeper and typist. He is widely travelled and, besides his Cabinet post, is also director of the ruling United National Independence Party's Youth Brigade and was formerly a senior party official on the Copperbelt.

The Transport portfolio is his second Cabinet appointment. He was Minister of Housing and Social Development in the 1964 Government.

LEWIS CHANGUFU

Lewis Changufu, Minister of Information and Postal Services, was one of the officials of Mr Harry Nkumbula's African National Congress who broke away from the party with President Kaunda in 1958 – the key political 'revolt' in the country.

Born in Kasama, northern Zambia, in 1927, he was educated locally and by correspondence. He entered politics in 1950 and was restricted together with a number of Zambian Congress leaders in 1959.

A key UNIP official, he was sent to Zanzibar by the party and deported from the island.

Mr Changufu also travelled to the USA where he took a course in public relations and leadership. He joined the 1964 Government as Parliamentary Secretary to the Prime Minister's Office and accepted the Information post on January 22, 1965.

Before going into full-time politics Mr Changufu was a businessman.

JUSTIN H. CHIMBA

Justin Henry Chimba was at 45 the oldest member of the Zambian Cabinet when he was appointed Minister of Commerce and Industry on January 22, 1965.

He was born in 1921 in Mporokoso, a remote part of northern Zambia and educated to school certificate level.

Mr Chimba was at one time employed by the Provincial Administration. After leaving Government employ he was selected as UNIP representative in Cairo and Dar es Salaam. The Commerce post is his second Cabinet appointment. He has also been Minister of Labour and Mines.

M. M. CHONA

Mathias Mainza Chona entered the Government in 1964 as Minister of Justice and was appointed Minister of Home Affairs. Apart from President Kaunda, he is the only other person to have held top rank in the United National Independence Party.

Born in southern Zambia in 1930, he was educated at mission schools and at Munali Secondary School, going to London to study law.

Already keenly interested in

politics, he telephoned Dr Kaunda one night while the future President was in Britain as an official of the African National Congress to urge him to take over from Congress chief Mr Harry Nkumbula. Kaunda replied he could not do so. The actual break came about a year later.

Mr Chona was called to the Bar at Gray's Inn and became his country's first African barrister.

When Dr Kaunda's party was banned in 1959, African politicians who had avoided detention formed new groups. These merged to form the United National Independence Party at the end of the year with Mainza Chona as president.

He made it clear, however, that he was only 'keeping the seat warm' for Dr Kaunda and stood down on the latter's release from prison.

Mr Chona became the party's national secretary.

SIR STEWART GORE-BROWNE

Sir Stewart Gore-Browne is one of East Africa's most remarkable 'white settlers'.

In 1966, the year of his 86th birthday, he was made a Grand Officer of the Companion Order of Freedom in independent Zambia's first Honours' List.

His long career has been closely linked with the political development of Zambia. Born in London in 1883 and educated at Harrow and the Royal Military Academy, Sandhurst, his first trip to Northern Rhodesia was in 1911 on a commission determining the boundary with the Congo.

He fought in World War I in France and returned to Northern Rhodesia in 1920 to begin his farm at Shiwa N'gandu and find

a place for eventual retirement.

Shiwa N'gandu, a 23,000-acre estate in the middle of the Zambian bush with a majestic Elizabethan-style farmhouse, is now a miniature welfare state. It has its own schools, hospital and post office. Many of the workers have been with Sir Stewart for more than 30 years and a large number are pensioned.

In his political career Sir Stewart was first allied with Sir Roy Welensky, former Federal Prime Minister, as one of the 'unofficials'–non-Colonial Office members of the Legislature.

But he split with Sir Roy over race questions and in 1946, a year after being knighted for his services to the Legislative Council, called for an end to all race discrimination.

He resigned from the Legislature in 1951 but continued to advise the country's African nationalists, becoming a close friend of the future President of the Republic.

He visited the United Nations with Dr Kaunda to advocate the cause of Zambian nationhood.

SOLOMON KALULU

Solomon Kalulu, Minister of Lands and Natural Resources (1966) is also national chairman of the ruling United National Independence Party.

Born in Lusaka in 1924, he trained in South Africa as a teacher and is a former headmaster. He has travelled widely in both Europe and America.

As Lands Minister, he became identified with Zambia's game conservation policy. In 1966 he warned in Parliament that the country's herds of Red Lechwe antelope faced extinction.

His warning was followed a few days later by a massive air and ground sweep against

Reuben Kamanga

Simon Kapwepwe

poachers which resulted in a large number of arrests.

REUBEN CHITANDIKA KAMANGA

A former clerk from eastern Zambia, Reuben Chitandika Kamanga became Vice-President when the Republic was formed. He is leader of the Government in Parliament (the President does not have a seat).

He was born on August 26, 1929 and was educated at mission schools and at Munali Secondary School, near Lusaka, the school that has produced so many members of the present Government.

He was involved in politics and the growing nationalist movement at a very early age. During the campaign against the Federation of Rhodesia he played a key role as representative of President Kaunda's United National Independence Party in Cairo. He became vice-president of the party.

He first entered the Government in January, 1964 as Minister of Transport and Communications. When the Rhodesia crisis flared up in November, 1965, his experience as Transport Minister stood him in good stead. He was given the chair of several committees responsible for Zambia's contingency planning, one big feature of which was building up routes which bypassed Southern Rhodesia.

SIMON KAPWEPWE

Outside the country the best-known Zambian politician, next to President Kaunda, Simon Mwansa Kapwepwe has the reputation of not being afraid to speak his mind.

During the London Commonwealth Conference in September, 1966, he made headlines in the world press when he accused the British Prime Minister, Mr Harold Wilson, of being a 'racialist' in his handling of the Rhodesia crisis.

The remark was reported to have angered Mr Wilson. Unperturbed, the tall, bearded Mr Kapwepwe repeated his remarks just as forcefully at four different press conferences on his way home.

Nor have African nationalists escaped his criticisms. He has told the Zambian Parliament that nationalists should take off their luxury clothes, roll up their sleeves and do something for their people.

Mr Kapwepwe has been closely associated with his country's independence movement since its birth and his career has closely followed that of Dr Kaunda.

He was born at Chinsali, in northern Zambia, on April 12, 1922, the son of a policeman. There were five children. He was the only one to receive an education as his parents could not afford to send the others to school. He went to Lubwa mission school, also attended by Dr Kaunda, and Bombay University.

In 1946 he was one of the founders of the African National Congress, one of the country's first nationalist groups. He supported Dr Kaunda when the split came with Nkumbula.

When the Zambia National Congress was banned, Mr Kapwepwe was detained. Describing his period in jail, he said, 'I was put in a cell with five murderers. It was a terrifying experience. They did not sleep, being troubled with dreams about their victims.'

Mr Kapwepwe was elected to Parliament in 1960. With the formation of an African Government he became Minister of African Agriculture, Minister of

Dr Kenneth Kaunda

Home Affairs in 1963 and Minister of Foreign Affairs with independence in 1964.

Political commentators have called him a spellbinding orator. Others have said he is a firebrand.

DR KENNETH KAUNDA

Dr Kenneth Kaunda was the youngest of eight children (four died while young). Born on April 28, 1924, his arrival was a surprise, and he was known in the family as *Buchizya*, 'the Unexpected One'.

His father was the Revd David Kaunda, a Church of Scotland missionary and teacher from Nyasaland, who died when he was eight.

His birthplace and early home was the Lubwa mission station in hilly country in northern Zambia. His childhood was calm and happy, surrounded by books. He went to Munali Secondary School, near Lusaka, then the only secondary school that accepted Africans. After taking a teacher's certificate, he tried farming in Lubwa, was unable to settle and, with another young man, Simon Kapwepwe, destined one day to be his Foreign Minister, went to Tanganyika and Southern Rhodesia in search of a satisfying job.

As a young teacher earning £5 a month he became interested in politics. Two incidents are thought to have influenced him powerfully. When he went into a white man's bookshop he was turned out and directed to the rear door for African 'boys'. On another occasion he was beaten up for using the whites' entrance to a cafe.

In 1949 he walked into the offices of Harry Nkumbula's African National Congress and took his first step on the road which led to the Presidency.

Cycling hundreds of miles through the bush, with a guitar to attract crowds to hear his 'freedom message', he organised nearly a hundred provincial branches.

His reputation in the party grew and in 1953 he was elected secretary-general of Congress and became Nkumbula's right-hand man.

A year later the two men were jailed for two months for possessing, at party headquarters, banned copies of a magazine which had been sent to them by a British Labour MP.

It was during this period that Kaunda formulated his political creed – faith in the common man and belief in non-violence, based on a study of Gandhi and a visit to India. The life of Abraham Lincoln also inspired him.

A split with Nkumbula came over the 1958 constitution, which gave 14 representatives to 70,000 Europeans but only eight to 2,500,000 Africans. Nkumbula accepted this as the best possible that could be obtained, but Kaunda led the agitation against it and formed the Zambia National Congress.

Within four months the new party was banned after organising a boycott of the registration of voters.

Kaunda was restricted to a remote part of Zambia, then he was sentenced to nine months' imprisonment. The main effect on him of Salisbury Central Prison was to make him more ascetic. When released he was a martyr in the eyes of his countrymen and took the leadership of the United National Independence Party formed in his absence.

Feeling on federation, the main issue in politics, became high.

Elijah Mudenda

John Mwanakatwe

Kaunda, however, firmly opposed violence, and when a white housewife was stoned to death on the Copperbelt, he condemned her murder saying, 'The battle is not anti-white, but anti-wrong. We can never fight racialism and be racialist ourselves.'

Passive resistance succeeded. Britain agreed that member states of the Federation could secede. Kaunda went as a member of the Legislature to a London conference and returned with an independence constitution in his briefcase.

An election enabled him and his party to win 52 out of 75 seats in the Legislative Assembly and he became Zambia's first Prime Minister in January, 1964, when the country began its period of internal self-government.

As President of the Republic he moved into State House, the spacious red-brick, Georgian style residence of former governors. He at once began what has been described as 'a ferocious work schedule that frequently alarms his colleagues and medical advisers'.

Beginning at 7 am, he lunches at 1.30 pm, starts again at 4 pm and goes on until midnight. For relaxation he plays hymns on a piano or picks up his guitar or plays snooker or table tennis.

Every day Dr Kaunda, a tall man with a friendly, charming smile, reads from a Bible given to him by Pope Paul. He is a member of the nonconformist United Church of Zambia, but cares little about denominational differences and worships happily in Anglican or Roman Catholic churches. He speaks with care and his speeches often have a biblical ring.

He has expressed a burning faith in his country as 'a potential paradise on earth'.

DR KABELEKE KONOSO

Dr Kabeleke Konoso, Minister of Justice, was Zambia's first African doctor; until he entered the Cabinet in 1966 he had a thriving practise in Lusaka.

Born in Barotse Province in 1930, Dr Konoso had an all-African education. His early schooling was in Northern Rhodesia, then he went to Makerere College in Uganda and obtained a science diploma.

After that he worked in Botswana to get money for school fees, then he went to Durban Medical School qualifying as a doctor in 1959. Dr Konoso is also a keen sportsman and has played first division soccer and held various athletic records.

In addition to his Cabinet appointment he is a member of the United National Independence Party's education committee.

ELIJAH MUDENDA

Elijah Mudenda, appointed Minister of Agriculture in 1964, is one of the Zambian Cabinet's technocrats.

Born in southern Zambia in 1927 he was educated in Zambia, Uganda, South Africa and Cambridge in Britain, graduating as an agriculturalist. He worked for the Government until 1962 as an agricultural research officer in plant breeding.

Then he entered politics and became Parliamentary Secretary for Agriculture in December, 1962, and Minister in 1964.

Mr Mudenda has written two books in the Tonga language.

JOHN MWANAKATWE

John Mupanga Mwanakatwe, Minister of Education, is another of the Zambian Cabinet's technocrats with an impressive list of 'firsts' in his career.

Harry Nkumbula

He was born at Chinsali, in northern Zambia, in 1926 and educated in Zambia and South Africa. He was the country's first African to obtain a degree and, in 1957, became the first Zambian principal of a secondary school.

He entered the Government as Parliamentary Secretary for Mines and Labour in 1962 but switched to the Cabinet with the Education post in 1964.

HARRY NKUMBULA

Harry Nkumbula, leader of the Opposition in the Zambian Legislature and head of the African National Congress, is President Kaunda's former political boss.

The son of a chief, Mr Nkumbula was born in 1916 in southern Zambia. He qualified as a teacher in 1934 and took a job on the Copperbelt. Already politically conscious, he joined the militant Kitwe African Society.

He was offered a government scholarship to Makerere College in Uganda, where he read history and geography, and went on to London with another scholarship to attend the London School of Economics.

In the British capital he joined the Africa Committee, composed of leading nationalists which had Jomo Kenyatta as chairman and Dr Nkrumah as secretary. Nkumbula was the typist.

His studies came to an end when his scholarship was withdrawn in 1950. Nkumbula said this was done because officials in the then Northern Rhodesia thought he was becoming too much of a political menace.

Back home he turned down the offer of a government job and instead spent 18 months travelling to and from the coast selling sea shells.

In 1951 he entered politics full time and was elected president of the Northern Rhodesia African National Congress, leading African opposition to the Rhodesian Federation and the colour bar.

He gathered round him a group of young men including Kenneth Kaunda, Reuben Kamanga and Simon Kapwepwe. He and Kaunda were jailed for three months in 1955 for possessing subversive literature.

Opposition to Nkumbula's leadership grew and at a conference in 1958 Kaunda and the main leaders of the party walked out to form the Zambia National Congress, leaving Nkumbula with the rump of the old party. His leadership was opposed as not being radical enough.

As the country advanced towards self-government an election in October, 1962, left Nkumbula's party the minority group but the dominant party. A Federalist group controlled 15 seats, Kaunda's party had 14 and Congress five. Dr Kaunda's party, however, won a majority of votes.

After lengthy talks, Mr Nkumbula joined his fellow-African and former secretary-general in forming a coalition. He took office as Minister of African Education and set to work on the gradual elimination of racial discrimination in education, a satisfying job for the ex-schoolteacher.

But differences between Dr Kaunda and Mr Nkumbula were profound and Kaunda likened the Government to a three-legged man trying to run, the legs being the two African parties and the Colonial Office.

Then in 1963 came British agreement to the end of the Rhodesian Federation, the winding up of the Federation and new elections to give self-government under an African Prime Minister.

Congress lost heavily. They won only 10 of the 75 seats. Mr Nkumbula was left a joint-leader of the Opposition with John Roberts, whose party was later dissolved.

Nkumbula maintained that he still had a role to play. Congress accused some officials of the ruling party of intimidation and of making appointments in the Civil Service. 'The ANC will fight against any form of slavery,' he said.

To many political observers, however, Mr Nkumbula and his group appear a waning political force. They have been accused, though Nkumbula denied it, of drawing their strength from tribal affiliations, mainly in the southern part of the country.

In addition Mr Nkumbula's leadership was openly questioned by some of his colleagues. Local government elections in 1966 under universal suffrage, left President Kaunda's party with overwhelming wins in nearly all parts of the country though Congress did retain some wards, mainly in southern Zambia.

WESLEY NYIRENDA

Speaker of the Zambian Parliament, Wesley Nyirenda has won respect from both Government and Opposition members for his firm handling of debates and decisive rulings.

Family poverty prevented him from becoming Zambia's first doctor. He was born on January 23, 1924, the first of five children, to parents who were both teachers. Part of his education was at the Church of Scotland's mission school at Lubwa, where Dr Kaunda and Simon Kapwepwe were also taught. He

went to South Africa for further studies, financing himself during the holidays by scrubbing ships in the docks. In 1949 he matriculated and won a scholarship to study medicine at the University of Witwatersrand in Johannesburg.

But a letter arrived from home telling him that his brothers would be forced to leave school if he did not return to help. Throwing up his chance to be the first African doctor in Northern Rhodesia he took a job as a teacher.

Every afternoon after school hours he used to go into the bush with a bundle of books under his arm. As a result of hard study he won an arts degree, though his eyesight failed temporarily through overwork two months before his examination.

By 1960 he was principal of a secondary school. It was Dr Kaunda who persuaded him to stand for Parliament the following year. He was three years a back bencher before becoming deputy Speaker.

'I took my duties very seriously, but very innocently,' says Nyirenda. 'I criticised almost every project in the development plans and I was being cheered by the Opposition.'

H. J. ROBERTS

Herbert John Roberts, former joint-leader of the Opposition in the Zambian legislature, is a one-time political colleague of former Rhodesian Federal Prime Minister, Sir Roy Welensky.

A farmer, Mr Roberts was born in Wolverhampton, England, in 1919 but was taken to South Africa as a child and went to Northern Rhodesia in 1928.

He began farming in Broken Hill in 1949. He entered politics

493

Munu Sipalo

Arthur Wina

as a supporter of Federation and was at one time Minister of Labour and Mines in a Northern Rhodesian administration.

After the Federation was broken up the Federal group became the National Progress Party and Mr Roberts headed its ten-strong group in Parliament. In mid-1966, however, announced its dissolution as being no longer appropriate to present-day Zambia.

The members, elected on a special franchise with seats reserved for whites, mostly continued to sit in Parliament as Independents, including Mr Roberts.

MUNU SIPALO

Munukayumbwa (Munu) Sipalo, Minister of Labour, (appointed January 22, 1965) is a close associate of President Kaunda from Congress days and the fight against the Rhodesian Federation.

He was born in Barotseland in 1929 and, after secondary education in Northern Rhodesia, studied economics at Delhi University.

Mr Sipalo was secretary-general of the Zambia African National Congress, forerunner of UNIP and was jailed with President Kaunda when the party was banned. Later he also served as secretary-general of UNIP until 1961.

He is widely travelled and has held two Cabinet posts: Natural Resources and his present portfolio.

J. J. SKINNER

James John Skinner, Zambia's Attorney-General (January 22, 1965), was born in Dublin, though he is now a Zambian citizen, and was one of the first white members of the United

National Independence Party, which he joined in 1960.

He was born in 1923 and was called to the Irish Bar in 1946 and to the English Bar in 1950. He went to Northern Rhodesia in 1951 and set up a law practice advising on legal matters and helping the party in elections.

He became Parliamentary Secretary for Justice in 1964 then Attorney-General in the following year.

ARTHUR WINA

Arthur Wina, Zambian Finance Minister, and one of two brothers in the Cabinet, is one of the United National Independence Party's foremost intellectuals and one of the Government's leading negotiators.

Christened Arthur Nutuluti Lubinda Wina, he was born in Barotse Province on July 21, 1929, the eldest son of the Ngambela, roughly equivalent to prime minister in the Paramount Chief's government.

He was educated at local mission schools and recalls that his early education in politics came from eavesdropping on meetings attended by his father. His father was dismissed by the Paramount Chief for his radical views.

Arthur was sent to secondary school at Munali, near Lusaka, his first glimpse of 'white man's Northern Rhodesia' and quickly became involved in politics.

He went to Makerere College, in Uganda, obtained an arts degree and joined the Northern Rhodesia Government first in the administration and then as an educationist.

His political involvement continued and he was frequently warned. By 1959 his position had become untenable and he took a scholarship to study in America.

Sikota Wina

Alexander G. Zulu

In 1960 he was appointed US representative of the United National Independence Party, travelling on speech-making trips around the country and making three appearances before the United Nations. He also obtained two masters degrees from the University of California.

He returned home in 1962, stood for Parliament and won. He was appointed Parliamentary Secretary for Finance in 1962 and Minister in 1964.

Mr Wina quickly won a reputation as a Minister who knew his portfolio intimately and the major part of his budget speeches are always written by himself rather than by Civil Service officials.

As Finance Minister he became a leading member of President Kaunda's Government. He was one of Zambia's chief delegates at the 1966 Commonwealth Conference in London.

SIKOTA WINA

Sikota Wina, Minister of Local Government and Housing, is the younger of the two Wina brothers in the Zambian Cabinet.

Born 18 months after his brother Arthur, Sikota Wina has been politically conscious since student days.

He was expelled from Fort Hare University in South Africa for his political activities and joined the Northern Rhodesia Government in the Information Department, but left to become editor of a Copperbelt newspaper.

He was detained during a ban on the Zambia National Congress – led by Dr Kaunda and forerunner to the present United National Independence Party.

He joined UNIP as publicity director on his release.

Since the formation of an African government he has served as Parliamentary Secretary for Local Government, Minister of Health and Minister for Local Government and Housing.

He is married to an American Negro journalist, the former Miss Glenda MacCoo, and has travelled widely on party and government business.

He is generally considered to take a more radical political line than his brother.

As Minister of Housing he has spearheaded a drive to rid Zambia of bad housing and been pictured driving a bulldozer demolishing slum dwellings.

ALEXANDER G. ZULU

Alexander Grey Zulu, Minister of Mines and Cooperatives, (January 22, 1965) is one of the pioneers of the cooperative movement in Zambia.

He was born at Fort Jameson in eastern Zambia in 1924 and after secondary education joined the Government as a water development assistant.

In 1954 he became the first manager of one of the territory's key African cooperatives in the centre of the country. He also started an independent night school.

Mr Zulu has held one other Cabinet post besides Mines, that of Commerce and Industry.

Acknowledgements

Reuters and the Publishers wish to thank the following
for permission to reproduce passages from works
published by them:
Frank Cass & Co Ltd, London (*The Ghana Coup*, by
Colonel A. A. Afrifa, first published in 1966).
The Pall Mall Press Ltd (Publishers), London, and
Frederick A. Praeger Inc, New York (*African Tightrope*,
by Major-General H. T. Alexander, first published in
1965).
They also wish to thank the Government departments of
the African countries which are the subject of this book
for their help in providing information and photographs,
and the following organisations, photographic agencies
and photographers:
Associated Press Ltd
Camera Press Ltd
J. Allen Cash
Central Office of Information (Crown Copyright
    Reserved)
Richard Costain Ltd
East African Standard Newspapers Ltd
Keystone Press Agency
Paul Popper Ltd
Press Association Photos Ltd
Radio Times Hulton Picture Library
Sport and General Press Agency
United Nations

Index to Biographies

56